The Beatles

The Beatles

The Ultimate Recording Guide

Allen J. Wiener

Facts On File
New York • Oxford

The Beatles: The Ultimate Recording Guide

Published by special arrangement with McFarland & Company, Inc., Publishers, Jefferson, North Carolina

Facts On File, Inc.   Facts On File Limited
460 Park Avenue South   c/o Roundhouse Publishing Ltd.
New York NY 10016   P.O. Box 140
USA   Oxford OX2 7SF
                             United Kingdom

Library of Congress Cataloging-in-Publication Data
Wiener, Allen J., 1943–
    The Beatles : the ultimate recording guide / Allen J. Wiener.
      p.   cm.
    Includes bibliographical references and index.
    ISBN 0-8160-2511-8
    1. Beatles—Discography.   2. Beatles—Video catalogs.—I. Title.
  ML156.7.B4W53   1992
  016.78~~42166~0972~—dc20   91-40635

A British CIP catalogue record for this book is available from the British Library.

Facts On File books are available at special discounts when purchased in bulk quantities for businesses, associations, institutions or sales promotions. Please call our Special Sales Department in New York at 212/683-2244 (dial 800/322-8755 except in NY, AK or HI) or in Oxford at 865/728399.

Text design by Ron Monteleone
Jacket design by Catherine Rincon Hyman
Composition by Ron Monteleone/Facts On File, Inc.
Manufactured by R.R. Donnelley & Sons, Inc.
Printed in the United States of America

10 9 8 7 6 5 4 3 2 1

This book is printed on acid-free paper.

To my father, who loved music, cowboys, laughter, and us

Contents

Acknowledgments

No work of this scope would be possible without the generous help and advice of many others. I am greatly indebted to each of the following individuals.

A very special "thank you" must go to Mark Wallgren for providing an almost continuous flow of valuable Beatles record information over a period of many years. Mark also spent considerable time reviewing the draft manuscript and provided many valuable suggestions. Even more important, perhaps, Mark constantly challenged me with innovative conceptual ideas from which I benefited considerably. He has not only been a valuable source, he has been that rarest of creatures: a real friend.

Special thanks to Mark Lewisohn for giving generously of his time during lengthy telephone conversations and for reviewing sections of the draft manuscript. The wealth of knowledge found in Mark's books, the product of years of meticulous, painstaking research, is more than gold to anyone researching The Beatles.

Allan Kozinn gave generously of his time and made an extra effort to review and double check many recordings, especially those listed in the "Alternate Versions and Bonus Tracks" section.

Arno Guzek made an extensive and time-consuming review of the manuscript, provided lengthy, detailed notes and generously contributed valuable information from his own files.

Scott "Belmo" Belmer, Supreme Publisher of *Belmo's Beatleg News*, generously shared his Beatles collection, reviewed parts of the manuscript, and contributed valuable suggestions.

Jim Berkenstadt provided something very special—perspective. By reminding me repeatedly that some people "just take this whole thing too seriously," he helped to keep my feet reasonably close to the ground. Jim also provided many rare Beatles recordings and valuable discography information.

A special thanks must go to Skip Groff and his staff at *Yesterday and Today Records* in Rockville, Maryland, and to Jeff Tamarkin, editor of *Goldmine* magazine.

I am very grateful to my agent, Carol Mann, for her hard work in bringing about this volume. My editor, Gary Krebs, deserves high praise for lending both an expert and caring eye to the manuscript. It was a kind fate that sent me an editor who is also a Beatles fan.

Others who have contributed to the completion of this work include Richard Buskin, Paul Altobell, Tim McGee, Ray Schweighardt, John Guisinger, Thomas A. Canova of Pennie & Edmonds, Jack Bennett, Bob and Linda Weiss, Michael Greisman, Harry Weinberg, Peter Coan, Perry Cox and Marjorie Sampson.

To all of those who have written and sent information over the years, and who are simply too numerous to mention here, a heartfelt "thank you" for caring.

A generous measure of gratitude is due Susan Gorsky, Courtney Tucker and Evans Wiley, my fellow members of "The Cabal," each of whom subjected themselves to my frequently irrational ravings.

Finally, the two individuals who have sacrificed more than anyone for this book are my wife, Kathy, and our daughter, Amanda. Yes, it's finished.

Introduction

Somewhere, in an earlier incarnation, I began to compile a "little checklist" of Beatles recordings that would help me complete and organize my collection. This, I reasoned, shouldn't be too difficult. To the unsuspecting newcomer, the group's recordings appeared to be manageable and finite in number. Some decades later the list has become the volume you are holding, and I have had to face the harsh fact that there is, and probably never will be, an end to the process of documenting Beatles recordings. Despite the number of years I have spent delving into their professional lives, I remain constantly surprised by how much Beatles material exists, and by how frequently new tapes of unreleased recordings find their way into circulation among collectors. The longer one works in this area, the more acute the sensation of the world slipping from one's grasp.

The book begins with a "General Chronology," a day-by-day account of the comings and goings of John, Paul, George and Ringo with heavy emphasis on events that were recorded on tape, film or disc. Other significant events are also noted in order to lend perspective to the group's development. Many entries are preceded by the code letter "r" or "b." The "r" denotes an event that was recorded and that appeared on a commercially available record or CD; the "b" indicates recordings that have not been officially released, many of which have appeared on underground, bootleg records and CDs. More detailed information about the "r" and "b" entries is found in the "Recording Chronology" and in the "Bootlegs and Unreleased Recordings Chronology" later in the book.

Throughout the book, notes list only an author's last name. Where more than one work by an author is listed, the note also contains the year of the work in question. Full information on the written source is found in the reference list.

The "General Chronology" is followed by several additional sections, each documenting a specific segment of Beatles recordings. The "Recording Chronology" documents all of the officially released Beatles recordings in the order in which they were made. In addition to their studio work, many interviews and other documentary discs are included in that listing.

The U.S. and U.K. discographies list the official record and CD releases in those countries in the order in which they were issued. The "Special Release Discography" adds records and CDs that were issued on a limited basis and that contain unique Beatles recordings. The "Alternate Versions and Bonus Tracks" section details recordings that have appeared in more than one version and songs that were issued, at least initially, only as B sides of singles, as bonus tracks on extended singles, EPs or compilation albums that contain the work of several artists. The "Bootlegs and Unreleased Recordings" section lists all known recordings that remain officially unreleased and notes bootleg records and CDs on which many of them can be found.

Appendix A, "The Beatles as Supporting Players," lists records by other artists that include some supporting participation by one or more members of The Beatles. The list includes songs written by members of The Beatles that the group never recorded but were given to other artists. Appendix B, "Video-cassettes and Laser Discs," lists all Beatle films and appearances released for home use.

Every effort has been made to verify the information contained herein, but in a work of this scope and volume some errors are unavoidable, if regrettable. The author welcomes any supplemental information, which may be sent in care of the publisher. Send all inquiries c/o Allen Wiener to: Facts On File, Inc., 460 Park Avenue South, New York, NY 10016.

Readers and prospective researchers are cautioned that there appears to be no end in sight to the discovery of previously unheard Beatles recordings. Moreover, George, Ringo and Paul continue to pursue their individual careers, yielding still more new material. Thus it is with some sense of trepidation that I offer the chronicle that follows.

General Chronology

1902

Jul 7: James McCartney, father of Paul McCartney, was born.

1909

May 28: Harold Harrison, father of George Harrison, was born.

1911

Mar 10: Louise French, mother of George Harrison, was born.

1912

Dec 14: Alfred "Freddie" Lennon, father of John Lennon, was born in England. His parents (John's paternal grandparents) were Jack Lennon and Mary McQuire.

1914

Mar 16: Julia Stanley, mother of John Lennon, was born.

1930

May 20: Harold Harrison and Louise French, parents of George Harrison, were married at Brownlow Hill Register Office.

1933

Feb 18: Yoko Ono, future second wife of John Lennon, was born.

1934

Sep 19: Brian Epstein, future manager of The Beatles, was born in England.

1936

That year: Richard Starkey and Elsie Gleave, parents of Richard Starkey (Ringo Starr), were married.

1938

Dec 3: Alfred "Freddie" Lennon and Julia Stanley, parents of John Lennon, were married at the Mount Pleasant Register Office, Liverpool.

1940

Jun 23: Stuart Sutcliffe was born in Edinburgh, Scotland.

July 7: Richard Starkey (Ringo Starr) was born at Royal Liverpool Children's Hospital, Liverpool. His parents resided on Madryn Street in the Dingle, the poorest section of Liverpool.

Oct 9: John Winston Lennon was born at Oxford Street Maternity Hospital, Liverpool, England.

1941

Nov 24: Randolph Peter Best (Pete Best) was born in Madras, India.

That year: James McCartney and Mary Patricia Mohin, parents of Paul McCartney, were married.

1942

Jun 18: James Paul McCartney was born at Walton Hospital, Liverpool, England. His family rented an apartment in Anfield.

1943

Feb 25: George Harrison was born at 12 Arnold Grove, Waretree, Liverpool, England. He was the fourth and youngest of the Harrison children.

Dec: John Lennon's father, Alfred, jumped ship in America while employed as a steward, and deserted his wife, Julia, and his son John.

That year: Ringo's parents, Richard and Elsie Gleave Starkey, were divorced. For a time, Elsie worked as a barmaid to support herself and her son.

1945

That year or 1946: John's mother, Julia, placed John in the care of her sister, Mimi Stanley Smith, and her husband, George Smith, at 251 Menlove Avenue, Woolton, a suburb of Liverpool.

1946

Jul: Freddie Lennon reemerged and took John on a holiday to Blackpool during which he tried to persuade his son to leave the country with him. Although given the choice of living with his father, John chose to remain with his Aunt Mimi, so he could be closer to his mother, Julia. By 1949 Julia resided with her common-law husband, John Dykins, whom John nicknamed "Twitchy."

That year: Ringo was taken to Myrtle Street Children's Hospital suffering from a burst appendix and peritonitis. He remained in a coma for several weeks and spent nearly a year in the hospital.

1953

Apr 17: Ringo's mother, Elsie, married Harry Graves, who became Ringo's stepfather.

1955

Jun 5: John's uncle, George Smith, died suddenly, leaving John to be raised by his aunt Mimi.

1956

Oct 31: Paul McCartney's mother, Mary Patricia Mohin McCartney, died.

Early that year: John Lennon, 16, formed a skiffle group, first dubbed The Black Jacks, but quickly renamed The Quarry Men, named for John's school, Quarry Bank High School, consisting of himself on guitar and his friend Pete Shotton on washboard. Bill Smith was one of several friends who would join the group, many on an intermittent basis. Skiffle was a form of music played on washboards and other instruments, many of them homemade, to create a kind of country music sound. John and Pete were soon joined by Nigel Whalley and Ivan Vaughan, who took turns playing the tea chest bass. Rod Davis (banjo), Colin Hanton (drums) and Eric Griffiths (guitar) also joined. The actual membership of the band varied from day to day, depending on who showed up and who didn't. Len Garry, a friend of Ivan Vaughan's, also joined the group and became its permanent bass player when Nigel Whalley decided to devote all of his time to managing The Quarry Men.

That year: Paul McCartney wrote his first song, "I Lost My Little Girl."

1957

Jun 9: The Quarry Men auditioned at Carroll Levis' "TV Star Search" at Liverpool's Empire Theater. This talent contest was conducted before a live audience; winners appeared on Levis' ATV "Discoveries" television show. The Quarry Men did poorly, and the winners were The Sunnysiders, a group that featured Nicky Cuff, a midget, on vocals and tea chest bass.

Jun 22: The Quarry Men played at an outdoor party on Rosebery Street in Liverpool, doing afternoon and evening sets from the back of a coal truck.

Jul 6: An annual summer garden fete, sponsored by St. Peter's Parish Church, was held in the town of Woolton. The various forms of entertainment included afternoon and evening performances by The Quarry Men, whose sets included "Cumberland Gap," "Railroad Bill" and "Maggie Mae." At the invitation of Ivan Vaughan Paul McCartney attended, saw The Quarry Men perform, and was introduced to John, who was slightly drunk at the time. Paul joined the others in a jam session after the fete and did his versions of Little Richard's "Long Tall Sally" and "Tutti Frutti." He demonstrated his ability to tune a guitar and memorize complete lyrics to rock and roll songs, skills that none of The Quarry Men had yet mastered; he also wrote out the words to "Twenty Flight Rock" and "Be-Bop-a-Lula." John could see Paul's obvious talent and felt he had two choices: either to remain the strongest member of the group by keeping Paul out or to make the group stronger by bringing Paul in.

Jul 20: John invited Paul to join The Quarry Men. Paul's entry into the band did strengthen it, as John had predicted. Bookings for the group improved when promoter Charlie McBain hired them to play at dances at the Broadway Conservative Club and the Wilson Hall in Garston.

Aug 7: Nigel Whalley booked The Quarry Men into the Cavern Jazz Club on Matthew Street, Liverpool for one night only. The club offered mostly jazz entertainment and occasionally skiffle but did not allow rock and roll. The Quarry Men played some Elvis Presley and Chuck Berry numbers but were quickly ordered to desist.

Oct 18: Paul McCartney made his debut with The Quarry Men at the Conservative Club's New Clubmoor Hall, Liverpool, where he botched his guitar solo during "Guitar Boogie."

Nov 7–Dec 7: The Quarry Men performed at Wilson Hall, Garston (Nov 7, Dec 7); Stanley Abattoir Social Club, Liverpool (Nov 16); and the Conservative Club's New Clubmoor Hall (Nov 23).

Middle of that year: John entered the Art College of Liverpool Institute on Hope Street, Liverpool.

Late that year: Rod Davis left The Quarry Men. Nigel Whalley, a victim of tuberculosis, resigned as their manager.

1958

Jan 10–Mar 13: The Quarry Men played the New Clubmoor Hall (Jan 10); the Cavern Club (Jan 24); Wilson Hall, Garston (Feb 6); and the Morgue Skiffle Cellar, Liverpool, on its opening night (Mar 13).

Feb 6: The Quarry Men again appeared at Wilson Hall, Garston. It was perhaps at this appearance that Paul McCartney's friend George Harrison met The Quarry Men. After filling in on guitar with the group more frequently, George was eventually accepted as a member, which now included John, Paul, George, Len Garry, Eric Griffiths and occasionally John "Duff" Lowe on piano. Eventually Garry and Griffiths would drop out.

Jul 15: John Lennon's mother, Julia, was killed when she was struck by a car driven by a drunken off-duty policeman. She had been waiting for a bus after a visit with John and Mimi. While John continued to reside with his aunt, his two half sisters, Julia and Jacqui, were sent to live with their aunt Harriet, youngest sister of John's mother.

Dec 20: The Quarry Men, whose bookings had rapidly dried up, played at the wedding of George Harrison's brother Harry in Liverpool.

(b) Middle of that year: The Quarry Men, including John, Paul, George, Colin Hanton and John "Duff" Lowe, recorded "That'll Be the Day" and "In Spite of All the Danger," the latter a McCartney/Harrison composition, at Liverpool's Kensington Recording Studio for 25 shillings. The only copy of this recording is the original shellac disc, now owned by Paul McCartney. Part of "That'll Be the Day" was aired on BBC2 television on Sep 12, 1985 with Paul's voice-over narration.

Late that year: The Quarry Men failed an audition for ABC Television in South Manchester.

1959

Jan 1: The Quarry Men played Wilson Hall, Garston. Shortly thereafter Colin Hanton—furious with the others—quit the group following a row that occurred after a particularly drunken, wild engagement. The loss of Quarry Men drummers would remain a chronic problem.

Jan 24: The Quarry Men appeared at the Woolton Village Club in Liverpool.

Aug 29: The Quarry Men began performing at Mona Best's Casbah Coffee Club in the Bests' basement in West Derby, Liverpool and continued to play there each Saturday into October. They also reportedly performed under the name "The Rainbows." Mona's son, Pete, later was a drummer with a group called The Blackjacks. Ken Browne performed with John, Paul and George for a very short time here.

Oct 10: Ken Browne quit The Quarry Men, and the group left the Casbah for a time following a dispute over wages. The other members objected to Mona Best paying Browne. The group played the Casbah again in Dec 1960, and from then until the club closed in Jun 1962.

Middle of Oct: The Quarry Men's name was changed to Johnny and The Moondogs, and the group again auditioned for Carroll Levis' "TV Star Search" at Liverpool's Empire Theater, still in search of a spot on his "Discoveries" television show. They again finished behind Nicky Cuff's group, now called The Connaughts, but qualified for the final round of competition on Nov 15.

Nov 15: The Moondogs performed in the final round of Carroll Levis' "TV Star Search." Without lodgings for the night, they were forced to return home before the final vote (a measure of audience applause) was taken.

Late that decade: A letter written by Paul, noted in Davies lists the following compositions by him and John: "Looking Glass," "Catswalk," "Winston's Walk" (instrumental), "Thinking of Linking," "The One After 909," "Years Roll Along" and "Keep Looking That Way." By this time, the Lennon/McCartney "catalog" also included Paul's "I Lost My Little Girl," and "That's My Woman," "Just Fun," "Too Bad About Sorrows," "Love Me Do," "Hello Little Girl," "When I'm Sixty-Four" and "Hot As Sun." Several would be recorded later, but most have been lost except for improvisational versions heard during the *Let It Be* filming sessions in Jan 1969. Paul's letter also noted the following titles covered by the group: "Ain't She Sweet," "You Were Meant for Me," "Home," "Moonglow" and "You Are My Sunshine." See Lewisohn (1986) for a complete early repertoire.

1960

Jan: John's friend Stuart Sutcliffe, an art student, joined The Quarry Men, having acquired a bass guitar that he never really learned to play. He had purchased it with £65 earned from the sale of one of his paintings.

Apr 23–24: Billed as The Nerk Twins, John and Paul performed on each of these dates at the Fox and Hounds pub, Caversham, Berkshire.

May: John asked Allan Williams to manage The Moondogs. Williams owned the Jacaranda Coffee Bar, where The Moondogs often congregated, and had begun promoting shows that included The Moondogs. Although he was unimpressed with them, he agreed to manage them. He found them a drummer named Tommy Moore, who was far older than the others. The Moondogs were allowed to practice at the Jacaranda while doing odd jobs for Williams, and occasionally played fill-ins.

■ The Silver Beetles were attacked after a show by a gang, and Stu received a severe kick to the head.

May 10: Promoter Larry Parnes sought musicians for tours of north England and Scotland as backing groups allegedly for his star attractions. Through Allan Williams, Parnes set up auditions for Liverpool groups to back Billy Fury, one of his top stars. Fury, a Liverpudlian himself, attended the audition. In reality, however, Parnes wanted to find backing groups who would work for low wages behind his lesser attractions. The announced audition to back Fury brought out every group in Liverpool, including The Moondogs. While preparing for the audition, The Moondogs decided that they needed a new name. Stu suggested "Beetles," modeled after Buddy Holly's group, The Crickets. John changed the "e" to an "a" to create a pun on the word "beat," or "Beatles." Williams strongly disapproved of the new name, and he suggested "Long John and the Silver Beatles" instead. John cut it to "The Silver Beatles" for the Parnes audition. The group experimented with several names at this time, including "Silver Beats," "Silver Beetles" and "Beatals." Parnes thought that—except for drummer Tommy Moore—The Silver Beatles had potential. Indeed, Tommy had arrived late for the audition and was replaced by drummer Johnny "Hutch" Hutchinson of Cass and The Casanovas.

May 14: The group played at Lathom Hall, Liverpool, as The Silver Beats.

May 18: Larry Parnes offered Lennon's group backup work for Johnny Gentle, one of the least known of Parnes' singers, on a nine-day tour of Scotland. Three of The Silver Beatles changed their names for this tour. McCartney became Paul Ramon, George was Carl Harrison and Stu changed his last name to deStael.

May 20–28: The Silver Beetles' tour of Scotland backing Johnny Gentle took place. They played the Town Hall, Alloa, Clackmannanshire (May 20); Northern Meeting Ballroom, Inverness (May 21); Dalrymple Hall, Aberdeen (May 23); St. Thomas' Hall, Deith, Banffshire (May 25); Town Hall, Forres, Morayshire (May 26); Regal Ballroom, Nairn, Nairnshire (May 27); and Rescue Hall, Peterhead, Aberdeen (May 28).

May 23: Prior to the Aberdeen show, the group was involved in an auto accident in which Tommy Moore lost several teeth. Gentle had been driving at the time.

May 30: The first of several Monday night fill-ins for The Silver Beetles at Allan Williams' Jacaranda Coffee Bar in Liverpool.

Jun 2: A 16-year-old boy was nearly kicked to death during a performance by The Silver Beetles at The Neston Institute.

Jun 4: Performance at the Grosvenor Ballroom, Liscard.

Jun 6: The Silver Beetles performed at a dance promoted by Les Dodd at the Grosvenor Ballroom, with Gerry and The Pacemakers.

Jun 9: Performance at the Neston Institute.

Jun 11: Performance at the Grosvenor Ballroom. Lacking a drummer, Lennon asked the rowdy crowd for a volunteer to sit in. One frighteningly burly hooligan named Ronnie took him up on the offer and "played" drums during the performance. Lennon summoned Allan Williams to resolve the "drumming" predicament.

Jun 13: Tommy Moore's last performance on drums with The Silver Beetles at Williams' Jacaranda. He returned to his job driving a forklift. Without a drummer, The Silver Beetles' only steady work was at Williams' strip club, backing a stripper named Janice. Soon afterward Williams became aware of a demand for music groups in Hamburg, Germany. After visiting Hamburg with his friend "Lord Woodbine," Williams decided to send The Silver Beetles there for an engagement.

June 16–Jul 30: Performances at the Neston Institute (Jun 16, Jun 23, Jun 30, Jul 7); Grosvenor Ballroom, Liscard (Jun 18, Jun 25, Jul 2, Jul 9, Jul 16, Jul 23, Jul 30).

Jul 2: Johnny Gentle made a surprise appearance, doing a few numbers with The Silver Beetles at the Grosvenor Ballroom.

July: The Silver Beetles employed Norman Chapman, an amateur, as their drummer for a few shows.

Aug 12: John, Paul and George auditioned Pete Best, Mona Best's son, and invited him to travel to Hamburg with them and become their permanent drummer. Pete's group, The Blackjacks, had recently disbanded. The Silver Beetles were signed for a two-month engagement but ultimately remained in Hamburg for more than three months. Sometime prior to this trip the group again changed its name, shortening it to "The Beatles."

Aug 17–Oct 3: In Hamburg, The Beatles played at The Indra Club, one of Bruno Koschmider's lesser establishments. They were to play a total of eight weeks for four and one-half hours on weeknights and six hours on weekends. Their lodgings consisted of one shared room located behind the screen of a moviehouse called The Bambi-Filmkunsttheater. At the Indra, the clientele consisted of a few prostitutes and their customers, all of them in various states of intoxication. Koschmider urged The Beatles to put more zest into their act, shouting "Make it a show, boys" ("*Mach Shau*"). Lennon went into contortions, began to scream, shout and leap wildly about the stage, and even throw microphones in a rough impersonation of Gene Vincent. The other Beatles began to follow their leader's example, banging their guitars on the stage, lying on the floor and kicking objects around the stage. John would sometimes appear only in his underwear and, on at least one occasion, performed with a toilet seat around his neck. The Beatles also ate, drank, smoked and fought on stage, all of which seemed to add to their appeal. Their wild antics

Quarrymen Rehearse with Stu Sutcliffe Spring 1960 and *Liverpool May 1960* (bootlegs). Two different bootleg releases of a 1960 Beatles rehearsal session, most likely taped in Germany.

began to draw larger crowds, while the long hours of performing improved their abilities as musicians. They got little sleep and, except for Pete Best, used drugs as a stimulant. The audience, which understood little English, laughed and applauded when John shouted "Sieg Heil" and called them "fucking Nazis."

(b) **Aug 17–Nov 20:** The Beatles taped themselves during a rehearsal in Germany. Originally reported as a spring 1960 recording, many believe the tape originated during this period in Hamburg. Songs include: "I'll Follow the Sun," "Hallelujah I Love Her So," "The One After 909," "Movin' and Groovin'," "I Will Always Be in Love With You," "Matchbox," "Wildcat," "That's When Your Heartaches Begin," "Rebel Rouser," "Hello Little Girl" and a number of unidentified songs.

Sep–Oct: In Hamburg, The Beatles became friends with Astrid Kirschher and Klaus Voorman. Voorman was a rock fan and wanted to design record album covers. Both were part of a group of existentialist intellectuals and artists known as "exis." Astrid and Stu soon fell in love and became engaged sometime in Nov or Dec. Astrid, an accomplished photographer, spent many sessions photographing the group.

Oct 4–Nov 30: The Beatles were moved to The Kaiserkeller, Koschmider's top club, after the police closed the Indra. Here, The Beatles continued performing seven days a week. The Kaiserkeller was a vast improvement with audiences of several hundred, though it was often violent. It was at this time that The Beatles became friendly with Richard Starkey, known professionally as Ringo Starr, the drummer for Rory Storm and The Hurricanes, another group on the bill. Pete Best had never fit in with The Beatles, on stage or off, and took no part in their use of drugs or other antics. After hearing Ringo play, the others thought less of Pete's drumming.

(b) **Oct 15:** Paul, John and George were recorded as a backing group for Walter Eymond (stage name: "Lou Walters," but everyone knew him as "Wally") of the Rory Storm group at the tiny Akustic Studio behind Hamburg's train station. Ringo Starr, also from that group, substituted for Pete Best as drummer. Thus this was the first session that included all four Beatles together. The songs recorded included "Summertime," "Fever" and "September Song"; while Ringo performed on all three, the other Beatles only played on "Summertime."

Nov: The Beatles began appearing at Peter Eckhorn's new Top Ten Club during their off hours and breaks from the Kaiserkeller. Koschmider quickly learned of the deception and said this was a violation of their contract.

Nov 21: George Harrison was deported from Germany for being underage and ineligible for work in nightclubs after midnight. Koschmider may have informed the police of Harrison's age as retaliation for The Beatles' desertion to the Top Ten Club.

Nov 29: While moving to new quarters provided by Eckhorn, Paul and Pete accidentally set their room at the Bambi-Filmkunsttheater on fire; when Koschmider learned of this, he had the two arrested for arson. The two were deported the next day and arrived back in Liverpool on Dec 1. John followed on Dec 10 but Stu remained until Feb 1961. Prior to leaving Hamburg, The Beatles concluded a verbal agreement to Eckhorn to play the Top Ten Club the following April—if their immigration difficulties could be resolved.

Dec 17: The Beatles played the Casbah in West Derby where Chas Newby began a short tenure with the group on bass. He was soon replaced by Paul, who would remain on bass throughout The Beatles' existence.

Dec 24: Concert at Grosvenor Ballroom, Liscard.

Dec 27: The Beatles performed at a "Welcome Home Concert" at Liverpool's Litherland Town Hall, promoted by Brian Kelly. They were a smash hit and mobbed by fans afterward. Whatever harm Hamburg may have done The Beatles was offset by a vast improvement in their stage act. The hundreds of hours of playing in Germany had honed their skills to a razor sharpness and given them a confidence and charisma that radiated directly to their audience. Disc Jockey Bob Wooler was so impressed with them that he urged promoters to book them and promoted them himself on his radio shows. Wooler began to M.C. their live performances and signaled their entrances with the overture from "William Tell." He also had them begin playing before the curtain was raised. Their popularity with young girls caused this introduction to result in a screaming rush to the stage. Ironically, much of this adulation was for Pete Best. Once girls nearly pulled him off the stage.

Dec 31: The Beatles again played the Casbah. During that month Neil Aspinall, an accounting student and friend of Pete Best, abandoned his studies to chauffeur The Beatles to and from their performances. Neil later became a permanent assistant and close companion to The Beatles.

1961

Jan 5–30: Performances at the Litherland Town Hall (Jan 5, 26); St. John's Hall, Bootle, Lancashire (Jan 6); Aintree Institute, Liverpool (Jan 7, 13, 14, 18, 21, 27, 28); Casbah Coffee Club, West Derby (Jan 8, 15, 22, 29); Alexandra Hall, Liverpool (Jan 19); Lathom Hall, Seaforth (Jan 20, 21, 28, 30); and Hambleton Hall, Liverpool (Jan 25).

Feb 1–28: Performances at Hambleton Hall, Huyton (Feb 1, 8, 15, 22); Litherland Town Hall (Feb 2, 14, 16, 21, 28); St. John's Hall, Bootle (Feb 3); St. John's Hall, Tuebrook, Liverpool (Feb 17); Lathom Hall, Seaforth (Feb 4, 6, 10, 11, 25); Blair Hall, Walton, Liverpool (Feb 5); Aintree Institute (Feb 8, 10, 15, 18, 22, 25); Cassanova Club, Liverpool (Feb 11, 14, 16, 21, 28); Casbah Coffee Bar (Feb 12, 19, 26); Cavern Club, Liverpool (Feb 21); and Grosvenor Ballroom, Liscard (Feb 24).

Feb 21: The Beatles returned to the Cavern Club in an afternoon appearance. The club was owned by Ray McFall and was located below ground beneath a warehouse at 10 Matthew Street, Liverpool, where the atmosphere was damp and hot. The Cavern had begun a slight shift from jazz to rock and roll music with noontime shows catering to young Liverpool workers on their lunch break. The Beatles would not perform an evening set at the Cavern until Mar 21. The Beatles' repertoire (in both Hamburg and Liverpool) was unlike that of other groups, encompassing the latest top 20 hits, big-band and early U.S. rock and roll classics by Elvis Presley, Buddy Holly, Chuck Berry, Fats Domino, Little Richard, Jerry Lee Lewis, Carl Perkins and others. The Cavern engagement was one of three on this date, the other two occurring at the Cassanova Club and the Litherland Town Hall. Multiple shows on a single day would become routine for The Beatles.

Mar 1–24: Performances at Aintree Institute (Mar 1, 4, 8, 11), Litherland Town Hall (Mar 2); St. John's Hall, Bootle (Mar 3); St. John's Hall, Tuebrook (Mar 10); Casbah Coffee Club, West Derby (Mar 5, 19); Cavern Club (Mar 6, 8, 10, 14, 15, 16, 20, 21 [first evening appearance], 22, 24); The Liverpool Jazz Society (Mar 6, 11, 13, 15, 17); Cassanova Club (Mar 7, 12); Hambleton Hall, Huyton (Mar 8, 20); Grosvenor Ballroom (Mar 10); and Mossway Hall (Mar 17).

Mar 11: After performing at Aintree Institute, The Beatles appeared at an all-night, 12-hour concert, "Rock Around the Clock," the first of several Big Beat Sessions promoted by Sam Leach, at The Liverpool Jazz Society (the once and future Iron Door Club). Other groups on the bill included Kingsize Taylor and The Dominoes, Rory Storm and The Hurricanes, and Gerry and The Pacemakers.

Mar 27–Jul 2: The Beatles returned to Hamburg and began an engagement at the Top Ten Club. They played seven hours per night, eight hours on weekends, with one 15-minute break per hour. Stu Sutcliffe, now plagued with violent headaches and painfully aware of his inadequacies as a musician, decided to quit The Beatles and return to painting. The Beatles also severed their ties with Allan Williams, and sent him a rather crude and tersely worded letter to that effect. Astrid had reorchestrated Stu's appearance by changing his hairstyle and clothing. Although the others ridiculed it at first, all but Pete Best adopted what would eventually become The Beatles' haircut.

May 12: The Beatles met with German orchestra conductor Bert Kaempfert and signed a recording and publishing contract with him.

(rb) **Jun 22–24:** The Beatles served as a backing group for vocalist Tony Sheridan on six songs and recorded two additional songs by themselves, "Ain't She Sweet" and "Cry for a Shadow." Bert Kaempfert produced the sessions, the first under the group's contract. When the first single was issued, Polydor renamed the group "The Beat Brothers" because the word "Beatles" sounded too much like "peedles," a German obscenity. Tony Sheridan claims that he and Paul wrote the unreleased song "Tell Me If You Can."

Jul: Stu Sutcliffe decided to remain in Hamburg when the other Beatles returned to Liverpool, where they found that "beat" music was now the rage.

■ Tony Sheridan's single, "My Bonnie"/"The Saints," was released for the first time in Germany on the Polydor label, by Tony Sheridan and "The Beat Brothers."

Jul 6: The first issue of *Mersey Beat*, a biweekly Liverpool beat music newspaper published by Bill Harry, was printed. The issue contained a satirical article by John, "Being a Short Diversion on the Dubious Origins of Beatles."

Jul 13–31: Performances at St. John's Hall, Tuebrook (Jul 13, 20, 27); Cavern Club (Jul 14 [2 shows], 17, 19 [2 shows], 21, 25 [2 shows], 26, 27, 31); Litherland Town Hall (Jul 17, 24, 31); Holyoake Hall, Liverpool (Jul 15, 22); Blair Hall, Walton (Jul 16, 23, 29, 30); Aintree Institute (Jul 21, 28).

Jul 14: A "Welcome Home" night was held for The Beatles at the Cavern Club.

Jul 20: The second issue of Bill Harry's *Mersey Beat* featured The Beatles on the cover and a report on their recording session with Tony Sheridan in Germany. Brian Epstein ordered 144 copies for his NEMS record shop. Brian began writing record reviews in *Mersey Beat* in Issue 3 on Aug 3 under the title "Stop the World—And Listen to Everything In It: Brian Epstein of NEMS."

Aug 2–31: Performances at the Cavern Club (Aug 2 [2 shows], 4, 5 ["Fabulous All-Night Session"], 8, 9, 10, 11, 14, 16, 18, 21, 23 [2 shows], 25, 28, 29, 30); Aintree Institute (Aug 4, 12, 18, 19, 26); Casbah Coffee Club (Aug 6, 13, 27); Litherland Town Hall (Aug 7); St. John's Hall, Tuebrook (Aug 3, 10, 17, 24, 31); Hambleton Hall (Aug 20); aboard MV *Royal Iris*, River Mersey (Aug 25).

Aug 17: The first Beatles fan letters were printed in *Mersey Beat*.

Sep 1–29: Performances at Cavern Club (Sep 1 [2 shows], 5, 6, 7, 11, 13 [2 shows], 15, 19, 20, 21, 25, 27 [2 shows], 29); Aintree Institute (Sep 2, 9, 16, 23); Hambleton Hall (Sep 3, 17); Litherland Town Hall (Sep 7, 14, 21, 28); St. John's Hall, Tuebrook (Sep 8); Casbah Coffee Bar (Sep 10, 24); Grosvenor Ballroom (Sep 15); Village Hall, Knotty Ash (Sep 15, 22, 29).

Sep 14: Lennon's column, "Around and About," began appearing in *Mersey Beat*. John wrote under the pseudonym "Beat Comer."

Sep: *Mersey Beat* reported the formation of the first Beatles fan club by Bernard Boyle. Also that month, the EP *Tony Sheridan & the Beat Brothers* was released in Germany, marking the first release of "Why" and "Cry for a Shadow," recorded by Sheridan with The Beatles.

Oct 1–14: John and Paul vacationed together in Paris.

Oct 15–31: Performances at the Albany Cinema, Maghull (Oct 15); Hambleton Hall (Oct 15, 29); Cavern Club (Oct 16, 18 [2 shows], 20, 21, 23, 26, 30); David Lewis

Club, Liverpool (Oct 17); Village Hall, Knotty Ash (Oct 27); Casbah Coffee Club (Oct 22); Aintree Institute (Oct 28); Litherland Town Hall (Oct 19, 31).

Oct 19: During their show at the Litherland Town Hall, The Beatles did "Whole Lotta Shakin' Goin' On," "What'd I Say?," "Red Sails in the Sunset" and "Hit the Road, Jack," together with Gerry and The Pacemakers, the two groups spontaneously dubbing themselves "The Beatmakers." Karl Terry of The Cruisers also joined in.

Oct 28: Legend would have us believe that on this date a youth named Raymond Jones attempted to purchase the record "My Bonnie" at Brian Epstein's NEMS record store in Liverpool. The shop was part of the larger department store owned by Epstein's father, with Brian managing the record shop. According to this story, Epstein had never heard of this song or of The Beatles. But Bill Harry claims that he discussed The Beatles and other local groups with Epstein and that Brian was aware of their popularity as reported in *Mersey Beat*. As noted on Aug 3, Brian had even begun writing record reviews for *Mersey Beat* and ordered many copies of the paper for his shop. Moreover, Lewisohn (1986) adds that, by Oct 27, Epstein had begun selling tickets to Sam Leach's Operation Big Beat, and the tickets bore The Beatles' name at the top of a list of groups.

Nov 1–29: Performances at the Cavern Club (Nov 1 [2 shows], 3, 4, 7 [2 shows], 8, 9, 13, 14, 15 [2 shows], 17, 18, 21, 22, 23, 27, 29 [2 shows]); at the Merseyside Civil Service Club, Liverpool (Nov 7, 14, 21, 28); Litherland Town Hall (Nov 9); Tower Ballroom, New Brighton (Nov 10, 24); Casbah Coffee Club (Nov 19, 24); Aintree Institute (Nov 11); Hambleton Hall (Nov 12, 26); Village Hall, Knotty Ash (Nov 10, 17).

Nov 9: Brian Epstein and his assistant, Alistair Taylor, visited the Cavern. After seeing The Beatles, Brian's interest in them extended far beyond finding their record.

Nov 10: The Beatles performed two sets at the Tower Ballroom, New Brighton, as part of Sam Leach's Operation Big Beat. Between those two sets they appeared at the Village Hall in Knotty Ash. They commuted back and forth that night with Neil Aspinall, who had graduated to the status of The Beatles' road manager.

Nov 24: Following a show at the Casbah, The Beatles appeared at Sam Leach's Operation Big Beat II at New Brighton's Tower Ballroom. They were joined on stage for a time by American R&B singer Davy Jones (not to be confused with Davy Jones of The Monkees).

Dec 1–29: Performances at the Cavern Club (Dec 1, 2, 5, 6, 8, 11, 13 [2 shows], 15, 16, 19, 20, 21, 23, 27, 29, 30); Tower Ballroom, New Brighton (Dec 1, 8, 15, 26); Casbah Coffee Club (Dec 3, 17); Palais Ballroom, Aldershot (Dec 9); Blue Gardenia Club, London (Dec 9—unscheduled); Hambleton Hall (Dec 10).

Dec 3: At their first formal meeting with Brian Epstein, The Beatles discussed Brian's proposal to act as their manager, but The Beatles would not commit themselves and a second meeting was arranged.

Dec 6: The Beatles met with Brian Epstein for a second time. Lennon, as leader of the group, accepted Brian's proposal to act as the group's manager, but no formal contract had yet been prepared.

Dec 8: The Beatles performed at the Cavern Club and later at the Tower Ballroom, New Brighton, performing their own sets and also backing Davy Jones at both venues.

Dec 9: As part of a tour close to London, The Beatles were booked at Palais Ballroom, Aldershot. The advertising that Sam Leach had paid for in a local paper was not run, and as a result only 18 people showed up for the concert. The Beatles, at first reluctant to play at all, were spurred on by Paul, who told them, "Let's show we're professionals." They performed a high-powered two-hour, nonstop session, after which a raucous party involving The Beatles and Sam Leach took place including an impromptu "football match." The noisy affair resulted in the police being summoned and Leach and The Beatles were asked to leave town. The group then retired to The Blue Gardenia, a London night club, where The Beatles played a few numbers to an enthusiastic crowd.

Dec 10: The Beatles informally agreed to a contract making Brian Epstein their manager, pending his showing an ability to obtain a recording contract for them. Epstein also promised to obtain their release from their recording contract with Bert Kaempfert in Hamburg. Epstein instructed The Beatles to be more punctual and physically appealing. They began to play a planned program during performances rather than choosing songs at random, and they ceased shouting at people in the audience and eating, drinking and fighting on stage. Eventually, they would be dressed in stylish collarless suits. Through his influence as a large record retailer, Brian persuaded Decca Records to send someone to see The Beatles at the Cavern Club.

Middle of Dec: Mike Smith, A&R (Artists and Repertoire) manager for Decca Records, visited the Cavern Club and saw The Beatles. He agreed to audition them in London.

(b) That year: Several titles of unreleased Beatles numbers were noted during the Aug 28, 1986 auction at Sotheby's, including several written by Stu Sutcliffe and a 1961 Beatles play list.

1962

(rb) Jan 1: The Beatles auditioned for Mike Smith, A&R man for Decca Records in London, recording 15 songs.

Jan 3–31: Performances at the Cavern Club (Jan 3 [2 shows], 5, 6, 9, 10, 11, 12, 15, 17 [2 shows], 19, 20, 22, 24 [2 shows], 26 [2 shows], 30, 31); Casbah Coffee Club (Jan 7, 14, 21, 28); Hambleton Hall (Jan 13); Tower Ballroom (Jan 12, 19, 26); Kingsway Club, Southport (Jan 22, 29); Aintree Institute (Jan 27).

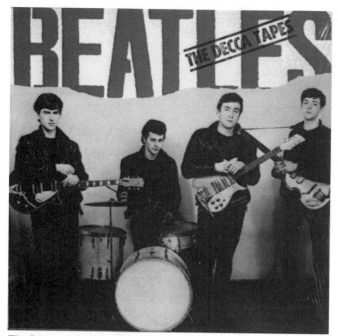

The Decca Tapes (bootleg). Bootleggers offered all 15 songs from The Beatles' failed audition for Decca. Virtually all other releases omit the three Lennon/McCartney numbers.

Jan 4: A *Mersey Beat* poll of 5,000 readers found that The Beatles were Liverpool's most popular group. Gerry and The Pacemakers finished second.

Jan 5: Single "My Bonnie"/"The Saints" released in the U.K.

Jan 24: The Beatles signed a contract making Brian Epstein their manager. He was to receive 25 percent of their earnings. Alistair Taylor witnessed the contract, which Brian did not actually sign.

Feb 1–28: Performances at the Cavern Club (Feb 1, 3, 7 [2 shows], 9 [2 shows], 13, 14, 15, 17, 19, 21 [2 shows], 23, 24, 27, 28); the Beatle Club, a venue rented by Brian Epstein in West Kirby for this one occasion (Feb 1); the Oasis Club, Manchester (Feb 2); Casbah Coffee Club (Feb 4, 11, 18, 25); Technical College Hall, Birkenhead (Feb 9, 16, 23); Youth Club, St. Paul's Presbyterian Church Hall, Birkenhead (Feb 10); Tower Ballroom (Feb 15, 16, 23); YMCA, Wirral (Feb 24); Floral Hall, Southport (Feb 20); Kingsway Club, Southport (Feb 26).

Feb 12: The Beatles auditioned for BBC Radio in Manchester.

Feb 20: Brian Epstein wrote to Bert Kaempfert in Hamburg requesting that he release The Beatles from their May 1961 recording contract. Kaempfert graciously agreed in a Mar 3 letter to Epstein, requesting only that The Beatles agree to record for Polydor during their spring engagement in Hamburg.

Mar 1–31: Performances at the Cavern Club (Mar 1, 3, 5, 6, 9 [2 shows], 13, 14, 15, 16, 20, 21, 22, 23 [2 shows], 26, 28 [2 shows], 30 [2 shows]); the Storyville Jazz Club, Liverpool (Mar 1, 8, 15); St. John's Hall, Bootle (Mar 2); Tower Ballroom, New Brighton (Mar 2); Casbah Coffee Club (Mar 4, 11, 18, 25); the Kingsway Club, Southport (Mar 5); Youth Club, Tranmere (Mar 10); Heseall Jazz Club, Wirral (Mar 24); Odd Spot Club, Liverpool (Mar 29); Village Hall, Knotty Ash (Mar 17); Subscription Rooms, Stroud, Gloucestershire (Mar 31).

(b) Mar 7: The Beatles recorded songs for the BBC Radio Light Programme, "Teenager's Turn (Here We Go)," aired the following day, at the Playhouse Theater, Manchester, marking their radio debut.

Mar 17: The Beatles performed at a dance promoted by Sam Leach at the Village Hall, Knotty Ash, with Rory Storm and The Hurricanes. Leach's engagement party followed the performances, attended by both groups, and lasted well into the next day.

Mar: 24 The Beatles began wearing suits as their stage costume at the Heswall Jazz Club show.

Mar: Decca's head of A&R, Dick Rowe, turned down The Beatles and signed Brian Poole and The Tremoloes instead. Brian Epstein, however, used The Beatles' Decca audition tape to seek further recording auditions.

■ **(b)** The Beatles recorded themselves rehearsing a few songs, reportedly at the Cavern Club. The songs include the unreleased "Catswalk," later retitled "Cat Call." The tape may actually date from later in the year.

Apr 1–7: Performances at the Casbah Coffee Club (Apr 1, 7); Cavern Club (Apr 2, 4 [2 shows], 5, 6, 7); Tower Ballroom (Apr 6), Liverpool Pavilion (Apr 2).

Apr 5: The Beatles' Fan Club presented "The Beatles for Their Fans, or an Evening with George, John, Paul, and Pete" at the Cavern Club.

Apr 7: George missed two performances due to illness.

Apr 10: In Hamburg, following a series of violent headaches, Stu Sutcliffe died in an ambulance on the way to the hospital at the age of 22. His death was attributed to a brain hemorrhage. All of The Beatles, except George who followed later, arrived in Hamburg the next day to begin another engagement running through Jun.

(r) Apr 13–May 31: The Beatles' undertook a seven-week engagement in Hamburg at the new Star-Club. In Apr The Beatles again served as a backing group during a Tony Sheridan recording session.

Apr 23: Single "My Bonnie"/"The Saints" released in the U.S. on the Decca label.

Apr–May: When Brian had the Decca tape cut onto acetate discs, the recording engineer liked what he heard and sent Epstein to EMI (Electrical and Musical Industries) Records' publishing company, Ardmore and Beechwood, headed by Sidney Coleman. Coleman offered to publish two of the songs, both written by Lennon and McCartney—"Love of the Loved" and "Hello Little Girl"—and sent Brian to see George Martin, head of A&R at EMI's subsidiary, Parlophone Records. Brian met with George Martin on May 9. Martin liked the Decca recordings enough to give The Beatles an audition upon their return from Hamburg.

Jun 4: Brian concluded a tentative agreement in which George Martin agreed to give The Beatles an audition with Parlophone. The agreement was most likely not an actual contract, and Martin held off any final decision on signing the group until after he had actually seen them. Epstein sent the following telegram to The Beatles in Hamburg: "Congratulations boys, EMI requests recording session. Please rehearse new material."

(b) Jun 6: The Beatles auditioned for George Martin at EMI's Number 3 studio on Abbey Road in North London. The Beatles and Martin liked each other, but at first Martin did not care for their selections, thought their own compositions were weak and felt that they had no future as songwriters. He also found Pete Best unacceptable as a drummer but was prepared to use a studio drummer for Beatles recording sessions.

Jun 9–30: Performances at the Cavern Club (Jun 9, 16, 25, 29, and 2 shows each on Jun 12, 13, 15, 19, 20, 22, 27); Tower Ballroom (Jun 21, with Bruce Channel, Jun 29); (Victory) Memorial Hall, Northwich (June 23); Casbah Club (Jun 24); Plaza Ballroom, St. Helens (Jun 25); Majestic Ballroom, Birkenhead (Jun 28); Heswall Jazz Club (Jun 30).

(b) Jun 11: The Beatles recorded songs for BBC Radio's "Here We Go," aired Jun 15.

Jun 23: Brian Epstein formed NEMS Enterprises, exclusively to administer The Beatles' affairs.

Jun 24: The Beatles' final appearance at the Casbah Club, which closed at the end of the month.

That summer: John and his girlfriend, Cynthia Powell, decided to marry after they learned that Cynthia was pregnant.

Jul: George Martin offered The Beatles a recording contract with Parlophone Records. For the initial year the contract paid Brian and The Beatles combined one penny per double-sided record for four titles. Four further one-year options were open each carrying an increase in royalties of one farthing per record. Pete Best was never told of the recording contract, and Paul and George had begun to urge Brian Epstein to fire Pete.

(b) Jul 1: The Beatles performed at the Cavern Club with Gene Vincent. A bootlegged recording of Vincent doing "What'd I Say" at the Cavern reportedly includes The Beatles among his backing musicians. During this month, a crude 1¾ i.p.s. tape of The Beatles was recorded by a fan at the Cavern and included several unreleased songs. Paul purchased the tape at Sotheby's auction for £2,100 on Aug 29, 1985.

Jul 1–30: Performances at the Cavern Club (Jul 1, 3, 4, 8, 10, 11, 12, 15, 16, 18 [2 shows], 20, 22, 24, 25 [2 shows], 28, 30); Plaza Ballroom, St. Helens (Jul 2, 9, 16); Majestic Ballroom, Birkenhead (Jul 5, 12, 19, 28); Riverboat Shuffle aboard the MV *Royal Iris*, another waterborne concert (Jul 6); a Golf Club Dance, Birkenhead (Jul 7); Tower Ballroom, New Brighton (Jul 13, 21, 27); Regent Dansette, Flintshire, Wales (Jul 14); McIlroy's Ballroom, Swindon (Jul 17); Kingsway Club, Southport (Jul 23); Cabaret Club, Liverpool (Jul 25); Cambridge Hall, Southport (Jul 26); the Blue Penguin Club, Bootle (Jul 30).

Aug 1–30: Performances at the Cavern Club (Aug 1 [2 shows], 5, 7 [2 shows], 9, 12, 13, 15 [2 shows], 19, 22 [2 shows], 24, 26, 28, 30); Grafton Rooms, Liverpool, with Gerry and The Pacemakers and The Big Three (Aug 3); Victoria Hall, Wirral (Aug 4); Co-op Ballroom, Doncaster (Aug 8); waterborne show aboard the MV *Royal Iris*, with Johnny Kidd and The Pirates and The Dakotas (Aug 10); Odd Spot Club, Liverpool (Aug 11); Riverpark Ballroom, Chester (Aug 16, 23, 30); Majestic Ballroom, Birkenhead (Aug 17, 24); Tower Ballroom, New Brighton (Aug 17); Horticulture Society Dance, Birkenhead (Aug 18); Majestic Ballroom, Crewe (Aug 13, 20); Marine Hall Ballroom, Fleetwood (Aug 25); Floral Hall (Aug 29); Town Hall, Lydney (Aug 31).

Aug 15: Pete Best's final appearance with The Beatles took place at the Cavern Club.

Aug 16 John, Paul and George gave Brian Epstein the unenviable assignment of telling Pete Best that the other boys wanted him out of the group. Best's longtime friend Neil Aspinall decided to quit as The Beatles' road manager, but later changed his mind and decided to stay with the group, largely at Best's insistence. Pete Best was replaced by Ringo Starr of Rory Storm and The Hurricanes, whom The Beatles had met in Germany.

■ A few hours after the firing of Pete Best, The Beatles performed the first of four Thursday sessions at the Riverpark Ballroom in Chester. Johnny "Hutch" Hutchinson (now of The Big Three) once again served as a Beatles substitute drummer on this and the following day.

Aug 18: Ringo Starr made his debut as a Beatle.

Aug 19: Ringo made his Cavern Club debut with The Beatles. The performance was greeted with hostility by a vocal pro-Pete Best faction, and George ended up with a black eye when the group was attacked by fans while entering the club.

(b) Aug 22: Granada TV filmed The Beatles during one of their two shows at the Cavern Club singing "Some Other Guy" and "Kansas City" for its "Know the North" show, scheduled to be aired Nov 7. The film was not shown, however, perhaps due to poor sound quality. While both film clips survive, the soundtrack for "Kansas City" was destroyed.

Aug 23: John and Cynthia were married at Mount Pleasant Register Office, Liverpool, the same place where John's parents had been married.

■ *Mersey Beat* announced The Beatles' change in drummers, and the reaction from Pete's fans was violent. Protest petitions were signed and The Beatles were jeered while on stage at the Cavern Club.

Sep 1–30: Performances at the Subscription Rooms, Stroud (Sep 1); the Cavern (Sep 2, 3, 6, 9, 10, 12, 13, 16, 17, 19, 20, 23, 26 [2 shows], 28, 30); Queen's Hall, Widnes (Sep 3, 10, 17); Rialto Ballroom, Liverpool (Sep 6); Newton Dancing School, Wirral (Sep 7); YMCA, Birkenhead (Sep 8); Majestic Ballroom, Birkenhead (Sep 8, 22); Riverpark Ballroom, Chester (Sep 13); Tower Ballroom (Sep 14, 21); Memorial Hall, Norwich

(Sep 15); Heswall Jazz Club (Sep 25); aboard MV *Royal Iris* (Sep 28); Oasis Club, Manchester (Sep 29).

(rb) Sep 4: The Beatles' first formal recording session with George Martin took place at EMI's number 2 studio at Abbey Road. They recorded "Love Me Do" (Version I) with Ringo on drums, and the unreleased "How Do You Do It?" Although strongly opposed to recording the latter, they did so at George Martin's insistence.

(rb) Sep 11: The Beatles recorded "Love Me Do" (Version II) and "P.S. I Love You," both with session drummer Andy White on drums and Ringo on tambourine and maracas. A slow version of "Please Please Me" was recorded, but the tape has not survived.

Sep 12: Cavern Club appearance with Freddie and The Dreamers. The Beatles also served as a backing group for vocalist Simone Jackson.

Sep 14: The Beatles appeared at the Tower Ballroom, New Brighton in Sam Leach's Operation Big Beat V. Also on the bill were Rory Storm and The Hurricanes, Gerry and The Pacemakers, Bill J. Kramer with The Coasters, and others.

Oct 1: The Beatles signed a formal, legally binding contract with Brian Epstein for five years. As their manager, Brian was to receive 25% of The Beatles' earnings.

Oct 2–28: Performances at the Cavern Club (Oct 2, 3, 4, 7, 10 [2 shows], 12, 13, 17 [2 shows], 19, 21, 26); Hulme Hall, Port Sunlight (Oct 6, 27); Rialto Ballroom, Liverpool (Oct 11); Tower Ballroom, New Brighton (Oct 12); Majestic Ballroom, Birkenhead (Oct 15); La Scala Ballroom, Runcorn (Oct 16); Majestic Ballroom, Hull (Oct 20); Queen's Hall, Widnes (Oct 22); Public Hall, Lancashire (Oct 26); Empire Theatre, Liverpool (Oct 28).

Oct 5: The Beatles' first single "Love Me Do"/"P.S. I Love You," was released in the U.K. Brian bought 10,000 copies, the number he had learned was needed for a top 20 hit. Radio Luxembourg played the record on this date.

Oct 6: The Beatles autographed copies of "Love Me Do" at Dawson's Music Shop in Widnes.

Oct 8: The Beatles recorded an appearance on Radio Luxembourg's "Friday Spectacular" show, aired Oct 12.

Oct 12: The Beatles were second on the bill to Little Richard at the Tower Ballroom in New Brighton.

Oct 17: Between Cavern shows, The Beatles made their television debut with a live appearance on Granada TV's "People and Places" show transmitted from Manchester.

Oct 25: The Beatles recorded "Love Me Do," "A Taste of Honey" and "P.S. I Love You" for BBC's "Here We Go" show in Manchester, aired on Oct 26.

(r) Oct 27: An interview with The Beatles was recorded by members of a boy's club for a hospital radio station in Cheshire and was aired the following day. The interview was done just prior to The Beatles' performance at a Saturday night Recreations Association Dance. The interview was released on a flexi disc with Mark Lewisohn's 1986 *The Beatles Live!*

Oct 28: The Beatles performed on a bill topped by Little Richard at Liverpool's Empire Theater.

Oct: Release of EP *Ya Ya* in Germany, the first release of "Sweet Georgia Brown."

Nov 1–14: The Beatles' fourth engagement in Hamburg, a two-week booking at the Star-Club. They returned to London on Nov 15.

Nov 16: The Beatles recorded their second "Friday Spectacular" show, aired Nov 23 on Radio Luxembourg.

Nov 17–30: Performances at Matrix Hall, Conventry (Nov 17); the Cavern (Nov 18, 19, 21 [2 shows], 25, 28, 30); Majestic Ballroom, Birkenhead (Nov 22, 29); Adelphi Ballroom, West Bromwich (Nov 19); Floral Hall, Southport (Nov 20); Royal Lido Ballroom, Prestatyn (Nov 24); the "Young Idea Dance" at Lewis' Department Store, Liverpool (Nov 28); Town Hall, Earlstown (Nov 30); Tower Ballroom, New Brighton (Nov 23).

Nov 23: The Beatles auditioned for BBC Television, which they failed. They also gave an evening performance at the Arts Ball held at the Tower Ballroom in New Brighton in aid of a children's charity.

(rb) Nov 26: The Beatles recorded "Please Please Me" and "Ask Me Why." George Martin informed the group on the spot that "Please Please Me" would be their first number one, which it eventually was. The Beatles also recorded "Tip of My Tongue," but the tape has not survived.

Nov 27: The Beatles recorded an appearance on BBC Radio's "Talent Spot," aired on Dec 4. They did "Love Me Do," "P.S. I Love You" and "Twist and Shout."

Late Nov: On George Martin's advice, Brian Epstein retained Dick James as publisher for original Beatles songs.

Dec 1–16: Performances at the (Victory) Memorial Hall, Northwich (Dec 1); Peterborough (Dec 2); Tower Ballroom (Dec 1, 7); Majestic Ballroom, Birkenhead (Dec 15 [2 shows]); the Cavern (Dec 5 [2 shows], 7, 9, 10, 12 [2 shows], 16); Club Django, Queen's Hotel, Southport (Dec 6); Oasis Club, Manchester (Dec 8); La Scala Ballroom, Runcorn (Dec 11); Embassy Cinema, Peterborough (Dec 2); Corn Exchange, Bedford (Dec 13); Music Hall, Shrewsbury (Dec 14).

Dec 2: The Beatles bombed badly during an appearance in Peterborough on the bill with Frank Ifield.

Dec 3: The Beatles appeared on a live telecast of "Discs-a-GoGo," transmitted from the TWW studios in Bristol.

Dec 4: The Beatles appeared on a live telecast of Associated-Rediffusion's "Tuesday Rendezvous," transmitted from Kingsway studios in London. They sang "Love Me Do."

Dec 9: George Martin attended The Beatles' evening session at the Cavern to assess the feasibility of recording a live album there.

Dec 15: The Beatles did two shows at the Majestic Ballroom in Birkenhead, one celebrating the *Mersey*

Beat poll winners, which had found The Beatles voted the top local group for the second consecutive year.

Dec 17: The Beatles appeared live on Granada TV's "People and Places" show.

Dec 18: The Beatles left Liverpool for their fifth and final Hamburg engagement, again at the Star-Club, ending on Jan 1, 1963. The engagement was arranged before their recent success with EMI, and they resented going.

Dec 27: "Love Me Do" reached number 17 on "Record Retailer's" top 50 chart.

(rb) Dec 31: Ted "Kingsize" Taylor of The Dominoes made an audiotape of a Beatles' performance at the Star-Club. This recording, or portions of it, was released beginning in 1977 on a variety of LPs and singles. A total of 30 Beatles songs recorded during this performance became available on records. A recording of The Beatles singing "Red Hot" (usually mistitled "My Girl Is Red Hot"), never released but available on bootlegs, also appears to be from this performance.

1963

Jan 1: The Beatles returned to London.

Jan 2–6: The Beatles made a brief tour of Scotland, including performances at Two Red Shoes Ballroom, Elgin (Jan 3); Town Hall in Dingwall (Jan 4); Museum Hall in Bridge of Allan (Jan 5); Beach Ballroom in Aberdeen (Jan 6).

Jan 8: The Beatles appeared on a live telecast of STV's "Round-Up," transmitted from Glasgow; they sang "Please Please Me."

Jan 10–30: Performances at the Cavern (Jan 11, 17, 20, 23, 30, 31); Majestic Ballroom, Birkenhead (Jan 17, 31); Grafton Rooms, Liverpool (Jan 10); Plaza Ballroom, Old Hill (Jan 11); Invicta Ballroom, Chatham (Jan 12); Wolverham Welfare Association Dance, Wirral (Jan 14), Floral Ballroom, Morecambe (Jan 18); Town Hall Ballroom, Whitchurch (Jan 19); Assembly Hall, Mold, Wales (Jan 24); Cooperative Hall, Darwen (Jan 25); El Rio Club, Macclesfield (Jan 26); King's Hall, Stoke-on-Trent (Jan 26); Three Coins Club, Manchester (Jan 27); Majestic Ballroom, Newcastle-upon-Tyne (Jan 28).

Jan 11: Single "Please Please Me"/"Ask Me Why" released in the U.K.

Jan 13: The Beatles were filmed as they mimed to "Please Please Me" for an appearance on ABC-TV's "Thank Your Lucky Stars," aired Jan 19. When the show was aired The Beatles were a tremendous hit, with both the show and their latest single receiving rave reviews. They were, at last, interviewed and written up in the London papers. Their sharp wit and unique appearance rapidly increased their popularity, and The Beatles were finally on their way.

Jan 16: The Beatles recorded "Chains," "Please Please Me," "Ask Me Why" and "Three Cool Cats" for BBC Radio's "Here We Go" at the Playhouse Theater in Manchester. The show aired on Jan 25, with "Three Cool Cats" cut from the broadcast.

Jan 21: Vee Jay Records signed The Beatles for U.S. releases.

■ The Beatles recorded "Chains," "Please Please Me" and "Ask Me Why" for Radio Luxembourg's "The Friday Spectacular," aired Jan 25.

(b) Jan 22: The Beatles recorded appearances on BBC Radio's "Saturday Club," aired Jan 26, and "The Talent Spot," aired Jan 29. Finally, they were interviewed live on the BBC show "Pop Inn."

Feb 1–28: Performances at Assembly Rooms, Tamworth (Feb 1); Maney Hall, Sutton Coldfield (Feb 1); the Gaumont, Bradford (Feb 2); the Cavern (Feb 3, 4 [final Cavern lunchtime session], 19); Doncaster's Gaumont (Feb 5); Bedford's Granada (Feb 6); Wakefield's Regal (Feb 7); Carlisle's ABC (Feb 8); Sunderland's Empire (Feb 9); Azena Ballroom, Sheffield (Feb 12); Astoria Ballroom, Oldmam (Feb 12); Majestic Ballroom, Hull (Feb 13); Locarno Ballroom, Liverpool (Feb 14); Ritz Ballroom, King's Heath (Feb 15); Carfax Assembly Rooms, Oxford (Feb 16); Queen's Hall, Widnes (Feb 18); St. James Street Swimming Baths, Doncaster (Feb 20); Majestic Ballroom, Birkenhead (Feb 21); Oasis Club, Manchester (Feb 22); Mansfield's Granada (Feb 23); Coventry Theater (Feb 24); Casino Ballroom, Leigh (Feb 25); Taunton's Gaumont (Feb 26); York's Rialto (Feb 27); Shrewsbury's Granada (Feb 28).

Feb 2–Mar 3: The Beatles performed their first nationwide tour for the bottom-of-the-bill fee of £80 per week. The bill was headed by Helen Shapiro.

(rb) Feb 11: In a single 10-hour session The Beatles recorded 10 new songs for their first album, *Please Please Me*. George Martin chose numbers from their Cavern Club act in an effort to capture the excitement of their live performances.

Feb 17: The Beatles recorded an appearance on "Thank Your Lucky Stars," televised on Feb 23, and sang "Please Please Me."

Feb 20: The Beatles appeared on BBC Radio's "Parade of the Pops" show and sang "Love Me Do" and "Please Please Me."

Feb 22: Beatles song publisher Dick James formed Northern Songs Ltd. exclusively for Beatles compositions.

Feb 23: "Please Please Me" reached number one on *Disc's* chart in the U.K., becoming The Beatles' first number-one hit. It reached Number one in *New Musical Express* on Mar 1 and on the following day in *Melody Maker*.

Feb 25: Single "Please Please Me"/"Ask Me Why" released in the U.S. on the Vee Jay label but made no showing on any of the pop charts.

Mar 1–31: Performances at Southport's Odeon (Mar 1); Sheffield's City Hall (Mar 2); Hanley's Gaumont (Mar 3); Plaza Ballroom, St. Helens (Mar 4); Elizabethan Ballroom, Nottingham (Mar 7); Royal Hall, Harrogate (Mar 8); East Ham's Granada (Mar 9); Hippodrome Theatre, Birmingham (Mar 10); Bedford's Granada (Mar 12); York's Rialto (Mar 13); Wolverhampton's Gaumont (Mar 14); Bristol's Colston Hall (Mar 15);

Please Please Me (© Apple Corps Ltd.). This version of The Beatles' first album is the stereo half-speed master edition issued by Mobile Fidelity Sound Labs.

Sheffield's City Hall (Mar 16); Petersborough's Embassy (Mar 17); Gloucester's Regal (Mar 18); Cambridge's Regal (Mar 19); Romford's ABC (Mar 20); West Croydon's ABC (Mar 21); Doncaster's Gaumont (Mar 22); Newcastle's City Hall (Mar 23); Liverpool's Empire (Mar 24); Mansfield's Granada (Mar 26); Northampton's ABC (Mar 27); Exeter's ABC (Mar 28); Lewisham's Odeon (Mar 29); Portsmouth's Guildhall (Mar 30); Leicester's De Montfort Hall (Mar 31).

(rb) Mar 5: The Beatles began recording "From Me to You" and "Thank You Girl," both completed later, and unreleased recordings of "The One After 909."

Mar 6: The Beatles recorded "Misery," "Do You Want to Know a Secret," "Please Please Me" and "I Saw Her Standing There" for BBC Radio's "Here We Go," aired Mar 12 with the last song cut from the broadcast.

Mar 7: The Beatles performed at a *Mersey Beat* Showcase, the first of several shows organized by Brian Epstein under that title, each featuring several acts.

Mar 9: The Beatles began a U.K. tour with a show at East Ham's Granada. They were to appear in support of Chris Montez and Tommy Roe, but they quickly were given top billing.

Mar 11: The Beatles recorded their third (and last) "Friday Spectacular" show for Radio Luxembourg, aired Mar 15.

Mar 12: John missed the Granada concert and the next two Beatles appearances due to illness.

(b) Mar 16: The Beatles appeared live on BBC Radio's "Saturday Club."

Mar 21: The Beatles recorded "Misery," "Do You Want to Know a Secret" and "Please Please Me" for BBC Radio's "On the Scene," aired Mar 28.

Mar 22: LP *Please Please Me* released in the U.K.

Mar: NEMS Enterprises signed its second group, Gerry and The Pacemakers. Their first recording was a song The Beatles had rejected, "How Do You Do It?" which reached number one on Mar 22.

(b) Apr 1: The Beatles recorded an appearance for BBC Radio's "Side by Side" show, aired May 13.

(b) Apr 3: The Beatles recorded an appearance on BBC Radio's "Easy Beat," aired Apr 7.

(b) Apr 4: The Beatles recorded songs for BBC Radio's "Side by Side" show, aired Jun 24.

Apr 4–27: Performances at the Stowe School, Buckinghamshire (Apr 4); Leyton Swimming Baths (Apr 5); Pavilion Gardens Ballroom, Buxton (Apr 6); Savoy Ballroom, Southsea (Apr 7); Gaumont State Cinema, Kilburn (Apr 9); Majestic Ballroom, Birkenhead (Apr 10); Cooperative Hall, Middleton (Apr 11); Cavern Club (Apr 12); Riverside Dancing Club, Tenbury Wells (Apr 15); Majestic Ballroom, Luton (Apr 17); Royal Albert Hall, London (Apr 18); King's Hall, Stoke-on-Trent (Apr 19); Mersey View Pleasure Grounds Ballroom, Frodsham (Apr 20); Empire Pool, Wembley (Apr 21); Pigalle Club, Piccadilly, London (Apr 21); Floral Hall, Southport (Apr 23); Majestic Ballroom, Finsbury Park (Apr 24); Fairfield Hall, Croydon (Apr 25); Shrewsbury Music Hall (Apr 26); (Victory) Memorial Hall, Northwich (Apr 27).

Apr 5: A private Beatles concert for EMI executives at EMI House in London, during which the group was presented with its first silver disc, for "Please Please Me," presented by *Disc* magazine.

Apr 8: Cynthia Lennon gave birth to a boy, John Charles Julian Lennon.

Apr 9: The Beatles appeared live on BBC Radio's "Pop Inn" and on AR-TV's "Tuesday Rendezvous" televised from Kingsway studios, London.

Apr 11: Single "From Me to You"/"Thank You Girl" released in the U.K.

Apr 13: The Beatles recorded an appearance on BBC-TV's "The 625 Show," at London's Lime Grove Studios, aired Apr 16, marking the group's BBC television debut. They sang "From Me to You," "Thank You Girl" and "Please Please Me."

Apr 14: The Beatles recorded "From Me to You" for U.K. TV's "Thank Your Lucky Stars," aired Apr 20. Following the session they attended a performance by a new group called The Rolling Stones at the Crawdaddy Club in Richmond.

Apr 16: The Beatles appeared live from Granada TV's Manchester Studio on "Scene at 6:30."

(b) Apr 18: The Beatles appeared live on BBC Radio's "Swinging Sound '63" show, broadcast from Royal Albert Hall. They were billed second behind Del Shannon.

Apr 19: Another appearance at one of Epstein's *Mersey Beat* Showcase shows.

Apr 21: The Beatles performed at the *New Musical Express* Poll Winner's Concert at Empire Pool, Wembley.

Apr 28: John and Brian Epstein began a short vacation in Spain. Paul, George and Ringo left for Santa Cruz, Tenerife. All of them returned on May 9.

May 5: "From Me to You" reached number one in the top 20 of *Music Week* and remained at number one for seven weeks, The Beatles' second number-one hit.

May 10: George served as a judge at the Lancashire and Cheshire Beat Group Contest in Liverpool.

May 11–31: Performances at the Imperial Ballroom, Nelson (May 11); Sunderland's Rink Ballroom (May 14); Chester's Royalty (May 15); Grosvenor Rooms, Norwich (May 17); Slough's Adelphi (May 18); Hanley's Gaumont (May 19); Southampton's Gaumont (May 20); Ipswich's Gaumont (May 22); Nottingham's Odeon (May 23); Walthamstow's Granada (May 24); Sheffield's City Hall (May 25); Liverpool's Empire (May 26); Cardiff's Capitol (May 27); Worcester's Gaumont (May 28); York's Rialto (May 29); Manchester's Odeon (May 30); Southend's Odeon (May 31).

May 12: The Beatles were filmed singing "From Me to You," aired May 18 on U.K. TV's "Thank Your Lucky Stars."

(b) **Middle of May:** John recorded a demo of "Bad to Me," to be recorded the following month by Billy J. Kramer.

May 16: The Beatles appeared live on "Pops and Lenny" on BBC-TV, aired from BBC Television Theatre in Shepherd's Bush Green. They reportedly sang "From Me to You," "Please Please Me," "After You've Gone" and joined in with other performers on the show's theme.

May 18: The Beatles began a concert tour of Britain with a performance at the Adelphi in Slough. Also on the bill were Roy Orbison and Gerry and The Pacemakers. This was the first tour on which The Beatles were featured at the top of the bill. They always entered to a hail of screams and soft jelly babies candy, which George had publicly mentioned that he liked. Prior to the show, Gerry Marsden of The Pacemakers presented The Beatles with their second silver disc, for "From Me to You."

(b) **May 21:** The Beatles recorded appearances for BBC's "Saturday Club" and "Steppin' Out," aired May 25 and Jun 3 respectively.

(b) **May 24:** The Beatles recorded the first of 15 weekly half-hour BBC Radio shows called "Pop Go The Beatles," aired Jun 4.

May 27: Single "From Me to You"/"Thank You Girl" released in the U.S. on the Vee Jay label and made no showing on the charts. Its highest *Billboard* position in 1963 was 116.

(b) **Jun 1:** The Beatles recorded songs for two more "Pop Go The Beatles" shows, aired Jun 11 and 18.

Jun 1–30: Performances at Tooting's Granada (Jun 1); Brighton's Hippodrome (Jun 2); Woolwich's Granada (Jun 3); Birmingham's Town Hall (Jun 4); Leeds's Odeon (Jun 5); Glasgow's Odeon (Jun 7); Newcastle's City Hall (Jun 8); Blackburn's King George's Hall (Jun 9); Bath's Pavilion (Jun 10); Grafton Rooms, Liverpool (Jun 12); Palace Theatre Club, Offerton (Jun 13); Southern Sporting Club, Manchester (Jun 13); Tower Ballroom, New Brighton (Jun 14); Salisbury City Hall (Jun 15); Romford's Odeon (Jun 16); Guildford's Odeon (Jun 21); Abergavenny's Town Hall, Wales (Jun 22); Astoria Ballroom, Middlesbrough (Jun 25); Majestic Ballroom, Newcastle (Jun 26); Queen's Hall, Leeds (Jun 28); Great Yarmouth's ABC (Jun 30).

Jun 12: The Beatles performed a charity concert for the National Society for Prevention of Cruelty to Children at Liverpool's Grafton Rooms.

(b) **Jun 17:** The fourth "Pop Go The Beatles" was recorded and aired Jun 25.

Jun 18: While in a violent, drunken stupor, John severely beat Bob Wooler during a 21st birthday party held for Paul at his Auntie Gin's house. John's attack was prompted when Wooler hinted that John and Brian Epstein may have had a homosexual affair during their recent vacation in Spain. Wooler subsequently sued John, but the matter was settled out of court when John apologized to Wooler and paid him £200.

(b) **Jun 19:** The Beatles recorded an appearance on BBC's "Easy Beat" radio show, aired Jun 23.

Jun 22: John recorded an appearance for BBC-TV's "Juke Box Jury," aired Jun 29.

Jun 23: The Beatles recorded an appearance on "Lucky Stars (Summer Spin)," aired Jun 29.

(b) **Jun 24:** The Beatles recorded an appearance on "Saturday Club," aired Jun 29.

Jun 27: Paul attended a recording session of Billy J. Kramer with The Dakotas, who were cutting two Lennon/McCartney numbers, "Bad to Me" and "I Call Your Name."

(b) **Middle of that year:** A reel-to-reel tape of George composing "Don't Bother Me" was auctioned at Sotheby's in 1989 but did not sell. The tape also reportedly contains some guitar exercises recorded at a Bournemouth hotel in Aug 1963.

(r) **Jul 1:** The Beatles recorded "She Loves You" and "I'll Get You."

(b) **Jul 2:** The Beatles recorded another edition of "Pop Go The Beatles," aired Jul 16.

Jul 3: The Beatles recorded "From Me to You," "A Taste of Honey" and "Twist and Shout" for BBC Radio's "The Beat Show," aired the following day.

Jul 5–31: Performances at Old Hill's Plaza Ballroom (Jul 5); (Victory) Memorial Hall, Northwich (Jul 6); Blackpool's ABC (Jul 7, 14); Winter Gardens, Margate (Jul 8–13 [2 shows each night]); Ritz Ballroom, Rhyl, Wales (Jul 19, 20); Blackpool's Queens (Jul 21); Weston-super Mare's Odeon (Jul 22–27); Great Yarmouth's ABC (Jul 28); Imperial Ballroom, Nelson (Jul 31).

(b) **Jul 10:** The Beatles recorded songs for BBC Radio's "Pop Go The Beatles" shows aired July 23 and 30.

Jul 12: EP *My Bonnie* released in the U.K.

■ EP *Twist and Shout* released in the U.K.

(b) **Jul 16:** The Beatles recorded 18 songs for BBC Radio's "Pop Go The Beatles" shows aired Aug 6, 13, and 20.

(b) **Jul 17:** The Beatles recorded an appearance on BBC Radio's "Easy Beat," aired Jul 21.

(rb) **Jul 18:** The Beatles recorded "You Really Got a Hold on Me," "Money (That's What I Want)" and "(There's a) Devil in Her Heart." They also recorded unreleased takes of "Till There Was You."

(b) **Jul 22–27:** The Beatles' concert series at Weston-super Mare's Odeon. The Beatles made several unreleased recordings on a reel-to-reel machine with Gerry Marsden, of The Pacemakers at the time, including readings from the Bible. Film of The Beatles was shot in Weston-super Mare by Dezo Hoffman on Jul 27 and aired nearly 20 years later, on Dec 3, 1982, on BBC Channel 4's "The Tube."

- LP *Introducing The Beatles* released in the U.S. by Vee Jay. A second version, with slightly altered contents, was issued on Jan 27, 1964.

(b) **Jul 24:** A reel-to-reel tape made at Abbey Road during The Fourmost's recording of "Hello Little Girl," attended by The Beatles, was auctioned at Sotheby's in 1989 for £5,720.

Jul 26: The Lennon/McCartney composition "Bad to Me" was released on a single in the U.K. by Billy J. Kramer with The Dakotas. Released in the U.S. Sep 23.

(b) **Jul 30:** The Beatles taped an interview with Phil Tate for "Non Stop Pop," aired by BBC on Aug 30. They also recorded "Long Tall Sally," "She Loves You," "Glad All Over," "Twist and Shout," "You Really Got a Hold on Me" and "I'll Get You" for BBC Radio's "Saturday Club," aired Aug 24.

- *(rb)* The Beatles recorded "It Won't Be Long," "Till There Was You," "Please Mr. Postman" and "Roll Over Beethoven."

Beatles at the Beeb Vol. 1 (bootleg). One of many bootlegs featuring songs recorded exclusively for BBC Radio, including many never officially released by The Beatles.

(b) **Aug 1:** The Beatles recorded the 11th and 12th editions of "Pop Go The Beatles," aired Aug 27 and Sep 3 respectively.

- *The Beatles Book*, a British monthly fan magazine devoted entirely to The Beatles, published its first issue in the U.K.

Aug 2–31: Performances at Liverpool's Grafton Rooms (Aug 2); Cavern Club (Aug 3); Blackpool's Queens (Aug 4); Abbotsfield Park, Urmston (Aug 5); Springfield Ballroom, St. Savior, Jersey (Aug 6, 7, 9, 10); Auditorium, Candie Gardens, St. Peter Port, Guernsey (Aug 8); Blackpool's ABC (Aug 11, 25); Llandudno's Odeon, Wales (Aug 12–17); Princess Theater, Torquay (Aug 18); Bournemouth's Gaumont (Aug 19–24); Southport's Odeon (Aug 26–31).

Aug 3: The Beatles performed for the last time at the Cavern Club.

Aug 11: Mal Evans met The Beatles at Manchester Airport, when they returned from the Channel Islands. Evans would remain assistant road manager to Neil Aspinall throughout The Beatles' group years.

Aug 14: The Beatles recorded an appearance on Granada Television's "Scene at 6:30," aired Aug 19.

Aug 18: The Beatles filmed an appearance on the U.K. TV show "Lucky Stars (Summer Spin)," aired Aug 24.

Aug 23: The single "She Loves You"/"I'll Get You" was released in the U.K. and went immediately to number one based on advance orders of 500,000 copies. It was The Beatles' third number-one hit. The *New Musical Express* carried an article in which Ringo mentioned that he had written a song called "Don't Pass Me By," which The Beatles would not record until 1968.

(b) **Aug 27–28:** The Beatles recorded a special appearance for the BBC-TV documentary "The Mersey Sound," aired Oct 9 in the U.K. A clip from the film was aired in the U.S. on "The Jack Paar Show" on Jan 3, 1964. Filming was done at BBC's Manchester studios with a live concert recorded on the first day at Southport's Little Theatre.

Sep 1: The Beatles recorded an appearance on ABC-TV's "Big Night Out," aired Sep 7.

(b) **Sep 3:** The Beatles recorded their final three "Pop Go The Beatles" shows for BBC Radio, which aired Sep 10, 17, and 24 respectively.

Sep 4–15: Performances at Worcester's Gaumont (Sep 4); Taunton's Gaumont (Sep 5); Luton's Odeon (Sep 6); Croydon's Fairfield Hall (Sep 7); Blackpool's ABC (Sep 8); Preston's Public Hall (Sep 13); (Victory) Memorial Hall, Northwich (Sep 14); Royal Albert Hall, London (Sep 15 "Great Pop Prom").

Sep 6: EP *The Beatles Hits* released in the U.K.

(b) **Sep 7:** The Beatles recorded songs for BBC Radio show "Saturday Club" aired Oct 5, the fifth anniversary edition of that show.

Sep 10: John and Paul attended a Rolling Stones rehearsal and offered the group their song "I Wanna Be Your Man," finishing the composition on the spot. Earlier in the day The Beatles received an award as the top vocal group of the year at a Variety Club luncheon. The next day *Melody Maker* announced that The Beatles had been voted the most popular recording artists in Britain.

(r) Sep 11: The Beatles recorded "All I've Got to Do" and "Not a Second Time."

(rb) Sep 12: The Beatles recorded "Don't Bother Me," "Little Child," "Hold Me Tight" and "I Wanna Be Your Man." They also recorded four messages for Australian radio.

Sep 16: Single "She Loves You"/"I'll Get You," turned down by Capitol, was released in the U.S. by a small New York label, Swan. It did not reach the top 100 in *Billboard* in 1963, but did so in 1964.

■ The Beatles embarked on a two-week vacation. George and his brother Peter flew to Benton, Illinois to visit their sister, Louise. George thus became the first of The Beatles to visit the U.S. John and Cynthia went to Paris, while Paul and Ringo visited Greece.

Sep 19: *Cashbox* magazine in the U.S. selected "She Loves You" as its "Newcomer of the Week."

Oct 4: The Beatles made their first live appearance on the Associated-Rediffusion TV show "Ready, Steady, Go." They mimed to their recordings of "Twist and Shout," "I'll Get You" and "She Loves You." The appearance was released on videocassette *Ready, Steady, Go! Volume 2* in May 1984.

Oct 5–29: Performances at Glasgow's Concert Hall (Oct 5); Carlton Theatre, Kirkcaldy (Oct 6); Dundee's Caird Hall (Oct 7); Trentham Gardens (Oct 11); London Palladium (Oct 13); Southport's Floral Hall (Oct 15); Pavilion Gardens Ballroom, Buxton (Oct 19); Karlaplan Studio, Stockholm, Sweden (Oct 24 [radio show recording]); Sundsta Laroverk, Karlstad, Sweden (Oct 25); Kungliga Hallen, Stockholm (Oct 26 [2 shows]); Goteborg, Sweden (Oct 27 [3 shows]); Boras, Sweden (Oct 28); Eskilstuna, Sweden (Oct 29).

Oct 9: On John's 23rd birthday, The Beatles taped "She Loves You" for BBC Radio's "The Ken Dodd Show," aired Nov 3. BBC-TV aired the documentary film *The Mersey Sound*, which included film of The Beatles shot on Aug 27 and 28.

Oct 11: "She Loves You" became The Beatles first U.K. gold disc with sales surpassing 1 million copies.

(b) Oct 13: The Beatles appeared live on ATV's "Sunday Night at the London Palladium" before a TV audience of 15 million. The term "Beatlemania" is said to date from press coverage following this highly successful appearance.

(b) Oct 16: The Beatles recorded an appearance on BBC Radio's "Easy Beat," aired Oct 20. The Beatles were also chosen to appear in the Royal Command Variety Performance in London on Nov 4. Although they were Britain's best-selling pop group, their income was relatively small and would remain so for a long time, under their original Parlophone contract.

■ John cut a demo of "I'm in Love" for the Fourmost around this time.

(r) Oct 17: The Beatles recorded "I Want to Hold Your Hand" and "This Boy." They also recorded the first of their annual fan club Christmas records, *The Beatles Christmas Record*. The U.S. Fan Club did not receive this record until Dec 18, 1970 when it was included on the album *The Beatles Christmas Album*.

Oct 18: The Beatles made a surprise, live appearance on Granada TV's "Scene at 6:30."

Oct 20: The Beatles recorded an appearance for the U.K. TV show "Thank Your Lucky Stars," aired Oct 26.

(b) Oct 24: The Beatles began a tour of Sweden with a performance before a live audience at Karlaplan studio in Stockholm, which was broadcast later on the Swedish radio show "Pop '63."

(b) Oct 30: The Beatles recorded an appearance on the Swedish TV show "Drop In," aired Nov 3.

Oct 31: The Beatles arrived home at London's Heathrow Airport and were greeted by hundreds of screaming fans. The Beatles themselves now finally realized the extent of their popularity and of "Beatlemania." American TV host Ed Sullivan was at Heathrow Airport and later met with Brian Epstein to set a tentative booking for The Beatles on his U.S. TV show for early 1964. Businessmen began seeking out Brian to get The Beatles' endorsements on any number of products. The firm Stramsact, was set up in the U.K. and an affiliate, Seltaeb (Beatles spelled backward), was to assign Beatles' merchandising rights in the U.S. Brian also received an offer from United Artists for The Beatles to make their first feature film. The Beatles would receive £25,000 each and 7½% of the picture's earnings.

Nov 1: Lennon/McCartney's "I'll Keep You Satisfied," by Billy J. Kramer with The Dakotas, was released as a single in the U.K.; released in the U.S. on Nov 11.

■ EP *The Beatles (No. 1)* released in the U.K.

Nov 1–Dec 14: A Beatles tour of the U.K. included performances at Cheltenham's Odeon (Nov 1); Sheffield's City Hall (Nov 2); Leeds' Odeon (Nov 3); Prince of Wales Theater, London (Nov 4 [Royal Variety Show, not part of tour]); Slough's Adelphi (Nov 5); Northampton's ABC (Nov 6); Adelphi, Dublin, Ireland (Nov 7); Ritz Cinema, Belfast (Nov 8); East Ham's Granada (Nov 9); Birmingham's Hippodrome (Nov 10); Plymouth's ABC (Nov 13); Exeter's ABC (Nov 14); Bristol's Colston Hall (Nov 15); Bournemouth's Winter Gardens Theatre (Nov 16); Coventry Theater (Nov 17); Wolverhampton's Gaumont (Nov 19); ABC Cinema, Ardwick, Manchester (Nov 20); Carlisle's ABC (Nov 21); The Globe, Stockton-on-Tees (Nov 22); Newcastle's City Hall (Nov 23); Hull's ABC (Nov 24); Cambridge's Regal (Nov 26); York's Rialto (Nov 27); Lincoln's ABC (Nov 28); Huddersfield ABC (Nov 29); Sunderland's Empire (Nov 30); Leicester's De Montfort Hall (Dec 1); Grosvenor House Hotel, London (Dec 2); Portsmouth's Guildhall (Dec 3); Empire Theater, Liverpool (Dec 7); Liverpool's Odeon (Dec 7); Lewisham's Odeon (Dec 8); Southend's Odeon (Dec 9); Doncaster's Gaumont (Dec 10); Scarborough's Futurist (Dec 11); Nottingham's

Odeon (Dec 12); Southampton's Gaumont (Dec 13); Wimbledon Palais (Dec 14).

Nov 3: The Beatles were interviewed on BBC Radio's "The Public Ear." Part of this was heard in 1988 on episode 7 of "The Beeb's Lost Beatles Tapes" BBC Radio series.

(b) **Nov 4:** The Beatles performed at the Royal Variety Show at the Prince of Wales Theater in London before an audience that included the Royal Family. The sang "From Me to You," "She Loves You," "Till There Was You" and "Twist and Shout." Prior to the last number, John encouraged those in the cheap seats to join in by clapping, while the rest could just "rattle your jewelry." The performance was filmed and aired on Nov 10 on the ATV network and was a huge success throughout Britain.

Nov 5: Brian Epstein flew to New York to begin promoting The Beatles in the U.S.

Nov 7: An interview by Frank Hall was filmed at Dublin Airport where The Beatles arrived for a concert.

Nov 8: The Beatles recorded an appearance on BBC Ulster's television show "Six O'Clock," aired the same evening. The appearance, taped at the Ritz Cinema in Belfast prior to their concert there, included one number and an interview.

Nov 9: George signed a five-year music publishing contract with Northern Songs Ltd., which he would not renew upon its expiration.

Nov 10: Following their concert at Birmingham's Hippodrome, The Beatles left the theater disguised as policemen.

Nov 11: In New York, following the success of "I Want to Hold Your Hand," Brian Epstein was able to get top billing for The Beatles on Ed Sullivan's U.S. TV show in exchange for them appearing on two shows, Feb 9 and 16, 1964 and taping more songs for a subsequent show. The Beatles' fee was $3,500 each per show and $3,000 for taping.

Nov 12: Paul was stricken with gastric flu. The Beatles' date at Portsmouth's Guildhall and their TV appearance on "Day by Day" were both canceled and rescheduled for Dec 3.

Nov 18: Sir Joseph Lockwood of EMI presented The Beatles with gold and silver discs for the singles "She Loves You" and "I Want to Hold Your Hand," and for the LP *With The Beatles*.

Nov 19: ABC-TV in the U.S. ran its first feature on The Beatles.

(b) **Nov 20:** The Beatles' concert was filmed by Pathe News at the ABC, Ardwick, Manchester. Their performance included "Twist and Shout" and "She Loves You." The 8½-minute film, *The Beatles Come to Town*, began running in movie theaters on Dec 22. The footage was also used in the film *Pop Gear*, released in the U.K. Apr 18, 1965.

Nov 21: All three major U.S. TV networks' evening news broadcasts featured reports and film footage from The Beatles' Nov 16, 1963 Bournemouth show.

Nov 22: The second Beatles LP, *With The Beatles*, was released in the U.K. As with their first album, this one was not released solely to capitalize on a single hit record but was sold on the strength of its overall content.

Advance orders alone totaled 250,000, more than Elvis Presley's largest-selling LP, *Blue Hawaii*.

Nov 26: The Beatles performed at the Regal in Cambridge before an audience of hundreds of fanatical, screaming teenage girls. These scenes had been commonplace for six months, but now the newspapers widely reported them and extensively interviewed The Beatles, who delighted everyone with their verbal wit and charm. Parliament even debated the cost of police protection for The Beatles.

Nov 27: The Beatles appeared on Granada Television's "Scene at 6:30." In addition to performing some songs, they were interviewed by Ken Dodd.

Nov 29: The Beatles' fifth single, "I Want to Hold Your Hand"/"This Boy," was released in the U.K. Advance orders of 1 million placed it instantly at number one, The Beatles' fourth number-one hit.

(b) **Dec 2:** The Beatles recorded an appearance on ATV's "Morecambe and Wise Show," including a rendition of "On Moonlight Bay," and a sketch, aired Apr 18, 1964.

Dec 3: The Beatles appeared on Southern TV's "Day by Day" show.

Dec 4: The Beatles Film Productions Ltd. was formed.

Dec 6: *The Beatles Christmas Record* was released to fan club members in the U.K. only. Beatles records occupied five of the top 20 positions in *New Musical Express*.

(b) **Dec 7:** The Beatles recorded an appearance on BBC-TV's "Juke Box Jury," aired later that evening. The appearance was recorded at the Empire Theater in Liverpool just before the group performed a special concert for members of their fan club. The BBC filmed the concert and aired it as a 30-minute TV special "It's The Beatles!" later that evening.

With The Beatles (© Apple Corps Ltd.). The Beatles' second album in the U.K. The same cover photo was used for their first U.S. Capitol Album, *Meet The Beatles*.

(rb) Dec 10: An interview was recorded with The Beatles prior to their Doncaster show.

Dec 13: Capitol Records signed an agreement giving it first refusal rights to future Beatles releases in the U.S.

Dec 14: The Beatles performed at their Southern Fan Club Convention at Wimbledon Palais.

(b) Dec 15: The Beatles recorded an appearance on a special Christmas version of U.K. TV show "Thank Your Lucky Stars," aired Dec 21.

(b) Dec 17: The Beatles recorded an appearance on "Saturday Club," aired Dec 21.

(b) Dec 18: The Beatles recorded songs for the BBC Radio show "From Us to You," aired Dec 26. This was the first in a series of five holiday specials, four of them with this title and a final one called "The Beatles Invite You to Take a Ticket to Ride."

Dec 20: The *New Musical Express* 12th International Popularity Poll listed The Beatles as number-one group and "She Loves You" as the record of the year. The Beatles were also seen singing "This Boy" on Granada TV's "Scene at 6:30."

Dec 21: The Beatles' NEMS Christmas Show had a preview performance at the Gaumont in Bradford, and on the following day previewed at the Empire in Liverpool.

Dec 24: A second Beatles' film company, Subafilms Ltd., was created.

Dec 24–Jan 11, 1964: The Beatles' NEMS Christmas Show ran during these dates at the Finsbury Park Astoria Theater in London. The Beatles performed sketches and sang nine songs. By this time "She Loves You" had sold 1.3 million copies and "I Want to Hold Your Hand," 1.25 million.

Dec 26: The single "I Want to Hold Your Hand"/"I Saw Her Standing There" was rush released in the U.S. by Capitol Records. Originally scheduled for release on Jan 13, 1964, the release date was moved up in response to large advance orders.

Dec 27: John Lennon and Paul McCartney were named "Outstanding Composers of 1963" by the music critics of the *London Times*.

Dec 29: *Sunday Times* music critic Richard Buckle called Lennon and McCartney the "greatest composers since Beethoven."

Late that year: EMI increased the royalty rate for The Beatles from one penny to two pennies per single. *New Musical Express* reported that 7 million Beatles LPs, EPs and singles had been sold in the U.K.

(b) That year: A reel-to-reel tape made by The Beatles sometime during 1963 was put up for auction, but did not sell, at Sotheby's in 1989. The tape reportedly featured John and Paul singing several tunes including "Over the Rainbow."

1964

(b) Early that year: A reel-to-reel tape dated as early 1964 was auctioned at Sotheby's in 1989 but did not sell. The tape features demos of "If I Fell." Paul cut at least one demo of "A World Without Love" at about this time for Peter and Gordon.

Jan 3: A film clip of The Beatles taken from the BBC documentary film *The Mersey Sound* was aired on U.S. TV on "The Jack Paar Show" on NBC-TV.

(b) Jan 7: The Beatles recorded an appearance on BBC Radio's "Saturday Club," aired Feb 15.

(b) Jan 12: The Beatles made their second live appearance on the U.K. TV show "Sunday Night at the London Palladium."

Jan 15: Vee Jay Records sued Capitol Records and Swan Records in New York over the rights to manufacture and distribute Beatles records in the U.S. In Chicago, Capitol was granted an injunction restraining Vee Jay from continuing to manufacture and distribute Beatles records. Vee Jay countersued on Jan 17.

■ Concert at the Cyrano Theater in Versailles, France.

(b) Jan 16–Feb 4: The Beatles performed a series of concerts in Paris at the Olympia Theater with Trini Lopez and Sylvie Vartan. One of three Jan 19 shows was aired on French radio station Europe 1 and was heard in the U.K. The Jan 22 show was filmed by French TV company ORTF-TV. The Beatles were not particularly popular or even well-known in Paris, and their reception there was far cooler than anywhere else. On Jan 16 they received a telegram announcing that "I Want to Hold Your Hand" had reached number one in *Cashbox* in the U.S. Demos of Lennon/McCartney's "One and One Is Two," composed during this trip were recorded.

Jan 20: LP *Meet The Beatles* released in the U.S. by Capitol.

(b) Jan 24: The Beatles recorded an interview for the British Forces Network.

Jan 27: Single "My Bonnie"/"The Saints" released in the U.S. on MGM label.

(rb) Jan 29: George Martin flew to Paris to supervise German-language recordings of "She Loves You" and "I Want to Hold Your Hand," "Komm, Gib Mir Deine Hand"/"Sie Liebt Dich," released as a single in Germany and later in the U.S. and U.K.

Jan 30: Single "Please Please Me"/"From Me to You" released in the U.S. by Vee Jay.

Jan 31: Single "Sweet Georgia Brown"/"Nobody's Child" released in the U.K.

Late Jan: An associate of New York promoter Sid Bernstein made a deal with Brian Epstein for The Beatles to perform at Carnegie Hall, New York, twice on Feb 12 for a flat fee of $3,500 each.

(r) Early Feb: The Beatles recorded an open-end interview, released in the U.S. in late Feb as a promo.

Feb 3: LP *The Beatles with Tony Sheridan & Their Guests* released in the U.S. on MGM label.

Feb 4: The Beatles appeared on the cover of *Newsweek* magazine in the U.S.

Feb 7: The Beatles arrived in New York. Throughout the morning, radio stations proclaimed their impending arrival and spent almost all of their air time describing the events of the day. The Beatles were shocked at the turnout at JFK Airport, where between 3,000 to 5,000 fans awaited them. They also held their first U.S. press conference on this date and interviews, later released, were recorded. While the U.S. had previously seemed largely uninterested in The Beatles, just after Christmas 1963 "I Want to Hold Your Hand" caught on throughout the country; by Jan 1964, 1.5 million copies of the record had already been sold in the U.S. The first U.S. Beatles Capitol LP, *Meet The Beatles*, went to number one immediately upon its release. It was similar to the U.K. LP *With The Beatles*, but contained fewer songs. This would become standard procedure for Capitol, which was determined to squeeze as much money out of The Beatles' recordings as possible. At least five different labels were now releasing Beatles records in the U.S.: Capitol, Vee Jay, MGM, Tollie and Swan. Seltaeb, the U.S. merchandising subsidiary of Stramsact, was deluged with applications for licenses to market Beatles merchandise.

■ EP *All My Loving* released in the U.K.

(rb) Feb 7–10: The Beatles were interviewed several times by D.J. Murray Kaufman ("Murray The K") and by Ed Rudy.

Feb 8: The Beatles rehearsed for CBS-TV's "The Ed Sullivan Show." They were interviewed live by telephone from New York by Brian Matthew during a broadcast of BBC Radio's "Saturday Club."

(b) Feb 9: The Beatles spent part of the morning rehearsing for "The Ed Sullivan Show" without George, who was ill with a sore throat. In the afternoon they taped a performance with George for the Sullivan show to be aired Feb 23. That evening they made their first appearance live on "The Ed Sullivan Show" and were seen by an estimated 73 million people, or 60 percent of all U.S. TV viewers.

Feb 10: The Beatles held a press conference at the Plaza Hotel in New York.

(rb) Feb 11: The Beatles traveled from New York to Washington, D.C. by train during a blizzard. They were greeted at Washington's Union Station by 3,000 teenagers, screaming as usual, and throwing themselves against a 20-foot-high platform gate. Their first U.S. concert took place at Washington Coliseum before 7,000 fans. The performance was at least partly filmed by CBS-TV and a concert film was screened on a closed circuit basis at movie theaters on Mar 14 and 15. Washington, D.C. disc jockey Carroll James hosted The Beatles' Washington concert and also interviewed the group on radio station WWDC. James claimed to be the first U.S. disc jockey to play "I Want to Hold Your Hand" on the air. The Beatles' visit to the British Embassy on the same day was very unpleasant. During it they were insulted and pushed around by the diplomatic corps and their wives.

(b) Feb 12: Two Beatles concerts promoted by Sid Bernstein were performed at New York's Carnegie Hall, both sellouts. The performance was reportedly taped, but no recording of it has surfaced to date. In England,

Granada TV aired a documentary *Yeah, Yeah, Yeah—The Beatles in New York.*

Feb 13: The Beatles flew to Miami for their second appearance on "The Ed Sullivan Show." They were greeted by 7,000 fans who smashed windows and glass doors in the Miami airport terminal. The Beatles' hotel, the Deauville—like New York's Plaza—became another prison where the group was besieged by thousands of screaming, hysterical teenage girls.

Feb 14: The Beatles rehearsed for their upcoming appearance on "The Ed Sullivan Show."

Feb 15: The Beatles again rehearsed for "The Ed Sullivan Show." For the first time in history, *Billboard* magazine listed five songs by one group (The Beatles) in the top 100: "I Want to Hold Your Hand," "I Saw Her Standing There," "She Loves You," "Please Please Me" and "My Bonnie"; and three LPs on the album chart: *Meet The Beatles* (number one), *Introducing The Beatles* and *With The Beatles*. *Billboard* also described The Beatles as the vanguard of a British pop music invasion.

(rb) Feb 16: In Miami, The Beatles were interviewed by Detroit D.J. Lee Alan at the Deauville Hotel.

■ The Beatles held an afternoon dress rehearsal, taped before a live audience, for "The Ed Sullivan Show." The evening show, aired live from the Deauville Hotel, was seen by an estimated 75 million viewers, the largest TV audience ever up to that time.

(rb) Feb 21: Shortly before leaving the U.S., George was interviewed by phone by Ed Rudy and the group recorded a "Farewell to Miami" message for Miami radio station WQAM. The Beatles were also filmed improvising a tune called "Guitar Blues," and the footage was used in the documentary film, *What's Happening: The Beatles in the U.S.A.*

(b) Feb 22: The Beatles returned to England. A press conference was filmed at London Airport and aired later on BBC-TV's "Grandstand." The group was also interviewed live by telephone during a broadcast of BBC Radio's "Saturday Club."

(b) Feb 23: The Beatles were filmed at Teddington Studios miming to several released recordings; the film aired on Feb 29 in the U.K. on ABC-TV's "Big Night Out." Their Feb 9 taped appearance was aired in the U.S. on "The Ed Sullivan Show."

(r) Feb 25: On George's 21st birthday, The Beatles recorded "You Can't Do That."

(r) Feb 26: The Beatles recorded "I Should Have Known Better."

■ LP *Jolly What! The Beatles & Frank Ifield on Stage* released in U.S. by Vee Jay.

(r) Feb 27: The Beatles recorded "And I Love Her," "Tell Me Why" and "If I Fell."

(b) Feb 28: The Beatles recorded the BBC Radio show "From Us to You" (second in the series of four holiday specials), aired Mar 30. Single "Why"/"Cry for a Shadow" released in the U.K.; released in the U.S. on Mar 27.

(r) **Mar 1:** The Beatles recorded "I'm Happy Just to Dance with You," "Long Tall Sally" and "I Call Your Name."

(b) **Mar 2–Apr 24:** The Beatles shot their first feature film, *A Hard Day's Night*, produced by Walter Shenson, directed by Richard Lester and written by Alun Owen. The film's title was taken from one of Ringo's off-the-cuff remarks.

Mar 2: Single "Twist and Shout"/"There's a Place" released in the U.S. on Tollie label.

Mar 5: Single "Komm Gib Mir Deine Hand"/"Sie Liebt Dich" released in Germany on Odeon label.

Mar 11: It was announced that The Beatles had won the Carl Allen Awards as 1963's best beat group and for best single ("She Loves You"). The awards were presented by Prince Philip on Mar 23.

Mar 13: U.S. sales of LP *Meet The Beatles* reached a record 3.5 million copies. *Billboard* reported that sales of Beatles singles constituted 60% of the market.

Mar 16: Single "Can't Buy Me Love"/"You Can't Do That" was rush-released in the U.S. by Capitol with advance orders for 2 million copies, a U.S. record. It was originally scheduled for release on Mar 30. It was issued in the U.K. on Mar 20.

Mar 18: The Beatles recorded an interview for the BBC Light program, "The Public Ear," aired Mar 22. Portions were aired in 1988 on episode 10 of "The Beeb's Lost Beatles Tapes."

Mar 19: The Beatles were taped miming to "You Can't Do That" and "Can't Buy Me Love," aired Mar 25 on BBC-TV's "Top of the Pops." The Beatles were presented an award as show business personalities of the year for 1963.

(b) **Mar 20:** The Beatles appeared live on the Associated-Rediffusion TV show "Ready, Steady, Go!" The appearance was included on the 1984 home videocassette *Ready, Steady, Go! Volume 1*. The group also received an award from *Billboard* for having the top three songs on the magazine's chart.

Mar 21: "She Loves You" reached number one in the U.S.

Mar 23: John's first book, *In His Own Write*, was published in the U.K. and received good reviews. The book was a collection of short comical works that showcased Lennon's humorous side, his talent for word play and his ability as a cartoonist. Lennon was interviewed by Kenneth Allsop on BBC-TV's "Tonight."

■ "Can't Buy Me Love" reached number one in both the U.K. and U.S. EP *The Beatles: Souvenir of Their Visit to America* and single "Do You Want to Know a Secret"/"Thank You Girl" released in the U.S. by Vee Jay.

Mar 27: In Australia, six of the top-10 hits belonged to The Beatles.

(b) **Mar 31:** The Beatles recorded songs for BBC Radio's "Saturday Club," aired Apr 4. John was also interviewed for the BBC Home Service show, "A Slice of Life," aired May 2.

Mar: Effigies of The Beatles were placed on display in Madame Tussaud's Wax Museum in London. The Beatles were the first rock-and-roll performers to be so honored.

(r) **Early Mar:** Bernice Lumb recorded interviews with John, George, Ringo and Brian Epstein.

Apr 1: John and his father, Freddie Lennon, met for the first time in 17 years.

Apr 4: The Beatles became the only artists in history to have the top five songs on *Billboard* magazine's Hot 100 chart in the U.S. The five songs had been released on a total of four different labels, an equally unique event: (1) "Can't Buy Me Love" (Capitol), (2) "Twist and Shout" (Tollie), (3) "She Loves You" (Swan), (4) "I Want to Hold Your Hand" (Capitol), (5) "Please Please Me" (Vee Jay). The group placed a total of 14 songs in the Hot 100 the following week.

Apr 5: Filming of scenes for *A Hard Day's Night* took place at Marylebone Station in London.

Apr 9: In an out-of-court settlement, Capitol and Vee Jay ended their legal struggle over rights to manufacture and distribute Beatles records, with Capitol obtaining those rights. Vee Jay was permitted to continue releasing Beatles records for a short time.

Apr 10: LP *The Beatles Second Album* released in the U.S.

(rb) **Apr 16:** The Beatles recorded "A Hard Day's Night." An interview with Ed Sullivan was shot on the *A Hard Day's Night* film set and aired on his U.S. TV show on May 24.

(r) **Apr 18:** The Beatles were interviewed by telephone by Art Roberts and Ron Riley of Chicago radio station WLS.

(b) **Apr 19:** The Beatles recorded songs for the TV special *Around the Beatles*. Actual rehearsals and filming of

The Beatles' Second Album (© Apple Corps. Ltd.). One of Capitol's early Beatles albums, all of which contained fewer tracks, different song lineups and different covers from those issued in the U.K.

the show took place during Apr 27 and 28, with The Beatles miming to these prerecorded tracks. The show was aired on May 6.

Apr 23: John received the Literary Prize for *In His Own Write* at Foyle's Literary Luncheon held at the Dorchester Hotel in London. His entire acceptance speech was: "Thank you very much, and God bless you." He did not say "You've got a lucky face," contrary to reports claiming that he did. He made that remark during the Apr 27–28 filming of "Around The Beatles."

(r) **Apr 24:** The Beatles were interviewed by telephone as they concluded filming *A Hard Day's Night*. The interview was edited into an open-ended one—with the questions left out—and released on a Capitol promo disc.

(r) **Apr 25:** Interviews with The Beatles were recorded.

(rb) **Apr 26:** The Beatles were filmed performing during the *New Musical Express* Poll Winners' Concert at the Empire Pool, Wembley. The film was aired in the U.K. on May 10 on ABC-TV's "Big Beat '64," the second of two specials with that title featuring performances from the concert, and the only one to feature The Beatles. A film clip from the show was aired in the U.S. on May 24 along with film of Ed Sullivan interviewing The Beatles on the set of *A Hard Day's Night* on Apr 16. Interviews were also recorded.

Apr 27: Single "Love Me Do"/"P.S. I Love You" released in the U.S. on Tollie label.

■ John's book, *In His Own Write*, was published in the U.S.

Apr 27–28: The Beatles spent these two days rehearsing and filming the Redifussion TV show "Around The Beatles" which aired May 6. They mimed to songs they had recorded on Apr 19. Approximately 20 minutes of The Beatles' musical portion of the show were released on Apr 29, 1985 on the video *The Beatles Live!* The show was repeated on Jun 8, and portions were aired on ABC-TV in the U.S. on Nov 15. In addition to other songs, The Beatles are seen singing "Shout" with all four sharing lead vocal. They also performed a comic Shakespearean sketch, released on the videocassette *Fun with The Fab Four.*

Apr 29: Concert at the ABC in Edinburgh, Scotland.

Apr 30: Concert at the Odeon in Glasgow, Scotland.

■ LenMac Enterprises Ltd., a Beatles music publishing company, was formed.

(b) **May 1:** The Beatles recorded the BBC Radio show "From Us to You" (third in this series of five holiday specials), aired May 18.

May 2: *The Beatles Second Album* reached number one in the U.S.

May 11: EP *Four by The Beatles* released in the U.S. by Capitol.

May 17: Radio Luxembourg's second "This Is Their Life" Beatles special was aired.

May 18: A recorded interview with Paul by David Frost was aired on the U.K. TV show "A Degree of Frost."

May 21: Single "Sie Liebt Dich"/"I'll Get You" released in the U.S.

(rb) **May 24:** An interview with George, Paul and Ringo concerning the filming of *A Hard Day's Night* took place on this date. It was released in Mar 1982 in the U.S. only on promo copies of "The Beatles Movie Medley," where it was titled "Fab Four on Film." Commercial copies intended for release were also pressed, but these were never officially issued. The "Movie Medley" was finally issued with "I'm Happy Just to Dance with You" as the B side. Other interviews were also recorded.

May 29: Single "Ain't She Sweet"/"If You Love Me Baby" released in the U.K. Paul attended recording sessions by Billy J. Kramer with The Dakotas, who were cutting Paul's composition "From a Window."

May 30: "Love Me Do" reached number one in the U.S., nearly two years after The Beatles had recorded it.

May 31: The Beatles performed in one of a series of concerts titled Pops Alive, at the Prince of Wales Theatre in London. The Beatles taped an interview for Australian TV.

(r) **Jun 1:** The Beatles recorded "I'll Cry Instead," "I'll Be Back," "Matchbox" and "Slow Down."

■ Single "Sweet Georgia Brown"/"Take Out Some Insurance on Me Baby" released in the U.S. on ATCO label nearly three years after it was recorded.

(r) **Jun 2:** The Beatles recorded "Anytime at All," "Things We Said Today" and "When I Get Home."

Jun 3: Ringo collapsed during a Beatles photo session and missed the first part of the group's world tour. Recording sessions for this date were canceled abruptly. Ringo, who was suffering from tonsillitis and pharyngitis, would rejoin The Beatles in Australia on Jun 15. His tonsils were not removed until Dec 2.

(b) **Jun 4:** The Beatles performed two concerts at the K.B. Hallen, Copenhagen, Denmark, opening their world tour.

Jun 4–Nov 10: The Beatles' world tour of over 50 cities on four continents took place. Ringo was temporarily replaced by drummer Jimmy Nicol.

(rb) **Jun 5:** A Beatles performance and interview were videotaped by Dutch TV (VARA Broadcasting Co.) at the Zaal Treslong Studio in Hillegom. The show was aired as *The Beatles* on Dutch TV Jun 8 and repeated Jul 18. A press conference was also held. The Beatles mimed to their released recordings, but their microphones were also turned on so a double-track effect was created.

(r) **Jun 6:** The Beatles performed at the Blokker Exhibition Hall (Veilinghal) in the Netherlands. They flew to Hong Kong on the following day.

Jun 9: The Beatles performed two concerts at Hong Kong's Princess Theater.

(r) **Jun 10:** George composed the unreleased song "You'll Know What to Do." No recordings have yet surfaced. The Beatles were interviewed by Bob Rogers and later took an evening flight from Hong Kong to Australia.

(r) Jun 11: The Beatles arrived in Australia at Darwin Airport at 2 A.M. and were interviewed there by John Edwards. They then flew to Sydney's Mascot Airport and later held a press conference at Sydney's Sheraton Hotel. The next day they flew to Adelaide, where they made an appearance on the balcony of their suite at the South Australian Hotel.

(b) Jun 12–13: The Beatles performed two concerts at Adelaide's Centennial Hall on each of these dates. Film of the Jun 12 show was aired on Australian television on Jun 13.

(r) Jun 14: The Beatles flew from Adelaide to Melbourne. Ringo arrived in Sydney and also departed for Melbourne. After his arrival, The Beatles held a press conference in Melbourne. The following day, The Beatles were greeted by more than 250,000 fans along the route to their hotel in Melbourne.

(rb) Jun 15–17: Ringo returned to The Beatles, who performed two concerts at Melbourne's Festival Hall on each of these dates. Songs from a Jun 16 show were aired Jul 1 on the Australian NTN TV special "The Beatles Sing for Shell." The Beatles were guests at the Jun 16 Lord Mayor's Reception.

(r) Jun 18–20: The Beatles flew to Sydney on Jun 18 where they celebrated Paul's 22nd birthday at the Sheraton Hotel. They performed two concerts at Sydney Stadium on each of these three dates.

Jun 19: EP *Long Tall Sally* and LP *The Beatles First* released in the U.K.

(r) Jun 21–23: The Beatles flew from Sydney to Wellington on Jun 21 and performed two concerts each on Jun 22 and 23 at Wellington Town Hall.

(r) Jun 24–25: The Beatles flew from Wellington to Auckland (Jun 24) where they were interviewed. They performed two concerts on each date at Auckland Town Hall.

(r) Jun 26: The Beatles flew from Auckland to Dunedin where they were again interviewed.

■ LP *A Hard Day's Night* released in the U.S. on United Artists label.

(r) Jun 26–30: New Zealand performances at Dunedin's Town Hall (Jun 26 [2 shows]); Christchurch's Majestic Theatre (Jun 27 [2 shows]); Brisbane, Australia's Festival Hall (Jun 29, 30 [2 shows each]). The Beatles flew from Christchurch, New Zealand to Brisbane, Australia via Sydney on Jun 28. During one of The Beatles' two Jun 29 concerts in Brisbane, a group of people threw rotten eggs at them. Police intervened to save the culprits from angry Beatles fans.

(r) Jul 1: The Beatles flew from Brisbane to Sydney, marking the end of their Australia/New Zealand tour. They were interviewed during the day. They departed Sydney for London via Singapore and Frankfurt.

Jul 2: The Beatles arrived at London Airport. Paul played piano on Cilla Black's recording of Lennon/McCartney's "It's for You," recorded on this date. Released in the U.K. on Jul 31 and in the U.S. on Aug 17.

Jul 6: The Beatles' first feature film, *A Hard Day's Night*, premiered in London and was an instant success;

The Beatles attended the premiere. Single "Ain't She Sweet"/"Nobody's Child" released in the U.S. on ATCO label.

Jul 7: The Beatles filmed an appearance on "Top of the Pops," aired the following day. They mimed to released versions of "Long Tall Sally" and "A Hard Day's Night."

Jul 10: The *A Hard Day's Night* LP was released in the U.K., the first Beatles album to contain only Lennon/McCartney songs. The U.S. version of the LP was much different, containing fewer Beatles songs and filled out with several of George Martin's instrumentals from the film score.

■ Single "A Hard Day's Night"/"Things We Said Today" released in the U.K. and in the U.S. on Jul 13 with "I Should Have Known Better" as the B side.

■ The Beatles arrived in Liverpool where they were greeted by approximately 1,500 fans. A formal public ceremony honoring the group was held in front of the Liverpool Town Hall. Following this tribute, the film *A Hard Day's Night* was screened at Liverpool's Odeon Cinema.

Jul 11: The Beatles recorded an appearance on the U.K. TV show "Lucky Stars (Summer Spin)," aired Jul 18.

Jul 12: Concert at Brighton's Hippodrome with The Fourmost and Jimmy Nicol.

(b) Jul 14: The Beatles recorded an appearance on the premiere of BBC Radio's "Top Gear" show, aired Jul 16. Paul was also interviewed for the BBC Overseas Service Show "Highlight," which was broadcast on Jul 18. The interview was repeated on "A Beatle's Eye View" on Sep 11. During the interview Paul sang a bit of "Don't Pass Me By"; he and Ringo mentioned that Starr had written

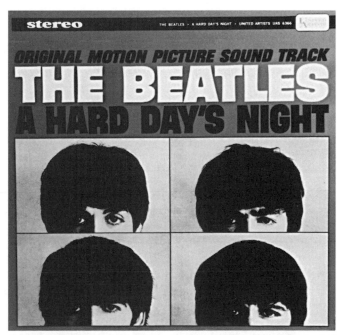

A Hard Day's Night (U.S.) (© Apple Corps Ltd.). Both stereo and mono editions of the U.S. album contained *mono* versions of The Beatles' songs and some unique mixes and edits not released elsewhere.

the words to the song and McCartney the tune. The Beatles did not record it until 1968.

(b) Jul 17: The Beatles recorded a Bank Holiday Show, the fourth in their "From Us to You" series of holiday specials and the last one with the "From Us to You" title. It was broadcast on Aug 3.

Jul 18: LP *A Hard Day's Night* reached number one in the U.K.

Jul 19: The Beatles appeared on the TV show "Blackpool Night Out," aired live from the Blackpool ABC Theatre.

Jul 20: Singles "I'll Cry Instead"/"I'm Happy Just to Dance With You" and "And I Love Her"/"If I Fell" and LP *Something New* released in the U.S.

Jul 23: The Beatles performed at a charity concert, Night of 100 Stars, at the London Palladium.

Jul 25: George appeared on the BBC-TV show "Juke Box Jury," and Ringo recorded an appearance on the same show that was aired Aug 1.

■ LP *A Hard Day's Night* reached number one in the U.S. and the single "A Hard Day's Night" reached number one in the U.K.

Jul 26: Concert at Blackpool's Opera House.

Jul 28–29: The Beatles performed concerts at the Ice Hockey Stadium, Stockholm, Sweden.

Jul 29: John recited his poem "Good Dog Nigel" during an appearance on Stockholm television. An ATV special, "Fans, Fans, Fans!" documenting fan reaction to The Beatles, was aired in the U.K.; an earlier, discarded title for the show was "The Road to Beatlemania."

Aug 2–16: Performances at Bournemouth's Gaumont (Aug 2); Scarborough's Futurist (Aug 9); and the Blackpool Opera House (Aug 16).

Aug 3: A 30-minute TV special, "Follow The Beatles," documenting the filming of *A Hard Day's Night* and The Beatles recording in Abbey Road Studios, was aired in the U.K. on BBC-TV.

Aug 11: The Beatles' film *A Hard Day's Night* was released in the U.S. to favorable reviews. Several critics compared The Beatles to the Marx Brothers.

(rb) Aug 14: The Beatles recorded "I'm a Loser" and "Mr. Moonlight," and the unreleased "Leave My Kitten Alone."

Aug 16: Concert at the Blackpool Opera House. Also on the bill were The Kings and The High Numbers.

(rb) Aug 18–Sep 20: The Beatles arrived in San Francisco to begin their tour of the U.S. and Canada. Many interviews and press conferences during this period were later released on several different records. The Beatles quickly saw that Americans had become even more Beatle- crazed than they had been in Feb. Their film had already earned $1.3 million in the U.S. in its first week. At San Francisco airport The Beatles were taken from their plane to a protective iron cage; they were removed just before a mob crushed it. Charles O. Finley, owner of the Kansas City Athletics baseball team, paid The Beatles $150,000 to add a Kansas City concert to the tour. Appearing with The Beatles were Jackie

DeShannon, The Righteous Brothers, The Bill Black Combo and The Exciters. The tour comprised concerts at San Francisco's Cow Palace (Aug 19); Las Vegas' Convention Center (Aug 20); Seattle's Coliseum (Aug 21); Vancouver's Empire Stadium (Aug 22); Los Angeles' Hollywood Bowl (Aug 23); Denver's Red Rocks Ampitheater (Aug 26); Cincinnati's Gardens (Aug 27); New York's Forest Hills Tennis Stadium (Aug 28, 29); Atlantic City's Convention Hall (Aug 30); Philadelphia's Convention Hall (Sep 2); Indianapolis' State Fair Coliseum (Sep 3); The Arena, Milwaukee (Sep 4); Chicago's International Ampitheater (Sep 5); Detroit's Olympia Stadium (Sep 6); Toronto's Maple Leaf Gardens (Sep 7); Montreal's Forum (Sep 8); Jacksonville's Gator Bowl (Sep 11); Boston's Boston Gardens (Sep 12); Baltimore's Civic Center (Sep 13); Pittsburgh's Civic Arena (Sep 14); Cleveland's Public Auditorium (Sep 15); New Orleans' City Park Stadium (Sep 16); Kansas City's Municipal Stadium (Sep 17); Dallas' Memorial Coliseum (Sep 18); Brooklyn's Paramount Theater, New York (Sep 20). Songs performed on the tour included "Twist and Shout," "You Can't Do That," "All My Loving," "She Loves You," "Things We Said Today," "Roll Over Beethoven," "Can't Buy Me Love," "If I Fell," "I Want to Hold Your Hand," "Boys," "A Hard Day's Night" and "Long Tall Sally." (Some shows opened with "I Saw Her Standing There," dropped "She Loves You" and closed with "Twist and Shout").

(b) Aug 22: The concert at Empire Stadium, Vancouver, British Columbia, Canada was filmed while also being recorded from the public address system and from radio broadcasts.

(rb) Aug 23: The Beatles' first Hollywood Bowl Concert took place in Los Angeles. George Martin had flown there to record the concert. Six cuts were released, with seven tracks from their 1965 concert at the same venue, on *The Beatles at The Hollywood Bowl* in 1977. A bit of "Twist and Shout" from the 1964 show is heard on *The Beatles Story* released Nov 23 in the U.S. only.

Aug 24: Single "Slow Down"/"Matchbox" released in the U.S.

Sep 9–10: The Beatles spent two days off at the Key Webster Hotel in Key West, Florida. On Sep 10 they took part in a jam session at their hotel with The Bill Black Combo, Clarence "Frogman" Henry, and The Exciters.

Sep 11: George Harrison formed his own music publishing company, Mornyork Ltd.

Sep 15: During their Cleveland concert, police asked The Beatles to leave the stage for 15 minutes to allow hysterical fans to calm themselves.

Sep 20: The Beatles were seen on U.S. TV on "The Ed Sullivan Show." Their U.S. tour ended with a charity concert for the Cerebral Palsy Fund at Brooklyn's Paramount Theater, New York. The Beatles returned to England the following day.

Sep 25: A group of U.S. businessmen offered Brian Epstein $3.5 million for The Beatles, but Brian declined the offer.

Sep 27: Ringo served as one of the judges for the Oxfan Beat Contest at the Prince of Wales Theatre in London's West End.

(r) Sep 29: The Beatles recorded "I Don't Want to Spoil the Party."

(r) Sep 30: The Beatles recorded "No Reply" and "Every Little Thing."

Oct: Brian Epstein's book *A Cellarful of Noise*, written with Derek Taylor's help, was published.

Oct 1: LP *The Beatles vs. The Four Seasons* released in the U.S. by Vee Jay.

(b) Oct 3: The Beatles recorded three songs for the U.S. TV show "Shindig," aired Jan 20, 1965, before a live audience at the Granville Theatre, Fulham.

(r) Oct 6: The Beatles recorded "Eight Days a Week," with minor work completed on Oct 18.

(rb) Oct 8: The Beatles recorded "She's a Woman."

Oct 9–Nov 10: The Beatles conducted a concert tour of the U.K. with Mary Wells and Tommy Quickly, the final leg of the world tour that had begun on Jun 4 and had taken them through Hong Kong, Denmark, the Netherlands, Australia, New Zealand, Sweden, the U.S., Canada and finally back to England. Performances at Bradford's Gaumont (Oct 9); Leicester's De Montfort Hall (Oct 10); Birmingham's Odeon (Oct 11); Wigan's ABC (Oct 13); the Ardwick ABC, Manchester (Oct 14); Stockton's Globe (Oct 15); Hull's ABC (Oct 16); Edinburgh's ABC (Oct 19); Dundee's Caird Hall (Oct 20); Glasgow's Odeon (Oct 21); Leeds' Odeon (Oct 22); Kilburn's Gaumont (Oct 23); Walthamstow's Granada (Oct 24); Brighton's Hippodrome (Oct 25); Exeter's ABC (Oct 28); Plymouth's ABC (Oct 29); Bournemouth's Gaumont (Oct 30); Ipswich's Gaumont (Oct 31); Finsbury Park's Astoria (Nov 1); Belfast's King's Hall (Nov 2); Luton's Ritz (Nov 4); Nottingham's Odeon (Nov 5); Southampton's Gaumont (Nov 6); Cardiff's Capitol (Nov 7); Liverpool's Empire (Nov 8); Sheffield's City Hall (Nov 9); Bristol's Colston Hall (Nov 10).

Oct 12: LP *Songs, Pictures and Stories of The Fabulous Beatles* released in the U.S. by Vee Jay.

Oct 14: The Beatles performed at the Ardwick ABC, Manchester. They also recorded an appearance on Granada TV's "Scene at 6:30," aired Oct 16.

Oct 16: The Beatles appeared live on the U.K. TV show, "Ready, Steady, Go."

(rb) Oct 18: The Beatles recorded "I Feel Fine," "Kansas City"/"Hey Hey Hey Hey," "I'll Follow the Sun," "Everybody's Trying to Be My Baby," "Rock and Roll Music," "Words of Love."

Oct 25: The Beatles received the following five Ivor Novello Awards for 1963 presented by the British Music Industry: (1) Most Outstanding Contribution to Music in 1963; (2) Most Broadcast Song: "She Loves You"; (3) Top-Selling Record: "She Loves You"; (4) Second Top-Selling Record: "I Want to Hold Your Hand"; (5) Second Most Outstanding Song: "All My Loving."

(rb) Oct 26: The Beatles recorded "Honey Don't" and "What You're Doing." They also recorded their second

annual Christmas record, *Another Beatles Christmas Record*, distributed free to members of their fan club.

Nov 4: EP *Extracts from the Film A Hard Day's Night* released in the U.K.

Nov 6: EP *Extracts from the Album A Hard Day's Night* released in the U.K.

Nov 14: The Beatles recorded an appearance on the U.K. TV show "Thank Your Lucky Stars," aired Nov 21.

Nov 15: Portions of The Beatles TV show, "Around the Beatles," were seen on ABC-TV in the U.S. The show was originally aired in the U.K. on May 6.

Nov 16: The Beatles taped an appearance on BBC-TV's "Top of the Pops," aired Dec 3. They mimed to "I Feel Fine" and "She's a Woman."

(b) Nov 17: In Manchester, The Beatles recorded an appearance on BBC Radio's "Top Gear" show, aired Nov 26.

(b) Nov 23: LP *The Beatles Story* released in the U.S. by Capitol.

■ Single "I Feel Fine"/"She's a Woman" released in the U.S. Released Nov 27 in the U.K.

■ The Beatles recorded an appearance on the TV show "Ready, Steady, Go," aired Nov 27, and released Nov 5, 1984 on videocassette *Ready, Steady, Go! Volume 3.*

Nov 24: Paul's father, James McCartney, married Angela Williams, following a one-week courtship.

(b) Nov 25: The Beatles recorded their final appearance on BBC Radio's "Saturday Club," aired Dec 26.

Nov 29: John taped an appearance on BBC-TV's "Not Only . . . But Also" with Dudley Moore and Peter Cook, and read some of his poems. The show aired on Jan 9, 1965 on BBC2.

Dec 2: Ringo's tonsils were surgically removed at University College Hospital, London.

Dec 4: LP *Beatles for Sale* released in the U.K. only.

Dec 7: George changed the name of his Mornyork Ltd. company to Harrisongs Ltd.

Dec 9: Paul visited Ringo in University College Hospital. Ringo was discharged the following day.

Dec 12: The LP *Beatles for Sale* and the single "I Feel Fine" both reached number one in the U.K.

Dec 15: LP *Beatles '65* released in the U.S.

Dec 18: *Another Beatles Christmas Record* released to fan club, the first Christmas record issued to U.S. members.

Dec 24–Jan 16, 1965: The second annual Beatles three-week Christmas show, "Another Beatles Christmas Show," ran during these dates at the Odeon in Hammersmith. Songs performed included "Twist and Shout," "I'm a Loser," "Baby's in Black," "Everybody's Trying to Be My Baby," "Can't Buy Me Love," "Honey Don't," "I Feel Fine," "She's a Woman," "A Hard Day's Night," "Rock and Roll Music" and "Long Tall Sally."

Dec 26: The single "I Feel Fine" reached number one in the U.S.

Beatles for Sale (U.K.) and *Beatles '65* (U.S.) (© Apple Corps. Ltd.). British and American Beatles albums released in the respective countries in Dec 1964. Capitol would not adopt the British album formats until *Sgt. Pepper* in 1967.

1965

Jan 9: The LP *Beatles '65* reached number one in the U.S.

Jan 27: Maclen (Music) Ltd., a music company was formed with John, Paul and Brian as directors.

Jan 29: Single "If I Fell"/"Tell Me Why" released in the U.K.

Feb 1: EP *4 by The Beatles* released in the U.S.

Feb 4: Paul and Jane Asher departed for a holiday in North Africa.

Feb 11: Ringo and Maureen Cox were married at Caxton Hall Register Office, London, by Registrar D. A. Boreham. John, George and Brian attended, but Paul was on vacation in Africa at the time.

Feb 15: Single "Eight Days a Week"/"I Don't Want to Spoil the Party" released in the U.S.

■ **(rb)** The Beatles recorded "Ticket to Ride," "Another Girl" and "I Need You."

(rb) Feb 16: The Beatles recorded "Yes It Is."

(r) Feb 17: The Beatles recorded "The Night Before" and "You Like Me Too Much." They also won the Carl Allen Award for best group of 1964.

(rb) Feb 18: The Beatles recorded "You've Got to Hide Your Love Away" and "Tell Me What You See." They also recorded the unreleased "If You've Got Trouble." Public sale of Northern Songs Ltd. began on the London Stock Exchange.

(rb) Feb 19: The Beatles recorded "You're Going to Lose That Girl."

(b) Feb 20: The Beatles recorded two takes of the unreleased song "That Means a Lot." They recorded the song again on Mar 30.

(r) Feb 22–Mar 12: The Beatles departed England on Feb 22 for the Bahamas where they began filming *Help!*, their second feature film, on Feb 23. Approximately 1,400 fans bid them farewell at Heathrow Airport. Walter Shenson and Richard Lester again served as producer and director, respectively, as they had on *A Hard Day's Night*, but filmed in color this time and set a far more ambitious schedule in several countries. The screenplay was penned by Marc Behm and Charles Wood from Behm's story. The non-Beatles musical score was composed by Ken Thorne.

Mar 10: The Beatles left the Bahamas for England.

Mar 13: The single "Eight Days a Week" reached number one in the U.S.

Mar 15–20: Filming of *Help!* continued in Austria.

Mar 17: The tentative title for The Beatles' new film was announced as *Eight Arms to Hold You*.

Mar 20: The Beatles were interviewed by phone from Austria on BBC Radio's "Saturday Club" show.

Mar 22: LP *The Early Beatles* released in the U.S.

Mar 24–Apr 30: Filming of *Help!* continued at Twickenham Film Studios in England.

Mar 28: The Beatles recorded an appearance for the U.K. TV show "Thank Your Lucky Stars" at the Birmingham Alpha Studios, aired Apr 3.

(b) Mar 30: The Beatles recorded five more takes of the unreleased song "That Means a Lot."

Apr 6: EP *Beatles for Sale* released in the U.K.

Apr 9: Single "Ticket to Ride"/"Yes It Is" released in the U.K. Released on Apr 19 in the U.S.

Apr 10: The Beatles filmed an appearance on BBC's "Top of the Pops," aired Apr 15. They mimed to "Ticket to Ride" and "Yes It Is."

(b) Apr 11: The Beatles performed at the *New Musical Express* Poll Winner's Concert at Empire Pool, Wembley. The appearance was aired, at least in part, on Apr

18 during the 85-minute U.K. TV special "Big Beat '65." Following the show, The Beatles appeared live on "The Eamonn Andrews Show" on ABC-TV.

■ The single "Ticket to Ride" reached number one in the U.K.

(rb) Apr 13: The Beatles recorded "Help!" They were also interviewed live on BBC's "Pop Inn" during the filming of *Help!* at Twickenham Studios.

Apr 14: The title *Eight Arms to Hold You* was discarded and The Beatles' new film was officially dubbed *Help!*

Apr 16: John and George were interviewed live on the U.K. TV show "Ready Steady Goes Live!"

Apr 19: The Beatles received 1964 Grammy Awards for best vocal performance by a group ("A Hard Day's Night") and for best new artists.

May 3: *Help!* filming continued at Salisbury Plain and at Knighton Down, Larkhill, Wiltshire. Filming resumed at Twickenham Studios on May 6.

May 9: The Beatles attended a Bob Dylan concert at London's Royal Festival Hall. Dylan's music impressed them, particularly John and George, and it had an impact on future Beatles compositions and recordings.

(r) May 10: The Beatles recorded "Dizzy Miss Lizzie" and "Bad Boy."

(b) May 13: The Beatles completed filming *Help!*

May 18: The Beatles did some postproduction work on *Help!* They also appeared in a prerecorded segment on NBC-TV during which they were interviewed by actor Peter Sellers.

(b) May 20: The Beatles recorded the BBC Radio show "The Beatles (Invite You to Take a Ticket to Ride)," aired Jun 7. This was the last BBC Radio show with songs especially recorded by The Beatles, the last in their series of five holiday specials and the only one without the "From Us to You" title. Their first BBC appearance had been on "Teenagers Turn," recorded Mar 7, 1963 and aired the following day.

May 22: The single "Ticket to Ride" reached number one in the U.S. The Beatles appeared on "Dr. Who" on U.K. TV.

(b) May: John appeared briefly in D.A. Pennebaker's documentary film *Eat the Document*, which chronicled Bob Dylan's U.K. tour.

Jun 4: EP *Beatles for Sale (No. 2)* released in the U.K.

Jun 12: It was announced that The Beatles would receive the MBE: Membership of the Most Excellent Order of the British Empire. The prime minister drew up the list, which was then routinely signed by the queen. Several previous recipients were outraged and returned their medals in protest.

(rb) Jun 14: The Beatles recorded "Yesterday," "I'm Down" and "I've Just Seen a Face." Only Paul and George were present during the recording of "Yesterday."

■ LP *Beatles VI* released in the U.S.

(r) Jun 15: The Beatles recorded "It's Only Love."

Middle of Jun: Brian Matthew taped several interviews with The Beatles during their U.S. tour. They were aired Aug 30 on the BBC Radio special, "The Beatles Abroad." Excerpts were heard on episode 12 of the 1988 BBC Radio series "The Beeb's Lost Beatles Tapes."

(b) Jun 16: John recorded an interview for BBC Radio's "The World of Books," aired Jul 3, during which he read his poem "The Fat Budgie" and discussed his new book, *A Spaniard in the Works*.

(r) Jun 17: The Beatles recorded "Wait" and "Act Naturally."

(b) Jun 18: John appeared on BBC1's "Tonight" show to promote his book *A Spaniard in the Works*, and read several selections.

(rb) Jun 20–Jul 3: The Beatles performed two shows on Jun 20 at the Palais des Sports in Paris, France. The second show was aired live by radio station Europe 1 and was filmed by French television. The shows marked the start of a European tour extending through Jul 3 with performances at Palais d'Hiver, Lyons, France (Jun 22 [2 shows]); Velodromo Vigorelli, Milan, Italy (Jun 24 [2 shows]), Palazzo dello Sport, Genoa (Jun 25 [2 shows]); Teatro Adriano, Rome (Jun 27, 28 [2 shows each date]); Palais des Fêtes, Nice, France (Jun 30); Plaza de Toros de Madrid, Madrid, Spain (Jul 2); Plaza de Toros Monumental, Barcelona, Spain (Jul 3). Interviews recorded with The Beatles during the tour were later released on several records.

Jun 24: John's second book, *A Spaniard in the Works*, was published in the U.K. It was issued in the U.S. on Jul 1. John was also interviewed in a prerecorded segment of the U.K. "Today" radio show.

Jul 5: A prerecorded interview with John was aired on the BBC Light show "Teen Scene."

Jul 11: The LP *Beatles VI* reached number one in the U.S.

Jul 19: Single "Help!"/"I'm Down" released in the U.S.

Jul 25: The single "Help!" reached number one in the U.K.

Jul 29: Royal premiere of film *Help!* held at London Pavilion.

(b) Aug 1: The Beatles appeared live on U.K. TV's "Blackpool Night Out" from ABC Theatre in Blackpool. The Beatles' numbers included "I Do Like to Be Beside the Seaside."

Aug 6: LP *Help!* released in the U.K. A radically different version was released in the U.S. on Aug 13, with fewer Beatles songs and incidental music from the Ken Thorne film score.

Aug 8: The LP *Help!* reached number one in the U.K.

(r) Aug 13–31: The Beatles arrived in the U.S. on Aug 13 at New York's Kennedy International Airport for a tour of North America. Performing with them were The King Curtis Band, Brenda Holloway, and Sounds Incorporated. Songs performed included: "Twist and Shout," "She's a Woman," "I Feel Fine," "Dizzy Miss Lizzy," "Ticket to Ride," "Everybody's Trying to Be My Baby," "Can't Buy Me Love," "Baby's in Black," "Act Naturally," "A Hard Day's Night," "Help!" "I'm Down" (or "I Wanna Be Your Man" at some shows). A number of interviews and press conferences recorded during the tour were later released on several records.

(b) Aug 14: The Beatles recorded six songs before a live audience for "The Ed Sullivan Show" aired Sep 12.

(b) Aug 15: The Beatles' tour began with their first Shea Stadium concert in New York, attended by approximately 56,000 fans. The Beatles performed 12 songs in 30 minutes. The performance was filmed and a documentary movie, *The Beatles at Shea Stadium*, premiered on BBC-TV Mar 1, 1966. ABC-TV aired it on Jan 10, 1967 as a special that included only 10 of the 12 songs. Bob Dylan later visited The Beatles at their hotel.

(b) Aug 17–31: Concerts at Maple Leaf Garden, Toronto (Aug 17 [2 shows]); Atlanta Stadium, Atlanta (Aug 18); Sam Houston Coliseum, Houston (Aug 19 [2 shows]); Comiskey Park, Chicago (Aug 20 [2 shows]); Metropolitan Stadium, Minneapolis (Aug 21); Memorial Coliseum, Portland, Oregon (Aug 22 [2 shows]); Balboa Stadium, San Diego (Aug 28); Hollywood Bowl, Los Angeles (Aug 29, 30); the Cow Palace, San Francisco (Aug 31 [2 shows]).

Aug 22: During the flight to Portland, The Beatles' plane caught fire, but no one aboard was injured.

(b) Aug 23: The film *Help!* opened in the U.S.

Aug 27: The Beatles attended a Byrds recording session and later met Elvis Presley at Presley's Beverly Hills mansion. A jam session took place to the accompaniment of a juke box, but little conversation took place. No recordings or photographs of the visit have ever surfaced.

(rb) Aug 30: Seven songs from The Beatles' Hollywood Bowl concert were released in 1977, with six songs from their Aug 23, 1964 appearance at the same venue, on *The Beatles at the Hollywood Bowl*. In England, BBC

Radio aired "The Beatles Abroad," a 45-minute special of tapes Brian Matthew recorded in the U.S.

(r) Aug: An interview with John and Paul was recorded by Capitol's *Teen Set* magazine. George Martin left EMI after 15 years and formed his own Associated Independent Recordings Company (AIR).

Sep 1: The Beatles returned to England.

Sep 4: The single "Help!" reached number one in the U.S.

Sep 12: The LP *Help!* reached number one in the U.S.

Sep 13: Single "Yesterday"/"Act Naturally" released in the U.S.

Sep 25: A weekly half-hour Beatles cartoon series, "The Beatles," began in the U.S. on ABC-TV, airing each Saturday from 10:30 to 11:00 A.M. The series ran through Sep 7, 1969 and featured actual Beatles recordings "performed" by cartoon caricatures of The Beatles. Voices were supplied by Paul Frees (John and George) and Lance Percibal (Paul and Ringo). The series was produced by Al Brodax, who would later produce The Beatles' film *Yellow Submarine*, and was distributed by King Features Syndicate.

Oct 9: The single "Yesterday" reached number one in the U.S.

(rb) Oct 12: The Beatles recorded "Run for Your Life."

(r) Oct 13: The Beatles recorded "Drive My Car."

(rb) Oct 16: The Beatles recorded "Day Tripper."

(r) Oct 16 & 18: The Beatles recorded George's "If I Needed Someone."

(r) Oct 18: The Beatles recorded "In My Life," with the piano solo by George Martin overdubbed on Oct 22.

(rb) Oct 20: The Beatles recorded "We Can Work It Out," with additional vocal overdubs added on Oct 29.

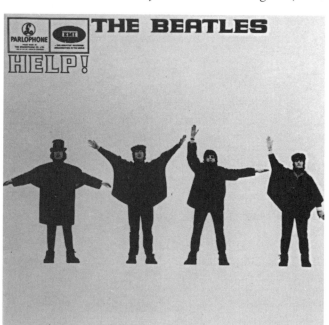

Help! (U.K. and U.S.) (© Apple Corps. Ltd.). Radically different soundtrack albums were issued in the U.K. and the U.S. for The Beatles' second film.

(rb) Oct 21: The Beatles recorded "Norwegian Wood (This Bird Has Flown)." Unreleased takes of "Nowhere Man" were also recorded.

(r) Oct 22: The Beatles recorded "Nowhere Man."

(b) Oct 24: The Beatles recorded an unreleased take of "I'm Looking Through You"; more unreleased takes were recorded on Nov 6. The released version was cut Nov 10 and 11.

Oct 26: The Beatles were presented with MBE medals by Queen Elizabeth at Buckingham Palace. Shortly before the presentation, The Beatles had secretly smoked marijuana in one of the royal bathrooms.

(b) Oct 28: A rough mix of "We Can Work It Out" was made for The Beatles to mime to when they appeared on Granada TV's special *The Music of Lennon and McCartney*, videotaped Nov 1 and 2. A separate mix of "Day Tripper" was prepared for the TV special on the following day.

Early Nov: John and George were interviewed by Brian Matthew for separate broadcasts of BBC's "Pop Profile" show, aired later in the fall. Excerpts were heard in 1988 on episodes 10 and 14 respectively of BBC Radio's "The Beeb's Lost Beatles Tapes."

Nov 1–2: A 50-minute TV special, *The Music of Lennon and McCartney*, was filmed at Granada TV's Manchester studio and aired Dec 17 in the U.K. During the show, Paul and Marianne Faithfull did a duet of "Yesterday" and The Beatles mimed to recordings of "We Can Work It Out" and "Day Tripper" recorded in Oct. Other artists did their versions of Beatles songs.

(b) Nov 4: The Beatles recorded two takes of "12-Bar Original," an unreleased instrumental.

(rb) Nov 8: The Beatles were recorded during rehearsals for "Think for Yourself." While never released on disc, a six-second clip of them practicing harmony vocals did appear in the film *Yellow Submarine*. They also recorded the released version on this date. Late in the evening, The Beatles recorded *The Beatles Third Christmas Record*, issued free to members of their fan club.

(r) Nov 10: The Beatles recorded "The Word."

(r) Nov 10–11: The Beatles recorded "I'm Looking Through You," their third attempt at the song; unreleased versions had been recorded Oct 24 and Nov 6.

(r) Nov 11: The Beatles recorded "Girl" and "You Won't See Me."

Dec 1: Several of John's drawings were included in an art exhibit at the Nell Gwynne Club in London.

(b) Dec 2: Promo films for "Day Tripper" and "We Can Work It Out" were seen on BBC's "Top of the Pops" show.

Dec 3: LP *Rubber Soul* and single "Day Tripper"/"We Can Work It Out" released in the U.K. *Rubber Soul* showed a remarkable progression in The Beatles' music and the influences to which it had been subjected, including the music of Bob Dylan. The album included far more thoughtful and introspective lyrics than any previous Beatles album, new instruments, including the sitar, and ground-breaking recording techniques. As innovative as all of this was, it only offered an inkling of what was to come on the next two Beatles albums, *Revolver* and *Sgt. Pepper's Lonely Hearts Club Band*.

Dec 3–12: The Beatles' final British tour took place; also on the bill were The Moody Blues (then including Denny Laine, later of Wings). Songs performed included "Dizzy Miss Lizzie," "I Feel Fine," "She's a Woman," "If I Needed Someone," "Ticket to Ride," "Act Naturally," "Nowhere Man," "Baby's in Black," "Help!" "We Can Work It Out," "Day Tripper" and "I'm Down." The tour included performances at Glasgow's Odeon (Dec 3); Newcastle City Hall (Dec 4); Liverpool's Empire (Dec 5); Ardwick's ABC (Dec 7); Sheffield's Gaumont (Dec 8); Birmingham's Odeon (Dec 9); Hammersmith's Odeon (Dec 10); Finsbury Park Astoria, London (Dec 11); Capitol's Cardiff (Dec 12). By this time The Beatles had come to detest live concerts. Touring had become both punishing and tiresome, and they saw their music suffering, since little of it was heard above the screaming audiences.

Dec 5: The Beatles' last concert in their native Liverpool took place at the Empire.

■ The single "Day Tripper"/"We Can Work It Out" became a two-sided number-one hit in the U.K.

■ The LP *Rubber Soul* reached number one in the U.K.

Dec 6: The LP *Rubber Soul* and the single "We Can Work It Out"/"Day Tripper" released in the U.S. EP *The Beatles Million Sellers* (aka *Beatles' Golden Discs*) released in the U.K.

Dec 12: The Beatles' last British tour ended with a performance at the Capitol in Cardiff. Their last U.K. concert would take place on May 1, 1966.

Dec 13: The Beatles rejected *A Talent for Loving* as their third feature film; Brian Epstein had purchased the rights to it.

Dec 17: *The Beatles Third Christmas Record* released to The Beatles Fan Club.

Dec 25: The Beatles were heard in prerecorded interview clips on "Saturday Club," parts of which were aired on episode 13 of BBC Radio's 1988 series "The Beeb's Lost Beatles Tapes." A specially recorded Christmas message by the group was aired on Radio Caroline, and film of the group doing "I Feel Fine," "Help!," "Ticket to Ride" and "Day Tripper" was seen on "Top of the Pops."

Dec 26: A prerecorded interview with Paul was aired on Radio Caroline's "Pop's Happening."

(b) Dec: Four copies of a special Christmas record were recorded by Paul called *Paul's Christmas Album*. Each of The Beatles received one copy and no other copies were ever made.

■ John's short story "Toy Boy" appeared in *McCall's* magazine.

1966

Jan 6: A taped performance of The Beatles singing "Day Tripper" and "We Can Work It Out" was shown on the U.S. TV show "Hullabaloo."

Jan 8: The single "We Can Work It Out" and the LP *Rubber Soul* both reached number one in the U.S.

Jan 21: George and Patricia (Pattie) Boyd were married at Esher Register Office, Surrey.

Feb 21: Single "Nowhere Man"/"What Goes On" released in the U.S.

Feb 28: The Cavern Club closed. Protests followed on Mar 1.

Feb: In an interview with journalist Maureen Cleave of the London *Evening Standard*, John was asked for his views on organized religion. His response was: ". . . We're more popular than Jesus now. I don't know which will go first—rock and roll or Christianity." While this remark was not particularly noticed in England, where it appeared in the London *Evening Standard* on Mar 4, it was reprinted in the U.S. on Jul 29 on the cover of the teenage magazine *Datebook*. John was quoted as claiming The Beatles were "Bigger than Jesus Christ," which caused violent anti-Beatles reactions.

Mar 4: EP *Yesterday* released in the U.K.

Mar 6: A petition with 5,000 signatures requesting that the Cavern Club be reopened was presented to Britain's prime minister, Harold Wilson.

(r) Mar 25: Tom Lodge of Radio Caroline recorded an interview with The Beatles.

(b) Mar: John cut six demos of "She Said She Said," tentatively titled "He Said He Said."

(rb) Apr 6–7: The Beatles recorded "Tomorrow Never Knows."

(r) Apr 7–8: The Beatles began recording "Got to Get You into My Life."

(rb) Apr 11–29: The Beatles recorded "Love You To," "Paperback Writer," "Rain," "Dr. Robert," "Taxman," "And Your Bird Can Sing," "I'm Only Sleeping" and "Eleanor Rigby."

May 1: The Beatles' last U.K. concert appearance took place at the *New Musical Express* Poll Winner's Show at the Empire Pool, Wembley. Only the award ceremony was filmed; it aired May 15.

(r) May 9: Paul and Ringo began recording "For No One."

(b) May 19–20: The Beatles were filmed while miming to recordings of "Paperback Writer" and "Rain" at EMI Studios and Chriswick House, London. The film was aired on "The Ed Sullivan Show" in the U.S. on Jun 5 and on "Top of the Pops" in the U.K. on Jun 2.

May 23: Single "Paperback Writer"/"Rain" released in the U.S. Released in the U.K. on Jun 10.

(r) May 26 & Jun 1: The Beatles recorded "Yellow Submarine."

May 27: John and George attended a Bob Dylan concert at the Royal Albert Hall in London, during which Dylan and The Band, which was backing him, were booed for using electric instruments during part of the show.

May: Paul and Ringo were interviewed by Brian Matthew for separate broadcasts of BBC Radio's "Pop Profile." Excerpts were aired on episodes 11 and 12 respectively of BBC Radio's 1988 series "The Beeb's Lost Beatles Tapes."

(r) Jun 2: The Beatles recorded "I Want to Tell You."

Jun 4: A prerecorded interview with The Beatles was aired on the 400th edition of BBC Radio's "Saturday Club."

(r) Jun 8–9: The Beatles recorded "Good Day Sunshine."

Jun 15: LP *Yesterday and Today* was released by Capitol in the U.S. The original cover photo showed The Beatles dressed as butchers, surrounded by dismembered dolls and slabs of raw meat and blood. The now-famous (and much-coveted) "butcher sleeve" was quickly withdrawn. New covers, with a bland photo of the group, were simply pasted over the existing butcher sleeves, and used for all subsequent pressings. The butcher photo had been intended as a picture sleeve for the "Paperback Writer" single too, and it appeared in U.K. newspaper ads, but was ultimately withdrawn there as well.

Jun 16: The Beatles appeared live on "Top of the Pops," and mimed to "Paperback Writer" and "Rain."

(rb) Jun 16–17: The Beatles recorded "Here, There and Everywhere."

Jun 20: LP *Yesterday and Today* rereleased with new cover in the U.S. only.

(r) Jun 21: The Beatles recorded "She Said She Said."

Jun 22: The Beatles attended a preopening party at Sibylla's, a new London club in which George owned a 10% share.

(b) Jun 23: The Beatles' last tour began with three dates in Hamburg, Germany. Appearing with The Beatles on this tour were Cliff Bennett and The Rebel Rousers and Peter and Gordon. The Beatles were presented with the 1966 Bravo award, and George made an acceptance speech in German.

(b) Jun 24: The Beatles' second show at Circus-Krone-Bau, Munich, was videotaped by German national TV station, ZDF.

(r) Jun 24–Aug 29: Several interviews and press conferences recorded during The Beatles' world tour were later released on a variety of records. Songs performed on the tour included "Rock and Roll Music," "She's a Woman," "If I Needed Someone," "Baby's in Black," "Day Tripper," "I Feel Fine," "Yesterday," "I Wanna Be Your Man," "Nowhere Man," "Paperback Writer" and either "Long Tall Sally" or "I'm Down." They performed at Circus-Krone-Bau, Munich, Germany (Jun 24 [2 shows]); the Grugahalle, Essen (Jun 25 [2 shows]); Ernst Merch Halle, Hamburg (Jun 26 [2 shows]); Nippon Budokan Hall, Tokyo, Japan (Jun 30; Jul 1 and 2 [2 shows each]); Rizal Memorial Football Stadium, Manila, the Philippines (Jul 4 [2 shows]); Chicago's International Ampitheater (Aug 12 [2 shows]); Olympia Stadium, Detroit (Aug 13 [2 shows]); Municipal Stadium, Cleveland (Aug 14); D.C. Stadium, Washington, D.C. (Aug 15); Connie Mack Stadium (aka Shibe Park), Philadelphia (Aug 16); Maple Leaf Gardens, Toronto (Aug 7 [2 shows]); Suffolk Downs Racetrack, Boston (Aug 18); Mid South Coliseum, Memphis (Aug 19 [2 shows]); Crosley Field, Cincinnati (Aug 21 [afternoon]); Busch Stadium, St. Louis (Aug 21 [evening]); Shea Stadium, New York (Aug 23); Seattle Coliseum, Washington (Aug 25 [2 shows]); Dodger Stadium, Los Angeles (Aug 28); Candlestick Park, San Francisco (Aug 29).

Jun 25: The single "Paperback Writer" reached number one in the U.S. and the U.K. The final edition of the U.K. TV show "Thank Your Lucky Stars" was aired and included a screening of the "Paperback Writer" promo film.

(b) Jun 30–Jul 2: The Beatles did five concerts over three days at Nippon Budokan Hall, Tokyo. The Jun 30 show was filmed in color by Japanese TV (NTV) and aired the following day. One of the Jul 2 shows was also filmed but not aired.

Jul 3: The Beatles flew to Manila, the Philippines. In a *New York Times Sunday Magazine* article, Maureen Cleave quoted an unnamed Beatle as saying "Show business is an extension of the Jewish religion." John later freely admitted that he had made the statement.

Jul 4–Jul 5: In Manila, The Beatles performed two shows at the Rizal Memorial Football Stadium. During the day, The Beatles failed to appear at a palace reception by President Marcos' family, who had not been informed that The Beatles had declined the invitation due to their performance commitment. The Philippine media misrepresented this as a deliberate snub by The Beatles. As a retaliation against The Beatles' "snub," the Philippine government provided no police protection for the group as they prepared to leave the country the following day. They were kicked and punched as they ran for their aircraft prior to their departure.

Jul 8: EP *Nowhere Man* released in the U.K.

Jul 23: British Prime Minister Harold Wilson presided over the reopening of the Cavern Club, under new management, in Liverpool.

Jul 29: The U.S. teenagers' magazine *Datebook* printed the Maureen Cleave interview with John, originally published in the London *Evening Standard* on Mar 4. Within days Beatles records were publicly burned in the southern U.S. at bonfires promoted by disc jockeys who took offense to John's remarks about Christianity. A ban on Beatles records was also begun by a Birmingham, Alabama D.J. Other stations, especially in the South, followed suit.

Jul 30: LP *Yesterday and Today* reached number one in the U.S.

Aug 1: Paul taped an interview aired Aug 6 on BBC Radio's "David Frost at the Phonograph."

Aug 5: LP *Revolver* released in the U.K. The new turn that The Beatles' music had taken was most evident on the final, drug-related number, "Tomorrow Never Knows" by John. The Beatles would later say that *Rubber Soul* was influenced by their use of marijuana and *Revolver* by LSD experimentation. On *Revolver*, George emerged as a creditable songwriter with three tracks of his own ("Taxman," "Love You To," "I Want to Tell You"). Paul produced some of The Beatles' most cele-

brated love songs and ballads on this album, including "Yesterday" and "Eleanor Rigby," in addition to the well-received "For No One" and "Here, There and Everywhere" (two songs John particularly liked). John's numbers ("She Said She Said," "And Your Bird Can Sing," "Tomorrow Never Knows") were rougher, more introspective and reflective of his drug experiments.

■ Single "Eleanor Rigby"/"Yellow Submarine" released in both the U.S. and U.K.

Aug 6: John and Paul were interviewed at Paul's house by Keith Fordyce for the one-hour BBC Radio special, *The Lennon and McCartney Songbook*, which was broadcast on Aug 29, even as The Beatles were performing the last concert of their career, in San Francisco's Candlestick Park. Excerpts from the radio broadcast were heard during episode 12 of BBC Radio's 1988 series "The Beeb's Lost Beatles Tapes."

Aug 8: LP *Revolver* released in the U.S. Radio play of Beatles records was banned in South Africa.

(r) Aug 11: At a press conference in Chicago, John attempted to explain (or "apologize" for) his "bigger than Jesus" remark as reprinted in the U.S. teen magazine *Datebook*. He was visibly nervous and shaken by the hate mail he had been receiving and by how sour the tour had gone because of the adverse publicity.

Aug 12: One of The Beatles' Chicago concerts was filmed.

Aug 13: The LP *Revolver* reached number one in the U.K.

Aug 14: After sponsoring a public bonfire of Beatles records, a Longview, Texas radio station was knocked off the air when struck by a bolt of lightning.

Aug 15: The Beatles' concert at D.C. Stadium (later RFK Stadium) in Washington, D.C. was filmed.

Aug 17: At a press conference in Toronto, John encouraged Americans to move to Canada if they wanted to avoid fighting in Vietnam and expressed admiration for those who had resisted the U.S. draft. The Beatles performed two concerts at Maple Leaf Gardens, Toronto.

Aug 19: During one of two shows in Memphis, firecrackers and other objects were thrown at The Beatles by attendees who, apparently, disapproved of John's remarks about Christianity. The performance was picketed by the Ku Klux Klan.

Aug 20: The Beatles scored another two-sided number-one hit in the U.K. with "Yellow Submarine"/"Eleanor Rigby."

Aug 21: Afternoon concert at Crosley Field, Cincinnati postponed from the previous day due to rain. That evening The Beatles performed at Busch Stadium, St. Louis, where it rained heavily throughout the show.

Aug 22: During a New York press conference, The Beatles criticized the U.S. war effort in Vietnam, although Brian Epstein had unsuccessfully urged them not to make political statements of this kind.

Aug 23: The Beatles' second Shea Stadium concert took place in New York. Attendance was approximately

45,000, about 10,000 fewer than their first Shea concert on Aug 15, 1965.

(b) Aug 29: The last scheduled Beatles' concert took place at Candlestick Park San Francisco. They returned to England on Aug 31, never to tour again.

(r) Sep 5: John arrived in Germany to begin filming Richard Lester's *How I Won the War*. The following day his hair was cut short by German hairdresser Klaus Baruch for his role as Muskateer Gripweed. Filming would extend into November. "How I Won the War," an instrumental film theme, included a line or two of John's film dialogue. John was the first of The Beatles to work professionally without the other members of the group, but had no wish to act in additional films. Afterward, he kept his hair short, as in the film, and began wearing wire-rimmed granny glasses. (Despite severe myopia, John had previously shunned glasses.) He now experimented frequently with LSD, which had a great influence on his songs. John became heavily involved with art and was pursued by publishers, print engravers and greeting card companies to write and sketch.

Sep 10: The LP *Revolver* reached number one in the U.S.

Sep 14–Oct 22: George and his wife, Pattie, vacationed in India where George met sitar master Ravi Shankar and began taking lessons in the instrument from him. He and Pattie also began practicing yoga. George had become increasingly resentful of being kept in the background in The Beatles. He felt John and Paul dominated the music, leaving him little room for creativity. John and Paul later said that they did not consider George's music good enough for Beatles records at first but that it improved in later years. The sitar provided George with his first unique contribution to The Beatles; the instrument was used on the LP *Rubber Soul* and even more so on *Revolver*.

Sep 18: Filming of *How I Won the War* resumed in Carboneras, Spain.

(b) Early Nov: John cut at least four demos of "Strawberry Fields Forever."

Nov 7: John returned to England after completing filming *How I Won the War*.

Nov 9: The Indica Gallery in London featured an exhibition entitled "Unfinished Painting and Objects by Yoko Ono." John first met Yoko at a special preview of this show, on this date.

(rb) Nov 24–Dec 29: The Beatles recorded John Lennon's "Strawberry Fields Forever."

(rb) Nov 25: The Beatles recorded their fourth annual Christmas record in a basement studio at the London office of their music publisher, Dick James. It was later issued to fan club members.

Nov 27: John filmed an appearance on "Not Only . . . But Also," with Dudley Moore and Peter Cook, aired Dec 26. He appeared in a sketch as the doorman of a night club located in a public restroom.

Nov–Dec: The score for the film soundtrack and LP *The Family Way*, written by Paul, was recorded by the George Martin Orchestra.

(b) Dec 6: The Beatles recorded special Christmas and New Year greetings for Radio London and Radio Caroline, two offshore British pirate radio stations. The messages were aired by the stations during the holiday season.

(r) Dec 6 & 8: The Beatles recorded "When I'm Sixty Four," with overdubs added later.

Dec 10: LP *A Collection of Beatles Oldies* released in the U.K.

Dec 16: *The Beatles Fourth Christmas Record* ("Everywhere It's Christmas") released to fan club.

Dec 18: The film *The Family Way*, featuring Paul's musical score, premiered in London. It opened in the U.S. in New York on Jun 28, 1967.

(rb) Dec 29–Jan 17, 1967: The Beatles recorded "Penny Lane."

Late that year–early 1967: The Beatles had begun to record an LP reflecting their Liverpool childhood with "Penny Lane" and "Strawberry Fields Forever." Paul, who wrote "Sgt. Pepper's Lonely Hearts Club Band," suggested doing the whole LP as a continuous stage show. The album became *Sgt. Pepper's Lonely Hearts Club Band*. It cost £25,000 to make, 20 times the cost of the first Beatles LP in 1963.

1967

(b) Early that year: John cut a demo of "You Know My Name (Look Up the Number)." The released studio recording was begun on May 17 and Jun 7 and 8 but was not completed until Apr 30, 1969, almost two years later.

(b) Jan 5: The Beatles recorded an unreleased 14-minute experimental sound effects track for the theatrical production *Carnival of Light*.

(rb) Jan 19–Feb 22: The Beatles recorded "A Day in the Life."

Jan 27: The Beatles signed a new nine-year contract with EMI under which they would receive 10% of the wholesale price of their records in the U.K. and 17.5% in the U.S.

Jan 30–31: The Beatles shot a promo film for "Strawberry Fields Forever" in Sevenoaks, Kent.

(r) Feb 1: The Beatles recorded the title song for the *Sgt. Pepper's Lonely Hearts Club Band* LP.

Feb 5 & 7: The Beatles shot a promo film for "Penny Lane" in Stratford, East London and Sevenoaks, Kent.

(rb) Feb 8–Mar 29: The Beatles recorded "Good Morning Good Morning."

(r) Feb 9: The Beatles recorded "Fixing a Hole" at Regent Sound Studio, the first time they had recorded outside of Abbey Road during their EMI years. Promotional clips of "Strawberry Fields Forever" and "Penny Lane" were seen on the U.K. TV show "Top of the Pops."

Feb 13: Single "Penny Lane"/"Strawberry Fields Forever" released in the U.S. Released in the U.K. on Feb 17.

(r) **Feb 13–Mar 14:** The Beatles recorded "Only a Northern Song," with work concluded on Apr 20. The song was not released until 1969, when it appeared on the *Yellow Submarine* LP.

(r) **Feb 17–Mar 31:** The Beatles recorded "Being for the Benefit of Mr. Kite!"

Feb 19: John and Ringo attended a London concert featuring Chuck Berry and Del Shannon.

(b) **Feb 22:** The Beatles recorded the unreleased "Anything" (aka "Drum Track"), a 22:10 track of Ringo drumming and playing tambourine and congas.

(r) **Feb 23–Mar 21:** The Beatles recorded "Lovely Rita."

Feb 25: Promotional clips of "Strawberry Fields Forever" and "Penny Lane" were seen in the U.S. on the TV show "Hollywood Palace." The same clips were also seen on "The Ed Sullivan Show" that month.

(r) **Mar 1–2:** The Beatles recorded "Lucy in the Sky with Diamonds."

(r) **Mar 9–23:** The Beatles recorded "Getting Better."

Mar 11: The Beatles received three Grammy Awards from the American National Academy of Recording Arts and Sciences for 1966: (1) Song of the Year—Composition, "Michelle"; (2) Best Contemporary Solo Vocal Performance, "Eleanor Rigby" (Paul); (3) Best Sleeve Design, LP, *Revolver* (partially done by Klaus Voorman).

(r) **Mar 15–Apr 4:** George recorded "Within You Without You" with a number of outside musicians.

(r) **Mar 17 & 20:** The Beatles recorded "She's Leaving Home."

Mar 18: The single "Penny Lane" reached number one in the U.S.

(b) **Mar 20:** John and Paul were interviewed by Brian Matthew on BBC Radio's "Top of the Pops" during recording sessions at Abbey Road. Part of the interview was heard on episode 14 of BBC Radio's 1988 series "The Beeb's Lost Beatles Tapes." A spoken-word tape titled "Beatle Talk," recorded at Abbey Road, was removed from the studio by George Martin; contents are unknown.

Mar 25: The Beatles received two Ivor Novello Awards for 1966 from the British Music Industry: Most Performed Work, "Michelle," and Top-Selling Single, "Yellow Submarine."

(r) **Mar 29–30:** The Beatles recorded "With a Little Help from My Friends." On Mar 30 a photo session was held for the cover of the *Sgt. Pepper* album.

(r) **Apr 1:** The Beatles recorded "Sgt. Pepper's Lonely Hearts Club Band (reprise)."

Apr 19: The Beatles signed a new partnership agreement creating The Beatles & Company, with a 10-year life span, thus legally binding the four members of the group for that period.

(rb) **Apr 21:** The edit pieces comprising the sounds of gibberish heard in the runout groove at the end of the U.K. pressing of the *Sgt. Pepper* album (sometimes known as "Sgt. Pepper Inner Groove") were assembled and added to the LP masters. A high-pitch dog whistle was also added just prior to the runout groove. Both items were eliminated from subsequent reissues but were restored to the 1987 CD release and the accompanying cassette releases and, in the U.S., to a vinyl LP. An unreleased mono mix of "Only a Northern Song" was also created on this date.

(r) **Apr 25–May 3:** The Beatles recorded "Magical Mystery Tour," the title song for a planned television special.

(b) **May 4:** An alternate mix of "Magical Mystery Tour" was made for the film but was not released on any official records.

(b) **May 9:** The Beatles recorded an untitled 16-minute rambling instrumental jam.

(r) **May 11:** The Beatles recorded "Baby, You're a Rich Man" at Olympic Sound Studios.

(r) **May 12:** The Beatles recorded "All Together Now," not released until 1969.

(b) **May:** D.J. Kenny Everett taped an interview with The Beatles on the upcoming release of the *Sgt. Pepper* LP while at a dinner party at Brian Epstein's home. This may be part of the May 20 "Where It's At" broadcast.

May 15: Paul met Linda Eastman during a Georgie Fame performance at London's Bag O'Nails nightclub.

(r) **May 17:** The Beatles recorded instrumental rhythm tracks and sound effects for "You Know My Name (Look Up the Number)." They continued these sessions on Jun 7 and 8, with Brian Jones of the Rolling Stones adding alto saxophone on Jun 8. Nearly two years would pass before John and Paul were to add their vocals, on Apr 30, 1969.

May 18: John and Paul provided backing vocals during The Rolling Stones' recording of "We Love You." Released in the U.K. on Aug 18 and in the U.S. on Aug 28.

May 20: On BBC Radio's "Where It's At," Kenny Everett previewed the *Sgt. Pepper* album and played a prerecorded interview with Paul. The BBC banned The Beatles' "A Day in the Life" because it felt the lyrics encouraged drug use.

(rb) **May 25–Jun 2:** The Beatles recorded "It's All Too Much" at De Lane Lea Music Recording Studios under the working title "Too Much."

May 26: *Sgt. Pepper's Lonely Hearts Club Band* was rush-released in the U.K., although the announced release date of Jun 1 is traditionally observed as the official release date.

(b) **Jun 1:** *Sgt. Pepper's Lonely Hearts Club Band* was officially released in the U.K. It was released a day later in the U.S. It was greeted by rave reviews portraying it as a revolution in recorded music. *The New York Times* called it "a new and golden Renaissance of song." Although in later years seen as something of a period piece, it clearly marked a startling revolution in recorded music. Reactions to the album in the U.K. and the U.S. were often fanatical. Many saw it as the product of The Beatles' drug experiences, and some prescribed it to enhance listeners' drug experiences. At the opposite extreme, right-wing fanatics saw it as sacrilegious and were convinced that The Beatles were Communist sub-

Sgt. Pepper's Lonely Hearts Club Band (© Apple Corps Ltd.). This monumental album showed how far The Beatles had come since 1964, and changed rock and roll considerably.

versives. The Beatles, however, disliked the practice of seeking messages in their songs. John denied that there was any motive behind his lyrics; "I just shove a lot of sounds together, then shove some words on," he said. It was clear, however, that the group's groundbreaking recording innovations and concepts were at the forefront of the popularization of psychedelic rock and roll, which would soon sweep both shores of the Atlantic. The first credits given to The Beatles' company, Apple, appeared on the *Sgt. Pepper* sleeve. Although no actual company yet existed, Paul had already suggested the idea of a totally Beatles-owned business organization, and planning had begun.

Jun 5: The LP *Sgt. Pepper's Lonely Hearts Club Band* reached number one in the U.K.

(rb) **Jun 14:** The Beatles recorded "All You Need Is Love."

Jun 19: Paul told *Life* magazine that he had taken LSD, thus becoming the first Beatle to admit it publicly. Later John, George and Brian also admitted that they had taken the drug.

(b) **Jun 25:** The Beatles appeared live on a televised program called "Our World" beamed around the world by satellite. The show was made up of attractions from many nations. The Beatles represented England, and they were seen recording "All You Need Is Love," with a number of celebrities present, including members of The Rolling Stones, Eric Clapton and Graham Nash. The television audience was estimated at 400 million. Paul had written "Hello Goodbye" for this TV special, but it was passed over in favor of John's "All You Need Is Love."

Jul 3: The LP *Sgt. Pepper's Lonely Hearts Club Band* reached number one in the U.S.

Jul 7: Single "All You Need Is Love"/"Baby You're a Rich Man" released in the U.K. and in the U.S. on June 17 when it also reached number one in the U.K.

Jul 24: An advertisement in the *London Times*, signed by all four Beatles and Brian Epstein, urged that the British government legalize marijuana.

Jul 31: Ringo recorded a "farewell message" to pirate radio station Radio London, aired on Aug 5, the station's final day on the air.

Aug 7: George and Pattie Harrison strolled through Golden Gate Park in San Francisco's Haight-Ashbury section, where George gave a spontaneous serenade on a borrowed guitar. He later voiced disapproval of the hippy lifestyle, which he termed wasteful.

Aug 19: The single "All You Need Is Love" reached number one in the U.S.

(rb) **Aug 22:** The Beatles recorded "Your Mother Should Know."

Aug 24: The Beatles met Maharishi Mahesh Yogi while attending one of the guru's lectures at the Hilton Hotel in London. The guru taught a technique known as Transcendental Meditation, which involved the silent repetition of a mantra (a word, sound or short phrase). Meditating for 20 minutes twice a day was said to reduce stress and produce calmness and energy throughout the day. The next day, at the invitation of the Maharishi, The Beatles traveled with the guru to North Wales for more lectures.

Aug 26: The Beatles held a press conference with the Maharishi at University College in Bangor, North Wales. They formally announced that they had become disciples of the Maharishi and that they had abandoned all use of drugs.

Aug 27: Brian Epstein was found dead in bed at his home. Paul received the news by telephone while The Beatles were with the Maharishi. Afterward, The Beatles consulted the Maharishi and were told that death was not to be feared or mourned. The Beatles soon became members of the Maharishi's Spiritual Regeneration Movement, which required them to donate a week's earnings per month to the organization. They planned to visit the guru's academy in Rishikesh, North India, to meditate, study and ultimately become teachers of Transcendental Meditation.

Aug 29: Brian Epstein's funeral was held in Liverpool. Only family members were present; The Beatles did not attend.

(rb) **Sep 5–8:** The Beatles recorded "I Am the Walrus," "Blue Jay Way," and "Flying," an instrumental written by all four Beatles, originally titled "Aerial Tour Instrumental."

■ Brian Epstein's death was ruled accidental suicide from the gradual accumulation of the barbiturate Carbrital over two to three days.

Sep 11: Filming of *Magical Mystery Tour* began. The Beatles lacked a clear idea of what they would do and proceeded without a script. The project was poorly directed and chaotic from start to finish. They embarked on a bus but had no specific destination, and were constantly hounded by the press and fans. They spent another 11 weeks taking turns repeatedly editing and reediting the film. NEMS ultimately sold the British rights to BBC-TV, where it premiered on Dec 26, in black and white. A subsequent showing was aired in color. (For critical reaction, see Dec 26).

Sep 13: George was interviewed by Miranda Ward for BBC Radio One's "Scene and Heard" show, aired in two parts on Sep 30 and Oct 7. Excerpts were heard on episode 14 of BBC Radio's 1988 series "The Beeb's Lost Beatles Tapes." The Beatles formed an electronics company called Fiftyshapes Ltd. and appointed John Alexis Mardas, known as "Magic Alex," as its director.

(b) Sep 16: The Beatles recorded 11 unreleased takes of "Your Mother Should Know."

(r) Sep 25–27: The Beatles recorded "The Fool on the Hill."

Sep 29: John and George were interviewed on U.K. Radio's "The David Frost Show," aired Sep 30.

Sep: The Beatles hired a three-member Dutch designer company called The Fool for £100,000 to design a boutique. The Fool was to stock the boutique with its own designs. At Paul's suggestion, the new establishment was named Apple. Before long members of The Fool had to be warned repeatedly about taking Apple merchandise without paying for it.

■ The Beatles appeared on the cover of *Time* magazine in the form of a papier-mâché caricature of the group created by British cartoonist Gerald Scarfe.

(rb) Oct 2–Nov 2: The Beatles recorded "Hello, Goodbye" under the working title "Hello Hello."

Oct 4: John and George were again interviewed on U.K. Radio's "The David Frost Show."

Oct 7: Sid Bernstein, who had promoted The Beatles' 1964 Carnegie Hall concerts, offered the group $1 million to perform another concert. The Beatles turned down the offer.

Oct 11: A Yoko Ono art exhibit, Yoko Plus Me, sponsored by John, opened at the Lisson Gallery in London and ran through Nov 14.

(b) Oct 12: Instrumental music, "Shirley's Wild Accordion," was recorded for the *Magical Mystery Tour* film but was not used.

Oct 13: Single "How I Won the War" (voice: John Lennon) non-Beatles B side, "Aftermath," released in the U.K.

Oct 17: All of The Beatles attended a memorial service for Brian Epstein at the New London Synagogue, Abbey Road.

Oct 18: World premiere of the film *How I Won the War*, featuring John, at the London Pavilion. It opened in the U.S. in New York on Nov 8.

Oct 30: Paul filmed the "Fool on the Hill" sequence in Nice, completing the *Magical Mystery Tour* film.

(b) Oct: The Beatles recorded "Jessie's Dream," instrumental music used in the *Magical Mystery Tour* film but never released on record.

Nov 10: The Beatles shot three promotional films for "Hello Goodbye," directed by Paul, at the Saville Theatre.

(r) Nov 22–23: George worked on English titles for the film score for *Wonderwall*.

Nov 23: A film clip from the film *A Hard Day's Night* was screened on "Top of the Pops" while The Beatles' recording of "Hello Goodbye" was played. The "Hello Goodbye" films were not used due to a British ban on miming.

(b) Nov 24: Single "Hello Goodbye"/"I Am the Walrus" released in the U.K. Released in the U.S. on Nov 27. John was quite irritated that his song was relegated to the B side of what he considered an inane McCartney A side.

■ A prerecorded interview with John, taped by Kenny Everett and Chris Denning, was aired on BBC Radio One's "Where It's At." Part of the interview was heard during episode 14 of the 1988 series "The Beeb's Lost Beatles Tapes." John appeared on the show to promote the *Magical Mystery Tour* EP.

Nov 26: One of the "Hello Goodbye" promo films was aired in the U.S. on "The Ed Sullivan Show."

Nov 27: LP *Magical Mystery Tour* released in the U.S.

(rb) Nov 28: The Beatles recorded their fifth annual Christmas disc, including the original song "Christmas Time (Is Here Again)," issued to the fan club Dec 15. The fan club disc itself only contained short excerpts of the song; the full version runs 6:37.

Dec 3: Ringo flew to Rome to begin filming *Candy*.

Dec 7: George and John attended The Beatles' Apple boutique opening at 94 Baker Street, London, which was one month later than planned. Pete Shotton, childhood friend of John Lennon and former member of The Quarry Men, was appointed manager of the boutique, which lost money from the start. It quickly became a shoplifter's paradise with garments disappearing regularly, often in the hands of personnel of The Fool.

Dec 8: EP *Magical Mystery Tour* released in the U.K.

Dec 9: The single "Hello Goodbye" reached number one in the U.K.

Dec 11: Apple Music signed its first act—dubbed Grapefruit by John. The group, with slightly different membership, had been signed previously by NEMS as Tony Rivers and The Castaways.

Dec 15: *Christmas Time (Is Here Again)* released to the fan club. John and Ringo designed the front of the sleeve; John's son Julian the back.

Dec 17: Ringo returned to London after completing the film *Candy*.

Dec 21: The Beatles held a party at the Royal Lancaster Hotel during which their film *Magical Mystery Tour* was previewed.

Dec 25: Paul and his longtime actress girl friend, Jane Asher, announced their engagement.

Dec 26: BBC-TV aired *Magical Mystery Tour* in black and white. The film was criticized as being little more than an overdone home movie and was panned. A U.S. TV deal for the film was canceled as a result of its poor reception in the U.K. The BBC also banned "I Am the Walrus," which it saw as drug-related. For the first time, The Beatles had produced an unmitigated flop.

Dec 27: Paul appeared on U.K. TV's "The David Frost Show" and defended the *Magical Mystery Tour* film.

Dec 30: The single "Hello Goodbye" reached number one in the U.S.

Dec: In London only one performance was given of the play *Scene II Act II*, based on John's book, *In His Own Write*.

(b) **Late that year:** Ringo recorded the unreleased ad lib "Daddy's Little Sunshine Boy," and he and John taped the unreleased "Chi Chi's Cafe" (a comical improvisation) reportedly at John's home, possibly around this time, along with Ringo's "Sailor Come Back to Me" and John's "El Tango Terrible," and "Cry Baby Cry" demos.

1968

Jan 5: The film *Magical Mystery Tour* was aired in color on BBC-TV.

Jan 6: The LP *Magical Mystery Tour* reached number one in the U.S.

Jan 7: George left England on a trip to India. He returned on Jan 18.

(r) **Jan 9–17:** George recorded the Indian titles for the *Wonderwall Music* soundtrack album at EMI's Bombay, India recording studio.

(r) **Jan 12:** George recorded the instrumental tracks for "The Inner Light" in Bombay, India; vocals were done at Abbey Road Studios on Feb 6 and 8.

- The names of The Beatles Film Productions Ltd. and Apple Music Ltd. were changed to Apple Films Ltd. and Apple Corps Ltd. respectively.

Jan 22: The Beatles opened offices at 95 Wigmore Street, London, housing Apple—and its many subsidiary companies. It was a haven for crackpots, including self-styled electronics wizard "Magic Alex," who in-cluded plans for a flying saucer among his credentials. His flights of fancy included construction of a recording studio that would feature 72-track tape machines.

Jan: John Lyndon replaced Pete Shotton as manager of the Apple Boutique. Shotton became John's personal assistant.

(b) **Early that year:** An interview with The Beatles recorded by two fans was auctioned many years later and purchased by the Hard Rock Cafe chain in London.

(rb) **Feb 3 & 6:** The Beatles began recording "Lady Madonna."

(rb) **Feb 4:** The Beatles recorded "Across the Universe," with minor overdubs completed on Feb 8. Backing vocals were provided by Lizzie Bravo and Gayleen Pease, two Beatles fans recruited spontaneously from the front steps of EMI's studio.

(b) **Feb 6:** Ringo appeared live as a guest on Cilla Black's TV show "Cilla."

(r) **Feb 11:** The Beatles recorded "Hey Bulldog." The song was written and recorded specifically for the *Yellow Submarine* film, but most prints of that film omitted the number.

Feb 15: John, George and their wives traveled to Rishikesh, India to study Transcendental Meditation with the Maharishi. Paul and Jane Asher and Ringo and Maureen followed on Feb 19, but the Starkeys left after only 10 days, bored with the routine and sick of the food. Paul lasted until Mar 26, when he and Jane returned to England. After 11 weeks John was told that the Maharishi was attempting to seduce actress Mia Farrow, who was also attending the sessions. The charge appears to have been untrue, but by Apr 12 John and George also decided to leave.

Magical Mystery Tour (U.S. and German) (© Apple Corps Ltd.). The original 1967 album appeared in the U.S. with some songs only in mono; an abbreviated double EP was issued in the U.K. The German album appeared later with all songs in true stereo; that version would appear on CD many years later.

(b) Feb: Paul recorded a demo of "Step Inside Love," commercially recorded by Cilla Black, and John cut demos of "Hey Bulldog."

(b) Late Feb: A jam session in India that included The Beatles, The Beach Boys, Donovan and others was filmed and aired at a later date on Italian television.

Mar 9: The Beatles received four Grammy Awards for 1967 for their LP *Sgt. Pepper's Lonely Hearts Club Band*: Best Album, Best Contemporary Album, Best Album Cover and Best Engineered Recording.

Mar 15: Single "Lady Madonna"/"The Inner Light" released in the U.K. Released in the U.S. on Mar 18.

■ **(b)** In Rishikesh, India, The Beatles were recorded during a loose jam session.

■ A promotional film of The Beatles singing "Lady Madonna" was shown on BBC-TV's "All Systems Freeman." It was seen in the U.S. on "Hollywood Palace" on Mar 30.

Mar 30: The single "Lady Madonna" reached number one in the U.K.

Mar: Apple hired Ken Partride, a design consultant, to stop the financial losses at the Apple Boutique.

That spring: George composed one verse for Donovan's song "Hurdy Gurdy Man," but the verse was not used on the released recording. A Donovan concert version, *with* the Harrison-composed verse, was released in 1990.

Apr 16: Apple Publicity Ltd. was formed.

Apr 20: Apple Music ran ads soliciting tapes from unknown artists, and the company was quickly swamped with submissions. Financial grants were given to many applicants, often with little regard to merit. John hired an astrologer named Caleb to consult the *I Ching Book of Changes* regarding business decisions. The music side of Apple's business was somewhat more successful, and the company would eventually sign Badfinger (originally called The Iveys), Grapefruit, James Taylor, Mary Hopkin, Jackie Lomax, The Modern Jazz Quartet, Steve Miller, Family, Donovan, Trash (aka White Trash), Billy Preston, John's "Plastic Ono Band," The Radha Krishna Temple, The Hot Chocolate Band, Doris Troy, John Tavener, Yoko Ono, Ronnie Spector, Bill Elliot, Ravi Shankar, David Peel, Chris Hodge, The Sundown Playboys, Elephant's Memory, and Lon and Derek Van Eaton.

May 11: John and Paul arrived in the U.S. to begin promoting Apple Corps Ltd. They also renounced their affiliation with the Maharishi.

(b) May 15: John and Paul appeared on the "Tonight Show" on NBC-TV, guest-hosted by Joe Garagiola. John later said that the event was one of the most embarrassing of his career; he had expected Johnny Carson to host the show, and Garagiola stupidly asked which of the two was Ringo. John and Paul also discussed Apple on the U.S. TV show "Newsfront." During their U.S. visit, John and Paul held Apple's first business conference on board a Chinese junk that navigated the waters surrounding Manhattan.

May 16: John and Paul returned to England. Apple Management Ltd. was created.

■ The film *Wonderwall*, containing George's musical score, had its world premiere at the Cannes Film Festival.

(b) May 20: The Beatles began rehearsal sessions at George's home in Esher, known as Kinfauns, during which they recorded demos of virtually all of the songs that would appear on *The Beatles* (aka the "White Album"), and some unreleased songs.

May 22: A recorded interview of John and Paul was aired on radio station WNET in New York.

May 23: An interview with Paul and Ringo was filmed at Abbey Road studios and aired Oct 31 on BBC-TV's documentary, "All My Loving." A second Apple boutique was opened, at 161 Kings Road in Chelsea. It closed within a year.

(r) May 30–June 21: The Beatles recorded "Revolution 1." At several sessions during this period, John and Yoko Ono assembled a variety of sound effects, tape loops and other audio items into the wild "Revolution 9," released on *The Beatles*.

May: As work on what would become *The Beatles* progressed, the presence of Yoko Ono, who was constantly at John's side, interrupted the communication that had previously existed between John and Paul during recording sessions. Their collaboration was a loose one, primarily driven by a strong but productive rivalry between the two. Each man essentially wrote most of his songs alone, but then subjected them to the other's input once studio work began. Often, however, only one or two of The Beatles were present at "White Album" sessions. At one point Ringo announced that he was quitting the group and went home. (He returned later.) The Beatles worked on the album for five months. Although George Martin pleaded with them to cut the work to a single album containing only the best songs, they refused, and *The Beatles* was issued as a double LP, even retaining John's experimental "Revolution 9," despite the others' protests.

(r) Late May: John and Yoko recorded "Two Virgins" for their experimental album *Unfinished Music No. 1— Two Virgins*.

(r) Jun 5–6: Kenny Everett recorded a radio interview with The Beatles at Abbey Road during recording sessions for "Don't Pass Me By." The interview was heard in edited form on "The Kenny Everett Show" on Jun 9 in the U.K. and was later released by Apple only in Italy.

Jun 8–17: During a visit to Los Angeles, George and Ringo took part in a jam session at the home of Peter Tork (of The Monkees).

(rb) Jun 11: Paul recorded "Blackbird" alone.

Jun 15: John and Yoko held an "Acorn Event" consisting of two acorns labeled with their names being buried at Coventry Cathedral to symbolize peace and simplicity. Beatles' fans quickly dug up and removed the acorns as souvenirs. Two more acorns were then buried and a security guard posted around the clock. This was the first of many such exhibits and "events" staged by the couple. John and Yoko were now hounded by the press with questions regarding their extra-marital relationship and about their respective spouses.

Jun 18: A one-act play, *In His Own Write*—based on John's two books—was performed by the National Theatre Company and opened in London at the Old Vic Theatre. The play was adapted by John, Adrienne Kennedy and actor Victor Spinetti (who directed). John and Yoko attended the opening.

Jun 21: Apple Corps Ltd. purchased offices at 3 Savile Row, London. Paul and other Apple officials attended the Capitol Records convention in Hollywood, California where they screened a film promoting Apple Records and singer Mary Hopkin, and announced that Beatles' records would henceforth appear on the Apple label.

Jun 22: John was interviewed on the BBC-2 TV show "Release." He discussed the play *In His Own Write*.

Jun 24–26: George produced Jackie Lomax recording sessions.

(r) **Jun 27–Jul 23:** The Beatles recorded "Everybody's Got Something to Hide Except Me and My Monkey."

Jun 30: In Yorkshire, Paul produced the recording of the TV theme "Thingumybob" by The Black Dyke Mills Brass Band. It became one of the first four records released on the Apple label on Aug 26.

(b) **That summer:** John recorded the unreleased, rambling, narrative-style "The Maharishi Song," a critical summation of his experience with the title character while in India and a Lennon/Ono recording called "I Want You" (not The Beatles' song), also largely improvised.

(b) **Jul:** An alternate acoustic version of "Helter Skelter" was recorded and aired on Dutch television's "Vara's Puntje" on Sep 27.

Jul 1: John held an art exhibition titled "You Are Here" at the Robert Fraser Gallery in London. Featured was John's sculpture "Built Around," which invited visitors to add to it whatever they liked. Lennon launched the show by letting loose 365 balloons.

(b) **Jul 3–5:** The Beatles cut an alternate version of "Ob-La-Di, Ob-La-Da,"; it was slated for official release by EMI in 1985 as the B side of the canceled "Leave My Kitten Alone" single, which was to have been issued in connection with the scrapped *Sessions* album.

(r) **Jul 8–15:** The Beatles recorded the released version of "Ob-La-Di, Ob-La-Da."

(rb) **Jul 10–12:** The Beatles recorded "Revolution," released as a single.

(b) **Jul 15:** An unreleased mono mix of "Ob-La-Di, Ob-La-Da" was made. Apple Corps Ltd. moved into its new offices at 3 Savile Row in London, and Ringo formed his own music company, Startling Music Ltd.

(r) **Jul 16 & 18:** The Beatles recorded "Cry Baby Cry."

Jul 17: The world premiere of the film *Yellow Submarine* took place at the London Pavilion and was attended by all four of The Beatles. The Beatles actually had very little to do with the production of this animated, feature-length cartoon, and appeared on screen only for a few minutes at the end. The voices for the film's cartoon Beatles were provided by Peter Battan (George), Paul Angelus (Ringo), John Clive (John) and Geoffrey Hughes (Paul). The film was directed by George Dunning and featured several previously released Beatles songs. Despite The Beatles' lack of interest in the effort, *Yellow Submarine* was one of the most popular and enduring of all Beatle-related productions. Its release spawned a new round of Beatlemania, accompanied by high sales of novelties patterned after the film's psychedelic motif. John later accused the film's producer, Al Brodax, of stealing from him most of the film's ideas (including the Vacuum Cleaner Monster and the Sea of Holes). The Beatles held a party at the Royal Lancaster Hotel in London to mark the film's opening.

(b) **Jul 18:** The Beatles recorded three lengthy alternate unreleased takes of "Helter Skelter," one lasting a staggering 27 minutes.

(b) **Jul 19:** Lennon did an impromptu ballad about The Beatles' late manager—dubbed "Brian Epstein Blues" by the bootleggers who released the recording. The group also recorded an unreleased 6-minute instrumental version of "Summertime" and a take of "Sexy Sadie" with off-color lyrics.

Jul 20: Paul and his longtime girlfriend, Jane Asher, broke their engagement, which had been announced the past Dec. Soon afterward Paul began seeing Linda Eastman, daughter of Lee Eastman, a prestigious attorney and head of the New York law firm of Eastman and Eastman (not of Eastman/Kodak). Linda was a professional photographer who specialized in candid photographs of rock musicians.

(rb) **Jul 22:** The Beatles recorded "Good Night."

■ An alternate mono mix of "Don't Pass Me By" was created and reportedly included on a tape of mono *White Album* tracks given to actor/comedian Peter Sellers by Ringo.

(b) **Jul 23:** A slightly different mono mix of "Everybody's Got Something to Hide Except Me and My Monkey" was made.

(b) **Jul 25:** George recorded an unreleased acoustic version of "While My Guitar Gently Weeps."

(b) **Jul 29:** The Beatles recorded unreleased rehearsals of "Hey Jude."

(b) **Jul 30:** The Beatles were filmed rehearsing "Hey Jude." The film was aired in August 1968 on the "Experiment in TV" show.

Jul 31: The Apple Boutique was closed and The Beatles relinquished control of Apple's second boutique located on Kings Road. John and Paul decided to close the original facility by simply giving away the remaining merchandise. The Beatles had spent £200,000 in less than eight months on this losing venture.

(r) **Jul 31–Aug 1:** The Beatles recorded "Hey Jude" at Trident Studios.

(b) **Jul–Aug:** During recording sessions for *The Beatles* album, three tapes containing studio outtakes and con-

versation, titled "Beatles Chat," were compiled. The Beatles also worked on songs that would not be recorded for release until later, including "Something," "Let It Be" and "The Long and Winding Road."

(b) **Aug 7–12:** The Beatles recorded an unreleased version of "Not Guilty." George later rerecorded the song for his *George Harrison* album.

(r) **Aug 9 & 20:** Paul recorded "Mother Nature's Son" alone. The song had once tentatively been titled "Maharishi."

(r) **Aug 13–14:** The Beatles recorded "Yer Blues."

(rb) **Aug 13 & 21:** The Beatles recorded "Sexy Sadie."

(b) **Aug 14:** John, George and Yoko Ono recorded the unreleased "What's the New Mary Jane."

(rb) **Aug 15:** The Beatles recorded "Rocky Raccoon."

(rb) **Aug 20:** Paul recorded "Wild Honey Pie," little more than an improvisation, and the unreleased "Etcetera."

(b) **Aug 21:** Five alternate mono mixes of "Sexy Sadie" were made. Final overdubs for the released version were completed on this date.

Aug 22: Cynthia Lennon filed suit for divorce from John. Earlier in the summer, Cynthia had returned home unexpectedly from a vacation in Greece to find Lennon and Ono living together.

(r) **Aug 22–23:** The Beatles recorded "Back in the USSR," without Ringo. Capping what had been an acrimonious series of sessions, Ringo became fed up with what he considered abusive treatment by the other members of the group and announced that he was quitting The Beatles. Ringo would return to the group on Sep 4 for the filming of "Hey Jude" and "Revolution" promo films and would resume recording sessions the following day. His outburst, however, was indicative of the general mood among the members of the group during the *"White Album"* sessions.

(b) **Aug 23:** A rare mono mix of "Back in the USSR" was made on this date, and released only on the U.K. mono version of *The Beatles*.

Aug 26: Single "Hey Jude"/"Revolution" released in the U.S. At an EMI sales conference, Derek Taylor screened unreleased, rare film footage of Paul performing with Mary Hopkin.

(rb) **Aug 28–30:** The Beatles recorded "Dear Prudence" at Trident Studios.

(b) **Sept 4:** The Beatles recorded promotional films before a live audience of 300 people singing "Hey Jude," aired Sep 8 on ITV's "Frost on Sunday" show, and "Revolution," aired Sep 19 on BBC-TV's "Top of the Pops." "Hey Jude" was aired in the U.S. on Oct 6 and "Revolution" on Oct 13 on "The Smothers Brothers Comedy Hour."

(rb) **Sept 5–6:** Ringo returned to the studio, and The Beatles recorded "While My Guitar Gently Weeps" for *The Beatles*, with Eric Clapton adding a guitar solo overdub.

(r) **Sep 9–10:** The Beatles recorded "Helter Skelter."

Sep 10: Film of Paul and Mary Hopkin was aired on the ITV children's show "Magpie."

(r) **Sep 11–Oct 10:** The Beatles recorded "Glass Onion."

Sep 14: A documentary film, *All My Loving*, was aired on U.K. TV and included interviews with The Beatles by Tony Palmer.

■ The single "Hey Jude" reached number one in the U.K.

(rb) **Sep 16–17:** The Beatles, minus George, recorded "I Will."

(r) **Sep 18:** The Beatles recorded "Birthday." Pattie Boyd Harrison and Yoko Ono contributed some of the backing vocals on this track.

■ George was interviewed by Alan Smith for BBC Radio One's "Scene and Heard," aired Sep 28.

(r) **Sep 19–20:** The Beatles recorded "Piggies."

(r) **Sep 23–25:** The Beatles recorded "Happiness Is a Warm Gun."

Sep 28: The single "Hey Jude" reached number one in the U.S. and remained there for nine weeks.

Sep: The Beatles announced plans for a live TV show and three live concerts. Paul was quoted in the British press as saying that he loved the idea of renewing live concerts and felt sure the other Beatles shared his interest. The concerts were tentatively scheduled for London during the week of Dec 14, but never took place.

(r) **Oct 1–4:** The Beatles recorded "Honey Pie" at Trident Studios.

(r) **Oct 3–14:** The Beatles recorded "Savoy Truffle" at Trident Studios and at Abbey Road.

(r) **Oct 4–5:** "Martha My Dear" was recorded at Trident Studios.

(r) **Oct 7–9:** The Beatles recorded "Long Long Long."

(r) **Oct 8:** The Beatles recorded "I'm So Tired" and "The Continuing Story of Bungalow Bill." One line of lead vocal, "Not when he looked so fierce," was sung by Yoko Ono, and Maureen Starkey sang on the track as well.

(r) **Oct 9–10:** Paul and Ringo recorded "Why Don't We Do It in the Road."

Oct 10: George formed Singsong Ltd., yet another music publishing company.

(r) **Oct 13:** John recorded "Julia" alone, the last track for *The Beatles*.

Oct 18: John and Yoko were arrested for possession of marijuana while staying at Ringo's house. The following day their case was adjourned until Nov 28 and they were freed on bail. (See Nov 28 for further details.)

Oct: John and Yoko's films *Smile* and *Two Virgins* premiered in Chicago.

Middle of Oct: John took nude photos of Yoko and himself with a delayed shutter-release while staying at Ringo's home at 34 Montague Square, London. The photos were eventually used for the front and back covers of the LP *Unfinished Music No. 1—Two Virgins*.

(b) **Oct–Nov:** John cut an acoustic demo of "Everybody Had a Hard Year," a song he never actually finished but which was later incorporated into "I've Got a Feeling."

(r) Nov 4–25: John and Yoko recorded songs that became side two of their LP *Unfinished Music No. 2: Life with the Lions*. The recordings were made in Room No. 1, Second West Ward, Queen Charlotte Hospital, Hammersmith, as John and Yoko awaited the birth of their child.

Nov 8: Cynthia Lennon was granted a divorce from John following an uncontested suit. George did not renew his Northern Songs Ltd. songwriting contract, which expired on this date.

Nov 11: John and Yoko's LP *Unfinished Music No. 1: Two Virgins* was released in the U.S. and in the U.K. on Nov 29, with nude photographs of them on the front and back covers. The LP arrived in record stores in a plain brown wrapper.

Nov 13: New York premiere of the film *Yellow Submarine*.

Nov 21: Yoko Ono suffered a miscarriage at Queen Charlotte's Hospital. A photograph taken of John and Yoko in the hospital later became the front cover of the LP *Unfinished Music No. 2: Life with the Lions*.

Nov 22: *The Beatles* or the "White Album" released in the U.K. Released in the U.S. on Nov 25.

Nov 24: Grapefruit, the first group signed by Apple, left The Beatles' company and eventually signed with Dunhill Records.

Nov 28: John and Yoko appeared before Marylebone Magistrates court on charges of possession of cannabis resin. John pleaded guilty in exchange for charges against Yoko being dropped; he was fined £150 and costs. This drug conviction caused John's later problems in seeking permission to remain in the U.S. in the 1970s. Throughout his life, John was certain that the drugs had been planted deliberately and that the arrest was a frame-up instigated by a disreputable policeman (later fired) who made a habit of arresting celebrities on drug possession charges. John and Yoko were photographed outside the court by the *Daily Mirror*. One of the photos was used on the back cover of the LP *Unfinished Music No. 2—Life with the Lions*.

Nov 30: The LP *The Beatles* reached number one in the U.K.

(rb) Nov: Each member of The Beatles separately recorded his portion of *The Beatles 1968 Christmas Record*, released to the fan club Dec 20. Tiny Tim recorded "Nowhere Man" for the disc while visiting George in the U.S.

(b) Nov–Jan 1969: During sessions for Mary Hopkin's *Post Card* album, produced by Paul, Donovan Leitch and McCartney were recorded running through several songs.

(b) Dec 10–11: Rehearsals (Dec 10) and filming (Dec 11) of The Rolling Stones' unreleased TV film *Rock and Roll Circus* took place, with John performing "Yer Blues."

Dec 17: The film *Candy*, featuring Ringo, premiered in New York.

Dec 18: John and Yoko appeared in a large white bag at London's Royal Albert Hall at the underground Christmas party called "Alchemical Wedding."

Dec 20: *The Beatles 1968 Christmas Record* was released to fan club.

Dec 28: The LP *The Beatles* reached number one in the U.S.

(b) Dec: John recorded demos of the unreleased "A Case of the Blues," and "Don't Let Me Down" and "Oh My Love."

(b) Late that year–early 1969: Paul cut a demo of "Goodbye" for Mary Hopkin.

1969

(r) Early that year: George recorded the instrumental tracks "No Time or Space" and "Under the Mersey Wall" for the experimental LP *Electronic Sound*.

Jan: The Beatles had begun negotiations to buy Nemperor Holdings, Brian Epstein's old NEMS Enterprises. Triumph Investment Trust offered £1 million for the 90% of Nemperor owned by the Epstein family; the remaining 10% was owned by The Beatles. Under a 1967 contract, all Beatles royalties went through Nemperor until 1977. Nemperor was to take its 25% of these earnings and then give the remainder to The Beatles through Apple.

(b) Jan 2–16: Work on a new Beatles project began at Twickenham Film Studios. The film was intended as a television documentary of the group at work, and the project was to culminate in a live concert. Along the way, the formal concert would be scrapped and the TV special converted into a theatrical film. The project was largely a compromise between Paul, who wanted to begin touring again, and the other Beatles, who were reluctant to do so. The album, to be produced by George Martin, would eliminate all of the sound effects, overdubbing, and other innovations that The Beatles had used in recent recordings, in order to create an "honest" rock-and-roll album. The project was initially titled *Get Back* to symbolize The Beatles' attempt to return to their rock-and-roll roots. However, the project quickly deteriorated into acrimony. During the sessions, Paul found it necessary to urge the others on constantly. Besides their new material, The Beatles often warmed up with many of their old songs and even older rock standards. Many unreleased songs and fragments were recorded during the filming; the *Let It Be* album contains only a tiny fraction of the work. The Beatles ended this month-long effort with 28 hours of film footage and so weary that they didn't want to hear, let alone edit, the music tracks. John wanted to release an early version of the album, mixed by Glyn Johns and titled *Get Back*. He said, "It'll tell people, 'This is us with our trousers off, so will you please end the game now?'" The live concerts that Paul had envisioned ended up as a single impromptu jam session on Jan 30 on the roof of the Apple building and was stopped by the police after local residents and merchants complained about the noise.

Jan 3: Newark, New Jersey police confiscated 30,000 copies of John and Yoko's LP *Two Virgins* claiming that the nude cover photo was pornographic. A Chicago record store was closed down after displaying the cover.

Jan 10: George announced that he was fed up with Paul "getting at" him and said that he was quitting The Beatles. He returned a few days later.

Jan 12: London premiere of film *Wonderwall*, which featured George's musical score.

Jan 13: LP *Yellow Submarine* released in the U.S. Released in the U.K. on Jan 17.

Jan 18: John was quoted in *Disc and Music Echo* as saying that if Apple continued losing money at its present rate, The Beatles would be "broke in the next six months." He said that the Apple concept had failed due to a lack of experienced business personnel. George was so angered by John's remarks that the two nearly came to blows, and the *Get Back* sessions soured even more. Allen Klein, a New York accountant, read John's remarks and was prompted to renew earlier bids he had made to become The Beatles' manager.

(b) Jan 20–31: The Beatles moved operations from Twickenham to their recording studio at Apple's headquarters at 3 Savile Row. There they concluded filming and recording for the *Let It Be* project. They found that "Magic Alex" had installed none of his promised recording facilities, and they had to bring in rented equipment.

(r) Jan 21: Ringo was interviewed by David Wigg for BBC Radio One's "Scene and Heard," aired on Jan 25 and later released on LP *The Beatles Tapes*.

(b) Jan 22: Joined for the first time by organist Billy Preston, The Beatles recorded songs later included on Glyn Johns' first unreleased *Get Back* album mix.

(b) Jan 23: An untitled one-minute blues instrumental improvisation was recorded.

(rb) Jan 24: The Beatles recorded "Maggic Mae." They also worked on "Dig It," then called "Can You Dig It?"

(rb) Jan 25: The Beatles recorded "For You Blue" under the working title "George's Blues."

■ Government officials in Union County, New Jersey banned the sale of *Two Virgins* because of its nude cover photos of John and Yoko. Mountainside, New Jersey police confiscated more than 20,000 copies of the LP. The city of Cleveland also ruled that the cover was obscene and, therefore, its sale illegal.

(rb) Jan 26: The Beatles recorded "Dig It," which ran 12:25 in its entirety, but was cut to about 50 seconds on the *Let It Be* album; a slightly longer clip appears in the *Let It Be* film.

(rb) Jan 27–28: The Beatles recorded "Get Back." Several takes were recorded, and it is not clear on which date the released version was recorded.

(rb) Jan 28: The Beatles recorded "Don't Let Me Down." John visited Allen Klein without telling the other Beatles and soon hired him to handle his business and financial affairs. This surprised the other Beatles, who thought the group had settled on the firm of Linda Eastman's father, Eastman and Eastman, Inc., as Paul had advocated. By now Paul planned to marry Linda Eastman and, while George and Ringo were willing to listen to Klein, Paul was not. The Eastmans warned Paul that Klein was disreputable, had a bad reputation and faced numerous lawsuits as well as charges of failing to file income tax returns. For a time The Beatles allowed the two companies to share management of their business affairs in an attempt to clear up the Apple financial mess. Paul later refused to allow Klein to represent him, however, and would not attend meetings with Klein and the other three Beatles, sending a lawyer to represent him instead. This irreconcilable difference was a leading factor in the eventual demise of The Beatles.

(b) Jan 29: The Beatles recorded several unreleased songs.

(rb) Jan 30: The Beatles' rooftop concert atop their Apple building took place and lasted 42 minutes, about half of it serving as the end of the *Let It Be* film. Some songs were released on the *Let It Be* LP.

(rb) Jan 31: The Beatles recorded "Two of Us" and "The Long and Winding Road." They also recorded "Let It Be" with various overdubs added on Apr 30 and Jan 4, 1970, which was the last recording session ever held by The Beatles as a group.

Feb 2: Yoko Ono and Anthony Cox were divorced. Cox received £6,700 as a divorce settlement, and Yoko retained custody of the couple's daughter, Kyoko.

Feb 3: Paul, billed as Paul Ramon, assisted Steve Miller in his recording of "My Dark Hour." The Beatles formally hired Allen Klein as their business manager. The Eastmans (Eastman and Eastman) were appointed general counsel for Apple on the following day in an attempt at compromise with Paul, but this dual arrangement never worked out. Klein entered into the negotiations between Apple and Nemperor despite the fact that Clive Epstein, who headed the company, had already said that The Beatles would have the first chance to buy the company. Klein's abrasiveness prompted Epstein to renew talks with Triumph Investment Trust, to whom the company was eventually sold.

Feb 7: George was admitted to University College Hospital in London, where his tonsils were removed the following day. George left the hospital on Feb 15.

Feb 12: Paul formed Adagrose Ltd. He would later rename the company McCartney Productions Ltd. (MPL).

Feb 20: World premiere of the film *Candy*, featuring Ringo, in London.

(rb) Feb 22–Aug 11: The Beatles recorded "I Want You (She's So Heavy)."

Feb 23: Paul introduced Mary Hopkin on U.S. TV's "The David Frost Show."

Feb 24: Nemperor Holdings was sold to Triumph Investment Trust. As controlling owners of NEMS, it would now collect Brian Epstein's old 25% of Beatles' performance royalties. The Beatles then instructed EMI to pay all royalties directly to Apple Corps, not to NEMS, and informed Triumph that NEMS no longer represented The Beatles. Triumph objected, claiming that there still existed a nine-year contract with EMI signed Jan 27, 1967, by which all record royalties were to go through NEMS no matter who owned it. Triumph sued The Beatles and EMI froze £1.3 million in royalties (scheduled to be paid to The Beatles) pending the outcome of the case.

(b) Feb 25: George recorded unreleased versions of "Old Brown Shoe," "All Things Must Pass" and "Something" without the other Beatles.

(r) Mar 1: Ringo began shooting the film *The Magic Christian* with filming completed in May. "The Hunting Scene," featuring Ringo and Peter Sellers, was included on the soundtrack LP *The Magic Christian*.

■ Paul acted as producer during Mary Hopkin's recording sessions.

(r) Mar 2: John and Yoko recorded "Cambridge 1969" live at Lady Mitchell Hall, Cambridge, England; released on LP *Unfinished Music No. 2: Life with the Lions*. This is really a nonstop Ono screaming track with no real sign of John, who provided guitar feedback as "background" to Ono's "music."

Mar 4: George was interviewed by David Wigg for BBC Radio One's "Scene and Heard," aired in two parts on Mar 8 and Apr 12. A small part was released on LP *The Beatles Tapes*.

Mar 12: Paul and Linda were married at Marylebone Register Office, London. The other Beatles did not attend. On the same day, the police raided George's house and arrested him and Pattie for possession of 570 grams of cannabis. On Mar 18 they were released on bail pending trial set for Mar 31.

Middle of Mar: Dick James sold his 23% of Northern Songs stock to Associated Television (ATV), owned by Sir Lew Grade, for over £1 million. Although Northern Songs, set up by James in 1963 exclusively for Lennon/McCartney compositions, owned The Beatles song catalog, James made the sale without telling The Beatles. Neither ATV nor The Beatles owned sufficient shares to establish control of the company, and the two competing entities began a frantic race to buy up additional shares in order to obtain majority control. Paul secretly bought so many shares in Northern Songs that he had 100,000 more shares than John. John felt that he had been treated underhandedly by Paul, whose action would later be seen as contributing to the group's demise. The Beatles, however, continued the race with ATV to gain control of Northern Songs, and John compared the experience to "playing Monopoly with real money."

Mar 20: John and Yoko were married at the British Consulate in Gibraltar. They announced that they were going to stage many "events" and "happenings," their wedding being one of them.

(rb) Mar 25–31: John and Yoko's honeymoon consisted of spending a week in bed at the Amsterdam Hilton Hotel. The press misguidedly thought they intended to make love in public during their "bed-in," generally considered their actions to be self-indulgent and saw no relevance in them to the Vietnam war or the cause of peace as the couple had said they intended. The bed-in was filmed by Apple Films but remained unreleased until 1991, when it appeared on video cassette and laser disc as *John and Yoko: The Bed-In (All We Are Saying Is Give Peace a Chance)*. During the bed-in, John and Yoko recorded "Amsterdam," later released on LP *Wedding Album*. They also recorded the unreleased jingle "Radio Peace."

Mar 31: John and Yoko's second "happening" occurred when they held a press conference while they lay inside a giant white bag on a table in the Sacher Hotel's Red Salon in Vienna. The press conference dealt with the world premiere of their film *Rape* (on this date) on Austrian National Television. Thus, "bagism," or "total communication," was demonstrated. In noting Lennon's actions, the *Daily Mirror* lamented that "a not inconsiderable talent . . . seems to have gone completely off his rocker."

■ George and Pattie pleaded guilty to charges of marijuana possession stemming from their arrest Mar 12. They were fined £250 each.

Apr 1: John and Yoko made an April Fool's Day appearance on the U.K. TV show, "Today," hosted by Eamonn Andrews.

Apr 11: Single "Get Back"/"Don't Let Me Down" released in the U.K., with the label crediting The Beatles and Billy Preston. Released in the U.S. on May 5.

(r) Apr 14: John and Paul recorded "The Ballad of John and Yoko."

(b) Apr 16: George recorded unreleased takes of "Something."

(r) Apr 16 & 18: The Beatles recorded "Old Brown Shoe."

(r) Apr 20–Aug 11: The Beatles recorded "Oh! Darling."

Apr 21: John and Yoko founded Bag Productions; it was dissolved in 1979.

(r) Apr 22: In a formal ceremony held on the roof of Apple's Savile Row headquarters, John's middle name was changed from Winston to Ono, although under British law "Winston" had also to be retained as part of his name.

■ John and Yoko recorded the 22-minute track "John and Yoko" in studio two at Abbey Road, released on their LP *Wedding Album*.

Apr 24: The Beatles-Triumph case was settled out-of-court through cash payments and a realignment of royalty disbursements.

Apr 25: John and Yoko's film *Rape* was screened at a television festival in Montreaux, Switzerland.

(r) Apr 26–Jul 18: The Beatles recorded "Octopus's Garden."

(r) Apr 30: John and Paul added vocals and additional sound effects to "You Know My Name (Look Up the Number)." The rhythm tracks and many sound effects had been recorded in 1967. See May 17, 1967 for additional details.

Apr–May: Paul, still anxious to give live performances, suggested that The Beatles make a series of unannounced appearances at small clubs. Although George and Ringo seemed receptive, John was not. By fall John had told Paul that he intended to leave The Beatles and wanted a divorce from them, "Like my divorce from Cynthia." Acrimonious meetings of this kind took place throughout the fall, but John's plans were kept secret in order to give Allen Klein enough time to negotiate a higher royalty with Capitol Records in the U.S. Capitol eventually agreed to 69 cents on each Beatles LP sold in the U.S., an unprecedented royalty. Klein's success in this area did not win over Paul, as Klein had hoped it would.

(r) May 2–Aug 15: The Beatles recorded "Something."

May 3: Single "Get Back" reached number one in the U.K.

May 5: ATV gained effective control of Northern Songs and thus of the Lennon/McCartney song catalog. ATV also obtained Lenmac Enterprises Ltd. in the deal. The acquisition became final on Sep 25.

(r) May 6–Jul 31: The Beatles recorded "You Never Give Me Your Money."

May 8: Allen Klein concluded a contract with John, George and Ringo making his company, ABKCO, manager of several Apple Corps companies. Paul refused to allow Klein to represent him and continued to deal through the Eastmans. John was interviewed by David Wigg for BBC Radio One's "Scene and Heard," aired in two parts May 11 and 18. Part of it was released on LP *The Beatles Tapes*.

May 9: John and Yoko's LP *Unfinished Music No. 2— Life with the Lions* and George's LP *Electronic Sound* were released in the U.K. on The Beatles' short-lived experimental Zapple label. They were released in the U.S. on May 26.

May 16: John was refused a visa by the U.S. Embassy in London due to his 1968 U.K. drug conviction.

■ Ringo and family left England aboard the *Queen Elizabeth II* with the cast of the film *The Magic Christian*. They arrived in New York on May 22.

May 19: The Beatles received the Ivor Novello Award for "Hey Jude," Britain's top-selling single in 1968.

May 20: Public announcement was made that Allen Klein had become The Beatles' manager. Klein then moved into the Apple offices on Savile Road, where he ruthlessly "cleaned house," firing executives and hangers-on en masse. Both the productive and those whom John Lennon called "spongers" and "hustlers" (presumably including "Magic Alex") were dismissed. Klein was able to stop the drain of money from Apple, and his main concern now was to obtain higher record royalties for The Beatles.

May 24: Single "Get Back" reached number one in the U.S.

(b) May 25: John taped a pre-bed-in recording of "Give Peace a Chance" at the King Edward Hotel in Toronto during an interview.

(b) May 26–Jun 2: John and Yoko's second bed-in took place in room 1742 of the Queen Elizabeth Hotel, Montreal. They were heavily involved in the anti-Vietnam war movement, and John was still barred from entering the U.S. because of his 1968 U.K. drug conviction. The bed-in consisted largely of broadcasts to U.S. and Canadian radio stations, and culminated with the live recording of John's composition "Give Peace a Chance" on Jun 1, which became an anthem for the peace movement and marked the start of a two-month media blitz by John and Yoko to spread their views through various demonstrations. For once John felt he was able to use constant media attention for his own purposes or, as he put it, to do a "commercial for peace."

(r) May 29: John was interviewed by telephone during the Montreal bed-in by Tom Campbell and Bill Holley of KYA Radio in San Francisco, later released as "The KYA 1969 Peace Talk."

May 30: The single "The Ballad of John and Yoko"/"Old Brown Shoe" was released in the U.K. Released in the U.S. on Jun 4. The A side was banned from many stations due to the refrain, containing the name of "Christ." On some radio stations the word "Christ" was re-edited so that it was played backward whenever the songs was aired.

(rb) Jun 1: "Give Peace a Chance" was recorded by John and Yoko at their bed-in. The chorus included Timothy Leary, The Smothers Brothers, Petula Clark, Derek Taylor, a local Canadian rabbi and the Canadian Radha Krishna Temple. A rehearsal version was also recorded. D.J. Murray "The K" Kaufman did not participate in the recording but was present.

Jun 7: John and Yoko returned to England from Canada.

"Give Peace a Chance" (© Apple Corps Ltd.). This German 12-inch maxi single was the full version with John's count-in.

Jun 14: John and Yoko appeared on the U.K. TV show "The David Frost Show."

Jun 21: Single "The Ballad of John and Yoko" reached number one in the U.K.

Jul 1: John, Yoko, Julian and Kyoko were hospitalized after an auto accident while they were vacationing in Golspie, Scotland. Recording sessions for *Abbey Road* began without John.

(rb) **Jul 2:** Paul recorded "Her Majesty."

(rb) **Jul 2–Aug 15:** The Beatles recorded "Golden Slumbers/Carry That Weight."

Jul 3: Ringo and Maureen substituted for John and Yoko, who were recovering from their auto accident, at a press conference at the Chelsea Town Hall dealing with the release of "Give Peace a Chance."

Jul 4: Single "Give Peace a Chance" (John)/"Remember Love" (Yoko) released in the U.K. Released in the U.S. on Jul 7.

(r) **Jul 7–Aug 19:** The Beatles recorded "Here Comes the Sun."

(r) **Jul 9:** A pregnant Yoko Ono and her bed were carted into the Abbey Road recording studio, where they resided throughout the remaining *Abbey Road* sessions.

(rb) **Jul 9–Aug 6:** The Beatles recorded "Maxwell's Silver Hammer."

(b) **Jul 11:** Paul, George and Ringo recorded background vocals for "Maxwell's Silver Hammer." Work also continued on George's "Something."

(b) **Jul 11–23:** Several unreleased recordings were made at Abbey Road.

(r) **Jul 21–30:** The Beatles recorded "Come Together."

(r) **Jul 23–Aug 18:** The Beatles recorded "The End" on which Ringo performed the only drum solo of his Beatles career released on record. "The End" proved to be an ironic title indeed, representing the final song on the final Beatles album—aside from "Her Majesty," which was actually an afterthought.

(b) **Jul 24:** Paul recorded a demo of "Come and Get It," which was scheduled for release on EMI's scrapped 1985 *Sessions* album. The demo was recorded for Badfinger, who would record the song the following week with Paul as producer.

(rb) **Jul 24–29:** The Beatles recorded "Sun King"/"Mean Mr. Mustard" as one recording.

(rb) **Jul 25–30:** The Beatles recorded "Polythene Pam" and "She Came in Through the Bathroom Window." A prefinal mix of the *Abbey Road* medley was made.

(rb) **Aug 1–5:** The Beatles recorded "Because."

Aug 8: Photo session with Iain MacMillan for the cover of the *Abbey Road* album, with The Beatles crossing the zebra walk in front of the studio.

(b) **Aug 14:** A short, bouncy version of "Mean Mr. Mustard" was recorded, possibly during an interview with John recorded on this date by Kenny Everett at Abbey Road. The recording may have been made by Everett himself, with no Beatles involvement at all.

Aug 21: Paul changed the name of his company from Adagrose Ltd. to McCartney Productions Ltd. (MPL).

Aug 27: Each of The Beatles sold their remaining shares in NEMS Enterprises Ltd.

Aug 28: Paul and Linda's first child, Mary McCartney, was born.

(b) **Aug:** John recorded the unreleased instrumental "Rock Peace."

Sep 1: John, George and Ringo attended a Bob Dylan concert on the Isle of Wight.

Sep 7: "The Beatles" U.S. cartoon series was canceled. The series had first aired on Sep 19, 1965.

Sep 8: Ringo was admitted to Middlesex Hospital for treatment of intestinal problems. He was released on Sep 11.

Sep 10: John and Yoko's films *Rape*, *Self Portrait*, *Honeymoon*, *Two Virgins* and *Smile* were screened at the Institute of Contemporary Arts in London. The two appeared in a white bag and remained there throughout the show.

(r) **Sep 13:** John and Yoko were recorded live at The Rock and Roll Revival at Varsity Stadium in Toronto, where they appeared with a hastily assembled Plastic Ono Band that also included Eric Clapton, Klaus Voorman and Alan White. The performance was later issued on LP *Plastic Ono Band: Live Peace in Toronto—1969*, and on video cassette as *Live Rock & Roll Revival—Toronto*, the footage taken from a much longer film made by D.A. Pennebacker but cut from that release.

(r) **Sep 19:** Paul was interviewed by David Wigg for BBC Radio One's "Scene and Heard," aired in two parts on Sep 21 and 28, and released on the LP *The Beatles Tapes*.

Sep 20: Allen Klein completed a new Beatles contract with EMI/Capitol that called for higher royalties. John appointed Klein manager of Bag Productions.

(rb) **Sep 25:** John recorded "Cold Turkey."

Sep 26: LP *Abbey Road* released in the U.K. Released in the U.S. on Oct 1. This, the group's final album, is generally regarded as one of their best, showcasing the four individual talents and culminating in the medley on side two. George's expanding abilities are demonstrated on "Here Comes the Sun" and "Something," the latter also his first Beatles single A side. Ringo contributed the characteristic "Octopus's Garden," while Paul flexed his vocal muscles with "Oh! Darling," added the tongue-in-cheek "Maxwell's Silver Hammer" and was primarily responsible for the medley. John's songs were indicative of the rougher blues-oriented musical path he was then treading ("Come Together," "I Want You [She's So Heavy]"), but also included the lighter "Because" and "Mean Mr. Mustard" and "Polythene Pam," which were two key ingredients in the medley, despite Lennon's later stated dislike of that segment.

(b) **Early Sep:** John cut several demos of "Cold Turkey." While he wanted to record the song for the *Abbey Road* album, the other Beatles rejected it, and Lennon then decided to release the song as a solo number, recording the released take on Sep 25.

(r) That fall: The Beatles separately recorded tracks for *The Beatles Seventh Christmas Record* (their last fan club Christmas disc).

Oct: Rumors began circulating that Paul was dead and that his death was being covered up by use of a look-alike double named William Campbell. The myth was reportedly begun by Detroit D.J. Russ Gibb, who allegedly received a phone call noting a number of "clues" regarding Paul's "death" that could be found on Beatles records, including the following: Paul wore no shoes on the *Abbey Road* cover (people in England are buried without shoes); Paul's back is turned on the *Sgt. Pepper* cover; Paul is the only one wearing a black carnation on *Magical Mystery Tour*; if played backward, "Revolution 9" allegedly reveals John saying "Turn me on, dead man" twice; the end of "I'm So Tired," if played backward, sounds like John saying "Paul is dead; miss him, miss him"; at the end of "Strawberry Fields Forever" John is supposedly heard to say "I buried Paul" (John later told interviewers that he had said "cranberry sauce"); the "28 IF" Volkswagen license plate on the *Abbey Road* cover indicates the age Paul would have reached were he still alive (he actually would not reach 28 until Jun 18, 1970). This well-publicized nonsense drove the sale of Beatles records to a new high. *Abbey Road* alone would initially sell 5 million copies, 1 million more than *Sgt. Pepper*.

(b) Oct 2: John was interviewed on BBC Radio and discussed the *Abbey Road* album.

Oct 4: The LP *Abbey Road* reached number one in the U.K.

Oct 6: Single "Something"/"Come Together" released in the U.S., featuring George's first Beatles A side. Released in the U.K. on Oct 31.

(r) Oct 8: George was interviewed by David Wigg for BBC Radio One's "Scene and Heard," aired in two parts on Oct 12 and 19, and released on the LP *The Beatles Tapes*.

Oct 9: Yoko Ono entered the hospital, where she would suffer a miscarriage on Oct 12.

Oct 20: John and Yoko's LP *Wedding Album* released in the U.S. Released on the U.K. on Nov 7.

■ Single "Cold Turkey" (John)/"Don't Worry Kyoko" (Yoko), featuring Ringo on drums, released in the U.S. Released in the U.K. on Oct 24.

Oct 21: John was interviewed by David Wigg for BBC Radio One's "Scene and Heard," aired Oct 26.

(rb) Oct 27–Dec: Ringo recorded songs for his album *Sentimental Journey*.

(b) Oct 31: George, Eric Clapton, Ric Grech and Denny Laine recorded unreleased tracks at Olympic Sound Studios in London.

(b) Late Oct: A Lennon-Ono recording called "John & Yoko's Happy Xmas Ditty" may date from around this time when the two recorded material for *The Beatles 1969 Christmas Record*.

■ John and Yoko's film *Apotheosis (Balloon)* premiered at the Institute of Contemporary Arts, The Mall, London.

Nov 1: The LP *Abbey Road* reached number one in the U.S.

Nov 3: The Institute of Contemporary Arts in London held another evening of John and Yoko film screenings.

Nov 6: John and Yoko's film *Rape—Part II* was screened at the Mannheim Film Festival in Germany.

Nov 10: The Institute of Contemporary Arts again ran a program of John and Yoko films.

Nov 25: John renounced his MBE, returning it to the queen with the following note: "I am returning this MBE in protest against Britain's involvement in the Nigeria-Biafra thing, against our support of America in Vietnam and against 'Cold Turkey' slipping down the charts."

Nov 26: A TV special, "John Lennon: A Tribute," was aired by the Canadian Broadcasting Company.

Nov 29: The single "Come Together" reached number one in the U.S.

Dec 1: The 77th and last issue of the original *Beatles Book* was published. It would resume publication in May 1976.

Dec 2–5: George appeared with Delaney and Bonnie and Friends at Colston Hall in Bristol (Dec 2), at City Hall in Sheffield (Dec 3), at the City Hall in Newcastle (Dec 4) and with Eric Clapton joining the group at the Empire Theatre in Liverpool (Dec 5).

Dec 5: Badfinger's single, "Come and Get It," written and produced by Paul, was released in the U.K. Released in the U.S. on Jan 12, 1970.

Dec 6: Ringo appeared on "The David Frost Show" on U.K. TV.

Dec 7: Delaney and Bonnie and Friends performed at Croydon's Fairfield Hall backed by George and Eric Clapton. The performance was released on LP *Delaney and Bonnie on Tour*.

■ John appeared on BBC-TV's "The Question Why."

(b) Dec 8: At Abbey Road, Ringo recorded a new vocal for "Octopus's Garden" for the George Martin TV special "With a Little Help from My Friends," aired by the IBA network in England on Dec 24.

Dec 9: John and Yoko announced their support for a public investigation into the execution for murder of James Hanratty in England in Apr 1963. They also announced plans for a film about Hanratty.

Dec 10: Ringo appeared on the BBC show "Late Night Line Up."

(b) Dec 10–14: The Delaney and Bonnie and Friends group extended their tour into Scandinavia for a few days with George and Eric Clapton.

Dec 11: Ringo's film *The Magic Christian* had its world premiere at the Odeon in Kensington. John and Yoko arrived in their white Rolls-Royce carrying a sign that read "Britain Murdered Hanratty."

Dec 12: The LP *Plastic Ono Band Live Peace in Toronto—1969* was released in both the U.S. and the U.K.

■ LP *No One's Gonna Change Our World* released in U.K. only containing the first version of "Across the Universe."

Dec 14: Ringo taped an additional segment for the TV special *With a Little Help from My Friends*, aired Dec 24.

(r) Dec 15: John and Yoko performed at the Lyceum Ballroom, London, with a group that included George Harrison, thus marking the first live appearance by more than one member of The Beatles since the group's final concert on Aug 29, 1966 and the Jan 30 Apple rooftop appearance. The concert was organized to benefit UNICEF and was dubbed "Peace for Christmas." John's performance of "Cold Turkey" and Ono's "Don't Worry Kyoko" were released on LP *Some Time in New York City*. Also appearing with the group were Eric Clapton, Billy Preston, Keith Moon (drummer of The Who) and members of the Delaney and Bonnie and Friends tour. The group was billed as The Plastic Ono Supergroup. BBC 1's documentary "24 Hours" was devoted to coverage of John and Yoko and included unreleased interview and other film footage.

Dec 16: John and Yoko purchased ads on billboards in several large cities proclaiming "War Is Over! If You Want It—Happy Xmas from John and Yoko."

(b) Dec 17: In Toronto, John and Yoko held a press conference and announced plans for a peace festival to be held Jul 3–5, 1970. It was canceled in Feb 1970.

Dec 19: An interview with John and Marshall McLuhan was filmed by CBS-TV in the U.S. *The Beatles Seventh Christmas Record* (their last) was released to the fan club. The front sleeve was photographed by Ringo and the back sleeve was drawn by his son, Zak.

Dec 21: John and Yoko held a press conference at the Chateau Champlain Hotel in Montreal.

Dec 23: John and Yoko met with Canadian Prime Minister Pierre Trudeau to discuss their plan to make 1970 "Year One for Peace." They returned to England the next day, where they joined a sit-in/fasting demonstration for peace in Kent.

Dec 25: A prerecorded spot by Ringo for the British Wireless for the Blind was aired on BBC Radio One.

(b) Dec 29: John and Yoko flew to Aalborg, Denmark to visit Yoko's daughter, Kyoko, who was ill, at the home of Kyoko's father, Anthony Cox and his wife, Melinda. During this visit two Canadian hypnotists hypnotized the Lennons in an effort to force them to give up smoking. Apparently the "cure" did not work since the two were still heavy smokers at the time of John's death. The Lennons were also taped at a press conference where they joined in on "O Kristelighed" ("O Christianity"), written nearly 100 years earlier by a Danish priest named Grundtvig.

(b) Dec 30: ITV aired a one-hour special called "Man of the Decade," featuring segments on John Lennon, Mao Tse-tung and John F. Kennedy. The 20-minute segment on Lennon featured a new interview with him. *Rolling Stone* magazine also named John as its Man of the Year.

Dec: The *Let It Be* project was finally resolved. Allen Klein sold the film rights to United Artists. The album tapes, nearly a year old by then, were edited and the album produced by Phil Spector, who had briefly replaced Peter Asher at Apple. While The Beatles had become indifferent toward the project, Paul was upset with Spector's addition of choirs and lavish instrumental overdubs to some of his songs. John, however, had nothing but praise for Spector's work and pointed out that no one else had been willing to take on the job of editing the tapes.

■ **(r)** John recorded a two-sided promo disc for Ronnie Hawkins' record "Down in the Alley," "John Lennon on Ronnie Hawkins."

Late that year: Paul told John that he too was leaving The Beatles and was planning to release an album of his own. John was pleased to hear this, but no public announcement of the group's demise was made, in accordance with John's agreement to remain silent about leaving the group.

■ John Dykins, former common-law husband of John's late mother, Julia, was killed in an automobile accident.

That year: John and Yoko appeared in a cameo part in the film *Dynamite Chicken*.

1970

(r) Jan 3: George, Paul and Ringo recorded "I Me Mine." The three returned the following day to add overdubs, marking the final studio appearance of The Beatles as a group.

Jan 15: An exhibit of 14 of John's lithographs, some of them erotic, were exhibited at the London Arts Gallery under the title "Bag One." The following day eight were confiscated by Scotland Yard detectives for possible violation of Britain's Obscene Public Act. The lithographs were ruled not obscene at a court hearing on Apr 27 and were returned to John. Many of the lithographs have brought high prices at auctions and have toured in exhibition since John's death.

Jan 20: John and Yoko cut off most of their hair to auction at Sotheby's with the proceeds to be donated to the London Blackhouse run by activist Michael Abdul Malik, known as Michael X. John and Yoko were strong supporters of Michael X and had helped to fund his Blackhouse. On Feb 4 they instead traded their hair for a used pair of Muhammed Ali's boxing trunks, which they planned to auction to raise money for Malik's legal defense. Michael X would hang for murder in Trinidad on Dec 29, 1975 despite efforts by John, Yoko and others to prevent the execution.

(r) Jan 22–Mar: Paul recorded songs for his first solo album, *McCartney*. Some sessions for this LP were held at Abbey Road, during which Paul used the pseudonym "Billy Martin."

(r) Jan 27: John wrote, recorded and mixed "Instant Karma (We All Shine On)" in one day.

■ Ringo appeared in the U.S. on NBC-TV's "Rowan & Martin's Laugh In."

Jan 29: Ringo's film *The Magic Christian* had its U.S. premiere in Los Angeles. Allen Klein was convicted of

10 different tax violations in New York Federal District Court.

(rb) Feb 3–Mar 13: Ringo concluded recording of his *Sentimental Journey* album.

Feb 6: Single "Instant Karma (We All Shine On)" (John; featuring George on guitar)/"Who Has Seen the Wind" (Yoko; produced by John) released in the U.K. Released in the U.S. on Feb 20.

(b) Feb 11: John recorded a performance of "Instant Karma," aired on BBC-TV's "Top of the Pops" the following day. Yoko, Klaus Voorman, Alan White and Mal Evans joined in.

■ Soundtrack LP *The Magic Christian*, containing dialogue by Ringo and Peter Sellers and Paul's composition "Come and Get It," performed by Badfinger and produced by Paul, was released in the U.S. Released in the U.K. on Apr 10.

(r) Feb 18: John was interviewed by David Wigg for BBC Radio One's "Scene and Heard," aired Feb 22 and later released on LP *The Beatles Tapes*.

(r) Feb 18–19: Ringo recorded "It Don't Come Easy" and "Early 1970."

Feb 23: Ringo again appeared on the U.S. TV show "Rowan & Martin's Laugh In."

■ LP *Hey Jude* (aka *The Beatles Again*) released in the U.S.

Feb 25: John canceled his participation in the scheduled Toronto Peace Festival following a dispute regarding admission policy. The festival never took place.

Mar: Paul intended to release his *McCartney* album in Apr, but Allen Klein disapproved the date since Ringo's *Sentimental Journey* was scheduled for release in late Mar, as was the *Let It Be* album. When Ringo visited Paul to explain the problem, McCartney lost his temper and threw him out. Ringo, however, sympathized with Paul and persuaded John and George to let Paul's album be released in Apr, after Ringo's, with *Let It Be* to be released later.

■ John and Yoko went through three weeks of intensive primal scream therapy in London with Arthur Janov.

Mar 1: A film of The Beatles singing "Two of Us" and "Let It Be" was shown in the U.S. on "The Ed Sullivan Show."

Mar 6: Single "Let It Be"/"You Know My Name (Look Up the Number)" released in the U.K. Released in the U.S. on Mar 11.

Mar 11: George recorded interviews for BBC Radio One's "Scene and Heard," aired Mar 15, and for a one-hour special, "The Beatles Today," aired Mar 30. The latter broadcast included selections from the original unreleased *Get Back* album.

Mar 15: Ringo filmed a promotional clip for the title track from his *Sentimental Journey* album, including some different vocals. The clip was seen on "The David Frost Show" on Mar 29 and on "The Ed Sullivan Show" on May 17.

(r) Mar 20: Ringo was interviewed by David Wigg for BBC Radio One's "Scene and Heard," aired Mar 20 and later released on LP *The Beatles Tapes*.

Mar 23: Phil Spector began remixing the Jan 1969 "Get Back" tracks into the *Let It Be* album.

Mar 27: Ringo's LP *Sentimental Journey* released in the U.K. Released in the U.S. on Apr 24.

Mar 28: John was interviewed by Kenny Everett on Radio Luxembourg.

(r) Apr 1: The final day of overdub and mixing sessions for the *Let It Be* album, supervised by Phil Spector, with Ringo adding drum tracks, marked the final studio appearance by any member of The Beatles on a Beatles studio recording. John and Yoko issued an April Fool's press release announcing that they would have dual sex-change operations.

Apr 9: Paul sang "Maybe I'm Amazed" during a five-minute spot on "London Weekend" on U.K. TV.

Apr 10: Paul publicly announced the breakup of The Beatles and said that the band would never work together again. His announcement took the form of a printed "self-interview" included with advance promotional copies of the *McCartney* album. Thus it was Paul who unilaterally broke The Beatles' mutual agreement of silence regarding their breakup, despite the fact that he had—more than anyone else—tried to keep the group together. Paul later admitted that John had wanted to be the first to announce the breakup, but said that he didn't really consider this self-interview an official announcement, claiming to have simply filled in the answers to questions that had been prepared by Apple aide Peter Brown.

Apr 11: The single "Let It Be" reached number one in the U.S.

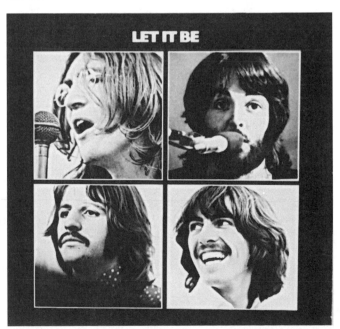

Let It Be (© Apple Corps Ltd.). The last album released by The Beatles, it was originally titled *Get Back* and sported a different mix, different songs and a different cover. Bootleggers ended up with the original; the public got *Let It Be* instead, remixed by Phil Spector, who added noticeable overdubs.

Apr 14: Paul purchased rights to the cartoon character Rupert the Bear.

Apr 17: LP *McCartney* was released in the U.K. Released in the U.S. on Apr 20.

Apr–Aug: John underwent an additional several months of primal scream therapy at Arthur Janov's Primal Institute in Los Angeles.

(b) May 1: George and Bob Dylan recorded several unreleased songs including "I'd Have You Anytime" (jointly composed) and "When Everybody Comes to Town" in Nashville during Dylan's *Self Portrait* sessions. A Dylan take of "If Not for You" with George on slide guitar was released in 1991 on Dylan's *The Bootleg Series Volumes 1–3 [Rare and Unreleased] 1961–1991.*

May 8: LP *Let It Be* released in U.K. as a deluxe boxed set with the book *Get Back*. The album was rereleased on Nov 6 in a regular sleeve and without the book. The original issue with the book is now one of the most valuable Beatles collectibles. The standard LP only was released in the U.S. on May 18.

May 11: Single "The Long and Winding Road"/"For You Blue" released in the U.S.

May 13: The New York premiere of the film *Let It Be* took place. It opened in the U.K. on May 20, with none of The Beatles in attendance.

May 23: The LP *McCartney* (Paul) reached number one in the U.S.

(rb) May 26–Aug: George recorded songs for his three-LP set *All Things Must Pass* with Ringo on drums.

Jun 6: The LP *Let It Be* reached number one in the U.K.

Jun 13: The single "The Long and Winding Road" and the LP *Let It Be* both reached number one in the U.S. on the same day.

(r) Jun 30–Jul 1: Ringo recorded songs for his LP *Beaucoups of Blues* in Nashville. He also recorded "Coochy-Coochy" (originally 28 minutes long), released only in the U.S. on a single with "Beaucoups of Blues."

Jun: In San Francisco, John and Yoko, with Jann Wenner, editor of *Rolling Stone* magazine, and his wife, Jane, attended an afternoon screening of *Let It Be* in an otherwise empty theater.

(b) That summer: John recorded several demos prior to studio sessions for his *John Lennon/Plastic Ono Band* album.

Jul 7: George's mother, Louise Harrison, died of cancer in Liverpool.

(b) Jul 26: John cut several demos of "God."

Sep 22: John and Yoko appeared on "The Dick Cavett Show" on U.S. TV with Dr. Arthur Janov.

Sep 25: Ringo's LP *Beaucoups of Blues* released in the U.K. Released in the U.S. on Sep 28.

(rb) Sep 26–Oct 27: John recorded songs for his LP *John Lennon/Plastic Ono Band.*

(b) That fall: Ringo recorded a special song for John's 30th birthday (Oct 9) and sent it to him as a greeting.

Oct 5: Ringo's single "Beaucoups of Blues"/"Coochy-Coochy" released in the U.S.

Nov 11: Ringo and Maureen's daughter, Lee Parkin, was born at Queen Charlotte's Hospital, London.

Nov 23: George's single "My Sweet Lord"/"Isn't It a Pity" released in the U.S. Released in the U.K. on Jan 15, 1971.

Nov 27: George's *All Things Must Pass* LP released in the U.S. Released in the U.K. on Nov 30.

Dec 8: Interviews with John were conducted in New York by Jann Wenner of *Rolling Stone* magazine. The interviews were printed in two parts in *Rolling Stone*, on Jan 21 and Feb 4, 1971. The entire interview was also published in the book *Lennon Remembers.*

Dec 11: John's LP *John Lennon/Plastic Ono Band* released in the U.S. and U.K. Ringo is featured on drums. Yoko's LP *Yoko Ono/Plastic Ono Band* also released in the U.S. and U.K. John is featured on guitar, and the LP was co-produced by John and Yoko.

Dec 18: *The Beatles Christmas Album* (U.K. title *From Then to You*) released to fan club and included all seven Beatles Christmas records.

Dec 26: George's single "My Sweet Lord" reached number one in the U.S.

Dec 28: John's single "Mother"/"Why" (Yoko) released in the U.S.

Dec 31: Paul brought suit in London High Court seeking an end to The Beatles & Company. To do so required that he also dissolve his association with the other three Beatles. Paul's suit requested that a receiver for Apple be appointed until the case was settled, and charged Allen Klein with mismanagement of Apple funds. The other three Beatles opposed Paul's action and the case continued until Mar 13, 1971.

(b) Late that year: John recorded a number of home demos, some of the songs never released, during this period, including an early stab at "I'm the Greatest." John would ultimately give the song to Ringo in 1973 for the *Ringo* LP. An interview was taped with Paul including discussion of Jimi Hendrix's death.

1971

Jan 2: George's LP *All Things Must Pass* reached number one in the U.S.

Jan 13: John and Yoko traveled to Japan.

Jan 19: The Beatles & Company partnership case opened in the Chancery Division of the London High Court and was adjourned; it was adjourned again on Jan 26.

Jan 20: John met Yoko Ono's parents for the first time. The Lennons returned to England the following day.

(rb) Jan 22: John recorded "Power to the People."

Jan 30: George's single "My Sweet Lord" and his LP *All Things Must Pass* reached number one in the U.K. on the same day.

(r) Jan–Mar: Paul recorded "Another Day" and "Oh Woman, Oh Why." Paul and Linda also recorded songs for their LP *Ram*. John interpreted Paul's "Too Many People" and "Dear Boy" on *Ram* as personal attacks on him; John, George and Ringo viewed "3 Legs" as attacks on them. John would retaliate with "How Do You

Sleep?" and "Crippled Inside" on his LP *Imagine*. Paul also recorded "Get on the Right Thing," later released on LP *Red Rose Speedway*.

Feb 15: George's single "What Is Life"/"Apple Scruffs" released in the U.S.

Feb 19: Paul's single "Another Day"/"Oh Woman, Oh Why" released in the U.K. Released in the U.S. on Feb 22. Arguments began in London High Court in The Beatles & Company case with a day of acrimony on all sides. Paul testified on Feb 26; the other Beatles submitted affidavits.

(r) Feb: George worked on songs later released on his *Living in the Material World* and *Extra Texture—Read All About It* LPs.

Mar 3: The South African Broadcasting Company lifted its ridiculous 1966 ban on Beatles records. A ban on John's solo recordings, however, remained in effect.

Mar 12: John's single "Power to the People"/"Open Your Box" (aka "Hirake") (Yoko) released in the U.K. only.

■ A court ruling granted Paul's request that a receiver be appointed to control the finances of The Beatles & Company.

Mar 16: The Beatles received a Grammy Award for 1970's Best Original Score Written for a Motion Picture or Television Special for their LP *Let It Be*.

Mar 20: Paul's single "Another Day" reached number one in the U.K.

Mar 22: John's single "Power to the People"/"Touch Me" (Yoko) released in the U.S. only.

Apr 9: Ringo's single "It Don't Come Easy"/"Early 1970" released in the U.K. Released in the U.S. on Apr 16. George produced the A side, on which he also played guitar.

Apr 15: The Beatles received an Oscar from the U.S. Academy of Motion Picture Arts and Sciences for 1970 Best Film Music—Original Film Score for *Let It Be*.

Apr 23: In Majorca, John and Yoko were taken into police custody and questioned regarding their alleged abduction of Yoko's daughter Kyoko from the child's father, Anthony Cox. Yoko had been awarded custody in the U.S. when she and Cox were divorced.

Apr 25: Ringo appeared live with Cilla Black on the BBC-TV show "Cilla," aired from Scandinavia.

May 15: Two films by John and Yoko, *Apotheosis (Balloon)* and *Fly*, were screened at the Cannes Film Festival. The audience reportedly booed *Apotheosis (Balloon)*.

May 17: Paul and Linda's LP *Ram* released in the U.S. Released in the U.K. on May 28.

(rb) Jun 1: John recorded "Do the Oz," released on single with Bill Elliot's "God Save Us." The recording was credited to The Elastic Oz Band. John cut a studio demo of "God Save Us" over which Elliot recorded his vocal.

(rb) Jun 6: John and Yoko performed live with Frank Zappa and The Mothers of Invention at New York's Fillmore East. The performance was released on LP *Some Time in New York City*.

■ John appeared on Howard Smith's U.S. radio talk show on WPLJ radio.

Jun: Ringo began filming *Blindman*, completed in Aug 1971.

Early that summer: John was interviewed by Peter McCabe and Robert D. Schonfeld, who would go on to write *Apple to the Corps*, published in 1972, describing the decay of The Beatles' Apple "empire." The interview, however, was not published until 1984, when it appeared in the book *John Lennon: For the Record*.

(rb) Jun–Jul: John recorded songs for his LP *Imagine*. A previously unreleased demo of "Imagine" was released in 1988 on the *Imagine: John Lennon* compilation LP. The sessions were filmed and planned for release as *Working Class Hero*, but the film was not issued. Some of the footage was used in the 1988 documentary *Imagine: John Lennon*. A completely different film, *Imagine*, consisting largely of promotional clips for the album's songs, was released, and later issued on video cassette.

(b) Middle of that year: John recorded a demo of "How?" and the earliest demo of "Aisemussen."

(rb) Early Jul: George recorded "Bangla Desh" and "Deep Blue."

Jul 3: McCartney's LP *Ram* reached number one in the U.K.

(b) Jul 16: John made a statement in support of *Oz* magazine and sang "The End of the Road" during a press conference dealing with the *Oz* magazine obscenity case in England. The recording was released as a flexi disc included with *Oz* magazine.

Jul 17: John and Yoko appeared on the U.K. TV show "Parkinson."

Jul 28: George's single "Bangla Desh"/"Deep Blue" released in the U.S. Released in the U.K. on Jul 30.

(b) Jul: John cut demos of "I'm the Greatest." Ringo would record the song in 1973 for his *Ringo* album, at which time John cut additional demos of the song.

(rb) Aug 1: George and Ringo appeared at the Concerts for Bangla Desh at Madison Square Garden in New York. Two concerts, afternoon and evening, were held, with most of the evening concert released on LP *The Concert for Bangla Desh*. Also appearing were Bob Dylan, Eric Clapton, Klaus Voorman, Billy Preston, Leon Russell and Ravi Shankar. The concert was also filmed; the movie premiered in New York Mar 23, 1972.

Aug 2: Paul and Linda's single "Uncle Albert-Admiral Halsey"/"Too Many People" released in the U.S.

Aug 3: Paul announced that he had formed a band called Wings consisting of himself, Linda, drummer Denny Seiwell and former Moody Blues guitarist Denny Laine.

Aug 11: John and Yoko took part in a London demonstration protesting British policy in Northern Ireland and the prosecution of the editors of *Oz* magazine on obscenity charges.

Aug 11–31: Five of John and Yoko's films were screened during the London Art Spectrum at Alexandra

Palace: *Cold Turkey, The Ballad of John and Yoko, Give Peace a Chance, Instant Karma* and *Up Your Legs Forever.*

Aug 13: Paul and Linda's single "Back Seat of My Car"/"Heart of the Country" released in the U.K.

Aug: Ringo completed filming *Blindman,* which premiered in Rome on Nov 15.

(b) Late that summer: Extremely short clips of Paul doing "Bip Bop," "Hey Diddle" and "Lucille," filmed around this time, were seen in the 90-minute "Wings over the World" television special, first broadcast on Mar 16, 1979 by CBS-TV in the U.S. Wings also cut a different version of "Lucille," possibly around this time.

Sep 3: John and Yoko left England for America. John would never again return to his native country.

■ Ringo and designer Robin Cruikshank formed a furniture design company, Ringo or Robin Ltd.

Sep 4: Wings' single "Uncle Albert-Admiral Halsey" reached number one in the U.S.

Sep 9: John's LP *Imagine* was released in the U.S. Released in the U.K. on Oct 8. John and Yoko taped an appearance on "The Dick Cavett Show" for ABC-TV in the U.S., aired on Sep 23.

Sep 13: Paul and Linda's second child, Stella Nina McCartney, was born.

(rb) Sep: Paul recorded songs for Wings' LP *Wild Life.* Paul's unreleased recording of "Tragedy" may date from this period; it was one of the tracks he later planned to release on *Cold Cuts.*

■ **(rb)** Ringo recorded "Back Off Boogaloo" and "Blindman." "Back Off Boogaloo" appeared in the films *Born to Boogie* and *That'll Be the Day.*

■ **(b)** John and Yoko recorded the soundtrack for the film *Clock* in a room at the St. Regis Hotel in New York, including many unreleased songs sung by John. The film was screened at Yoko's Oct 9 Syracuse, N.Y., art exhibit.

■ A promotional film for John's LP *Imagine* was released by John and Yoko's Joko Productions. The film was made by and starred the Lennons and featured cameo appearances by George, Fred Astaire, Dick Cavett and Andy Warhol. It was released many years later on videocassette.

(b) That fall: John recorded several unreleased songs at home.

(r) Oct 8: John and Yoko held a press conference in Syracuse, N.Y., filmed and later released on disc in the U.S.

(b) Oct 9: On John's 31st birthday, Yoko held an art exhibit, "This Is Not Here," at the Everson Museum of Art in Syracuse, N.Y. The show was taped and aired on U.S. TV on May 11, 1972 as "John and Yoko in Syracuse, New York." The exhibit ran through Oct 27. During the exhibit, John and Yoko joined some Onondaga tribespeople protesting the government takeover of their land for highway construction. A jam session celebrating John's birthday took place at a Syracuse hotel and included Ringo, Phil Spector, Klaus Voorman, Allan Ginsberg, Jim Keltner and possibly Eric Clapton, Mal Evans and Neil Aspinall. Lennon and Yoko were also

interviewed by a Japanese journalist. Part of the interview was aired on "The Lost Lennon Tapes" where it was dubbed "the argument interview," owing to an unusual degree of acrimony between the two during the proceedings.

Oct 11: John's single "Imagine"/"It's So Hard" released in the U.S.

Oct 14: John and Yoko appeared on the TV show "Free Time" on New York public TV station WNET-TV.

(b) Middle of Oct: Lennon cut a demo of "Happy Xmas (War Is Over)."

(r) Oct 25: John was interviewed by David Wigg for BBC One's "Scene and Heard," aired in three parts on Nov 13, 20 and 27, and later released on LP *The Beatles Tapes.*

(rb) Oct 28–29: John and Yoko recorded "Happy Xmas (War Is Over)" with the Harlem Community Choir.

Oct 30: John's LP *Imagine* reached number one in the U.S.

Nov 10: The film *200 Motels,* featuring Ringo, opened in New York.

(b) Nov 12: John recorded several demo takes of "Luck of the Irish."

Nov 15: The film *Blindman,* featuring Ringo, had its world premiere in Rome.

Nov 23: *Raga,* a documentary film about Ravi Shankar featuring George, opened in New York.

■ George accompanied Gary Wright on the song "Two Faced Man" on "The Dick Cavett Show" on U.S. TV.

Nov 30: John's LP *Imagine* reached number one in the U.K.

Dec 1: John and Yoko's single "Happy Xmas (War Is Over)"/"Listen the Snow Is Falling" (Yoko) released in

"Happy Xmas (War Is Over)" (© Apple Corps Ltd.). Italian release of John's single.

the U.S. Released in the U.K. almost a year later, on Nov 24, 1972.

(b) Dec 3: George appeared on "The David Frost Show" on U.S. TV.

Dec 4: John made a public attack on Paul in a letter published in *Melody Maker*.

Dec 5: The London High Court appointed a receiver for Maclen (Music) Ltd.

Dec 7: Wings' first album, *Wild Life*, released in the U.S. and the U.K.

(b) Dec 10: John and Yoko performed at a benefit concert in Ann Arbor, Michigan for John Sinclair, a radical activist who had been sentenced to 10 years imprisonment for attempting to sell two marijuana joints. Sinclair was freed three days later. The performance was also filmed, but the movie *Ten for Two* was not released until Apr 1, 1989, more than 17 years later.

(b) Dec 17: John performed a benefit concert for the families of victims of the riot at New York's Attica State Prison at the Apollo Theater in New York, during which he did acoustic versions of "Imagine" and "Attica State."

Dec 20: U.S. release of LP *Concert for Bangla Desh*. Released in the U.K. on Jan 10, 1972.

(r) Late that year: Paul produced an instrumental version of his *Ram* album, titled *Thrillington*, under the pseudonym "Percy 'Thrills' Thrillington."

1972

(r) Early that year: Paul recorded "Mary Had a Little Lamb" and "Little Woman Love."

■ **(b)** Approximately 25 hours of unreleased Lennon tapes were reportedly given to Bruce Bierman by John during recording of David Peel's *The Pope Smokes Dope* album, produced by Lennon.

Jan 6: John and Yoko formed Joko Films Ltd.

Jan 10: John assisted at Yoko's concert in Alice Tully Hall in New York's Lincoln Center.

Jan 12: The film *Blindman*, featuring Ringo, had its U.S. premiere in Chicago.

(b) Jan 13: John and Yoko appeared with David Peel and The Lower East Side Band on "The David Frost Show" on U.S. TV.

(rb) Feb 1: Wings recorded "Give Ireland Back to the Irish" (vocal and instrumental versions). The song was a rare political message from Paul, and the BBC immediately banned the record. Wings was also filmed rehearsing the song.

Feb 4: A secret memo to U.S. Attorney General John Mitchell from Senator Strom Thurmond suggested that John Lennon should be deported as an undesirable alien, because of his political views and activism.

Feb 5: John and Yoko joined a demonstration in New York at the offices of British Overseas Airways in support of a union boycott of British exports in protest of British policy in Northern Ireland.

Feb 9: Henry McCullough, formerly with The Grease Band, joined Wings.

(b) Feb 9–23: Wings conducted a tour of unannounced U.K. dates on a bill topped by singer Brinsley Schwarz, including shows at Nottingham University (Feb 9); York University (Feb 10); Hull University (Feb 11); Newcastle-upon-Tyne (Feb 13); Lancaster (Feb 14); Leeds' Town Hall (Feb 16); Sheffield (Feb 17); Manchester (Feb 18); Birmingham University (Feb 21); Swansea University (Feb 22); Oxford University (Feb 23).

(b) Feb 14–18: John and Yoko served as guest hosts on "The Mike Douglas Show," performing several songs with Elephant's Memory, and with John dueting with Chuck Berry on Feb 16 on "Memphis" and "Johnny B. Goode." John introduced Berry as "my hero."

Feb 17: The Lennons' only screening of their James Hanratty film took place in the crypt of St. Martin-in-the-Fields Church, London.

Feb 25: U.K. release of Wings' single "Give Ireland Back to the Irish." Released in the U.S. on Feb 28.

Feb 29: John and Yoko's nonimmigrant U.S. visas expired. They were given 15-day extensions, but this began what would become a three-and-a-half-year struggle by John to gain permission to remain in the U.S. The government's opposition to his request was allegedly based on John's 1968 U.K. drug conviction, but later evidence showed that he was targeted by the Nixon administration as a political enemy.

Feb: George and Pattie Harrison were involved in an accident in which their car struck a light pole during an electrical blackout.

(rb) Mar 1–20: John and Yoko recorded songs for the LP *Some Time in New York City*.

Mar 3: Yoko Ono's legal custody of her daughter, Kyoko, was again granted, but by this time the girl's father, Anthony Cox, had fled with the child. One of John's arguments for remaining in the U.S. was that he and Yoko wanted desperately to find the girl.

Mar 6: John and Yoko's visa extensions were canceled by the U.S. Immigration and Naturalization Service only five days after being granted.

Mar 16: John and Yoko were served with deportation orders by the U.S. Immigration and Naturalization Service; they filed an immediate appeal.

Mar 17: Ringo's single "Back Off Boogaloo"/"Blindman" released in the U.K. Released in the U.S. on Mar 20. George produced the A side on which he plays guitar. Ringo and Klaus Voorman produced the B side.

Mar 18: Ringo began shooting his documentary film *Born to Boogie* by directing the filming of a T. Rex concert at the Empire Pool, Wembley. Ringo was seen in a jam session sequence filmed on this date. Filming was concluded in Apr. The film dealt with Marc Bolan of T. Rex and premiered in London on Dec 18.

Mar 23: The film *Concert for Bangla Desh* opened in New York.

Mar 31: The Beatles' Fan Club was terminated.

(r) Mar: Paul recorded "My Love."

(rb) Middle of Mar: Wings recorded songs for the LP *Red Rose Speedway*. Recordings for the LP were finalized in Oct. Wings also recorded "I Would Only Smile," released later by Denny Laine alone.

Apr 18: An Immigration and Naturalization Service hearing was held in New York regarding deportation proceedings against John. Other hearings followed on May 12 and 17. Evidence later showed that the Nixon administration feared Lennon would lead demonstrations at the upcoming Republican National Convention in Miami, but John never went to the convention site.

Apr 22: John addressed the National Peace Rally in New York.

Apr 24: John's single "Woman Is the Nigger of the World"/"Sisters O Sisters" (Yoko) released in the U.S. only. Although most U.S. radio stations refused to play this record, it still managed to reach number 57 in *Billboard*.

Apr 27: Lennon publicly charged that deportation proceedings against him were politically motivated.

(b) May 11: John sang "Woman Is the Nigger of the World" on "The Dick Cavett Show" on U.S. TV, appearing with Elephant's Memory. During this show, John claimed that his phones were being tapped and that he was being followed. By this time a National Committee for John and Yoko had collected petitions urging the U.S. government to halt its deportation proceedings against John.

May 12: Wings' single "Mary Had a Little Lamb"/"Little Woman Love" released in the U.K. Released in the U.S. on May 29.

May 13: John took part in anti-Vietnam war protests in New York.

Jun 5: UNICEF, the United Nations' children's fund, awarded its "Child Is the Father of the Man" award to George and Ravi Shankar for their efforts to help Bangla Desh.

Jun 12: LP *Some Time in New York City* (John, Yoko and Elephant's Memory) released in the U.S. Released in the U.K. on Sep 15.

Jun 28: A promo clip of Wings' "Mary Had a Little Lamb" was aired on "Top of the Pops" in the U.K.

(r) Middle of that year: An interview with John was recorded by an unknown person about his relationship with musician David Peel. The interview was released in 1980 on the limited edition disc "The David Peel Interview."

(b) That summer: Lennon ran through several acoustic numbers reportedly during a television news segment.

Jul 1: The film *Concert for Bangla Desh* opened in London.

(b) Jul 9: Wings performed a concert at Theatre Antique, Chateauvallon, France. This marked the start of the Wings over Europe tour extending through Aug 24. Songs included "Smile Away," "The Mess," "Hi Hi Hi," "Mumbo," "Bip Bop," "Say You Don't Mind" (by Denny Laine), "Seaside Woman" (Linda), "I Would Only Smile," "Blue Moon of Kentucky," "Give Ireland Back to the Irish," "Henry's Blues" (Henry McCullough), "1882," "I Am Your Singer," "Eat at Home," "Maybe I'm Amazed," "My Love," "Mary Had a Little Lamb,"

"Soily," "Best Friend," "Long Tall Sally," "Wild Life" and "Cottonfields." The lineup varied slightly from one concert to the next. This was basically a "tryout" to sharpen Wings' act. Paul produced a film of this tour that included animated footage of a cartoon character named Bruce McMouse as well as concert footage. The film, *The Bruce McMouse Show*, was never released.

(b) Jul 12–Aug 24: Paul and Wings performed at Juan Les Pins, France (Jul 12); Theatre Antique, Arles, France (Jul 13); Olympia, Paris (Jul 16 [2 shows]); Circus Krone, Munich, Germany (Jul 18); Offenbach Halle, Frankfurt (Jul 19); Kongresshaus, Zurich, Switzerland (Jul 21); Pavilion, Montreux, Switzerland (Jul 22); K.B. Hallen, Copenhagen, Denmark (Aug 1); Messuhalli, Helsinki, Finland (Aug 4); Kupittaan Urheiluhalli, Turku, Finland (Aug 5); Kungliga Hallen, Stockholm, Sweden (Aug 7); Idretshalle, Orebro, Sweden (Aug 8); Oslo, Norway (Aug 9); Scandinavium Hall, Goteborg, Sweden (Aug 10); Olympean, Lund, Sweden (Aug 11); Fyns Forum, Odense, Denmark (Aug 12); Vejlby Risskov Hallen, Aarhus, Denmark (Aug 14); Hanover, Germany (Aug 16); Doelen, Rotterdam, the Netherlands (Aug 17); Evenementenhall, Groningen, the Netherlands (Aug 19); Concertgebouw, Amsterdam, the Netherlands (Aug 20); Congresgebouw, The Hague, the Netherlands (Aug 21); Antwerp, Belgium (Aug 22); Deutschlandhalle, Berlin, Germany (Aug 24).

Jul 14: A scheduled Wings concert in Lyons, France was canceled due to poor ticket sales.

Aug 10: Following Wings' Goteborg, Sweden show, Paul, Linda and Denny Seiwell were arrested on charges of drug possession and were fined the equivalent of $1,000, $200 and $600 respectively.

(b) Aug 18: Lennon and his band rehearsed for the One to One Concert; other rehearsals were held on Aug 21 and 22.

(rb) Aug 21: Paul and Wings were recorded singing "The Mess" during their concert at the Congresgebouw, The Hague, the Netherlands, later released on a single with "My Love."

(rb) Aug 30: John performed two One to One Benefit Concerts at Madison Square Garden, New York with Elephant's Memory. Afternoon and evening shows were performed for the benefit of the Willowbrook School for Children. Songs performed were released on LP *John Lennon: Live in New York City*. A short excerpt of "Give Peace a Chance" appeared on the LP *Shaved Fish*. Both concerts were filmed, and an excerpt featuring seven of the songs performed at the evening concert was aired on ABC-TV on Dec 14; a one-hour videocassette, *John Lennon: Live in New York City* was released at the same time as the LP. It contained different edits of some of the songs and added some of Yoko's numbers (the full concert film originally ran 70 minutes). The concert, organized by TV reporter Geraldo Rivera, also featured Stevie Wonder, Roberta Flack and Sha Na Na. John purchased $60,000 worth of tickets and gave them away to volunteer fund-raisers. The event raised over $1.5 million.

(r) Aug: Ringo began filming *Son of Dracula*, completed in Oct; the film would not premiere until Apr 19, 1974. Some of Ringo's dialogue and the songs "Daybreak" and "At My Front Door" from the film were released on the soundtrack album *Son of Dracula*.

(b) Sep 6: John and Yoko appeared live with Elephant's Memory on the TV special "Jerry Lewis Muscular Dystrophy Telethon."

Sep 20: Police found cannabis plants in a greenhouse at Paul's farm in Campbeltown, Scotland, and he was again charged with drug violations. He pled guilty on Mar 8, 1973, and was fined £100 plus court costs.

Sep 27: Rory Storm, leader of Ringo's old group, The Hurricanes, committed suicide.

(r) Sep: Ringo recorded "Fiddle About" and "Tommy's Holiday Camp" with the London Symphony Orchestra and Chamber Choir for the LP *Tommy*. The all-star recording cast also included The Who, Steve Winwood, Richie Havens, Rod Stewart, Richard Harris, Maggie Bell, Sandy Denny, Graham Bell and Merry Clayton.

Oct 12: A promo clip of Wings' "Mary Had a Little Lamb" was seen on "The Flip Wilson Show" on U.S. TV.

Oct 16: Ringo began filming *That'll Be the Day*, completed in Jan 1973. It premiered in London on Apr 12, 1973.

(r) Oct: Paul and Wings recorded "Hi Hi Hi" (banned by the BBC because of what were termed "sexually suggestive lyrics"), "C Moon," "Country Dreamer," "Live and Let Die" and "I Lie Around." Recording of *Red Rose Speedway*, begun in Mar, was also concluded.

(b) Nov 2: A copyright was registered for "You've Gotta Stay With Me," written by Paul L. Woodall (words, music, arrangement) and George Harrison (music and arrangement).

Nov 24: LP *Tommy* containing songs by Ringo released in the U.K. Released in the U.S. on Nov 27.

Dec 1: Paul's single "Hi Hi Hi"/"C Moon" (Wings) released in the U.K. Released in the U.S. on Dec 4.

Dec 12: Ringo appeared live on the ITV children's show "Magpie."

Dec 14: Ringo's film *Born to Boogie* premiered in London with Ringo present.

- ABC-TV aired a film shot at John and Yoko's One to One Concert of Aug 30.

Dec 23: World premiere of John and Yoko's film *Imagine* on U.S. television. The film was released on videocassette in 1985.

Dec 28: Ringo appeared live on BBC 2's "Late Night Line-Up."

(b) Dec: George was seen in the U.S. on "The David Frost Show."

- **(b)** George recorded an unreleased demo of "Sue Me, Sue You Blues." He would record the song again the following year.

1973

(r) Jan 3: Ringo was interviewed by David Wigg for BBC Radio One's "Scene and Heard," aired on Jan 6; released later on LP *The Beatles Tapes*.

Jan 22: Northern Songs Ltd. and Maclen (Music) Ltd. charged John with improperly placing recent copyrights with Ono's music company, Ono Music Ltd.

(r) Jan–Apr: George recorded "Give Me Love" and "Miss O'Dell." On "Miss O'Dell," George bursts into laughter several times, but he did not bother to rerecord the song. George also recorded additional songs for his LP *Living in the Material World*.

Mar 3: The LP *The Concert for Bangla Desh* was awarded a Grammy as Album of the Year for 1972.

(b) Middle of Mar: During taping for his TV special "James Paul McCartney," aired Apr 16, Paul did an unreleased acoustic medley of "Bluebird"/"Mama's Little Girl"/"Michelle"/"Heart of the Country," which was not included in the special. A similar medley, without "Mama's Little Girl," was featured on the show.

(b) Mar 18: Paul recorded a special live performance for his TV special "James Paul McCartney." That evening Wings performed a surprise concert for the benefit of Release, a drug abuse program, at London's Hard Rock Cafe.

Mar 23: Single "My Love"/"The Mess" (Paul and Wings) released in the U.K. Released in the U.S. on Apr 9.

- U.S. Immigration and Naturalization Service Judge Ira Fieldsteel ruled that John had to leave the U.S. within 60 days or face deportation. Yoko was granted permanent residency. John filed an appeal.

Mar 31: Allen Klein's management contract with John, George and Ringo expired and was not renewed, although the three ex-Beatles would not formally fire Klein until Nov.

Mar: Release of 4-LP box set *Alpha Omega (Volume One)* and *(Volume Two)* in U.S. including Beatles group and solo songs. These were unauthorized releases sold through TV and radio advertising, and they prompted Apple to rush release its own Beatles "greatest hits" anthologies on two double albums.

(b) That spring: John recorded several unreleased demos prior to *Mind Games* sessions.

Apr 1: Appropriately on April Fool's Day, Lennon and Ono held a press conference in New York announcing the birth of their conceptual country, Nutopia, and reading through the country's "constitution." Part of this was aired many years later on the "Lost Lennon Tapes" radio series.

(rb) Apr 1–15: Ringo recorded "Down and Out" and songs for his LP *Ringo*. John recorded demos of "I'm the Greatest." Ringo also recorded an antidrug radio spot released on a special LP *Get Off* issued to radio stations by the National Association of Progressive Radio Announcers.

Apr 2: Two Beatles greatest hits albums, *The Beatles 1962–1966* and *The Beatles 1967–1970* were released in the U.S., widely known as the "Red" and "Blue" albums. They were released in the U.K. on Apr 19.

- At a press conference in New York City, John and Yoko discussed their appeal, filed the same day, to the Mar 23 decision by the U.S. Immigration and Naturalization Service to deport John.

Apr 12: The film *That'll Be the Day*, starring Ringo, had its world premiere in London.

(b) **Apr 16:** Paul's TV special "James Paul McCartney" was aired in the U.S. on ABC-TV. It was aired in the U.K. by ATV on May 10.

- Elliot Mintz taped an interview with the Lennons on this date, clips from which were aired throughout the "Lost Lennon Tapes" U.S. radio series.

(br) **Apr 16–30:** Ringo concluded the recording of his album *Ringo* with sessions in England for Paul and Linda McCartney's composition "Six O'Clock." All of The Beatles appear on the album. John wrote "I'm the Greatest," and both he and George participated during the song's recording. Paul also played on "You're Sixteen"; George co-authored "Photograph" with Ringo and "You and Me (Babe)" with Mal Evans. George also wrote "Sunshine Life for Me" and played on each of these recordings. The LP and spinoff singles were smash hits, showing that The Beatles still were a winning combination.

Apr 26: George founded The Material World Charitable Foundation Trust.

Apr 30: Wings' LP *Red Rose Speedway* released in the U.S. Released in the U.K. on May 4.

(b) **May 1:** A copyright was registered for the unreleased song "Only One More Kiss," written by Paul McCartney.

May 7: George's single "Give Me Love (Give Me Peace on Earth)"/"Miss O'Dell" released in the U.S. Released in the U.K. on May 25.

(b) **May 11–Jul 10:** Wings toured Britain, performing "Big Barn Bed," "Soily," "When the Night," "Wild Life," "Seaside Woman" (Linda), "Go Now" (Denny Laine), "Little Woman Love," "C Moon," "Live and Let Die," "Maybe I'm Amazed," "Say You Don't Mind" (Denny Laine), "My Love," "The Mess," "Hi Hi Hi," "Long Tall Sally." The tour included shows at Bristol's Hippodrome (May 11); Oxford's New Theatre (May 12); Cardiff's Capitol (May 13); Bournemouth's Winter Gardens (May 15); Manchester's Hard Rock (May 16, 17); the Empire in Liverpool (May 18); Leeds University (May 19); Preston's Guildhall (May 21); Newcastle's Odeon (May 22); Edinburgh's Odeon (May 23); Green's Playhouse, Glasgow (May 24); Hammersmith's Odeon (May 25, 26, 27); Sheffield's City Hall (Jul 4); Birmingham's Odeon (Jul 6); Leicester's Odeon (Jul 9); Newcastle City Hall (Jul 10).

May 19: The LP *The Beatles 1967–1970* reached number one in the U.K. It reached number one in the U.S. on May 26.

May 27: The Cavern Club in Liverpool finally closed for good; it was displaced by an underground railway. Above ground, the site was covered with a parking lot.

In 1984 a shopping center called Cavern Walks opened on the site and included a new Cavern Club designed to look like the original and built with the club's original bricks.

May 30: U.S. release of George's LP *Living in the Material World*. Ringo is featured on drums. Released in the U.K. on Jun 22.

Jun 1: Wings' single "Live and Let Die"/"I Lie Around" released in the U.K. Released in the U.S. on Jun 18.

Jun 2: Wings' single "My Love" and LP *Red Rose Speedway* both reached number one in the U.S.

Jun 3: John and Yoko attended the International Feminist Planning Conference at Harvard University where they were interviewed by Danny Schechter. Excerpts from the taped interview were aired on "The Lost Lennon Tapes" radio series.

Jun 9: The LP *The Beatles 1962–1966* reached number one in the U.K.

Jun 23: George's LP *Living in the Material World* reached number one in the U.S.

Jun 28: John and Yoko took part in protest demonstrations at the South Vietnamese embassy in Washington, D.C.

Jun 29: The film *Live and Let Die*, containing the title track by Wings, opened in New York. It would open in London on Jul 5.

- John and Yoko attended the Senate Watergate hearings in Washington, D.C.

Jun 30: George's single "Give Me Love (Give Me Peace on Earth)" reached number one in the U.S.

Jul 2: Soundtrack LP *Live and Let Die*, including the title track by Paul and Wings, was released in the U.S. Released in the U.K. on Jul 6.

Jul 25: George paid £1 million in taxes owed to the British government on revenues from the Bangla Desh concert and album.

Jul 26: Ringo formed Wobble Music Ltd.

(rb) **July–Aug:** John recorded songs for his LP *Mind Games*.

(rb) **Aug 4:** During *Mind Games* sessions, John recorded "Rock & Roll People," ultimately omitted from the album but released posthumously on *Menlove Ave*. After omitting the track from his album, John gave the song to Johnny Winter, who released his version on the LP *John Dawson Winter III*. Winter also released a live concert version of the number on *Johnny Winter Captured Live*.

Aug 9: Henry McCullough and Denny Seiwell quit Wings on the eve of the band's departure for Lagos, Nigeria. Paul, Linda and Denny Laine—all that remained of Wings—went on to Lagos anyway, where they recorded *Band on the Run*, far and away the group's most popular and successful album.

(rb) **Aug 10–Sep 22:** Wings recorded songs for the LP *Band on the Run* in Lagos, Nigeria. The U.S. release of *Band on the Run* included "Helen Wheels," as did the compact disc release many years later, but the original U.K. album did not contain that track. Wings also recorded "Seaside Woman" and "B Side to Seaside," later

issued as a single. Linda and Wings recorded "Oriental Nightfish," used in the May 1978 animated film of the same title.

Sep 23: Wings returned from Lagos, Nigeria having completed *Band on the Run*.

Sep 24: Ringo's single "Photograph"/"Down and Out" released in the U.S. George and Ringo co-wrote the A side on which George contributed guitar and backing vocals; George co-wrote and produced the B side. Released in the U.K. on Oct 19.

Sep 30: John's favorable review of Spike Milligan's book, *The Goon Show Scripts*, appeared in the *New York Times Book Review*.

(r) Sep: Wings recorded "Helen Wheels" and the instrumental, "Zoo Gang."

Early Oct: John and Yoko Ono separated and Lennon began living with Ono's secretary, May Pang, in Los Angeles. The cause of the separation is vague, but May Pang published her version of this period in her 1983 book, *Loving John*.

Oct 24: John sued the U.S. Immigration and Naturalization Service under the Freedom of Information Act in an effort to obtain documentary evidence that would show prejudgment in his deportation case and of illegal wiretapping of his phones. An appeal hearing was held on Oct 31.

Oct 26: Wings' single "Helen Wheels"/"Country Dreamer" released in the U.K. Released in the U.S. on Nov 12.

Oct 29: John's single "Mind Games"/"Meat City" released in the U.S. Released in the U.K. on Nov 16.

■ The film *That'll Be the Day*, starring Ringo, opened in Los Angeles.

(rb) Oct–Dec: John began work on an album of old rock and roll standards in Los Angeles with Phil Spector producing. Only three tracks from these disorderly sessions would see official release on the LP *Rock 'N' Roll*. Following the Los Angeles sessions, Spector vanished with the tapes. He returned them to Lennon the following year when Lennon completed the album. During the Spector sessions John also recorded "Here We Go Again," written with Spector; later released on *Menlove Ave.*, which contains "My Baby Left Me" and "To Know Her Is to Love Her," also from these sessions. John's recordings of "Angel Baby" and "Be My Baby were not included on *Rock 'N' Roll*, but did appear on the unauthorized LP *John Lennon Sings the Great Rock and Roll Hits [Roots]*, commonly known as *Roots*, released only in the U.S. by mail order (see Feb 1975). "Angel Baby" was officially released on *Menlove Ave.* and the *Lennon* CD boxed set, where it was artificially extended.

Nov 2: John, Ringo and George fired Allen Klein and sued ABKCO (his company) in High Court over payments due The Beatles. Klein then countersued for $19 million claiming that he was due unpaid fees. When the suits were settled on Jan 10, 1977, Klein paid The Beatles $800,000 and The Beatles paid ABKCO between $1 million and $5 million. Klein had also sued Paul for $34 million, but that suit was thrown out of court. Klein was later sentenced in New York to two months prison and a $5,000 fine for tax offenses. Klein's approaching departure from Apple ushered in a period of renewed goodwill among The Beatles.

■ Ringo's LP *Ringo* released in the U.S. Released in the U.K. on Nov 23. John, Paul and George all participated in the recording of this album. (See Mar–Jul for details.)

■ John's LP *Mind Games* was released in the U.S. Released in the U.K. on Nov 16.

Nov 24: Ringo's single "Photograph" reached number one in the U.S.

Dec 3: Ringo's single "You're Sixteen"/"Devil Woman" released in the U.S. Released in the U.K. on Feb 8.

Dec 5: Wings' LP *Band on the Run* released in the U.S., including "Helen Wheels," omitted on the Dec 7 U.K. release. Viewed by critics as a marked improvement for Paul, *Band on the Run* was named Album of the Year by *Rolling Stone* magazine, and quickly reached number one. Over the next three years, it sold 5 million copies, was still on the charts and became one of the most popular Beatles solo LPs.

Dec 26: Paul and Linda co-hosted the "Disney Time" Christmas TV show on BBC 1.

(b) Dec: John produced an unreleased recording of "Too Many Cooks," with Mick Jagger doing lead vocal, at the Record Plant West in Los Angeles.

1974

(b) Early that year: John recorded an acoustic demo of "What You Got."

Jan 26: Ringo's single "You're Sixteen" reached number one in the U.S.

Ringo (© Apple Corps Ltd.). Far and away Ringo's most popular solo LP, the album was aided immeasurably by contributions of John, Paul and George. This was the closest the world ever came to a Beatles reunion album.

Jan 28: Wings' single "Jet"/"Mamunia" released in the U.S.

Jan: John is reported to have asked the Queen of England for a royal pardon of his drug conviction stemming from his arrest on Oct 18, 1968, which had led to his immigration problems in the U.S.

Feb 6: Ringo taped an appearance on BBC Radio One's "My Top Twelve," aired Apr 7.

Feb 15: Wings' single "Jet"/"Let Me Roll It" released in the U.K. Released in the U.S. on Feb 18.

Feb 18: Ringo's single "Oh My My"/"Step Lightly" released in the U.S.

Mar 1: In U.S. district court, John asked for a temporary restraining order of the Immigration and Naturalization Service appeal ruling on his deportation case. John's request was denied on May 1.

Mar 12: In Los Angeles, John and Harry Nilsson heckled The Smothers Brothers during their performance at the Troubadour Club and were thrown out. A club waitress claimed that Lennon assaulted her, but that charge was later dismissed. The Smothers Brothers later explained that the incident was partly their own fault for engaging in banter with Lennon, who was quite drunk. The Brothers also said that the newspapers blew the incident out of proportion. John and Nilsson later sent flowers to The Smothers Brothers and apologized to them. The incident was part of a six-month binge of drinking and carousing by John and Nilsson.

Mar 28: George founded Oops Publishing Ltd.

(b) Mar–Apr: John produced Harry Nilsson's LP *Pussy Cats*, wrote "Mucho Mungo" for the LP and recorded several demos of the song. Ringo is featured on drums on the album, released Aug 19 in the U.S. and Aug 30 in the U.K. An unreleased jam session including John and Paul and Linda McCartney (who were visiting) was also recorded.

Apr 1: The soundtrack album *Son of Dracula* was released in the U.S. and contained excerpts from Ringo's film dialogue, and Nilsson's songs "Daybreak" (Ringo on drums; George on cowbell) and "At My Front Door" (Ringo on drums). Released in the U.K. on May 24.

Apr 8: Wings' single "Band on the Run"/"Nineteen Hundred and Eighty Five" released in the U.S. only.

Apr 19: The film *Son of Dracula*, starring Ringo and Harry Nilsson, premiered in Atlanta, Georgia, a year and a half after filming was completed.

Apr 26: Paul held auditions to find a new drummer, ultimately selecting Geoff Britton.

May 17–18: John donated his time during these two days as a guest disc jockey for Philadelphia radio station WFIL's Helping Hand Marathon fund-raising drive.

May 23: George founded his own record company, Dark Horse Records Ltd.

Jun 8: Wings' single "Band on the Run" reached number one in the U.S.

Jun 15: Guitarist Jimmy McCulloch and drummer Geoff Britton joined Wings.

(b) Jun 19: A copyright was registered for the unreleased "Where Are You Going?" written by Ringo and Billy Lawrie.

(b) Early that summer: John recorded several demos prior to *Walls and Bridges* sessions.

(br) Jun–Jul: In Nashville, Wings recorded "Junior's Farm," "Sally G." and the instrumentals "Walking in the Park with Eloise" (written by Paul's father, James McCartney, many years earlier) and "Bridge over the River Suite" with Chet Atkins and Floyd Cramer joining in, the entire group billed as "The Country Hams." Paul also recorded the unreleased cuts "Hey Diddle," "Wide Prairie," "Send Me the Heart" and "Proud Mum."

(b) Middle of that year: Paul taped demos of several songs that he and Wings would later record for the *Venus and Mars* album.

Jul 6: Wings' LP *Band on the Run* reached number one in the U.K.

(rb) Jul 15: John recorded "Move Over Ms. L." He also wrote "Incantation" with Roy Cicala, but no recording of the song has surfaced; a copyright for the title was registered on Nov 15. Several rehearsals, outtakes and prefinal mixes of *Walls and Bridges* songs, reportedly from Jul 14 and 15, have been bootlegged.

Jul 17: A U.S. Immigration and Naturalization Service board denied John's Oct 31, 1973 appeal of the deportation order against him and ordered that he leave the U.S. within 60 days. John again filed an appeal.

(b) Jul 21: John and others were recorded while listening to studio playbacks of *Walls and Bridges* tracks before final overdubbing and mixing.

(r) Jul: John returned to New York and began recording sessions by cutting "Whatever Gets You Through the Night" (with Elton John on piano, organ and harmony vocals) and "Beef Jerky" (instrumental). John also recorded additional songs, released on his LP *Walls and Bridges*. Alternate versions of several songs were released on *Menlove Ave.* in 1986. Elton John elicited a promise from Lennon to appear with him at his Thanksgiving concert at New York's Madison Square Garden if "Whatever Gets You Through the Night" reached number one. John agreed to this, feeling certain the song would not reach number one "in a million years." It did, however.

(rb) That summer: Ringo recorded songs for his LP *Goodnight Vienna*. John recorded demos of "It's All Down to Goodnight Vienna" earlier for Ringo and supervised recording of the song in Los Angeles. While there, he also cut a studio demo of "Only You," which Ringo then recorded for the album at John's suggestion. On his way home from Los Angeles, John stopped at Elton John's Caribou Ranch in Colorado to do backup work on Elton's recording of "Lucy in the Sky with Diamonds."

(b) That summer–fall: Paul and Wings recorded several songs for the unreleased documentary film *One Hand Clapping*. The film was partly shot earlier in Nashville, but screen credits state that it was video recorded at EMI in England in fall 1974, directed by David Litchfield. One segment of the film "The Backyard" was edited into a separate unreleased film.

Aug 31: John testified in U.S. Federal Court that officials of the Nixon administration sought to deport him on trumped-up charges strictly because of John's anti-Vietnam war activities and fear that he would lead demonstrations in Miami at the 1972 Republican National Convention.

Sep 23: John's single "Whatever Gets You Through the Night"/"Beef Jerky" released in the U.S. Released in the U.K. on Oct 4.

■ Ravi Shankar's *Music Festival from India*, produced by George and filmed and recorded by Dark Horse Records, took place at the Royal Albert Hall in London. The film was not released.

Sep 26: John's LP *Walls and Bridges* released in the U.S. Released in the U.K. on Oct 4.

(b) Sep 27: John was a guest D.J. on Los Angeles radio station KHJ-AM.

(b) Sep 28: An interview with John by Dennis Elsas was recorded when he appeared as a guest D.J. on New York radio station WNEW-FM.

Sep: John was interviewed by Tom Donahue on San Francisco radio station KSAN-FM. Excerpts from the interview were aired on "The Lost Lennon Tapes" radio series.

(rb) Sep–Oct: George recorded "I Don't Care Anymore" and songs for his LP *Dark Horse*. George was suffering from laryngitis, which was obvious on the recordings. The condition would seriously hurt the album, as well as George's tour in Nov and Dec, during which his voice deteriorated still further.

■ George and Patti's marriage ended when Pattie ran off with George's friend Eric Clapton. It was also rumored that George had had an affair with Ringo's wife, Maureen. George wrote new lyrics to the old Everly Brothers song "Bye, Bye, Love" criticizing Eric and Pattie for their conduct and then had them join in on the recording of the song for his LP *Dark Horse*. George soon found a new girlfriend, Olivia Trinidad Arias.

Oct 18: Single "Walking in the Park with Eloise"/"Bridge Over the River Suite" released in the U.K., with Paul, Wings, Floyd Cramer and Chet Atkins billed as "The Country Hams." Released in the U.S. on Dec 2.

(rb) Oct 21–25: John recorded several new tracks for his LP *Rock 'N' Roll*. The songs were also included on the unauthorized U.S. LP *John Lennon Sings the Great Rock & Roll Hits [Roots]*. Several unreleased studio jams were also recorded.

Oct 25: Wings' single "Junior's Farm"/"Sally G." released in the U.K. Released in the U.S. on Nov 4.

Oct 28: Allen Klein lost his legal case against John, George and Ringo.

Nov 1: John requested court permission to question the Immigration and Naturalization Service regarding its motivation for deporting him and regarding former U.S. Attorney General John Mitchell's role in the proceedings.

(b) Nov 2–Dec 20: George toured North America, and many of his shows were benefits. Appearing with him were Billy Preston, Tom Scott, Chuck Findley, Jim Horn, Robben Ford, Andy Newmach, Willie Weeks and Emil Richards. Songs performed included "Hari's on Tour (Express)," "The Lord Loves the One (That Loves the Lord)," "For You Blue," "Something," "Sue Me, Sue You Blues," "Maya Love," "Sound Stage of Mind," "Dark Horse," "Give Me Love," "In My Life," "While My Guitar Gently Weeps," "What Is Life" and "My Sweet Lord." Unfortunately, George had almost completely lost his voice at this time, and the tour was generally panned and considered a failure; George was sometimes greeted by disappointed or even hostile fans. The tour included performances at Pacific Coliseum, Vancouver (Nov 2); Seattle, Washington (Nov 4); the Cow Palace, San Francisco (Nov 6, 7); Oakland Coliseum (Nov 8 [2 shows]); Long Beach Arena (Nov 10); Los Angeles Forum (Nov 11 [1 show], 12 [2 shows]); Tucson's Community Center, Arizona (Nov 14); Salt Palace, Salt Lake City (Nov 16); Denver's Coliseum (Nov 18 [2 shows]); St. Louis Arena (Nov 20); Tulsa Assembly Center, Oklahoma (Nov 21); Fort Worth, Texas (Nov 22); Houston's Hofheinz Pavilion (Nov 24); Baton Rouge, Louisiana (Nov 26); Mid-South Coliseum, Memphis (Nov 27); the Omni, Atlanta (Nov 28 [2 shows]); Chicago, Illinois (Nov 30 [2 shows]); Olympia Stadium, Detroit (Dec 4 [2 shows]); Toronto's Maple Leaf Gardens (Dec 6 [2 shows]); Montreal's Forum (Dec 8 [2 shows]); Boston Garden (Dec 10 [2 shows]); Providence Civic Center, Rhode Island (Dec 11); Largo, Maryland (Dec 13 [2 shows]); Nassau Coliseum, Uniondale, Long Island (Dec 15 [2 shows]); Philadelphia's Spectrum (Dec 16 [1 show], Dec 17 [2 shows]); New York's Madison Square Garden (Dec 19 [1 show], Dec 20 [2 shows]).

Nov 6: Paul and Linda appeared on Thames TV's "This Is Your Life" in the U.K., with light-heavyweight boxer John Conteh the guest of honor.

Nov 8: Ringo appeared live on BBC Radio One's "Rockspeak."

Nov 11: Ringo's single "Only You (and You Alone)"/"Call Me" released in the U.S. Released in the U.K. on Nov 15.

(b) Nov 15: A copyright was registered for the unreleased song "Incantation," written by John and Roy Cicala during John's summer 1974 *Walls and Bridges* sessions.

■ Ringo's LP *Goodnight Vienna* released in the U.K. Released in the U.S. on Nov 18.

Nov 16: John's single "Whatever Gets You Through the Night" reached number one in the U.S., his first American solo number one. *Walls and Bridges* also reached number one in the U.S. on this date.

Nov 18: George's single "Dark Horse"/"I Don't Care Anymore" released in the U.S.

Nov 20: Wings taped a performance of "Junior's Farm" for "Top of the Pops," aired the following day by BBC-TV. They also backed David Essex on "I'm Gonna Make You a Star" during the show.

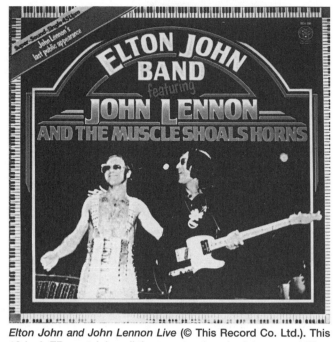

Elton John and John Lennon Live (© This Record Co. Ltd.). This 12-inch EP, containing all three songs done by Lennon and Elton John on Thanksgiving 1974, appeared outside the U.S. and U.K. This one was released in Germany.

(b) Nov 24: Lennon and Elton John rehearsed songs for Elton's Nov 28 Thanksgiving concert at New York's Madison Square Garden.

(b) Nov 27: Paul and Linda provided backing vocals on "Mine for Me," written by Paul, performed by Rod Stewart during a live performance at the Odeon Cinema, Lewisham, South London. The performance was aired in the U.S. on "Midnight Special" on Apr 25, 1975.

(r) Nov 28: Keeping his promise, John performed three numbers with Elton John at Elton's Thanksgiving concert in New York's Madison Square Garden, "Whatever Gets You Through the Night," "Lucy in the Sky with Diamonds" and "I Saw Her Standing There." Although Lennon and Ono have repeatedly claimed that John did not know that Yoko was in attendance, May Pang claims in her book, *Loving John*, that not only did Lennon know well in advance, but he had secured Ono's tickets and that Ono had phoned him more than once to complain about the location of her seats.

(b) Nov: Paul began recording sessions with Wings for his *Venus and Mars* album at Abbey Road Studios. The sessions resumed in New Orleans in Jan 1975.

Dec 5: *Rolling Stone* magazine printed a copy of the Feb 4, 1972 secret memo to former U.S. Attorney General John Mitchell from Senator Strom Thurmond and charged that John's deportation case was political.

Dec 6: George's single "Ding Dong, Ding Dong" (Ringo on drums)/"I Don't Care Anymore" released in the U.K.

(b) Dec 9: John appeared on ABC-TV's "Monday Night Football" and was briefly interviewed by Howard Cosell.

■ George's LP *Dark Horse* released in the U.S. and in the U.K. on Dec 20. Ringo is featured on drums on "Ding Dong, Ding Dong" and "So Sad."

Dec 11: Ringo changed the name of his company from Reckongrade Ltd. to Pyramid Records Ltd.

(rb) Dec 13: George's live version of "For You Blue," recorded at the Capitol Center in Largo, Maryland, was released Feb 15, 1988 on the limited edition CD and vinyl EP *Songs by George Harrison*, issued with Harrison's book of the same title. The concert location is almost always mistakenly listed as Washington, D.C. (including on this record sleeve).

■ George, his father, Ravi Shankar, Billy Preston and Jim Keltner lunched with U.S. President Gerald Ford at the White House.

Dec 16: John's single "No. 9 Dream"/"What You Got" released in the U.S. Released in the U.K. on Jan 31, 1975.

Dec 20: John was scheduled to join George on stage during his second Madison Square Garden show, but the two had an argument prior to the show and John did not perform (he may have been backstage during the show). After the show, the two settled their argument and were interviewed together in George's hotel room by KHJ radio, Los Angeles. The interview was aired as a one-hour special some months later. This is the only known radio interview with more than one Beatle recorded after the group's demise. George held a party at New York's Hippopotamus Nightclub to celebrate the end of his American tour, and John and Yoko, arriving separately, were among the guests.

Dec 23: George's single "Ding Dong, Ding Dong" (Ringo on drums)/"Hari's on Tour (Express)" released in the U.S.

Dec: On BBC-TV's "Rutland Weekend Television," British comedian Eric Idle of Monty Python and Neil Innes presented their original "Rutles" sketch based on The Beatles. A clip from the sketch was aired on the U.S. TV show "Saturday Night Live" on Oct 2, 1976.

■ John was interviewed by Kenny Everett on Capital Radio in the U.K.

(b) Dec–Feb 1975: John cut several demos of "Tennessee." The song went through a number of later incarnations under different titles, including "Memories" and "Howling at the Moon," with different lyrics. Part of "Memories" later evolved into "Watching the Wheels." Other reported working titles for the song include "Emotional Wreck" and "People." Lennon also wrote a song called "Popcorn" during this period, described by May Pang as a funny, catchy tune.

(b) Late that year: George appeared on the U.K. Radio show "Rock Around the World" with Alan Freeman.

■ The film *Little Malcolm and His Struggle Against the Eunuchs*, for which George served as executive producer, had its world premiere at the Berlin Film Festival.

1975

Early that year: John and Yoko were permanently reunited and returned to their apartment in New York's Dakota building overlooking Central Park.

Jan 2: U.S. district court Judge Richard Owen ruled in New York City that John and his attorneys were to be permitted access to U.S. Immigration and Naturalization Service files dealing with John's deportation case. John was also permitted to question INS officials. The ruling was designed to give John the opportunity to determine whether the deportation proceedings against him were really based on his 1968 U.K. drug conviction or on opposition to his U.S. political activities.

Jan 9: The last remaining legal links binding the four Beatles together were finally severed when The Beatles & Company partnership was formally dissolved at a private hearing in London High Court. The ruling came four years after Paul had originally requested that the partnership be dissolved.

(rb) Jan 16–Feb 24: Wings recorded songs for the LP *Venus and Mars* in New Orleans. Wings also cut the unreleased tracks "Karate Chaos" and an instrumental, "Sea Dance." After Feb 24, Wings moved on to Los Angeles where recording sessions were concluded. This was Paul's first LP for Capitol under his new contract.

Jan 27: Ringo's single "No No Song"/"Snookeroo" released in the U.S.

Jan: Geoff Britton left Wings.

Feb 8: LP *John Lennon Sings the Great Rock & Roll Hits [Roots]* was released only in the U.S. via mail-order advertising. John had been sued by Chuck Berry's publisher, Morris Levy, for plagiarizing Berry's song "You Can't Catch Me" on The Beatles' recording of "Come

Rock 'N' Roll (© EMI Records Ltd.). Lennon's oldies album was rush-released following the unauthorized release of *Roots* in the U.S.

Together." As part of an out-of-court settlement, John gave Levy a prefinal mix tape of his oldies recording sessions. The tape was used by Levy without Lennon's permission to create *Roots*. John then sued Levy, charging that the release was illegal. In Jul 1975 John was awarded $144,700 in damages. While of inferior sound quality, *Roots* contains "Be My Baby" and "Angel Baby," omitted from the *Rock 'N' Roll* album. The other tracks on *Roots* are the same recordings found on *Rock 'N' Roll* with some differences in mixing and editing. Release of *Rock 'N' Roll* was moved up in reaction to the release of *Roots*.

(rb) Feb 12: Wings recorded "My Carnival" during sessions in New Orleans for *Venus and Mars*. It was not released until 1985 when it became the B side of "Spies Like Us." While in New Orleans, Paul appeared on stage with The Tuxedo Jazz Band and sang "Baby Face." That performance was filmed and appears on underground copies of the 1974 unreleased McCartney film *One Hand Clapping*.

Feb 17: John's LP *Rock 'N' Roll* released in the U.S. Released in the U.K. on Feb 21.

Feb 21: Ringo's single "Snookeroo"/"Oo Wee" released in the U.K.

Feb 24: Single "Philadelphia Freedom" (Elton John)/"I Saw Her Standing There" (John and Elton John live at Madison Square Garden Nov 28, 1974) released in the U.K. and the U.S.

Feb 28: George's single "Dark Horse"/"Hari's on Tour" released in the U.K.

(rb) Feb: Wings recorded the instrumental medley "Lunch Box-Odd Sox."

■ A copyright for the instrumental version of Paul's "Tomorrow" was registered. A vocal version had originally appeared on Wings' *Wild Life* album in Aug 1971.

■ Joe English replaced Geoff Britton as Wings' drummer.

Mar 1: John and Paul Simon served as award presenters on the Grammy Awards show, televised from Los Angeles. Paul received two 1974 Grammys for his Wings LP *Band on the Run*: Best Pop Vocal Performance By a Group and Best Produced Non-Classical Recording.

Mar 2: Police stopped Paul and Linda's car in Los Angeles for running a red light. Linda was subsequently charged with possession of marijuana after police found six to eight ounces of it in her purse.

Mar 6: Lennon issued a press release announcing that he was returning to Yoko Ono, adding that their separation "hadn't worked out."

■ John's single "Stand By Me"/"Move Over Ms. L" released in the U.S. Released in the U.K. on Apr 18.

Mar 17: Keith Moon's LP *Two Sides of the Moon* released in the U.S. Ringo is featured as the announcer on "Solid Gold" and on drums and "rap" on "Together." Released in the U.K. on May 23.

Mar 26: During a U.S. telecast of the premiere of the film *Tommy*, Paul and Linda were interviewed by David Frost.

(b) Mar: John recorded the line "Voulez-vous couchez avec moi ce soir" from Labelle's hit, "Lady Marmalade," during an interview.

■ Final sessions for Wings' *Venus and Mars* album in Los Angeles. Paul held a party in Long Beach, California celebrating the end of *Venus and Mars* recording sessions aboard the ocean liner *Queen Mary*. Guests included George Harrison, which marked the first time that he and Paul were seen socializing together since the breakup of The Beatles.

Apr 4: Ringo formed a new record company, Ring O' Records.

(b) Apr 18: John appeared on the TV show "Old Grey Whistle Test," aired on BBC 2 and taped earlier in New York.

Apr 19–20: Dave Herman recorded a two-hour interview with George Harrison, aired on May 24 by the DIR syndication network.

(b) Apr 28: Ringo appeared on NBC-TV's "The Smothers Brothers Comedy Hour" and sang "No No Song" with the Brothers.

■ John and his lawyer Leon Wildes were interviewed on NBC-TV's "Tomorrow Show" by Tom Snyder. A commercial videotape of a Dec 9, 1980 rebroadcast of this show was released under the title "The John Lennon Interview."

Apr 29: John appeared on the "Today" show on U.S. TV.

May 2: Apple Records closed down.

May 16: Wings' single "Listen to What the Man Said"/"Love in Song" released in the U.K. Released in the U.S. on May 23.

May 21: A TV special, "Beatles Special with Host David Frost" was seen on U.S. TV.

May 27: Wings' LP *Venus and Mars* released in the U.S. Released in the U.K. on May 30.

(r) May–June: George recorded songs for his LP *Extra Texture—Read All About It*.

Jun 2: Ringo's single medley: "It's All Down to Goodnight Vienna"-"Goodnight Vienna" (reprise)/"Oo-Wee" released in the U.S.

(b) Jun 13: A prerecorded John Lennon performance was seen on the TV special "A Salute to Sir Lew Grade," aired in the U.S. on this date, marking Lennon's final stage appearance. John's backing group wore two-faced masks as an expression of Lennon's opinion of Sir Lew, owner of Associated Communications Corporation in the U.K. John's group was billed as "John Lennon and Etcetera" for the performance.

Jun 19: John brought suit against former Nixon administration attorneys General John Mitchell and Richard Kleindienst and officials of the U.S. Immigration and Naturalization Service in Federal Court in Manhattan. The suit charged that John had been singled out for selective prosecution because of his political views and that he was not being deported, as stated by the U.S.

government, because of his 1968 drug conviction in England.

Jun 28: Wings' LP *Venus and Mars* reached number one in the U.K.

Jul 17: Maureen was granted a divorce from Ringo on grounds of adultery.

Jul 19: Wings' single "Listen to What the Man Said" and LP *Venus and Mars* both reached number one in the U.S.

Sep 5: Wings' single "Letting Go"/"You Gave Me the Answer" released in the U.K. Released in the U.S. on Sep 29.

Sep 6: Wings performed live at Elstree Film Studios for 1,200 EMI employees prior to the start of their world tour.

(b) Sep 9–Nov 14: Paul and Wings toured Britain and Australia. Songs performed on the tour included "Venus and Mars," "Rock Show," "Jet," "Let Me Roll It," "Little Woman Love," "C Moon," "Maybe I'm Amazed," "Lady Madonna," "The Long and Winding Road," "Live and Let Die," "Picasso's Last Words," "Bluebird," "I've Just Seen a Face," "Blackbird," "Yesterday," "You Gave Me the Answer," "Magneto and Titanium Man," "Call Me Back Again," "My Love," "Listen To What the Man Said," "Letting Go," "Junior's Farm," "Band on the Run," "Hi, Hi, Hi" and "Soily." U.K. dates: Southampton's Gaumont (Sep 9); Bristol's Hippodrome (Sep 10); Cardiff's Capitol (Sep 11); Manchester's Free Trade Hall (Sep 12); Birmingham's Hippodrome (Sep 13); Liverpool's Empire (Sep 15); Newcastle's City Hall (Sep 16); Hammersmith's Odeon (Sep 17, 18); Edinburgh's Usher Hall (Sep 20); Glasgow's Apollo (Sep 21); Aberdeen's Capitol (Sep 22); Dundee's Caird Hall (Sep 23). Australia dates: Perth's Entertainment Centre (Nov 1); Adelaide's Apollo Stadium (Nov 4, 5); Sydney's Horden Pavilion (Nov 7, 8); Brisbane's Festival Hall (Nov 10, 11); Melbourne's Myer Music Bowl (Nov 13, 14).

Sep 12: George's single "You"/"World of Stone" released in the U.K. Released in the U.S. on Sep 15.

Sep 22: George's LP *Extra Texture—Read All About It* released in the U.S. Released in the U.K. on Oct 3.

Sep 23: The U.S. government suspended deportation proceedings against John pending the termination of Yoko Ono's pregnancy.

Oct 7: John finally won his three-and-a-half-year battle to remain in the U.S. when a three-judge U.S. court of appeals in New York City overturned the order to deport him. The court ruled that John's 1968 U.K. drug conviction was contrary to U.S. understanding of due process of law and did not justify deportation. The ruling noted that "Lennon's four-year battle to remain in our country is a testimony to his faith in [the] American dream." The court ordered the Immigration and Naturalization Service to reconsider Lennon's request for resident status.

Oct 9: On John's 35th birthday, Yoko gave birth to their son, Sean Taro Ono Lennon in New York. Elton John served as the child's godfather.

Oct 10: The film *Lisztomania*, featuring a cameo by Ringo, premiered in New York. It opened in London on Nov 13.

Oct 24: John's compilation LP *Shaved Fish* released in the U.K. and the U.S. His single "Imagine"/"Working Class Hero" released in the U.K.

Oct 27: Wings' single medley: "Venus and Mars"-"Rock Show"/"Magneto and Titanium Man" released in the U.S. Released in the U.K. on Nov 28.

(b) **Nov 13:** Wings' concert at Myer Music Bowl, Melbourne was taped and aired on Australian television.

Nov 25: Ringo's compilation LP *Blast from Your Past* released in the U.S. Released in the U.K. on Dec 12.

■ George's single "This Guitar (Can't Keep from Crying)"/"Maya Love" released in the U.S. Released in the U.K. on Feb 6, 1976.

(b) **Dec 26:** George appeared in a prerecorded segment on the U.K. TV show "Rutland Weekend Television Christmas Show." He sang "The Pirate Song," which he had written with Eric Idle, and which pokes fun at George's legal problems concerning his recording of "My Sweet Lord." George had been charged with plagiarism of that song by Bright Tunes, the publishers of "He's So Fine," a 1963 Chiffons hit. "He's So Fine" composer Ronnie Mack was dead, but Bright Tunes pressed the suit. During trial testimony George maintained that he never intended to plagiarize "He's So Fine" and actually had the spiritual "Oh Happy Day" in mind when he composed the song. On Sep 7, 1976, George was found guilty of "subconscious plagiarism" and ordered to pay $587,000 in composition royalties. The fine was paid on Feb 26, 1981, ironically to then former Beatles manager Allen Klein's company, ABKCO, which had purchased rights to "He's So Fine" in 1980.

Shaved Fish (© Apple Corps Ltd.). This Lennon anthology was released in the U.S. and in the U.K. in Oct 1975.

Dec 29: Michael Abdul Malik, known as Michael X, was executed by hanging in Trinidad for the murder of Joseph Skerritt. John and Yoko had been supporters of Michael X and had worked for a reversal of his conviction and commutation of his death sentence.

(b) **Late that year–early 1976:** John cut an acoustic home recording of "Mucho Mungo," which he had originally written in 1974 for Harry Nilsson.

(b) **Middle of the decade:** Paul recorded the unreleased songs "Thank You Darling," "Great Cock and Seagull Race," "When I Was In Paris" and "Rode All Night," the last possibly a working title for "Giddy," later given to Roger Daltry.

■ John recorded a number of unreleased songs at home during a period in which he claimed to have never touched a guitar.

1976

(b) **Jan 1:** During an interview taped by Elliot Mintz—who did not seem able to face Lennon without a tape recorder in hand—John twice ad-libbed lines from "As Time Goes By" and sang a line from the chorus of "What's the New Mary Jane," also explaining a little about the song's history.

Jan 5: Mal Evans, former Beatles' assistant, bodyguard and one of the few individuals who was truly close to The Beatles, was shot and killed by police in a Los Angeles motel. In a drugged stupor, he had become uncontrollably violent, appeared to be attempting suicide and had apparently pointed a loaded rifle at policemen who then shot him.

Jan 9: Ringo's single "Oh My My"/"No No Song" released in the U.K.

Jan 25: Ringo appeared with Bob Dylan and The Band as a "surprise" guest at an all-star benefit concert for convicted murderer and ex-boxer Rubin "Hurricane" Carter at Houston's Astrodome.

Jan 26: The Beatles' nine-year contract with EMI expired. While Paul remained with the company, George signed with A&M Records and Ringo with Atlantic in the U.S. and Polydor elsewhere. John did not sign a new contract.

(r) **Jan–Feb:** Wings recorded songs for the LP *Wings at the Speed of Sound*.

Feb: Bill Sargent, a U.S. promoter, offered The Beatles $50 million if they would perform one reunion concert. The Beatles declined to do so.

Mar 8: Single "Yesterday"/"I Should Have Known Better" released in the U.K.

Mar 18: Paul's father, James McCartney, died.

(b) **Mar 20–26:** Wings conducted a short European tour with concerts at the Falkoner Theater, Copenhagen (Mar 20, 21); Deutschlandhalle, Berlin (Mar 23); Ahoy Sport Paleis, Rotterdam (Mar 25); Pavillion, Paris (Mar 26).

Mar 25: LP *Wings at the Speed of Sound* released in the U.S. Released in the U.K. on Apr 9.

(b) Mar 26: Wings' tour concluded with a show at Pavillion in Paris, after which guitarist Jimmy McCulloch broke his finger, causing a three-week postponement of Wings' U.S. tour.

Apr 1: Wings' single "Silly Love Songs"/"Cook of the House" released in the U.S. Released in the U.K. on Apr 30.

■ John's father, Alfred "Freddie" Lennon, died in England. John had not enjoyed much of a relationship with his father, who had deserted him as a boy and later returned to obtain what he could of John's Beatles-acquired wealth. The two apparently reconciled somewhat during the final days of Freddie's life.

Apr 7: Paul changed the name of McCartney Productions Ltd. to MPL Communications Ltd.

Apr 20: George appeared with the Monty Python comedy group at New York's City Center during the "Lumberjack Song." The performance appears on several bootlegs masked as a track from George's 1974 tour.

Apr 24: The LP *Wings at the Speed of Sound* reached number one in the U.S.

(rb) Apr–May: Ringo recorded songs for his LP *Ringo's Rotogravure*. Ringo also cut the unreleased tracks "Where Are You Going," "All Right" and "It's Hard to Be Lovers" during these sessions. John assisted in the recording of his composition, "Cookin' (in the Kitchen of Love)," his last studio work until 1980's *Double Fantasy*, although he remained busy recording new songs at home.

(rb) May 3–Jun 23: Wings' tour of the U.S. took place. The tour included shows at Fort Worth's Tarrant Country Convention Hall (May 3); Houston's Summit (May 4); Detroit's Olympia (May 7, 8); Toronto's Maple Leaf Gardens (May 9); Cleveland's Richfield Coliseum (May 10); Philadelphia's Spectrum (May 12, 14); Largo, Maryland's Capitol Center (May 15, 16); Atlanta's Omni (May 18, 19); Long Island's Nassau Coliseum (May 21); Boston Garden (May 22); New York's Madison Square Garden (May 24, 25); Cincinnati's Riverfront Stadium (May 27); Kansas City's Kemper Arena (May 29); Chicago, Illinois (Jun 1, 2); St. Paul, Minnesota's Civic Center (Jun 4); Denver's McNichols Arena (Jun 7); Seattle's Kingdome (Jun 10); San Francisco's Cow Palace (Jun 13, 14); San Diego's Sports Arena (Jun 16); Tucson's Community Forum (Jun 18); Los Angeles' Forum (Jun 21, 22, 23).

May 22: Paul's single "Silly Love Songs" reached number one in the U.S. It reached number one in the U.K. on Jun 19.

(r) May 24–Sep 13: George recorded his LP *Thirty Three & 1/3*.

May 31: Single "Got to Get You into My Life"/"Helter Skelter" released in the U.S.

(b) Jun 10: Wings performed a concert in Seattle's Kingdome. Most of Paul's official concert tour film, *Rockshow*, was shot at this show; it premiered in New York on Nov 26, 1980 and was later released on videocassette.

■ Double LP *Rock and Roll Music* released in the U.K. Released in the U.S. on Jun 11.

(b) Jun 23: Wings' final concert at Los Angeles' Forum, concluding the Wings over America tour. Ringo took the stage during the group's final number and presented Paul with some flowers.

Jun 25: Single "Back in the U.S.S.R."/"Twist and Shout" released in the U.K.

(b) Jun 28: Paul, Linda and Wings were interviewed by Geraldo Rivera on his U.S. late-night TV show "Goodnight America" on ABC-TV. Excerpts from the Jun 10 Wings Seattle concert were shown. Clips from the show were seen the following day on ABC-TV's "Good Morning America."

■ Wings' single "Let 'Em In"/"Beware My Love" released in the U.S. Released in the U.K. on Jul 23.

Jul 23: George failed to produce a new album due to A&M Records under terms of his contract. After beginning the recording of *Thirty Three & 1/3* early in 1976, a serious bout with hepatitis caused delay in the album's completion.

Jul 27: John's application to remain in the U.S. was approved. He was formally issued his "green card" (# 17-597-321) permitting him to remain permanently in the U.S. and enabling him to apply for citizenship in 1981. The ceremony took place at the New York offices of the U.S. Immigration and Naturalization Service, where Judge Ira Fieldsteel handed John the green card. It was he who had handed down the decision ordering John to leave the U.S. on Mar 23, 1973.

Jul 30: LP *The Beatles Tapes* released in the U.K., containing David Wigg's interviews with The Beatles for BBC Radio's "Scene and Heard" show. Ringo and George sought to block release of the album but failed to do so.

Aug: Wings' LP *Band on the Run* was released in the Soviet Union on the Melodiya label.

(b) That summer: Denny Laine's LP *Holly Days* was recorded. Paul played most of the instruments on this album, provided backing vocals and produced the sessions.

Sep 7: Paul staged the first "Buddy Holly Week" celebration on the 40th anniversary of Holly's birth. The celebration would become an annual event. Paul had purchased the Edward H. Morris Music Publishing Company, thus acquiring publishing rights to the Buddy Holly music catalog.

Sep 17: Ringo's LP *Ringo's Rotogravure* released in the U.K. Released in the U.S. on Sep 27. John wrote "Cookin' (in the Kitchen of Love)" (on which he plays piano); Paul wrote "Pure Gold" (on which he contributes backing vocals); George wrote "I'll Still Love You."

Sep 19–27: Wings conducted a short European tour including performances in Vienna, Austria (Sep 19); Zagreb, Yugoslavia (Sep 21); Venice, Italy (Sep 25); Munich, Germany (Sep 27).

Sep 20: Ringo's single "A Dose of Rock and Roll"/"Cryin'" released in the U.S. Released in the U.K. on Oct 15.

Sep 25: Wings performed a UNESCO benefit concert in St. Mark's Square, Venice, Italy and raised $50,000 to help restore the city of Venice.

Sep 28: A&M Records sued George for $10 million charging that he had failed to comply with the terms of his contract by not completing an LP by the July 26 deadline. The matter was resolved by both parties agreeing to end the contract. George subsequently retained Warner Brothers to distribute his Dark Horse label.

Oct 2: On the U.S. TV show "Saturday Night Live," Eric Idle screened a clip of "I Must Be in Love" from the "Rutles" sketch, originally seen in the U.K. in Dec 1974 on BBC-TV's "Rutland Weekend Television." The success of this early film led to the full-blown Rutles TV special "All You Need Is Cash," aired in the U.S. Mar 22, 1978. "The Rutles" were an imaginary group whose career comically paralleled that of The Beatles.

Oct 19–21: A three-day concert engagement by Wings took place at Empire Pool, Wembley.

(b) Oct 29: Ringo recorded the unreleased track "I Can Hear You Calling."

Oct–Nov: George's promotional film for the songs "Crackerbox Palace," "True Love" and "This Song" was released.

Nov 8: George's LP *The Best of George Harrison* released in the U.S. Released in the U.K. on Nov 20.

■ Single "Ob-La-Di, Ob-La-Da"/"Julia" released in the U.S.

Nov 15: George's single "This Song"/"Learning How to Love You" released in the U.S. Released in the U.K. on Nov 19.

(rb) Nov 19: George and Paul Simon recorded several songs for the U.S. TV show "Saturday Night Live," aired Nov 20, including "Here Comes the Sun" and "Homeward Bound." Promo videos of George's "Crackerbox Palace" (directed by Eric Idle) and "This Song" (directed by George) were also aired.

■ George's LP *Thirty Three & 1/3* released in the U.K. Released in the U.S. on Nov 24.

■ The LP *Magical Mystery Tour* was released in the U.K. The album was originally released in the U.S. in 1967.

Nov 22: Ringo's single "Hey Baby"/"Lady Gaye" released in the U.S. Released in the U.K. on Nov 29.

Nov 24: Ringo appeared with The Band at the Winterland in San Francisco, The Band's final concert, dubbed The Last Waltz. A film of the concert was later released and also issued on videocassette.

Nov 30: George appeared on BBC 2's TV show "Old Grey Whistle Test."

Dec 10: Wings' LP *Wings over America* was released in the U.K. and U.S.

Dec 25: George's single "My Sweet Lord"/"What Is Life" released in the U.K.

1977

(b) Early that year: George recorded a message for a Warner Brothers promo film intended for viewing by the company's sales personnel.

(b) Early–middle of that year: During sessions for his LP *London Town* Paul recorded the unreleased "Boil Crisis."

Jan 22: *Wings over America* reached number one in the U.S.

Jan 24: George's single "Crackerbox Palace"/"Learning How to Love You" released in the U.S.

Feb 4: Wings' single "Maybe I'm Amazed" (live version)/"Soily" released in the U.K. Released in the U.S. in Feb 7.

(b) Feb 5: Ringo recorded the unreleased songs "Lover Please" and "Wild Shining Stars" at Cherokee Studios in Los Angeles.

(r) Feb 7–Mar 31: Wings recorded "London Town" and "Deliver Your Children."

Feb 11: George's single "True Love"/"Pure Smokey" released in the U.K.

Feb 19: Ringo was a guest presenter on the Grammy Awards show televised in the U.S.

(r) Mar: Wings recorded "Girl's School" (completed in Aug).

Apr 4: John's single "Stand by Me"/"Woman Is the Nigger of the World" and George's "Dark Horse"/"You" released in the U.S.

Apr 6: The Beatles, through Apple, lost their bid to halt the commercial release of the LP *The Beatles Live! At the Star Club in Hamburg, Germany: 1962* containing recordings made on a portable tape recorder during their Dec 31, 1962 appearance. The LP was released in Germany on Apr 8.

Apr 29: LP *Thrillington* released in the U.K., Paul's instrumental version of *Ram* produced under the pseudonym "Percy 'Thrills' Thrillington." A single, "Uncle Albert-Admiral Halsey"/"Eat at Home," was also issued in the U.K. LP released in the U.S. on May 17.

Apr: Neil Innes sang his Rutles number "Cheese and Onions" on the U.S. TV show "Saturday Night Live," hosted by Eric Idle. The recording has been bootlegged and the vocal erroneously credited to John Lennon. The same song was re-recorded by Innes for the full-blown Rutles TV special, "All You Need Is Cash," aired Mar 22, 1978 and released on the LP *The Rutles*.

May 1: U.K. release of LP *The Beatles Live! At the Star Club in Hamburg, Germany: 1962*. Another version of the LP, with a different song lineup, was released in the U.S. on Jun 13; neither album contained all of the songs.

May 6: U.K. and U.S. releases of LP *The Beatles at the Hollywood Bowl*, recorded at The Beatles' concerts of Aug 23, 1964 and Aug 30, 1965.

May 13: U.K. release of Roger Daltry's LP *One of the Boys*, which includes "Giddy," written by Paul. Released in the U.S. on Jun 16.

May 31: George's single "It's What You Value"/"Woman Don't You Cry for Me" released in the U.K.

■ Single "Seaside Woman"/"B Side to Seaside" released in the U.S. Linda McCartney wrote the A side on which she and Paul share lead vocal, and Paul wrote the B side featuring Linda on lead vocal. The artists are billed as "Suzy and The Red Stripes," a name taken from a brand of Jamaican beer. Paul also produced the record, which was not released in the U.K. until Aug 10, 1979.

(rb) May: Wings recorded songs for the LP *London Town* aboard the yacht *Fair Carol* off the Virgin Islands. Paul also recorded unreleased titles including the instrumental "El Toro Passing."

Jun 9: George and Pattie Harrison were granted a divorce. Pattie would later marry (and subsequently divorce) George's friend Eric Clapton, while George would later wed Olivia Arias.

Jun 25: The LP *The Beatles at the Hollywood Bowl* reached number one in the U.K.

(rb) Jun: Ringo recorded "Just a Dream" and songs for his LP *Ringo the 4th*. Ringo also cut the unreleased titles "By Your Side," "Duet—Nancy & Ringo," and "Nancy, Ringo, Vinnie & Friends"; the latter two appear to be inexact titles for informal studio recordings. All of these sessions took place at Atlantic Studios in New York. During this period, however, Ringo shifted to Cherokee Studios in Los Angeles for a time where he recorded the unreleased "Birmingham" and "The Party" and an alternate take of "Just a Dream."

■ John, Yoko and their son, Sean began a four-month visit to Japan.

That summer: Ringo recorded songs for the children's album *Scouse the Mouse*. Although planned as an animated TV film, that part of the project was never done due to trade union problems.

Aug 25: Ringo's single "Wings"/"Just a Dream" released in the U.S.

(r) Aug: Paul recorded "Mull of Kintyre."

Sep 4: A 60-minute interview with Ringo by D.J. Dave Herman took place.

Sep 8: Jimmy McCulloch left Wings and joined the re-formed group Small Faces.

Sep 12: Paul and Linda's son James Louis McCartney was born.

Sep 16: Ringo's single "Drowning in a Sea of Love"/"Just a Dream" released in the U.K. Released in the U.S. on Oct 18.

Sep 20: Ringo's LP *Ringo the 4th* released in the U.K. Released in the U.S. on Sep 26.

(b) That fall: John recorded demos of the unreleased "Mirror Mirror (on the Wall)." The song was one of several intended for a planned stage musical called *The Ballad of John and Yoko*.

Oct 4: John and Yoko held a press conference in Japan at the end of a four-month vacation there. John announced that his highest priority for the next several years would be raising his son Sean and that artistic endeavors would be secondary.

Oct 19: By an 11 to 9 vote the Liverpool City Council rejected a plan to build a monument to The Beatles in Liverpool.

Oct 21: LP *Love Songs* released in the U.S. Released in the U.K. on Nov 19.

(r) Oct 25–Dec 14: Wings held more recording sessions for *London Town* at EMI's Abbey Road studios.

(b) Oct: Paul taped an interview with Melvin Bragg, aired on the first broadcast of London Weekend Television's "The South Bank Show," broadcast on Jan 14, 1978. During the interview several unreleased songs were heard.

■ Single "Girl"/"You're Going to Lose That Girl" released in the U.S.

Nov: Joe English left Wings.

Nov 11: Wings' single "Mull of Kintyre"/"Girl's School" released in the U.K. Released in the U.S. on Nov 14 with A and B sides reversed.

Dec 3: Wings' single "Mull of Kintyre" reached number one in the U.K. and remained there for nine weeks.

Dec 3–14: Wings held several recording sessions for *London Town* at George Martin's AIR studios.

Dec 9: Ringo's LP *Scouse the Mouse* released in the U.K. only.

■ A promo clip of "Mull of Kintyre" was seen on "Midnight Special" on U.S. TV.

Dec 10: Wings taped an appearance on U.K. TV's "Mike Yarwood Christmas Show," aired Dec 25 on BBC 1. The group performed a sketch, and a promotional clip of "Mull of Kintyre" was screened.

Dec 17: George performed at a pub near his home in Henley-on-Thames.

(r) Late that year: Ringo recorded songs for his LP *Bad Boy*.

(b) That year: Ringo recorded the songs for "Simple Life" and "I Love My Suit" for four TV commercials in which he appeared for Simple Life Japanese leisure suits.

(rb) Dec–Jan 1978: Wings recorded songs for the LP *London Town*, including "Name and Address," said to be a tribute to the style of Elvis Presley, one of The Beatles' earliest and strongest influences, who had passed away on Aug 16, 1977. Paul also recorded the unreleased "Waterspout."

■ **(b)** John recorded demos of the unreleased "One of the Boys."

1978

(b) Early that year: Paul recorded a number of songs, including many unreleased titles, while seated at the piano at home.

(r) Jan 4–23: Wings held final recording sessions for *London Town*.

Jan 14: Wings' "Mull of Kintyre" became the largest-selling single in U.K. history with sales of over 1,667,000. It had sold 2 million copies in the U.K. by the end of January and eventually the total reached 2.5 million. It did not, however, go over well in the U.S. Its U.K. record was finally surpassed in Dec 1984 by Band Aid's charity single "Do They Know It's Christmas"/"Feed the World," the B side of which included two spoken messages from Paul.

Jan 25: George was a surprise guest on ITV's "This Is Your Life," honoring motorcyclist Barry Sheene.

Feb 19: A TV special about The Beatles, "All You Need Is Love," was aired in the U.S.

Mar 20: Wings' single "With a Little Luck"/"Backwards Traveller"-"Cuff Link" released in the U.S. Released in the U.K. on Mar 23.

Mar 22: The TV special "All You Need Is Cash" was telecast in the U.S. Telecast in the U.K. on Mar 27. This was a spoof of The Beatles' career tracing the history of a mythical group called The Rutles, portrayed by Eric Idle, Neil Innes, Rikki Fataar and John Halsey. George Harrison appeared briefly as a television reporter. Mick Jagger also appeared. Most of the songs were commercially released on an LP *The Rutles*; additional songs were later added to the CD release and the show has also been issued on videocassette.

Mar 31: Wings' LP *London Town* released in the U.K. and U.S.

(r) Mar: George recorded "Flying Hour," included on the original, unreleased version of the *Somewhere in England* album but omitted from the released version. The song was later remixed and released worldwide on the bonus EP and CD, *Songs by George Harrison*, issued with George's book of the same title on Feb 15, 1988.

(r) Apr 11–Oct 12: George recorded songs for his LP *George Harrison*. He also recorded "Circles" (written in 1968) during these sessions, released in 1982 on LP *Gone Troppo*.

(b) Apr 17: Ringo appeared on "The Mike Douglas Show" on U.S. TV.

Apr 18: Ringo's single "Lipstick Traces"/"Old Time Relovin'" released in the U.S.

Apr 21: Ringo's LP *Bad Boy* released in both the U.K. and U.S.

(b) Apr 26: Ringo appeared on his own TV special, "Ringo," aired in the U.S. only. The show was a modern comic/musical version of Mark Twain's "The Prince and the Pauper" and was narrated by George Harrison. Ringo played a character named Ognir Rrats (Ringo Starr spelled backward). The cast included Art Carney, Angie Dickinson, Mike Douglas, Carrie Fisher, Vincent Price and John Ritter.

May 14: A 30-minute interview with Paul, dealing with the release of Wings' LP *London Town*, was aired on BBC Radio.

May: Linda McCartney's song "Oriental Nightfish" was featured in the animated film *Oriental Nightfish* at the Cannes Film Festival. The film was included on Paul's *Rupert and the Frog Song* video releases.

■ George's father, Harold Harrison, died.

Jun 12: Wings' single "I've Had Enough"/"Deliver Your Children" released in the U.S. Released in the U.K. on Jun 16.

(rb) Jun 29–Nov 30: Wings recorded songs for the LP *Back to the Egg*. During these sessions guitarist Laurence Juber and drummer Steve Holly joined Wings, completing the group's final lineup. The unreleased "Crawl of the Wild" (with Dave Mason) was also recorded as was "Maisie," later released by Juber on his solo LP *Standard Time*, and alternate takes of several songs. Denny Laine later released "Weep for Love" from these sessions on his solo LP *Japanese Tears* (aka *In Flight*). Paul recorded "Same Time Next Year," originally intended for the movie of the same title but ultimately not used. Paul also recorded "Mama's Little Girl," possibly during *Back to the Egg* sessions. The latter two songs were not released until Feb 5, 1990 when they appeared only in the U.K. on "Put It There" CD and 12-inch singles.

(b) Middle of that year: Wings may have recorded an early version of "Ballroom Dancing" during *Back to the Egg* sessions. Laurence Juber referred in an interview to an unreleased Wings recording of this song, which Paul later rerecorded for his *Tug of War* album.

Jul 6: Ringo's single "Heart on My Sleeve"/"Who Needs a Heart" released in the U.S.

Jul 21: Ringo's single "Tonight"/"Old Time Relovin'" released in the U.K.

(rb) Jul 23: Paul recorded "Spin It On."

Aug 1: Olivia Arias, George's girlfriend, gave birth to their son, Dhani (the Indian word for "wealthy" or "wealthy person") in Windsor, England.

Aug 14: Single "Sgt. Pepper's Lonely Hearts Club Band"—"With a Little Help from My Friends"/"A Day in the Life" released in the U.S. Released in the U.K. on Sep 30.

Aug 21: Wings' single "London Town"/"I'm Carrying" released in the U.S. Released in the U.K. on Aug 26.

Sep 2: George and Olivia Arias were married, four weeks after their son's birth, in a secret ceremony at Henley-on-Thames Register Office.

(rb) Sep 11–20: Paul and Wings recorded songs for the LP *Back to the Egg*

(rb) Oct 3: Wings was joined at EMI studios by a large "super group" of guest musicians, the entire assembly billed as Rockestra, which recorded "Rockestra Theme" and "So Glad to See You Here," released on LP *Back to the Egg*. In addition to Wings, Rockestra included Dave Gilmour, Hank Marvin, Pete Townshend, John Bonham, Kenney Jones, John Paul Jones, Tony Ashton, Speedy Acquaye, Tony Carr, Ray Cooper, Morris Pert, Howie Casey, Tony Dorsey, Steve Howard and Thaddeus Richard.

Oct 6: Ringo was interviewed on the U.S. TV show "Everyday."

(rb) **Oct–Nov:** Wings recorded more songs for *Back to the Egg*.

Nov 22: Wings' LP *Wings Greatest* released in the U.S. Released in the U.K. on Dec 1.

(b) **Late Nov:** John Lennon ad-libbed a Dylan parody while watching a TV news broadcast around this time. He simply used the news reports to create spontaneous lyrics. The track is known as "News of the Day (from Reuters)."

Dec: LP *Rarities* released in the U.S. This LP was later scrapped and a revised version was issued on Mar 24, 1980.

■ George appeared at a benefit concert in the town of Pisshole, England. He performed with Mick Ralphs, Boz Burrell, Simon Kirke, Ian Paice and Jan Lords. The group billed itself as The Pisshole Artists.

(rb) **Late Dec:** Wings recorded "Goodnight Tonight" and "Daytime Nightime Suffering." An extended version of "Goodnight Tonight" was also later released.

That year: LP *The Beatles Tapes* was released in the U.S.

■ Ringo appeared in the film *Sextette* with Mae West. The film was issued on videocassette in the U.K. on Sep 20, 1982.

1979

Feb 9: George appeared live on BBC Radio One's "Roundtable."

Feb 14: LP *George Harrison* released in the U.S. Released in the U.K. on Feb 16.

■ George's single "Blow Away"/"Soft Hearted Hana" released in the U.S.

Feb 16: George's single "Blow Away"/"Soft Touch" released in the U.K.

Feb 19: George was interviewed briefly by Nicky Horn outside the Thames Studios. A two-minute film of the interview was aired the same day.

Mar 15: Wings' single "Goodnight Tonight"/"Daytime Nightime Suffering" released in the U.S. Released in the U.K. on Mar 23.

Mar 16: The 90-minute film *Wings over the World*, featuring highlights of Wings' 1975 and 1976 tours, was aired on U.S. TV. It was aired in the U.K. on Apr 8.

Mar 26: An extended 12-inch version of Paul's "Goodnight Tonight" was released with "Daytime Nightime Suffering" in the U.S. Released in the U.K. on Apr 3. This was Paul's first 12-inch extended mix release.

Apr 1: The NBC Radio show "An Afternoon with Paul McCartney" was aired in the U.S.

Apr 3: A promo clip for "Goodnight Tonight" was filmed at Hammersmith Palais in London.

Apr 6: A promo clip of George's "Blow Away" was aired on "Midnight Special" on U.S. TV.

Apr 20: George's single "Love Comes to Everyone"/"Soft Hearted Hana" released in the U.K.

Apr 27: Allen Klein was found guilty of tax evasion and sentenced to prison.

Late Apr: Ringo became seriously ill while living in Monte Carlo. His ailment was a recurrence of peritonitis from which he had suffered as a child. He underwent surgery for intestinal blockage at Princess Grace Hospital in Monte Carlo. Laser beam surgery was part of the treatment.

May 11: George's single "Love Comes to Everyone"/"Soft Touch" released in the U.S.

■ LP *Hey Jude* (aka *The Beatles Again*) released in the U.K., originally released in the U.S. on Feb 26, 1970.

May 19: While attending a party celebrating Eric Clapton's marriage to Pattie, George, Paul and Ringo staged an impromptu concert. They ran through old rock-and-roll hits and Beatles standards. Except for John, it was a Beatles reunion. Others joining in included Mick Jagger, Denny Laine, Eric Clapton himself, Lonnie Donegan and Ginger Baker.

May 24: Wings' LP *Back to the Egg* released in the U.S. Released in the U.K. on Jun 8.

May 26: George, Ringo and racing driver Jackie Stewart were interviewed on ABC-TV's "Wide World of Sports" in Monaco.

Jun 1: Wings' single "Old Siam, Sir"/"Spin It On" released in the U.K.

Jun 5: Wings' single "Getting Closer"/"Spin It On" released in the U.S.

Jun 8: Ringo played drums behind Stones' guitarist Ron Wood on "Buried Alive" on NBC-TV's "Midnight Special" in the U.S.

(rb) **Jul:** Paul recorded "Wonderful Christmastime" and "Rudolph the Red Nosed Reggae."

■ Paul recorded "Coming Up" (studio version).

(rb) **That summer:** Paul recorded songs for his LP *McCartney II* and other tracks. Paul originally planned this as a double album with several additional songs, including "All You Horseriders," running more than 80 minutes; test pressings of that version were made.

Jul 30: George's single "Faster"/"Your Love Is Forever" released in the U.K.

Aug 10: U.K. release of single "Seaside Woman"/"B Side to Seaside." Originally issued in the U.S. on May 31, 1977.

Aug 14: Wings' single "Arrow Through Me"/"Old Siam, Sir" released in the U.S.

Aug 16: Wings' single "Getting Closer"/"Baby's Request" released in the U.K.

Aug 22: George's limited edition book *I Me Mine* was published and sold for £148 per copy, with only 2,000 copies printed. An inexpensive edition appeared later. The book detailed all of George's musical writing and included lyrics to all of his songs. John was quite upset about the scant mention of his role in the development of George's music.

Sep 3: Ringo appeared on the TV special "Jerry Lewis Muscular Dystrophy Telethon" with Bill Wyman, Todd Rundgren, Doug Kershaw and Kiki Dee. Songs performed included "Money," "Twist and Shout" and "Jumpin' Jack Flash." Ringo also spent time taking phone pledges for the fund drive. A promo clip of Paul's "Getting Closer" was aired during the telecast.

(b) Sep 5: John began tape recording a verbal memoir, including his earliest childhood memories, his reaction to seeing his mother Julia performing oral sex on "Twitchy" Dykins, his low opinion of Dykins, and considerable criticism of Paul McCartney, Mick Jagger, and Bob Dylan, whom he viewed as "company men."

(b) Sep 14: Paul performed live at the Hammersmith Odeon as part of the fourth annual Buddy Holly Week celebration. The concert was filmed by Paul's MPL Communications and aired in the U.S. under the title "The Music Lives On" on MTV on Sep 8, 1984.

Sep 27: Former Wings guitarist Jimmy McCulloch was found dead in London at the age of 26, reportedly of a drug overdose.

That fall: Premiere of the film *Monty Python's Life of Brian*, produced by George. George's $5.5 million investment resulted in a profit of $65 million. The film was produced by George's HandMade Films, although George would not formally found the company until Aug 1980.

Oct 8: U.S. release of the soundtrack LP *Monty Python's Life of Brian* featuring "Always Look on the Bright Side of Life," mixed by George and Phil MacDonald. Released in the U.K. on Nov 9.

Oct 12: LP *The Beatles Rarities* released in the U.K.

Oct 15: John and Yoko contributed $1,000 to a fund to purchase bulletproof vests for New York City police officers.

Oct 24: Paul was honored by, and included in, the *Guinness Book of Records* as the most successful composer and recording artist of all time. He was awarded a rhodium-plated disc noting his enormous record sales, including 43 million-sellers, 60 gold records and more total record sales worldwide than any other artist. A party was held in Paul's honor on this date at the Les Ambassadeurs Club in London.

(rb) Oct 30–Oct 30, 1980: George recorded most of the songs for his LP *Somewhere in England*. The album was scheduled for release on Nov 2, 1980, but the finished album was rejected by Warner Brothers, which wanted four songs replaced. The original album, with the four discarded songs, has been bootlegged, and three of the rejected songs were eventually released officially ("Lay His Head" [recorded in Apr 1980], "Flying Hour" [recorded earlier in Mar 1978] and "Sat Singing" [recorded in Mar 1980]) with "Tears of the World" still unreleased.

Nov 1: Paul and Linda were interviewed by Geraldo Rivera on ABC-TV's "20/20."

Nov 16: Paul's single "Wonderful Christmastime"/"Rudolph the Red Nosed Reggae" released in the U.K. Released in the U.S. on Nov 20.

(b) Nov 23–26: Wings performed on four consecutive nights at Liverpool's Royal Court Theater. The Nov 23 show was a free warm-up concert, held for an invited audience of handicapped children, and students and employees of the Liverpool Institute, Paul's alma mater.

(b) Nov 23–Dec 17: Wings toured the U.K., performing "Got to Get You into My Life," "Getting Closer," "Every Night," "Again and Again and Again," "I've Had Enough," "No Words," "Cook of the House," "Old Siam, Sir," "Maybe I'm Amazed," "The Fool on the Hill," "Let It Be," "Hot as Sun," "Spin It On," "Twenty Flight Rock," "Go Now," "Arrow Through Me," "Wonderful Christmastime," "Coming Up," "Goodnight Tonight," "Yesterday," "Mull of Kintyre" and "Band on the Run." The tour included shows at Liverpool's Royal Court Theater (Nov 23–26); Apollo in Ardwick, Manchester (Nov 28, 29); Southampton's Gaumont (Dec 1); Brighton's New Conference Centre (Dec 2); Lewisham's Odeon (Dec 3); Rainbow Theater, Finsbury Park (Dec 5); Empire Pool, Wembley (Dec 7–10); Birmingham's Odeon (Dec 12); Newcastle City Hall (Dec 14); Edinburgh's Odeon (Dec 15); Glasgow's Apollo (Dec 16, 17).

Nov 28: Ringo's Hollywood Hills home was destroyed by fire and many of his most prized Beatles mementos were lost.

Nov–Dec: A syndicated 30-minute Wings TV special, "Back to the Egg," was aired in the U.S.

(b) Dec 5: Paul and Linda were interviewed by Tom Snyder on the U.S. TV show "Tomorrow" just prior to their performance at the Rainbow Theater, Finsbury Park.

(r) Dec 17: Wings was recorded singing "Coming Up" (live version) during their second night at the Apollo in Glasgow, ending Wings' tour of Britain.

Dec 20: Paul and Linda were again interviewed on the U.S. TV show "Tomorrow" by Tom Snyder.

(rb) Dec 29: Wings' final concert appearance took place at a special benefit performance at Hammersmith's Odeon on the final night of the Concerts for Kampuchea, which had begun on Dec 26. Some songs were released on LP *Concerts for the People of Kampuchea* in 1981. A TV film of the performance, *Rock for Kampuchea*, was also made and was aired in January 1981.

Dec 31: John and Yoko's Bag Productions Ltd. and Joko Films Ltd. were dissolved along with most of the couple's companies.

Late that year: Paul and Linda donated $10,000 to the New York Times Neediest Fund that annually raises money for the poor at Christmas.

That year: Ringo was seen in The Who documentary film *The Kids Are Alright*. He also recorded several radio spots promoting the film.

(b) Late that decade: John recorded several demos, including several unreleased titles.

■ Paul recorded songs and narration for a planned full-length *Rupert the Bear* animated film to be shot by Oscar Grillo. The film was never made, but test pressings of an album containing Paul's music and narration were made.

1980

Jan 16: Wings arrived in Tokyo, Japan for a scheduled tour of 11 concerts between Jan 21 and Feb 2. Upon their arrival, however, Paul was arrested for possession of marijuana and the tour was subsequently canceled. Other members of Wings were so angered at Paul's behavior that the incident appears to have ensured the group's demise, although they continued to work together throughout the year. Denny Laine was particularly upset; his recording of "Japanese Tears" is a critical account of the incident. Laine, however, would continue working with McCartney into 1981.

Jan 21: Wings, except for Paul, who remained in jail, and Linda, left for home.

Jan 25: After spending 10 days in a Tokyo jail, Paul was released and deported from Japan.

Feb 18: Ringo began shooting the film *Caveman* in Durango, Mexico. During filming he met actress Barbara Bach, whom he would later marry. Filming was completed in Mar.

Feb 20: Paul was interviewed in *Rolling Stone* magazine.

Feb 26: Paul attended the British Rock and Pop Awards at the Cafe Royale in London where he received an award as the Outstanding Music Personality of 1979.

Feb 27: Paul's "Rockestra Theme" was awarded a Grammy in the U.S.

Mar 24: The LP *The Beatles Rarities* was released by Capitol in the U.S. This was the first authorized release of Version I of "Love Me Do" (with Ringo on drums) in the U.S., coming nearly 17 years after its initial U.K. release.

(r) Mar: George recorded "Sat Singing," originally planned for *Somewhere in England*, but not released until 1988.

(r) Apr: George recorded "Lay His Head," also planned for *Somewhere in England* but not released until 1987.

Apr 11: Paul and Wings' single "Coming Up" (studio version)/"Coming Up" (live version)—"Lunch Box-Odd Sox" released in the U.K. Released in the U.S. on Apr 15.

(r) Early May: Paul was interviewed by Vic Garbarini for *Musician* magazine. A recording of the interview was later released as *The McCartney Interview*.

May 16: Paul's LP *McCartney II* was released in the U.K.

May 17: Paul's video for "Coming Up" had its U.S. premiere on "Saturday Night Live" in the U.S. It was introduced by Paul and Linda live via satellite from England.

May 19: Ringo and Barbara Bach escaped serious injury when they were involved in a car accident in South London.

May 20: An interview was recorded with Paul and aired on a special devoted to his career on BBC Radio One on May 26.

May 21: Paul's LP *McCartney II* was released in the U.S. and included a one-sided promo of "Coming Up" (live version). The bonus disc was not included with the U.K. release.

May 31: Paul's LP *McCartney II* reached number one in the U.K.

May: Oscar Grillo's five-minute animated film *Seaside Woman*, including Linda McCartney's song of the same title, won first prize in the short film category at the Cannes Film Festival.

Jun 13: Paul's single "Waterfalls"/"Check My Machine" released in the U.K. Released in the U.S. on Jul 22.

Jun 28: Wings' single "Coming Up" (live version) reached number one in the U.S.

(b) Jun–Jul: John spent several weeks in Bermuda with his son Sean, during which time he cut a number of demos of songs that would later be recorded during the *Double Fantasy/Milk and Honey* sessions.

(b) Middle of that year: Many demos were recorded by Lennon during this post-Bermuda period, most of them cut in preparation for the *Double Fantasy* sessions.

(rb) Jul 7–31: Ringo recorded songs for his LP *Stop and Smell the Roses*. The album was originally titled *Can't Fight Lightning*, and initially contained several unreleased songs, including "Can't Fight Lightning," "Brandy" and "Waking Up" and some different mixes of the released tracks.

Jul 10: General release of the five-minute animated film *Seaside Woman* began in the U.K.

Aug 1: George formally founded HandMade Films (Productions) Ltd.

(rb) Aug 4–Sep 8: John recorded tracks for the *Double Fantasy* album as well as those that appeared on the posthumously released *Milk and Honey* album, issued in 1984. John recorded a harmony vocal track for Yoko's song, "Every Man Has a Woman Who Loves Him," released in 1984 without Ono's vocal, thus appearing to be a Lennon solo, on the LP *Every Many Has a Woman*.

(b) Aug 6: Unreleased studio takes of John's "I'm Stepping Out" were recorded.

(b) Aug 7: Unreleased takes of John's "Borrowed Time" and "Gone from This Place" were recorded.

(r) Sep 8–28: A series of interviews with John was recorded by David Sheff for *Playboy* magazine; excerpts were released in 1983 on LP *Heart Play—Unfinished Dialogue*. Additional clips were aired in the U.S. on "The Lost Lennon Tapes." The interview appeared in the December issue of *Playboy*.

Sep 19: Paul's 12-inch single "Temporary Secretary"/"Secret Friend" released in the U.K.

Sep 29: An interview with John appeared in *Newsweek* magazine in the U.S.

(b) That fall: Paul laid down a set of demos, possibly in preparation for his *Tug of War* and *Pipes of Peace* sessions, although some of the songs did not appear on either album and five of them remain unreleased.

■ **(rb)** John recorded several demos of "Real Love," a song he had begun composing in the late 1970s, with take 6 released in 1988 on the *Imagine: John Lennon* compilation soundtrack album. The same recording was again released in 1990 on the *Lennon* 4-CD boxed set, but it appeared there under the title "Girls and Boys." John also recorded several unreleased songs, including demos of "Serve Yourself," a parody of Bob Dylan's "Gotta Serve Somebody," recorded several times throughout 1980 beginning in the spring with the final take recorded on Nov 14.

Oct 13: LP *The Beatles Ballads—20 Original Tracks* released in the U.K.

Oct 15: George founded HandMade Films (Distribution) Ltd. to serve his HandMade Production Company founded in Aug.

Oct 24: Single "(Just Like) Starting Over" (John)/"Kiss Kiss Kiss" (Yoko) released in the U.K. Released in the U.S. on Oct 27.

(r) Oct 31–Nov 3: Paul recorded "We All Stand Together" (vocal and humming versions), later used in the 1984 animated film *Rupert and the Frog Song* and released as a single on Nov 12, 1984 only in the U.K.

Oct: Wings' final recording session was devoted to previously recorded but still unreleased tracks, intended for Paul's *Cold Cuts* album, which he has tinkered with and reconfigured many times but never released.

(b) Early Nov: John recorded a demo of the unreleased song "Dear John," one of the last songs he composed, perhaps the very last. He goes into the lyrics of "September Song" on the demo, lyrics all the more poignant given the events that were soon to follow.

Nov 3: *The Beatles Box*, a set of eight LPs containing 126 Beatles recordings, several of them in rare mixes, was released in the U.K. through EMI's mail order division, World Records.

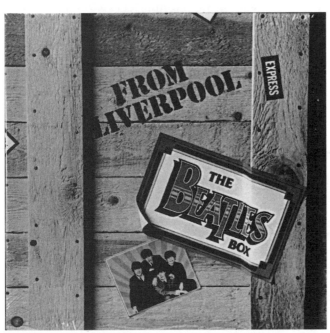

The Beatles Box (© EMI Records Ltd.). **This unique eight-LP collection featured 126 Beatles songs, several of them rare versions.**

(b) Nov 14: During one of his final home taping sessions, John recorded demos of "You Saved My Soul (with Your True Love)," "Pop Is the Name of the Game" and the final demo of "Serve Yourself."

Nov 17: John and Yoko's LP *Double Fantasy* released in the U.S. and U.K.

Nov 26: The film *Rockshow* premiered at the Ziegfield Theater in New York. The film was shot at Wings' Jun 10, 1976 Seattle concert. It premiered in the U.K. in Apr 1981 and was also issued on videocassette.

Nov 28: In a legal deposition, John stated that he and the other former Beatles did indeed plan to stage a reunion concert that would be filmed and included as the finale of a Beatles-made autobiographical documentary film, *The Long and Winding Road*, originally scheduled for a mid-1980s release. The deposition was taken for a lawsuit by Apple Corps Ltd. against the producers of the stage show *Beatlemania*. The suit was settled on Jun 4, 1986 with Apple being awarded $10.5 million. At that time the contents of John's deposition were revealed.

(r) Nov: An unidentified interview with John, videotaped at the Hit Factory after the release of *Double Fantasy*, was issued in Oct 1990 in the U.K. on *John Lennon—Interview 80*.

(r) Nov–Jan 16, 1981: George concluded recording of *Somewhere in England*, recording four new tracks to replace those rejected by Warner Brothers. One of them, "Blood from a Clone," is an attack on Warner Brothers for rejecting his first version of the album. While George had produced the earlier album sessions, Ray Cooper was brought in to co-produce with George during this period.

Dec 4: The LP *The McCartney Interview* was released in the U.S. The interview was recorded in May by Vic Garbarini for *Musician* magazine. Released in the U.K. on Feb 23, 1981.

Dec 5: An interview with John was taped by Jonathan Cott of *Rolling Stone* magazine; excerpts were aired on "The Lost Lennon Tapes" U.S. radio series.

(r) Dec 6: John Lennon was interviewed at length by Andy Peebles of the BBC. The interview formed the heart of a five-hour radio special and was later released on a CD.

(r) Dec 8: John and Yoko were interviewed during the morning in their Dakota apartment by Dave Sholin, Laurie Kaye, Ron Hummel and Bert Keane of RKO Radio in New York. John said that he was speaking to people of his generation on *Double Fantasy* who had shared with him the social and political events of the 1960s and 1970s. Only hours before his death, John seemed to be imparting a final message to his generation when he said, "Maybe in the '60s we were all naive . . . The thing the '60s did was show us the possibility, and the *responsibility* that we all had. It wasn't the answer, it just gave us a glimpse of the possibility. . . ." Following the interview, photographer Annie Liebovitz arrived at the Dakota for a photo session, producing many shots that would appear in the Jan 22, 1981 issue of *Rolling Stone* magazine, including a nude shot of John that appeared on the magazine's cover.

■ John Lennon was shot and killed by a "fan" in front of his home at New York's Dakota apartment building when he and Yoko returned from a recording session at approximately 10:50 P.M. They had been mixing Yoko's recording "Walking on Thin Ice" earlier that evening. John was rushed to St. Luke's Roosevelt Hospital where he was pronounced dead at 11:07 P.M. The murderer, Mark David Chapman, had apparently legally purchased a handgun near his home in Hawaii, traveled with it by air to New York and waited for more than a day outside John's home before killing him. Earlier in the day John was photographed autographing a copy of *Double Fantasy* for Chapman. John's body was cremated without ceremony on Dec 10.

(r) **Dec 9:** Paul and Denny Laine worked in the studio, recording at least part of "Rainclouds." Unable to verbalize his feelings regarding John's death he avoided a prolonged meeting with the press. Paul offhandedly remarked to reporters, "It's a drag, i'n it?" The comment was widely mistaken as a flippant one. Ringo visited Yoko and Sean at the Dakota, Paul telephoned there to convey his grief and George issued a press release in reaction to the shocking murder of John Lennon.

Dec 14: Crowds ranging in size from a few dozen to tens of thousands gathered in cities throughout the world to observe a day of mourning for John Lennon. At Yoko's request, 10 minutes of silence was observed at all of these locations at 2 P.M. EST. During the 10-minute period, many radio stations around the world ceased broadcasting. Two of the largest gatherings were in Liverpool and New York. In Liverpool, Sam Leach, one of The Beatles' first promoters, led 100,000 mourners in a seven-hour tribute to John Lennon outside Liverpool's St. George's Hall. The ceremony ended with the 10-minute silent vigil requested by Yoko.

Dec 27: John's single "(Just Like) Starting Over" and the LP *Double Fantasy* both reached number one in the U.S. They reached number one in the U.K. on Jan 3, 1981.

(rb) **Dec:** George recorded "Dream Away" for the film *Time Bandits*. The recording was later remixed for George's 1982 LP *Gone Troppo*.

(b) **That year:** George reportedly wrote the unreleased song "Sooty Goes to Hawaii."

(r) **Late that year–early 1981:** George recorded "All Those Years Ago," a tribute written for John Lennon, although the song may have originally had different lyrics. A drumming track by Ringo and backing vocals by Paul and Linda McCartney were overdubbed onto "All Those Years Ago," thus including all three surviving Beatles on the Lennon tribute. It was released as a single and on *Somewhere in England*.

1981

Jan 4: A TV film of highlights from the Kampuchea concerts of Dec 26–29, 1979, *Rock for Kampuchea*, was aired and included footage of Paul and Wings' performance of Dec 29.

Jan 10: John's single "Imagine" reached number one in the U.K. This was not a rerelease; rather the record reemerged on the charts after John's death. The original single, first released Oct 24, 1975 in the U.K., had never been deleted and had remained available. The single was originally released in the U.S. on Oct 11, 1971.

Jan 12: John's single "Woman"/"Beautiful Boys" (Yoko) released in the U.S. Released in the U.K. on Jan 16.

Feb 1: Paul arrived at George Martin's AIR Studios in Montserrat to begin work on a new album. In fact, two albums (*Tug of War* and *Pipes of Peace*) would emerge from these sessions.

(rb) **Feb 2–Mar 3:** Paul recorded songs for his albums *Tug of War* and *Pipes of Peace*.

(r) **Feb 16–18:** Paul recorded "Take It Away" (Ringo on drums).

Feb 20: LP *Hear The Beatles Tell All* released in the U.K.; originally released in the U.S. on Sep 14, 1964.

(rb) **Feb 21–25:** Paul recorded "Get It," with Carl Perkins sharing lead vocal on the number, released on LP *Tug of War*. Paul and Carl also composed the unreleased "My Old Friend" and recorded several unreleased tracks.

(r) **Feb 26–27:** Paul and Stevie Wonder recorded "What's That You're Doing?" which they co-wrote. On Feb 27 they recorded a duet of "Ebony and Ivory."

Mar 4: Paul and Linda flew back to England following the conclusion of recording sessions in Montserrat.

Mar 13: U.K. release of EP *Elton John Band Featuring John Lennon and the Muscle Shoals Horns*, with live recordings from the Nov 28, 1974 concert. A 12-inch single and Elton John album with these songs were released in several countries outside the U.K. and U.S.

■ John's single "Watching the Wheels"/"Yes I'm Your Angel" (Yoko) released in the U.S. Released in the U.K. on Mar 27.

Mar 30: LP *Concerts for the People of Kampuchea* was released in the U.S. and included songs recorded live on Dec 29, 1979 by Paul, Wings and Rockestra. Released in the U.K. on Apr 3.

Mar 31: Ringo and Barbara Bach were interviewed by Barbara Walters on "20/20" on ABC-TV in the U.S.

Apr 10: World premiere of Ringo's film *Caveman* in New York.

Apr 16: The LPs *Dawn of the Silver Beatles* and *Lightning Strikes Twice* were released in the U.S. via mail order. Combined, they contained the 15 songs recorded by The Beatles at their Decca Records audition on Jan 1, 1962. The releases were of questionable legality.

Apr 27: Ringo and Barbara Bach were married at Marylebone Register Office, London. Paul and George attended.

■ Paul officially announced that Wings was dissolved.

May 11: George's single "All Those Years Ago"/"Writing's on the Wall" released in the U.S. Released in the U.K. on May 15.

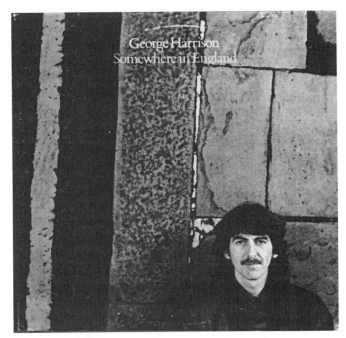

Somewhere in England (both versions) (© Dark Horse Records). The original version of George's album featured a different cover and four songs that were replaced on the released version.

Jun 1: George's LP *Somewhere in England* released in the U.S. Released in the U.K. on Jun 5.

Jun 10: "Back to the Egg," a series of promotional videos for the Wings album of that title, was aired on BBC 1, the first U.K. showing of the film.

Jun 12: Wings' single "Silly Love Songs"/"Cook of the House" released in the U.S.

(r) **Middle of that year:** Paul recorded more songs released on the *Tug of War* and *Pipes of Peace* albums. Paul also recorded "Say Say Say" (written and recorded with Michael Jackson) and "Ode to a Koala Bear."

Jul 6: John's single "(Just Like) Starting Over"/"Woman" released in the U.S.

Jul 23: Ringo's film *Caveman* premiered in London.

Jul 24: George's single "Teardrops"/"Save the World" released in the U.S. Released in the U.K. on Jul 31.

Jul: The film *Time Bandits* opened in London. It was produced by George's HandMade Films and included George's recording of "Dream Away," played over the closing credits, which was later remixed and released on *Gone Troppo*.

Aug 25: John Lennon's murderer, Mark David Chapman, received a 20 years-to-life sentence in U.S. court.

Oct 27: Ringo's LP *Stop and Smell the Roses* released in the U.S. Paul wrote and produced "Private Property" and "Attention" and contributed bass, piano, vocals and percussion to these cuts and to "Sure to Fall," which he also produced. George wrote and produced "Wrack My Brain" on which he played guitar and did backing vocals. He also produced "You Belong to Me" on which he played lead guitar. Released in the U.K. on Nov 20.

- Ringo's single "Wrack My Brain"/"Drumming Is My Madness" released in the U.S. Released in the U.K. on Nov 13.

Oct 28: A play about John Lennon, *Lennon*, opened at the Everyman Theater in Liverpool.

Nov 4: George's single "All Those Years Ago"/"Teardrops" released in the U.S. John's single "Watching the Wheels"/"Beautiful Boy (Darling Boy)" released in the U.S.

Nov: John's single "Happy Xmas"/"Beautiful Boy (Darling Boy)" released in the U.S.

(b) **Dec 12:** Ringo appeared on the "Parkinson" TV show in the U.K. He was joined by Tim Rice, Jimmy Tarbuck and Michael Parkinson in an impromptu version of "Singing the Blues."

That year: Paul and Yoko joined in a bid to purchase ATV Music, owners of the copyrights to the Northern Songs Lennon/McCartney song catalog. Their bid of £21 million was turned down.

1982

(r) **Early that year:** An interview with Pete Best was recorded.

Jan 11–15: *The Cooler*, a promotional film for three of the songs on Ringo's *Stop and Smell the Roses* album, was produced by Paul's MPL company. Paul, Ringo and their wives all appeared in the film, which premiered May 24 at the Cannes Film Festival.

Jan 13: Ringo's single "Private Property"/"Stop and Take the Time to Smell the Roses" released in the U.S.

(b) **Jan 30:** Paul appeared on BBC Radio Four's "Desert Island Discs" where he sang along with parts of The Coasters' recording of "Searchin'" and John's "Beautiful Boy (Darling Boy)."

Feb 24: John and Yoko were awarded a 1981 Grammy Award for Album of the Year for *Double Fantasy*.

(b) Mar 7: BBC Radio aired a special two-hour show, "The Beatles at the Beeb," reviewing and playing tapes of The Beatles' BBC Radio appearances in the early 1960s. The broadcast marked the 20th anniversary of the recording of The Beatles' first BBC Radio appearance.

Mar 22: LP *Reel Music* released in the U.S. Released in the U.K. on Mar 29.

■ Single "The Beatles Movie Medley"/"I'm Happy Just to Dance with You" released in the U.S. Released in the U.K. on May 24.

Mar 29: Paul's single "Ebony and Ivory" (with Stevie Wonder)/"Rainclouds" released in the U.K. Released in the U.S. on Apr 2. A U.K. 12-inch single (also released on Apr 16 in the U.S.) added Paul's solo version of "Ebony and Ivory."

(r) That spring: Paul recorded "The Girl Is Mine" with Michael Jackson. Written by Jackson, it was released as a single with Jackson's "Can't Get Outta the Rain" and on Jackson's *Thriller* album.

Apr 20: A section of New York's Central Park, partly funded by Yoko Ono, was officially dedicated as "Strawberry Fields" in John's memory.

Apr 26: Paul's LP *Tug of War* released in the U.S. and U.K. Ringo is featured on drums on "Take It Away."

May 1: The single "Ebony and Ivory" (Paul and Stevie Wonder) reached number one in the U.K.

(r) May 5–Aug 27: George recorded songs for his LP *Gone Troppo*. "Circles," written in 1968 and recorded in 1978, also appeared on this album.

May 15: The single "Ebony and Ivory" (Paul and Stevie Wonder) reached number one in the U.S. Paul's LP *Tug of War* reached number one in the U.K.

May 29: The radio special "The Beatles at the Beeb" was aired in the U.S. throughout the Memorial Day weekend.

■ Paul's LP *Tug of War* reached number one in the U.S.

Jun 21: Paul's single "Take It Away" (featuring Ringo on drums)/"I'll Give You a Ring" released in the U.K. Released in the U.S. on Jul 3.

(b) Jun 23: Paul filmed a promo for "Take It Away" before a live audience of his U.K. Fan Club at Elstree Film Studios. Paul's miniconcert also included several rock oldies. Ringo and George Martin were among those in his backing group.

(r) That summer: Ringo recorded songs for his album *Old Wave*. Although released in Germany on Jun 16, 1983, where a single was also released of "In My Car"/"As Far As We Can Go," and in Canada on Jun 24, 1983, the album was not released in the U.S. or the U.K. It was issued in several other countries as well. Four songs were released in the U.S. on Feb 24, 1989 on the CD *Starr Struck: Best of Ringo Starr Vol 2*.

Jul 5: Paul's 12-inch single "Take It Away"/"I'll Give You a Ring"-"Dress Me Up as a Robber" released in the U.K. Released in the U.S. on Jul 26.

Jul 15: Paul's "Take It Away" video premiered on "Top of the Pops" in the U.K.

Sep 17–19: The radio special "John Lennon: Rock and Roll Never Forgets" was syndicated in the U.S. by Westwood One.

Sep 20: Paul's single "Tug of War"/"Get It" released in the U.K. Released in the U.S. on Sep 26.

(b) Sep 28: Ringo recorded a television appearance for "Parkinson in Australia," aired Oct 8. He played drums and did some vocals on "Honey Don't" and a medley of "Honey Don't"/"Blue Suede Shoes," sung by Glenn Shorrock.

Sep: Mobile Fidelity Sound Labs released a 13-album boxed set of original stereo U.K. Beatles albums on half-speed mastered discs, plus a half-speed mastered version of the U.S. *Magical Mystery Tour* album.

■ Bettina Huebers, a 20-year-old German woman, filed a paternity suit claiming that Paul McCartney was her father.

(r) That fall: Paul recorded songs for the LP *Pipes of Peace*.

Oct 4: EMI issued 7-inch vinyl and picture disc singles with "Love Me Do" and "P.S. I Love You" as a 20th-anniversary commemorative. The singles, however, included the *album* version of "Love Me Do," not the original single version with Ringo on drums. On Nov 1, a 12-inch single was issued with both versions of "Love Me Do" and "P.S. I Love You." All original Beatles U.K. singles would be issued on the 20th anniversary of their release.

Oct 15: LP *The Beatles—20 Greatest Hits* released in the U.S. Released in the U.K. on Oct 18.

Oct 25: Single "The Girl Is Mine" (Paul and Michael Jackson)/"Can't Get Outta the Rain" (M. Jackson) released in the U.S. Released in the U.K. on Oct 29.

Oct 27: George's LP *Gone Troppo* released in the U.S. Released in the U.K. on Nov 8.

■ George's single "Wake Up My Love"/"Greece" released in the U.S. Released in the U.K. on Nov 8.

Oct: Release of the documentary film *The Compleat Beatles* on videocassette.

Nov 1: LP *The John Lennon Collection* released in the U.K. Released in the U.S. on Nov 8.

Nov 2: Yoko Ono's LP *It's Alright (I See Rainbows)* released in the U.S. John's shouts are heard on "Never Say Goodbye."

(rb) Nov 5–May 8 1983: Paul recorded songs during filming of *Give My Regards to Broad Street*, which began at Elstree Studios and would be released on the *Give My Regards to Broad Street* soundtrack. The documentary film *The Making of Give My Regards to Broad Street* was also shot during the filming and aired Oct 14, 1984 in the U.K. on "The South Bank Show."

Nov 11: John's single "Happy Xmas (War Is Over)"/"Beautiful Boy (Darling Boy)" rereleased in the U.S.

Nov 15: John's single "Love"/"Gimme Me Some Truth" released in the U.K.

Nov 29: Michael Jackson's LP *Thriller* released in the U.S. featuring his duet with Paul, "The Girl Is Mine." Released in the U.K. on Dec 3.

Dec 3: BBC Channel 4's "The Tube" show aired film of The Beatles shot by Dezo Hoffmann on Jul 27, 1963 while the group was in Weston-super-Mare.

Dec 25: LP *The John Lennon Collection* reached number one in the U.K.

Dec 27: BBC repeated the radio special "The Beatles at the Beeb" with some songs from the original broadcast replaced by others not included in the earlier version of the show.

(b) **Late that year:** Paul discussed John's death and their partnership during a taped interview.

1983

Jan 2: Ringo's TV special "Ringo" was aired in the U.K. The show was first seen in the U.S. on Apr 26, 1978.

Jan 25: Yoko Ono's single "Never Say Goodbye" (featuring John's shouts)/"Loneliness" released in the U.S. only.

Feb 7: George's single "I Really Love You"/"Circles" released in the U.S.

Feb: Paul received an award as the Best British Male Artist from the British Record Industry.

Mar: Under a Freedom of Information Act request, Jon Wiener of the University of California, Irvine, obtained heavily censored FBI files relating to the agency's actions against John Lennon in 1972. Wiener also received 26 pounds of immigration data dealing with John's fight to remain in the U.S. Wiener sued the FBI to obtain the information deleted from the files, and he used the information he obtained in his book *Come Together*, published in 1984. In 1991 a court ruling ordered the FBI to turn over the deleted files to Wiener.

(b) **That spring:** Paul recorded the unreleased "Theme From *Twice in a Lifetime*," heard at the close of the film.

Apr 6: Paul won some of the first American Video Awards (AVA), including one for the best soul video for "Ebony and Ivory" with Stevie Wonder, a video produced for Paul by KEEFCO. A second award was given to Paul as the first inductee into the Video Hall of Fame.

■ A German court ordered Paul to pay the equivalent of $282 per month to Bettina Huebers, the 20-year-old German woman who had filed a paternity suit in Sep 1982 claiming that she was Paul's illegitimate daughter. Paul offered to submit to blood tests or to any other tests dictated by the court to disprove the woman's claim. Although he insisted he was not Ms. Huebers' father, the court ordered that he make the payments until the case was settled. Ms. Huebers later posed nude for a German magazine claiming she needed the money because Paul had not made any payments to her. Blood tests later proved that Paul was not the woman's father.

May 8: Filming at Elstree Studios for *Give My Regards to Broad Street* was completed, with final shooting concluded on Jul 26. Paul had written the script and starred in the film with Linda, Ringo and Barbara Bach (Mrs. Starr). Twentieth Century-Fox released the film Oct 25, 1984 in the U.S. and Nov 28, 1984 in the U.K.

May 29: The radio special "The Beatles at the Beeb" was rebroadcast in U.S. syndication and included some songs that had not been heard on the original broadcasts.

May: The McCartney/Stevie Wonder hit "Ebony and Ivory" received the "International Hit of the Year" award at the annual Ivor Novello Awards ceremony at the Grosvenor Hotel, London. McCartney also received an award for his LP *Tug of War* at the German Phono-Academy Awards.

Middle of that year: Paul again signed with CBS Records for two more albums including *Pipes of Peace*, the sequel to *Tug of War*.

Jun 4: Ringo began a 26-week radio series in the U.S. on the ABC Radio Network called "Ringo's Yellow Submarine," acting as D.J. One show featured Ringo playing the original 1964 Beatles open-end interview promo while providing the questions himself. The final broadcast on Nov 26 was a live call-in show with listeners asking Ringo questions directly.

Jun 16: Ringo's *Old Wave* album was released in Germany. A single was released the same day—"In My Car"/"As Far As We Can Go." The LP was also released in Canada on Jun 24 and several other countries but not in the U.S. or U.K.

(b) **Jun 17:** Paul was interviewed on BBC Radio One and also sang the Radio One jingle.

Jul 11: EMI's Abbey Road Studio announced the "finding" of the following "previously undiscovered" Beatles recordings: "How Do You Do It," "That Means a Lot," "If You've Got Trouble" and "Leave My Kitten Alone."

(b) **Jul 18:** EMI opened Abbey Road's Number 2 studio to the public for a special program, "The Beatles at Abbey Road," presented three times per day for a limited period extending to Sep 11. The tour included a two-hour multimedia presentation of The Beatles' career and the playing of many unreleased tracks.

Jul 25: Paul, George and Ringo were seen enjoying a drink together in the bar of the Gore Hotel in Queen's Gate, Kensington, London.

Jul 26: Filming of *Give My Regards to Broad Street* was concluded.

Aug 22: Several Public Broadcasting Stations in the U.S. aired the film *The Beatles at Shea Stadium*.

That summer: Johnny Carson's Carson Productions announced plans for a three-hour TV film about John Lennon's years with Yoko Ono, tentatively titled *Imagine: The Story of John and Yoko*, but eventually released in Dec 1985 as *John and Yoko: A Love Story*.

Sep: The film *Bullshot* opened in London. It had been made by George's HandMade Films Company.

Sep 12: George made a brief appearance on the BBC TV show "Film '83" and discussed his new HandMade movie *Bullshot*.

Sep 13–14: A play about The Beatles called *John, Paul, George, Ringo* was staged at London's Young Vic Theater.

That fall: Paul was interviewed on Radio GOSH, a British hospital radio station at the Great Ormond Street Hospital for Sick Children. He also recorded a one-hour special for the British Hospital Radio Association.

Oct 3: Paul's single "Say Say Say" (with Michael Jackson)/"Ode to a Koala Bear" released in the U.S. and the U.K. along with the 12-inch single "Say Say Say" (extended remix with Michael Jackson)/"Say Say Say" (instrumental)—"Ode to a Koala Bear."

Oct 4–6: Paul's video for "Say Say Say" was shot in California.

Oct 14: Paul taped an interview aired the following day on BBC Radio One's "Saturday Live Show."

Oct 17: Paul's LP *Pipes of Peace* released in the U.K. Ringo is featured on drums. Released in the U.S. on Oct 26.

Oct 28: Paul and Michael Jackson's "Say Say Say" video was shown for the first time on U.K. TV on Channel Four's "The Tube" show.

Oct 29: Paul and Linda appeared on BBC-TV's "Late Late Breakfast Show" and screened the "Say Say Say" video.

Oct: U.K. videocassette release of *The Concert for Bangla Desh* film.

Nov 7: Ringo was interviewed briefly on U.S. TV's "Entertainment Tonight."

■ Ringo and his wife, Barbara Bach, appeared in part two of the U.S. made-for-TV trash film, *Princess Daisy*.

Nov 11: Ringo was seen during a special TV show on T. Rex's Marc Bolan, aired on BBC's Channel Four in the U.K.

Nov 21: EMI Music Video and Dave Clark International released the video compilation *Ready, Steady, Go—Volume One*, which included The Beatles' Mar 20, 1964 appearance.

Dec 1: Paul was interviewed on the U.S. TV show "Entertainment Tonight."

■ A meeting took place in London's Dorchester Hotel among Yoko, Paul, Ringo and George, reportedly in order to conclude the affairs of Apple.

Dec 3: Paul was interviewed for one hour on BBC Radio One by Simon Bates. He said that he had burned his copy of former Beatles' aide Peter Brown's tell-all Book *The Love You Make*.

Dec 5: LP *Heart Play—Unfinished Dialogue* (excerpts from September 1980 *Playboy* interview with John) released in the U.S. Released in the U.K. on Dec 16.

■ The single "Say Say Say" (Paul and Michael Jackson) reached number one in the U.S. Paul's single "So Bad"/"Pipes of Peace" released in the U.S. and, with the A and B sides reversed, in the U.K.

Dec 13: Paul appeared on ITV's "Razzamatazz" children's show in the U.K.

Dec 14: Paul appeared on Russell Harty's "Harty" talk show with George Martin from Martin's AIR Studio.

Dec 16: Paul appeared on Channel 4's "The Tube" U.K. TV show.

Dec 18–24: London Wavelength's "BBC Rock Hour" aired a one-hour interview with Paul.

Dec 24: The first half of a taped interview with Paul was show on NBC-TV's "Friday Night Videos" in the U.S. Videos of "Say Say Say" and "Pipes of Peace" were also shown. The second half of the interview was aired on Jan 27, 1984.

Dec 26: A one-hour special, "The Beatles at Christmas," was aired on BBC Radio Two.

Dec: Ringo signed to narrate 26 five-minute U.K. TV episodes of an animated children's show called "Thomas the Tank Engine and Friends" for Central Television.

Late that year: A poor-audio-quality CD release of *Abbey Road* was issued in Japan by EMI-Toshiba several years before official EMI Beatles CDs were released and was technically the first Beatles album released on CD; it was deleted in 1985.

1984

Early that year: Paul made a brief cameo appearance in Tracy Ullman's video for "They Don't' Know About Us."

■ It was announced that Paul and The Rolling Stones' Bill Wyman would narrate a 12-part TV series on the history of rock music on U.K. TV.

Jan 1: Granada TV's 45-minute documentary film *The Early Beatles: 1962–1965* premiered on U.K. TV.

Jan 5: John's single "Nobody Told Me"/"O'Sanity" (Yoko) released in the U.S. Released in the U.K. on Jan 9.

Jan 15: While vacationing in Barbados, Paul and Linda's villa was raided by local police who found 10 grams of marijuana on Paul and 7 grams on Linda. The McCartney's were charged with drug possession. The following day they pleaded guilty and were fined $200 each.

Jan 17: No sooner had the McCartneys arrived at London's Heathrow Airport when still more marijuana was discovered in Linda's baggage, and she was again charged with possession.

Jan 19: John and Yoko's LP *Milk and Honey* released in the U.S. Released in the U.K. on Jan 23.

Jan 24: Linda McCartney was fined a small sum for marijuana possession.

Jan 27: The second half of a taped interview with Paul was shown on NBC-TV's "Friday Night Videos" in the U.S. Paul's "So Bad" video was also shown and featured Paul, Linda and Ringo and guitarist Eric Stewart.

■ An article written by Paul appeared in the London magazine *Time Out*. Paul recommended legislation legalizing marijuana.

Jan: Paul's single "Pipes of Peace" reached number one in the U.K.

Feb 3: French television TF-1 aired the film of John's One to One Concert of Aug 30, 1972.

Feb 4: George's appearance of Nov 20, 1976 on "Saturday Night Live" was aired in the U.K. by London Weekend Television.

Feb 10: "Friday Night Videos" included an appearance by Paul and an "I Want to Hold Your Hand" video.

Feb 21: Paul's "Pipes of Peace" video received the award for Best Video of 1983 during the British Rock and Pop Awards live broadcast on BBC TV. Paul did not attend the ceremony but left a prerecorded video message that was screened during the ceremony.

Feb 29: U.S. CD release of Paul's *Tug of War*.

Feb: The Mar 1984 issue of *Playboy* magazine featured an extensive report on the theft of many of John's belongings from his Dakota apartment only days after his death, including his diary and tapes of unreleased songs. Former Lennon employee Fred Seaman and his accomplice, Bob Rosen, were charged with the theft and were later apprehended. Most of the stolen items were recovered. According to the story, Seaman had kept 10 notebooks in which he detailed his intent to use information contained in the stolen items in a book, ostensibly of his own personal recollections. Seaman and Rosen also supposedly planned to plant false stories in the news media casting aspersions on Yoko Ono's sanity, character and sexual habits, and they even allegedly purchased illegal drugs claiming that they were for Ono. Following a falling out between the two, Rosen testified against Seaman, who was ultimately convicted and sentenced to 5 years probation. Seaman's book deal with Simon and Schuster fell through when the publisher learned of the deception, and then sued Seaman for $47,500 in advances already paid to him plus $1 million in punitive damages. Birch Lane Press issued Seaman's book, *The Last Days of John Lennon*, in Sep 1991, with most of the "damaging" material omitted.

■ *(b)* A planned single that would have included Paul and Michael Jackson's "The Man" backed with the unreleased "Blackpool" was canceled. The record was to have been issued in both 7-inch and 12-inch formats (Parlophone R and 12R 6066). Whether or not "Blackpool" is the same song found on the unreleased McCartney film The Backyard is not known, nor is the recording date of this version. The 12-inch release would also have contained an unreleased instrumental version of "The Man."

Mar 9: John's single "Borrowed Time"/"Your Hands" (Yoko) released in the U.K. Released in the U.S. on May 11.

Mar 15: John's single "I'm Stepping Out"/"Sleepless Night" (Yoko) released in the U.S.

Mar 16: NBC-TV's "Friday Night Videos" aired its first telecast of John's "I'm Stepping Out" video. MTV aired the video on the same night, including a bit of nudity cut by NBC.

■ The video for John's "Borrowed Time" had its world premiere on BBC 2's "Old Grey Whistle Test."

Mar 21: A teardrop-shaped memorial garden within New York's Central Park, designated "Strawberry Fields" in John's memory, was officially dedicated.

Apr 2: A New York State Supreme Court jury ruled that Yoko Ono must pay record producer Jack Douglas $2,524,809 plus three years' interest for work he did on the LP *Double Fantasy* and that she would also have to pay Douglas a percentage of the earnings from the LP *Milk and Honey* for his work on that album.

Apr 3: Liverpool's first Beatles' statue was unveiled above the doorway of The Beatles Shop on Mathew Street. The statue was done by David Hughes, a former student at the Liverpool College of Art, John Lennon's alma mater.

Apr 12: Lawyers for Mark David Chapman, John Lennon's murderer, told a New York appeals court that Chapman was mentally incompetent when he pleaded guilty in 1981 and that his sentence should be vacated. The appeal was denied.

Apr 26: John Doubleday's statue of The Beatles was dedicated by Paul's brother, Mike McCartney, on Mathew Street near the location of the old Cavern Club in Liverpool. The statue was to be the centerpiece of a $12.6 million shopping complex.

■ Paul was seen in a cameo appearance in Bob Marley's "One Love" video on BBC's "Top of the Pops" show.

Apr: Several U.S. TV stations ran the "On and Off Camera" series' 30-minute episode "Paul McCartney: The Man, His Music, and His Movies."

May 2: Queen Elizabeth II officially opened the Beatle Maze at the Liverpool International Garden Festival. The queen also stepped aboard a life-size yellow submarine docked nearby.

May 18: A sneak preview of Paul's film *Give My Regards to Broad Street* was held in Atlanta, Georgia at the Phipps Plaza Cinema.

May: The videocassette *Ready Steady Go! Volume 2* was released containing footage of The Beatles' Oct 4, 1963 appearance.

Jun 3: World premiere of the 30-minute video compilation "Milk and Honey" on MTV, featuring the first U.S. showings of videos for "Borrowed Time" and "Grow Old with Me" and the previously seen "Nobody Told Me" and "I'm Stepping Out" videos.

(b) **Jun 9:** Paul and Tracy Ullman were guests on the U.K. TV show "Aspel and Company." They did a duet of "That'll Be the Day."

Jun 17: Stuart Colman conducted an interview with Paul on BBC Radio London's "Echoes" show.

Jun: U.S. videocassette release of *The Concert for Bangla Desh* film.

(b) **That summer:** Paul recorded a demo of "On the Wings of a Nightingale," which he had written for the Everly Brothers.

(r) **Jul 4:** Ringo performed at two U.S. Fourth of July concerts. In the afternoon he appeared with The Beach Boys on The Mall in Washington, D.C., drumming on

"Back in the USSR." He also performed with The Beach Boys at an evening concert in Miami, Florida.

Jul 5: The film of the concerts for Kampuchea, *Rock for Kampuchea*, was shown by Home Theater Network in the U.S.

Jul 6: U.S. release of *A Hard Day's Night* on videocassette and video laser disc.

Jul 15: John's single "I'm Stepping Out"/"Sleepless Night" (Yoko) released in the U.K.

Sep 8: MTV in the U.S. aired the documentary film *The Music Lives On*, produced by Paul's MPL Communications. The 14-minute film included Paul's Sep 14, 1979 performance of "It's So Easy" and "Bo Diddley." It aired on the same date in the U.K. on Channel Four at 1:30 A.M., unannounced, and was repeated later that morning on London Weekend Television.

Sep 13: LP *Every Man Has a Woman*, containing John's harmony vocal recorded for Yoko's original version of "Every Man Has a Woman Who Loves Him," released in the U.S. John's track is presented here as his solo version of the song. Released in the U.K. on Sep 21.

Sep 16–17: The U.S. made-for-television film *Princess Daisy* was aired in the U.K. on ITV. The film featured Ringo and Barbara Bach.

Sep 24: Paul's single "No More Lonely Nights" (ballad)/"No More Lonely Nights" (playout version 3:56) released in the U.K. A 12-inch edition featured "No More Lonely Nights" (extended playout version 8:10)/"No More Lonely Nights (ballad)-"Silly Love Songs." They were issued in the U.S. on Oct 5 and Oct 2 respectively.

That fall: The marathon radio special "Sgt. Pepper's Lonely Hearts Club Band: A History of the Beatle Years 1962–1970" was aired in the U.S. and the U.K., and

"No More Lonely Nights" (© MPL Communications Ltd.). The new B side for the second edition of this single was noted on the revised U.K. picture sleeve. The sleeve remained unchanged in the U.S.

featured many rare Beatles recordings, including a 1962 Cavern rehearsal, the Jun 6, 1962 EMI recording of "Besame Mucho," cuts from the Oct 24, 1963 concert aired on Swedish radio's "Pop '63" show, Lennon's "Bad to Me" demo, "Shout!" and the medley from "Around the Beatles" (Apr 19, 1964).

Early Oct: A secret agreement was reached by which Northern Songs, owned by Associated Communications Corporation's ATV, paid John Lennon's estate and Paul McCartney approximately £2 million and increased the ex-Beatles' royalty rates. No further details were available due to a "no-publicity" agreement among the parties involved. It was reported, however, that ATV Music, owner of the Lennon/McCartney song catalog copyrights, had been put up for sale by Associated Communications. Northern was sold to Michael Jackson for $47.5 million in Aug 1985. Paul, Ringo, George and Yoko also sued EMI over audit and royalty matters, especially in the U.S.

Oct 2: Paul's video for "No More Lonely Nights" had its world premiere on MTV in the U.S.

Oct 5: Paul's single "No More Lonely Nights" (ballad)/"No More Lonely Nights" (playout version 3:56) released in the U.S. The B side was later changed to the Arthur Baker "Special Dance Mix" but, while the labels were reworded, the U.S. picture sleeve remained unchanged. No official announcement of the change in this single was ever made.

■ John's single "Every Man Has a Woman Who Loves Him"/"It's Alright" (Sean Ono Lennon) released in the U.S. Released in the U.K. on Nov 16.

Oct 9: Ringo appeared on TV-AM's "Good Morning Britain" in the U.K. He was interviewed, took part in the show's cooking segment and promoted the new animated TV series "Thomas the Tank Engine and Friends," which he narrated. The 13-week series premiered on U.K. TV the same day and featured 26 five-minute segments.

Oct 14: London Weekend Television's "The South Bank Show" aired a one-hour program devoted to Paul and the film *Give My Regards to Broad Street*. The show marked the first public airing of Paul's new versions of "Eleanor Rigby," "For No One" and "Yesterday." The show was aired in the U.S. as "The Making of *Give My Regards to Broad Street*."

Oct 15: Paul arrived in New York and began a busy schedule of promotional activities for *Give My Regards to Broad Street*, including several taped interviews and appearances on U.S. TV shows. Paul was honored at an ASCAP luncheon held at New York's Jockey Club.

Oct 18: Paul's "No More Lonely Nights" video was shown on the U.K. TV show "Top of the Pops."

Oct 22: Paul's soundtrack LP *Give My Regards to Broad Street* released in the U.S. and U.K.

Oct 23: Paul appeared on the "Tonight Show" on U.S. TV. Toward the end of the show he did a mock-drunken version of a few lines from "Yesterday" and also sang "You Are My Sunshine."

Oct 24: Paul appeared on the U.S. radio call-in show "Rockline."

Oct 25: Paul's film *Give My Regards to Broad Street* had its world premiere at the Gotham Theater in New York and began running nationally the following day with the animated short *Rupert and the Frog Song*, produced by MPL. U.S. reviews of the film were almost universally negative, many of them brutally so. *Washington Post* critic Paul Attanasio closed his review by saying "You don't have to play this movie backwards to believe that Paul is dead."

■ "Friday Night Videos" taped separate interviews with Paul and Julian Lennon at New York's Carlyle Hotel. The two met briefly during the taping, their first meeting in 10 years. The interviews were aired on Nov 16.

Oct 25–31: Paul appeared on five consecutive "Good Morning America" weekday shows on U.S. TV.

Oct 29: Remixed 7-inch and 12-inch versions of the "No More Lonely Nights" singles were released in the U.K., replacing the original Sep releases. Several unique mixes of "No More Lonely Nights," including the "Mole Mix," were also released as promos.

Oct: The film of The Beatles' first 1966 Tokyo concert was released by The Beatles Collector's Shop, a Japanese video company, on home videocassette under the title *The Beatles Live in Japan*.

■ Paul's soundtrack LP *Give My Regards to Broad Street* reached number one in the U.K.

Nov 2: Paul was seen on the U.S. TV show "Entertainment Tonight."

■ Paul and Linda appeared on the U.S. TV show "A.M. Chicago." Paul sang a verse of his earliest composition, "I Lost My Little Girl."

Nov 5: Videocassette *Ready Steady Go! Volume 3* was released containing The Beatles' performance of Nov 27, 1964.

Nov 12: Paul's single "We All Stand Together"/"We All Stand Together" (humming version) released in the U.K. only. The tune is from the MPL animated short *Rupert and the Frog Song*. Paul was heard on Radio Radio's "Top 30 U.S.A." and on "Rock Notes."

Nov 16: Paul appeared on U.S. TV's "New York Hot Tracks."

Nov 19: Paul was featured on the U.S. TV show "P.M. Magazine."

(r) Nov 25: Paul joined with many other British rock stars in donating time to record the special Christmas single "Do They Know It's Christmas?"/"Feed the World." All proceeds went to benefit starving African drought victims. Two brief spoken messages by Paul are heard on the B side. The charity single eventually became the largest-selling record in U.K. history, breaking the record held by Paul's "Mull of Kintyre," released on Nov 11, 1977.

Nov 26: Paul was interviewed on BBC Radio One by Russel Harty.

Nov 26–28: A three-part interview with Paul by Simon Bates was aired on BBC Radio One.

Nov 27: Paul was featured on "Entertainment Tonight" on U.S. TV.

Nov 28: The U.K. premiere of *Give My Regards to Broad Street* took place at the Odeon Cinema in Liverpool, where *A Hard Day's Night* had premiered in 1964. Paul accepted the Freedom of the City Council award, presented to all of The Beatles by the Liverpool City Council. George joined Derek Taylor in New Zealand to aid in promoting Taylor's limited edition book, *Fifty Years Adrift*.

Nov 29: Paul's film *Give My Regards to Broad Street* had its London premiere at the Empire Theatre in Leicester Square. George's HandMade Films' production *A Private Function* premiered during the same week. Paul was heard on BBC Radio Two's "Star Sound Extra."

Nov: Paul and Linda were interviewed by Joan Goodman for the Dec issue of *Playboy* magazine. Paul said he resisted discussing John's death, since he still considered it a shock and felt that he could never really put his feelings about it into words. Paul revealed that he had been severely depressed for some time following The Beatles' demise but that he felt John did not miss the group.

Dec 3: BBC 2 TV aired the documentary film *Horizon* which detailed the struggle by 43-year-old Ivan Vaughan, the original Quarry Man who introduced John Lennon and Paul McCartney, against Parkinson's disease. Paul offered the filmmakers free use of the song "Blackbird" for the film.

Dec 3–16: An interview with Paul on Westwood One Radio's "Star Trak Profiles" was syndicated in the U.S. during these dates.

Dec 6: The 25-minute TV special, "Paul McCartney: The Man, His Music, His Movies," was aired in parts of the U.K. by ITV.

Dec 7: The special Christmas single, "Do They Know It's Christmas?"/"Feed the World," including messages from Paul on the B side, was released in the U.S. and U.K. A 12-inch edition was issued on Dec 14. Channel Four's "The Tube" show in the U.K. included a 15-minute interview with Paul by hostess Paula Yates.

Dec 8: 10-minute tribute to John, "Remembering John," was aired on MTV. Paul was briefly seen on "Solid Gold" on U.S. TV. He gave a tongue-in-cheek introduction to the song "Disco Duck." A 30-minute interview with Paul was seen on TV-AM's "Good Morning Britain."

■ **(b)** Ringo appeared on "Saturday Night Live" on NBC-TV in the U.S. He read an opening monologue, appeared in a few comic sketches and did some songs.

Dec 13: The high court in London resolved the 1979 lawsuit involving unpaid royalties by EMI to Apple Corps Ltd. Apple had claimed that The Beatles were owed $2.5 million in royalties unpaid from 1966 to 1979. A complete audit was ordered. In a separate U.S. suit Apple asked $42.5 million from Capitol Records, including $20 million in back royalties. This suit also dated from 1979. This date's action merely added each ex-Beatle and Yoko by name as plaintiffs with Apple and asked that The Beatles be released from any remaining legal ties to Capitol. Capitol, in turn, filed a $1.5 million countersuit claiming that The Beatles had failed to deliver two albums required by their contract. Capitol also stated that John's LP *Some Time in New York City* did not count as one of the required albums.

(b) Dec 14: George Harrison appeared as a surprise guest with Deep Purple on stage in Sydney, Australia. He was introduced as "Arnold Grove from Liverpool" (12 Arnold Grove was the Harrisons' address at the time of George's birth). Paul appeared on Rick Dee's "Weekly Top 40" radio show in the U.S.

Dec 16: Paul was interviewed on MTV in the U.S.

(rb) Late that year: George recorded "I Don't Want to Do It," written by Bob Dylan, released on the *Porky's Revenge* film soundtrack album. A slightly different mix was released as a single in the U.S. only. George also recorded a new vocal with slightly different lyrics for "Save the World," released on the charity LP *Greenpeace* in 1985.

■ Paul recorded "We Got Married" during sessions co-produced by Paul and David Foster. It was released on *Flowers in the Dirt* in 1989. Two other songs recorded with Foster remain unreleased, including "Lindiana." Despite reports that Foster and McCartney produced four songs, Foster said in an early 1990 interview on Canada's "Much Music" that he had recorded only three titles with McCartney. He called "We Got Married" the weakest of the group.

1985

Jan 6: An interview with Paul was aired on MTV's "The Tube" in the U.S.

Jan 9: BBC-TV aired the Wings animated film *Seaside Woman*.

Jan 18: World premiere in London of the film *Water* produced by George's HandMade Films. The film featured cameo appearances by George, Ringo and Eric Clapton during the performance of "Freedom" by Billy Connolly, Christopher Tumming and The Singing Rebels Band. This clip was also used as a promotional video. Two other songs in the film, "Celebration" and "Focus of Attention," were co-written by George and performed in the film by Jimmy Helms with George on guitar. "Freedom" and "Celebration" were released as a single in the U.K.

Jan 19: Paul was featured on "Night Flight" on USA TV in the U.S. and several of his videos were shown.

Jan 22: Ringo's son Zak was married to Sarah Menikides at a private ceremony at the registry office in Bracknell, Berkshire. Parents of the couple were not informed and did not attend the ceremony. Ringo and his wife, Barbara, hosted a small wedding reception for the couple on Jan 24.

Jan 26: George played slide guitar and did backing vocals on the recording "Children of the Sky." It was not released until Nov 7, 1986, and then only in the U.K., as

a single and on Mike Batt's concept LP *The Hunting of the Snark*.

Jan: The National Coalition on Television Violence commended John (posthumously) and Paul for their "pro-social" music videos.

Feb 1: George was interviewed on BBC-TV's "Newsnight" show and noted that he had some fears for his safety following John's murder.

Feb 4: A 21-track special videocassette was released in the U.K. as a benefit fund-raiser for the Ethiopian Appeal Fund. It included Paul's rare video for the disco version of "No More Lonely Nights."

Feb 22: The Metromedia TV special "Visions of Yesterday and Today" featured segments on The Beatles and included a black-and-white film clip of "Give Peace a Chance" filmed at John and Yoko's Jun 1969 bed-in.

Feb 25: It was reported that George, Ringo and Yoko had filed an $8.6 million suit against Paul for breach of contract, related to the fact that Paul was earning more royalties from Beatles records than the others.

Feb: The first licenses were issued for Beatles songs to be used in TV ads, surely a new low in Beatles' cover versions. "Help!" the first victim, was to be used by Lincoln-Mercury in the U.S. for a fee of $100,000 for six months; Hewlett-Packard shelled out £45,000 to use "We Can Work It Out" for spots in the U.K.; Schweppes paid $11,000 to use "She Loves You" on Spanish television. Cover artists were used instead of the original Beatles recordings since licenses would thus be much cheaper. The Beatles' recording of "Revolution" was later used in a Nike commercial.

Mar 1: New York premiere of *A Private Function*, produced by George's HandMade Films.

Mar 11: Ringo appeared in a nonmusical cameo during filming of a charity video, *Willie and the Poor Boys—The Video*, released by PolyGram Music Video on May 25.

Mar 13: Paul received an Ivor Novello Award for "We All Stand Together" as Best Film Theme of 1984.

Mar 14: U.S. release of soundtrack LP *Porky's Revenge* with George's "I Don't Want to Do It." Released in the U.K. on Jul 1.

Mar: In one of the more serious Beatles false alarms, EMI announced that a new Beatles album containing previously unreleased tracks would be released. The album, unimaginatively titled *Sessions*, was killed almost as soon as the rumor began, although bootleg copies quickly appeared. A single of "Leave My Kitten Alone" was also planned with an alternate take of "Ob-La-Di, Ob-La-Da" as the B side in the U.S. and an alternate take of "Hello Goodbye" as the U.K. B side; neither was released.

(rb) Mar–May: Paul recorded his *Press to Play* album, produced by Hugh Padgham. Sessions resumed in Oct and concluded in Dec. A tape of Paul doing several songs from *Press to Play* includes the unreleased song "Yvonne."

Apr 29: Release of the videocassette *The Beatles Live: Ready, Steady Go Special Edition* containing approxi-

Sessions (both bootlegs). Two bootleg versions of the *Sessions* album planned for release by EMI in 1985 but ultimately scrapped.

mately 20 minutes of The Beatles' musical performance during the May 6, 1964 "Around The Beatles" TV special. A Beatles comedy sketch from the show was omitted.

(rb) Early May: In the U.S., Ringo portrayed the Mock Turtle and recorded "Nonsense" (written by Steve Allen) during filming of the TV musical *Alice in Wonderland*, aired Dec 9 and 10 on CBS TV. Clips of Ringo's dialogue, but not the song, later appeared on the soundtrack LP *Alice in Wonderland*.

May 6: *People* magazine carried a story copyrighted by the *Liverpool Daily Post and Echo* in which John's half sister, Julia Dykins Baird, related details regarding John's family which included two other half sisters: Julia and Jacqueline Gertrude Dykins were fathered by John Albert Dykins, common-law husband of John's mother. A third half sister, Victoria Elizabeth Lennon, of an unknown father, was given up for adoption shortly after her birth.

(r) Middle of May: Paul recorded a 17-second message of sympathy for the victims of a May 11 football stadium fire in Bradford City. The message was included on the B side of Gerry Marsden's charity single, "You'll Never Walk Alone"/"Messages" (credited to "The Crowd"), released on May 24 in the U.K. only. A 12-inch edition was issued on Jun 7.

May: A single with a different mix of George's recording "I Don't Want to Do It," from the film *Porky's Revenge* was released in the U.S.

Jun 4: U.K. release of special LP *Greenpeace* containing George's new recording of "Save the World." Released in the U.S. on Aug 19.

Jun 18: John's single "Nobody Told Me" received a BMI award.

Jun 25: Mark Lindsay was notified that he was being dropped from the role of John Lennon in the NBC-TV film *John and Yoko: A Love Story* less than a week after he had been hired for the part. The NBC decision to fire Lindsay came after it was learned that the actor's real name—Mark Chapman—was the same as that of John Lennon's killer. The decision to fire Lindsay was reportedly made by Yoko Ono after she had learned the actor's real name. Lindsay was replaced by Mark McGann.

Jul 13: Paul was one of many top rock stars to perform at London's Wembley Stadium before 90,000 people as part of the Live Aid concert. The all-day event was organized by Bob Geldof, of the group Boomtown Rats, who had also organized the "Do They Know It's Christmas?"/"Feed the World" charity single late in 1984. Like that single, the concert was aimed at raising funds for starving people in Africa. Another concert in Philadelphia was held simultaneously, and the entire event was televised live worldwide throughout the day and also broadcast on radio. This was the most elaborate and largest all-star rock show ever staged, and it attracted the largest worldwide television audience in history (over 1.5 billion people). Paul's appearance came at the close of the Wembley concert when he sang "Let It Be" while seated at a piano, but his microphone failed to function during the first half of his number.

(b) Jul 14: The day after he appeared at the Live Aid concert singing "Let It Be," Paul recorded a studio version of the song as an overdub for the live performance if it ever was released (it never was).

Aug 10: Michael Jackson purchased ATV Music (and thus Northern Songs) for $47.5 million, thereby acquiring ownership of the Lennon/McCartney song catalog. The sale became final on Sep 6. All Lennon/McCartney songs except "Love Me Do," "P.S. I Love You" (owned by McCartney's MPL), "Please Please Me," "Don't Bother Me" and "Ask Me Why" (owned by Dick James) were included along with approximately 4,000 other song titles.

(b) Sep 12: The 1958 Quarry Men recording of "That'll Be the Day" was aired in part on MPL/BBC-TV special *Buddy Holly* on BBC 2, with the latter part obscured by Paul's voiceover narration. The program aired in the U.S. as *The Real Buddy Holly Story*.

Sep 20: Twenty-eight posthumous song title copyrights were registered in John Lennon's name and their "date of creation" listed as 1980. Two of the copyrights were made in error, since Lennon had nothing to do with either "Lullaby for a Lazy Day," actually recorded as "Lullaby" by Grapefruit, or "Have You Heard the Word." The latter title, written by Steve Kipner and Steve Groves, appears on a number of bootlegs where it is mistakenly listed as an unreleased song by the Bee Gees and Lennon. Most of the other titles exist as demos and were aired on "The Lost Lennon Tapes" radio series; most of them have also appeared on bootlegs. The titles are: "Girls and Boys" (officially released under this title and also as "Real Love," another working title), "Dear John," "When a Boy Meets a Girl," "Across the River," "Whatever Happened to . . .?" "She Is a Friend of Dorothy's," "Help Me to Help Myself," "Boat Song," "I Don't Want to Lose You," "Not for Love Nor Money," "Gone from This Place," "Hold On, I'm Coming," "Sally and Billy," "Dream Time," "Pill," "Free as a Bird," "He Got the Blues," "The Happy Rishikesh Song," "Man Is Half of Woman (Woman Is Half of Man)," "You Saved My Soul (with Your True Love)," "Memories," "Don't Be Afraid," "One of the Boys," "Life Begins at Forty," "Serve Yourself" and "A Case of the Blues." The 1980 creation date is obviously in error since Lennon worked on several of these titles well before that year, including "Pill," "A Case of the Blues," "Memories," "Sally and Billy" and others.

(r) Sep: Paul recorded "Spies Like Us" for the film of the same name.

(r) Oct 1–Dec 6: Paul resumed recording sessions for his *Press to Play* album.

Oct 9: The section of New York's Central Park dedicated to John Lennon and called Strawberry Fields was completed and officially opened to the public on the 45th anniversary of John's birth.

■ Paul filmed the video for "Spies Like Us" with Dan Aykroyd and Chevy Chase; it aired Nov 16 in the U.K. on "The Noel Edmonds Late Late Breakfast Show," on which Paul appeared live, and in the U.S. on MTV on Nov 17.

(b) Oct 21: George and Ringo appeared with Carl Perkins, Eric Clapton, Roseanne Cash, Dave Edmunds and former members of Stray Cats before an audience of 250 at Limehouse Studios, London, during taping of the Perkins TV special "Blue Suede Shoes: A Rockabilly Session with Carl Perkins and Friends" aired Jan 1, 1986 in the U.K. on BBC Channel 4 and on Jan 5, 1986 in the U.S. on Cinemax.

Oct: Paul re-signed with Capitol Records in the U.S. after having been with Columbia Records since 1979.

■ Ringo rerecorded the narration for eight of the 26 "Thomas the Tank Engine" TV shows for commercial release on audio cassettes in the U.K. only as part of Pickwick Records' Tell-a-Tale series, in association with Ladybird Books. Each cassette contained two stories and came with a book.

Nov 11: The film *Imagine* was released on videocassette in the U.K. and in the U.S. the following year.

■ Two more audio cassettes, with specially recorded "Thomas the Tank Engine" stories read by Ringo, were released in the U.K.

Nov 14: Release of MPL's *Rupert and the Frog Song* on videocassette, also containing the animated films *Seaside Woman* and *Oriental Nightfish*.

Nov 18: U.S. and U.K. release of Paul's single "Spies Like Us"/"My Carnival" in 7-inch and 12-inch formats.

■ U.K. release of John's single "Jealous Guy"/"Going Down on Love"; the 12-inch release also included "Oh Yoko!" A four-minute video promo taken from the film *Imagine* was also released.

Nov 18–Dec 20: Ringo recorded narration for 26 additional "Thomas the Tank Engine" episodes to be aired in the fall of 1986. He also recorded the narration for a "Thomas" Christmas show to be aired in Dec 1986.

Dec 2: World premiere of the made-for-TV film *John and Yoko: A Love Story* on NBC-TV in the U.S.

Dec 5: Compilation videocassette *Greenpeace: Non-Toxic Video Hits* featuring George's "Save the World," released in the U.K. Released in the U.S. on Apr 16, 1986. George does not appear in it.

Dec 6: Paul recorded an interview with Alan Grimadell of the National Association of Hospital Broadcasting Organizations. The interview was titled "Paul McCartney: The Man" and was intended for U.K. broadcast to hospital patients.

Dec 7: Paul appeared on BBC 1's "Saturday Superstore" where he took part in an audience phone-in segment and screened promos for "Spies Like Us" and "We All Stand Together." He was also interviewed by David Frost on "TV-am."

Dec 8: On the fifth anniversary of John Lennon's death, Paul was interviewed on ITV's "Good Morning Britain" in the U.K. He called John "the best collaborator I have ever worked with."

Dec 9: Part I of the TV musical film *Alice in Wonderland*, featuring Ringo as the Mock Turtle, premiered on CBS-TV in the U.S. Ringo appeared only in part I and sang "Nonsense."

Dec 11: Ringo appeared live on Thames' TV's "This Is Your Life" show honoring show business photographer Terry O'Neill.

Dec 18: A videotaped message by Paul was seen in the U.K. on the "This Is Your Life" TV show honoring Gerry Marsden.

Dec 22: A lengthy interview with Paul by Janice Long was aired by Radio One in the U.K.

Dec 25: A taped message from Paul was seen on "TV-am" in the U.K.

Dec 26: RTE TV in Ireland aired a filmed interview with The Beatles conducted on Nov 7, 1963 by Frank Hall at Dublin Airport.

Dec 30: "The Music of Lennon and McCartney" was rebroadcast in the U.K. on Channel 4. The 50-minute special was part of the 30th anniversary celebration of Granada Television. It had originally been aired on Dec 17, 1965.

Dec: Paul withdrew from the legal battle between Apple and Capitol/EMI over unpaid Beatles royalties. His action may have been related to his new recording contract with Capitol. George, Ringo and Yoko continued the legal action, however, and increased their demand to $30 million in compensatory damages and $50 million in punitive damages and sought custody of all Beatles master tapes.

(b) That year: George reportedly co-wrote the unreleased song "Shelter in Your Love" with Alvin Lee.

1986

Jan 19: An intruder reportedly lowered himself from the roof of the Dakota building and entered Yoko Ono's apartment through an open window. He left several notes, a photograph and a letter to Yoko, who was asleep at the time. The intruder was later arrested by New York City police.

Jan 23: John's sons, Julian and Sean Lennon, presented the award commemorating Elvis Presley's induction at the first Rock and Roll Hall of Fame induction ceremony, held at the Waldorf-Astoria Hotel in New York. The two read a letter John had written praising Elvis.

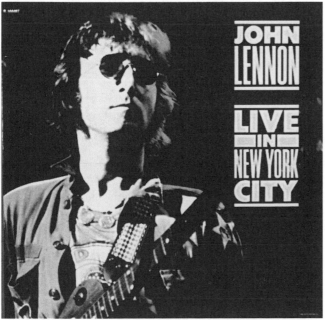

John Lennon Live in New York City (© Capitol Records Inc.). Posthumous release of Lennon's 1972 Madison Square Garden show, also issued on video.

Jan 24: U.S. release of LP and videocassette *John Lennon: Live in New York City* released in the U.K. the following month, from John's Aug 30, 1972 One to One Concert. George's HandMade films production *A Private Function* was issued on videocassette.

Jan 26: George received an award on behalf of his HandMade Films for the company's contribution to the British film industry at the London Standard Film Awards ceremony.

Jan 27: Paul received a special Award of Merit at the 13th annual American Music Awards in Los Angeles. Paul accepted the award from Phil Collins at the London nightclub The Hippodrome, where he was viewing the ceremony.

Jan 31: Ringo was featured on CBS Radio's "Top 30 U.S.A."

Early Feb: World premiere of the film *John Lennon: Live in New York City* took place at the Library of Performing Arts at New York's Lincoln Center.

Feb 1: Dick James, original and longtime publisher of The Beatles' songs, died of a heart attack at his home in St. John's Wood, London. He was 67.

Feb 4: "Come Together," from the film *John Lennon: Live in New York City*, premiered in the U.S. as a video on MTV.

Feb 8–9: Paul was featured on UK TV's "Rick Dee's Weekly Top 40."

Feb 14: U.K. release of 60-minute videocassette *British Rock: The First Wave*. The documentary included footage from the color Pathé film shot live in Manchester in Nov 1963, The Beatles' Swedish TV appearance of Oct 1963, two songs from *New Musical Express* Poll Winner's Concerts ("Can't Buy Me Love" from 1964 and "She's a Woman" from 1965), an interview with Brian Epstein, one song from the Feb 1964 Washington, D.C. concert, part of John's Aug 11, 1966 "Apology," the Apple Boutique opening party and the premiere of the film *Yellow Submarine*.

Feb 24: U.K. release of *John Lennon: Live in New York City*.

(r) Feb: Paul recorded "Simple as That" for the U.K. charity album *The Anti-Heroin Project: It's a Live-in World*.

Mar 6: George appeared at a press conference with Madonna in London to smooth relations between the press and Madonna and her husband, Sean Penn. The "poison Penns" were filming *Shanghai Surprise*, produced by George's HandMade Films, and their alleged poor behavior toward the press and unprofessional conduct on the set had alarmed George.

Mar 7: George was interviewed by Paul Yates on Channel 4's "The Tube" show in the U.K., postponed from Feb 14.

Mar 14: The world TV premiere of *John Lennon: Live in New York City*, filmed at the Aug 30, 1972 One to One Concert, took place on the Showtime U.S. cable TV station. Showtime also aired the *Let It Be* film, clips from the 1969 Montreal bed-in and three tracks from the *Imagine* film. The entire evening was billed as "The Lennon Legacy: Two Generations of Music." The *Live in New York City* portion was simulcast nationally in the U.S. via Westwood One Radio.

(b) Mar 15: George joined in the all-star finale at the Heartbeat '86 marathon charity rock concert at the National Exhibition Centre in Birmingham. He shared lead vocal on "Money" and "Johnny B. Goode" with Denny Laine and Robert Plant. The concert was held to raise money for the Birmingham Children's Hospital. It was filmed by BBC-TV and aired Aug 2 on BBC 1.

■ The film of the Kampuchea concert of Dec 1979, *Rock for Kampuchea*, was aired on U.S.A. cable TV in the U.S.

Mar 26: EMI paid £2,832,264 in back royalties as the result of an earlier London High Court ruling. The court now ruled that The Beatles, through Apple, should be entitled to review overseas accounts, which could result in an additional £2 million.

Mar 29: The first legitimate release of Beatles records in the Soviet Union took place, although black-market Beatles records had been circulating there for years. A deal between Soviet recording company Melodiya and EMI resulted in the release of 300,000 copies of albums titled *A Hard Day's Night* and *A Taste of Honey* (a compilation LP), each selling for 3.5 rubles (about £6).

That spring: Ringo recorded a new narration for Harry Nilsson's animated film *The Point*, released in May 1986 on home videocassette.

Apr 4: Paul was seen performing an unidentified original tune on the 100th edition of U.K. Channel Four's "The Tube" show, repeated Apr 8.

Apr 14, 16–18: George appeared on the U.S. TV show "Today" on each of these dates. He had been scheduled to appear on all five shows during this week, but the Apr 15 show was given over to full-time coverage of a crisis news story.

Apr 22: George and Ringo appeared briefly on BBC-TV show "Film Night" and discussed HandMade Film's *Mona Lisa*.

Apr 28: U.K. release of the compact disc *John Lennon: Live in New York City*.

Apr: Paul recorded a spoken message to be used later in the year on a U.S. TV special commemorating Peggy Lee's 40 years in show business.

May 1: New York premiere of play *Liverpool Fantasy* at Charas New Assembly Theater, hypothesizing what might have become of each of The Beatles had they never found success as a band.

May 15: A picture of John was featured on a 70-laree postage stamp by the Maldive Islands.

May 19: MTV broadcast a 10-part, twice-weekly series "In My Life: The John Lennon File" in the U.S.

May 22: U.S. release of the one-hour *Imagine* film on home videocassette.

May 26: Paul was one of the first six inductees into the *Guinness Book of Records* Hall of Fame, enshrined during a televised ceremony. Guinness listed Paul as the most successful musician of all time. Paul was also seen on BBC 1's "Video Jukebox" show.

May 28: ASCAP presented an award to Paul for "No More Lonely Nights" as the most performed song of the year beginning Oct 1, 1984. Hal David accepted the award for Paul at a Los Angeles ceremony.

May: An exhibit of John's lithographs and sketches called "This Is My Story Both Humble and True" opened in San Francisco and Beverly Hills. It was later moved to the Dyansen Gallery in New York.

Jun 4: Los Angeles Superior Court Judge Paul Breckenridge ordered producers of the *Beatlemania* stage show and film to pay $10.5 million to Apple Corps Ltd., ruling that *Beatlemania*'s primary purpose was to commercially exploit The Beatles' popularity. *Beatlemania* was a stage show in which four Beatles look-alikes performed the group's songs against a backdrop of 1960s film clips and slides.

Jun 13: The film *Mona Lisa*, produced by George's HandMade Films, premiered in New York.

Jun 17: Four members of Elephant's Memory joined in a $104 million contract fraud lawsuit previously filed by their fellow member, Adam Ippolito, against Yoko Ono and the John Lennon estate. The suit claimed that Yoko had improperly made financial profits from the record album and cable TV and videocassette release of the One to One Concert film. Elephant's Memory had served as John's backup band at the concert and claimed to have worked at the charity event for free. The band also charged that during the concert, Yoko had pretended to play keyboards that were actually being played by Ippolito. Yoko asked the court to dismiss the suit; her spokesman called it a "nuisance case" filed by "10th rate" backup musicians. He also termed "scandalous" the band's charge that Yoko faked her keyboard playing.

Jun 19: George attended a Trafalgar Square rally protesting the deployment of nuclear weapons.

(r) Jun 20: Paul performed at the Prince's Trust Birthday Party concert at Wembley Arena, singing "Long Tall Sally," "I Saw Her Standing There" and "Get Back." A film of the concert was seen in the U.K. on BBC 2 on Jun 28 and again on Dec 31, and it was heard on BBC Radio One on Jul 6. The film was also released on videocassette in the U.S. and U.K.

Jun 23: Brief clips of the Jun 20 Prince's Trust concert were seen on "Entertainment Tonight" on U.S. TV along with an interview with Paul by Selina Scott.

Jun 25: The 1968 film *Music!* was aired by Channel 4 in the U.K., including the clip of The Beatles rehearsing "Hey Jude." It was shown with excellent color and sound quality, unlike most previous broadcasts.

Jun 27: Paul was interviewed by Noel Edmonds on U.K. TV.

Early Jul: The video for Paul's single "Press" was filmed mostly in the Bond Street tube station, directed by Phillip Downey; world premiere on Jul 5 on BBC's Channel 4; U.S. premiere on Jul 20 on MTV.

(b) Jul 12: The premiere of the MPL film *Blankit's First Show* took place on BBC 2 and was repeated Nov 6. An unscheduled repeat broadcast occurred on May 10, 1989 on BBC 2. The 25-minute film is about an Appaloosa horse owned by Linda McCartney and features Paul's unreleased "All You Horseriders."

■ ITV broadcast of "I Feel Fine," one of a series of Granada TV shows, including an appearance by Ringo.

Jul 14: U.S. and U.K. release of Paul's single "Press"/"It's Not True."

Jul 16: Selina Scott recorded an interview with Paul at MPL's London offices. It was televised the following day on BBC 1's "Breakfast Time" show.

Jul 18: A lengthy interview with Paul was filmed at Abbey Road studios and aired as "McCartney" on BBC 1 TV on Aug 29. It was repeated Dec 20 on BBC 2.

■ Ringo appeared on the U.S. syndicated radio show "Ticket to Ride" with Scott Muni.

(rb) Jul: Paul recorded an alternate vocal for "Press" while being filmed for a BBC-TV special, released in 1989 on home videocassette as *The Paul McCartney Special*.

■ George recorded "Zig Zag," an instrumental from the *Shanghai Surprise* film soundtrack. He also recorded several other songs for the film that remain unreleased.

Aug 1: Paul appeared live on BBC 1's "Wogan" TV show.

Aug 18–22: Paul taped a number of interviews for *Press to Play* in the U.S.

Aug 22: U.S. release of Paul's *Press to Play* album, issued in the U.K. on Sep 1. The CD contained additional songs; two variations of the album appeared in the U.K., each featuring a different mix of "Press."

Aug 25–28: An interview with Paul taped the previous week was shown in installments over four days on the "Today" show on NBC-TV in the U.S.

(b) Aug 25–29: Paul recorded some unreleased songs in New York with members of Billy Joel's band, with Phil Ramone producing.

Aug 26: U.K. release of videocasette *The Real Buddy Holly Story*, including a partial playing of the 1958 Quarry Men recording of "That'll Be the Day." Released in the U.S. Sep 21, 1987. The video was an extended version of the MPL/BBC co-production originally aired in Sep 1985 on BBC 2's "Arena" show. This 90-minute version added 30 minutes of new footage and was sold with two audio cassettes containing 28 Buddy Holly recordings.

Aug 29: World premiere, in New York, of HandMade Films' *Shanghai Surprise* with songs by George and score by George and Michael Kamen, and a cameo appearance by George.

(r) Aug: Ringo, John Cleese and Bill Oddie recorded the comic track "Naughty Atom Bomb," released only in the U.K. on Nov 24 on the charity album *The Anti-Heroin Project: It's a Live-in World*. Ringo also recorded the spoken-work track "You Know It Makes Sense," released only in the U.K. on a 12-inch single and on *The Anti-Heroin* album.

Sep 5: Premiere of HandMade Films' *Mona Lisa*.

Sep 20: *Rupert and the Frog Song* was aired on the Disney Channel in the U.S.

Sep 24: *The Real Buddy Holly Story* was aired on Cinemax in the U.S. In the U.K. ITV began a second

series of 26 "Thomas the Tank Engine and Friends" episodes, all narrated by Ringo.

(rb) Sep: Paul was interviewed by Chris Salewicz for *Q* magazine; the recording was later released on disc.

■ Paul composed a song for his wife's birthday titled simply "Linda" and recorded two versions of it. Only one copy of a special single was pressed with one version of the song on each side.

(r) Oct 6: Ringo held a press conference in Atlanta, Georgia as a promotion for The Brasserie, a restaurant located there in which he owned a part interest.

■ John's book *Skywriting by Word of Mouth* appeared in bookstores; the official publication date was Oct 9.

Oct 7: A documentary on the making of *Shanghai Surprise* was aired on BBC Channel 4. The film included interviews with George and footage of him recording the musical score.

Oct 10: U.S. release of *Double Fantasy* CD.

Oct 16: Paul received the 1985 Best Selling Video award for *Rupert and the Frog Song* during the British Video Awards ceremony in London.

Oct 27: U.S. release of John's posthumous LP *Menlove Ave.*, which featured alternate takes from *Walls and Bridges* and other previously unreleased songs. Released in the U.K. on Nov 3.

■ Paul's single "Pretty Little Head"/"Write Away" released in the U.K.

■ Ringo's "You Know It Makes Sense" released on a 12-inch single only in the U.K.

Oct 29: Paul's single "Stranglehold"/"Angry" released in the U.S.

Nov 17–19: Paul filmed a promotional video for "Only Love Remains" at Pinewood Studios in Buckingham.

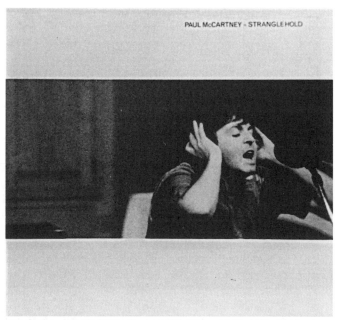

"Stranglehold" (© MPL Communications, Ltd.). U.S. McCartney single from *Press to Play*. The same picture sleeve was used for the U.K. "Pretty Little Head" single.

(b) Nov 24: Paul performed "Only Love Remains" at the Royal Variety Show, held at London's Theatre Royal. Paul's number was televised in the U.K. on Nov 29 by BBC 1.

- U.K. release of *The Anti-Heroin Project: It's a Live-in World*, an anti-drug album including tracks by Paul and Ringo.

Dec 1: U.S. release of *Wings Greatest* CD. U.K. release of Paul's single "Only Love Remains"/"Tough On a Tightrope," released in the U.S. on Jan 17, 1987.

Dec 11: Paul recorded an appearance on BBC Channel 4's "The Tube," aired Dec 12.

(b) Dec: Ringo filmed and recorded several television and radio commercials for Sun Country Wine Coolers, and appeared in magazine ads for the product as well.

1987

Early that year: U.K. CD release of John's *Some Time in New York City*. It was quickly withdrawn due to poor sound quality, and reissued on Aug 10.

(rb) Jan 5–Mar 31: George recorded songs for his *Cloud Nine* album. The unreleased "Vatican P2 Blues" was also recorded.

Jan 28: U.S. video laser disc and videocassette release of *Help!*; videocassette released in the U.K. on Mar 26, 1990.

(b) Feb: Ringo recorded songs for a planned album at Chips Moman's 3 Alarm Studio in Memphis, Tennessee, with Moman serving as producer. A second set of sessions were held in late Apr. The album was not released, however. In mid-1989 Ringo sued Moman to halt a planned release of the album. Ringo claimed Moman was attempting to capitalize on Ringo's All Starr concert tour, then underway. Ringo also charged that the album was done under the influence of alcohol, which he had by then given up after undergoing treatment for alcoholism. In his testimony of Nov 15, 1989, Ringo noted that he objected mostly to the timing of the release of the album (Aug 1989), and claimed that he wanted more time to overdub his own drum tracks. Ringo hadn't played the drums during the sessions and had required help from Moman's wife, Toni, to complete his vocals.

Feb 2: Paul held recording sessions at Audio International in London.

Feb 4: Duane Eddy recorded a cover version of Paul's "Rockestra Theme" for his *Duane Eddy* album at Paul's Sussex studio. Paul produced the track and provided bass and backing vocals. Eddy also recorded "The Trembler" and "Theme for Something Really Important" for that album at George's home studio shortly thereafter, with George playing slide guitar on both tracks. The album was released on Jun 19.

(b) Feb 19: George, Bob Dylan, John Fogerty and Jesse Ed Davis joined singer Taj Mahal on stage during his performance at the Palomino Club in North Hollywood. The performance was videotaped on the house video system.

Feb 26: Worldwide release of the first four Beatles compact discs, *Please Please Me*, *With The Beatles*, *A Hard Day's Night* and *Beatles for Sale*. All four were mono, which caused a considerable furor among Beatles fans and audiophiles. Seemingly endless audio analysis of the CDs appeared on the pros and cons of the mono releases and the quality of the digital transfers. A frequently heard accusation held that these four were hurriedly and poorly prepared for release in order to meet the EMI timetable that would have the *Sgt. Pepper* CD released on Jun 1, the observed 20th anniversary of the album's original release. EMI claimed to have prepared stereo CD releases of these albums, but said that when George Martin was called in to review them, he found their sound quality to be so bad that he remixed all four in mono in time for the scheduled release date.

Mar 4: Paul and Linda filmed a cameo spot in the film *Eat the Rich* on location in Moor Park Hertfordshire.

Apr 8: A portion of The Beatles' $80 million suit was dismissed. The ruling was, however, reversed on May 17, 1988.

Apr 13: U.K. CD release of John's *Menlove Ave.*

Apr 24: U.K. release of *Prince's Trust Tenth Anniversary Birthday Party* album including a free bonus McCartney single not included with the U.S. album, released on May 11.

Apr 27: U.K. CD release of Paul's *McCartney* and *Ram* albums.

Apr 30: Worldwide CD release of original stereo British versions of *Help!*, *Revolver* and *Rubber Soul*.

(b) Late Apr: Ringo held additional recording sessions with Chips Moman in Memphis. Bob Dylan participated in at least one recording on Apr 29.

May 18: U.K. CD release of George's *All Things Must Pass* and *Best of George Harrison*.

May 26: U.S. and U.K. CD release of John's *Shaved Fish*. U.K. CD release of Ringo's *Blast from Your Past*, John's *Rock 'N' Roll* and *Imagine*, and Paul's *Wings over America*.

May: U.S. release of black-and-white videocassette *Fun with The Fab Four* containing a variety of newsreel footage but no music.

Jun 1: Worldwide CD release of *Sgt. Pepper's Lonely Hearts Club Band* on the day when it could almost be said that "It was twenty years ago today" (the album had actually been rush released on May 26, 1967 in the U.K.). Granada TV aired its two-hour documentary *It Was Twenty Years Ago Today*, chronicling the 1960s, including a good deal of Beatles footage and new filmed interviews with George and Paul. The film was aired by PBS in the U.S. on Nov 11.

(rb) Jun 2–30: Paul recorded "Once upon a Long Ago" and "Loveliest Thing" during sessions produced by Phil Ramone. Both were released only in the U.K. Paul's sessions with Ramone yielded a complete album that remains unreleased.

■ *(r)* Paul recorded "Back on My Feet," co-written with Elvis Costello and released only in the U.K. Paul also recorded "P.S. Love Me Do," a new arrangement of The Beatles' "Love Me Do," and "P.S. I Love You." The track was officially released in Mar 1990 only on a special double CD release of *Flowers in the Dirt* issued in Japan.

(r) **Jun 5–6:** George and Ringo performed on both of these dates at the Prince's Trust Rock Gala concerts. Their numbers were released on *The Prince's Trust Concert 1987* album only in the U.K. During the first night's concert, George and Ringo joined Ben E. King on stage for "Stand by Me." Highlights from both shows were edited into a TV special aired in the U.K. on Jun 20; a radio special was aired on Jan 1, 1988 on BBC Radio One. A videocassette of the performance was issued on Jun 14, 1988.

(b) **Jun–Jul:** Paul recorded a special version of "Sgt. Pepper's Lonely Hearts Club Band" in honor of U.K. disc jockey Alan Freeman's 60th birthday. The song was aired on Jul 6, by Capitol Radio in London.

(r) **Jul 1:** Paul recorded overdubs for three songs, including "Once upon a Long Ago," with George Martin at Abbey Road Studios.

Jul 20: U.K. CD release of John's *Walls and Bridges*.

(r) **Jul 20–21:** Paul recorded several rock-and-roll oldies during two days of studio jamming. Most of them were released in 1988 in the Soviet Union on the album *CHOBA B CCCP (Back in the USSR,* or *Again in the USSR).* Some appeared as bonus tracks on various singles prior to the entire album being issued on CD, with one additional track, as *CHOBA B CCCP (The Russian Album)* on Sep 30, 1991 in the U.K. and Oct 29, 1991 in the U.S.

(r) **Late Jul:** Paul recorded "I Wanna Cry," released only in the U.K.

Aug 3: U.K. CD release of John's *Mind Games*.

Aug 10: U.K. CD rerelease of John's *Some Time in New York City*.

Aug 14: U.K. release of *The Prince's Trust Concert 1987*, containing George and Ringo's live recordings from the Jun 5–6 Prince's Trust concerts.

Aug 24: Worldwide CD release of *The Beatles* (aka "The White Album") and *Yellow Submarine*.

Aug 28: *Yellow Submarine* was released on videocassette in the U.K. The "Hey Bulldog" number, originally released on U.K. copies of the film, was omitted. Released in the U.S. on Oct 20.

Aug 31: Ringo appeared in the spoof documentary *Bruce Willis—The Return of Bruno* on BBC 2.

(b) **Aug:** Paul completed mixing and editing another version of his unreleased *Cold Cuts* album with producer Chris Thomas and engineer Bill Price.

(b) **Sep 9:** An impromptu jam at London's Dolphin Brasserie took place during Buddy Holly Week. Paul performed with Mick Green (once of Johnny Kidd and the Pirates), Alvin Stardust, and U.K. DJ Tony Prince.

Sep 21: Worldwide CD release of *Magical Mystery Tour*.

Sep 26: Ringo took part in a jam session that included Jerry Lee Lewis and several other musicians during the grand opening of The London Brasserie.

(rb) **That summer–fall:** Paul recorded "My Brave Face," co-written with Elvis Costello. The two also recorded several unreleased songs. Paul recorded three more songs written with Costello for *Flowers in the Dirt*.

(r) **That fall:** Ringo recorded "When You Wish upon a Star" with Herb Alpert, released in 1988 on the album *Stay Awake*.

Oct 5: U.K. CD release of Paul's *Red Rose Speedway*, *McCartney II* and *Wild Life* albums.

Oct 12: U.K. release of George's single "Got My Mind Set on You"/"Lay His Head." Released in the U.S. on Oct 16. A 12-inch edition, released only in the U.K., featured an extended mix of the A side.

(b) **Oct 17:** George made an impromptu appearance with Bob Dylan on stage at Dylan's Wembley Arena concert.

Oct 19: Worldwide CD release of *Abbey Road* and *Let It Be*.

Oct 21: George, Ringo and Paul spent the evening dining together and relaxing at an empty London house owned by Paul.

Oct 23: The film *Eat the Rich*, featuring a cameo by the McCartneys, premiered in London.

Nov 2: U.S. and U.K. release of George's *Cloud Nine* album.

■ U.K. release of Paul's *All the Best*, a greatest hits collection. Released in the U.S. on Dec 5. The respective U.S. and U.K. releases featured different song lineups.

Nov 6: *The Paul McCartney Special* was released on videocassette in the U.S. Released in the U.K. on Nov 27.

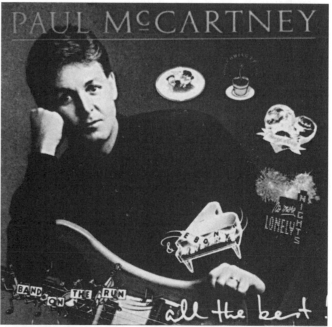

All the Best (© MPL Communications Ltd.). Different versions appeared in the U.S. and U.K. Only the U.K. edition featured the new song "Once upon a Long Ago."

Nov 16: U.K. videocassette release of the first 26 episodes of *Thomas the Tank Engine and Friends*, narrated by Ringo. Several book/audio cassette packs were also released featuring Ringo's reading of "Thomas" stories.

■ U.K. 7-inch, 12-inch and CD releases of Paul's single "Once upon a Long Ago"/"Back on My Feet." Two different 12-inch singles were issued. There was no U.S. release.

(b) **Nov 17:** Paul taped a performance of "Once upon a Long Ago" before an audience of children, aired Nov 24 on the Tyne Tees "The Roxy" U.K. television show.

(b) **Nov 19:** Paul and Linda taped an appearance as the only guests on the "Wogan" U.K. TV show, aired the following day.

(b) **Nov 27:** Paul appeared live on "The Last Resort with Jonathan Ross" on BBC Channel 4.

Nov 30: Release of three-volume videocassette *Queen: Magic Years*; Paul appears in volume 1, *The Foundations*; Ringo appears in volume 2, *Live Killers in the Making*.

Late Nov: Paul mimed to the released recording of "Once upon a Long Ago" for a satellite transmission to Japan.

Dec 1: U.S. CD release of Paul's *Band on the Run*.

Dec 2: Paul taped a performance of "Once upon a Long Ago," aired on BBC 1 the following day on "Top of the Pops." He and Linda also taped a sketch for the BBC 1 fund-raising Comic Relief special aired on Feb 5, 1988.

Dec 6: Paul and his band appeared on a Paris charity TV show.

Dec 7: Release of Paul's "Once upon a Video" worldwide, except North America.

Dec 12: Paul made a surprise visit with his son James on the U.K. TV show "Going Live." He took call-in questions on the air and performed "Once upon a Long Ago" with his full band, including Stan Salzman and Nigel Kennedy.

(b) **Dec 14–19:** Paul recorded a new Rupert the Bear song with George Martin.

Dec 18: George, Ringo and Elton John shot a video for George's "When We Was Fab."

Dec 20: Paul and his band appeared on a German music game show and performed a live version of "Once upon a Long Ago."

Dec 27: George appeared on BBC Radio One in a *Cloud Nine* special. During the show, George played the unreleased recording, "Hottest Gong in Town," from the *Shanghai Surprise* film soundtrack.

Dec 30: George appeared on the U.S. radio show "Rockstars" on KLOS-FM, Los Angeles.

(r) **Dec–Jan 1988:** Paul recorded "Ou Est Le Soleil?," "Figure of Eight," "Rough Ride" and "How Many People," all released on *Flowers in the Dirt*.

1988

Early that year: Film clips of mid-1960s interviews with The Beatles were included on the U.S. videocassette release *Casey Kasem's Rock 'n' Roll Gold Mine: The Sixties*.

Jan 4: U.K. mid-price CD release of Paul's *Press to Play*.

Jan 16: George's "Got My Mind Set on You" reached number one in *Billboard* in the U.S.

Jan 17: U.S. CD release of Ringo's *Blast from Your Past*, and Paul's *McCartney*, *Wings over America*, *Ram* and *Tug of War*.

Jan 18: The Westwood One syndicated radio network began broadcasting "The Lost Lennon Tapes" in the U.S. This series, originally scheduled to run for one year, ran for over four and its content was unprecedented. Week after week, the series initially featured unreleased Lennon and Beatles' recordings, studio outtakes, alternate mixes, home demos and many interviews and clips. The unreleased Lennon tapes were provided by Yoko Ono.

(b) **Jan 20:** The Beatles were inducted into the Rock and Roll Hall of Fame during ceremonies at New York's Waldorf-Astoria. George and Ringo attended, and Yoko, Sean and Julian represented John. Paul, however, elected not to attend and sent a prepared statement in which he cited still-existing business differences among The Beatles as the reason for his absence. Paul later received a tongue lashing for his actions from Mike Love of The Beach Boys during their induction at the ceremony. George and Ringo joined Bob Dylan, Mary Wilson, Mick Jagger, Bruce Springsteen and others in an informal jam following the ceremony.

Jan 24: Premiere of George's "When We Was Fab" video, which also included Ringo. Although George remarked during his Feb 10 "Rockline" radio interview that the character of the Walrus was played by Paul, he must have been joking. Whoever did play the part was holding a standard right-handed Rickenbacher bass, although he (or she) was holding it upside down in order to appear to be playing left-handed.

Jan 25: U.S. and U.K. release of George's single "When We Was Fab"/"Zig Zag." CD and 12-inch singles were issued only in the U.K. with additional tracks.

(b) **Feb 10:** George appeared on the U.S. live call-in radio show "Rockline," originating from KLOS-FM in Los Angeles. George did impromptu versions of several songs, some with Jeff Lynne.

Feb 12: George appeared live via satellite from Los Angeles on BBC 1's "Wogan" TV show.

Feb 15: George published *Songs by George Harrison*, his second limited edition book (*I Me Mine* had been the first), available only by mail order for £235. Each copy of the book was signed by George and included either a 7-inch vinyl EP or 5-inch CD (purchasers chose one) with four Harrison songs, three of them previously unreleased.

Feb 21: U.S. CD release of George's *All Things Must Pass*.

Feb 24: George appeared on Dutch television's "Countdown" show.

Feb 26: George received the award for Best Video of the Year, for "When We Was Fab," at the San Remo Music Festival in Italy.

Feb 28: Paul and his band headlined the Song Festival at San Remo, Italy. The band now included Hamish Stuart (guitar/bass), Chris Whitten (drums), Gary Barnacle (sax), Andrew Chater (violin) and Linda McCartney (keyboards).

Mar 3: George and Ringo joined host Michael Aspel to tape an appearance on London Weekend Television's "Aspel & Company," the first joint television appearance by two former Beatles, aired Mar 5. John and George had appeared together during a radio interview following George's final concert on his 1974 tour.

Mar 8: Worldwide release of two separate CDs, *Past Masters Vol. 1* and *Past Masters Vol. 2*, with packaging as unimaginative as the title. These CDs, also issued as a double LP, contained all of The Beatles' songs not included on their original British albums or on the *Magical Mystery Tour* album, and thus not yet issued on CD. Thus collectors could now obtain the complete Beatles releases on compact disc (except for the countless rarities or variations in stereo and mono releases that had appeared over the years).

Mar 17: U.S. CD release of John's *Imagine*.

Mar 21: Unauthorized U.S. videocassette release of *The Beatles at Shea Stadium*, one of a series of four videocassettes sold by more than one distributor at budget prices; Apple later sued to halt the sales. The other titles were *The Beatles in Tokyo, The Beatles in Washington, D.C.* and *The Beatles in Magical Mystery Tour.* The Shea Stadium and Tokyo films had been issued several years earlier by MEDA but were withdrawn at the request of Apple.

■ U.K. release of videocassette *John and Yoko: The Complete Story* originally aired in the U.S. in 1985 as a made-for-TV movie titled *John and Yoko: A Love Story.* The videocassette was released in the U.S. on Dec 21, 1989 with the original film title.

Mar 22: U.S. CD release of George's *The Best of George Harrison* and John's *Mind Games*.

(b) Late Mar: George wrote a song for one of a series of U.K. five-minute animated TV shows called "Bunburys," which was not scheduled to premiere until fall 1992, at which time album and video releases were also planned.

Apr: George filmed a cameo appearance in HandMade Films' *Checking Out* in Los Angeles.

Apr 5: U.S. and U.K. CD release of *John Lennon/Plastic Ono Band*.

Apr 16: In New York, Les Paul presented McCartney with a custom-made guitar. He had intended to make the presentation at the Jan 20 Rock and Roll Hall of Fame ceremony, but McCartney declined to attend that event.

Apr 19: U.S. CD release of John's *Walls and Bridges* and *Rock 'N' Roll*.

(r) That spring: George recorded "Handle with Care" with Bob Dylan, Roy Orbison, Tom Petty and Jeff Lynne, a group that was to soon record an album together as The Traveling Wilburys.

May 2: U.S. release of George's single "This Is Love"/"Breath Away from Heaven." Released in the U.K. on Jun 13.

May 17: U.S. and U.K. rerelease of John's *Shaved Fish* on CD. The first issue was withdrawn due to poor sound quality.

■ The New York State Supreme Court overturned the Apr 8, 1987 ruling that dismissed an $80 million portion of The Beatles' suit against Capitol/EMI.

(r) May: Paul and Johnny Cash recorded "New Moon over Jamaica" released on Cash's *Water from the Wells of Home* album. Paul also co-wrote and produced the record.

(rb) Middle of May: Most of *The Traveling Wilburys Volume One* album was recorded during the two middle weeks of May. The Wilburys, and their assumed names, were: George Harrison (Nelson Wilbury), Roy Orbison (Lefty), Bob Dylan (Lucky), Tom Petty (Charlie T. Jnr.) and Jeff Lynne (Otis). George and Lynne produced the album.

■ Film of The Traveling Wilburys recording their first album was shot and screened as *Whatever Wilbury Wilbury* at a convention of Warner Brothers Records officials later in the year. The film, which runs about 15 minutes, was never officially released and, although shot in color, was printed in black and white.

Jun 14: The videocassette *The Prince's Trust Rock Gala* was released in the U.K. containing George and Ringo's appearance at the Jun 5–6, 1987 Prince's Trust concerts.

Jun 24: Paul received the Silver Clef Award for Outstanding Achievement in the World of British Music, sponsored by the Nordoff-Robbins Music Therapy Centre.

Jun 26–27: Paul and Linda shot cameo appearances in the BBC 1 comedy series "Bread," aired Oct 30.

(r) Jun–Jul: Paul recorded "The First Stone," released only in the U.K. He also recorded songs released on *Flowers in the Dirt* and "Flying to My Home," released as the "My Brave Face" B side.

(b) Early that summer: Paul recorded the unreleased "Indigo Moon."

Jul 12: Paul received an honorary doctorate from the University of Sussex in Brighton during graduation ceremonies.

Aug 2: Paul conducted some filming for a video at the Liverpool Institute, his alma mater.

(b) Sep 7: McCartney joined The Crickets on stage at Stefano's restaurant in London for a Buddy Holly luncheon.

Sep 16: U.K. release of videocassette *Music, Memories and Milestones*, with assorted Beatles footage.

Sep 19: U.S. release of John's "Jealous Guy"/"Give Peace a Chance" single, issued in connection with the *Imagine: John Lennon* film and compilation album.

Sep 22: U.S. videocassette release of *The Long Good Friday*, a film produced by Harrison's HandMade Films; George is executive producer.

- U.S. videocassette release of *Time Bandits*. George provided music for the soundtrack of this film, including his song "Dream Away."
- U.S. videocassette release of *Monty Python's Life of Brian*, which includes a cameo appearance by George.

Sep 30: A star honoring John Lennon was unveiled on Hollywood's Walk of Fame.

(r) Sep–Oct: Paul recorded "Good Sign," released only in the U.K., and "Motor of Love."

Oct 1: BBC Radio began a 14-part weekly series of half-hour shows, "The Beeb's Lost Beatles Tapes," including some new interview tapes never heard on the 1982 "Beatles at the Beeb" radio retrospective.

- A party celebrating the 10th anniversary of George's HandMade Films was held at Shepperton Film Studios. Film of the event, including George's speech and a music set with Carl Perkins and Joe Brown, were seen in a one-hour Granada TV special *The Movie Life of George*, aired Jan 8, 1989 in the U.K. and Feb 25, 1990 in the U.S. on the Discovery Channel. Songs included "Honey Don't" and "That's All Right (Mama)." The film also featured footage of George, Ringo and Eric Clapton performing during the "Freedom" musical number from the film *Water*.

Oct 4: Premiere of the documentary film *Imagine: John Lennon* in New York. The U.K. premiere was Oct 25; general release was Oct 28.

- U.K. release of compilation album *Imagine: John Lennon*, issued as a soundtrack album for the film of the same title. Release in the U.K. on Oct 10.

Oct 9: The U.S. cable TV network Cinemax aired film of John's Live Peace in Toronto concert appearance; it was later released on home videocassette. Lennon's footage had been cut from the film's original 1972 release for legal reasons. The film was shot by D.A. Pennebaker at the Sep 13, 1969 Toronto concert.

Oct 10: U.S. release of Johnny Cash album *Water from the Wells of Home*, including his duet with Paul on "New Moon over Jamaica." Released in the U.K. on Nov 14.

Oct 11: Ringo and his wife, Barbara, traveled to the U.S. to undergo treatment for alcoholism in a Tucson, Arizona clinic. They completed treatment on Nov 25 and returned to England.

Oct 17: U.S. and U.K. release of Traveling Wilburys single "Handle with Care"/"Margarita."

Oct 18: U.S. release of *The Traveling Wilburys Volume One* featuring George, Roy Orbison, Bob Dylan, Tom Petty and Jeff Lynne. Released in the U.K. on Oct 24.

- U.S. release of *Stay Awake* album, including Ringo's recording with Herb Alpert of "When You Wish upon a Star." Released in the U.K. on Oct 24.

Oct 26: U.S. videocassette release of 1967 film *Magical Mystery Tour*, released in the U.K. on Mar 26, 1990, the first video release by Apple Corps Ltd.

- Paul appeared on BBC 1's documentary *The Power of Music*, in which he is seen visiting a therapy center for

CHOBA B CCCP (© MPL Communications Ltd.). In 1988 Paul released this oldies album in the Soviet Union.

mentally retarded children operated by the Nordoff-Robbins organization.

Oct 31: Paul's album *CHOBA B CCCP* (*Back in the USSR* or *Again in the USSR*) was released in the Soviet Union containing 11 songs from his Jul 1987 studio oldies jam. A second Soviet edition, with 13 songs, was issued on Dec 24. A 14-song edition was released on CD on Sep 30, 1991 in the U.K. and Oct 29, 1991 in the U.S.

Nov 2: U.S. release of *Porky's Revenge* soundtrack on CD, including George's "I Don't Want to Do It."

Nov 25: U.S. videocassette release of The Who's film *Tommy*, featuring Ringo.

Nov 28: EMI began reissuing all of The Beatles' original U.K. singles on 3-inch CDs. Once again, however, EMI used the album version of "Love Me Do," which features Andy White, not Ringo, on drums.

- U.K. release of single "Imagine"/"Jealous Guy" as a tie-in to the *Imagine: John Lennon* compilation album.

Nov: U.S. CD release of Paul's *Red Rose Speedway*, *Venus and Mars* and *McCartney II*.

Dec 6: Roy Orbison, legendary rock performer and fellow Traveling Wilbury to George Harrison, died suddenly of a massive heart attack at the age of 52.

Dec: George and his fellow Traveling Wilburys shot a video for "End of the Line" in California. The video premiered worldwide on Jan 20, 1989.

1989

Jan 23: U.S. release of Traveling Wilburys single "End of the Line"/"Congratulations." Released on Feb 20 in the U.K., where 12-inch and CD editions featured an extended mix of the A side.

Traveling Wilburys Vol. 1 (© T. Wilbury & Co.). In 1988 George joined with some old friends—Tom Petty, Jeff Lynne, Roy Orbison and Bob Dylan—to form The Traveling Wilburys.

Jan 26: Paul appeared live on the Soviet radio show "Granny's Chest" answering questions, from a London studio, telephoned from the Soviet Union. Only British Prime Minister Margaret Thatcher had previously done this, having taken Soviet calls in 1988.

Jan 29: The Public Broadcasting System in the U.S. began airing a new children's show called "Shining Time Station," with Ringo appearing as the 18-inch-tall Mr. Conductor, who narrates animated stories about Thomas the Tank Engine and Friends. Ringo had been providing narration for these stories in the U.K. for some time.

- EMI/Capitol issued John's *Double Fantasy* on CD and LP in the U.S. and U.K., having finally obtained the album from Geffen Records.

Feb 24: U.K. videocassette release of 1966 film *The Family Way*, with musical score by Paul.

- The film *The Magic Christian* was released on video laser disc in the U.S. and videocassette in the U.K. The 1969 film featured Ringo and the song "Come and Get It," composed by McCartney and sung by Badfinger.

- U.S. release of *Starr Struck: Best of Ringo Starr Vol. 2*, a Ringo greatest hits compilation not issued in the U.K. It marked the first U.S. release of several of Ringo's *Old Wave* tracks.

(rb) Feb–Apr: Paul and his band were filmed rehearsing and recording several songs. The film *Put It There* was aired as a 50-minute special, Jun 10 on BBC 1 in the U.K. and Nov 11 on Showtime in the U.S. A 65-minute version was later issued on videocassette. During filming, Paul also recorded new versions of "The Long and Winding Road" and "Rough Ride," released only in the U.K. His recording of "Party Party" was later released

on 7-inch vinyl and 3-inch CD singles issued with the World Tour Pack editions of *Flowers in the Dirt* and, in different edits, on U.S. and U.K. promo discs.

(r) Mar 5: Ringo was one of many artists contributing vocals to "Spirit of the Forest," a record sold to raise funds for preservation of the planet's rain forests.

Mar 22: George and Ringo shot a video with Tom Petty for Petty's "I Won't Back Down"; George was featured on the recording but Ringo was not. Filming continued on the following day without Ringo.

(b) Mar 25–May 13: BBC Radio One presented an eight-part series titled "McCartney on McCartney," comprising a marathon interview with Paul. It was aired in edited form in the U.S. during the Memorial Day weekend, May 27–29.

(r) Mar 27: Ringo and Buck Owens recorded a new version of "Act Naturally" at Abbey Road Studios, a song each of them had done years earlier. Ringo's version had been recorded with The Beatles.

(r) Mar: George recorded "Cheer Down," released on the *Lethal Weapon 2* soundtrack album and as a single. The song was originally written for Eric Clapton for his *Journeyman* album in early 1989, but Clapton rejected the song and Harrison recorded it himself, with Jeff Lynne producing.

- Ringo appeared in the video for Jan Hammer's "Too Much to Lose."

Apr 1–2: World premiere of the Lennon/Ono film *Ten for Two*, shot at the Dec 10, 1971 John Sinclair benefit concert with screenings at Royal Oak Music Theater and Michigan Theater, Ann Arbor.

Apr 2: U.K. videocassette release of the 1986 TV special "The Paul McCartney Special." The 60-minute cassette and a video laser disc were released in the U.S. on Jun 21. The film includes an interview with McCartney taped by Richard Skinner at Abbey Road in Jul 1986.

Apr 4: Paul received an Outstanding Services to British Music award at the Ivor Novello luncheon ceremony.

Apr 13: Paul completed filming of a video for "My Brave Face."

(r) Apr 20: Paul was one of several artists who contributed vocals to a new recording of "Ferry 'Cross the Mersey," once a hit for Gerry and the Pacemakers, released only in the U.K. on May 8 as a special charity single. Income from the record went to the Hillsborough Disaster Fund, organized to help families of victims of a soccer stadium disaster.

Apr 21: U.K. release of videocassette *Cool Cats*, a 96-minute compilation including some footage of The Beatles.

Apr 28: U.K. release of videocassette *John Lennon & the Plastic Ono Band Live Rock & Roll Revival, Toronto*. The cassette, released in the U.S. on May 1, was a new, edited version of the D.A. Pennebaker film of John's Sep 13, 1969 Toronto concert.

■ U.S. videocassette release of documentary film *Imagine: John Lennon*. The video was issued in the U.S. on May 8.

(r) **Apr–Jun:** George recorded "Cockamamie Business" and "Poor Little Girl," both released as bonus tracks on the *Best of Dark Horse 1976–1989* album. "Poor Little Girl" was also released as a single in the U.K.

May 1: U.K. release of videocassette *Rock 'n' Roll—The Greatest Years*. Sales were halted in Jul due to Harrison's objection to his Bangla Desh Concert version of "My Sweet Lord" being included. Existing copies were not withdrawn, however. The tape also includes Ringo's original promo film for "It Don't Come Easy," the first time that one of Ringo's promos had been released commercially.

May 8: U.K. release of Paul's single "My Brave Face"/"Flying to My Home." Released in the U.S. on May 10.

■ U.K. release of charity single "Ferry 'Cross the Mersey" including Paul's vocals.

May 10: Paul appeared in a pre-recorded TV segment on "Rapids" on BBC 2.

May 13: Paul mimed to "My Brave Face" on the French TV show "Champs Elysee."

May 17: Paul and his band appeared on the Dutch TV show "Countdown."

(b) **May 18:** Paul appeared on the West German TV show "Mensch Meir."

(b) **May 19:** Paul appeared on the BBC 1 TV show "Wogan."

(b) **May 24:** Paul appeared live on NED 2's "Countdown" show, aired on Dutch television.

May 29: Paul appeared on the U.S. live call-in radio show "Rockline," which originated from KLOS-FM in Los Angeles.

May 31: U.S. release of Tom Petty's videocassette compilation *A Bunch of Videos and Some Other Stuff*, including "I Won't Back Down" with George and Ringo appearing. Issued in the U.K. on Aug 11.

Jun 5: U.S. release of charity 12-inch single, and U.K. release of 7-inch single "Spirit of the Forest," including some lead vocal lines by Ringo.

■ U.K. release of Paul's *Flowers in the Dirt* album; released in the U.S. on the following day.

(b) **Jun 13:** Ringo appeared on stage with Bob Dylan at the latter's concert at Les Arenes in Frejus, France, and joined in on two songs.

(r) **Jun 15:** Excerpts of Paul's Rome press conference on this date were later released on disc in the U.K.

■ *(b)* Paul recorded songs before a live audience at the Teatro delle Vittorie in Rome to which he mimed on the following day's broadcast of the "Saint Vincent Estate '89" TV show, aired by RAI TV.

Jun 20: U.S. CD release of Paul's *Wild Life*, *Pipes of Peace*, *London Town*, *Back to the Egg* and *Wings at the Speed of Sound*.

■ At a New York press conference, aired live by Westwood One, Ringo announced plans for his first solo concert tour. Ringo later appeared on "The David Letterman Show."

Jun 24: Ringo and Buck Owens shot a video for their recording of "Act Naturally."

Jun 30: The Beatles' suit against Dave Clark (London) Ltd. was settled out of court with Clark (one-time leader and drummer of The Dave Clark Five) retaining the right to market videocassettes of *Ready Steady Go!* television shows containing Beatles' appearances.

Jun: U.S. CD release of *Tommy* album containing two tracks by Ringo.

Early Jul: A second video for "This One" was shot by Paul, directed by Dean Chamberlain. The earlier promo, known as the "Eastern" one, had been directed by Tim Pope and filmed at Albert Wharf Studio, London.

Jul 5: U.S. single release of Ringo and Buck Owens' duet of "Act Naturally."

■ Ringo and his new band met in Los Angeles to begin rehearsals for his tour. The "All-Starr" band included Clarence Clemmons, Jim Keltner, Billy Preston, Levon Helm, Dr. John, Joe Walsh, Rick Danko and Nils Lofgren.

Jul 10: U.K. CD release of Paul's *Wings at the Speed of Sound*.

Jul 14: Paul completed shooting of a video for "Ou est le Soleil?" at Griphouse Studios, London.

Jul 17: U.K. release of Paul's single "This One"/"The First Stone," issued only as a cassette single in the U.S. on Aug 2.

"This One" (© MPL Communications Ltd.). One of several U.K. singles featuring the same A side and an assortment of B sides and bonus tracks. Such multiple releases became the rule in England. U.S. Beatles fans would remain largely limited to cassette singles.

Jul 21: Ringo and his band continued rehearsals in Los Calinas, Texas.

(b) Jul 23–Sep 4: Ringo conducted his first solo tour, a swing through North America, accompanied by his All-Starr Band. Each member of the band did at least one number at each show, and Ringo's tour repertoire included "It Don't Come Easy," "The No-No Song," "Honey Don't," "You're Sixteen," "Photograph," "Yellow Submarine," "Act Naturally," "Boys," "With a Little Help from My Friends" and either "I Wanna Be Your Man" or "Back Off Boogaloo." The tour included concerts at Park Central Amphitheater, Dallas (Jul 23); Poplar Creek Music Theater (near Chicago) (Jul 25); Deer Creek Amphitheater, Indianapolis (Jul 26); Riverfest, Minneapolis (Jul 28); Alpine Valley Music Theater, East Troy, Wisconsin (Jul 29); Pine Knob Music Theater, Clarkston (near Detroit) (Jul 30); Blossom Music Center, Cuyahoga Falls (near Cleveland) (Jul 31); Lake Compounce Amusement Park, Bristol, Connecticut (Aug 2); Performing Arts Center, Saratoga Springs, New York (Aug 4); Garden State Arts Center, Holmdel, New Jersey (Aug 5, 11); Bally's Grand Hotel, Atlantic City (Aug 6); Merriweather Post Pavillion, Columbia, Maryland (Aug 8); Mann Music Center, Philadelphia (Aug 9); Jones Beach Amphitheater, Wantaugh, New York (Aug 12, 13); Great Woods Center, Mansfield (near Boston), Massachusetts (Aug 15); Kingston Concert Grounds, Kingston, New Hampshire (Aug 16); Memorial Auditorium, Buffalo, New York (Aug 18); CNE, Toronto (Aug 19); Castle in Charlevoix, Michigan (Aug 20); Winnipeg, Canada (Aug 22); Saskatoon, Saskatchewan, Canada (Aug 23); Olympic Saddledome, Calgary (Aug 24); Northlands Coliseum, Edmonton (Aug 25); PNE Pacific Coliseum, Vancouver, B.C. (Aug 27); Cal Expo Amphitheater, Sacramento (Aug 29); Aladdin Theater, Las Vegas (Aug 30); Shoreline Amphitheater, Mountain View, California (Sep 1); Pacific Amphitheater, Costa Mesa, California (Sep 2); the Greek Theater, Los Angeles (Sep 3, 4).

Jul 24: Ringo appeared on the U.S. live radio call-in show "Rockline."

■ U.K. release of Paul's limited boxed edition single "This One"/"The Long and Winding Road." U.K. CD release of Paul's *Back to the Egg*.

■ Ringo obtained a court order from Judge Ralph Hicks in Fulton County Supreme Court, Georgia, barring producer Chips Moman and CRS Records from releasing the album Ringo had recorded with Moman in 1987. The ruling blocked Moman from releasing the album for 30 days pending a final ruling on the case.

■ Paul and his band began four days of rehearsals at the Playhouse Theater in London. They had been rehearsing for several months in East Sussex. The band now included Paul, Linda, guitarists Hamish Stuart and Robbie McIntosh, keyboard player Paul "Wix" Wickens and drummer Chris Whitten.

Jul 25: Paul and his band taped appearances on several children's shows and for "Top of the Pops," aired Aug 3.

(b) Jul 26: Paul performed the first of two surprise concerts at London's Playhouse Theatre before invited audiences; the second show was held the following evening. The shows were previews of his tour, which would begin on Sep 26.

■ U.S. release of 12-inch and cassette maxi single with three alternate mixes of Paul's "Ou Est le Soleil?"

(rb) Jul 27: McCartney performed a brief music set at a U.K. press conference at London's Playhouse Theatre prior to his second preview show.

Jul 28: Paul made an unbilled appearance on the BBC 1 children's show "The O Zone."

Aug 2: A 7-inch 45 RPM vinyl promo of Paul's "This One" was issued in the U.S. It is very likely the last McCartney vinyl single ever to be released there. The release coincided with Capitol's announcement that it was discontinuing most 7-inch vinyl singles. (A Capitol vinyl single was released in Canada.)

Aug 3: U.K. release of *Porky's Revenge* videocassette, including George's recording of "I Don't Want to Do It."

Aug 4: A segment featuring Paul was seen on the U.K. TV show "Notte Rock," including part of a performance of "Twenty Flight Rock."

Aug 10: U.S. release of *Lethal Weapon 2* soundtrack album, including George's "Cheer Down." Released in the U.K. on Sep 4.

Aug 11: Bruce Springsteen appeared on stage as a surprise guest during Ringo's Holmdel, New Jersey show at the Garden State Arts Center, and joined in on "Get Back," "Long Tall Sally" (neither among the regular tour song lineup), "Photograph" and "With a Little Help from My Friends." Ringo's son Zak played drums on the final two numbers, while Springsteen's drummer, Max Weinberg, played on the first three. Zak also drummed on "You're Sixteen," which did not include Springsteen.

(b) Aug 12–13: Ringo performed on both of these dates at the Jones Beach Amphitheater in Wantaugh, New York. Paul McCartney reportedly attended one show and watched from the wings but never appeared on stage; his presence has not been confirmed.

Aug 21–24: Paul rehearsed his band for their upcoming tour.

Aug 22: Two of the recordings from Ringo's 1987 sessions with Chips Moman, "Whiskey and Soda" and "I Can Help," were played in court to weigh Ringo's charge that the recordings were subpar due to the use of alcohol during the sessions. On Aug 24 the court granted Ringo another extension of the order barring Moman from releasing the 1987 album.

(b) Aug 24: Paul conducted a brief press conference, aired live by Westwood One, at the Lyceum Theater in New York, performing several songs. Later in the evening Paul performed a show for an invited audience at the Lyceum.

■ U.S. release of George's single "Cheer Down"/"That's What It Takes."

Aug 25: A U.S. TV commercial for Oldsmobile with Ringo and his daughter, Lee Starkey, was aired.

Aug 29: U.K. CD release of Paul's *London Town*.

That summer: George reportedly taped an appearance on a new U.K. television show, "Beyond the Groove," devised and co-produced by The Eurythmics' Dave Stewart. The show was not aired and remains unreleased.

(r) Early Sep: Paul recorded a completely new version of "Figure of Eight," later released as a single in eight different formats in the U.K. and as a cassette single in the U.S.

Sep 2: A televised BBC tribute "Network East Tribute to Ravi Shankar," celebrating the 50th anniversary of Shankar's first public recital, included footage of George.

(rb) Sep 3–4: Ringo performed on two consecutive nights at the Greek Theater in Los Angeles, concluding his North American tour. Four songs from the Sep 3 show and three from Sep 4 were released on *Ringo Starr and His All-Starr Band*, and "Boys" was aired live on Sep 3 in the U.S. on the "Jerry Lewis Muscular Dystrophy Telethon."

Sep 4–21: Paul and his band rehearsed at Elstree Film Studios near London.

Sep 11: U.S. release of Paul's "My Brave Face" CD single.

Sep 21: Paul conducted a secret, pretour concert at Elstree Studios. The standing-room-only audience of approximately 750 saw the full 30-song lineup, the 11-minute Richard Lester documentary film and all of the visual effects that would be used during the tour. The song lineup would be altered periodically during the 10-month tour. This show was filmed and recorded, as Paul planned to do at most shows on the tour.

Sep 26: Paul performed at Drammenshalle in Dramen, Norway. This was not a full-fledged concert but rather the final tuneup before the start of Paul's tour. The first official concert took place on Sep 28 in Goteborg, Sweden. For the Dramen show, Paul did: "Figure of Eight," "Jet," "Rough Ride," "Got to Get You into My Life," "Band on the Run," "Ebony and Ivory," "We Got Married," "Maybe I'm Amazed," "The Long and Winding Road," "The Fool on the Hill," "Sgt. Pepper's Lonely Hearts Club Band," "Good Day Sunshine," "Can't Buy Me Love," "Put It There," "Hello Goodbye" (ending only, tacked onto "Put It There"), "Things We Said Today," "Eleanor Rigby," "Back in the USSR," "I Saw Her Standing There," "This One," "My Brave Face," "Twenty Flight Rock," "Coming Up," "Let It Be," "Live and Let Die," "Hey Jude," "Yesterday," "Get Back," "Golden Slumbers," "Carry That Weight," "The End." The latter three were done as an encore. The Richard Lester film was not shown. The booklet included with the CD release of Paul's tour album, *Tripping the Live Fantastic*, lists the location of this show as Oslo, not Dramen, and refers to this show as the official start of the tour.

Sep 27: Worldwide video release of *Yellow Submarine* with a "digitally enhanced stereo hi-fi soundtrack."

(rb) Sep 28–Oct 30: McCartney concerts at the Scandinavium, Goteborg, Sweden (Sep 28); Johanneshovs Isstadion, Stockholm (Sep 29, 30); Sportshalle, Hamburg (Oct 3, 4); Festehalle, Frankfurt (Oct 6, 7); Palais Omnisport De Bercy, Paris (Oct 9, 10, 11); Westfallenhalle, Dortmund, Germany (Oct 16, 17); Olympiahalle, Munich (Oct 20, 21, 22); Palaeur, Rome (Oct 24); Palatrussardi, Milan (Oct 26, 27); Zurich, Switzerland (Oct 29, 30). Some tracks from several shows and soundchecks were released on *Tripping the Live Fantastic*. Paul's unreleased "Church Mice" was among several pre-recorded instrumentals played at each concert prior to the start of the show.

Oct 1: U.S. release of Buck Owens' *Act Naturally* album, including his duet with Ringo on "Act Naturally." Released in the U.K. on Feb 19, 1990.

Oct 3: U.K. CD release of Paul's *Wings at the Speed of Sound*.

Oct 10: U.S. videocassette release of *Wonderwall*, containing George's film score.

Oct 12: Hurriedly edited film shot at Ringo's Sep 3 Los Angeles concert was aired at the MIPCOM trade fair in Cannes, France.

Oct 17: U.S. release of George's *Best of Dark Horse: 1976–1989*. Released in the U.K. on Oct 23.

Oct 23: U.K. CD release of *The John Lennon Collection*.

(rb) Oct 27: Paul performed "All My Trials" only once during his 1989–1990 world tour, on this date during his Milan, Italy show. The song was later released on several U.K. records after being edited and remixed. It appeared in the U.S. only on a special record club vinyl edition of *Tripping the Live Fantastic Highlights!*

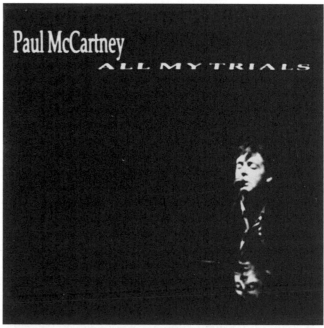

"All My Trials" (© MPL Communications Ltd.). One of two U.K. CD single releases of this live McCartney track, also issued on 12-inch and 7-inch U.K. singles. In the U.S. the song appeared only on a record club vinyl edition of *Tripping the Live Fantastic Highlights!* never on a single.

Oct 30–Nov 8: Ringo conducted a short tour of Japan. His songs included "It Don't Come Easy," "No No Song," "Yellow Submarine," "Act Naturally," "Honey Don't," "I Wanna Be Your Man," "Boys," "Photograph," "You're Sixteen," "With a Little Help from My Friends." Billy Preston also did "Get Back." Concerts were given at Rainbow Hall, Nagoya (Oct 30); Castle Hall, Osaka (Oct 31); Sun Plaza, Hiroshima (Nov 2); Kyushi (Nov 3); Nippon Budokan Hall, Tokyo (Nov 6, 7); Yokohama Arena (Nov 8).

(rb) Nov 2–29: McCartney concerts at Palacio de Sportes, Madrid (Nov 2,3); Lyon, France (Nov 5); Ahoy Sportpaleis, Rotterdam (Nov 7, 8, 10, 11); the Los Angeles Forum (Nov 23, 24, 27, 28, 29). Some songs from these shows were released on *Tripping the Live Fantastic*. Recordings of interviews and press conferences were also released.

Nov 3: U.K. videocassette release of *Water* and *A Private Function*, both produced by George's HandMade Films. *Water* features George and Ringo during the "Freedom" musical number.

Nov 8: Settlement was at last reached in the 20-year-old legal case pitting The Beatles against EMI/Capitol and involving many issues, not the least of which was the amount of record royalties due to The Beatles. While all parties agreed not to reveal the terms of the agreement, it was widely reported that EMI/Capitol agreed to pay The Beatles approximately £100 million in back royalties. The Beatles also obtained full control over the use of their recordings, including record cover artwork. The settlement resolved business differences between Paul and the other Beatles, but public bickering between George and Paul would soon begin anew.

■ **(rb)** Preconcert rehearsals and film footage from Paul's Rotterdam concerts were aired Nov 21 in the U.K. on BBC Channel 4's "Big World" show, repeated on Nov 24.

Nov 11: An interview taped with Paul in Rotterdam was added to the final part of a U.K. radio rebroadcast of "McCartney on McCartney," aired Dec 25 to Jan 4, 1990 on BBC Radio One.

Nov 13: U.K. release of Paul's single "Figure of Eight"/"Ou Est le Soleil?" released Nov 15 in the U.S. only as a cassette single with shorter edits of both songs. Eight different "Figure of Eight" singles were issued in the U.K.

Nov 15: In Atlanta, Ringo testified that his performance on the unreleased 1987 Chips Moman-produced sessions was below par, partly due to excessive use of alcohol by band members during recording sessions, and that Moman was trying to rush-release an album to capitalize on Ringo's successful All-Starr tour. He noted that no label had been interested in releasing the record during its two-year dormancy and that Moman had formed his own CRS label for that purpose. The court issued an injunction blocking release of the album for the time being.

Nov 23: U.K. release of *Flowers in the Dirt* (World Tour Pack), a limited edition repackaging of Paul's album, including a bonus one-track single with the previously unreleased song "Party Party." Released in the U.S. on Jan 15, 1990.

(rb) Nov 27: During Paul's Los Angeles Forum show, Stevie Wonder joined him on stage for a duet of their hit "Ebony and Ivory." During a press conference, later released in the U.K., Paul referred to the recent Beatles/Apple settlement with EMI and said The Beatles might perform together again. He added that he had never written with George and would like to do so. Ringo had no comment on the statement, but George issued one on Nov 28 saying that there would be no Beatles reunion "as long as John Lennon remains dead."

■ U.K. release of George's single "Cheer Down"/"Poor Little Girl."

Dec 3: Paul ad-libbed a bit of "Chicago" during his Rosemont Horizon show, as he had done during his 1976 Chicago concerts. Most of the CBS-TV "48 Hours" special, aired Jan 25, 1990, was shot during Paul's stay in Chicago.

(rb) Dec 3–15: McCartney concerts at Rosemont Horizon (near Chicago) (Dec 3, 4); the Skydome, Toronto (Dec 7); Montreal Forum (Dec 9); Madison Square Garden, New York (Dec 11, 12, 14, 15). Some songs were released on *Tripping the Live Fantastic* or as bonus tracks on McCartney singles.

(r) Dec 18–24: During a break in his tour, Paul recorded the score for a film about artist Honore Daumier, produced by MPL.

Dec 19: U.S. videocassette and laser disc release, and U.K. videocassette release, of *Put It There*, a 65-minute version of the TV special, originally running only 50 minutes. The outer box boasted four additional songs not included in the TV broadcast of this film but in fact only one, "Fool on the Hill," was actually included. The packaging in the U.S. was changed to eliminate the false claim.

Dec 21: U.S. video laser disc release of *Imagine*, the original Lennon video compilation film. Released in the U.K. in Aug 1991. U.S. release of video laser discs *John Lennon: Live in New York City* and Paul's 1976 concert film *Rockshow*.

Dec 27: BBC 2 aired the documentary film *25 x 5: The Continuing Adventures of The Rolling Stones*, which included footage from Pathe newsreel film *The Beatles Come to Town*, shot backstage at the Manchester Ardwick ABC in Nov 1963, and footage from the "Our World" Jun 1967 TV special and other clips of The Beatles. Released on videocassette Mar 19, 1990.

Dec: U.K. release of *The Royal Concert*, containing tracks from the 1986 and 1987 Prince's Trust shows by Paul and George respectively.

■ Ringo took part in the U.K. radio campaign "Recording Artists Against Drunk Driving."

Late that year: U.S. video laser disc release of Paul's films *Give My Regards to Broad Street* and *Rupert and the Frog Song*.

The Royal Concert (© The Prince's Trust and A&M Records). U.K. double album and CD with two of Paul's 1986 numbers and two by George from 1987 but, alas, no Ringo.

1990

(r) **Jan 2–26:** McCartney U.K. concerts at NEC International Arena, Birmingham (Jan 2, 3, 5, 6, 8, 9) and at Wembley Arena (Jan 11, 13, 14, 16, 17, 19, 20, 21, 23, 24, 26). Some tracks were released on *Tripping the Live Fantastic.*

Jan 5: A court ruling granted Ringo's request stopping Chips Moman from releasing the album he had produced for Starr in 1987. Ringo was ordered to pay Moman $74,354, less than half the $162,600 in production costs that Moman had sought.

Jan 22–26: "Good Morning Britain" ran a five-part series on McCartney's tour, which included a soundcheck performance of The Rolling Stones' "Honky Tonk Woman."

Jan 25: The U.S. TV series "48 Hours" expanded from 60 to 90 minutes with a documentary special show devoted entirely to Paul's tour, shot mostly in Chicago. It was later edited and rebroadcast at 60 minutes.

(r) **Feb 1–19:** McCartney concerts at the Palace of Auburn Hills (near Detroit) (Feb 1, 2); Pittsburgh (Feb 4, 5); Centrum, Worcester, Massachusetts (Feb 8, 9); Riverfront Coliseum, Cincinnati (Feb 12); Indianapolis, Indiana (Feb 14, 15); the Omni, Atlanta (Feb 18, 19). Some songs were released on *Tripping the Live Fantastic.* Recordings of press conferences were also released.

Feb 4–5: Paul omitted several songs from both of his Pittsburgh shows due to illness that had strained his voice.

Feb 5: U.K. release of Paul's single "Put It There"/"Mama's Little Girl"; U.K. CD and 12-inch editions added "Same Time Next Year." Released in the U.S. on May 1 only as a cassette single.

Feb 8: U.S. videocassette and laser disc release of *Lethal Weapon 2,* including George's "Cheer Down." Videocassette issued in the U.K. on Mar 16.

Feb 19: U.S. release of *The John Lennon Collection* on CD.

Feb 21: Paul received the Lifetime Achievement Grammy Award during the Academy of Recorded Arts and Sciences televised award ceremony. Paul accepted in person and made a short speech that included a plea for a cleaner environment. *The Traveling Wilburys Volume One* and Tom Petty's *Full Moon Fever,* both featuring George, were nominated for Album of the Year; *Volume One* was also nominated for Best Rock Performance by a Duo or Group with Vocal; Ringo's duet with Buck Owens on "Act Naturally" was nominated for Best Country Vocal Collaboration. Paul's *Flowers in the Dirt* and *Full Moon Fever* were nominated for Best Engineered Album. None of them won any Grammys.

(rb) **Mar 1:** At the start of a Tokyo press conference at the MZA Ariake Theater, Paul sang "Matchbox."

(rb) **Mar 3–31:** McCartney concerts at Tokyo Dome (Mar 3, 5, 7, 9, 11, 13); Seattle's Kingdome (Mar 29); Berkeley, California (Mar 31). Some songs were released on *Tripping the Live Fantastic* or on McCartney singles. At three Tokyo shows Paul added his new medley "P.S. Love Me Do."

Mar 5: U.K. release of 20th-anniversary single "Let It Be"/"You Know My Name (Look Up the Number)," concluding the series of 20th-anniversary Beatles singles releases.

Mar 9: Paul's Tokyo show was broadcast live to closed-circuit TV outlets in 10 Japanese cities, all of which sold out.

Mar 24: U.K. release of *The Last Temptation of Elvis,* including Paul's "It's Now or Never," which was also issued on U.K. promos. The LP appeared in the U.S. as an import in Apr 1990.

Mar: U.S. video laser disc release of McCartney's *Put It There* documentary film.

(b) **Late Mar:** Ringo joined Joe Walsh, Tom Petty, Jeff Lynne and Jim Keltner to record and film a new version of "I Call Your Name," screened during the May 5 John Lennon Scholarship Concert in Liverpool. The video was officially released Apr 15, 1991 on the videocassette *Lennon: A Tribute.*

Apr 1: U.S. CD release of John's *Some Time in New York City.*

(rb) **Apr 1–21:** McCartney concerts in Berkeley, California (Apr 1); Tempe, Arizona (Apr 4); Texas Stadium, Irving, Texas (Apr 7); Rupp Arena, Lexington, Kentucky (Apr 9); Tampa Stadium, Tampa, Florida (Apr 12); Joe Robbie Stadium, Miami, Florida (Apr 14, 15); Maracana Stadium, Rio de Janeiro (Apr 20, 21). Some songs were later released.

Apr 2: A series of 40 videotapes was issued by Parkfield Entertainment in the U.S., including a tape of Pathe weekly newsreel footage for each year beginning with 1930 and running through 1969. The tapes for 1963 through 1969 each have Beatles footage. 1963: Variety Club awards luncheon (Sep). 1964: Kennedy Airport arrival and press conference; return to London Airport and press conference. 1965: airport shots; receiving Radio Caroline award from Simon Dee on *Help!* film set; return to London Airport form U.S. in Sep; Oct 26 at Buckingham Palace. 1966: Arrival at London Airport from Far East tour. 1967: no Beatles footage, but views of Lennon's car and Weybridge home. 1968: Rishikesh, India and 1964 flashback footage. 1969: Paul and Linda's wedding.

Apr 12: U.K. videocassette release *Concert for Bangla Desh*.

Apr 15: The British Satellite Broadcasting's Power Station aired a 90-minute special, *In Concert: Ringo Starr and His All-Starr Band*, comprising footage from Ringo's Sep 3, 1989 Los Angeles show.

Apr 16: George appeared in Jim Capaldi's video for "Oh Lord, Why Lord," for which George did backup work on Capaldi's LP *Some Come Running*. This was the only promo video screened at the Nelson Mandela concert at Wembley but was not aired during the telecast.

(r) Apr 20 & 21: Paul performed concerts at Rio de Janeiro's Maracana Stadium on each of these dates. The first show was originally scheduled for Apr 19 but was postponed due to rain. The Apr 21 show was certified by the *Guinness Book of Records* as the largest paying audience ever to see a rock concert by a single artist. Approximately 184,000 people attended; only 80,000 saw the Apr 20 show. The Apr 21 show was filmed and eight numbers from it were aired by TV Globo in Rio on Apr 23, plus the "We Got Married" and "Figure of Eight" videos in a special broadcast titled "Paul in Rio," which appeared almost immediately on bootleg videocassettes.

(rb) Late Apr–middle of May: The Traveling Wilburys reunited, without a replacement for the late Roy Orbison, to record their second album, and devoted a period from late Mar to mid-May to writing new songs. They recorded them over a three-week period during Apr and early May at a private home studio in Bel Air, California with work completed in Jul. The first release from these sessions was "Nobody's Child," a song that The Beatles had backed Tony Sheridan on in Jun 1961 in Hamburg during their first commercial studio session. It was released on the album *Nobody's Child: Romanian Angel Appeal*, a charity release to raise funds for Romanian orphanages and hospitals then dealing with an epidemic of AIDS among infants. The fund-raising had been organized by George's wife, Olivia, and involved other Beatles' wives as well. The song also appeared as a single. The Traveling Wilburys' second album was released as the numerically incorrect *The Traveling Wilburys Volume 3* (there had been no Volume 2). The album, produced by George and Jeff Lynne, did not contain any George Harrison solos; his only one, "Maxine," had been omitted. Harrison and Lynne used the new pseudonyms Spike and Clayton Wilbury, while Tom Petty and Bob Dylan took the monickers Muddy and Boo Wilbury respectively.

May 1: George joined Eric Clapton on stage at the L.A. Forum during the encore of Clapton's show, contributing guitar on Clapton's "Crossroads" and "Sunshine of Your Love."

May 5: A fund-raising memorial concert for John Lennon was held at Pier Head on the banks of the Mersey River in Liverpool. The concert was organized by Yoko and proceeds went to what she called the Greening of the World John Lennon Scholarship Fund. Ringo's new "I Call Your Name" video was screened, as was a film clip of Paul doing "P.S. Love Me Do" at one of his Tokyo shows, along with spoken messages from both ex-Beatles. Both videos were also seen during broadcast of the show on Dec 8 in the U.S. and U.K. Many performers participated in the show. A TV special, aired later on the night of May 5 in the U.K., included short clips from John's appearances on the Jan 9, 1965 BBC-TV "Not Only . . . But Also" show and the Jun 22, 1968 "Release" show. The concert was released on videocassette on Apr 15, 1991.

May 8: U.S. videocassette release of 55-minute *The Beatles: Alone and Together*, comprising news archive footage.

May 26–27: In the U.S., Westwood One syndicated the BBC Radio One series "The Beeb's Lost Beatles Tapes" during the Memorial Day weekend. Originally aired in the U.K. in late 1988 as 14 30-minute programs, it was edited for U.S. broadcast to a single six-hour special and retitled "The BBC's Beatles Tapes: The Original Masters."

May–Jun: During a break in his tour, Paul worked with Carl Davis at Olympic Sound Studios in southwest London on the composition of an oratorio built around his Liverpool childhood. It premiered Jun 28, 1991 in Liverpool, conducted by Davis.

Jun 7: U.S. release of the first two *Thomas the Tank Engine and Friends* videocassette with narration by Ringo.

■ U.K. videocassette release of HandMade Films' *Checking Out*, featuring a cameo appearance by George.

Jun 13: Paul appeared unannounced and live on BBC Radio One's "The Steve Wright Show" where he was interviewed, took questions, participated in the disc jockey's routines of weather and traffic reporting and did short acoustic versions of "Matchbox" and "Blackbird." A live version of "P.S. Love Me Do" was also played.

Jun 18: U.K. release of single "Nobody's Child" (the Traveling Wilburys)/"Lumiere" (Dave Stewart). Twelve-inch and CD editions added Ringo's Sep 4, 1989 live version of "With a Little Help form My Friends."

Jun 19–21: Paul and his band rehearsed at East Sussex during Jun 19 and 20 and in Glasgow on Jun 21.

Jun 20: George appeared on BBC Radio One's "The Simon Bates Show." While at BBC, George and his wife, Olivia, also taped an appearance aired Aug 1 by BBC Radio One as part of a one-hour Romanian Appeal documentary called *Nobody's Child*.

Jun 22: George and Olivia Harrison appeared on BBC 1's "Wogan." Part of the *Nobody's Child* video was also shown.

Jun 23: A 30-minute documentary about Paul, produced by Granada TV and MPL, aired on some IBA television stations in the U.K. The film included footage from Paul's world tour and served as promotion for upcoming shows in Liverpool and Glasgow.

(rb) Jun 23–Jul 29: McCartney concerts at Scottish Exhibition & Conference Centre, Glasgow (Jun 23); King's Dock, Liverpool (Jun 28); Knebworth, U.K. (Jun 30); RFK Stadium, Washington, D.C. (Jul 4, 6); Giants Stadium, East Rutherford, New Jersey (Jul 9, 11); Philadelphia, Pennsylvania (Jul 14, 15); Ames, Iowa (Jul 18); Cleveland, Ohio (Jul 20); Carter-Finley Stadium, Raleigh, North Carolina (Jul 22); Sullivan Stadium, Foxboro, Massachusetts (Jul 24, 26); Soldier Field, Chicago (Jul 29), concluding the world tour that had begun 10 months earlier. Several songs were later released.

Jun 25–26: Paul and his band held filming sessions at Twickenham Studios near London.

(rb) Jun 28: Paul's concert at King's Dock in Liverpool, billed as "Let It Be Liverpool," marked the debut of Paul's Lennon medley ("Strawberry Fields Forever"/"Help!"/"Give Peace a Chance"), his first public performance of Lennon compositions. About 75 minutes of the show was transmitted by BBC Radio One on Oct 27. It was also featured prominently in the TV special, "From Rio to Liverpool," aired in the U.K. in December and in the U.S. in Oct 1991 as "Paul McCartney—Going Home" on the Disney Channel.

■ A prerecorded interview with Paul was seen on "TV-am" in the U.K.

Jun 29: Paul and his band did a soundcheck at Knebworth a day prior to their appearance at the charity concert held there.

(rb) Jun 30: Paul did an abbreviated 45-minute set at the Knebworth benefit concert for the Nordoff-Robbins Music Therapy Center and the British Recording Industry Trust School for the Performing Arts. Some of his songs were later released. The concert was broadcast live on U.S. and U.K. radio and was filmed with footage aired in the U.S. on Jul 14 on MTV and in the U.K. on Aug 6 by ITV.

■ U.S. laser disc release of 90-minute version of *Ringo Starr and His All-Starr Band* taped at Ringo's Sep 3, 1989 Los Angeles show. A Jan 29, 1991 U.S. videocassette release also ran 90 minutes. Only a 60-minute cassette was issued in the U.K. on Jul 16. The U.S. releases include all of Ringo's songs except "You're Sixteen."

Jun: U.K. release of CD *Denny Laine Featuring Paul McCartney*, a copy of Laine's *Japanese Tears*.

Jul 2: C4 television in the U.K. aired the film *Eat the Rich*, which features a cameo appearance by Paul.

Jul 4 & 6: Paul performed concerts on each of these dates at Washington, D.C.'s RFK Stadium. At the July 4th show, Paul replaced the Lennon medley with "Birthday" and a rendition of "Happy Birthday" in honor of the nation's 214th birthday.

Jul 9: U.K. videocassette release of documentary film *Yoko Ono: Then and Now*, which includes footage of Lennon and The Beatles.

Jul 16: U.K. videocassette release of 1985 U.S. made-for-TV movie *Alice in Wonderland*, featuring Ringo as the Mock Turtle.

Jul 23: U.K. release of *Nobody's Child: Romanian Angel Appeal*, issued the following day in the U.S., including songs by George, Ringo and others.

Jul 25: In Foxboro, Massachusetts Paul and his band mimed to a recording from their Philadelphia show to provide a film crew with close-up shots to be used in the concert film. An invited audience of about 800 attended.

(r) Jul 29: Ten months after it began, Paul's world tour concluded with a concert at Chicago's Soldier Field. His Chicago press conference was also recorded.

Aug 6: U.S. and U.K. release of *Knebworth: The Album*, including two of Paul's Jun 30 concert tracks.

Aug 13: U.K. videocassette rerelease of *Lisztomania*, in which Ringo portrays the pope.

Aug 28: U.K. videocassette release *Knebworth: The Event (Volume One)*, including the same four McCartney numbers aired on TV specials of the Jun 30 event: "Coming Up," "Birthday," "Hey Jude" and "Can't Buy Me Love."

Aug: Video Collection International released a *Thomas the Tank Engine & Friends* compilation videocassette

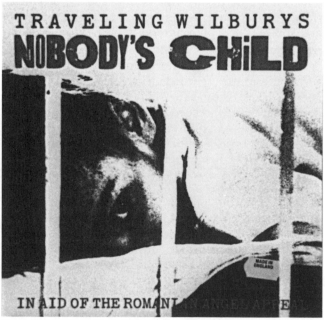

"Nobody's Child" (© T. Wilbury & Co.). U.K. charity single from George and the Wilburys; the song also appeared worldwide on a compilation album.

combining previously released cassettes, with 17 stories narrated by Ringo.

Sep 4: Paul performed at a Buddy Holly birthday celebration at New York's Lone Star Roadhouse. His brief appearance included "Oh Boy," "Rave On" and "Lucille." Although the annual Holly Week celebration sponsored by McCartney had taken place in England for the past 14 years, this year it was moved to New York to coincide with the Nov 4 opening of the Broadway musical Buddy.

Sep 10: U.K. release of *Thomas the Tank Engine & Friends* videocassette as part of "Watch & Play" series, with stories narrated by Ringo.

Sep 27: U.S. release of two Thomas the Tank Engine and Friends videocassettes: *Thomas and Turntables and Other Stories* and *Thomas Breaks the Rules and Other Stories*.

Oct 6: BBC radio began airing *In My Life: Lennon Remembered*, a series of 10 one-hour programs about John that included more than 20 new interviews taped with Paul, Yoko and many others who knew or worked with John.

Oct 8: U.K. release of Paul's single "Birthday"/"Good Day Sunshine" in several formats. Released in the U.S. Oct 16 only on cassette.

- U.K. release of *Ringo Starr and His All-Starr Band*, from Ringo's Sep 3 and 4, 1989 Los Angeles concerts. A bonus CD single was issued with the deluxe CD edition in the U.S. on Oct 12 but was not released in the U.K.

Oct 9: A special broadcast of John's recording of "Imagine" was reportedly carried simultaneously by approximately 1,000 radio stations in 50 countries (or 130, according to some sources). The broadcast, a celebration of John's 50th birthday, originated from the Trusteeship Council Chamber at the United Nations building in New York City. An excerpt from a Lennon interview was also included. Special prerecorded versions were also carried in Spanish and French.

Oct 26: U.K. videocassette release of *The Road*, containing 60 minutes of Beatles-era newsreel footage.

Oct 29: U.K. release of *The Traveling Wilburys Volume 3*, released in the U.S. the following day; the second album (despite the title) by this group that included George Harrison.

Oct 30: U.K. release of four-CD boxed set *Lennon*, containing the first CD release of many Lennon tracks. Also issued as an import in the U.S. An official U.S. release took place the following July.

Oct: U.K. videocassette release of *My Love Is Bigger Than a Cadillac*, a film about The Crickets that includes a brief appearance by Paul. The film was aired on U.S. TV on Aug 5 and 11.

Nov: Three artists completed an animated video for Paul's "Party Party" in 12 days, working 600 man-hours to draw approximately 4,500 images. The video, however, was hardly ever aired, which is not surprising since the song was released only on a bonus single included with *Flowers in the Dirt* World Tour Packs and on a very limited edition Japanese double CD pack.

Nov 5: U.S. and U.K. release of Paul's live concert album *Tripping the Live Fantastic*.

- U.K. release of Wilburys' single "She's My Baby"/"New Blue Moon," 12-inch and CD editions added bonus track "Runaway."

Nov 11: George was seen in a pretaped interview on London Weekend Television's "Sunday Sunday."

Nov 19: U.S. and U.K. release of the CD *Tripping the Live Fantastic: Highlights!* an abbreviated 17-track version of the tour album, which contained different track lineups in each country. The U.K. edition featured "All My Trials," omitted from the U.S. edition, which featured "Put It There" instead. In spring 1991, the Columbia House Record Club issued a 12-track vinyl *Highlights!* album in the U.S., with the only U.S. release of "All My Trials"; the vinyl edition also appeared in Australia.

Nov 26: Paul appeared on a two-hour syndicated broadcast of "Rockline" on U.S. radio.

- U.K. release of Paul's single "All My Trials"/"C Moon" in several formats. Twelve-inch and CD editions added "Mull of Kintyre" and "Put It There."

Nov 28: Paul appeared live and responded to questions during a one-hour pan-European call-in radio show aired by 17 U.K. ILR stations as well as outlets in 16 other countries.

(b) Nov: Paul recorded several unknown demos in preparation for a new album. He and his band were scheduled to begin studio sessions in Apr 1991.

- George's legal difficulties stemming from his conviction for plagiarism of "He's So Fine" on his recording of "My Sweet Lord" were apparently finally settled. Judge Richard Owen, in U.S. Federal Court in New York, ruled that Harrison would own rights to both songs in the U.S., the U.K. and Canada. ABKCO would own rights to the song outside of those countries. George would continue to own "My Sweet Lord," but ABKCO would continue to receive a percentage of the song's royalties. George was also ordered to pay ABKCO a net sum of $270,020.

Dec 3: U.K. release of the Lennon/Ono film *John and Yoko: The Bed-In*, the first official release of the Lennons' self-produced film of the May–Jun 1969 Montreal bed-in. It later appeared on laser disc in the U.K. and Japan; the cassette was also sold in the U.S. The film, subtitled *All We Are Saying Is Give Peace a Chance*, includes an unreleased acoustic version of "Because," most of Lennon's acrimonious confrontation with cartoonist Al Capp and other footage, some of which had appeared previously in various films and television specials.

- U.K. release of a second edition of Paul's CD single "All My Trials"/"C Moon," this one replacing the two bonus tracks with the "Lennon Medley."

Dec 5: George was interviewed on BBC 2 TV's "Rapido."

Dec 8: The May 5 Liverpool Lennon benefit concert was aired in the U.K. and in syndication throughout the

U.S. The telecast included videos by Paul ("P.S. Love Me Do") and Ringo ("I Call Your Name") that were screened during the concert.

Dec 9: BBC 2 TV aired a repeat of Dudley Moore and Peter Cook's "Not Only . . . But Also" show of Jan 9, 1965, which featured an appearance by John.

Dec 10: Paul received an award for the highest-grossing concert act in the U.S. in 1990 during the Billboard Music Awards, broadcast throughout the U.S. by the Fox Network. Paul appeared in a pretaped message and a concert clip.

Dec 12: Paul received *Q* Magazine's Merit Award for his outstanding and continued contribution to the music industry.

■ A broadcast of Paul's appearance on the U.S. TV show "After Hours" was scheduled by BBC 2 for this date.

Dec 13: Paul and his band filmed an appearance at Limehouse TV studios in Wembley before a live audience, aired Dec 26 in Denmark and later in Italy. Three numbers were videotaped: "Let It Be," "The Long and Winding Road" and "All My Trials." By this time Chris Whitten had left Paul's band and was replaced by drummer Blair Cunningham, formerly with Echo and the Bunnymen, and later of The Pretenders, which also once included Robbie McIntosh.

(b) Dec 14: Paul reunited with Elvis Costello, and the two wrote three new songs during the month.

■ Paul appeared on BBC 1's "Wogan," where he mimed to "All My Trials."

Dec 17: BBC Channel 4 aired a one-hour documentary on Paul's tour, *From Rio to Liverpool*. It aired in the U.S. Oct 13, 1991 on the Disney Channel as *Paul McCartney: Going Home*. It included footage from Rio, Philadelphia, Glasgow and Liverpool shows, soundchecks, and interviews.

Dec 22: Paul was seen in a pretaped interview and an excerpt from a promo video for "All My Trials" was shown on BBC 1's "Going Live!"

Dec 26: A promo film shot during Paul's concert tour of "Sgt. Pepper's Lonely Hearts Club Band" was seen on MTV in the U.S.

Dec: U.K. videocassette release of *Terry O'Neill: His England, His Ireland*, including an excerpt from Pathé News footage of The Beatles' Nov 20, 1963 Manchester show.

Late that year: *Amusement Business* magazine in the U.S. issued a year-end survey showing that Paul's shows included the top-grossing booking of the year, $3,550,560 for two sellout crowds at the University of California, Berkeley on Mar 31 and Apr 1. He also had the number 3, 6, 10, 11 and 12 rated shows (East Rutherford, Jul 9, 11; Philadelphia, Jul 14, 15; Miami, Apr 14, 15; Washington, D.C., Jul 4, 6; Foxboro, Jul 24, 26).

1991

(rb) Jan 25: Paul performed live before an invited audience of about 200 for a videotaping of MTV's "Unplugged" television series, aired in the U.S. on Apr 3 and

in the U.K. on Aug 18 on Channel 4. Most of the performance was later released on *Unplugged (the Official Bootleg)*.

Jan 28: Paul was featured on "The Live Show," syndicated by Radio Today in the U.S. Paul's "Lennon Medley" was aired. Since the show was distributed on CD, the disc represents something of a rarity in the U.S.: it is the only authorized domestic appearance of the "Lennon Medley" on disc.

Jan: U.S. release of 30-minute videocassette *Greatest Rock 'n Roll Legends—Elvis & The Fab Four*, containing newsreel footage and an interview with author Howard DeWitt.

Middle of Feb: U.S. release of videocassette *Better Late Than Never and Other Stories*, a compilation of Thomas the Tank Engine and Friends stories narrated by Ringo.

Feb 17: George attended Bob Dylan's concert at the Hammersmith Odeon in London and presented Dylan with some flowers. George reportedly attended all eight of Dylan's concerts at this venue.

Feb 18: U.K. reissue of video *Rock 'n' Roll—The Greatest Years: 1971*, first released in 1989.

Feb 20: John posthumously received the Lifetime Achievement Award at the annual Grammy Awards presentations, held at Radio City Music Hall in New York City, by the Academy of Recorded Arts and Sciences. Paul had received the same award on Feb 21, 1990.

Feb: Ringo participated in the shooting of Nils Lofgren's "Valentine" video, although he did not play on that track on Lofgren's *Silver Lining* album.

(b) Mar 3: George took the stage at a convention of George Formby fans held at the Winter Gardens in Blackpool. Armed with a ukulele, he sang Formby's "In My Little Snapshot Album." George also participated in a closing group play-and-singalong on this date and on the previous night.

Mar 4: U.K. CD release of Ringo's album *Ringo*. Released in the U.S. on May 6.

Mar 25: U.K. and U.S. release of Traveling Wilburys' single "Wilbury Twist"/"New Blue Moon" (instrumental), issued only in cassette format in the U.S. Several formats appeared in the U.K., some adding "Cool Dry Place."

Mar 26: U.S. CD release of Ringo's *Bad Boy* album.

(r) Mar: Ringo announced that he had signed a new recording contract with the Private Music label. His announcement came in the form of a videotaped message screened at the National Association of Record Merchandisers in San Francisco. Recording sessions began about this time on the *Time Takes Time* album released May 22, 1992, with tracks produced by Jeff Lynne, Phil Ramone, Don Was and Peter Asher. Sessions concluded in Feb 1992.

■ U.K. videocassette release of *Born to Boogie—The Movie* by PMI; the 1972 film was directed by Ringo. U.S. videocassette and laser disc release of *John Lennon: The Beatles and Beyond* by Fun House.

That spring: Release of the Columbia House Record Club vinyl LP edition of Paul's *Tripping the Live Fantastic*

Highlights! containing the only U.S. release of Paul's live version of "All My Trials." It was also the only U.S. or U.K. vinyl release of *Highlights!*

Apr 3: U.S. telecast of Paul's "Unplugged" appearance, taped Jan 25. The concert telecast was followed by a "Last Word" interview with Paul that included very brief film clips from his 1989–90 world tour. A radio simulcast in the U.S. was preceded by a 15-minute show that included brief interview clips with Paul.

Apr 15: Release of videocassette *Lennon: A Tribute*, filmed at the May 5, 1990 Lennon Liverpool tribute concert. First official release of Ringo's new recording of "I Call Your Name" and of Paul's "P.S. Love Me Do" video.

Apr: It was reported that Ringo performed on one or more tracks for a still-untitled Taj Mahal album produced by Skip Drinkwater for the Private Music label.

■ Ringo appeared as a guest voice and in the form of an animated caricature on the U.S. television series "The Simpsons."

May 1: Paul appeared live via telephone on BBC Radio One's "Simon Bates Show."

(b) May 8–Jul 24: Paul and his band played surprise concerts at the Zeleste Club, Barcelona, Spain (May 8); London's Mean Fiddler Club (May 10); Teatro Tendo, Naples, Italy (Jun 5); Cornwall Coliseum, St. Austell, U.K. (Jun 7); Cliffs Pavilion, Westcliff, U.K. (Jul 19); the Falkoner Theatre, Copenhagen, Denmark (Jul 24). Two sets were performed, one acoustic and one electric, at each show. The last four shows included the completely new McCartney song, "Down to the River."

May 20: U.K. release of Paul's album *Unplugged (The Official Bootleg)*, recorded live Jan 25. Released in the U.S. on Jun 4.

Unplugged (© MPL Communications Ltd.). Paul's preemptive strike at bootleggers; however, this official release of his "Unplugged" TV appearance omitted five songs from the performance.

May 31: Ringo joined Nils Lofgren on stage at the Roxy Club in Los Angeles, playing drums on Lofgren's version of The Beatles' "Anytime at All."

Jun 4: Chips Moman renewed his suit against Ringo in Georgia's Supreme Court, seeking the full $162,600 production costs he had originally sought for the unreleased 1987 album that he produced for Ringo. A Jan 5, 1989 ruling ordered that Ringo pay only $74,354.

Jun 11: U.S. CD releases of George's *Somewhere in England* and *Gone Troppo* albums.

Jun 25: U.S. CD release of George's *Thirty Three & 1/3* and *George Harrison* albums.

Jun 28: *The Paul McCartney Liverpool Oratorio*, composed by Paul and Carl Davis, received its world premiere at the Anglican Cathedral in Liverpool, performed by the Royal Liverpool Philharmonic, with Davis conducting. A second performance took place the following evening. The London premiere took place on Jul 7 at the Royal Festival Hall; the U.S. premiere on Nov 18 at New York's Carnegie Hall, with Paul attending. A recording of the Liverpool premiere was released Oct 7 in the U.K. and Oct 22 in the U.S. A videocassette of the performance was issued in the U.K. Oct 28 and video laser disc on Dec 9. A single, "The World You're Coming Into"/"Tres Conejos" was issued in the U.K. only Sep 20; a second single, "Save the Child"/"The Drinking Song," was released Nov 12 in the U.S. and Nov 18 in the U.K. The Liverpool performance was aired in the U.S. Oct 30 by PBS, and Dec 14 in the U.K. on Channel 4, with an accompanying BBC Radio Two special.

Jul 30: U.S. CD release of *The Concert for Bangla Desh*. Released in the U.K. on Aug 19.

Aug: It was announced that Ringo would no longer appear on the U.S. PBS children's TV series "Shining Time Station."

■ U.S. CD release of John and Yoko's *Two Virgins* album.

(r) Sep 14: Ringo recorded "You Never Know," played over the closing credits in the film *Curly Sue*, and released on the film soundtrack album Nov 26 in the U.S. and Jan 6, 1992 in the U.K.

Sep 18: World premiere of Paul's 1989–90 tour film, *Get Back*, in Hamburg, Germany; U.K. premiere on Sep 19, U.S. Oct. 25. Home video released Oct 21 in the U.K. and Dec 11 in the U.S.

Sep 30: U.K. CD release of Paul's *CHOBA B CCCP*, previously issued only on vinyl in the Soviet Union; CD issued in the U.S. on Oct 29.

Oct 4: BBC 1 aired *Ghosts of the Past*, a documentary film about the development of Paul's *Liverpool Oratorio*. It was shown in the U.S. by PBS, followed by the Oratorio, on Oct 30.

Oct 13: The film *Paul McCartney: Going Home* was aired in the U.S. on the Disney Channel. It originally aired in the U.K. Dec 17, 1990 under the title *From Rio To Liverpool*.

Oct 18: Paul appeared live on London Weekend Television's "Six O'Clock Live" show.

Nov 4–22: George rehearsed with Eric Clapton and his band at Bray Film Studios in Berkshire for his upcoming tour of Japan.

Nov 13: U.S. videocassette and laser disc release *The Beatles: The First U.S. Visit*, issued by Apple, including Feb 1964 "Ed Sullivan Show" and Washington, D.C. concert footage.

Dec 1–18: George toured Japan, backed by Eric Clapton and his band, appearing in Yokohama Arena (Dec 1); Castle Hall, Osaka (Dec 2, 3, 10, 11, 12); International Exhibition Hall, Nagoya (Dec 5); Sun Plaza, Hiroshima (Dec 6); Kokusai Center, Fukuoka (Dec 9); and Tokyo Dome (Dec 14, 15, 17). Songs included "Old Brown Shoe," "Taxman," "Give Me Love," "If I Needed Someone," "Here Comes the Sun," "What Is Life," "Piggies," "I Want to Tell You," "Cloud Nine," "My Sweet Lord," "Cheer Down," "Got My Mind Set on You," "All Those Years Ago," "Something," "Isn't It a Pity," "Love Comes to Everyone," "Devil's Radio," "Fish on the Sand," "Dark Horse," and encores of "While My Guitar Gently Weeps" and "Roll Over Beethoven." Clapton's numbers included "Badge," "Wonderful Tonight," "Pretending" and "Old Love."

Dec 5: CD release of George's albums *Living in the Material World*, *Extra Texture (Read All About It)* and *Dark Horse* in Japan; released worldwide, including U.S. and U.K., Jan 27, 1992.

Dec–Mar 1992: Paul scheduled band rehearsals and recording sessions for this period.

Recording Chronology

This section lists all commercially released Beatles recordings chronologically by recording date. For The Beatles' studio recording sessions as a group, all dates are taken from Lewisohn (1988). The exact dates for many post-Beatles era solo sessions are not known, but the closest approximate date is given for them using available information.

The first official release of each recording in the U.S. and in the U.K. is given, including album title, or B side if the release is a single, followed by the release date. In some cases first official release occurred in another country. Where appropriate, that release information is given before the U.S. and U.K. releases. For those few recordings that were never officially released in either the U.S. or U.K., full information is listed for releases in other countries, including the record label and serial number; these releases also appear in the "Special Releases Discography." For records issued *only* in the U.S. or *only* in the U.K., the phrase "released only in the U.S. (or U.K.)" is used. While many of these records have appeared in other countries, this book is essentially concerned only with U.S. and U.K. releases (except for foreign-only releases). The "released only in" phraseology should be understood in that context. The section also contains many nonmusical Beatles' recordings that have been released commercially on disc, notably interviews and press conferences.

1961

Jun 22–23: The Beatles recorded several songs in Hamburg as a backing group, billed as "The Beat Brothers," for vocalist Tony Sheridan, including "My Bonnie Lies over the Ocean" (released as "My Bonnie" with slow intros recorded in both German and English for separate releases) and "When the Saints Go Marching In" (released as "The Saints"). These two titles were released as a single in Germany in July (Polydor NH 24-673), in the U.K. Jan 5, 1962 and in the U.S. Apr 23, 1962; "Why," released in Germany in Sep on EP *Tony Sheridan & the Beat Brothers* (Polydor EPH-21610M), in the U.K. Jul 12, 1963 on EP *My Bonnie* and in the U.S. Feb 3, 1964 on LP *The Beatles with Tony Sheridan and Their Guests*; "Nobody's Child," released in the U.K. Jan 31, 1964 on a single with "Sweet Georgia Brown" and in the U.S. Jul 6, 1964 on a single with "Ain't She Sweet"; and "Sweet Georgia Brown," released in Germany in Oct 1962 on EP *Ya Ya* (Polydor EPH-21485). The original German release of "Sweet Georgia Brown" differed from all subsequent releases, which contain revised lyrics recorded later by Sheridan that refer to The Beatles. Another rare version, recorded by Sheridan in Dec 1961 without The Beatles, is said to exist (see this title in the "Alternate Versions and Bonus Tracks" section. See also Ingham and Mitsui [1987], a fascinating investigation into the background of this recording. The authors hypothesize that there are three different released versions of the song.). The Beatles also recorded two songs of their own, without Sheridan, "Ain't She Sweet," released in the U.K. on May 29, 1964 as a single with Sheridan's "Take Out Some Insurance on Me Baby," and in the U.S. Jul 6, 1964 as a single with Sheridan's

"Nobody's Child," and "Cry for a Shadow" (an instrumental), released in Sep in Germany on EP *Tony Sheridan & the Beat Brothers* (Polydor EPH-21610M), in the U.K. Jul 12, 1963 on EP *My Bonnie*, and in the U.S. Feb 3, 1964 on LP *The Beatles with Tony Sheridan and Their Guests*. "Ain't She Sweet" and "Cry for a Shadow" were the first formal studio recordings made by The Beatles.

Jun 24: The Beatles again backed Tony Sheridan on his recording of "Take Out Some Insurance on My Baby," released in the U.K. May 29, 1964 as a single with "Ain't She Sweet," and Jun 1, 1964 in the U.S. on single with "Sweet Georgia Brown."

1962

Jan 1: The Beatles recorded the following songs at their London audition for Decca Records: +"Love of the Loved," *"Money (That's What I Want)," *"Sure to Fall," *"Take Good Care of My Baby," *"Three Cool Cats," +"Like Dreamers Do," "Crying, Waiting, Hoping," *"Searchin'," "Till There Was You," *"Memphis," +"Hello Little Girl," "Besame Mucho," *"September in the Rain," "Sheik of Araby," and "To Know Her Is to Love Her," all released Apr 16, 1981 in the U.S. on LPs *Dawn of the Silver Beatles* and *Lightning Strikes Twice*, sold by mail order; Sep 10, 1982 in the U.K. on LP *The Complete Silver Beatles*, which included all but the three Lennon/McCartney compositions (+), as did *The Silver Beatles Volumes 1 and 2*, released Sep 27, 1982 in the U.S., on which seven songs (*) were artificially lengthened by repeating sections of the recordings.

Apr: The Beatles' final recording session with Tony Sheridan took place in Hamburg. They again served as his backing group, but no details about the sessions have survived. It has been speculated that The Beatles backed Sheridan on "Swanee River" or a new version of "Sweet Georgia Brown." See Jun 22, 1961 for more details.

Sep 4: The Beatles recorded "Love Me Do" (Version I 2:22), the first of two released versions of the song. This version features Ringo on drums and was released as a single in the U.K. with "P.S. I Love You" on Oct 5. It was not released in the U.S. until Mar 24, 1980 when it appeared on *The Beatles Rarities* album. A second version was recorded Sep 11.

Sep 11: The Beatles again recorded "Love Me Do" (Version II 2:19), this time with session man Andy White on drums and Ringo on tambourine. This is the more common version, which appeared on LPs and was also substituted for Ringo's version on later reissues of the single. They also recorded "P.S. I Love You," also with White on drums and with Ringo on maraca. Version II of "Love Me Do" was released in the U.K. Mar 22, 1963 on the *Please Please Me* album, while "P.S. I Love You" was first released in the U.K. as a single with "Love Me Do" (Version I) Oct 5. Both songs were first released in the U.S. on the LP *Introducing The Beatles* Jul 22, 1963.

Oct 27: The first known recorded interview with The Beatles was taped and aired the following day on a Cheshire hospital radio station. It was released on a special flexi disc included free with copies of Mark Lewisohn's 1986 book *The Beatles Live!*

Nov 26: The Beatles recorded "Please Please Me" and "Ask Me Why," first released as a single in the U.K. Jan 11, 1963 and in the U.S. Feb 25, 1963. Separate mono and stereo mixes of "Please Please Me" were prepared. The stereo mix, released on the U.K. *Please Please Me* album Mar 22, 1963, is noticeably different toward the end: John flubs a line and then chuckles slightly; that mix was first released in the U.S. on Jan 27, 1964 on a second pressing of *Introducing the Beatles*.

Dec 31: A live Beatles performance at the Star-Club in Hamburg, Germany was recorded on a small, portable recorder by Ted "Kingsize" Taylor of The Dominoes, who were also appearing at the Star-Club. The Beatles numbers included: "I Saw Her Standing There," "Twist and Shout," "Reminiscing," "Ask Me Why," "I'm Gonna Sit Right Down and Cry over You," "Where Have You Been All My Life," "Till There Was You," "Sheila," "Roll over Beethoven," "Hippy Hippy Shake," "Sweet Little Sixteen," "Lend Me Your Comb," "Your Feets Too Big," "Mr. Moonlight," "A Taste of Honey," "Besame Mucho," "Kansas City"/"Hey Hey Hey Hey," "Nothin' Shakin' (But the Leaves on the Trees)," "To Know Her Is to Love Her," "Little Queenie," "Falling in Love Again," *"Be-Bop-a-Lula," *"Hallelujah I Love Her So," "Red Sails in the Sunset," "Everybody's Trying to Be My Baby," "Matchbox," "I'm Talking About You," "Shimmy Shake," "Long Tall Sally," "I Remember You." *Vocal by waiter Horst Fascher.

"Hully Gully" often appears on Star-Club records but is not by The Beatles. On some releases "Reminiscing" is mistitled "Can't Help It/Blue Angel." These songs were released on the LP *The Beatles Live! At the Star Club in Hamburg, Germany: 1962* May 1, 1977 in the U.K. and Jun 13, 1977 in the U.S. Neither record contained all of the recordings, and the lineup on each was different. The recordings were rereleased many times on a variety of records in both countries; see "U.S. Discography" and "U.K. Discography." All 30 cuts were released on the LP *The Beatles: Historic Sessions* in the U.K. on Aug 14, 1981, and they have appeared on CD.

1963

Feb 11: The Beatles recorded the following songs, all released Mar 22 in the U.K. on the *Please Please Me* album and Jul 22 in the U.S. on *Introducing The Beatles*: "There's a Place," "I Saw Her Standing There," "A Taste of Honey," "Do You Want to Know a Secret," "Misery," "Anna (Go to Him)," "Boys," "Chains," "Baby It's You," "Twist and Shout."

Mar 5: The Beatles recorded "Thank You Girl" and "From Me to You," with work completed on Mar 13 and 14. The songs were released as a single on Apr 11 in the U.K. and May 27 in the U.S.

Jul 1: The Beatles recorded "She Loves You" and "I'll Get You," released as a single on Aug 23 in the U.K. and Sep 16 in the U.S.

Jul 18: The Beatles recorded "You Really Got a Hold on Me," "Money (That's What I Want)" and "(There's a) Devil in Her Heart." All were first released in the U.K. Nov 22 on the LP *With The Beatles* and Apr 10, 1964 in the U.S. on LP *The Beatles Second Album*. "Money" received piano overdubs by George Martin at later sessions.

Jul 30: The Beatles recorded the following songs: "It Won't Be Long," "Till There Was You," "Please Mr. Postman," "Roll over Beethoven," all released Nov 22, in the U.K. on LP *With The Beatles* and in the U.S. as follows: "It Won't Be Long" and "Till There Was You": LP *Meet The Beatles* Jan 20, 1964; the other two songs appeared on LP *The Beatles Second Album* Apr 10, 1964.

Sep 11: The Beatles recorded "All I've Got to Do" and "Not a Second Time," released Nov 22 in the U.K. on LP *With The Beatles* and Jan 20, 1964 in the U.S. on LP *Meet The Beatles*.

Sep 12: The Beatles recorded "Don't Bother Me," "Little Child," "Hold Me Tight" and "I Wanna Be Your Man," all released Nov 22 in the U.K. on LP *With The Beatles* and Jan 20, 1964 in the U.S. on LP *Meet The Beatles*. Work on "I Wanna Be Your Man" was finished during sessions on Sep 30 and Oct 3 and 23.

■ During sessions at Abbey Road, The Beatles recorded four messages for Australian radio, three of them directly addressed to Australian D.J. Bob Rogers and one that could be used by any station. One message was released as "Message from England" in 1981 in the U.S. and May 1, 1982 in the U.K. on the Australian LP *The Beatles Talk Downunder*.

Oct 17: The Beatles recorded the first of seven annual Christmas records to be distributed free to members of their fan club on flexi disc. The debut disc was simply titled *The Beatles Christmas Record* and it was released to the fan club in the U.K. only on Dec 6. The U.S. Fan Club did not receive this record until Dec 18, 1970, when it was included with all of the other Christmas recordings on *The Beatles Christmas Album* (U.K. title: *From Then to You*).

- The Beatles recorded "I Want to Hold Your Hand," released as a single Nov 29 in the U.K. and Dec 26 in the U.S. The U.K. B side was "This Boy"; in the U.S. it was "I Saw Her Standing There."
- The Beatles recorded "This Boy," released as a single with "I Want to Hold Your Hand" Nov 29 in the U.K. and on the LP *Meet The Beatles* Jan 20, 1964 in the U.S. The stereo mix was fairly hard to find until the release of the *Past Masters* album.

Dec 10: The Beatles were interviewed prior to their performance at the Gaumont in Doncaster, during which John read his poem "The Neville Club," released in the U.S. in 1985 on LP *The Beatles 'Round the World* and in Dec 1988 in the U.K. on CD *Beatles: Conversation Disc Series*.

1964

Jan 29: Recording of "Can't Buy Me Love" was completed while The Beatles were in Paris. It was released as a single with "You Can't Do That" Mar 16 in the U.S. and Mar 20 in the U.K.

- In Paris, The Beatles recorded "Sie Liebt Dich" and "Komm, Gib Mir Deine Hand," German-language versions of "She Loves You" and "I Want to Hold Your Hand" respectively. They were originally released as a single only in Germany on Mar 5 (Odeon 22671). "Sie Liebt Dich" was released on a single with "I'll Get You" in the U.S. May 21; "Komm, Gib Mir Deine Hand" first appeared in the U.S. Jul 20 on the *Something New* album; both songs were first released in the U.K. on Dec 2, 1978 on the *Rarities* album. Both songs later appeared on the *Past Masters* albums in mono, although the stereo mixes are readily available. "Komm, Gib Mir Deine Hand" used the same instrumental track cut in England for "I Want to Hold Your Hand" on Oct 17, 1963, but "Sie Liebt Dich" was a completely different recording from "She Loves You" and included a new instrumental track.

Early Feb: The Beatles taped an open-end interview, released in the U.S. in late Feb as a promo, *The Beatles Open-End Interview*, a disc that left blank space between The Beatles' answers for radio disc jockeys to dub in a printed list of questions supplied with the record. The D.J. would thus appear to be interviewing The Beatles on the air. The open-end interview also appeared in the U.S. in Mar 1983 on the 7-inch picture disc *Timeless II 1/2* and again in Nov 1984 on the LP *The British Are Coming*. It was released in the U.K. in Oct 1988 on the picture disc LP *The Gospel According To: The Beatles*. The U.S. releases falsely list the recording as an interview with Bob Miles, who simply dubs in the questions and

adds some narration on all three of these releases. During his U.S. radio series "Ringo's Yellow Submarine," Ringo once played the record and dubbed in the questions himself.

Feb 7–16: Several Beatles interviews and press conferences were recorded, including some with Fred Robbins (Feb 7), released in the U.S. in Feb 1984 on cassette only as *Historic Interviews: The Beatles' First Day in America*, issued by Beatlefest; by New York D.J. Murray "The K" Kaufman (Feb 8, 10, 12, 14), released in the U.S. in mid-1964 on EP *The Beatles & Murray the 'K': As It Happened*; by Ed Rudy (Feb 9), released in the U.S. Jun 9 on LP *The Beatles American Tour with Ed Rudy*; in Washington, D.C. by Carroll James (Feb 11), released in the U.S. Feb 1984 on EP *The Carroll James Interview with The Beatles*, sold via mail order; and by Detroit D.J. Lee Alan at the Deauville Hotel, Miami (Feb 16) released on a special disc "A Trip to Miami"/"A Trip to Miami Part 2."

Feb 21: While in Miami, George was interviewed by telephone by Ed Rudy, who released the interview in the U.S. on Jun 9 on his LP *The Beatles American Tour with Ed Rudy*. The interview also appears as an open-end one with Rudy's voice omitted. The most notable example is a version with Miami D.J. Charlie Murdock dubbing in the questions. The Murdock recording and a "Farewell to Miami," recorded by The Beatles for radio station WQAM, were released in 1984 on *The Beatles Talk Downunder (and All Over) Vol. 2* (Australia Raven RVLP-1013) also imported into the U.S. and U.K.

Feb 25: The Beatles recorded "You Can't Do That," released as a single with "Can't Buy Me Love" Mar 16 in the U.S. and Mar 20 in the U.K.

Feb 26: The Beatles recorded "I Should Have Known Better," released Jun 26 in the U.S. and Jul 10 in the U.K. on LP *A Hard Day's Night*.

Feb 27: The Beatles recorded "And I Love Her," "Tell Me Why" and "If If Fell," all released Jun 26 in the U.S. and Jul 10 in the U.K. on LP *A Hard Day's Night*.

Mar 1: The Beatles recorded "I'm Happy Just to Dance with You," "Long Tall Sally" and "I Call Your Name." The first was released Jun 26 in the U.S. and Jul 10 in the U.K. on LP *A Hard Day's Night*; the other two titles were first released in the U.S. Apr 10 on LP *The Beatles Second Album* and Jun 19 in the U.K. on EP *Long Tall Sally*.

Early Mar: Bernice Lumb interviewed John, George, Ringo and Brian Epstein; released in the U.S. and the U.K. in late 1984 on Australian LP *The Beatles Talk Downunder (and All Over) Vol. 2*.

Apr 16: The Beatles recorded "A Hard Day's Night," released Jun 26 in the U.S. and Jul 10 in the U.K. on LP *A Hard Day's Night*.

Apr 18: The Beatles were interviewed by telephone by Art Roberts and Ron Riley of Chicago radio station WLS, released in 1979 on the U.S. promo album *The Ultimate Radio Bootleg, Vol. III*.

Apr 24: The Beatles were interviewed by telephone as they concluded filming *A Hard Day's Night*. The interview was edited into an open-end one and released on the promo *The Beatles Second Open-End Interview*. It was again released in the U.S. in Mar 1990 on a limited edition black-and-white picture disc, *The Beatles Open-End Interview: A Hard Days Night*, as a promotion for the book *Picture Discs of the World Price Guide*.

Apr 25–26: The Beatles were interviewed by Murray "The K," released in the U.S. in mid-1964 on EP *The Beatles & Murray The 'K': As It Happened*. John read his poem "I Sat Belonely" (Apr 26); Gene Loving interviewed George (Apr 25) and all of The Beatles prior to their Wembley show (Apr 26), released Feb 8, 1986 in the U.S. on LP *All Our Loving*.

May 24: Murray "The K" taped an interview with The Beatles at Twickenham studio during *A Hard Day's Night* filming; released in the U.S. in mid-1964 on EP *The Beatles & Murray the 'K': As It Happened*. An interview with Paul, George and Ringo was also recorded and released in Mar 1982 on promo copies of "The Beatles Movie Medley," titled "The Fab Four on Film."

Jun 1: The Beatles recorded the following songs: "Matchbox" and "Slow Down," released Jun 19 in the U.K. on EP *Long Tall Sally* and Jul 20 in the U.S. on LP *Something New*; "I'll Be Back," released Jul 10 in the U.K. on LP *A Hard Day's Night* and Dec 15 in the U.S. on LP *Beatles '65*; and "I'll Cry Instead," recorded in two parts, Section A and Section B, released Jun 26 in the U.S. and Jul 10 in the U.K. on LP *A Hard Day's Night*. Due to different edits of the two sections of this recording, the released version runs 2:04 in the U.S. but only 1:44 in the U.K. The longer edit was also used in the original *A Hard Day's Night* film print but was ultimately cut from the movie. It did surface many years later as the background for a still-photo prologue on the home videocassette release of the film. The shorter U.K. edit also appeared on the stereo edition of the U.S. *Something New* album on Jul 20, where it was incorrectly listed as 2:04. The mono *Something New* contained the longer 2:04 edit.

Jun 2: The Beatles recorded "Any Time at All," "Things We Said Today" and "When I Get Home," released Jul 10 in the U.K. on LP *A Hard Day's Night* and Jun 20 in the U.S. on LP *Something New*.

Jun 5: The Beatles held a press conference and were interviewed on Dutch TV, where they also mimed to released recordings of "She Loves You," "All My Loving," "Twist and Shout," "Roll Over Beethoven," "Long Tall Sally" and "Can't Buy Me Love." The broadcast was aired Jun 8; the recordings were released Jun 9, 1984 in the Netherlands on LP *De Bietels Tussen de Bollen* (*The Beatles Among the Bulbs*), sold via mail order by "Beatles Unlimited," the Dutch Beatles Fan Club.

Jun 6: Instrumentals and audience singalong from The Beatles' evening concert at Blokker Exhibition Hall were recorded. The Beatles' vocals are not actually heard on these recordings, which are taken from the Dutch AVRO-KRO-VARA Radio/TV broadcast tapes and Polygon Movie archives: "I Saw Her Standing There," "I Want to Hold Your Hand," "All My Loving," "She Loves You," "Twist and Shout" and a very short excerpt of "Long Tall Sally"; released in the Netherlands Jun 9, 1984 on *De Bietels Tussen de Bollen*. The album also includes excerpts from "I Saw Her Standing There" from a Polygon Cinema News film and a "Twist and Shout" excerpt from a radio broadcast.

Jun 10–15: Several interviews and press conferences with The Beatles were taped. They were interviewed in Hong Kong by Bob Rogers (Jun 10), press conference and interview by John Edwards in Darwin (Jun 11), interview by Bob Rogers during their flight from Sydney to Adelaide and in Adelaide (Jun 12), interview with Ringo by Garvin Rutherford during the flight from Sydney to Melbourne and Ringo's Melbourne press conference (Jun 14), interview by Allan Lappin and Bob Rogers in Melbourne (Jun 15), Paul's announcement of Ringo's return during the Festival Hall concert in Melbourne (Jun 17) (same announcement appears to have been made at each Melbourne show), interviews at a 22nd birthday party for Paul in Sydney (Jun 18), interviews by Bob Rogers during The Beatles' flight from Sydney to Wellington, New Zealand (Jun 21) and in Wellington (Jun 22), Auckland (Jun 24), in Dunedin (Jun 26), by Tony McArthur in Brisbane (Jun 29), by Bob Rogers and Garvin Rutherford in Sydney (Jul 1); all released on the Australian albums *The Beatles Talk Downunder* (1981) and *The Beatles Talk Downunder (and All Over) Vol. 2* (1984). Other Melbourne interviews (Jun 15) and some recorded with The Beatles at Sydney's Mascot Airport (Jul 1) were released in the U.S. in Jul 1987 on LP *From Britain with Beat*. Excerpts from a Beatles Adelaide press conference (Jun 12) were released only in the U.K. on Mar 1, 1990 by Wax Records on black-and-white picture disc and color vinyl singles.

Aug 11: The Beatles recorded "Baby's in Black," released Dec 4 in the U.K. on LP *Beatles for Sale* and Dec 15 in the U.S. on LP *Beatles '65*.

Aug 14: The Beatles recorded "I'm a Loser" and "Mr. Moonlight," both released Dec 4 in the U.K. on LP *Beatles for Sale* and Dec 15 in the U.S. on LP *Beatles '65*. Takes 1–4 of "Mr. Moonlight" were cut on this date and takes 5–8 on Oct 18; the released version is a mix taken from takes 4 and 8.

Aug 18–20: Several interviews were recorded with The Beatles, including some by Larry Kane upon their airport arrival in San Francisco (Aug 18), a San Francisco press conference (Aug 19), Kane interviews with Paul, Ringo and George (Aug 20), all released in the U.S. Nov 1985 on LP *West Coast Invasion*; and an interview at the Seattle airport (Aug 20), released in the U.S. in Aug 1986 on LP *Things We Said Today*.

■ The Beatles were interviewed and held press conferences on numerous occasions during their North American tour. Excerpts from press conferences were released in the U.S. Nov 23 on *The Beatles Story* and in 1982 on *Like Dreamers Do*. The Beatles were interviewed by Ed Rudy during this tour, and a Beatles concert was also recorded and then overdubbed with other voices and released with the interviews in 1965 on LP *Ed Rudy with New U.S. Tour (The Beatles Great American Tour)*. An interview with The Beatles (incorrectly dated Mar 28) is on *Timeless II 1/2*, released in the U.S. in Mar 1983. Still another interview by Tom Clay was released in the fall of 1964 in the U.S. on the promo *Remember, We Don't Like Them We Love Them* listed as the Official IBBB Interview.

Aug 21: The complete Beatles Seattle press conference, running more than 14 minutes, was released in the U.S. Oct 9, 1989 on a 7-inch vinyl picture disc in a limited edition of 2,000, available only by mail order, titled "Seattle Press Conference." Proceeds went to the John Lennon Memorial Society and the Portland and Seattle Area Food Banks. A 6:52 excerpt from the press conference had also been released in the U.S. in Aug 1986 on the LP *Things We Said Today*, which includes an interview with Ringo taped upon The Beatles' arrival at the Seattle airport.

Aug 22–23: The Beatles held a press conference in Vancouver (Aug 22), released in the U.S. Nov 15, 1978 on LP *Beatle Talk*; often mistakenly listed as an interview by Red Robinson, who merely narrates this record; part of the interview was issued in the U.K. Jun 25, 1982 on *The Beatles Interviews*. John and Ringo were interviewed by Larry Kane (Aug 23), released in the U.S. Dec 1985 on *The Beatles 'Round the World* and in the U.K. in Dec 1988 on CD *The Beatles: Conversation Disc Series*.

Aug 23: The Beatles were recorded live during their first Hollywood Bowl concert: "Things We Said Today," "Roll over Beethoven," "Boys," "All My Loving," "She Loves You" and "Long Tall Sally," were released May 6, 1977 in the U.S. and U.K. on LP *The Beatles at the Hollywood Bowl*. A short bit of "Twist and Shout" was released Nov 23 in the U.S. only on the documentary LP *The Beatles Story*.

Aug 24–25: Jim Steck interviewed John and Dave Hull conducted several short interviews with all of The Beatles in Los Angeles (Aug 24, 25), released Sep 14 in the U.S. on LP *Hear The Beatles Tell All*. Interviews with John (Aug 25) were released in the U.S. in Dec 1965 on LP *The Beatles 'Round the World* and in Aug 1986 on LP *Not a Second Time*.

Aug 27–Sep 2: The Beatles were interviewed during their flight to New York by Larry Kane (Aug 27), who announced their being named recipients of a *Melody Maker* award; interviews were taped with Paul, George and Brian Epstein (Aug 28), with John, Paul and Ringo (Aug 29), with George (Sep 1), and with John and Ringo (Sep 2), all released in the U.S. in Nov 1985 on *East Coast Invasion*. An interview with John and Ringo (Sep 1, listed as Aug 23) was released in the U.S. in Nov 1985 on *West Coast Invasion* (part 1) and in Dec 1985 *The Beatles 'Round the World* (part 2).

Sep 4: Interviews with Paul, George and Ringo, and Paul's impromptu promo introductions for WFUN Radio, Miami, were released in the U.S. in Dec 1985 on *The Beatles 'Round the World* and in the U.K. in Dec 1988 on picture disc CD *Conversation Disc Series*. Another interview with Paul from this date was released in the U.S. in Aug 1986 on LP *Not a Second Time*.

Sep 5–18: Interviews were taped with John (Sep 5, 13), with George, Paul and Ringo (Sep 8), by Jean Morris in Jacksonville, Florida (Sep 11), and interviews and press conference in Dallas, Texas (Sep 18), all released in the U.S. in Aug 1986 on LP *Things We Said Today*. Interviews recorded with George, Paul and Ringo (Sep 17) were released in the U.S. in Jul 1987 on LP *From Britain with Beat*. The Sep 18 press conference was also released in the U.K. in Oct 1990, where it was mistakenly dated as 1966, on the 7-inch color vinyl single "Dallas Press Conference."

Sep 29: The Beatles recorded "I Don't Want to Spoil the Party," released Dec 4 in the U.K. on LP *Beatles for Sale* and Feb 15, 1965 in the U.S. as a single with "Eight Days a Week."

Sep 30: The Beatles recorded "No Reply" and "Every Little Thing," both released Dec 4 in the U.K. on LP *Beatles for Sale*; "No Reply" first appeared in the U.S. Dec 15 on LP *Beatles '65*; first U.S. release of "Every Little Thing" was Jun 14, 1965 on LP *Beatles VI*.

Oct 6: The Beatles recorded "Eight Days a Week," with minor work completed on Oct 18; it was released Dec 4 in the U.K. on LP *Beatles for Sale* and Dec 15, 1965 in the U.S. as a single with "I Don't Want to Spoil the Party."

Oct 8: The Beatles recorded "She's a Woman," released Nov 23 in the U.S. and Nov 27 in the U.K. as a single with "I Feel Fine." Different mono mixes were released in each country.

Oct 18: The Beatles recorded "I Feel Fine," released as a single with "She's a Woman" Nov 23 in the U.S. and Nov 27 in the U.K. Different mono mixes were released in each country.

■ The Beatles recorded (1) "Kansas City"/"Hey Hey Hey Hey," (2) "I'll Follow the Sun," (3) "Everybody's Trying to Be My Baby," (4) "Rock and Roll Music," (5) "Words of Love," all released Dec 4 in the U.K. on LP *Beatles for Sale* and as follows in the U.S.: numbers 2, 3, and 4 Dec 15 on LP *Beatles '65*; numbers 1 and 5 Jun 14, 1965 on LP *Beatles VI*.

Oct 26: The Beatles recorded "Honey Don't" and "What You're Doing," both released Dec 4 in the U.K. on LP *Beatles for Sale*; "Honey Don't" was first released in the U.S. Dec 15 on LP *Beatles '65*, while "What You're Doing" first appeared in the U.S. Jun 14, 1965 on LP *Beatles VI*.

■ The Beatles recorded their second annual Christmas record, *Another Beatles Christmas Record*, distributed free to members of their fan club Dec 18 in the U.S. and U.K.

1965

Feb 15: The Beatles recorded "Ticket to Ride," "Another Girl" and "I Need You"; minor overdubs were added to the latter two songs on Feb 16. "Ticket to Ride" was released as a single with "Yes It Is" Apr 9 in the U.K. and Apr 19 in the U.S.; "Another Girl" and "I Need You" were first released on the LP *Help!* Aug 6 in the U.K. and Aug 13 in the U.S.

Feb 16: The Beatles recorded "Yes It Is," released as a single with "Ticket to Ride" Apr 9 in the U.K. and Apr 19 in the U.S. Until the release of the *Past Masters* albums, the stereo mix of "Yes It Is" was fairly difficult to find.

Feb 17: The Beatles recorded "The Night Before" and "You Like Me Too Much," released Aug 6 in the U.K. on LP *Help!* "The Night Before" was released Aug 13 in the U.S. on LP *Help!* "You Like Me Too Much" first appeared in the U.S. on Jun 14 on LP *Beatles VI*.

Feb 18: The Beatles recorded "You've Got to Hide Your Love Away" and "Tell Me What You See," both released Aug 6 in the U.K. on LP *Help!* "You've Got to Hide Your Love Away" was first released in the U.S. Aug 13 on LP *Help!* while "Tell Me What You See" first appeared in the U.S. Jun 14 on LP *Beatles VI*.

Feb 19: The Beatles recorded "You're Going to Lose That Girl," released Aug 6 in the U.K. and Aug 13 in the U.S. on LP *Help!*

Feb 22: The Beatles were interviewed by Gene Loving on their arrival in the Bahamas, released Feb 8, 1986 in the U.S. on LP *All Our Loving*. Other interviews from this date were released in the U.S. in Dec 1985 on *The Beatles 'Round the World*.

Feb 24–Mar 9: Interviews taped with The Beatles during the Bahamas location filming of *Help!* were released Feb 8, 1986 in the U.S. on LP *All Our Loving*. Interviews conducted by Derek Taylor, then on assignment for Los Angeles radio station KRLA, were released in the U.S. in Nov 1986 on LP *Here There and Everywhere*. Other interviews were released in the U.S. in Apr 1987 on LP *Moviemania!* and in Jul 1987 on LP *From Britain with Beat*. Clips from a number of interviews with The Beatles taped between their filming dates in the Bahamas and the opening of the movie *Help!* were combined to create the promo disc *Help! Open-End Interview*, released in Aug 1965 to promote the film. An unedited version of the interview appeared on a special 7-inch disc, *Help!—Open End Interview '65* issued in Jun 1990 in the U.S. with the third edition of *The Beatles Price Guide for American Records*. The interview is also found on the 1985 Silhouette album, *The Golden Beatles* (later released on CD), with Wink Martindale dubbing in the questions, and on the U.K. CD *The Beatles: The Conversation Disc Series*.

Apr 13: The Beatles recorded "Help!" the title song for their second feature film. It was released as a single with "I'm Down" Jul 19 in the U.S. and Jul 23 in the U.K. Mono and stereo mixes of "Help!" were prepared on Apr

18 for United Artists, but only the mono mixes were used in the film. The mono and stereo mixes released on disc were done on Jun 18, and they contain noticeably different lead vocals by John with slightly different lyrics. The single release contained the mono mix. In the U.K., the two different mixes were released Aug 6 on the stereo and mono editions of the *Help!* LP. In the U.S., while separate stereo and mono editions of the *Help!* LP were released on Aug 13, both actually contained the stereo mix; the "mono" album simply combined the separate tracks from the stereo mix into one. Thus the mono mix appeared in the U.S. only on the single. That mix appeared again in the U.S. on the *The Beatles Rarities* album, released Mar 24, 1980.

May 10: The Beatles recorded "Dizzy Miss Lizzie" and "Bad Boy," released Jun 14 in the U.S. on LP *Beatles VI*; "Dizzy Miss Lizzie" was first released in the U.K. Aug 6 on LP *Help!*; "Bad Boy" did not appear in the U.K. until Dec 10, 1966, when it was released on the LP *A Collection of Beatles Oldies*.

Jun 14: The Beatles recorded "Yesterday," "I'm Down" and "I've Just Seen a Face." Only Paul and George were present during the recording of "Yesterday," which was released Aug 6 in the U.K. on the *Help!* album, and Sep 13 in the U.S. as a single with "Act Naturally"; "I'm Down" was released as a single with "Help!" Jul 19 in the U.S. and Jul 23 in the U.K.; "I've Just Seen a Face" was released Aug 6 in the U.K. on LP *Help!* and Dec 6 in the U.S. on LP *Rubber Soul*.

Jun 15: The Beatles recorded "It's Only Love," released Aug 6 in the U.K. on LP *Help!* and Dec 6 in the U.S. on LP *Rubber Soul*.

Jun 17: The Beatles recorded "Wait" and "Act Naturally," with further overdubs added to "Wait" on Nov 11. "Act Naturally" was released Aug 6 in the U.K. on LP *Help!* and Sep 13 in the U.S. as a single with "Yesterday." "Wait" was released Dec 3 in the U.K. and Dec 6 in the U.S. on LP *Rubber Soul*.

Jun 27: The Beatles held a press conference in Rome, part of which was released in the U.S. in Mar 1983 on the 7-inch picture disc *Timeless II 1/2: The Beatles Around the World*, where it is falsely listed as an interview with someone named Carmela Anna Fortunata, who may or may not have been a real person; it also appeared on the 1984 Australian LP *The Beatles Talk Downunder (and All Over) Vol. 2*, also sold in the U.S. and the U.K.

Jul 2–Aug 31: The following interviews and press conferences with The Beatles were taped: Toronto (Aug 17) and Los Angeles (Aug 29) press conferences, released in the U.S. in Aug 1986 on LP *Things We Said Today*; interviews with D.J. Jerry G. Bishop (Aug 18, 19, 22, 28, 29, 31), released in the U.S. in Aug 1983 on LP *The Beatles Talk with Jerry G. Volume 2*; Madrid interview with Graham Webb (Jul 2), and Minneapolis press conference (Aug 21), released in 1984 on Australian LP *The Beatles Talk Downunder (and All Over) Vol. 2*.

Aug 28: The Beatles and Mal Evans were interviewed by Jerry G. Bishop regarding their visit to the Bel-Air home of Elvis Presley on the previous day, released on the U.S. Aug 1983 on LP *The Beatles Talk with Jerry G. Volume 2.*

Aug 30: The following songs from The Beatles' Hollywood bowl concert were released May 6, 1977 in the U.S. and U.K. on LP *The Beatles at the Hollywood Bowl*: "Twist and Shout," "She's a Woman," "Dizzy Miss Lizzie," "Ticket to Ride," "Can't Buy Me Love," "A Hard Day's Night" and "Help!"

Aug: A short clip of an interview with John and Paul conducted by Capitol's *Teen Set* magazine (previously released on several bootlegs) was released in Mar 1983 on EP *Timeless II 1/2* and again in Nov 1984 on LP *The British Are Coming*; it is incorrectly listed on both records as a Nov 19, 1967 Los Angeles interview. It appeared again in Oct 1988 on the U.K. picture disc *The Gospel According to: The Beatles.*

That summer: An unidentified press conference held during the tour was released in the U.S. in 1982 on LP *Like Dreamers Do.*

Oct 12: The Beatles recorded "Run for Your Life," released on LP *Rubber Soul* Dec 3 in the U.K. and Dec 6 in the U.S.

Oct 13: The Beatles recorded "Drive My Car," released Dec 3 in the U.K. on LP *Rubber Soul* and Jun 15, 1966 in the U.S. on LP *Yesterday and Today.*

Oct 16: The Beatles recorded "Day Tripper," released as a single with "We Can Work It Out" Dec 3 in the U.K. and Dec 6 in the U.S.

Oct 16 & 18: The Beatles recorded "If I Needed Someone," with instrumental tracks completed on the first day and vocals recorded on the second; the song was released Dec 3 in the U.K. on LP *Rubber Soul* and Jun 15, 1966 in the U.S. on LP *Yesterday and Today.*

Oct 18: The Beatles recorded "In My Life," with the piano solo by George Martin overdubbed on Oct 22. The song was released Dec 3 in the U.K. and Dec 6 in the U.S. on LP *Rubber Soul.*

Oct 20: The Beatles recorded "We Can Work It Out," with additional vocal overdubs added on Oct 29. It was released as a single with "Day Tripper" Dec 3 in the U.K. and Dec 6 in the U.S.

Oct 21: The Beatles recorded "Norwegian Wood (This Bird Has Flown)," released Dec 3 in the U.K. and Dec 6 in the U.S. on LP *Rubber Soul.*

Oct 22: The Beatles recorded "Nowhere Man," released Dec 3 in the U.K. on LP *Rubber Soul* and Jun 15, 1966 in the U.S. on LP *Yesterday and Today.*

Nov 3: The Beatles recorded "Michelle," released Dec 3 in the U.K. and Dec 6 in the U.S. on LP *Rubber Soul.*

Nov 4: The Beatles recorded "What Goes On," released Dec 3 in the U.K. on LP *Rubber Soul* and Feb 21, 1966 in the U.S. as a single with "Nowhere Man." The Beatles had actually done this song in the studio as early as Mar 5, 1963, although no recordings of it were made then, and the song had actually been written much earlier.

Nov 8: The Beatles recorded "Think for Yourself," released Dec 3 in the U.K. and Dec 6 in the U.S. on LP *Rubber Soul.* The Beatles were also recorded during rehearsals for "Think for Yourself" and, while never released on disc, a six-second clip of them practicing harmony vocals for the song did appear in the film *Yellow Submarine*, which premiered on Jul 17, 1968. Late in the evening, The Beatles recorded *The Beatles Third Christmas Record*, issued free to members of their fan club on a flexi disc Dec 17.

Nov 10: The Beatles recorded "The Word," released Dec 3 in the U.K. and Dec 6 in the U.S. on LP *Rubber Soul.*

Nov 10–11: The Beatles recorded "I'm Looking Through You," released Dec 3 in the U.K. and Dec 6 in the U.S. on LP *Rubber Soul.* Instrumental tracks were recorded on Nov 10; vocals were added the next day. This was the group's third attempt at recording this song; unreleased versions had been recorded Oct 24 and Nov 6.

Nov 11: The Beatles recorded "Girl" and "You Won't See Me," released Dec 3 in the U.K. and Dec 6 in the U.S. on LP *Rubber Soul.*

1966

Mar 25: An interview with The Beatles was recorded by Tom Lodge of Radio Caroline in the U.K. released on the flexi disc "Sound of the Stars," offered free to readers of *Disc and Music Echo* magazine.

Apr 6–7: The Beatles recorded "Tomorrow Never Knows," with more overdubs added on Apr 22. The song was released Aug 5 in the U.K. and Aug 8 in the U.S. on LP *Revolver.* At this point, the song was known only by the working title "Mark I."

Apr 7–8: The Beatles began recording of "Got to Get You into My Life," with brass and vocal overdubs added on May 18 and other minor overdubs added on Apr 11 and Jun 17. The song was released Aug 5 in the U.K. and Aug 8 in the U.S. on LP *Revolver.*

Apr 11 & 13: The Beatles recorded "Love You To," under the working title "Granny Smith," released Aug 5 in the U.K. and Aug 8 in the U.S. on LP *Revolver.*

Apr 13–14: The Beatles recorded "Paperback Writer," released as a single with "Rain" May 23 in the U.S. and Jun 10 in the U.K.

Apr 14 & 16: The Beatles recorded "Rain," released as a single with "Paperback Writer" May 23 in the U.S. and Jun 10 in the U.K.

Apr 17 & 19: The Beatles recorded "Dr. Robert," released Jun 15 in the U.S. on LP *Yesterday and Today* and Aug 5 in the U.K. on LP *Revolver.*

Apr 21–22: The Beatles recorded "Taxman," released Aug 5 in the U.K. and Aug 8 in the U.S. on LP *Revolver.* Minor overdubs were added on May 16.

Apr 26: The Beatles recorded "And Your Bird Can Sing," released Jun 15 in the U.S. on LP *Yesterday and Today* and Aug 5 in the U.K. on LP *Revolver.*

Apr 27: The Beatles began recording "I'm Only Sleeping," with John's lead vocal added on Apr 29 and more overdubs done on May 5 and 6. The song was released Jun 15 in the U.S. on LP *Yesterday and Today* and Aug 5 in the U.K. on LP *Revolver*. At least four different mixes of "I'm Only Sleeping" were officially released, including different stereo mixes on the U.K. *Revolver* and U.S. *Yesterday and Today* albums; both of these are, in turn, different from the U.S. mono mix. The Fourth mix appeared on the mono U.K. *Revolver* LP and French EP *Strawberry Fields Forever* (Odeon MEO-134). The differences are in the location of the backward guitar effects.

Apr 28–29: The Beatles recorded "Eleanor Rigby." Orchestra recording was done the first day with lead and harmony vocals recorded the second. Paul's lead vocal, however, was completely done over on Jun 6 for the released recording. The song was released Aug 5 in the U.K. on LP *Revolver* and on the same day in the U.S. as a single with "Yellow Submarine."

May 9: Paul and Ringo began recording "For No One," with Paul's lead vocal being added on May 16 and french horn overdubs added on May 19. John and George were not involved in the recording. It was released Aug 5 in the U.K. and Aug 8 in the U.S. on LP *Revolver*.

May 26 & Jun 1: The Beatles recorded "Yellow Submarine," released Aug 5 in the U.K. on LP *Revolver* and on the same date in the U.S. as a single with "Eleanor Rigby."

Jun 2: The Beatles recorded "I Want to Tell You" under the working titles "Laxton's Superb" and "I Don't Know," with a bass overdub added on the following day. It was released Aug 5 in the U.K. and Aug 8 in the U.S. on LP *Revolver*.

Jun 8–9: The Beatles recorded "Good Day Sunshine" under the working title "A Good Day's Sunshine," released Aug 5 in the U.K. and Aug 8 in the U.S. on LP *Revolver*.

Jun 16–17: The Beatles recorded "Here, There and Everywhere," released Aug 5 in the U.K. and Aug 8 in the U.S. on LP *Revolver*. Studio work on the song began on Jun 14, but the released version was done during this two-day period.

Jun 21: The Beatles recorded "She Said She Said," released Aug 5 in the U.K. and Aug 8 in the U.S. on LP *Revolver*.

Late Jun: An interview with The Beatles was recorded in Tokyo and released in late 1984 on the Australian LP *The Beatles Talk Downunder (and All Over) Vol. 2*.

Aug 11: At a press conference in Chicago, John attempted to explain his "bigger than Jesus" remark as reprinted in the U.S. teen magazine *Date Book*. His comments are usually referred to as an "apology." The press conference was released in the fall of 1966 on the one-sided LP *I Apologize*, sold by mail order through a Chicago newspaper. Excerpts from the press conference also appeared on the U.S. LP *Beatle Views*, released Oct 14 by Ring Around the Pops, and on the U.K. LP *The Beatle Interviews*, released on Jun 25, 1982. A short

excerpt was released in the U.K. in Jun 1990 on a 7-inch picture disc, *Vancouver Press Conference/Interviews 64*, where it is mislabeled a 1964 Vancouver press conference.

Aug 12–30: Ken Douglas taped interviews with The Beatles (Aug 12, 16) and with Brian Epstein (Aug 30), and Jim Stagg taped a description of the crowd's wild, sometimes frightening behavior during the group's Cleveland concert (Aug 14), released Oct 14 in the U.S. on LP *Beatle Views*. Part of the Aug 12 interview appeared on *The Gospel According to: The Beatles*, released in the U.K. in Oct 1988. Interviews with spectators were recorded during The Beatles' second Shea Stadium concert (Aug 23) and released later in 1966 on LP *Beatles Blast Described by Erupting Fans*. The Beatles' Seattle press conference (Aug 25) was released Nov 15, 1978 in the U.S. on LP *Beatle Talk* and again in 1982 on LP *Timeless II*. Dates listed on some LPs and heard in Red Robinson's narration are wrong. The press conference is also frequently mistakenly labeled as a "Red Robinson interview," but Robinson merely serves as narrator on the record releases. Separate interviews by Dusty Adams with each of The Beatles were also released on *Timeless II* but under the erroneous date of Aug 20, 1964. The same interviews, in edited form, appear on the 1984 Australian LP *The Beatles Talk Downunder (and All Over) Vol. 2*. Only the Adams interview with John is on LP *The Beatles Interviews*, released in the U.K. Jun 25, 1982. The Beatles' Los Angeles press conference (Aug 28) was released in the U.S. in Nov 1985 on LP *West Coast Invasion*. During their U.S. tour, The Beatles were again interviewed by D.J. Jerry G. Bishop, with excerpts released in the U.S. in Oct 1982 on LP *Beatles Talk with Jerry G.* and in Aug 1983 on *Beatles Talk with Jerry G. Vol. 2*.

Sep 5: "How I Won the War," with a line of dialogue by John from the film soundtrack, released only in the U.K. Oct 13, 1967 as a single with non-Beatles instrumental B side "Aftermath."

Nov 25: The Beatles recorded their fourth annual Christmas record in a basement studio at the London office of their music publisher, Dick James. It was issued free to fan club members on Dec 16 under the title *Pantomime: Everywhere It's Christmas*, and included a number of individually titled segments and the song "Everywhere It's Christmas."

Nov 28–Dec 21: The Beatles recorded John Lennon's "Strawberry Fields Forever" in two series of sessions, each of which yielded a finished version. The released recording included about half of each. The sessions of Nov 28 and 29 yielded the first "final version" (take 7), but recording for the song was begun again on Dec 8 and ran through Dec 21; that period produced a second "final version" (take 26). Lennon liked both versions and couldn't decide which should be released. He requested that George Martin create a mix combining the first part of take 7 and the second part of take 26, even though they were in different keys and tempos. Martin completed this task by speeding up take 7 and slowing down take 26 to match the two as closely as possible. The song was released as a single with "Penny Lane" Feb 13, 1967 in the U.S. and Feb 17, 1967 in the U.K. Separate mono mixes were prepared for the U.K. (mono remix 12) and the U.S. (mono remix 13) on Dec 22 and Dec 29 respectively. The stereo mix released in Germany differs from that released in the U.S. and U.K. in that John's voice is not as slowed down and many of the backward effects and instrumental riffs are in different places. The German mix is also slightly longer.

Dec 6 & 8: The Beatles recorded "When I'm Sixty Four," with backing vocals and other overdubs added on Dec 20 and clarinets on Dec 21. It was released May 26, 1967 in the U.K. and Jun 2, 1967 in the U.S. on LP *Sgt. Pepper's Lonely Hearts Club Band.*

Dec 29–Jan 17, 1967: The Beatles recorded "Penny Lane" during several different sessions. It was released as a single with "Strawberry Fields Forever" Feb 13, 1967 in the U.S. and Feb 17, 1967 in the U.K. Mono mix 11, prepared on Jan 17, 1967, included a piccolo trumpet solo in the coda recorded as an overdub by David Mason of the New Philharmonia. That mix was sent to the U.S. where it was pressed onto promo copies that were distributed to radio stations. The commercially released recording, however, was pressed from mono mix 14, prepared on Jan 25, 1967, on which the trumpet solo ending was mixed out. No stereo mix was prepared until Sep 30, 1971; all commercial releases omit the solo trumpet ending.

1967

Jan 19–Feb 22: The Beatles recorded "A Day in the Life," with most of John's vocal work done on the first day. Paul's solo vocal was cut on Feb 3, after a discarded attempt at it was made on Jan 20. The massive orchestra overdubs were recorded on Feb 10, and the final resounding piano chord was recorded on Feb 22. The song was released on LP *Sgt. Pepper's Lonely Hearts Club Band* May 26 in the U.K. and Jun 2 in the U.S.

Feb 1–2: The Beatles recorded "Sgt. Pepper's Lonely Hearts Club Band," with brass and solo guitar overdubs added on Mar 3 and sound effects on Mar 6. It was released on the album of the same title May 26 in the U.K. and Jun 2 in the U.S.

Feb 8–Mar 29: The Beatles recorded "Good Morning Good Morning" at several sessions during this period. Lennon's lead vocal, his backing vocals with Paul and a lead guitar solo played by Paul were not recorded until Mar 28. That session was preceded by taping of the rhythm track and instrumental overdubs on Feb 8, 16 and Mar 13. The animal sound effects were also assembled on Mar 28, but they were not overdubbed onto the finished recording until the following day. The song was released on the LP *Sgt. Pepper.*

Feb 9: The Beatles recorded "Fixing a Hole" at Regent Sound Studio, the first time they had recorded outside of Abbey Road during their EMI years. Overdubs were added on Feb 21 and the song was released on *Sgt. Pepper.*

Feb 13–14: The Beatles recorded "Only a Northern Song," with work concluded on Apr 20. The song was not released until Jan 13, 1969, when it appeared on LP *Yellow Submarine* in the U.S. Released Jan 17, 1969 in the U.K.

Feb 17–Mar 31: The Beatles recorded "Being for the Benefit of Mr. Kite!" with the rhythm track and Lennon's lead vocal done on Feb 17 and various overdubs added on Feb 20 and Mar 28, 29 and 31. The song was released May 26 in the U.K. and Jun 2 in the U.S. on the LP *Sgt. Pepper.*

Feb 23–Mar 21: The Beatles recorded "Lovely Rita," with rhythm and lead vocal tracks completed on Feb 23 and 24; harmony vocal overdubs were added Mar 7 and George Martin's piano solo on Mar 21. It was released on LP *Sgt. Pepper.*

Mar 1–2: The Beatles recorded "Lucy in the Sky with Diamonds," released on LP *Sgt. Pepper.*

Mar 9–23: The Beatles recorded "Getting Better." Rhythm track and instrumental overdubs were recorded Mar 9 and 10. Ultimately discarded vocals were cut on Mar 21. The final vocals were recorded on Mar 23. The song was released on LP *Sgt. Pepper.*

Mar 15–Apr 4: George recorded "Within You Without You" with a number of outside musicians. No other Beatle took part in the sessions, which occurred on Mar 15 and 22 and Apr 3 and 4. The song was released on LP *Sgt. Pepper.*

Mar 17 & 20: The Beatles recorded "She's Leaving Home," released on LP *Sgt. Pepper.* No Beatles play instruments on this recording. The only instruments, strings, were recorded Mar 17. Paul's lead vocal and John's backing vocals were cut on Mar 20.

Mar 29–30: The Beatles recorded "With a Little Help form My Friends," released on LP *Sgt. Pepper.*

Apr 1: The Beatles recorded "Sgt. Pepper's Lonely Hearts Club Band (reprise)," completely different from the version that opened LP *Sgt. Pepper,* and released as the penultimate track on that album.

Apr 21: The edit pieces comprising the gibberish heard in the runout groove at the end of the U.K. pressing of LP *Sgt. Pepper* were assembled and added to the LP masters. A high-pitch dog whistle was also added just prior to the runout groove. Both were eliminated from the U.S. release and from subsequent U.K. reissues, but they were restored to the 1987 CD release and the accompanying cassette releases and, in the U.S., a vinyl LP.

Apr 25–May 3: The Beatles recorded "Magical Mystery Tour," the title song for a planned television special. An additional vocal line by Paul was overdubbed during final remixing on Nov 7, and the song was released Nov 27 in the U.S. on LP *Magical Mystery Tour* and Dec 8 in the U.K. on a double EP of the same title. The version used on the film soundtrack was different from the one released on disc.

May 11: The Beatles recorded "Baby, You're a Rich Man," released as a single with "All You Need Is Love" Jul 7 in the U.K. and Jul 17 in the U.S. The recording session was held at Olympic Sound Studios, not at Abbey Road. Mick Jagger attended the session and may have participated in some way on the recording (Lewisohn 1988, p. 111).

May 12: The Beatles recorded "All Together Now," released Jan 13, 1969 in the U.S. and Jan 17, 1969 in the U.K. on LP *Yellow Submarine*.

May 17: The Beatles recorded instrumental rhythm tracks and sound effects in five separate parts for "You Know My Name (Look Up the Number)." They continued these sessions on Jun 7 and 8, with Brian Jones of The Rolling Stones adding alto saxophone on Jun 8. One master take (take 30) was compiled and a rough mono mix was done on Jun 9, at which point the song ran 6:08. Nearly two years would pass before John and Paul were to add their vocals, on Apr 30, 1969, at which time more effects were also added, some with the help of Mal Evans. Three new mono mixes were then made, but the song still ran 6:08 and was shelved until Lennon edited one mix down to 4:19 on Nov 26, 1969, planning to release it as a Plastic Ono Band single with the still-unreleased "What's the New Mary Jane" as APPLES 1002. Copies of the single were pressed, but the record was never released. "You Know My Name" eventually appeared as the B side on the "Let It Be" single, released Mar 6, 1970 in the U.K. and Mar 11, 1970 in the U.S. Exact authorship of the song is vague. It seems to have been conceived by John, with substantial help from Paul, who once claimed to be proud to have written the song. The song has never been released in stereo, and there is no record of a stereo mix ever having been made.

May 25–Jun 2: The Beatles recorded "It's All Too Much" at De Lane Lea Music Recording Studios under the working title "Too Much." Most of the work was done on May 25 and 26, with brass and woodwind overdubs completed on Jun 2. The song was released on LP *Yellow Submarine* Jan 13, 1969 in the U.S. and Jan 17, 1969 in the U.K.

Jun 14–25: The Beatles recorded "All You Need Is Love," originally intended only as the group's contribution to the worldwide satellite television special "Our World," broadcast live on Jun 25. Shortly before the actual broadcast, however, it was decided also to release the song as a single. Much recording was done between Jun 14 and the actual broadcast; the entire rhythm track was completed and preliminary vocals and orchestra tracks recorded as well. On the evening of the telecast, The Beatles recorded Lennon's lead vocal, bass, lead guitar solo in the middle eight, and the orchestra live over the prerecorded rhythm track. Following the broadcast, some of Lennon's vocal was rerecorded and Ringo's opening snare drum roll was overdubbed. A mono mix was prepared and released as a single with "Baby You're a Rich Man" Jul 7 in the U.K. and Jul 17 in the U.S. A different mono mix, running 13 seconds

shorter than the single at 3:44, was used in the *Yellow Submarine* movie. A stereo mix was released on LP *Yellow Submarine*.

Aug 22–23: The Beatles recorded "Your Mother Should Know" at Chappell Recording Studios, released Nov 26 in the U.S. on LP *Magical Mystery Tour* and Dec 8 in the U.K. on EP *Magical Mystery Tour*. Final overdubs (Paul: bass; John: organ) were added on Sep 29. The Beatles recorded a complete remake of the song (11 takes) on Sep 16 at Abbey Road, but those recordings were not released.

Sep 5–6: Recording of "I Am the Walrus" was essentially completed. Overdubs were added on Sep 27 and the radio sound effects, including lines from a broadcast of *King Lear*, added during final mono mixing on Sep 29. The released version was an edit of two different mono mixes. The stereo mix, prepared on Nov 6 and 17, becomes mono from the point where the radio effects begin until the end of the song, since that part was recorded only in mono through a live radio feed. The song was released as a single with "Hello Goodbye" Nov 24 in the U.K. and Nov 27 in the U.S., where it was also released on the same day on LP *Magical Mystery Tour*.

Sep 6–7: Recording of "Blue Jay Way" was essentially completed, with cello and tambourine overdubs added on Oct 6. The song was released Nov 27 in the U.S. and Dec 8 in the U.K. on LP *Magical Mystery Tour* and EP respectively.

Sep 8: The Beatles recorded "Flying," an instrumental with a chanting vocal background, originally titled "Aerial Tour Instrumental." Additional overdubs were added on Sep 28, including some instrumentals and various sound effects. The song ran 9:36 before being edited down to 2:14 for release on the *Magical Mystery Tour* LP and EP, released Nov 27 in the U.S. and Dec 8 in the U.K. respectively.

Sep 25–27: The Beatles recorded "The Fool on the Hill," with some additional flute overdubs (with no Beatles playing) added on Oct 20. The song was released Nov 27 in the U.S. and Dec 8 in the U.K. on the *Magical Mystery Tour* LP and EP respectively. Although the song ran as long as 4:25 at one point, it was edited down drastically to 2:57 for release.

Oct 2–Nov 2: The Beatles recorded "Hello, Goodbye" under the working title "Hello Hello," released as a single with "I Am the Walrus" Nov 24 in the U.K. and Nov 27 in the U.S. Recording sessions for this song began with the rhythm track cut on the first day, guitar and vocal overdubs on Oct 19, viola overdubs (with no Beatles playing) on Oct 20, bass guitar overdubs on Oct 25 and Nov 2.

Oct: The Beatles recorded "Jessie's Dream," instrumental music used in *The Magical Mystery Tour* film but never released on record. The recordings were done privately, not at EMI's Abbey Road studio, and no recording details are available.

Nov 22–23: George worked on the following English-titled compositions for the film score of *Wonderwall*, released on the soundtrack LP *Wonderwall Music* on Nov 1, 1968 in the U.K. and Dec 2, 1968 in the U.S.: "Cowboy Music," "On the Bed," "Wonderwall to Be There," "Red Lady Too," "In the Park," "Drilling a Home," "Guru Vandana," "Greasy Legs" and "Dream Scene." He also recorded sound effects and songs with the working titles "India" and "Swordfencing," both of which would later be changed. No such titles were ever released, but the first one is doubtless the source of longstanding erroneous reports of an unreleased Beatles song called "India." George was also conducting sessions at this time at De Lane Lea Studios, and another session was held at Abbey Road on Jan 5, 1968, just before he left for India on Jan 7, 1968 where recording of Indian titles would commence on Jan 9.

Nov 28: The Beatles recorded their annual Christmas disc, their fifth, including the original song "Christmas Time (Is Here Again)," issued free to the fan club Dec 15. The fan club disc itself only contained short excerpts of the song, but the full version runs 6:37 and has appeared on some bootlegs.

1968

Jan 9–17: George recorded the following Indian titles for the *Wonderwall Music* soundtrack LP at EMI's Bombay, India recording studio; the album was completed back at Abbey Road on Jan 30: "Party Seacombe," "Love Scene," "Crying," "Fantasy Sequins," "Glass Box," "Singing Om," "Microbes," "Tabla and Pakavaj," "Skiing" and "Gat Kirwani." The album was released Nov 1 in the U.K. and Dec 2 in the U.S.

Jan 12: George recorded the instrumental tracks for "The Inner Light" in Bombay, India; vocals were done at Abbey Road Studios on Feb 6 and 8. It was released as a single with "Lady Madonna" Mar 15 in the U.K. and Mar 18 in the U.S. Prior to the release of *Past Masters*, the stereo version of the song was fairly difficult to find.

Feb 3 & 6: The Beatles began recording "Lady Madonna," released as a single with "The Inner Light" Mar 15 in the U.K. and Mar 18 in the U.S.

Feb 4: The recording of "Across the Universe" was done with minor overdubs completed on Feb 8. Backing vocals were provided by Lizzie Bravo and Gayleen Pease, two Beatles fans recruited spontaneously from the front steps of EMI's studio. Some bird sound effects were added and a stereo mix prepared on Oct 2, 1969, with no involvement by The Beatles; that mix was released only in the U.K. on Dec 12, 1969 on the charity LP *No One's Gonna Change Our World*, issued by the World Wildlife Fund. The same mix was later released on the U.K. and U.S. *Rarities* albums and on the *Past Masters* album. The same recording of "Across the Universe" was completely remixed, again in stereo, by Glyn Johns on Jan 5, 1970 for the second of two versions of the unreleased *Get Back* album, with all backing vocals and the bird sound effects omitted. The same recording was again remixed, this time by Phil Spector, on Mar 23, 1970, and orchestra and choral overdubs were added on Apr 1, 1970; Lennon's vocal was also slowed down noticeably by Spector, whose stereo mix was released on the *Let It Be* album May 8, 1970 in the U.K. and May 18, 1970 in the U.S. Although the two released versions were once thought to be completely different recordings, The Beatles recorded "Across the Universe" only once, and all releases are taken from that recording.

Feb 11: The Beatles recorded "Hey Bulldog," released on LP *Yellow Submarine* Jan 13, 1969 in the U.S. and Jan 17, 1969 in the U.K. This song was written and recorded specifically for the *Yellow Submarine* film, but most prints of that film omitted the number.

May 30–Jun 21: The Beatles recorded "Revolution 1" (Version II), released on *The Beatles* (aka the "*White Album*") Nov 22 in the U.K. and Nov 25 in the U.S. Specific session dates were May 30 and 31 and Jun 4 and 21. The first day's recording yielded a take lasting 10:17, including Lennon's first, unreleased vocal. The final six minutes of that take ended up on the bizarre "Revolution 9" track. Despite the fact that this version of "Revolution" was recorded first, it is labeled "Version II" since it was released nearly three months after Version I, which appeared a a single in Aug 1968.

- At several sessions during this period, John and Yoko Ono assembled a variety of sound effects, tape loops and other audio items into the wild "Revolution 9," released on *The Beatles*. The only other member of the group involved in this project was George, who made a relatively minor contribution to the final track including some spoken lines. The final six minutes from an unreleased 10:17 take of "Revolution 1," recorded on May 30, were used on "Revolution 9." Other sessions during which the final track was assembled took place on Jun 6, 10, 11, 20 and 21.

Late May: "Two Virgins" (14:02) and "Two Virgins" (15:00), recorded by John and Yoko, both released Nov 11 in the U.S. and Nov 29 in the U.K. on LP *Unfinished Music No. 1: Two Virgins*.

Jun 5–6: The Beatles recorded "Don't Pass Me By," with final overdubs added on Jul 12 and the introduction taped as an edit piece on Jul 22; the song was released on *The Beatles*. Ringo and Paul had been working on this song as early as 1963 and mentioned it during a BBC Radio interview in Jul 1964. Although the song's final title was mentioned on those earlier dates, it proceeded under two working titles in Jun 1968: "Ringo's Tune" and "This Is Some Friendly."

- Kenny Everett recorded an interview with The Beatles at Abbey Road during sessions for "Don't Pass Me By." The interview was heard in edited form on "The Kenny Everett Show" on Jun 9 on U.K. radio. Most of the interview was commercially released by Apple only in Italy on one of four EPs issued as a set, titled *Una Sensazionale Intervista Con I Beatles* (*A Sensational Interview with The Beatles*) (Apple DPR-108). The full interview, running nearly 13 minutes, was released in the U.S. in Jul 1985 on the LP *The Golden Beatles* and in the U.K. on Jan 30, 1987 on the LP *The Beatles:*

Interviews II. During the interview, John sang a short improvisational version of "Cottonfields."

Jun 11: Paul recorded "Blackbird" alone; it was released on LP *The Beatles*.

Jun 27–Jul 23: The Beatles recorded "Everybody's Got Something to Hide Except Me and My Monkey," released on *The Beatles*. Specific session dates were Jun 27 and Jul 1 and 23. The Beatles also rehearsed the song on Jun 26.

Jul 8–15: The Beatles recorded "Ob-La-Di, Ob-La-Da," released on *The Beatles*. Specific session dates included Jul 8, 9, 11 and 15, with an original and two remake versions being taped and Paul's released lead vocal cut on the final date.

Jul 10–12: The Beatles recorded "Revolution" (Version I), released as a single with "Hey Jude" on Aug 26 in the U.S. and Aug 30 in the U.K. This recording is very different from the version released on *The Beatles*, called "Revolution 1" (Version II), which had been recorded during May and Jun. While the single version was originally released only in mono, a stereo mix of the recording was released Feb 26, 1970 in the U.S. and May 11, 1979 in the U.K. on the *Hey Jude* LP (aka *The Beatles Again*). Despite the fact that this version of "Revolution" was recorded second, it is labeled "Version I" since it was released nearly three months before the album version.

Jul 16 & 18: The Beatles recorded "Cry Baby Cry," released on *The Beatles*. They had begun work on the song on Jul 15, but actual recording took place on these two days.

Jul 22: The Beatles recorded "Good Night" for *The Beatles*.

Jul 31– Aug 1: The Beatles recorded "Hey Jude" at Trident Studios, released as a single with "Revolution" Aug 26 in the U.S. and Aug 30 in the U.K. Work on the song had taken place on Jul 29 and 30, but the released version was done during this two-day period. Unreleased versions from Jul 29 included complete takes running 6:21, 4:30 and 5:25.

Aug 9 & 20: Paul recorded "Mother Nature's Son" for *The Beatles*.

Aug 13 & 21: The Beatles recorded "Sexy Sadie" for *The Beatles*. The song had once tentatively been titled "Maharishi," and The Beatles had worked on it on Jul 19, with the first "official" recording cut on Jul 24. The first day's session yielded unreleased takes running from 5:36 to 8:00, with 23 more unreleased takes cut on Jul 24.

Aug 13–14: Except for an edit piece added on Aug 20, The Beatles recorded "Yer Blues" during these two days for *The Beatles*.

Aug 15: The Beatles recorded "Rocky Raccoon" for *The Beatles*.

Aug 20: Paul recorded "Wild Honey Pie," little more than an improvisation, for *The Beatles*.

Aug 22–23: The Beatles recorded "Back in the USSR," without Ringo, for *The Beatles*.

Aug 28–30: The Beatles recorded "Dear Prudence" at Trident Studios for *The Beatles*.

Sep 5–6: The Beatles recorded "While My Guitar Gently Weeps" for *The Beatles*, with Eric Clapton adding a guitar solo overdub on Sep 6. An acoustic run-through was taped on Jul 25 and a first attempt at the recording was begun on Aug 16, with overdubs added on Sep 3 and 5, at which point George decided to do the song over completely.

Sep 9–10: The Beatles recorded "Helter Skelter" for *The Beatles*. The mono and stereo mixes, prepared on Sep 17 and Oct 12 respectively, are quite different. The longer stereo mix (4:29) includes a fade-down and -up concluding with Ringo shouting "I've got blisters on my fingers!" which is missing on the shorter (3:36) mono mix.

Sep 11–Oct 10: The Beatles recorded "Glass Onion" for *The Beatles* with specific sessions on Sep 11, 12, 13, 16, 26 (sound effects overdubs) and Oct 10.

Sep 16–17: The Beatles, minus George, recorded "I Will" for *The Beatles*.

Sep 18: The Beatles recorded "Birthday" for *The Beatles*. Pattie Boyd Harrison and Yoko Ono contributed some of the backing vocals on this track.

Sep 19–20: The Beatles recorded "Piggies" for *The Beatles*, with string overdubs added on Oct 10.

Sep 23–25: The Beatles recorded "Happiness Is a Warm Gun" for *The Beatles*. The song's original working title was "Happiness Is a Warm Gun in Your Hand."

Oct 1–4: The Beatles recorded "Honey Pie" at Trident Studios for *The Beatles*.

Oct 3–14: The Beatles recorded "Savoy Truffle" for *The Beatles* with sessions on Oct 3 and 5 at Trident Studios, and Oct 11 and 14 overdub sessions at Abbey Road.

Oct 4–5: The Beatles recorded "Martha My Dear" at Trident Studios for *The Beatles*. While session records cannot firmly establish whether Paul recorded the song alone, such appears to be the case.

Oct 7–9: The Beatles recorded "Long Long Long" under the working title "It's Been a Long Long Long Time," released on *The Beatles*.

Oct 8: The Beatles recorded "I'm So Tired" and "The Continuing Story of Bungalow Bill" (with a line by Yoko Ono), released on *The Beatles*.

Oct 9–10: Paul recorded "Why Don't We Do It in the Road," released on *The Beatles*. The only other Beatle involved in this recording was Ringo, who added a drum track overdub on Oct 10.

Oct 13: John recorded "Julia" alone for *The Beatles*, the final track to be recorded for that marathon double album.

Nov 4–25: John and Yoko recorded "No Bed for Beatle John," "Baby's Heartbeat," "Two Minutes of Silence," "Radio Play" all released May 9, 1969 in the U.K. and May 26, 1969 in the U.S. on LP *Unfinished Music No. 2: Life with the Lions*.

Nov: Each of The Beatles separately recorded his part of *The Beatles 1968 Christmas Record*. All of the recording was done outside of Abbey Road. Tiny Tim recorded "Nowhere Man" while visiting George in the U.S. The separate tracks were edited for release by disc jockey Kenny Everett, and the disc was issued to fan club members on Dec 20.

1969

Jan 2–16: The Beatles were filmed during rehearsal sessions at Twickenham Studios. The only recording ever officially released from these sessions was John's remark, "Queen says 'no' to pot-smoking FBI," which can be heard at the start of "For You Blue" on the *Let It Be* album, released May 8, 1970 in the U.K. and May 18, 1970 in the U.S.

Jan 21: Ringo was interviewed by David Wigg for BBC Radio One's "Scene and Heard," aired on Jan 25; released Jul 30, 1976 in the U.K. and 1978 in the U.S. on LP *The Beatles Tapes*.

Jan 24: The Beatles recorded "Maggie Mae," a spontaneous 38-second rendition that was released on *Let It Be*.

■ John's vocal ad lib, "That was 'Can You Dig It' by Georgie Wood, and now we'd like to do 'Hark the Angels Come . . .'" recorded during this date's sessions, was released on the *Let It Be* album where it was spliced onto the end of the brief excerpt of "Dig It," recorded Jan 26, that appears on that album.

Jan 25: The Beatles recorded "For You Blue" under the working title "George's Blues," released on *Let It Be*.

Jan 26: The Beatles recorded "Dig It," released on *Let It Be*. Although this track ran 12:25 in its entirety, only about 50 seconds of it appeared on the released album.

Jan 27: John's ad-lib remark "Sweet Loretta Fart she thought she was a cleaner but she was a frying pan" from this date's recording session was released on *Let It Be* where it was spliced onto the beginning of "Get Back."

Jan 27–28: The Beatles recorded "Get Back," released as a single with "Don't Let Me Down" Apr 11 in the U.K. and May 5 in the U.S. Although there were once thought to be two completely different released versions of this song (Lewisohn 1988), there really is only one. The respective mixes released on the single (Version I) and on the *Let It Be* album (Version II) differ noticeably since the album version was remixed by Phil Spector prior to release while the single was not. The original ending was omitted when the song faded out early on both releases, but that ending was used during the closing credits in the film *Let It Be*. It also closed out the unreleased *Get Back* album mixed by Glyn Johns. The guitar solo on "Get Back" was done by John, rather than by usual lead guitarist George. The Beatles recorded several takes of "Get Back" on both of these dates; it is not clear on which date the released version was recorded.

Jan 28: The Beatles recorded "Don't Let Me Down," released as a single with "Get Back" Apr 11 in the U.K. and May 5 in the U.S.

Jan 30: The Beatles' rooftop concert atop their Apple building took place and lasted 42 minutes, about half of it serving as the end of the *Let It Be* film. "I've Got a Feeling," "The One After 909" and "Dig a Pony" from the concert were all released on LP *Let It Be*.

Jan 31: The Beatles recorded "Two of Us" under the working title "On Our Way Home" and "The Long and Winding Road," both released on *Let It Be*. "The Long and Winding Road" underwent overdubbing on Apr 1, 1970.

■ The Beatles recorded "Let It Be" with various overdubs added on Apr 30 and Jan 4, 1970, the last recording session they ever held as a group. While two different mixes of "Let It Be" were officially released, they were both made from the same recording. The first mix (Version I) was released as a single with "You Know My Name (Look Up the Number)" on Mar 6, 1970 in the U.K. and Mar 11, 1970 in the U.S. A different mix (Version II), prepared by Phil Spector, was released on *Let It Be*.

Early that year: George recorded an instrumental album at his home, largely using a new Moog synthesizer. He released the recordings on the album *Electronic Sound* May 9 in the U.K. and May 26 in the U.S. The only titles on the album were "No Time or Space" and "Under the Mersey Wall."

Feb 22–Aug 11: The Beatles recorded "I Want You (She's So Heavy)," released Sep 26 and Oct 1 in the U.K. and U.S. respectively on the LP *Abbey Road*. The recording was a very complex one, including edits of different mixes. Recording began on Feb 22 at Trident Studios with an edit of three different takes (9, 20 and 32) assembled the following day. John and George added guitar overdubs at Abbey Road on Apr 18, a reduction mixdown was made, called take 1, and more overdubs were added to that. Still more overdubs were added on Apr 20. On Aug 8 John added effects and synthesizer overdubs to the original Trident master, and on Aug 20 a final master was created for release by editing together parts of different stereo remixes that were made separately from the Apr 18 take 1, and from the Trident master. Thus the released version comprised parts of both "final" versions.

Mar 1: "The Hunting Scene," a short bit of dialogue by Ringo and Peter Sellers from film *The Magic Christian*, was released Feb 11, 1970 in the U.S. and Apr 10, 1970 in the U.K. on soundtrack LP *The Magic Christian*.

Mar 2: John and Yoko recorded "Cambridge 1969" (26:30) live at Lady Mitchell Hall, Cambridge, England; released May 9 in the U.K. and May 26 in the U.S. on LP *Unfinished Music No. 2: Life with the Lions*. This is really a nonstop Yoko screaming track with no real sign of John.

Mar 4: George was interviewed by David Wigg for BBC Radio One's "Scene and Heard," aired in two parts on Mar 8 and 12, and a small part of which was released on LP *The Beatles Tapes* Jul 30, 1976 in the U.K. and in 1978 in the U.S.

Mar 26: During their bed-in, John and Yoko recorded "Amsterdam," consisting of conversations with the press and the following titles: "John, John (Let's Hope for Peace," "Goodbye Amsterdam, Goodbye," "Bed Peace" and "Good Night" (originally done by The Beatles for the *White Album*"), released on LP *Wedding Album* Oct 20 in the U.S. and Nov 7 in the U.K.

Apr 14: John and Paul recorded "The Ballad of John and Yoko," released as a single with "Old Brown Shoe" on May 30 in the U.K. and Jun 4 in the U.S.

Apr 16 & 18: The Beatles recorded "Old Brown Shoe," released as a single with "The Ballad of John and Yoko" May 30 in the U.K. and Jun 4 in the U.S. George had taped a demo of the song at Abbey Road on Feb 25; and another demo taped at the start of the Apr 16 sessions was erased when the final recording commenced.

Apr 20–Aug 11: The Beatles recorded "Oh! Darling," released on *Abbey Road* on Sep 26 in the U.K. and Oct 1 in the U.S. The specific session dates included Apr 20 (rhythm track), Jul 23 (Paul's lead vocal), Aug 8 (lead guitar and tambourine overdubs) and Aug 11 (harmony vocal overdub). Paul made several unsuccessful attempts at the lead vocal during this period as well.

Apr 22: John and Yoko recorded the 22-minute track "John and Yoko" in Studio 2 at Abbey Road, released on their LP *Wedding Album* Oct 20 in the U.S. and Nov 7 in the U.K.

Apr 26–Jul 18: The Beatles recorded "Octopus's Garden," released on LP *Abbey Road*. Specific session dates included Apr 26 and 29 and Jul 17 and 18.

Apr 30: John and Paul added vocals and additional sound effects to "You Know My Name (Look Up the Number)." The rhythm tracks and many sound effects had been recorded between May 17 and Jun 9, 1967. It was released as a single with "Let It Be" on Mar 6, 1970 in the U.K. and Mar 11, 1970 in the U.S. See May 17, 1967 for additional details.

May 2–Aug 15: The Beatles recorded "Something" for the *Abbey Road* album. Specific session dates included May 2 and 5 (at Olympic Sound Studio), Jul 11 and 16 and Aug 15. George had recorded a demo of the song on Feb 25 and 13 unreleased takes on Apr 16 before beginning the song completely anew with the May 2 remake session.

May 6–Jul 31: The Beatles recorded "You Never Give Me Your Money," released on LP *Abbey Road*. Specific session dates included May 6 (at Olympic Sound Studios) and Jul 1, 11, 15 and 31. Sound effects for the crossfade into "Sun King" were added on Aug 14.

May 8: John was interviewed by David Wigg for BBC Radio One's "Scene and Heard," aired in two parts May 11 and 18, and part of which was released Jul 30, 1976 in the U.K. and in 1978 in the U.S. on LP *The Beatles Tapes*.

May 29: John was interviewed by phone by Tom Campbell and Bill Holley of KYA Radio, San Francisco during his Montreal bed-in. Issued on a single "The KYA 1969 Peace Talk" by the station.

Jun 1: John, Yoko and many others recorded "Give Peace a Chance" live at the Queen Elizabeth Hotel, Montreal (credited to "Plastic Ono Band"); released Jul 4 in the U.K. and Jul 7 in the U.S. as a single with Ono's "Remember Love."

Jul 2: Paul recorded "Her Majesty," released on LP *Abbey Road*. While the song was initially eliminated from the album, when it was edited out of the early album mix its final chord was accidentally left on at the beginning of "Polythene Pam," which it would have preceded on the album at that point. "Her Majesty" appeared, with its final chord missing, at the end of *Abbey Road* by accident; the "omitted" track was haphazardly spliced onto the end of the same early album mix. When The Beatles heard it during a playback, after what they thought was the end of the album, they decided to leave the song there on the released version. The distinctive electric guitar chord that precedes "Her Majesty" on the album was also placed there by accident. It was the original *final* guitar chord from "Mean Mr. Mustard," which was accidentally cut out with "Her Majesty" when that song was removed from its original place in the album lineup.

Jul 2–Aug 15: The Beatles, without John, recorded "Golden Slumbers/Carry That Weight," released on LP *Abbey Road*. The song, which was recorded as one and is not an edit of two separate recordings, was originally known only as "Golden Slumbers," with the title and some of the lyrics taken from the work of Thomas Dekker, a 16th-century British poet whose original version had later been set to music as a nursery rhyme. "Carry That Weight" was a completely new creation of Paul's. Specific session dates included Jul 2, 3, 4, 30 and 31 and Aug 15.

Jul 7–Aug 19: The Beatles recorded "Here Comes the Sun," released on LP *Abbey Road*. Specific session dates included Jul 7, 8 and 16 and Aug 6, 11, 15 and 19.

Jul 9–Aug 6: The Beatles recorded "Maxwell's Silver Hammer," released on LP *Abbey Road*. Specific recording dates included Jul 9, 10 and 11 and Aug 6.

Jul 21–30: The Beatles recorded "Come Together" for LP *Abbey Road*, with specific session dates including Jul 21, 22, 23, 25, 29 and 30.

Jul 23–Aug 18: The Beatles recorded "The End" for LP *Abbey Road*. Specific session dates included Jul 23, during which Ringo recorded the only drum solo of his Beatles career, and Aug 5, 7, 8, 15 and 18. The track was initially known only as "Ending" and was specifically intended to complete the "Golden Slumbers/Carry That Weight" segment of the album. "The End" proved to be an ironic title indeed, representing the final song on the final Beatles album, if one considers "Her Majesty," which actually follows "The End," as an afterthought.

Jul 24–29: The Beatles recorded "Sun King/Mean Mr. Mustard" for LP *Abbey Road* as one recording, not an edit of two separate ones. The song began under the working title "Here Comes the Sun King" and had apparently originated as two separate John Lennon compositions.

Jul 25–30: The Beatles recorded "Polythene Pam," and "She Came in Through the Bathroom Window" as one, single recording, released on LP *Abbey Road*. This two-title track included one Lennon and one McCartney composition, one of the few examples of actual collaboration by the two; "A Day in the Life" and "I've Got a Feeling" are two other such instances.

Aug 1–5: The Beatles recorded "Because," released on LP *Abbey Road*.

Sep 13: John and Yoko were recorded live at the Rock and Roll Revival at Varsity Stadium in Toronto, where they appeared with a hastily assembled Plastic Ono Band also comprising Eric Clapton, Klaus Voorman and Alan White. John's songs were: "Blue Suede Shoes," "Money," "Dizzy Miss Lizzie," "Yer Blues," "Cold Turkey" and "Give Peace a Chance," released in the U.S. and U.K. Dec 12 on LP *Plastic Ono Band: Live Peace in Toronto—1969*.

Sep 19: Paul was interviewed by David Wigg for BBC Radio One's "Scene and Heard," aired in two parts on Sep 21 and 28 and released on the LP *The Beatles Tapes* (where it is listed as Mar 1970) on Jul 30, 1976 in the U.K. and in 1978 in the U.S.

Sep 25: John recorded "Cold Turkey," released as a single with Yoko Ono's "Don't Worry Kyoko" Oct 20 in the U.S. and Oct 24 in the U.K.

That fall: Each of The Beatles recorded his part of *The Beatles Seventh Christmas Record* (their last) separately outside of the Abbey Road studio. Disc jockey Kenny Everett edited the tapes, this time under his real name, Maurice Cole, and the record was issued free to members of the fan club on Dec 19.

Oct 8: George was interviewed by David Wigg for BBC Radio One's "Scene and Heard," aired in two parts on Oct 12 and 19, and released on LP *The Beatles Tapes* (where it is listed as Mar 1969) on Jul 30, 1976 in the U.K. and in 1978 in the U.S.

Oct 27–Dec: Ringo recorded the following tracks for his album *Sentimental Journey* released Mar 27, 1970 in the U.K. and Apr 24, 1970 in the U.S. (sessions resumed on Feb 3, 1970): "Night and Day," "Star Dust," "Blue Turning Grey over You," "Sentimental Journey," "I'm a Fool to Care," "Dream," "You Always Hurt the One You Love," "Have I Told You Lately That I Love You?" and "Let the Rest of the World Go By."

Dec 15: John, Yoko, George, Eric Clapton and members of the Delaney and Bonnie and Friends tour were recorded live during a benefit concert for UNICEF at the Lyceum Ballroom, London. John sang "Cold Turkey," released Jun 12, 1972 in the U.S. and Sep 15, 1972 in the U.K. on LP *Some Time in New York City*. Other musicians included Billy Preston, Keith Moon, Bonnie and Delaney Bramlett, Jim Gordon, Klaus Voorman, Alan White, Jim Price, Bobby Keyes, Bobby Whitlock, Carl Raddle, "Legs" Larry Smith and Dino Danelli. Nicky

Hopkins later added some electric piano overdubs to replace an inaudible Billy Preston organ track.

Dec: John recorded a promo for Ronnie Hawkins' "Down in the Alley," called "John Lennon on Ronnie Hawkins."

1970

Jan 3: George, Paul and Ringo recorded "I Me Mine," released on the LP *Let It Be* May 8 in the U.K. and May 18 in the U.S. George also did the song during the Twickenham *Let It Be* filming sessions. While it is heard in the film, no formal recordings of it were made until this date. This studio recording was mandated by the fact that the song was included in the released film, and thus it had to appear on the soundtrack album. The final studio version ran only 1:34, but in preparing it for release on *Let It Be*, Phil Spector reedited the track so that it ran 2:25 on the album, and added orchestral overdubs on Apr 1. George, Paul and Ringo would return to Abbey Road the following day, Jan 4, to add overdubs to "Let It Be," marking the last appearance in the studio by The Beatles as a group, and "I Me Mine" as the last song recorded by The Beatles.

Jan 22–Mar: Paul recorded the following songs, released Apr 17 in the U.K. and Apr 20 in the U.S. on LP *McCartney*: "The Lovely Linda," "That Would Be Something," "Valentine Day," "Every Night," medley: "Hot As Sun"/"Glasses," "Junk," "Man We Was Lonely," "Oo You," "Momma Miss America," "Teddy Boy," "Singalong Junk," "Maybe I'm Amazed," "Kreen-Akrore." A short, unlisted bit of "Suicide" was also recorded and is on the album.

Jan 27: John recorded "Instant Karma," released as a single with Ono's "Who Has Seen the Wind" Feb 6 in the U.K. and Feb 20 in the U.S.

Feb 3–Mar 13: Ringo concluded recording of his *Sentimental Journey* album with the following songs: "Whispering Grass (Don't Tell the Trees)," "Bye Bye Blackbird" and "Love Is a Many Splendored Thing," released Mar 27 in the U.K. and Apr 24 in the U.S.

Feb 18: John was interviewed by David Wigg for BBC Radio One's "Scene and Heard," aired Feb 22 and released Jul 30, 1976 in the U.K. and in 1978 in the U.S. on LP *The Beatles Tapes* (where it is listed as a Jun 1969 interview).

Feb 18–19: Ringo recorded "It Don't Come Easy" and "Early 1970," released as a single Apr 9, 1971 in the U.K. and Apr 16, 1971 in the U.S.

Mar 20: Ringo was interviewed by David Wigg for BBC Radio One's "Scene and Heard," aired Mar 29 and released on LP *The Beatles Tapes* (where it is listed as a Jul 1970 interview) Jul 30, 1976 in the U.K. and in 1978 in the U.S.

Apr 1: The final day of overdub and mixing sessions for the *Let It Be* album, supervised by Phil Spector. Orchestra overdubs for several songs were recorded with Ringo doing drum tracks. This marked the final studio appearance by any member of The Beatles on a Beatles studio recording.

May 26–Aug: George recorded the following songs for his LP *All Things Must Pass*: "My Sweet Lord" and "Isn't It a Pity" (Version I, begun on Jun 2), first released as a single in the U.S. Nov 23; and "I'd Have You Anytime," "Wah- Wah," "What Is Life," "If Not for You," "Behind That Locked Door," "Let It Down," "Run of the Mill," "Beware of Darkness," "Apple Scruffs," "Ballad of Sir Frankie Crisp (Let It Roll)," "Awaiting on You All," "All Things Must Pass," "I Dig Love," "Art of Dying," "Isn't It a Pity" (Version II), "Hear Me Lord," and *Apple Jam*, a bonus LP that includes "Out of the Blue," "It's Johnny's Birthday" (written for John's 30th birthday, Oct 9), "Plug Me In," "I Remember Jeep" and "Thanks for the Pepperoni." *All Things Must Pass* was released as a three-LP boxed edition Nov 27 in the U.S. and Nov 30 in the U.K.

Jun 30–Jul 1: Ringo recorded songs for his album *Beaucoups of Blues* in Nashville, released Sep 25 in the U.K. and Sep 28 in the U.S., including "Beaucoups of Blues," "Love Don't Last Long," "Fastest Growing Heartache in the West," "Without Her," "Woman of the Night," "I'd Be Talking All the Time," "$15 Draw," "Wine, Women and Loud Happy Songs," "I Wouldn't Have You Any Other Way," "Loser's Lounge," "Waiting," "Silent Homecoming." He also recorded "Coochy-Coochy" (originally 28 minutes long), released Oct 5 only in the U.S. as a single with "Beaucoups of Blues."

Sep 26–Oct 27: John recorded "Mother," "Hold on (John)," "I Found Out," "Working Class Hero," "Isolation," "Remember," "Love," "Well Well Well," "Look at Me," "God," and "My Mummy's Dead," all released Dec 11 in the U.S. and U.K. on LP *John Lennon/Plastic Ono Band*.

1971

Jan 22: John recorded "Power to the People," released in the U.K. on Mar 12 as a single with Ono's "Open Your Box" (later retitled "Hirake"), and in the U.S. on Mar 22 as a single with Ono's "Touch Me."

Jan–Mar: Paul recorded songs for his LP *Ram*, released May 17 in the U.S. and May 28 in the U.K., including "Another Day" and "Oh Woman, Oh Why," released as a single Feb 19 in the U.K. and Feb 22 in the U.S.; the other *Ram* songs are: "Too Many People," "3 Legs," "Ram On" (2:30), "Dear Boy," "Uncle Albert/Admiral Halsey," "Smile Away," "Heart of the Country," "Monkberry Moon Delight," "Eat at Home," "Long Haired Lady," "Ram On" (0:55); "Back Seat of My Car." Paul also recorded "Get on the Right Thing," released on LP *Red Rose Speedway* Apr 30, 1973 in the U.S. and May 4, 1973 in the U.K.

Feb: George recorded instrumentals for "Try Some, Buy Some," released on LP *Living in the Material World* May 30, 1973 in the U.S. and Jun 22, 1973 in the U.K., and instrumentals for "You" and "A Bit More of You" completed in May and Jun 1975. All of the recordings were completed later.

Jun 1: John recorded "Do the Oz" released with Bill Elliot's "God Save Us" as a single Jul 7 in the U.S. and Jul 16 in the U.K. Lennon did the original vocal on "God Save Us," but it was replaced by Elliott's vocal with the same basic instrumental track used for both vocal overdubs. The record was credited to The Elastic Oz Band.

Jun 6: John and Yoko performed "Well (Baby Please Don't Go)," "Jamrag," "Scumbag" and "Au," live with Frank Zappa and The Mothers of Invention at New York's Fillmore East, released on LP *Some Time in New York City* Jun 12, 1972 in the U.S. and Sep 15, 1972 in the U.K. Klaus Voorman later added a studio bass overdub.

Jun–Jul: John recorded the following songs for his LP *Imagine*, released Sep 9 in the U.S. and Oct 8 in the U.K.: "Imagine," "Crippled Inside," "Jealous Guy," "It's So Hard," "I Don't Want to Be a Soldier Mama, I Don't Want to Die," "Gimme Some Truth," "Oh My Love," "How Do You Sleep?" "How?" and "Oh Yoko!" Most of the album was recorded during Jun at John's home studio in England; some overdub sessions were held in New York in early Jul. A demo of "Imagine" was released on the *Imagine: John Lennon* album Oct 4, 1988 in the U.S. and Oct 10, 1988 in the U.K.

Jul: George recorded "Bangla Desh" and "Deep Blue," released as a single in the U.S. on Jul 28 and in the U.K. on Jul 30.

Aug 1: George and Ringo performed at two concerts for Bangla Desh in New York; the following numbers from the evening concert were released on LP *The Concert for Bangla Desh* in the U.S. Dec 20 and in the U.K. Jan 10, 1972: George's "Wah-Wah," "My Sweet Lord," "Awaiting on You All," "Beware of Darkness" (vocal-George with Leon Russell), "While My Guitar Gently Weeps," "Here Comes the Sun," "Something" and "Bangla Desh"; Ringo's "It Don't Come Easy."

Sep: Paul recorded "Mumbo," "Bip Bop," "Love Is Strange," "Wild Life," "Some People Never Know," "I Am Your Singer," "Tomorrow," "Dear Friend," and "Bip Bop" (unlisted reprise) released on Wings' LP *Wild Life* Dec 7 in the U.S. and U.K.

■ Ringo recorded "Back off Boogaloo" (Version I) and "Blindman," released as a single Mar 17, 1972 in the U.K. and Mar 20, 1972 in the U.S.

Oct 8: John and Yoko held a press conference in Syracuse, New York. Excerpts were released in the U.S. in 1976 on LP *The History of Syracuse Music Vol VIII/IX* and in 1980 on *The History of Syracuse Music Vol. X/XI*. The full recording (24:54) was released in 1986 on *The History of Syracuse Music Vol. XII/XIII*.

Oct 25: John was interviewed by David Wigg for BBC Radio One's "Scene and Heard," aired in three parts on Nov 13, 20 and 27, and released on LP *The Beatles Tapes* Jul 20, 1976 in the U.K. and in 1978 in the U.S.

Oct 28–29: John and Yoko recorded "Happy Xmas (War Is Over)" with the Harlem Community Choir, released as a single with Ono's "Listen the Snow Is Falling" Dec 1 in the U.S. and Nov 24, 1972 in the U.K.

Late that year: Paul produced an instrumental version of his *Ram* album, titled *Thrillington*, under the pseudonym "Percy 'Thrills' Thrillington," released Apr 29, 1977 in the U.K. and May 17, 1977 in the U.S., including "Too Many People, "3 Legs," "Ram On," "Dear Boy," "Uncle Albert/Admiral Halsey," "Smile Away," "Heart of the Country," "Monkberry Moon Delight," "Eat at Home," "Long Haired Lady" and "Back Seat of My Car"; the album adds an unlisted piano number as well.

1972

Early that year: Paul recorded "Mary Had a Little Lamb" and "Little Woman Love," released as a Wings single May 12 in the U.K. and May 29 in the U.S.

Feb 1: Paul recorded "Give Ireland Back to the Irish"; vocal and instrumental versions were released as a Wings single Feb 25 in the U.K. and Feb 28 in the U.S.

Mar 1–20: John recorded the following songs for his LP *Some Time in New York City*: "Woman Is the Nigger of the World" (first released as a single only in the U.S. on Apr 24 with Ono's "Sisters O Sisters"), "Attica State," "New York City," "Sunday Bloody Sunday," "Luck of the Irish," "John Sinclair" and "Angela." *Some Time in New York City* was released Jun 12 in the U.S. and Sep 15 in the U.K.

Mar: Paul recorded "My Love," released as a single with live version of "The Mess" (recorded Aug 21) on Mar 23, 1973 in the U.K. and Apr 9, 1973 in the U.S.

Mar–Oct: Paul recorded the following songs, released on the Wings LP *Red Rose Speedway* Apr 30, 1973 in the U.S. and May 4, 1973 in the U.K.: "Big Barn Bed," "One More Kiss," "Little Lamb Dragonfly," "Single Pigeon," "When the Night," "Loup (1st Indian on the Moon)," medley: "Hold Me Tight"/"Lazy Dynamite"/"Hands of Love"/"Power Cut."

Middle of that year: An interview with John was recorded by an unknown person regarding musician David Peel. The interview was released in 1980 on the limited edition disc "The David Peel Interview."

Aug 21: Paul's live version of "The Mess" was recorded at the Congresgebouw, The Hague, the Netherlands, released as a single with "My Love" Mar 23, 1973 in the U.K. and Apr 9, 1973 in the U.S.

Aug 30: John and Yoko performed two One to One Concerts at Madison Square Garden, New York, for the benefit of the Willowbrook School for Children. The following Lennon numbers were released on LP *John Lennon: Live in New York City* Jan 24, 1986 in the U.S. and Feb 24, 1986 in the U.K.: "Cold Turkey," "Hound Dog," "Give Peace a Chance" (excerpt), all from the evening show; and "New York City," "Come Together," "Imagine," "Instant Karma," "Mother," "It's So Hard," "Well Well Well" and "Woman Is the Nigger of the World," all from the afternoon performance. No complete recording of "Give Peace a Chance" has been released officially, and it is not even known if it was done at the afternoon show. A different excerpt from the song had appeared in 1975 on John's *Shaved Fish* album where it was tacked onto the end of "Happy Xmas (War Is Over)." Many of the songs were edited differently for

the respective album and accompanying videocassette releases. The spoken introductions to "Mother" and "Woman Is the Nigger of the World" are from the evening show, although the songs themselves are from the afternoon performance. "Hound Dog" is from the evening show but includes the afternoon introduction. Many tracks were shortened for release. "New York City," "Woman Is the Nigger of the World" and "Well Well Well" are shortened, and some of Lennon's comments are cut, including the end of his introduction to "Mother," during which he says, "That's why they're all junkies, right?" The LP has only the opening lines of "Give Peace a Chance," while the video has the intro and about the first quarter of the number. "New York City" is edited differently on the respective releases as well. Ono's numbers included "Sisters O Sisters," "Born in a Prison," "Don't Worry Kyoko" (afternoon only), "We're All Water," "Move on Fast" and "Open Your Box," none of which appear on the album.

Sep: Ringo recorded "Fiddle About" and "Tommy's Holiday Camp" with the London Symphony Orchestra and Chamber Choir, released on LP *Tommy* Nov 24 in the U.K. and Nov 27 in the U.S.

Oct: Wings recorded the following songs: "Hi Hi Hi" and "C Moon," released as a single Dec 1 in the U.K. and Dec 4 in the U.S.; "Country Dreamer," released as a single with "Helen Wheels" Oct 26, 1973 in the U.K. and Nov 12, 1973 in the U.S.; and "Live and Let Die" and "I Lie Around," released as a single Jun 1, 1973 in the U.K. and Jun 18, 1973 in the U.S.. Recording of the LP *Red Rose Speedway*, begun in Mar, was also concluded.

1973

Jan 3: Ringo was interviewed by David Wigg for BBC Radio One's "Scene and Heard," aired on Jan 6; released Jul 30, 1976 in the U.K. and 1978 in the U.S. on LP *The Beatles Tapes*.

Jan–Apr: George recorded "Give Me Love" and "Miss O'Dell," released as a single May 7 in the U.S. and May 25 in the U.K. George burst into spontaneous, giddy laughter three times while recording "Miss O'Dell," and released the song with the laughter intact. The following songs were released on LP *Living in the Material World*, May 30 in the U.S. and Jun 22 in the U.K.: "Sue Me, Sue You Blues," "The Light That Has Lighted the World," "Don't Let Me Wait Too Long," "Who Can See It," "Living in the Material World," "The Lord Loves the One (That Loves the Lord)," "Be Here Now," "Try Some, Buy Some" (begun in Feb 1971), "The Day the World Gets 'Round," "That Is All"; the LP also includes "Give Me Love."

Apr 1–15: Ringo recorded "Photograph" and "Down and Out," released as a single Sep 24 in the U.S. and Oct 19 in the U.K. He also recorded "I'm the Greatest," "Have You Seen My Baby," "Sunshine Life for Me (Sail Away Raymond)," "You're Sixteen," "Oh My My," "Step Lightly," "Devil Woman" and "You and Me (Babe)," all released on LP *Ringo* Nov 2 in the U.S. and Nov 23 in the U.K.

Apr 16–30: Ringo recorded "Six O'Clock," with Paul supervising; released on LP *Ringo* Nov 2 in the U.S. and Nov 23 in the U.K.

Jul–Aug: John recorded "Mind Games" and "Meat City," released as a single Oct 29 in the U.S. and Nov 16 in the U.K. The following titles were released on LP *Mind Games* Nov 2 in the U.S. and Nov 16 in the U.K.: "Tight A\$," "Aisumasen (I'm Sorry)," "One Day (at a Time)," "Bring on the Lucie (Freeda Peeple)," "Nutopian International Anthem" (3 seconds of silence), "Intuition," "Out the Blue," "Only People," "I Know (I Know)," "You Are Here."

Aug 4: During *Mind Games* sessions John recorded "Rock & Roll People," omitted from the album but released on LP *Menlove Ave.* Oct 27, 1986 in the U.S. and Nov 3, 1986 in the U.K.

Aug 10–Sep 22: Wings recorded the following songs in Lagos, Nigeria released on LP *Band on the Run* Dec 5 in the U.S. and Dec 7 in the U.K.: "Band on the Run," "Jet," "Bluebird," "Mrs. Vanderbilt," "Let Me Roll It," "Mamunia," "No Words," "Picasso's Last Words," "Nineteen Hundred and Eighty Five." Wings also recorded "Helen Wheels," released as a single with "Country Dreamer" (recorded Oct 1972) Oct 26 in the U.K. and Nov 12 in the U.S.; and "Zoo Gang" (an instrumental), released as a single with "Band on the Run" Jun 28, 1974 in the U.K. only. Wings recorded "Seaside Woman" and "B Side to Seaside," released as a single May 13, 1977 in the U.S. and Aug 10, 1979 in the U.K. Lead vocals by Linda McCartney.

Oct–Dec: John recorded "You Can't Catch Me," "Sweet Little Sixteen," "Bony Moronie," released Feb 17, 1975 in the U.S. and Feb 21, 1975 in the U.K. on LP *Rock*

'N' Roll, and with some tracks in different mixes and lengths on LP *John Lennon Sings the Great Rock & Roll Hits [Roots]*, released only in the U.S. Feb 8, 1975 via mail order. "Here We Go Again," "My Baby Left Me" and "To Know Her Is to Love Her" were released on *Menlove Ave.* Oct 27, 1986 in the U.S. and Nov 3, 1986 in the U.K. "Angel Baby" and "Be My Baby" were released on *[Roots]*. "Angel Baby" was also released on *Menlove Ave.* and again in 1990 on the CD boxed set *Lennon*, but it was artificially extended on both of those releases. The following table illustrates the different releases.

Lennon *Rock 'N' Roll* Songs

Song Title	Running Time	
	Rock 'N' Roll	*Roots*
"Sweet Little Sixteen"	3:00	2:57
"You Can't Catch Me"	4:51	4:02

The first half of "You Can't Catch Me" is the same on both albums, but on *Rock 'N' Roll* a sharp break and an edit follow that adds a repeat of the first verse before the final verse. *Roots* has a slightly longer fadeout. Lennon can be heard adding a few lines from Jimmy McCraklin's song "The Walk" during this number.

"Bony Moronie"	3:50	3:43
"Angel Baby"	not on LP	3:03

"Angel Baby" was also released on *Menlove Ave.* and CD boxed set *Lennon*, where it is artificially extended to a running time of 3:41 (listed as 3:39), 38 seconds longer than on *Roots*. The song runs longer because an additional repeat of the chorus was edited in before the final verse.

"Be My Baby"	not on LP	4:31

Parts of two different takes were used for this track.

1974

Jun–Jul: In Nashville, Wings recorded "Junior's Farm" and "Sally G.," released as a single Oct 25 in the U.K. and Nov 4 in the U.S. They also recorded two instrumentals, with Chet Atkins and Floyd Cramer joining Wings: "Walking in the Park with Eloise" (written by Paul's father, James McCartney, many years earlier) and "Bridge over the River Suite." The two instrumentals were released as a single Oct 18 in the U.K. and Dec 2 in the U.S.

Jul 15: John recorded "Move Over Ms. L," released as a single with "Stand by Me" Mar 10, 1975 in the U.S. and Apr 18, 1975 in the U.K.

Jul: John recorded "Whatever Gets You Through the Night" (with Elton John on piano, organ and harmony vocals) and "Beef Jerky" (an instrumental), released as a single Sep 23 in the U.S. and Oct 4 in the U.K. He also recorded the following songs, released on LP *Walls and Bridges* Sep 26 in the U.S. and Oct 4 in the U.K.: "Going Down on Love," "Old Dirt Road," "What You Got," "Bless You," "Scared," "No. 9 Dream," "Surprise, Sur-

Roots (© Adam VIII). Before John issued *Rock 'N' Roll*, he gave Morris Levy a prefinal mix of the album, which Levy issued on this unauthorized U.S. mail-order album. John was able to stop the sale of *Roots*, which contains different mixes of several songs and two omitted from *Rock 'N' Roll*.

prise (Sweet Bird of Paradox)" (also with Elton John doing harmony vocals), "Steel and Glass" (an attack on former Beatles' manager Allen Klein), "Nobody Loves You (When You're Down and Out)," "Ya Ya" (Version I, featuring John's son Julian on drums). Alternate versions of "Steel and Glass," "Scared," "Old Dirt Road," "Nobody Loves You (When You're Down and Out)" and "Bless You" were released on *Menlove Ave.* Oct 27, 1986 in the U.S. and Nov 3, 1986 in the U.K.

That summer: Ringo recorded "Only You (and You Alone)" and "Call Me," released as a single Nov 11 in the U.S. and Nov 15 in the U.K. He also recorded the following songs for his LP *Goodnight Vienna*, released Nov 15 in the U.K. and Nov 18 in the U.S.: "It's All Down to Goodnight Vienna," "Occapella," "Oo Wee," "Husbands and Wives," "Snookeroo," "All By Myself," "No No Song," "Skokiaan," "Easy for Me" and "Goodnight Vienna" (reprise).

Sep–Oct: George recorded "Dark Horse" and "I Don't Care Anymore," released as a single Nov 18 in the U.S., and "Ding Dong, Ding Dong," released Dec 6 as a single backed with "I Don't Care Anymore," in the U.K. He also recorded the following songs for LP *Dark Horse*, released Dec 9 in the U.S. and Dec 20 in the U.K.: "Hari's on Tour (Express)," "Simply Shady," "So Sad," "Bye Bye, Love," "Maya Love," "Far East Man" and "It Is 'He' (Jai Sri Krishna)." George's voice clearly showed the effects of laryngitis, which would continue to plague him during a fall tour.

Oct 21–25: John recorded more songs for his LP *Rock 'N' Roll*, released Feb 17, 1975 in the U.S. and Feb 21, 1975 in the U.K. The recordings largely comprised new lead vocals to replace unusable ones done with Phil Spector in the fall of 1973. Many of the instrumental backing tracks recorded with Spector, however, were retained on the released recordings. The new numbers included: "Just Because," "Stand by Me," "Be-Bop-a-Lula," medley: "Rip It Up"/"Ready Teddy," "Ain't That a Shame," "Do You Want to Dance," "Slippin' and Slidin'," "Peggy Sue," medley: "Bring It on Home to Me"/"Send Me Some Lovin'," "Ya Ya" (Version II). The songs were also included on the unauthorized LP *John Lennon Sings the Great Rock & Roll Hits [Roots]*, released Feb 8, 1975 only in the U.S. via TV mail order. The following table illustrates the two different releases of these tracks.

Lennon *Rock 'N' Roll* Songs

Song Title	Running Time	
	Rock 'N' Roll	*Roots*
"Be-Bop-a-Lula"	2:36	2:33
"Ain't That a Shame"	2:31	2:32

Roots has a slightly longer fadeout.

| "Stand by Me" | 3:28 (listed as 3:30) | 3:23 |

Parts of two different takes were used for this track.

Song Title	Running Time	
	Rock 'N' Roll	*Roots*
"Rip It Up"/"Ready Teddy"	1:32 (listed as 1:39)	1:31
"Do You Want to Dance"	2:53	2:56

Roots has a slightly longer fadeout.

"Peggy Sue"	2:02 (listed as 2:06)	2:01
"Bring It on Home to Me"/ "Send Me Some Lovin'"	3:40	3:36
"Slippin' & Slidin'"	2:16	2:17

The spoken lines heard at the end on *Roots* are missing on *Rock 'N' Roll*.

| "Just Because" | 4:25 | 4:19 |

The instrumental backing tracks from the 1973 sessions were retained, but Lennon's vocal was recorded during this period at the Record Plant East.

| "Ya Ya" | 2:17 | 2:14 |

Nov 28: John joined Elton John on stage at the latter's Thanksgiving concert at Madison Square Garden, New York. The two dueted on "Whatever Gets You Through the Night," "Lucy in the Sky with Diamonds" and "I Saw Her Standing There." The last title was released Feb 24, 1975 in both the U.S. and U.K. as the B side of Elton's "Philadelphia Freedom" single. All three tracks were released in the U.K. Mar 13, 1981 on the 7-inch EP *Elton John Band Featuring John Lennon and the Muscle Shoals Horns*. They also appeared on a German 12-inch (DJM 0934.006) and on Elton's European LP *Elton John Band Featuring John Lennon and the Muscle Shoals Horns* (DJM 0064.230). All three were officially released worldwide Oct 30, 1990 on the four-CD boxed set *Lennon*, marking the first U.S. release of the first two numbers.

Dec 13: George's live version of "For You Blue," recorded at the Capitol Center in Largo, Maryland, was released Feb 15, 1988 on the limited edition CD and vinyl EP *Songs by George Harrison*, issued with Harrison's book of the same title.

1975

Jan 16–Feb 24: Wings recorded songs for their LP *Venus and Mars* in New Orleans; recording sessions were concluded in Los Angeles. The album was released May 27 in the U.S. and May 30 in the U.K.: "Venus and Mars," "Rock Show," "You Gave Me the Answer," "Magneto and Titanium Man," "Letting Go," "Venus and Mars" (reprise), "Spirits of Ancient Egypt," "Medicine Jar," "Call Me Back Again," medley: "Treat Her Gently"/"Lonely Old People," "Crossroads Theme."

■ Wings recorded "Listen to What the Man Said" and "Love in Song," released as a single May 16 in the U.K. and May 23 in the U.S.

Feb 12: Wings recorded "My Carnival," released Nov 18, 1985 in the U.S. and U.K. on a single with "Spies Like

Us." A 12-inch release included a 6:00 "party mix" of "My Carnival."

Feb: Wings recorded the instrumental medley "Lunch Box–Odd Sox," released on a single with "Coming Up" (studio and live versions) Apr 11, 1980 in the U.K. and Apr 15, 1980 in the U.S.

May–Jun: George recorded "You" (begun in Feb 1971) and "World of Stone," released as a single Sep 12 in the U.K. and Sep 15 in the U.S. The following songs were released on his LP *Extra Texture—Read All About It* Sep 22 in the U.S. and Oct 3 in the U.K.: "The Answer's at the End," "This Guitar (Can't Keep from Crying)," "Ooh Baby (You Know That I Love You)," "A Bit More of You" (begun in Feb 1971), "Can't Stop Thinking About You," "Tired of Midnight Blue," "Grey Cloudy Lies," "His Name Is Legs (Ladies and Gentlemen)."

1976

Jan–Feb: Wings recorded songs for LP *Wings at the Speed of Sound,* released Mar 25 in the U.S. and Apr 9 in the U.K.: "Let 'Em In," "The Note You Never Wrote," "She's My Baby," "Beware My Love," "Silly Love Songs" (Version I), "Cook of the House," "Must Do Something About It," "San Ferry Anne," "Warm and Beautiful," "Time to Hide" and "Wino Junko."

Apr–May: Ringo recorded the following songs for his LP *Ringo's Rotogravure* released Sep 17 in the U.K. and Sep 27 in the U.S.: "A Dose of Rock and Roll," "Hey Baby," "Pure Gold," "Cryin'," "You Don't Know Me at All," "Cookin' (in the Kitchen of Love)," "I'll Still Love You" (working title: "When Every Song Is Sung"), "This Be Called a Song," "Las Brisas," "Lady Gaye" and the instrumental "Spooky Weirdness."

May 3–Jun 23: The following songs from Wings' concert tour were released on LP *Wings over America* Dec 10 in both the U.S. and the U.K.: "Lady Madonna," "The Long and Winding Road," "I've Just Seen a Face," "Blackbird," "Yesterday," "You Gave Me the Answer," "Live and Let Die," "Picasso's Last Words," "Richard Cory," "Bluebird," "Venus and Mars," "Rock Show," "Jet," "Let Me Roll It," "Spirits of Ancient Egypt," "Medicine Jar," "Maybe I'm Amazed," "Call Me Back Again," "Magneto and Titanium Man," "Go Now," "My Love," "Listen to What the Man Said," "Let 'Em In," "Time to Hide," "Silly Love Songs," "Beware My Love," "Letting Go," "Band on the Run," "Hi Hi Hi," "Soily." Although consisting of live recordings, with many tracks taped at the Jun 23 Los Angeles concert, the album reportedly underwent extensive rerecording in the studio before release.

May 24–Sep 13: George recorded "This Song" and "Learning How to Love You," released as a single Nov 15 in the U.S. and Nov 19 in the U.K. He also recorded the following songs for his LP *Thirty Three & 1/3,* released Nov 19 in the U.K. and Nov 24 in the U.S.: "Woman Don't You Cry for Me," "Dear One," "Beautiful Girl," "See Yourself," "It's What You Value," "True Love," "Pure Smokey" and "Crackerbox Palace."

Nov 19: George videotaped an appearance with Paul Simon for "Saturday Night Live," aired in the U.S. Nov 20. A Harrison/Simon duet of "Homeward Bound" was released Jul 23, 1990 in the U.K. and Jul 24, 1990 in the U.S. on the charity CD *Nobody's Child: Romanian Angel Appeal.*

1977

Feb 7–Mar 31: Wings recorded "London Town" and "Deliver Your Children," released on LP *London Town* Mar 31, 1978 in both the U.S. and U.K.

Mar: Paul and Wings recorded "Girls' School" (completed in Aug), released on a single with "Mull of Kintyre" Nov 11 in the U.K. and Nov 14 in the U.S.

May: Wings recorded "With a Little Luck" released as a single with "Backwards Traveller"/"Cuff Link" Mar 20, 1978 in the U.S. and Mar 23, 1978 in the U.K. They also recorded "Cafe on the Left Bank," "I'm Carrying," "I've Had Enough," "Famous Groupies," "Don't Let It Bring You Down" and "Morse Moose and the Grey Goose," all released on the LP *London Town* Mar 31, 1978 in both the U.S. and U.K.

Jun: Ringo recorded "Wings" and "Just a Dream," released as a single Aug 25 in the U.S., and "Drowning in a Sea of Love," released as a single with "Just a Dream" in the U.K. Sep 16. Ringo also recorded the following songs for his LP *Ringo the 4th,* released Sep 20 in the U.K. and Sep 26 in the U.S.: "Tango All Night," "Gave It All Up," "Out on the Streets," "Can She Do It Like She Dances," "Sneaking Sally Through the Alley," "It's No Secret," "Gypsies in Flight," "Simple Love Song."

That summer: Ringo recorded the following songs, released only in the U.K. Dec 9 on the LP *Scouse the Mouse*: "I Know a Place," "S.O.S.," "A Mouse Like Me," "Living in a Pet Shop," "Scouse's Dream," "Running Free," "Boat Ride," "Scouse the Mouse."

Aug: Paul recorded "Mull of Kintyre," released as a single with "Girl's School" Nov 11 in the U.K. and Nov 14 in the U.S.

Oct 25–Dec 14: Paul held more recording sessions for his LP *London Town* at EMI's Abbey Road studios.

Late that year: Ringo recorded "Lipstick Traces" and "Old Time Relovin'," released as a single Apr 18, 1978 in the U.S. only. He also recorded the following songs for his LP *Bad Boy,* released Apr 21, 1978 in the U.S. and U.K.: "Who Needs a Heart," "Bad Boy," "Heart on My Sleeve," "Where Did Our Love Go," "Tonight," "Hard Times," "Monkey See Monkey Do" and "A Man Like Me," the last song a remake of "A Mouse Like Me" from the *Scouse the Mouse* album.

Dec–Jan 1978: Wings recorded "Backwards Traveller"/"Cuff Link" released on a single with "With a Little Luck" Mar 20, 1978 in the U.S. and Mar 23, 1978 in the U.K. Wings also recorded: "Children Children," "Girlfriend" and "Name and Address," released on LP *London Town* Mar 31, 1978 in the U.S. and U.K.

1978

Jan 4–23: Wings concluded recording sessions for *London Town*.

Mar: George recorded "Flying Hour," included on the original, unreleased version of the *Somewhere in England* album but omitted on the released version. The song was later remixed and released worldwide on the bonus EP and CD *Songs by George Harrison*, issued with George's book of the same title on Feb 15, 1988.

Apr 11–Oct 12: George recorded the following songs for his LP *George Harrison*, released Feb 14, 1979 in the U.S. and Feb 16, 1979 in the U.K.: "Love Comes to Everyone," "Not Guilty," "Here Comes the Moon," "Soft Hearted Hana," "Blow Away," "Faster," "Dark Sweet Lady," "Your Love Is Forever," "Soft Touch" and "If You Believe." George also recorded "Circles," released on LP *Gone Troppo* Oct 27, 1982 in the U.S. and Nov 8, 1982 in the U.K. "Circles" was written in 1968 and originally intended for the *"White Album."*

Jun 29–Jul 27: Wings recorded the following songs in Scotland: "Old Siam, Sir," released on a single with "Spin It On" Jun 1, 1979 in the U.K. and on LP *Back to the Egg* May 24, 1979 in the U.S. and Jun 8, 1979 in the U.K.; and "Arrow Through Me," "To You," "Winter Rose" and "Again and Again and Again," all released on LP *Back to the Egg*. Wings also recorded "Same Time Next Year," originally planned for the movie of the same title but ultimately not used. It was later included on the unreleased *Cold Cuts* album. It was finally released on Feb 5, 1990, only in the U.K., as a bonus track on CD and 12-inch "Put It There" singles.

Jun 29–Nov 30: Wings recorded "Mama's Little Girl," possibly during *Back to the Egg* sessions. The song was not released until Feb 5, 1990 when it appeared only in the U.K. as a bonus track on CD and 12-inch "Put It There" singles. The song was included on the unreleased *Cold Cuts* album that Paul compiled in late 1980. Wings recorded this song in 1972, and the released version may be the 1972 recording. However, Chris Thomas is listed as McCartney's co-producer on the released version, and Thomas did not work with McCartney in 1972. He did, however, co-produce *Back to the Egg* with Paul in 1978. Thomas also worked on a still-unreleased revised *Cold Cuts* album in Aug of 1987, and may have produced the released version with Paul then or done some overdubbing and remixing that earned him the producer's credit. However, the released version sounds exactly the same as the one on *Cold Cuts*, and it is difficult to see what Thomas might have added to it in 1987.

Jul 23: Wings recorded "Spin It On," released as a single with "Old Siam, Sir" in the U.K. Jun 1, 1979, and on LP *Back to the Egg*.

Sep 11–20: Wings recorded "The Broadcast" (contains poems "The Sport of Kings" by Ian Hay and "The Little Man" by John Galsworthy, both read by Harold Margery, who is not mentioned on the album), "Recep-

tion," "We're Open Tonight," "Love Awake," "After The Ball—Million Miles," all released on LP *Back to the Egg*.

Oct 3: Wings and a large number of guest musicians, collectively billed as Rockestra, recorded "Rockestra Theme" and "So Glad to See You Here," both released on LP *Back to the Egg*.

Oct–Nov: Wings recorded "Getting Closer" and "Baby's Request" for LP *Back to the Egg*.

Late Dec: Wings recorded "Goodnight Tonight" and "Daytime Nightime Suffering," released as a single Mar 15, 1979 in the U.S. and Mar 23, 1979 in the U.K. An extended version of "Goodnight Tonight" was released as a 12-inch single Mar 26, 1979 in the U.S. and Apr 3, 1979 in the U.K.

1979

Jul: Paul recorded "Wonderful Christmastime" and "Rudolph the Red Nosed Reggae," released as a single Nov 16 in the U.K. and Nov 20 in the U.S.

■ Paul recorded "Coming Up" (studio version), released as a single with "Lunch Box-Odd Sox" and "Coming Up" (Dec 17, 1979 live version) Apr 11, 1980 in the U.K. and Apr 15, 1980 in the U.S.

That summer: Paul recorded the following songs for his LP *McCartney II*, released May 16, 1980 in the U.K. and May 21, 1980 in the U.S.: "Temporary Secretary," "On the Way," "Waterfalls," "Nobody Knows," "Front Parlour" (instrumental), "Summer's Day Song," "Frozen Jap" (instrumental), "Bogey Music," "Darkroom," "One of These Days." Paul also recorded "Check My Machine," released as a single with "Waterfalls" Jun 13, 1980 in the U.K. and Jul 22, 1980 in the U.S., and "Secret Friend," released on a 12-inch single with "Temporary Secretary" only in the U.K. on Sep 19, 1980.

Oct 30–Oct 30, 1980: George recorded the following songs for his LP *Somewhere in England*, released Jun 1, 1981 in the U.S. and Jun 5, 1981 in the U.K.: "Baltimore Oriole," "Hong Kong Blues," "Unconsciousness Rules," "Life Itself," "Save the World" and "Writing's on the Wall,"

Dec 17: Wings' live version of "Coming Up" was recorded in Glasgow at the Apollo, released as a single with "Coming Up" (studio version) and "Lunch Box-Odd Sox" Apr 11, 1980 in the U.K. and Apr 15, 1980 in the U.S.

Dec 29: Wings was recorded live at London's Hammersmith Odeon during the benefit Concerts for Kampuchea. They sang: "Got to Get You into My Life," "Every Night" and "Coming Up." Remaining songs performed by "Rockestra" (Wings plus 11 guest musicians): "Lucille," "Let It Be," "Rockestra Theme" (vocal by Paul and Robert Plant), all released on LP *Concerts for the People of Kampuchea* Mar 30, 1981 in the U.S. and Apr 3, 1981 in the U.K.

1980

Mar: George recorded "Sat Singing," included on the original, unreleased version of *Somewhere in England*.

The song was later remixed and released worldwide Feb 15, 1988 on the bonus EP and CD *Songs by George Harrison*, included with George's book of the same title.

Apr: George recorded "Lay His Head," included on the original, unreleased version of *Somewhere in England*. The song was later remixed and released as the B side of the "Got My Mind Set on You" single Oct 12, 1987 in the U.K. and Oct 16, 1987 in the U.S. It was also released worldwide Feb 15, 1988 on the bonus EP and CD *Songs by George Harrison*.

Early May: Paul was interviewed by Vic Garbarini for *Musician* magazine, released Dec 4 in the U.S. and Feb 23, 1981 in the U.K. on LP *The McCartney Interview*.

Jul 7–31: Ringo began sessions for the LP *Stop and Smell the Roses* with Paul at the Superbeat Studios in France, where he recorded two tracks Paul had written for him: "Private Property" and "Attention." The album was released Oct 27, 1981 in the U.S. and Nov 20, 1981 in the U.K. and also included "Wrack My Brain," "Drumming Is My Madness," "Stop and Take the Time to Smell the Roses," "Dead Giveaway," "You Belong to Me," "Sure to Fall," "Nice Way," "Back Off Boogaloo" (Version II).

Aug 4–Sep 8: John's tracks for the *Double Fantasy* album, released Nov 17 in both the U.S. and the U.K., and for the posthumously released *Milk and Honey* album, issued Jan 19, 1984 in the U.S. and Jan 23, 1984 in the U.K., were largely completed during this period. The songs include "(Just Like) Starting Over," released as a single with Ono's "Kiss Kiss Kiss" Oct 24 in the U.K. and Oct 27 in the U.S., and "Cleanup Time," "I'm Losing You," "Beautiful Boy (Darling Boy)," "Watching the Wheels," "Woman," "Dear Yoko," all released on *Double Fantasy*; "Nobody Told Me," released as a single with Ono's "O'Sanity" Jan 5, 1984 in the U.S. and Jan 9, 1984 in the U.K., and "Grow Old with Me," "I Don't Wanna Face It," "Borrowed Time," "(Forgive Me) My Little Flower Princess," and "I'm Stepping Out" (recorded Aug 6, 1980), all released on LP *Milk and Honey*. John also recorded a harmony vocal track for Ono's recording "Every Man Has a Woman Who Loves Him," released without Ono's vocal, thus appearing to be a Lennon solo, on the LP *Every Man Has a Woman* Sep 13, 1984 in the U.S. and Sep 21, 1984 in the U.K.

Sep 9–28: A series of interviews with John was recorded by David Sheff of *Playboy* magazine; excerpts were released on LP *Heart Play—Unfinished Dialogue*, Dec 5, 1983 in the U.S. and Dec 16, 1983 in the U.K.

That fall: John recorded several demos of "Real Love"; take 6 was released on *Imagine: John Lennon* Oct 4, 1988 in the U.S. and Oct 10, 1988 in the U.K. The same track was again released on the four-CD boxed set *Lennon* on Oct 30, 1990, but it appeared there under the title "Girls and Boys."

Oct 31–Nov 3: Paul recorded vocal and humming versions of "We All Stand Together," released only in the U.K. as a single Nov 12, 1984.

Nov–Jan 16, 1981: George recorded "Blood from a Clone," "Teardrops," "That Which I Have Lost" and "All Those Years Ago," the latter released as a single with "Writing's on the Wall" May 11, 1981 in the U.S. and May 15, 1981 in the U.K.; all of the songs were released on LP *Somewhere in England* Jun 1, 1981 in the U.S. and Jun 5, 1981 in the U.K.

Nov: An unidentified interview with John, recorded after the release of *Double Fantasy*, was issued in Oct 1990 in the U.K. on *John Lennon—Interview 80*, a 7-inch picture disc. The interview was taken from an unreleased home video shot at the Hit Factory, with a science fiction film soundtrack recording heard in the background.

Dec 6: Only two days prior to his death, John Lennon was interviewed at great length by Andy Peebles of the BBC. The interview formed the heart of a five-hour radio special that included musical tracks as well. The entire interview was released Nov 12,1990 in the U.K. on the CD and cassette *John and Yoko—The Interview*.

Dec 8: John was interviewed at his Dakota apartment by Dave Sholin, Laurie Kaye, Ron Hummel and Bert Keane of RKO Radio. Part of the interview was released in the U.S. on the LP *Reflections and Poetry* in April 1984; longer excerpts were released in the U.K. Jul 11, 1989 on LP and picture disc CD *The Last Word* and on Dec 14, 1990 on CD *Testimony*, which contains the longest released version of the interview.

Dec 9: Paul and Denny Laine recorded at least part of "Rainclouds," released as a single with "Ebony and Ivory" Mar 29, 1982 in the U.K. and Apr 2, 1982 in the U.S.

Dec: George recorded "Dream Away," released on LP *Gone Troppo* Oct 27, 1982 in the U.S. and Nov 8, 1982 in the U.K. The song was originally recorded for the film *Time Bandits* and later remixed for release on George's LP.

1981

Feb 2–Mar 3: Paul recorded "Ebony and Ivory" (Version II: solo), released on a 12-inch single with "Ebony and Ivory" (Version I: duet) and "Rainclouds" Mar 29, 1982 in the U.K. and Apr 16, 1982 in the U.S. He also recorded "Somebody Who Cares" and "The Pound Is Sinking," released on LP *Tug of War* Apr 26, 1982 in both the U.S. and in the U.K.

■ Paul recorded "Hey Hey" (instrumental), released on the LP *Pipes of Peace* Oct 17, 1983 in the U.K. and Oct 26, 1983 in the U.S.

Feb 16–27: Paul recorded "Take It Away" (Ringo: drums), released on LP *Tug of War*.

Feb 21–25: Paul and Carl Perkins recorded "Get It," released on LP *Tug of War*.

Feb 26–27: Paul and Stevie Wonder recorded "What's That You're Doing?" released on LP *Tug of War*.

Feb 27: Paul and Stevie Wonder recorded "Ebony and Ivory" (Version I: duet), released as a single with "Rainclouds" Mar 29, 1982 in the U.K. and Apr 2, 1982 in the U.S.

Middle of that year: Paul recorded the following tracks for his *Tug of War* album: "Dress Me Up As a Robber," "Tug of War," "Ballroom Dancing" (Version I),

"Wanderlust" (Version I), "Be What You See" and "Here Today." He recorded "I'll Give You a Ring" released as a single with "Take It Away" Jun 21, 1982 in the U.K. and Jul 3, 1982 in the U.S., and the following tracks, released on *Pipes of Peace*: "The Man," "Average Person," "Keep Under Cover" and "Sweetest Little Show." He also recorded "Say Say Say" with Michael Jackson, and "Ode to a Koala Bear" (an instrumental), released as a single Oct 3, 1983 in the U.S. and U.K. A dance mix of "Say Say Say" and an instrumental version of the song were released on a 12-inch single Oct 3, 1983 in both countries.

1982

Early that year: An interview with Pete Best was recorded and released on LP *Like Dreamers Do* in 1982 in the U.S.

That spring: Paul recorded "The Girl Is Mine" with Michael Jackson, released as a single with Jackson's "Can't Get Outta the Rain" Oct 25 in the U.S. and Oct 29 in the U.K.; it also appeared on Jackson's *Thriller* album Nov 29 in the U.S. and Dec 3 in the U.K.

May 5–Aug 27: George recorded "I Really Love You," "Wake Up My Love," "That's the Way It Goes," "Greece," "Gone Troppo," "Mystical One," "Unknown Delight," "Baby Don't Run Away," all released on LP *Gone Troppo* Oct 27 in the U.S. and Nov 8 in the U.K. A remix of "That's the Way It Goes" was released only in the U.K. as a bonus track on 12-inch and CD "When We Was Fab" singles Jan 25, 1988 and Feb 8, 1988 respectively.

That summer: Ringo recorded *"In My Car," "As Far As We Can Go," *"Hopeless," "Alibi," "Be My Baby," *"She's About a Mover," *"I Keep Forgettin'," "Picture Show Life," "Everybody's in a Hurry But Me" (instru-

Old Wave (© Monteco B.V.). Ringo could not get RCA to release *Old Wave* in the U.S. or U.K. It was issued in Germany, Canada and elsewhere.

mental) and "I'm Going Down," released on LP *Old Wave* Jun 16, 1983 in Germany and Jun 24, 1983 in Canada. There was no U.S. or U.K. release, but four songs (*) were released in the U.S. on Feb 24, 1989 on the CD *Starr Struck: Best of Ringo Starr Vol. 2*. *Old Wave* was also released in Brazil, Mexico, Japan, Australia and New Zealand. The single "In My Car"/"As Far As We Can Go" was also released in Germany.

That fall: Paul recorded the following songs for *Pipes of Peace*: "Pipes of Peace," "So Bad," "Tug of Peace," "The Other Me" and "Through Our Love."

Nov 5–May 8, 1983: Paul recorded "No More Lonely Nights" (4:38 ballad version), "No More Lonely Nights" (8:10 playout version) and "Silly Love Songs" (Version II), released on a 12-inch single Sep 24, 1984 in the U.K. and Oct 2, 1984 in the U.S.; the playout version also appeared in a 3:56 edit on a 7-inch single released with the ballad version on Sep 24, 1984 in the U.K. and Oct 5, 1984 in the U.S. On the *Give My Regards to Broad Street* soundtrack album, released Oct 22, 1984 in both countries, the ballad version is 4:50 and the playout version 4:17. Unlike many extended mix releases, the playout version of "No More Lonely Nights" and the ballad version are two completely different recordings.

- Paul recorded new versions of "Ballroom Dancing," "Eleanor Rigby," "For No One," "Good Day Sunshine," "Here, There and Everywhere," "The Long and Winding Road," "Wanderlust" and "Yesterday"; and the new titles "Not Such a Bad Boy" and "No Values," all released on the soundtrack LP *Give My Regards to Broad Street*.

- Paul recorded "So Bad" (Version II), released only on the CD and cassette editions of *Give My Regards to Broad Street*. The CD also added an instrumental, "Goodnight Princess," with Paul's spoken introduction. "Corridor Music" and "Eleanor's Dream," instrumental tracks written by Paul for the film soundtrack, also appear on all releases of the album (longer versions on CD and cassette). All of the recordings were done live during the filming of *Give My Regards to Broad Street*.

1984

Jul 4: Ringo backed The Beach Boys during their Washington, D.C. concert; "Back in the USSR" from this show was released in Dec 1986 only in the U.S. on the limited edition, mail order album *Fourth of July: A Rockin' Celebration of America*, released by the Love Foundation.

Nov 25: Paul recorded two very brief Christmas messages, included on the B side of the special benefit single "Do They Know It's Christmas?"/"Feed the World," released as a single Dec 7 in the U.S. and U.K.

Late that year: George recorded "I Don't Want to Do It," released on the *Porky's Revenge* soundtrack album Mar 14, 1985 in the U.S. and Jul 1, 1985 in the U.K. It was also released in a slightly different mix as a single only in the U.S. in May 1985. George also recorded a new vocal with slightly different lyrics for "Save the World," released (with the original backing track remixed) on the charity album *Greenpeace* Jun 4, 1985 in the U.K. and Aug 19, 1985 in the U.S.

■ Paul recorded "We Got Married" during sessions co-produced by Paul and David Foster. It was released on *Flowers in the Dirt* Jun 5, 1989 in the U.K. and Jun 6, 1989 in the U.S. New sections were recorded in summer 1988, when McCartney produced his own sessions, and Neil Dorfsman received an "additional production" credit for this track. Despite reports that Foster and McCartney produced a total of four songs, Foster said in an early 1990 interview on Canada's "Much Music" that he had recorded only three titles with McCartney and he called "We Got Married" the weakest of the group.

1985

Mar–May: Paul recorded his *Press to Play* album, produced by Hugh Padgham and released Aug 22, 1986 in the U.S. and Sep 1, 1986 in the U.K. Sessions resumed in Oct and concluded on Dec 6, with postproduction work completed during Jan–Feb 1986. The album included *"Stranglehold," "Good Times Coming"/"Feel the Sun," "Talk More Talk," *"Footprints," "Only Love Remains," "Press," *"Pretty Little Head," *"Move Over Busker," *"Angry" and *"However Absurd." The CD release added *"Write Away," *"Tough on a Tightrope" and "It's Not True" (Julian Mendelsohn remix). Paul also recorded the instrumental *"Hanglide," released on the "Press" 12-inch single Jul 14, 1986 in the U.S. and U.K. Most titles were co-written with Eric Stewart (*). "It's Not True" also appeared in a different mix as the B side of the "Press" single; "Write Away" was also released as the B side of "Pretty Little Head"; "Tough on a Tightrope" also appeared as the B side of "Only Love Remains" and was also released on the 12-inch single in a remix by Julian Mendelsohn; "Pretty Little Head" was remixed by John "Tokes" Potoker for release on a U.K. 12-inch single and remixed yet again by Larry Alexander for release as a U.K. 7-inch single; "Angry" was remixed by Larry Alexander for the U.K. "Pretty Little Head" 12-inch single and for the U.S. "Stranglehold" 7-inch single; "Only Love Remains" was remixed by Jim Boyer for release on a 7-inch single in the U.S. and U.K., and a 12-inch single in the U.K. only; "Talk More Talk" was remixed by McCartney and Jon Jacobs for release on the U.K. "Only Love Remains" 12-inch single. Two different mixes of "Press" were released. The original U.K. LP *Press to Play* appeared in two different versions; one included the Hugh Padgham mix of "Press" while the other contained a remix done by Bert Bevans and Steve Forward. The Padgham mix also appeared on the first edition of the U.K. 7-inch "Press" single, but that record was quickly replaced with a second edition that featured the Bevans/Forward mix and a new picture sleeve that added the designation "Video Edit." The Bevans/Forward mix appeared on all U.S. copies of the album, on

the U.S. single and on U.S. and U.K. "Press" 12-inch singles, where it was designated "Video Soundtrack." Both mixes appeared on a U.K. 10-inch single that also included the Julian Mendelsohn remix of "It's Not True."

Early May: Some of Ringo's dialogue from the TV movie *Alice in Wonderland* was released in the U.S. in Dec 1985 on the soundtrack album *Alice in Wonderland*; the album does not contain any of the film's songs.

Middle of May: Paul recorded a 17-second spoken message released on the B side of Gerry Marsden's charity single "You'll Never Walk Alone"/"Messages," issued only in the U.K. May 24; Paul's message was moved to the start of the A side on the extended mix version, released as a 12-inch single Jun 7 in the U.K.

Sep: Paul recorded "Spies Like Us" for the film of the same title, released as a single with "My Carnival" Nov 18 in the U.K. and the U.S. in both 7-inch and 12-inch formats. The 12-inch featured three alternate mixes of "Spies Like Us" and an extended version of "My Carnival."

Oct 1–Dec 6: Paul resumed recording sessions for his *Press to Play* album with Hugh Padgham producing; see Mar–May for song titles and release dates.

1986

Feb: Paul recorded "Simple as That," released Nov 24 only in the U.K. on the charity album *The Anti-Heroin Project: It's a Live-in World*. The song may have been composed much earlier.

Jun 20: Paul performed at the Prince's Trust Birthday Party concert at Wembley Arena, singing "Long Tall Sally," "I Saw Her Standing There" and "Get Back." "Get Back" was released on the LP *The Prince's Trust 10th Anniversary Birthday Party* Apr 24, 1987 in the U.K. and May 11, 1987 in the U.S. The other two songs were released in the U.K. as a bonus 7-inch single included with the album; "Long Tall Sally" and "Get Back" appeared on the CD release. "Get Back" and "Long Tall Sally" also appeared in the U.K. in Dec 1989 on *The Royal Concert* album along with two songs performed by George at the 1987 show.

Jul: George recorded "Zig Zag" (instrumental) from the *Shanghai Surprise* film soundtrack, released as a single with "When We Was Fab" Jan 25, 1988 in the U.S. and U.K.

Aug: Ringo, John Cleese and Bill Oddie recorded the comic track "Naughty Atom Bomb," released only in the U.K. Nov 24 on *The Anti-Heroin Project: It's a Live-in World*. Ringo's presence on this recording is difficult to detect, and Cleese told an interviewer in late 1990 that he recorded the track himself in the studio with Oddie producing. He also thought that Oddie had written the song, and he had no recollection of Ringo being involved.

Late Aug: Ringo recorded the spoken-word track "You Know It Makes Sense" at his home studio, released on a 12-inch single only in the U.K. with the non-Beatles "Live-in World" Oct 27. The song was also released Nov

24 only in the U.K., on *The Anti-Heroin Project: It's a Live-in World*.

Sep: Paul was interviewed by Chris Salewicz for *Q* magazine (the interview was later sold to *Musician* magazine); the recording was released on the picture disc album *Paul McCartney: Interview* in the U.K. in Jan 1987. The album was later reissued, also as a picture disc, as *Chat with the Stars: Paul McCartney*.

Oct 6: Ringo held a press conference in Atlanta, Georgia as a promotion for The Brasserie, a restaurant in which he owned a part interest. The press conference was released in the U.K. Mar 11, 1991 by Wax Records on colored vinyl and picture disc LPs and on a CD.

1987

Jan 5–Mar 31: George recorded the following songs for his *Cloud Nine* album, released Nov 2 in the U.S. and U.K.: "That's What It Takes," "This Is Love," "When We Was Fab," "Got My Mind Set on You," "Cloud 9," "Fish on the Sand," "Just for Today," "Devil's Radio," "Someplace Else," "Wreck of the Hesperus" and "Breath Away from Heaven." "Got My Mind Set on You" first appeared as a single on Oct 12 in the U.K. and Oct 16 in the U.S. with "Lay His Head." An extended version of "Got My Mind Set on You" was released only in the U.K. on a 12-inch single on Oct 12. A special mix of "When We Was Fab" (reverse ending) was released only in the U.K. on a 12-inch single Jan 25, 1988 and on a CD single Feb 8, 1988, both of which also contained a remix of George's previously released "That's the Way It Goes." Ringo played drums on this album. Other guest musicians included Eric Clapton, Elton John and Jeff Lynne; Lynne co-produced the album with George.

Jun 2–30: Paul recorded "Loveliest Thing" during sessions produced by Phil Ramone, released only in the U.K. on Nov 13, 1989 on the 5-inch "Figure of Eight" CD single (reissued Nov 27, 1989). It also appeared in Mar 1990 on a special double-CD *Flowers in the Dirt* released in Japan. Paul also recorded "Once upon a Long Ago," released as a 7-inch vinyl and CD single, only in the U.K., on Nov 16. A "long version" of the song was also released in the U.K. on Nov 16 on a 12- inch single; an "extended version" was released on a second 12-inch, also only in the U.K., on Nov 23. The original single version also appeared on the U.K. release of McCartney's greatest hits collection, *All the Best*, Nov 2; it has never been released in the U.S. Paul also recorded "Back on My Feet," co-written with Elvis Costello, released only in the U.K. on Nov 16 on 7-inch and 12-inch singles with "Once upon a Long Ago," and on a second edition of the 12-inch on Nov 23. It has never been released in the U.S. Paul also recorded "P.S. Love Me Do," a new arrangement of the two early Beatles songs "Love Me Do" and "P.S. I Love You." The track was officially released in Mar 1990 only on a special double CD release of *Flowers in the Dirt* issued in Japan.

Jun 5–6: George and Ringo performed on both of these dates at the Prince's Trust Rock Gala concerts,

doing the following numbers at both shows: "While My Guitar Gently Weeps" and "Here Comes the Sun" (George), and "With a Little Help from My Friends" (Ringo). All three were released on Aug 14, only in the U.K., on *The Prince's Trust Concert 1987* album. George's tracks were also released in the U.K. in Dec 1989 on *The Royal Concert*, which also included two of Paul's songs from the 1986 concert. During the first night's concert, George and Ringo joined Ben E. King on stage for "Stand by Me," but they did not appear during that number on the second night. The second night's performance was released on the *Prince's Trust* album.

Jul 1: Paul recorded overdubs for three songs, including "Once upon a Long Ago," with George Martin at Abbey Road Studios.

Jul 20: Paul recorded the following songs, released Oct 31, 1988 in the Soviet Union on the Album *CHOBA B CCCP* (*Back in the USSR*, or *Again in the USSR*): "Lucille," "Twenty Flight Rock," "That's All Right (Mama)," "Bring It on Home to Me," "Summertime," "Just Because," "I'm Gonna Be a Wheel Someday," "Midnight Special," "Kansas City" and "Lawdy Miss Clawdy." He also recorded "I'm in Love Again," omitted from the Soviet album but released Jul 17, 1989 in the U.K. as a bonus track on 12-inch and CD "This One" singles. It was also added to the 14-track CD *CHOBA* released Sep 30, 1991 in the U.K. and Oct 29, 1991 in the U.S. "Midnight Special," "Kansas City" and "Lawdy Miss Clawdy" also appeared on the 12-inch "Once upon a Long Ago" singles released only in the U.K. on Nov 16 and 23; "Kansas City" also appeared on the CD single released Nov 16. "I'm Gonna Be a Wheel Someday" also appeared on U.K. 12-inch, cassette and CD "My Brave Face" singles, released May 8, 1989; the CD single was released in the U.S. on Sep 11, 1989.

Jul 20–21: Paul recorded "It's Now or Never," omitted from the *CHOBA* album but released in the U.K. on Mar 24, 1990 on the charity album *The Last Temptation of Elvis*, initially released only by mail order through England's *New Musical Express*, with general release to follow later in the year. The album was also available in the U.S. as an import, but no official release took place.

Jul 21: Paul recorded more songs for *CHOBA B CCCP*, including "Crackin' Up," "Don't Get Around Much Anymore" and "Ain't That a Shame." "Don't Get Around Much Anymore" was first released in the U.K. on Nov 16 on the "Once upon a Long Ago" 12-inch and CD singles; it also appeared on a U.S. promo-only CD album, *Paul McCartney Rocks*, released Feb 20, 1990. "Ain't That a Shame" also appeared on "My Brave Face" 12-inch, CD and cassette singles released in the U.K. on May 8, 1989; the CD single was also released in the U.S. on Sep 11, 1989. All 14 tracks listed above were issued on the CD *CHOBA B CCCP (The Russian Album)* Sep 30, 1991 in the U.K. and Oct 29, 1991 in the U.S.

Late Jul: Paul recorded "I Wanna Cry," released Jul 17, 1989, only in the U.K., as a bonus track on "This One" 12-inch and CD singles.

That summer–fall: Paul recorded four songs co-written with Elvis Costello: "My Brave Face," released as a single with "Flying to My Home" May 8, 1989 in the U.K. and May 10, 1989 in the U.S., "Don't Be Careless Love," "That Day Is Done" and "You Want Her Too." All four were released on the *Flowers in the Dirt* album Jun 5, 1989 in the U.K. and Jun 6, 1989 in the U.S.

That fall: Ringo recorded "When You Wish upon a Star" with Herb Alpert, released on the *Stay Awake* album Oct 18, 1988 in the U.S. and Oct 24, 1988 in the U.K.

Dec–Jan 1988: Paul recorded "Ou Est Le Soleil?" which was released in a number of different mixes and edits. It originally appeared as a bonus track only on cassette and CD releases of *Flowers in the Dirt*. Three alternate mixes of the song, different from the album version, were released in the U.S. Jul 26, 1989 (and in Europe outside the U.K.) on a 12-inch and cassette maxi single (7:02, 4:25 instrumental, and 4:27 Tub Dub Mix, all done by Shep Pettibone). Shorter edits of the Pettibone remix were released on U.K. 7-inch (Nov 13, 1989), 12-inch (Nov 27, 1989), CD (Nov 27, 1989), and cassette (U.K. Nov 13, 1989; U.S. Nov 15, 1989) "Figure of Eight" singles. Paul also recorded "Figure of Eight" (Version I), "Rough Ride" (Version I) and "How Many People," all released on *Flowers in the Dirt*.

1988

That spring: George recorded "Handle with Care" with Bob Dylan, Roy Orbison, Tom Petty and Jeff Lynne, a group that would soon record an album as The Traveling Wilburys. The union came about when George and Jeff Lynne began recording a B side for one of the *Cloud Nine* singles at Bob Dylan's home studio in Malibu. Orbison and Petty were also present, and all five helped to compose and share lead vocal on the recording of "Handle with Care." The song was considered too good for a B side and was held over, later to be released as a Traveling Wilburys single with "Margarita" on Oct 17 in the U.S. and U.K.

Middle of May: In several recorded interviews, George mentioned that the entire *The Traveling Wilburys Volume One* album had been recorded during the two middle weeks of May. However, there are also reports that the album was recorded during Mar and Apr. It was released Oct 18 in the U.S. and Oct 24 in the U.K. The Wilburys, and their assumed names, were George Harrison (Nelson Wilbury), Roy Orbison (Lefty), Bob Dylan (Lucky), Tom Petty (Charlie T. Jnr.) and Jeff Lynne (Otis). George and Lynne produced the album. George does lead vocal on "Heading for the Light" and shares lead vocal on "End of the Line." He contributes backing vocals and instrumentals on the remaining tracks: "Dirty World," "Rattled," "Last Night," "Not Alone Any More," "Congratulations," "Margarita" and "Tweeter and the Monkey Man."

May: Paul and Johnny Cash recorded "New Moon over Jamaica," with June Carter, Linda McCartney and Tom T. Hall providing harmony vocals. The song was released on Cash's *Water from the Wells of Home* album Oct 10 in the U.S. and Nov 14 in the U.K. Paul's contribution is far more than a typical guest appearance. In addition to co-writing the song with Cash and Hall, and producing the record, Paul sang a virtual duet with Cash, even taking lead vocal himself at one point.

Jun–Jul: Paul recorded "The First Stone," released only in the U.K. on 7-inch, 12-inch and CD "This One" singles on Jul 17, 1989. He also recorded "Put It There," "Distractions" and "This One," all released on *Flowers in the Dirt*. A special "Club Lovejoys Mix" of "This One" was released initially only on a limited edition 12-inch, white label club DJ single in the U.K., and on Nov 13, 1989 on a U.K. 12-inch single with "Figure of Eight." Paul also recorded "Flying to My Home," released as a single with "My Brave Face" May 8, 1989 in the U.K. and May 10, 1989 in the U.S.

Sep–Oct: Paul recorded "Good Sign," released only in the U.K. on Jul 31, 1989 as a bonus track on a U.K. 12-inch single with "This One" and "The First Stone." He also recorded "Motor of Love," released on *Flowers in the Dirt*.

1989

Feb–Apr: Paul recorded a new version of "The Long and Winding Road" (Version III), released Jul 24 only in the U.K. on a special limited boxed edition "This One" single ("The First Stone" was the first edition B side). It also appeared on the U.K. 5-inch CD "Figure of Eight" single released Nov 13 and reissued Nov 27. "The Long and Winding Road" (Version III) is taken from the soundtrack of the TV special "Put It There," aired in the U.K. on Jun 10 and later released on videocassette. Paul also recorded "Party Party," released only on one-track etched 7-inch vinyl and 3-inch CD singles issued with the respective vinyl and CD "World Tour Pack" editions of *Flowers in the Dirt*, released in the U.K. on Nov 23. Only the CD edition was imported into the U.S. on Jan 15, 1990. A 3:40 edit of "Party Party" was released in the U.S. on the promo CD *Paul McCartney Rocks* on Feb 20, 1990. A special remix running 6:21 was issued on a U.K. 12-inch promo released only to club disc jockeys Nov 27, with the 5:36 single version on the other side. Finally, Paul recorded a new version of "Rough Ride" (Version II) during filming of the "Put It There" TV special, released Nov 27 only in the U.K. on a 3-inch CD single with "Figure of Eight" and "Ou Est le Soleil?"

Mar 5: Ringo was one of many artists contributing vocals to "Spirit of the Forest," released Jun 5 as a 12-inch single in the U.S. and a 7-inch single in the U.K.; Ringo does one line of lead vocal. The record was a fund-raiser for environmental groups.

Mar 27: Ringo and Buck Owens recorded a new version of "Act Naturally," a song each of them had done years earlier, Ringo's version having been recorded with The Beatles. The new duet was released Jul 5 in the U.S.

as a single, and Feb 19, 1990 in the U.K. on Owens' *Act Naturally*, released in the U.S. Oct 1.

Mar: George recorded "Cheer Down," released Aug 10 in the U.S. and Sep 4 in the U.K. on the *Lethal Weapon 2* soundtrack album. It appeared as a single with "That's What It Takes" on Aug 24 in the U.S.; the U.K. single was released on Nov 27 with "Poor Little Girl" as the B side; U.K. 12-inch and CD singles, also released Nov 27, added the previously released "Crackerbox Palace" as a bonus track.

Apr 20: Paul was one of several artists who contributed vocals to a new recording of "Ferry 'Cross the Mersey" (once a hit for Gerry and The Pacemakers), released only in the U.K. on May 8 as a special charity single (vinyl and CD) with Paul, Gerry Marsden, Holly Johnson and The Christians sharing vocals. Income from the single was to go to the Hillsborough Disaster Fund, organized to help families of victims of a soccer stadium disaster.

Apr–Jun: George recorded "Cockamamie Business" and "Poor Little Girl," both released on the *Best of Dark Horse 1976–1989* album on Oct 17 in the U.S. and Oct 23 in the U.K. "Poor Little Girl" was also released in the U.K. on 7- inch, 12-inch and CD singles with "Cheer Down" on Nov 27.

Jun 15: Portions of Paul's Rome press conference were released in the U.K. on Jan 22, 1990 by Wax Records on *Press Conferences Rome & London 1989*, issued in several formats.

Jul 27: Paul's press conference at London's Playhouse Theatre was released in the U.K. Jan 22, 1990 by Wax Records on *Press Conferences Rome & London 1989*, issued in several formats.

Early Sep: Paul recorded a new version of "Figure of Eight" (Version II), released in several edits only in the U.K. on eight different singles, as follows: Nov 13: 7-inch and cassette single with "Ou Est le Soleil?"; gatefold 5-inch CD single with bonus tracks "The Long and Winding Road" (Version III) and "Loveliest Thing"; 12-inch single with "This One" (Club Lovejoys Mix); Nov 20: 12-inch single with "Ou Est le Soleil?" (4:50 edit); Nov 27: 3-inch CD with "Rough Ride" (Version II) and "Ou Est le Soleil?" (4:50 edit); 12-inch single with bonus tracks "Ou Est le Soleil?" (full 7:10 Pettibone remix) and "Ou Est le Soleil?" (Tub Dub Mix); second edition of the 5-inch CD single, identical to Nov 13 release, but in standard jewel box instead of the gatefold cover. Only a cassette single was released in the U.S. Running times of "Figure of Eight" (Version II) vary and often differ from the times listed on the records and CDs. See "Alternate Versions and Bonus Tracks" section for more details.

Sep 3: Ringo performed on the first of two consecutive nights at the Greek Theater in Los Angeles. "The No No Song," "Honey Don't," "You're Sixteen" and "Photograph" from this show were released on Oct 8, 1990 in the U.K. and Oct 12, 1990 in the U.S. on *Ringo Starr and*

Ringo Starr and His All-Starr Band (© Monteco B.V.). Ringo's 1989 All-Starr tour rejuvenated his career. The album was taped at his Los Angeles shows.

His All-Starr Band, which includes songs by other band members.

Sep 4: Ringo's live version of "With a Little Help from My Friends," recorded during his encore at the Greek Theater, was released Jun 18, 1990 in the U.K. on the 12-inch and CD single releases of The Traveling Wilburys' "Nobody's Child," a fund- raising release for the Romanian Angel Appeal; Ringo's song is not featured on the 7-inch or cassette single releases. It was released Jul 23, 1990 in the U.K. and Jul 24, 1990 in the U.S. on the album *Nobody's Child: Romanian Angel Appeal.* "It Don't Come Easy" from this show was released on *Ringo Starr and His All-Starr Band* and "Act Naturally" was released only in the U.S. on a special CD single included with a deluxe edition of the *All-Starr* CD.

Sep 28–Dec 9: The following songs from Paul's concert tour were released worldwide Nov 5, 1990 on the album *Tripping the Live Fantastic*: "Put It There" and "Live and Let Die" (Sep 28), "Rough Ride" (Oct 10), "Got to Get You into My Life" (Oct 17), "Can't Buy Me Love" (Oct 21), "Things We Said Today" (Nov 2), "Ebony and Ivory" and "Maybe I'm Amazed" (Nov 8), "Figure of Eight" (Nov 10), "Crackin' Up" and "Sgt. Pepper's Lonely Hearts Club Band" (Nov 23), "Together" (Dec 5 soundcheck), "Golden Slumbers"/"Carry That Weight"/"The End" (Dec 7, listed on LP as Jan 13), "Yesterday" (Dec 9 show) and "Don't Let the Sun Catch You Crying" (Dec 9 soundcheck, listed on LP as Feb 9).

Oct 26: A recording of "C Moon" from Paul's Milan soundcheck was released in the U.K. only on Dec 3, 1990 on 7-inch, 12-inch, cassette and two different CD singles with "All My Trials," from the next day's show.

Oct 27: "All My Trials" was performed by Paul only once during his 1989–90 world tour, on this date during his Milan show. It was released following radical editing. The unedited track runs 4:41, has five verses and two instrumental breaks. The released edit runs 3:13, starts with the fourth verse, followed by the third, the first instrumental break and concludes with the fifth verse; the first two verses and the second instrumental break are omitted. The track was first released Nov 19, 1990 on the U.K. *Tripping the Live Fantastic Highlights!* album (the U.S. version of that album contained "Put It There" instead). It was released again in the U.K. on Dec 3, 1990 as a 7-inch, 12-inch, CD and cassette single, all with "C Moon"; the 12-inch and CD added "Mull of Kintyre" and "Put It There" as bonus tracks, all live tracks from the tour. A second, limited edition of the CD single replaced the last two titles with the Lennon medley of "Strawberry Fields Forever"/"Help!"/"Give Peace a Chance," recorded at Paul's Jun 28, 1990 Liverpool show. In the U.S., "All My Trials" appeared only on the Columbia House Record Club vinyl edition of *Highlights!* released in the spring of 1991.

Nov 2: Paul's Madrid press conference was released in England in Jul 1990 by Wax Records in several formats. Part of the press conference was released in the U.S. in Sep 1990 on LP *Press Conferences Madrid/L.A.*

Nov 7: Paul's Rotterdam press conference was released in Aug 1990 in England by Wax Records.

Nov 27: Paul's Los Angeles press conference was released in the U.K. in Jul 1990 by Wax Records in several formats, and in the U.S. in Sep 1990 on LP *Press Conferences Madrid/L.A.*

Dec 9: Paul's live version of "Good Day Sunshine" from his Montreal show was released on 7-inch, cassette, 12-inch and CD "Birthday" singles on Oct 8, 1990 in the U.K.; it was released only as a cassette single in the U.S. Oct 16, 1990.

Dec 18–24: Paul recorded the mostly instrumental soundtrack for a documentary film about artist Honore Daumier, produced by MPL.

1990

Jan 2–Jun 28: The following songs from Paul's concert tour were released worldwide Nov 5 on the album *Tripping the Live Fantastic*: "Inner City Madness" (Jan 2 soundcheck), "Fool on the Hill" and "Twenty Flight Rock" (Jan 13), "We Got Married" and "Band on the Run" (Jan 16), "Jet" (Jan 17), "My Brave Face" (Jan 19), "Matchbox" and "Sally" (a Gracie Fields World War II era number) (Jan 21 soundcheck), "This One" (Feb 1), "Eleanor Rigby" (Feb 8), "Yesterday" (Feb 9), "If I Were Not upon a Stage" and "Hey Jude" (Feb 12, listed on LP as Sep 26), "Coming Up" (Mar 3), "Back in the USSR" (Mar 5), "Ain't That a Shame" (Mar 9), "Get Back" (Mar 13), "Let It Be" (Apr 14), "The Long and Winding Road" (Apr 21, listed on LP as Apr 19) and "Birthday" (Jun 30, also issued as a single).

Feb 1: Paul's Detroit press conference was released in the U.K. in Jul 1990 by Wax Records in several formats.

Mar 1: Paul's Tokyo press conference was released in the U.K. in Dec 1991 on *Paul McCartney: Press Conferences Tokyo/Chicago 1990.*

Mar 5: "Let 'Em In" from Paul's Tokyo show was released as a bonus track only on U.K. 12-inch and CD "Birthday" singles on Oct 8. "Back in the USSR" from this show was released on *Tripping the Live Fantastic*.

Apr 21: "P.S. Love Me Do" from Paul's second Rio concert was released in the U.K. on Oct 8 as a bonus track on 12-inch and CD "Birthday" singles; "The Long and Winding Road" was released on *Tripping the Live Fantastic*, incorrectly listed as Apr 19.

Late Apr: The Traveling Wilburys—George, Bob Dylan, Tom Petty and Jeff Lynne—reunited without a replacement for the late Roy Orbison, to record their second album. They devoted a period from late Mar to middle of May first writing new songs, and then recording them over a three-week period during Apr and early May at a private home studio in Bel Air, California; final vocal overdub sessions took place in Jul. The first release from these sessions was "Nobody's Child," a song that The Beatles had backed Tony Sheridan on in Jun 1961 in Hamburg during their first commercial studio session. The Wilbury recording (more faithful than Sheridan's to its original country and western flavor) took place in late Apr and was released Jun 18 in the U.K. as a single backed with Dave Stewart's "Lumiere." The song was first released in the U.S. Jul 24 on the album *Nobody's Child: Romanian Angel Appeal*, also released in the U.K. a day earlier.

Late Apr–early May: The Traveling Wilburys recorded their second album, released as the numerically incorrect *The Traveling Wilburys Volume 3* (there had been no Volume 2) on Oct 29 in the U.K. and Oct 30 in the U.S. George shares lead vocals on "She's My Baby," "The Devil's Been Busy," "Where Were You Last Night?" and "Wilbury Twist," and contributes instrumental and vocal backing on "Inside Out," "If You Belonged to Me," "7 Deadly Sings," "Poor House," "Cool Dry Place," "New Blue Moon" and "You Took My Breath Away." As with *Volume One*, no specific composing credits were given for these songs; all were attributed to The Traveling Wilburys. The group also recorded "Runaway," which had been a number-one hit for Del Shannon in 1961. The Wilbury version was released only in the U.K. on Nov 5 as a bonus track on 12-inch and CD single editions of "She's My Baby." The instrumental track from "New Blue Moon" also appeared on those singles and as the B side on the 7-inch single. Although a promo CD single was released in the U.S., no commercial release of the single took place there.

Jun 23: Paul performed "Mull of Kintyre" only once during his world tour, during his concert at the Scottish Exhibition and Conference Centre in Glasgow on this date. The track was released only in the U.K. on Nov 26 as a bonus track on the 12-inch and first edition CD "All My Trials" singles.

Jun 28: The Lennon medley from Paul's concert at King's Dock in Liverpool ("Strawberry Fields Forever"/"Help!"/"Give Peace a Chance") was released in the U.K. on Dec 3 as a bonus track on the second of two "All My Trials" CD singles. Paul's preconcert Liverpool press conference was released in Dec in the U.K. on *Liverpool Press Conference June 1990* in several formats.

Jun 30: Paul performed live at a benefit concert in Knebworth. "Coming Up" and "Hey Jude" from this show were released on *Knebworth: The Album* on Aug 6 in the U.S. and U.K. "Birthday" was released Oct 16 as a cassette single in the U.S. and Oct 8 in the U.K. in 7-inch, 12-inch, cassette and CD single formats with a live version of "Good Day Sunshine"; "Birthday" also appeared on *Tripping the Live Fantastic*.

Jul 29: Paul's Chicago press conference was released in the U.K. in Dec 1991 on *Paul McCartney: Press Conferences Tokyo/Chicago 1990*.

1991

Jan 25: Paul taped an appearance for MTV's "Unplugged" television series before an invited audience of about 200, aired in the U.S. Apr 3. The telecast included "Be-Bop-a-Lula," "I Lost My Little Girl" (the first public performance of Paul's first composition, written at the age of 14), "Here, There and Everywhere," "Blue Moon of Kentucky" (slow and fast versions), "We Can Work It Out" (a breakdown and a complete runthrough), "I've Just Seen a Face," "Every Night," "She's a Woman," "And I Love Her," "That Would Be Something," "Blackbird," "Good Rockin' Tonight" and "Singing the Blues." An instrumental version of "Junk" was played over the closing credits. These numbers were released May 20 in the U.K. and Jun 4 in the U.S. on the album *Unplugged (The Official Bootleg)*, which added the unaired "San Francisco Bay Blues," "Hi-Heel Sneakers" and "Ain't No Sunshine" (vocal by Hamish Stuart). Paul also did the unaired and unreleased "Mean Woman Blues," "Matchbox," "Midnight Special," "The Fool" and "Things We Said Today."

Mar–Sep: Ringo recorded songs for *Time Takes Time*, the first album under his new contract with Private Music. The album includes "Weight of the World," "Don't Know a Thing About Love," "I Don't Believe You," "Runaways," "After All These Years," "In a Heartbeat," "Don't Go Where The Road Don't Go," "Golden Blunders," "All in the Name of Love," and "What Goes Around." Sessions were concluded in Feb 1992. The album was released May 22, 1992. "Don't Be Cruel" was issued as a CD single bonus track Apr 28, 1992 in U.S. and May 4, 1992 in U.K.

Sep 14: Ringo recorded "You Never Know," which was played over the closing credits in the film *Curly Sue*, and released on the soundtrack album Nov 26 in the U.S. and Jan 6, 1992 in the U.K.

Discographies

This section contains three separate discographies listing all Beatles records that have been officially released in the United States, in the United Kingdom and special, limited edition releases. Each entry includes the release date, the type of record (single, LP, EP, CD, cassette), the record title, label and serial number, and all song titles or other recordings found on the record. In addition to all Beatles group and solo song titles, the discographies contain a number of nonmusical Beatles recordings, including their annual Christmas records, interviews and press conferences. At the end of this section are listings of "Alternate Versions and Bonus Tracks" and "Notable Album Variations."

Entries also include the following information:
1. First release: Indicates that the material has never been released before anywhere.
2. First U.K. or first U.S. release: The material has been previously released in another country, but this is its first release in one of these two countries.
3. Previously released: The material has been issued before, at least in the country represented in the discography (U.S. or U.K.), but not necessarily in the other country. For example, a song may have been issued two or three times in the U.K. but never issued in the U.S.

The following abbreviations are used:
LP = 12-inch, long playing, vinyl album
CD = Compact disc, long playing album
EP = 7-inch, extended play, vinyl record
single = standard 7-inch vinyl single
CD single = single issued in CD format, usually including from two to four songs
12-inch single = vinyl release, usually including from two to four songs
10-inch single = rarely used vinyl format containing two to four songs
cassette = long-playing album issued in cassette format
cassette single = single issued on cassette

U.S. Discography

1962

Apr 23: Single "My Bonnie"/"The Saints" (Decca 31382). First U.S. release of both songs.

1963

Feb 25: Single "Please Please Me"/"Ask Me Why" (Vee Jay 448). First U.S. release of both songs.

May 27: Single "From Me to You"/"Thank You Girl" (Vee Jay 522). First U.S. release of both songs.

Jul 22: LP *Introducing The Beatles* (Vee Jay 1062; stereo and mono). First U.S. release of all 12 songs: "I Saw Her Standing There," "Misery," "Anna," "Chains," "Boys," "Love Me Do" (Version II 2:19), "P.S. I Love You," "Baby It's You," "Do You Want to Know a Secret," "A Taste of Honey," "There's a Place," "Twist and Shout."

Sep 16: Single "She Loves You"/"I'll Get You" (Swan 4152). First U.S. release of both songs.

Dec 26: Single "I Want to Hold Your Hand"/"I Saw Her Standing There" (Capitol 5112). First U.S. release of A side; B side previously released.

1964

Jan 20: LP *Meet The Beatles* (Capitol stereo: ST 2047; mono: T 2047). First U.S. release of "This Boy," "It Won't Be Long," "All I've Got to Do," "All My Loving," "Don't Bother Me," "Little Child," "Till There Was You," "Hold Me Tight," "I Wanna Be Your Man," "Not a Second Time." Also contains "I Want to Hold Your Hand" and "I Saw Her Standing There," both previously released.

Jan 27: LP *Introducing The Beatles* (Vee Jay 1062; stereo and mono). Same contents as Jul 22, 1963 release except "Love Me Do" and "P.S. I Love You" were replaced by "Please Please Me" and "Ask Me Why." All previously released.

■ Single "My Bonnie"/"The Saints" (MGM K13213). Both previously released.

Jan 30: Single "Please Please Me"/"From Me to You." Both previously released (Vee Jay 581).

Feb 3: LP *The Beatles with Tony Sheridan and Their Guests* (MGM SE-4215). First U.S. release of "Why" and "Cry for a Shadow." Also contains prior releases "My Bonnie" and "The Saints" plus non-Beatles material.

Feb 26: LP *Jolly What! The Beatles and Frank Ifield on Stage* (Vee Jay 1085). All previously released: "Please Please Me," "From Me to You," "Ask Me Why," "Thank You Girl" and non-Beatles cuts. (This is *not* a live recording.)

Mar 2: Single "Twist and Shout"/"There's a Place" (Tollie 9001). Both previously released.

Mar 16: Single "Can't Buy Me Love"/"You Can't Do That" (Capitol 5150). First release of both.

Mar 23: EP *The Beatles—Souvenir of Their Visit to America* (Vee Jay VJEP 1-903). All previously released: "Misery," "A Taste of Honey," "Ask Me Why," "Anna."

■ Single "Do You Want to Know a Secret"/"Thank You Girl" (Vee Jay 587). Both previously released.

Mar 27: Single "Why"/"Cry for a Shadow" (MGM K13227). Both previously released.

Apr 10: LP *The Beatles Second Album* (Capitol stereo: ST 2080; mono T 2080). First release of "Long Tall Sally," "I Call Your Name." First U.S. release of "Roll Over Beethoven," "You Really Got a Hold on Me," "Devil in Her Heart," "Money," "Please Mr. Postman." Contains prior releases "Thank You Girl," "You Can't Do That," "I'll Get You," "She Loves You."

Apr 27: Single "Love Me Do" (Version II 2:19)/"P.S. I Love You" (Tollie 9008). Both previously released.

May 11: EP *Four by The Beatles* (Capitol EAP-2121). "Roll Over Beethoven," "All My Loving," "This Boy," "Please Mr. Postman." All previously released.

May 21: Single "Sie Liebt Dich"/"I'll Get You" (Swan 4182). First U.S. release of A side; B side previously released.

Jun 1: Single "Sweet Georgia Brown"/"Take Out Some Insurance on Me, Baby" (ATCO 6302). First U.S. release of both.

Jun 9: LP *The Beatles American Tour with Ed Rudy* (Radio Pulsebeat News Documentary No. 2). First release: album with interviews taped during Feb 1964 U.S. visit.

Jun 26: LP *A Hard Day's Night* (United Artists stereo: UAS 6366; mono: UAL 6366). Despite the separate catalog numbers for stereo and mono editions, all releases of this album in the U.S. contain mono versions of The Beatles' songs. The stereo release features stereo versions only of George Martin's instrumental tracks from the film soundtrack. The contents did not change when the album was reissued on the Capitol label. Contains prior release "Can't Buy Me Love"; first release of: "A Hard Day's Night," "Tell Me Why," "I'll Cry Instead" (2:06), "I'm Happy Just to Dance with You," "I Should Have Known Better," "If I Fell," "And I Love Her." Also contains instrumentals.

Middle of that year: 33 1/3 EP *The Beatles & Murray the 'K': As It Happened* (BRS-1/2). Interviews of Feb 8, 10, 14 and May 24. First release of interviews.

■ LP *This Is The . . . Savage Young Beatles* (Savage BM-69). "Cry for a Shadow," "Take Out Some Insurance on Me, Baby," "Sweet Georgia Brown," "Why." All previously released.

Jul 6: Single "Ain't She Sweet"/"Nobody's Child" (ATCO 6308). First U.S. release of both.

Jul 13: Single "A Hard Day's Night"/"I Should Have Known Better" (Capitol 5222). Both previously released.

Jul 20: Single "I'll Cry Instead" (2:06)/"I'm Happy Just to Dance with You" (Capitol 5234). Both previously released.

■ Single "And I Love Her"/"If I Fell" (Capitol 5235). Both previously released.

■ LP *Something New* (Capitol stereo: ST 2108; mono: T 2108). First U.S. release of "Things We Said Today," "Anytime At All," "When I Get Home," "Slow Down," "Matchbox," "Komm, Gib Mir Deine Hand," "I'll Cry Instead." Contains previously released "Tell Me Why," "And I Love Her," "I'll Cry Instead" (1:44 U.K. edit on stereo LP, incorrectly listed as 2:04 on the LP and cover), "I'm Happy Just to Dance with You," "If I Fell."

Aug 10: Singles "Do You Want to Know a Secret"/"Thank You Girl" (Oldies 45 OL 149), "Please Please Me"/"From Me to You" (OL 150), "Love Me Do" (Version II)/" P.S. I Love You" (OL 151), "Twist and Shout"/"There's a Place" (OL 152), all previously released.

Aug 24: Single "Slow Down"/"Matchbox" (Capital 5255). Both previously released.

Sep 7: LP *The Big Hits from England and the USA* (Capitol DT 2125). Contains "Can't Buy Me Love" and "You Can't Do That," both previously released.

Sep 14: LP *Hear The Beatles Tell All* (Vee Jay VJ PRO-202). First release of Jim Steck interview with John, and Dave Hull's interview with all of The Beatles taped Aug 24 and 25.

Oct 1: Double LP *The Beatles Vs. The Four Seasons* (Vee Jay VJDX 30). All previously released: "I Saw Her Standing There," "Misery," "Anna," "Chains," "Boys," "A Taste of Honey," "There's a Place," "Twist and Shout," "Ask My Why," "Please Please Me," "Baby It's You," "Do You Want to Know a Secret." Other cuts by The Four Seasons.

Oct 5: LP *Ain't She Sweet* (ATCO SD 33-169). "Ain't She Sweet," "Sweet Georgia Brown," "Take Out Some Insurance on Me, Baby," "Nobody's Child." All previously released.

Oct 12: LP *Songs, Pictures, and Stories of The Fabulous Beatles* (Vee Jay VJLP 1092). "I Saw Her Standing There," "Misery," "Chains," "Boys," "Ask Me Why," "Please Please Me," "Baby It's You," "Do You Want to Know a Secret," "A Taste of Honey," "There's a Place," "Twist and Shout." All previously released.

Nov 23: Double LP *The Beatles Story* (Capitol stereo: STBO 2222; mono: TBO 2222). First release of documentary LP; few actual interview clips; mostly narration. A very brief clip of "Twist and Shout" from the Aug 23 Hollywood Bowl concert is heard.

■ Single "I Feel Fine"/"She's a Woman" (Capitol 5327). First release of both songs.

Dec 15: LP *Beatles '65* (Capitol stereo: ST 2228; mono: T 2228). First U.S. release of "No Reply," "I'm a Loser," "Baby's in Black," "Rock and Roll Music," "I'll Follow the Sun," "Mr. Moonlight," "Honey Don't," "I'll Be Back," "Everybody's Trying to Be My Baby." Includes prior releases "She's a Woman" and "I Feel Fine."

Dec 18: *Another Beatles Christmas Record* released to fan club. This was the first of The Beatles' annual Christmas records issued to the U.S. Fan Club.

1965

That year: LP *Ed Rudy with New U.S. Tour* (*The Beatles Great American Tour*) or *American Tour with Ed Rudy No. 3* (Radio Pulsebeat News L-1001/1002 Documentary No. 3). Interview LP made during second 1964 U.S. visit.

■ LP *The Great American Tour—1965 Live Beatlemania Concert* (Lloyds E.R.M.C. Ltd. Records). First release of Ed Rudy's so-called tribute LP features what amounts to a near-bootleg recording of a Beatles 1964 U.S. concert performance with vocals overdubbed by a group called the Liverpool Lads.

Feb 1: EP *4 by The Beatles* (Capitol R 5365). "Honey Don't," "I'm a Loser," "Mr. Moonlight," "Everybody's Trying to Be My Baby." All previously released.

Feb 15: Single "Eight Days a Week"/"I Don't Want to Spoil the Party" (Capitol 5371). First U.S. release of both.

Mar 22: LP *The Early Beatles* (Capitol stereo: ST 2309; mono: T 2309). Despite the separate stereo and mono releases, the mono version contains the stereo mix of these songs with the separate tracks combined into one: "Love Me Do" (Version II 2:19), "Twist and Shout," "Anna," "Chains," "Boys," "Ask Me Why," "Please Please Me," "P.S. I Love You," "Baby It's You," "A Taste of Honey," "Do You Want to Know a Secret." All previously released.

Apr 19: Single "Ticket to Ride"/"Yes It Is" (Capitol 5407). First U.S. release of both songs.

Jun 14: LP *Beatles VI* (Capitol stereo: ST 2358; mono: T 2358). First release of "You Like Me Too Much," "Bad

Beatles VI (© Apple Corps Ltd.). Another album with the title, cover and song lineup created by Capitol for the U.S. market; it too bore no resemblance to its British counterparts.

Boy," "Dizzy Miss Lizzie," "Tell Me What You See." First U.S. release of "Kansas City"/"Hey Hey Hey Hey," "Words of Love," "What You're Doing," "Every Little Thing." Contains previously released "Eight Days a Week," "I Don't Want to Spoil the Party," "Yes It Is."

Jul 19: Single "Help!" (Version I)/"I'm Down" (Capitol 5476). First release of both. This was the only U.S. release of the mono mix of "Help!" featuring a different Lennon vocal, until it appeared on the *Rarities* album on Mar 24, 1980.

Aug 13: LP *Help!* (Capitol stereo: SMAS 2386; mono: MAS 2386). As with *The Early Beatles* LP, the U.S. mono release of this album contained the stereo mix with the separate tracks combined into one. First U.S. release of "Help!" (Version II), "The Night Before," "You've Got to Hide Your Love Away," "I Need You," "Another Girl," "You're Going to Lose That Girl." Contains prior release "Ticket to Ride" and instrumentals from the film soundtrack.

Sep 13: Single "Yesterday"/"Act Naturally" (Capitol 5498). First U.S. release of both.

Oct 11: Singles "Twist and Shout"/"There's a Place" (Capitol Starline 6061), "Love Me Do" (Version II)/"P.S. I Love You" (6062), "Please Please Me"/"From Me to You" (6063), "Do You Want to Know a Secret"/"Thank You Girl" (6064), "Roll Over Beethoven"/"Misery" (6065), "Boys"/"Kansas City"/"Hey Hey Hey Hey" (6066), all previously released.

Dec 6: Single "We Can Work It Out"/"Day Tripper" (Capitol 5555). First U.S. release of both songs.

■ LP *Rubber Soul* (Capitol stereo: ST 2442; mono: T 2442). "I've Just Seen a Face," "Norwegian Wood (This Bird Has Flown)," "You Won't See Me," "Think for Yourself," "The Word," "Michelle," "It's Only Love," "Girl," "I'm Looking Through You," "In My Life," "Wait," "Run for Your Life." First U.S. release of all songs.

Dec 17: *The Beatles Third Christmas Record*. Released to fan club.

1966

Feb 21: Single "Nowhere Man"/"What Goes On" (Capitol 5587). First U.S. release of both songs.

May 23: Single "Paperback Writer"/"Rain" (Capitol 5651). First release of both songs.

Jun 15: LP *Yesterday and Today* (Capitol stereo: ST 2553; mono: T 2553). First release of "I'm Only Sleeping," "Dr. Robert," "And Your Bird Can Sing." First U.S. release of "Drive My Car," "If I Needed Someone." Contains previously released "Nowhere Man," "Yesterday," "Act Naturally," "We Can Work It Out," "What Goes On," "Day Tripper." Released in "Butcher Sleeve" cover on this date.

Jun 20: LP *Yesterday and Today* rereleased with new cover; contents unchanged.

Aug 5: Single "Eleanor Rigby"/"Yellow Submarine" (Capitol 5715). First release of both songs in U.S. and U.K. on same day.

Aug 8: LP *Revolver* (Capitol stereo: ST 2576; mono: T 2576). First U.S. release of "Taxman," "Love You To," "Here, There and Everywhere," "She Said She Said," "Good Day Sunshine," "For No One," "I Want to Tell You," "Got to Get You into My Life," "Tomorrow Never Knows." Contains previously released "Yellow Submarine" and "Eleanor Rigby."

Aug 15: LP *This Is Where It Started* (Metro MS 563). "My Bonnie," "Cry for a Shadow," "The Saints," "Why." All previously released.

Oct 17: LP *The Amazing Beatles and Other Great English Group Sounds* (Clarion 601). "Ain't She Sweet," "Take Out Some Insurance on Me, Baby," "Nobody's Child," "Sweet Georgia Brown." All previously released.

Nov 28: LP *The Original Discotheque Hits* (Clarion 609). "Take Out Some Insurance on Me, Baby." Previously released.

Dec 16: *The Beatles Fourth Christmas Record.* Released to fan club.

1967

Feb 13: Single "Strawberry Fields Forever"/"Penny Lane" (Capitol 5810). First release of both songs.

Jun 2: LP *Sgt. Pepper's Lonely Hearts Club Band* (Capitol stereo: SMAS 2653; mono: MAS 2653). "Sgt. Pepper's Lonely Hearts Club Band" (1:59), "With a Little Help from My Friends," "Lucy in the Sky with Diamonds," "Getting Better," "Fixing a Hole," "She's Leaving Home," "Being for the Benefit of Mr. Kite," "Within You Without You," "When I'm Sixty-Four," "Lovely Rita," "Good Morning Good Morning," "Sgt. Pepper's Lonely Hearts Club Band" (Reprise 1:20), "A Day in the Life." First U.S. release of all material.

Jul 17: Single "All You Need Is Love"/"Baby You're a Rich Man" (Capitol 5964). First U.S. release of both songs.

Nov 27: LP *Magical Mystery Tour* (Capitol stereo: SMAL 2835; mono: MAL 2835). First release of "Magical Mystery Tour," "The Fool on the Hill," "Flying," "Blue Jay Way," "Your Mother Should Know." First U.S. release of "Hello Goodbye" and "I Am the Walrus." Also contains previously released "Strawberry Fields Forever," +"Penny Lane," +"Baby You're a Rich Man," +"All You Need Is Love." (+ these tracks appear in mono even on the stereo release of this album. Later German LP, U.K. cassette, and worldwide CD editions were all stereo.)

■ Single "Hello Goodbye"/"I Am the Walrus" (Capitol 2056). Released in U.S. same day on LP *Magical Mystery Tour.*

Dec 15: *Christmas Time Is Here Again.* Released to fan club.

1968

Mar 18: Single "Lady Madonna"/"The Inner Light" (Capitol 2138). First U.S. release of both songs.

Aug 26: Single "Hey Jude"/"Revolution" (Version I) (Apple 2276). First release of both songs.

Nov 11: LP *Unfinished Music No. 1—Two Virgins* (John and Yoko) (Apple Tetragrammaton T-5001. Side one: Two Virgins (14:02); side two: Two Virgins (15:00); first release.

Nov 25: Double LP *The Beatles* (aka the "*White Album*") (Apple stereo only SWBO 101). "Back in the USSR," "Dear Prudence," "Glass Onion," "Ob-La-Di, Ob-La-Da," "Wild Honey Pie," "The Continuing Story of Bungalow Bill," "While My Guitar Gently Weeps," " Happiness Is a Warm Gun," "Martha My Dear," "I'm So Tired," "Blackbird," "Piggies," "Rocky Racoon," "Don't Pass Me By," "Why Don't We Do It in the Road?" "I Will," "Julia," "Birthday," "Yer Blues," "Mother Nature's Son," "Everybody's Got Something to Hide Except Me and My Monkey," "Sexy Sadie," "Helter Skelter," "Long Long Long," "Revolution 1" (Version II), "Honey Pie," "Savoy Truffle," "Cry Baby Cry," "Revolution 9," "Good Night." First U.S. release of all songs. Although this album was released in both stereo and mono in the U.K., only the stereo version was issued in the U.S.

Dec 2: LP *Wonderwall Music* (Apple ST 3350). First U.S. release of George's original soundtrack album.

Dec 20: *The Beatles 1968 Christmas Record.* Includes "Nowhere Man" sung by Tiny Tim. Released to fan club.

1969

Jan 13: LP *Yellow Submarine* (Apple SW 153). First release of "Only a Northern Song," "All Together Now," "Hey Bulldog," "It's All Too Much." Also contains previously released "Yellow Submarine" and "All You Need Is Love." Side two consists of instrumentals from the film score by George Martin.

May 5: Single "Get Back" (Version I)/"Don't Let Me Down" (Apple 2490). First U.S. release of both songs.

May 26: LP *Unfinished Music No. 2: Life with The Lions* (John and Yoko) (Zapple ST 3357). "Cambridge 1969," "No Bed for Beatle John", "Baby's Heartbeat," "Two Minutes of Silence," "Radio Play." First U.S. release.

■ LP *Electronic Sound* (George) (Zapple ST3358). "Under the Mersey Wall," "No Time or Space." First U.S. release.

May: LP *First Vibration* (US Mail Order—Do It Now Foundation 5000). Contains "Nowhere Man," previously released.

Jun 4: Single "The Ballad of John and Yoko"/"Old Brown Shoe" (Apple 2531). First U.S. release of both songs.

Jul 7: Single "Give Peace a Chance" (Version I) (John)/"Remember Love" (Yoko) (Apple 1809). First U.S. release of both songs.

Oct 1: LP *Abbey Road* (Apple SO 383). "Come Together," "Something," "Maxwell's Silver Hammer," "Oh! Darling," "Octopus's Garden," "I Want You (She's So Heavy)," "Here Comes the Sun," "Because," "You Never Give Me Your Money," "Sun King," "Mean Mr. Mustard," "Polythene Pam," "She Came in Through the Bathroom Window," "Golden Slumbers," "Carry That

Weight," "The End," "Her Majesty." First U.S. release of all songs.

Oct 6: Single "Something"/"Come Together" (Apple 2654). Both previously released.

Oct 20: LP *Wedding Album* (John and Yoko) (Apple SMAX 3361). Side 1: "John and Yoko"; Side 2: "Amsterdam" ["John, John (Let's Hope for Peace)," "Bed Peace," "Good Night," "Goodbye Amsterdam Goodbye"]. First release.

■ Single "Cold Turkey" (John)/"Don't Worry Kyoko" (Yoko) (Apple 1813). First release of both songs.

Dec 12: LP *The Plastic Ono Band Live Peace in Toronto—1969* (John) (Apple SW 3362). Recorded live at the Rock and Roll Revival, Toronto, Sep 13. "Introduction of the Band," "Blue Suede Shoes," "Money (That's What I Want)," "Dizzy Miss Lizzie," "Yer Blues," "Cold Turkey," "Give Peace a Chance," and Yoko's "Don't Worry Kyoko," "John, John (Let's Hope for Peace)." First release in both U.S. and U.K. on same day.

Dec 19: *The Beatles Seventh Christmas Record.* Released to fan club.

1970

Feb 11: LP *The Magic Christian* (Commonwealth United CU 6004). Original soundtrack album. "Hunting Scene" (Ringo and Peter Sellers dialogue from film soundtrack). Contains non-Beatles material. First release.

Feb 20: Single "Instant Karma (We All Shine On)" (John)/"Who Has Seen the Wind" (Yoko) (Apple 1818). First U.S. release of both songs.

Feb 26: LP *The Beatles Again* (Apple SO 385; also SW 385); later reissued as *Hey Jude* (Apple SW 385). Although all covers bore the *Hey Jude* title and the SW 385 catalog number, labels on early issues were titled *The Beatles Again* and had the SO 385 catalog number. "Can't Buy Me Love," "I Should Have Known Better," "Paperback Writer," "Rain," "Lady Madonna," "Revolution" (Version I), "Hey Jude," "Old Brown Shoe," "Don't Let Me Down," "The Ballad of John and Yoko." All previously released.

Mar 11: Single "Let It Be" (Version I)/"You Know My Name (Look Up the Number)" (Apple 2764). First U.S. release of both songs.

Apr 20: LP *McCartney* (Paul) (Apple STAO 3363). "The Lovely Linda," "That Would Be Something," "Valentine Day," "Every Night," medley "Hot As Sun"/"Glasses," "Junk," "Man We Was Lonely," "Oo You," "Momma Miss America," "Teddy Boy," "Singalong Junk" "Maybe I'm Amazed," "Kreen-Akrore"; a short, unlisted bit of "Suicide" is also included. First U.S. release of all material.

Apr 24: LP *Sentimental Journey* (Ringo) (Apple SW 3365). "Sentimental Journey," "Night and Day," "Whispering Grass (Don't Tell the Trees)," "Bye Bye Blackbird," "I'm a Fool to Care," "Star Dust," Blue Turning Grey Over You," "Love Is a Many Splendored Thing," "Dream," "You Always Hurt the One You Love," "Have I Told You Lately That I Love You," "Let the Rest of the World Go By." First U.S. release of all material.

May 11: Single "The Long and Winding Road"/"For You Blue" (Apple 2832). First U.S. release of both songs.

May 18: LP *Let It Be* (Apple AR 34001). Contains prior release "The Long and Winding Road" and "For You Blue." First U.S. release of "Let It Be" (Version II), "Across the Universe" (Version II), "Get Back" (Version II), "Two of Us," "Dig a Pony" (listed as *"I Dig a Pony"*), "I Me Mine," "Dig It," "Maggie Mae," "I've Got a Feeling," "One After 909."

Sep 28: LP *Beaucoups of Blues* (Ringo) (Apple SMAS 3368). "Beaucoups of Blues," "Love Don't Last Long," "Fastest Growing Heartache in the West," "Without Her," "Woman of the Night," "I'd Be Talking All the Time," "$15 Draw," "Wine, Women and Loud Happy Songs," "I Wouldn't Have You Any Other Way," "Loser's Lounge," "Waiting," "Silent Homecoming." First U.S. release of all material.

Oct 5: Single "Beaucoups of Blues"/"Coochy-Coochy" (Ringo) (Apple 2969/1826). First release of B side; A side previously released.

Nov 23: Single "My Sweet Lord"/"Isn't It a Pity" (Version I) (George) (Apple 2995). First release of both songs.

Nov 27: Triple LP *All Things Must Pass* (George) (Apple STCH 639). Contains previously released "My Sweet Lord" and "Isn't It a Pity" (Version I). First release of "I'd Have You Any Time," "Wah-Wah," "What Is Life," "If Not for You," "Behind That Locked Door," "Let It Down," "Run of the Mill," "Beware of Darkness," "Apple Scruffs," "Ballad of Sir Frankie Crisp (Let It Roll)," "Awaiting on You All," "All Things Must Pass," "I Dig Love," "Art of Dying," "Isn't It a Pity" (Version II), "Hear Me Lord." Apple Jam: "Out of the Blue," "It's Johnny's Birthday," "Plug Me In," "I Remember Jeep," "Thanks for the Pepperoni."

Dec 11: LP *John Lennon/Plastic Ono Band* (John) (Apple SW 3372). "Mother" (5:29), "Hold On (John)," "I Found Out," "Working Class Hero," "Isolation," "Remember," "Love," "Well Well Well," "Look at Me," "God," "My Mummy's Dead." First U.S. and U.K. release.

Dec 18: LP *The Beatles Christmas Album* (Apple SBC 100) (UK title: *From Then to You*). Contains all seven Beatles Christmas records. First U.S. release of 1963 Christmas Record; others previously released.

Dec 28: Single "Mother" (3:55) (John)/"Why" (Yoko) (Apple 1827). Both previously released.

1971

Feb 15: Single "What Is Life"/"Apple Scruffs" (George) (Apple 1828). Both previously released.

Feb 22: Single "Another Day"/"Oh Woman, Oh Why" (Paul) (Apple 1829). First U.S. release of both songs.

Feb: LP *Do It Now: 20 Giant Hits* (U.S. Mail Order—Do It Now Foundation LP 1001). Contains "Nowhere Man." Previously released.

Mar 22: Single "Power to the People" (John)/"Touch Me" (Yoko) (Apple 1830). First U.S. release A side; B side previously released.

Apr 16: Single "It Don't Come Easy"/"Early 1970" (Ringo) (Apple 1831). First U.S. release of both songs.

May 17: LP *Ram* (Paul and Linda McCartney) (Apple SMAS 3375). "Too Many People," "3 Legs," "Ram On" (2:30), "Dear Boy," "Uncle Albert/Admiral Halsey," "Smile Away," "Heart of the Country," "Monkberry Moon Delight," "Eat at Home," "Long Haired Lady," "Ram On" (reprise 0:55), "Back Seat of My Car." First release of all material.

Jul 7: Single "God Save Us" (Bill Elliot)/"Do the Oz" (John) (Apple 1835); record credited to The Elastic Oz Band. First release of both songs.

Jul 28: Single "Bangla Desh"/"Deep Blue" (George) (Apple 1836). First release of both songs.

Aug 2: Single "Uncle Albert-Admiral Halsey"/"Too Many People" (Paul and Linda) (Apple 1837). Both previously released.

Sep 9: LP *Imagine* (John) (Apple SW 3379). "Imagine," "Crippled Inside," "Jealous Guy," "It's So Hard," "I Don't Want to Be a Soldier Mama, I Don't Want to Die," "Gimme Some Truth," "Oh My Love," "How Do You Sleep?" "How?" "Oh Yoko." First release.

Oct 11: Single "Imagine"/"It's So Hard" (John) (Apple 1840). Both previously released.

Dec 1: Single "Happy Xmas (War Is Over)" (John/Ono)/ "Listen, the Snow Is Falling" (Ono) (Apple 1842). Released on green vinyl; first release of both songs.

Dec 7: LP *Wild Life* (Wings) (Apple SW 3386). "Mumbo," "Bip Bop," "Love Is Strange," "Wild Life," "Some People Never Know," "I Am Your Singer," "Bip Bop" (reprise), "Tomorrow," "Dear Friend." First release of all songs in U.S.

Dec 20: Triple LP *The Concert for Bangla Desh* (George, Ringo, others) (Apple STCX 3385). George: "Wah-Wah," "My Sweet Lord," "Awaiting on You All," "Beware of Darkness" (with Leon Russell), "While My Guitar Gently Weeps," "Here Comes the Sun," "Something," "Bangla Desh." Ringo: "It Don't Come Easy." Contains additional non-Beatles performances. Recorded live Aug 1. First release of all material.

1972

Feb 28: Wings' single "Give Ireland Back to the Irish" (vocal)/"Give Ireland Back to the Irish" (instrumental version) (Apple 1847). First U.S. release.

Mar 20: Single "Back Off Boogaloo" (Version I)/"Blindman" (Ringo) (Apple 1849). First U.S. release of both songs.

Apr 24: Single "Woman Is the Nigger of the World" (John)/"Sisters, O Sisters" (Yoko) (Apple 1848). First release of both songs; recorded with Elephant's Memory.

May 29: Wings' single "Mary Had a Little Lamb"/"Little Woman Love" (Apple 1851). First U.S. release of both songs.

Jun 12: Double LP *Some Time in New York City* (John and Yoko, Elephant's Memory, and others as noted) (Apple SVBB 3392). Contains previously released "Woman Is the Nigger of the World." First release of

John's "Attica State," "New York City," "Sunday Bloody Sunday," "The Luck of the Irish," "John Sinclair," "Angela." Also contains Yoko's "We're All Water," "Born in a Prison," and previously released "Sisters O Sisters." Recorded live Dec 15, 1969 at London's Lyceum Ballroom: "Cold Turkey" and Yoko's "Don't Worry Kyoko." Recorded live Jun 6, 1971 at New York's Fillmore East with Frank Zappa and The Mothers of Invention: "Well (Baby Please Don't Go)," "Jamrag," "Scumbag," "Au."

Nov 27: Double LP *Tommy* by London Symphony Orchestra and Chamber Choir (ODE SP 9001). Contains "Fiddle About" and "Tommy's Holiday Camp" (Ringo). First U.S. release of both songs.

Dec 4: Single "Hi Hi Hi"/"C Moon" (Wings) (Apple 1857). First U.S. release of both songs.

1973

Mar: Four-LP boxed set *Alpha Omega (Volume 1)* (Audio Tape Inc. ATRBH-3583; sold via TV advertising). "Act Naturally," "All I've Got to Do," "All My Loving," "And I Love Her," "Baby's in Black," "Yesterday," "The Ballad of John and Yoko," "Bangla Desh," "Can't Buy Me Love," "Come Together," "Day Tripper," "Do You Want to Know a Secret," "Eight Days a Week," "Eleanor Rigby," "Uncle Albert-Admiral Halsey," "I Should Have Known Better," "It Won't Be Long," "I Want to Hold Your Hand," "Lady Madonna," "Ticket to Ride," "Lucy in the Sky with Diamonds," "Michelle," "Mr. Moonlight," "I Feel Fine," "If I Fell," "I'll Be Back," "Hey Jude," "I'm a Loser," "I'm Happy Just to Dance with You," "I Saw Her Standing There," "Nowhere Man," "Ob-La-Di, Ob-La-Da," "Paperback Writer," "Penny Lane," "Help!" "Roll Over Beethoven," "Sgt. Pepper's Lonely Hearts Club Band," "Get Back" (Version I), "Hello Goodbye," "Revolution 1," "Here Comes the Sun," "I'll Follow the Sun," "Imagine," "Honey Don't," "We Can Work It Out," "With a Little Help from My Friends," "Yellow Submarine," "Baby You're a Rich Man," "You Can't Do That," "You've Got to Hide Your Love Away," "Maybe I'm Amazed," "A Hard Day's Night," "She Loves You," "Something," "Strawberry Fields Forever," "Tell Me Why," "The Long and Winding Road," "Let It Be" (Version I), "Everybody's Trying to Be My Baby." All previously released.

■ Four-LP boxed set *Alpha Omega (Volume 2)* (Audio Tape Inc. ATRBH; no catalog number). "Taxman," "She Said She Said," "All Together Now," "Pepperland" (soundtrack instrumental), "Crippled Inside," "Oh Yoko," "I'm Looking Through You," "Back in the USSR," "No Reply," "Rock & Roll Music," "Too Many People," "Heart of the Country," "Back Seat of My Car," "Magical Mystery Tour," "The Fool on the Hill," "Kansas City"/"Hey Hey Hey Hey," "Tell Me What You See," "I Don't Want to Spoil the Party," "Birthday," "Good Night," "Why Don't We Do It in the Road," "Across the Universe," "Another Girl," "All Things Must Pass," "Apple Scruffs," "Baby It's You," "A Taste of Honey," "She Came in Through the Bathroom

Window," "Maxwell's Silver Hammer," "Golden Slumbers," "Mean Mr. Mustard," "Love Me Do," "Twist and Shout," "Please Please Me," "Dizzy Miss Lizzie," "Rocky Racoon," "Helter Skelter," "You Never Give Me Your Money," "I've Just Seen a Face," "Norwegian Wood," "You Won't See Me," "The Lovely Linda," "Drive My Car," "Doctor Robert," "What Goes On," "My Sweet Lord," "Maggie Mae," "Two of Us," "I've Got a Feeling," "Dig a Pony," "All You Need Is Love," "I Am the Walrus," "Being for the Benefit of Mr. Kite," "Lovely Rita," "When I'm Sixty Four," "A Day in the Life," "Getting Better," "You've Got to Hide Your Love Away," "Good Day Sunshine," "P.S. I Love You." All previously released.

Apr 2: Double LP *The Beatles 1962–1966* (Apple SKBO 3403). "Love Me Do" (Version II), "Please Please Me," "From Me to You," "She Loves You," "I Want to Hold Your Hand" (mono), "All My Loving," "Can't Buy Me Love," "A Hard Day's Night" (mono), "And I Love Her," "Eight Days a Week," "I Feel Fine" (mono), "Ticket to Ride" (mono), "Yesterday," "Help!" (Version II; includes "James Bond Theme" omitted on U.K. release), "You've Got to Hide Your Love Away," "We Can Work It Out," "Day Tripper," "Drive My Car," "Norwegian Wood (This Bird Has Flown)," "Nowhere Man," "Michelle," "In My Life," "Girl," "Paperback Writer," "Eleanor Rigby," "Yellow Submarine." All previously released.

■ Double LP *The Beatles 1967–1970* (Apple SKBO 3404). "Strawberry Fields Forever," "Penny Lane" (mono), "Sgt. Pepper's Lonely Hearts Club Band," "With a Little Help from My Friends," "Lucy in the Sky with Diamonds," "A Day in the Life," "All You Need Is Love," "I Am the Walrus," "Hello Goodbye" (mono), "The Fool on the Hill," "Magical Mystery Tour," "Lady Madonna," "Hey Jude," "Revolution" (Version I), "Back in the USSR, "While My Guitar Gently Weeps," "Ob-La-Di, Ob-La-Da," "Get Back" (Version I), "Don't Let Me Down," "The Ballad of John and Yoko," "Old Brown Shoe," "Here Comes the Sun," "Come Together," "Something," "Octopus's Garden," "Let It Be" (Version I), "Across the Universe" (Version II), "The Long and Winding Road." All previously released. Some tracks on the U.S. editions of these two double albums appear in mono; U.K. and other foreign editions contain stereo versions of those songs.

Apr 9: Single "My Love"/"The Mess" (Paul and Wings) (Apple 1861). B side recorded live Aug 21, 1972. First U.S. release of both songs.

Apr 30: LP *Red Rose Speedway* (Paul and Wings) (Apple SMAL 3409). Contains previously released "My Love." First release of "Big Barn Bed," "Get on the Right Thing," "One More Kiss," "Little Lamb Dragonfly," "Single Pigeon," "When the Night," "Loup (1st Indian on the Moon)," medley "Hold Me Tight"/"Lazy Dynamite"/"Hands of Love"/"Power Cut."

May 7: Single "Give Me Love (Give Me Peace on Earth)"/"Miss O'Dell" (George) (Apple 1862). First release of both songs. "Miss O'Dell" is somewhat unique in that George's fits of giddy laughter are clearly heard during the song, which he did not bother to rerecord.

May 30: LP *Living in the Material World* (George) (Apple SMAS 3410). Contains previously released "Give Me Love (Give Me Peace on Earth)." First release of "Sue Me, Sue You Blues," "The Light That Has Lighted the World," "Don't Let Me Wait Too Long," "Who Can See It," "Living in the Material World," "The Lord Loves the One (That Loves the Lord)," "Be Here Now," "Try Some, Buy Some," "The Day the World Gets Round," "That Is All."

Jun 18: Single "Live and Let Die"/"I Lie Around" (Wings) (Apple 1863). First U.S. release of both songs.

Jul 2: LP *Live and Let Die* (soundtrack; United Artists UAS 100G). Contains Wings' "Live and Let Die." Previously released.

Sep 24: Single "Photograph"/"Down and Out" (Ringo) (Apple 1865). First release of both songs.

Oct 29: Single "Mind Games"/"Meat City" (John) (Apple 1868). First release of both songs.

Nov 2: LP *Ringo* (Ringo) (Apple SWAL 3413). Contains previously released "Photograph." First release of "I'm the Greatest," "Have You Seen My Baby," "Sunshine Life for Me (Sail Away Raymond)," "You're Sixteen," "Oh My My," "Step Lightly," "Six O'Clock" (4:05), "Devil Woman," "You and Me (Babe)." Cassette and 8-track tape editions have longer version of "Six O'Clock" (5:26), also released on some promo copies of the LP.

■ LP *Mind Games* (John) (Apple SW 3414). Contains previously released "Mind Games" and "Meat City." First release of "Tight A$," "Aisumasen (I'm Sorry)," "One Day (at a Time)," "Bring on the Lucie (Freeda Peeple)," "Nutopian International Anthem," "Intuition," "Out the Blue," "Only People," "I Know (I Know)," "You Are Here."

Nov 12: Single "Helen Wheels"/"Country Dreamer" (Paul & Wings) (Apple 1869). First U.S. release of both songs.

Dec 3: Single "You're Sixteen"/"Devil Woman" (Ringo) (Apple 1870). Both previously released.

Dec 5: LP *Band on the Run* (Paul and Wings) (Apple SOP 3415). Contains previously released "Helen Wheels." First release of "Band on the Run," "Jet," "Bluebird," "Mrs. Vanderbilt," "Let Me Roll It," "Mamunia," "No Words," "Picasso's Last Words (Drink to Me)," "Nineteen Hundred and Eighty Five." Note: U.K. version of LP did not include "Helen Wheels."

1974

Jan 28: Single "Jet"/"Mamunia" (Paul and Wings) (Apple 1871). Both previously released; deleted and reissued on Feb 18, 1974 with a new B side.

Feb 18: Single "Jet"/"Let Me Roll It" (Paul and Wings) (Apple 1871). Both previously released; second issue of single.

■ Single "Oh My My"/"Step Lightly" (Ringo) (Apple 1872). Both previously released.

Apr 1: LP *Son of Dracula* (Ringo/Harry Nilsson) (Rapple ABL 1-0220). Film soundtrack album includes dialogue by Ringo and "Daybreak" (George: cowbell; Ringo: drums), and "At My Front Door" (Ringo: drums). First release.

Apr 8: Single "Band on the Run"/"Nineteen Hundred and Eighty Five" (Paul and Wings) (Apple 1873). Both previously released.

Sep 23: Single "Whatever Gets You Through the Night"/"Beef Jerky" (John) (Apple 1874). First release of both songs.

Sep 26: LP *Walls and Bridges* (John) (Apple SW 3416). Contains prior releases "Whatever Gets You Through the Night" and "Beef Jerky." First release of "Going Down on Love," "Old Dirt Road," "What You Got," "Bless You," "Scared," "No. 9 Dream," "Surprise, Surprise (Sweet Bird of Paradox)," "Steel and Glass," "Nobody Loves You (When You're Down and Out)," "Ya Ya" (Version I).

Nov 4: Single "Junior's Farm"/"Sally G." (Paul and Wings) (Apple 1875). First U.S. release of both songs; A and B sides reversed on Jan 20, 1975.

Nov 11: Single "Only You (and You Alone)"/"Call Me" (Ringo) (Apple 1876). First release of both songs.

Nov 18: LP *Goodnight Vienna* (Ringo) (Apple SW 3417). Contains previously released "Only You (and You Alone)" and "Call Me." First U.S. release of "It's All Down to Goodnight Vienna," "Occopella," "Oo Wee," "Husbands and Wives," "Snookeroo," "All by Myself," "No No Song"/"Skokiaan," "Easy for Me," "Goodnight Vienna" (reprise).

■ Single "Dark Horse"/"I Don't Care Anymore" (George) (Apple 1877). First release of both songs.

Dark Horse (© Apple Corps Ltd.). This album and the 1974 tour that followed its release were dubbed "Dark Hoarse," a somewhat cruel reference to George's vocal condition at the time.

Dec 2: Single "Walking in the Park With Eloise"/"Bridge Over the River Suite" (Paul, Wings, Floyd Cramer, and Chet Atkins, all billed as "The Country Hams") (EMI 3977). Also released as a 7-inch picture disc. First U.S. release of both songs.

Dec 9: LP *Dark Horse* (George) (Apple SMAS 3418). Contains prior release "Dark Horse." First release of "Hari's on Tour (Express)," "Simply Shady," "So Sad," "Bye Bye Love," "Maya Love," "Far East Man," "It Is He (Jai Sri Krishna)." First U.S. release of "Ding Dong; Ding Dong."

Dec 16: Single "No. 9 Dream"/"What You Got" (John) (Apple 1878). Both previously released.

Dec 23: Single "Ding Dong; Ding Dong"/"Hari's on Tour (Express)" (George) (Apple 1879). Both previously released.

1975

Jan 27: Single "No No Song"/"Snookeroo" (Ringo) (Apple 1880). Both previously released.

Feb 8: LP *John Lennon Sings the Great Rock & Roll Hits [Roots]* (John) (Adam VIII A 8018). "Be-Bop-a-Lula," "Ain't That a Shame," "Stand by Me," "Sweet Little Sixteen," medley "Rip It Up"/"Ready Teddy" (listed only as "Rip It Up"), *"Angel Baby," "Do You Want to Dance," "You Can't Catch Me," "Bony Moronie," "Peggy Sue," medley: "Bring It on Home to Me"/"Send Me Some Lovin'" (listed only as "Bring It on Home to Me"), "Slippin' and Slidin'," *"Be My Baby," "Ya-Ya" (Version II), "Just Because." (* Two songs omitted from John's officially released *Rock 'N' Roll* album. The album was pressed using a prefinal mix advance tape of Lennon's *Rock 'N' Roll* album tracks. This unauthorized album was sold only in the U.S. via television mail order advertising. It was later withdrawn following Lennon's successful lawsuit. An artificially extended mix of "Angel Baby" was later officially released on the posthumous *Menlove Ave.* album and the CD boxed set *Lennon.* "Be My Baby" remains officially unreleased.

Feb 17: LP *Rock 'N' Roll* (John) (Apple SK 3419). "Be-Bop-a-Lula," "Stand by Me," "medley "Rip It Up"/"Ready Teddy," "You Can't Catch Me," "Ain't That a Shame," "Do You Want to Dance," "Sweet Little Sixteen," "Slippin' and Slidin'," "Peggy Sue," medley "Bring It on Home to Me"/"Send Me Some Lovin'," "Bony Moronie," "Ya Ya" (Version II), "Just Because." First release of all songs (excluding their release on the LP *Roots* listed above).

Feb 24: Single "Philadelphia Freedom" (Elton John)/"I Saw Her Standing There" (Lennon and Elton live Nov 28, 1974) (MCA 40364). First release in U.S.

Mar 10: Single "Stand by Me"/"Move Over Ms. L" (John) (Apple 1881). A side previously released; first release of B side.

May 23: Single "Listen to What the Man Said"/"Love in Song" (Wings) (Capitol 4091). First U.S. release of both songs.

May 27: LP *Venus and Mars* (Wings) (Capitol SMAS 11419). Contains previously released "Listen to What the Man Said" and "Love in Song." First release of "Venus and Mars," "Rock Show," "You Gave Me the Answer," "Magneto and Titanium Man," "Letting Go," "Venus and Mars" (reprise), "Spirits of Ancient Egypt," "Medicine Jar," "Call Me Back Again," medley "Treat Her Gently"/"Lonely Old People," "Crossroads Theme."

Jun 2: Single (medley) "It's All Down to Goodnight Vienna"-"Goodnight Vienna" (reprise)/"Oo-Wee" (Ringo) (Apple 1882). All previously released. A side is a unique edit combining two tracks from the *Goodnight Vienna* album; the edit was not released on other editions of the single throughout the world.

Sep 15: Single "You"/"World of Stone" (George) (Apple 1884). First U.S. release of both songs.

Sep 22: LP *Extra Texture—Read All About It* (George) (Apple SW 3420). Contains prior releases "You" and "World of Stone." First release of "The Answer's at the End," "This Guitar (Can't Keep From Crying)," "Ooh Baby (You Know That I Love You)," "A Bit More of You," "Can't Stop Thinking About You," "Tired of Midnight Blue," "Grey Cloudy Lies," "His Name Is Legs (Ladies and Gentlemen)."

Sep 29: Single "Letting Go"/"You Gave Me the Answer" (Wings) (Capitol 4145). Both previously released.

Oct 24: LP *Shaved Fish* (John) (Apple SW 3421). First U.S. and U.K. release of "Give Peace a Chance" (Version II), recorded live at Madison Square Garden, New York, Aug 30, 1972. Also contains "Give Peace a Chance" (Version I shortened to 0:59), "Cold Turkey," "Instant Karma (We All Shine On)," "Power to the People," "Mother," "Woman Is the Nigger of the World" (shortened to 4:37 from 5:15), "Imagine," "Whatever Gets You Through the Night," "Mind Games," "No. 9 Dream," "Happy Xmas (War Is Over)."

Oct 27: Single (medley) "Venus and Mars"-"Rock Show"/"Magneto and Titanium Man" (Wings) (Capitol 4175). All previously released. A side is a unique edit combining two songs from the *Venus and Mars* album.

Nov 25: LP *Blast from Your Past* (Ringo) (Apple SW 3422). "You're Sixteen," "No No Song," "It Don't Come Easy," "Photograph," "Back Off Boogaloo" (Version I), "Only You (and You Alone)," "Beaucoups of Blues," "Oh My My," "Early 1970," "I'm the Greatest." All previously released.

Dec 8: Single "This Guitar (Can't Keep from Crying)"/"Maya Love" (George) (Apple 1885). Both previously released.

1976

Mar 25: LP *Wings at the Speed of Sound* (Wings) (Capitol SW11525). "Let 'Em In," "The Note You Never Wrote," "She's My Baby," "Beware My Love," "Wino Junko," "Silly Love Songs" (Version I), "Cook of the House," "Time to Hide," "Must Do Something About It," "San Ferry Anne," "Warm and Beautiful." First release of all material.

Apr 1: Single "Silly Love Songs" (Version I)/"Cook of the House" (Wings) (Capitol 4256). Both previously released.

May 31: Single "Got to Get You Into My Life"/"Helter Skelter" (Capitol 4274). Both previously released.

Jun 11: Double LP *Rock and Roll Music* (Capitol SKBO 11537). All previously released. "Twist and Shout," "I Saw Her Standing There," "You Can't Do That," "I Wanna Be Your Man," "I Call Your Name," "Boys," "Long Tall Sally," "Rock and Roll Music," "Slow Down," "Kansas City"/"Hey Hey Hey Hey," "Money," "Bad Boy," "Matchbox," "Roll Over Beethoven," "Dizzy Miss Lizzie," "Anytime at All," "Drive My Car," "Everybody's Trying to Be My Baby," "The Night Before," "I'm Down," "Revolution" (Version I 3:22), "Back in the USSR," "Helter Skelter," "Taxman," "Got to Get You Into My Life," "Hey Bulldog," "Birthday," "Get Back" (Version II 3:09 listed as Version I 3:11).

Jun 28: Single "Let 'Em In"/"Beware My Love" (Wings) (Capitol 4293). Both previously released.

Sep 20: Single "A Dose of Rock and Roll"/"Cryin'" (Ringo) (Atlantic 3361). First U.S. release of both songs.

Sep 27: LP *Ringo's Rotogravure* (Ringo) (Atlantic SD 18193). Contains previously released "A Dose of Rock and Roll" and "Cryin'." First U.S. release of "Hey Baby," "Pure Gold," "You Don't Know Me at All," "Cookin' (in the Kitchen of Love)," "I'll Still Love You," "This Be Called a Song," "Las Brisas," "Lady Gaye," "Spooky Weirdness."

Nov 8: LP *The Best of George Harrison* (George) (Capitol ST-11578). "Something," "If I Needed Someone," "Here Comes the Sun," "Taxman," "Think for Yourself," "For You Blue," "While My Guitar Gently Weeps," "My Sweet Lord," "Give Me Love (Give Me Peace on Earth)," "You," "Bangla Desh," "Dark Horse," "What Is Life." All previously released.

■ Single "Ob-La-Di, Ob-La-Da"/"Julia" (Capitol 4347). Both previously released.

Nov 15: Single "This Song"/"Learning How to Love You" (George) (Dark Horse 8294). First release of both songs.

Nov 22: Single "Hey Baby"/"Lady Gaye" (Ringo) (Atlantic 3371). Both previously released.

Nov 24: LP *Thirty-Three & 1/3* (George) (Dark Horse DH 3005). Contains previously released "This Song" and "Learning How to Love You." First U.S. release of "Woman Don't You Cry for Me," "Dear One," "Beautiful Girl," "See Yourself," "It's What You Value," "True Love," "Pure Smokey," "Crackerbox Palace."

Dec 10: Triple LP *Wings Over America* (Wings) (Capitol SWCO 11593). "Venus and Mars," "Rock Show," "Jet," "Let Me Roll It," "Spirits of Ancient Egypt," "Medicine Jar," "Maybe I'm Amazed," "Call Me Back Again," "Lady Madonna," "The Long and Winding Road," "Live and Let Die," "Picasso's Last Words," "Richard Cory," "Bluebird," "I've Just Seen a Face," "Blackbird," "Yesterday," "You Gave Me the Answer," "Magneto and Titanium Man," "Go Now," "My Love," "Listen to What the

Man Said," "Let 'Em In," "Time to Hide," "Silly Love Songs," "Beware My Love," "Letting Go," "Band on the Run," "Hi Hi Hi," "Soily." Although this was intended to be a live album recorded during Wings' 1976 tour, studio overdubs were reportedly recorded for several tracks.

1977

Jan 24: Single "Crackerbox Palace"/"Learning How to Love You" (George) (Dark Horse 8313). Both previously released.

Feb 7: Single "Maybe I'm Amazed"/"Soily" (Wings) (Capitol 4385). Both previously released.

Apr 4: Single "Stand by Me"/"Woman Is the Nigger of the World" (John) (Capitol Starline 6244). Both previously released.

■ Single "Dark Horse"/"You" (George) (Capitol Starline 6245). Both previously released.

May 6: LP *The Beatles at the Hollywood Bowl* (Capitol SMAS 11638). "Twist and Shout," "She's a Woman," "Dizzy Miss Lizzie," "Ticket to Ride," "Can't Buy Me Love," *"Things We Said Today," *"Roll Over Beethoven," *"Boys," "A Hard Day's Night," "Help!" *"All My Loving," *"She Loves You," *"Long Tall Sally." First release in U.S. and U.K. of these tracks, recorded live *Aug 23, 1964 and Aug 30, 1965 at the Hollywood Bowl.

May 17: LP *Thrillington* (instrumental version of *Ram* album recorded by Paul under the pseudonym "Percy 'Thrills' Thrillington") (Capitol ST 11642). "Too Many People," "3 Legs," "Ram On," "Dear Boy," "Uncle Albert/Admiral Halsey," "Smile Away," "Heart of the Country," "Monkberry Moon Delight," "Eat at Home," "Long Haired Lady," "Back Seat of My Car." First U.S. release.

May 31: Single "Seaside Woman"/"B Side to Seaside" (Wings billed as Suzy and the Red Stripes) (Epic 8-50403).

Jun 13: Double LP *The Beatles Live! At the Star-Club in Hamburg, Germany: 1962* (Lingasong/Atlantic LS-2-7001). "I'm Gonna Sit Right Down and Cry Over You," "Where Have You Been All My Life," "Till There Was You," "Sheila," "Roll Over Beethoven," "Hippy Hippy Shake," "Sweet Little Sixteen," "Lend Me Your Comb," "Your Feets Too Big," "Mr. Moonlight," "A Taste of Honey," "Besame Mucho," "Kansas City/Hey Hey Hey Hey," "Nothin' Shakin' (But the Leaves on the Trees)," "To Know Her Is to Love Her," "Little Queenie," "Falling in Love Again," "Be-Bop-a-Lula," "Hallelujah I Love Her So," "Red Sails in the Sunset," "Everybody's Trying to Be My Baby," "Matchbox," "I'm Talking About You," "Shimmy Shake," "Long Tall Sally," "I Remember You." First U.S. release of these tracks recorded Dec 31, 1962 in Hamburg.

Aug 25: Single "Wings"/"Just a Dream" (Ringo) (Atlantic 3429). First release of both songs.

Sep 26: LP *Ringo the 4th* (Ringo) (Atlantic SD 19108). Contains previously released "Wings." First U.S. release of "Drowning in a Sea of Love," "Tango All Night," "Gave It All Up," "Out on the Streets," "Can She Do It Like She

Dances," "Sneaking Sally Through the Alley," "It's No Secret," "Gypsies in Flight," "Simple Love Song."

Oct 18: Single "Drowning in a Sea of Love"/"Just a Dream" (Ringo) (Atlantic 3412). Both previously released.

Oct 21: Double LP *Love Songs* (Capitol SKBL 11711). "Yesterday," "I'll Follow the Sun," "I Need You," "Girl," "In My Life," "Words of Love," "Here, There and Everywhere," "Something," "And I Love Her," "If I Fell," "I'll Be Back," "Tell Me What You See," "Yes It Is," "Michelle," "It's Only Love," "You're Going to Lose That Girl," "Every Little Thing," "For No One," "She's Leaving Home," "The Long and Winding Road," "This Boy," "Norwegian Wood," "You've Got to Hide Your Love Away," "I Will," "P.S. I Love You." All previously released.

Oct: Single "Girl"/"You're Gonna Lose That Girl" (Capitol 4506). Both previously released.

Nov 14: Single "Mull of Kintyre"/"Girl's School" (Wings) (Capitol 4504). First U.S. release of both songs.

1978

Mar 20: Single "With a Little Luck"/medley: "Backwards Traveller"-"Cuff Link" (Wings) (Capitol 4559). First release of both songs.

Mar 31: LP *London Town* (Wings) (Capitol SW 11777). Contains previously released "With a Little Luck," "Backwards Traveller," "Cuff Link." First release of "London Town," "Cafe on the Left Bank," "I'm Carrying," "Children Children," "Girlfriend," "I've Had Enough," "Famous Groupies," "Deliver Your Children," "Name and Address," "Don't Let It Bring You Down," "Morse Moose and the Grey Goose."

Apr 18: Single "Lipstick Traces"/"Old Time Relovin'" (Ringo) (Portrait 6-70015). First release of both songs.

Apr 21: LP *Bad Boy* (Ringo) (Portrait JR 35378). Contains previously released "Lipstick Traces" and "Old Time Relovin'." First release of "Who Needs a Heart," "Bad Boy," "Heart on My Sleeve," "Where Did Our Love Go," "Hard Times," "Tonight," "Monkey See-Monkey Do," "A Man Like Me."

Jun 12: Single "I've Had Enough"/"Deliver Your Children" (Wings) (Capitol 4594). Both previously released.

Jul 6: Single "Heart on My Sleeve"/"Who Needs a Heart" (Ringo) (Portrait 6-70018). Both previously released.

Aug 14: Single "Sgt. Pepper's Lonely Hearts Club Band"-"With a Little Help from My Friends"/"A Day in the Life" (Capitol 4612). Previously released tracks. B side is *not* a different mix of "A Day in the Life" with a clean introduction. It simply cuts the "Sgt. Pepper" cross fade lead-in that is heard on the *Sgt. Pepper* album. A real alternate mix of the song, with a clean introduction, later appeared on the *Imagine: John Lennon* soundtrack compilation album.

Aug 21: Single "London Town"/"I'm Carrying" (Wings) (Capitol 4625). Both previously released.

Aug: Capitol reissued the following albums: *Sgt. Pepper's Lonely Hearts Club Band* (SEAX-11840 Limited

Edition picture disc), *The Beatles* (SEBX-11841 Limited Edition white vinyl discs), *The Beatles 1962–1966* (SEBX-11842 Limited Edition red vinyl discs), *The Beatles 1967–1970* (SEBX-11843 Limited Edition blue vinyl discs).

Nov 15: LP *Beatle Talk* (Great Northwest Music Co. GWC-4007). Press conferences of Aug 22, 1964 in Vancouver and Aug 25, 1966 in Seattle. The LP is narrated by Red Robinson. First release.

Nov 22: LP *Wings Greatest* (Wings) (Capitol SOO-11905). "Another Day," "Silly Love Songs" (Version I), "Live and Let Die," "Junior's Farm," "With a Little Luck," "Band on the Run," "Uncle Albert-Admiral Halsey," "Hi Hi Hi," "Let 'Em In," "My Love," "Jet," "Mull of Kintyre." All previously released.

Dec : *The Beatles Collection* (EMI/Capitol BC-13 Limited Edition boxed set). Set of all 12 original U.K. Beatles LPs plus a LP *Rarities* (different versions of which were included with the U.S. and U.K. sets). Set contains all of the following Parlophone LPs: *Please Please Me* (PCS 3042), *With The Beatles* (PCS 3045), *A Hard Day's Night* (PCS 3058), *Beatles for Sale* (PCS 3062), *Help!* (PCS 3071), *Rubber Soul* (PCS 3075), *Revolver* (PCS 7009), *Sgt. Pepper's Lonely Hearts Club Band* (PCS 7027), *The Beatles* ("White Album") (PCS 7067), *Yellow Submarine* (PCS 7070), *Abbey Road* (PCS 7088), *Let It Be* (PCS 7096), *Rarities* (Capitol SPRO-8969 included with U.S. set). All material previously released.

■ LP *Rarities* (Capitol SPRO-8969). First U.S. release of "Across the Universe" (Version I). Also contains: "Yes It Is," "This Boy," "The Inner Light," "I'll Get You," "Thank You Girl," "I Want to Hold Your Hand," "You Know My Name (Look Up the Number)," "She Loves You," "Rain," "She's a Woman," "Matchbox," "I Call Your Name," "Bad Boy," "Slow Down," "I'm Down," "Long Tall Sally." This album was included with the boxed set of U.K. Beatles albums and was intended for separate release as Capitol SN-12009, but was not issued. Instead, *Rarities* was revised and issued as a separate U.S. release on Mar 24, 1980.

■ LP *Abbey Road* (Capitol SEAX-11900; Limited Edition picture disc). Reissue.

■ LP *Band on the Run* (Paul and Wings) (Capitol SEAX-11901; Limited Edition picture disc). Reissue.

That year: Double LP *The Beatles Tapes* (P.B.R. International 7005/7006). First U.S. release of interviews recorded by David Wigg for BBC Radio's "Scene and Heard." Interviews were recorded with Ringo (Jan 21, 1969, Mar 20, 1970, and Jan 3, 1973), George (Mar 4, 1969 and Oct 8, 1969), John (May 8, 1969, Feb 18, 1970, and Oct 25, 1971), and Paul (Sep 19, 1969). The recording dates of several interviews are listed incorrectly on the record and jacket.

1979

Jan 24: LPs *The Beatles: First Live Recordings Vol. I* and *Vol. II* (Pickwick SPC-3661 and 3662). Vol I: "Where Have You Been All My Life," "A Taste of Honey," "Your Feets Too Big," "Mr. Moonlight," "Besame Mucho," "I'm Gonna Sit Right Down and Cry Over You," "Be-Bop-a-Lula," "Hallelujah I Love Her So," "Till There Was You," "Sweet Little Sixteen," "Little Queenie," "Kansas City"/"Hey Hey Hey Hey," "Hully Gully" (not by The Beatles). Vol II: "Nothin' Shakin' (But the Leaves on the Trees)," "Everybody's Trying to Be My Baby," "Matchbox," "I'm Talking About You," "Long Tall Sally," "Roll Over Beethoven," "Hippy Hippy Shake," "Falling in Love Again," "Lend Me Your Comb," "Sheila," "Red Sails in the Sunset," "To Know Her Is to Love Her," "Shimmy Shake," "I Remember You." Recordings made at Star-Club in Hamburg, Germany Dec 31, 1962. All previously released.

Feb 14: LP *George Harrison* (George) (Dark Horse DHK-3255). "Loves Comes to Everyone," "Not Guilty," "Here Comes the Moon," "Soft Hearted Hana," "Blow Away," "Faster," "Dark Sweet Lady," "Your Love Is Forever," "Soft Touch," "If You Believe." First release of all songs.

■ Single "Blow Away"/"Soft Hearted Hana" (George) (Dark Horse DRC-8763). Songs released same day on LP *George Harrison*.

Mar 15: Single "Goodnight Tonight"/"Daytime Nighttime Suffering" (Wings) (Columbia 3-10939). First release of both songs.

Mar 26: 12-inch single "Goodnight Tonight" (extended version)/"Daytime Nighttime Suffering" (Wings) (Columbia 23-10940). A side is an extended remix of previously released track.

May 11: Single "Love Comes to Everyone"/"Soft Touch" (George) (Dark Horse DRC 8844). Both previously released.

May 24: LP *Back to the Egg* (Wings) (Columbia FC-36057). "Spin It On," "Old Siam, Sir," "Reception," "Getting Closer," "We're Open Tonight," "Again and Again and Again," "Arrow Through Me," "Rockestra Theme," "To You," "After the Ball-Million Miles," "Winter Rose"-"Love Awake," "The Broadcast" (which includes poems "The Sport of Kings" and "The Little Man," both read by Harold Margery), "So Glad to See You Here," "Baby's Request." First release of all songs.

May: Double LP *Monsters* (Warner Bros. PRO A796). Includes George's previously released "Not Guilty," sold via mail order.

Jun 5: Single "Getting Closer"/"Spin It On" (Wings) (Columbia 3-11020). Both previously released.

Aug 14: Single "Arrow Through Me"/"Old Siam, Sir" (Wings) (Columbia 1-11070). Both previously released.

Nov 20: Single "Wonderful Christmastime"/"Rudolph the Red Nosed Reggae" (Paul) (Columbia 1-11162). First U.S. release of both songs.

Dec 12: LP *Hear The Beatles Tell All* (Vee Jay PRO-202). Reissue.

Dec 28: LP *Abbey Road* (Mobile Fidelity Sound Lab/Capitol MFSL 1-023). Half-speed master recording.

Late that year: Double LP *British Rock Classics* (Sire R-234021). Includes previously released "My Bonnie."

1980

Mar 24: LP *The Beatles Rarities* (Capitol SHAL-12060). Includes the first U.S. release of "Love Me Do" (Version I), "I'm Only Sleeping" (U.K. stereo mix), mono versions of "Helter Skelter" and "Don't Pass Me By," "I Am the Walrus" (full version), "Across the Universe" (Version I), and "Sgt. Pepper Inner Groove" (untitled, unlisted 2 seconds of gibberish originally released only on the U.K. *Sgt. Pepper* album where it was placed on the runout groove); and previously released "Misery," "There's a Place," "Sie Liebt Dich," "And I Love Her," "Help!" (Version I), "Penny Lane" (with trumpet ending originally released only on U.S. promo), "The Inner Light," "You Know My Name (Look Up the Number)."

Apr 15: Single "Coming Up" (studio version; Paul)/"Coming Up" (live version; Paul and Wings)-"Lunch Box-Odd Sox" (Paul and Wings) (Columbia 1-11263). First U.S. release of all songs.

May 16: Double LP *The Historic First Live Recordings* (Pickwick PTP-2098). Another collection from the Dec 31, 1962 Star-Club recordings: "Where Have You Been All My Life," "A Taste of Honey," "Your Feets Too Big," "Mr. Moonlight," "Besame Mucho," "I'm Gonna Sit Right Down and Cry Over You," "Be-Bop-a-Lula," "Nothin' Shakin' (But the Leaves on the Trees)," "Everybody's Trying to Be My Baby," "Matchbox," "I'm Talking About You," "Long Tall Sally," "Roll Over Beethoven," "Hippy Hippy Shake," "Hallelujah I Love Her So," "Till There Was You," "Sweet Little Sixteen," "Little Queenie," "Kansas City"/"Hey Hey Hey Hey," "Falling in Love Again," "Lend Me Your Comb," "Sheila," "Red Sails in the Sunset," "To Know Her Is to Love Her," "Shimmy Shake," "I Remember You." Also includes "Hully Gully" (not by The Beatles). All previously released.

May 21: LP *McCartney II* (Paul) (Columbia FC-36511). Contains previously released "Coming Up" (studio version). First U.S. release of "Temporary Secretary," "On the Way," "Waterfalls," "Nobody Knows," "Front Parlour" (instrumental), "Summer's Day Song," "Frozen Jap" (instrumental), "Bogey Music," "Darkroom," "One of These Days." The album included a special one-sided promo single of the previously released live version of "Coming Up" (Columbia AE7-1204). This disc was not included with the U.K. LP.

May 22: Columbia reissued the following McCartney/ Wings albums: *McCartney* (FC-36478), *Ram* (FC-36479), *Wild Life* (FC-36480), *Red Rose Speedway* (FC-36481), *Band on the Run* (FC-36482).

Jul 22: Single "Waterfalls"/"Check My Machine" (Paul) (Columbia 1-11335). A side: prior release. B side: first U.S. release.

Aug: LPs *A Hard Day's Night* (Capitol SW-11921) and *Let It Be* (SW 11922). Reissues.

Sep 25: LP *Venus and Mars* (Wings) (Columbia FC-36801). Reissue.

Oct 27: Single "(Just Like) Starting Over" (John)/"Kiss Kiss Kiss" (Yoko) (Geffen GEF-49604). First U.S. release of both songs.

■ LPs *Rock 'n' Roll Music—Vol. 1* (Capitol SN-16020), and *Rock 'n' Roll Music—Vol. 2* (SN-16021). Contents identical to 2-LP set released Jun 11, 1976.

Oct: Capitol reissued the following albums: *Dark Horse* (George) (SN-16055), *Mind Games* (John) (SN-16068), *Rock 'n' Roll* (John) SN-16069), *Ringo* (Ringo) (SN-16114).

Nov 17: LP *Double Fantasy* (John and Yoko) (Geffen GHS-2001). Contains previously released "(Just Like) Starting Over" (John) and "Kiss Kiss Kiss" (Yoko). First release in U.S. and U.K. of "Cleanup Time," "I'm Losing You," "Beautiful Boy (Darling Boy)," "Watching the Wheels," "Woman," "Dear Yoko" (all by John); and "Every Man Has a Woman Who Loves Him," "Hard Times Are Over," "Give Me Something," "I'm Moving On," "(Yes) I'm Your Angel," "Beautiful Boys" (all by Yoko).

Dec 4: LP *The McCartney Interview* (May 1980 interview with Paul by Vic Garbarini for *Musician* magazine) (Columbia PC-36987 Limited Edition). First commercial release; released as promo in May.

■ Single "My Love" (Paul and Wings)/"Maybe I'm Amazed" (Paul) (Columbia Hall of Fame 13-33407). Both previously released.

■ Single "Uncle Albert-Admiral Halsey" (Paul & Linda)/"Jet" (Paul/Wings) (Columbia Hall of Fame 13-33408). Both previously released.

■ Single "Band on the Run"/"Helen Wheels" (Paul and Wings) (Columbia Hall of Fame 13-33409). Both previously released.

■ Single "Getting Closer"/"Goodnight Tonight" (Wings) (Columbia Hall of Fame 13-33405). Both previously released.

That year: LP *The American Tour with Ed Rudy* (INS Radio News Documentary 2). Reissue of Jun 9, 1964 release.

1981

Jan 12: Single "Woman" (John)/"Beautiful Boys" (Yoko) (Geffen GEF-49644). Both previously released.

Jan 30: LP *Magical Mystery Tour* (Mobile Fidelity Sound Lab/Capitol MFSL 1-047). Half-speed master recording.

Feb: Capitol reissued the following LPs: *Living in the Material World* (George) (SN-16216), *Extra Texture (Read All About It)* (George) (SN-16217), *Sentimental Journey* (Ringo) (SN-16218), *Goodnight Vienna* (Ringo) (SN-16219) (with "Easy for Me" listed as *Easier* for Me on label and album cover).

■ Double LP *The Beatles Live at the Star Club, 1962, Hamburg, Germany* (Hall of Music HMI 2200). Eighteen songs from the Star-Club tape of Dec 31, 1962: "Roll Over Beethoven," "Hippy Hippy Shake," "Sweet Little Sixteen," "A Taste of Honey," "Till There Was You," "I Saw Her Standing There," "Ask Me Why,"

"Reminiscing," "Twist and Shout," "Kansas City"/ "Hey Hey Hey Hey," "Mr. Moonlight," "Long Tall Sally," "Little Queenie," "Be-Bop-a-Lula," "Red Sails in the Sunset," "Everybody's Trying to Be My Baby," "Matchbox," "I'm Talking About You." All previously released; sold via mail order.

Mar 1: LP *Timeless* (Silhouette Music SM-10004-Limited Edition Picture Disc). Previously issued press conference excerpts from Vancouver, Canada, 1964 and Chicago, 1966; Newscast about John Lennon; additional tracks featuring cover versions and tributes by studio musicians.

Mar 13: Single "Watching the Wheels" (John)/"Yes I'm Your Angel" (Yoko) (Geffen 49695). Both previously released.

Mar 30: Double LP *Concerts for the People of Kampuchea* (Atlantic SD 2-7005). Includes live performance by Paul and Wings and Rockestra Dec 29, 1979: "Got to Get You Into My Life," "Every Night," "Coming Up," "Lucille," "Let It Be," "Rockestra Theme," and material by other performers at the concerts. First release of these recordings.

Apr 16: LPs *Dawn of The Silver Beatles* (PAC Records UDL 2333-Limited Edition) and *Lightning Strikes Twice* (UDL 2382). First LP contains "Love of the Loved," "Money," "Sure to Fall," "Take Good Care of My Baby," "Three Cool Cats," "Like Dreamers Do," "Crying, Waiting, Hoping," "Searchin'," "Till There Was You," "Memphis." Second LP adds "Hello Little Girl," "Sheik of Araby," "To Know Her Is to Love Her," "September in the Rain," "Besame Mucho," all from The Beatles' Jan 1, 1962 Decca audition. Sold via mail order, these records are of dubious legality.

Apr 24: LP *Band on the Run* (Paul and Wings) (Columbia HC-46982). Half-speed master recording.

May 11: Single "All Those Years Ago"/"Writing's on the Wall" (George) (Dark Horse DRC 49725). First release of both songs.

Jun 1: LP *Somewhere in England* (George) (Dark Horse DHK 3492). Contains previously released "All Those Years Ago" and "Writing's on the Wall." First release of "Blood from a Clone," "Unconsciousness Rules," "Life Itself," "Baltimore Oriole," "Teardrops" (4:04, "That Which I Have Lost," "Hong Kong Blues," "Save the World."

Jun 12: Single "Silly Love Songs" (Version I)/"Cook of the House" (Wings) (Columbia 18-02171). Both previously released.

Jul 6: Single "(Just Like) Starting Over"/"Woman" (John) (Geffen GGEF 0408). Both previously released.

Jul 13: LP *Wings at the Speed of Sound* (Wings) (Columbia FC 37409). Reissue.

Jul 24: Single "Teardrops" (3:20)/"Save the World (George) (Dark Horse DRC 79825); also listed as released Jul 15 and Jul 20 as DRC 49785. Both songs previously released.

Sep: Capitol reissued Ringo's *Beaucoups of Blues* (SN-16235) and *Blast from Your Past* (SN-162366).

Oct: LP *The Beatles Featuring Tony Sheridan—In the Beginning (Circa 1960)* (Polydor 24-4504). Reissue of May 4, 1970 release with slightly altered title.

Oct 27: LP *Stop and Smell the Roses* (Ringo) (Boardwalk NB1-33246). "Private Property," "Wrack My Brain," "Drumming Is My Madness," "Attention," "Stop and Take the Time to Smell the Roses," "Dead Giveaway," "You Belong to Me," "Sure to Fall," "Nice Way," "Back Off Boogaloo" (Version II). First release.

■ Single "Wrack My Brain"/"Drumming Is My Madness" (Ringo) (Boardwalk NB7-11-130). Both released same day on *Stop and Smell the Roses*.

Nov 4: Single "All Those Years Ago"/"Teardrops" (George) (Dark Horse GDRC 0410). Both previously released.

■ Single "Watching the Wheels"/"Beautiful Boy (Darling Boy)" (John) (Geffen GGEF 0415). Both previously released.

Nov 30: Capitol reissued the following singles on its Starline label: "I Want to Hold Your Hand"/"I Saw Her Standing There" (A-6278); "Can't Buy Me Love"/"You Can't Do That" (A-6279); "A Hard Day's Night"/"I Should Have Known Better" (A-6281); "I'll Cry Instead"/"I'm Happy Just to Dance with You" (A-6282); "And I Love Her"/"If I Fell" (A-6283); "Matchbox"/"Slow Down" (A-6284); "I Feel Fine"/"She's a Woman" (A-6286); "Eight Days a Week"/"I Don't Want to Spoil the Party" (A-6287); "Ticket to Ride"/"Yes It Is" (A-6288); "Help!"/"I'm Down" (A-6290); "Yesterday"/"Act Naturally" (A-6291); "We Can Work It Out"/"Day Tripper" (A-6293); "Nowhere Man"/"What Goes On" (A-6294); "Paperback Writer"/"Rain" (A-6296); "Yellow Submarine"/"Eleanor Rigby" (A-6297); "Penny Lane"/"Strawberry Fields Forever" (A-6299); "All You Need Is Love"/"Baby You're a Rich Man" (A-6300). All previously released.

Nov: Single "Happy Xmas"/"Beautiful Boy (Darling Boy)" (John) (Geffen 29855). Both previously released.

That year: LP *The Beatles Talk Downunder* (Raven Records PVC 8911). Interviews recorded during tour of Australia (Jun 10–Jul 1, 1964). First U.S. release.

1982

That year: LP *Timeless II* (Silhouette Music S.M. 10010). 12-inch picture disc contains previously released interviews by Murray "The K" recorded early in 1964; the Aug 25, 1966 Seattle press conference; first release of Aug 25, 1966 interviews by Dusty Adams (mislabeled Vancouver, Aug 20, 1964).

■ LP *Double Fantasy* (John and Yoko) (Nautilus NR-47). Half-speed master recording.

Jan 7: Double LP *The Beatles* (Mobile Fidelity Sound Labs Capitol MFSL 2-072). Half-speed master recording.

Jan 13: Single "Private Property"/"Stop and Take the Time to Smell the Roses" (Ringo) (Boardwalk NB7-11-134). Both previously released.

Mar 22: Single "The Beatles Movie Medley"/"I'm Happy Just to Dance with You" (Capitol B-5107). A side is a medley made up of bits from released recordings; B side also previously released.

■ LP *Reel Music* (Capitol SV-12199). "A Hard Day's Night," "I Should Have Known Better," "Can't Buy Me Love," "And I Love Her," "Help!," "You've Got to Hide Your Love Away," "Ticket to Ride," "Magical Mystery Tour," "I Am the Walrus," "Yellow Submarine," "All You Need Is Love," "Let It Be" (Version II), "Get Back" (Version II), "The Long and Winding Road." All previously released.

Apr 2: Single "Ebony and Ivory" (Paul and Stevie Wonder)/"Rainclouds" (Paul) (Columbia 18-02860). First U.S. release of both songs.

Apr 16: 12-inch single "Ebony and Ivory" (Paul and Stevie Wonder)/"Rainclouds" (Paul)-"Ebony and Ivory" (solo version by Paul) (Columbia 44-02878). First U.S. release of solo version of "Ebony and Ivory"; other titles previously released.

Apr 26: LP *Tug of War* (Paul) (Columbia TC 37462). Contains previously released "Ebony and Ivory" (Paul and Stevie Wonder). First release of "Take It Away" (4:13), "Dress Me Up as a Robber," "Tug of War," "Somebody Who Cares," "What's That You're Doing?," "Here Today," "Ballroom Dancing" (Version I), "The Pound Is Sinking," "Wanderlust" (Version I), "Get It," "Be What You See."

May: Three-album set *Like Dreamers Do* (Backstage BSR 1111). Two picture discs and one white vinyl disc that was identical in contents to one of the picture discs; includes a 1982 interview with Pete Best, 1964 and 1965 Beatles press conferences, and 10 previously released cuts from the Jan 1, 1962 Decca audition: "Like Dreamers Do," "Money," "Take Good Care of My Baby," "Three Cool Cats," "Sure to Fall," "Love of the Loved," "Memphis," "Crying, Waiting, Hoping," "Till There Was You," "Searchin'." First release of Pete Best interview; reissued as a 2-LP set with same contents in Oct 1982.

That summer: Series of 15 singles containing cuts from the Dec 31, 1962 Star-Club tapes was issued on the Collectibles label: "I'm Gonna Sit Right Down and Cry Over You"/"Roll Over Beethoven" (1501); "Hippy Hippy Shake"/"Sweet Little Sixteen" (1502); "Lend Me Your Comb"/"Your Feets Too Big" (1503); "Where Have You Been All My Life"/"Mr. Moonlight" (1504); "A Taste of Honey"/"Besame Mucho" (1505); "Till There Was You"/"Everybody's Trying to Be My Baby" (1506); "Kansas City"-"Hey Hey Hey Hey"/"Nothin' Shakin' (But the Leaves on the Trees)" (1507); "To Know Her Is to Love Her"/"Little Queenie" (1508); "Falling in Love Again"/"Sheila" (1509); "Be-Bop-a-Lula"/"Hallelujah I Love Her So" (1510); "Red Sails in the Sunset"/"Matchbox" (1511); "I'm Talking About You"/"Shimmy Shake" (1512); "Long Tall Sally"/"I Remember You" (1513); "Ask Me Why"/"Twist and Shout" (1514); "I Saw Her Standing There"/Reminiscing" (1515—listed incorrectly as "Can't Help It (Blue Angel)").

Jul 3: Single "Take It Away" (3:59)/"I'll Give You a Ring" (Paul) (Columbia 18-03018). First U.S. release of

B side; A side previously released. Single features clean opening on A side; album version is sequed from previous track.

Jul 26: 12-inch single "Take It Away"(3:59)/"I'll Give You a Ring"-"Dress Me Up As a Robber" (Paul) (Columbia 44-03019). All previously released.

Sep 26: Single "Tug of War"/"Get It" (Paul) (Columbia 38-03235). Both previously released.

Sep 27: LPs *The Silver Beatles Vol. 1* and *Vol. 2* (Phoenix PHX 352 and 353). Contains 12 of the 15 songs performed at the Decca audition, Jan 1, 1962. Volume 1: +Memphis," "The Sheik of Araby," +"Three Cool Cats," "Till There Was You," "Besame Mucho," +"Searchin'," +"Sure to Fall." Volume 2: "To Know Her Is to Love Her," +"September in the Rain," +"Money," +"Take Good Care of My Baby," "Crying, Waiting, Hoping"; also repeats +"Searchin'" and "Three Cool Cats." All previously released; + denotes seven tracks artificially lengthened on these albums; they are unaltered on the single LP *The Complete Silver Beatles*, released Sep 10 in the U.K. and Sep 27 in the U.S.

■ LP *The Complete Silver Beatles* (Audio Rarities AR-2452). Contains the same 12 songs listed above from the Decca audition of Jan 1, 1962, but none were artificially extended on this LP.

Sep: LP *Sgt. Pepper's Lonely Hearts Club Band* (Mobile Fidelity Sound Labs UHQR 1-100). Half-speed master recording.

■ 13-LP boxed set *The Beatles: The Collection* (no number: Mobile Fidelity Sound Labs). Half-speed master recordings of all 12 original stereo U.K. Beatles albums plus U.S. *Magical Mystery Tour* LP.

Oct 15: LP *The Beatles—20 Greatest Hits* (Capitol SV-12245). "She Loves You," "Love Me Do" (Version II), "I Want to Hold Your Hand," "Can't Buy Me Love," "A Hard Day's Night," "I Feel Fine," "Eight Days a Week," "Ticket to Ride," "Help!," "Yesterday," "We Can Work It Out," "Paperback Writer," "Penny Lane," "All You Need Is Love," "Hello Goodbye," "Hey Jude" (short version), "Get Back" (Version I), "Come Together," "Let It Be" (Version I), "The Long and Winding Road." All previously released.

Oct 25: Single "The Girl Is Mine" (Paul and Michael Jackson)/"Can't Get Outta the Rain" (Michael Jackson) (EPIC 34-03288). First release of both songs. One-sided single "The Girl Is Mine" also released (Epic ENR-03372).

Oct 27: LP *Gone Troppo* (George) (Dark Horse 23734-1). "Wake Up My Love," "That's the Way It Goes," "I Really Love You," "Greece," "Gone Troppo," "Mystical One," "Unknown Delight," "Baby Don't Run Away," "Dream Away," "Circles." First release of all songs.

■ Single "Wake Up My Love"/"Greece" (George) (Dark Horse 7-29864). Released same day as LP *Gone Troppo*.

Oct: 2 LPs *Like Dreamers Do* by "The Silver Beatles" (Backstage Records BSR 2-201). 2-LP reissue of 3-LP set released May 1982.

- LP *The Beatles Talk with Jerry G.* (Backstage BSR 1165). Interviews with D.J. Jerry G. Bishop held during 1965 and 1966 U.S. tours. First release.

Nov 8: LP *The John Lennon Collection* (John) (Geffen GHSP 2023). "Give Peace a Chance," "Instant Karma," "Power to the People," "Whatever Gets You Through the Night," "No. 9 Dream," "Mind Games," "Love," "Imagine," "Jealous Guy," "(Just Like) Starting Over," "Woman," "I'm Losing You," "Beautiful Boy (Darling Boy)," "Dear Yoko," "Watching the Wheels." U.S. LP release omits "Happy Xmas (War Is Over)" and "Stand by Me," both included on the U.S. cassette edition and on U.K. releases. All previously released.

Nov 11: Single "Happy Xmas (War Is Over)" (John, Yoko, and others)/"Beautiful Boy (Darling Boy)" (John) (Geffen 7-29855). Both previously released.

Nov 19: Single "Love Me Do"/"P.S. I Love You" (Capitol B-5189). Previously released.

Nov 29: LP *Thriller* by Michael Jackson (Epic QE 38112). Includes "The Girl Is Mine" (Paul and Jackson).

Nov: LP *The Silver Beatles* (Audio Rarities AR 30-003; picture disc). 10 cuts from Jan 1, 1962 Decca audition: "Besame Mucho," "Searchin'," "Three Cool Cats," "Crying, Waiting, Hoping," "September in the Rain," "Sure to Fall," "To Know Her Is to Love Her," "Take Good Care of My Baby," "Memphis," "Sheik of Araby." All previously released.

Dec: LP *Christmas Reflections* (Desert Vibrations Heritage Series HSRD-SP1) and LP *Happy Michaelmas* (The Adirondack Group A.G. 8146). Reedited portions of 1963–69 Beatles Christmas records.

1983

Feb 7: Single "I Really Love You"/"Circles" (George) (Dark Horse 29744). Both previously released.

Mar: Seven-inch picture disc *Timeless II 1/2: The Beatles Around the World* (Silhouette Music S.M. 1451): The Capitol promotional open-end interview from Feb 1964, falsely listed as a Feb 9, 1964 interview by Bob Miles of WKNX Underground Radio, Venus, New York; Jun 27, 1965 Rome press conference clip, falsely listed as a Jun 24, 1965 interview by "Carmela Anna Fortunata"; Aug 1964 interview clip (interviewer listed as Deutcher Bovick; date incorrectly listed as Feb 28, 1964). Short interview clip with John and Paul from Aug 1965 *Teen Set* interview, falsely listed as a Los Angeles interview of Nov 19, 1967.

Aug: LP *The Beatles Talk with Jerry G. Vol. 2* (Backstage BRS 1175). Includes 1965 and 1966 interviews recorded by D.J. Jerry G. Bishop. First release.

Oct 3: Single "Say Say Say" (Paul and Michael Jackson)/"Ode to a Koala Bear" (Paul) (Columbia 38-04168). First U.S. and U.K. release of both songs.

- 12-inch single "Say Say Say" (extended dance remix; Paul and Michael Jackson)/"Say Say Say" (instrumental), (both remixed by John "Jellybean" Benitez)-"Ode to a Koala Bear" (Paul) (Columbia 44-04169). First

U.S. and U.K. release of "Say Say Say" instrumental and extended remix.

Oct 26: LP *Pipes of Peace* (Paul) (Columbia 39149). Contains previously released "Say Say Say" (with Michael Jackson). First U.S. release of "The Man" (also with Michael Jackson), "Pipes of Peace," "The Other Me," "Keep Under Cover," "So Bad" (Version I), "Sweetest Little Show," "Average Person," "Hey Hey," "Tug of Peace," "Through Our Love."

Dec 5: LP *Heart Play—Unfinished Dialogue* (Lennon interview LP) (Polydor/PolyGram 817 238-1 Y-1). Contains first release of excerpts from a long series of interviews taped by David Sheff for *Playboy* magazine in Sep 1980.

- Single "So Bad" (Version I)/"Pipes of Peace" (Paul) (Columbia 39149). Both previously released.

Dec 19: Single "Ain't She Sweet"/"Sweet Georgia Brown" (Atlantic 13243). Both previously released.

1984

Early Jan: Single "I Want to Hold Your Hand"/"I Saw Her Standing There" (Capitol 5112). Reissue of Dec 26, 1963 release with slightly altered picture sleeve.

Jan 5: Single "Nobody Told Me" (John)/"O'Sanity" (Yoko) (Polydor/PolyGram 817 254-7). First release.

Jan 19: LP *Milk and Honey* (John and Yoko) (Polydor/PolyGram 817 160-1 Y-1). Contains previously released "Nobody Told Me." First release in U.S. and U.K. of "Grow Old with Me," "I Don't Wanna Face It," "Borrowed Time," "I'm Stepping Out," "(Forgive Me) My Little Flower Princess" (John), plus the following six cuts by Yoko: "Sleepless Night," "Don't Be Scared," "O'Sanity" (previously released), "Your Hands," "Let Me

"Nobody Told Me" (© PolyGram). U.S. 12-inch promo of a *Milk and Honey* single.

Count the Ways," "You're the One." All songs were recorded in Aug and Sep 1980 during the *Double Fantasy* sessions.

- CD *Milk and Honey* (John) (Polydor 817 160-2).

Feb 29: The following McCartney CDs were released: *Pipes of Peace* (Columbia CK 39149), *Wings over America* (2 CDs) (Columbia CK-37990/1), *Venus and Mars* (Columbia CK-36801), *Band on the Run* (Columbia CK-36482) (includes "Helen Wheels"), *Tug of War* (Columbia CK 37462).

Mar 15: Single "I'm Stepping Out" (John)/"Sleepless Night" (Yoko) (Polydor/PolyGram 821 107-7). Both previously released.

Apr: Double LP *Reflections and Poetry* (Silhouette Music—S.M. 10014). Contains first release of excerpts of Dec 8, 1980 interview with John recorded by RKO Radio, and previously released recordings of John reading some poetry. This album was withdrawn following legal action by Yoko, but longer versions of the interview were later released in the U.K. on CDs *The Last Word* and *Testimony*.

May 11: Single "Borrowed Time" (John)/"Your Hands" (Yoko) (Polydor 821-204-7). Both previously released.

Jul 9: LP *Let's Beat It* (K-tel TU-2200). Includes previously released "Say Say Say" (Paul and Michael Jackson).

Sep 13: LP *Every Man Has a Woman* (Polydor 823-490-1-Y-1). Contains first release of John's vocal harmony track for "Every Man Has a Woman Who Loves Him," presented here as a solo recording of the song.

Oct 2: 12-inch single "No More Lonely Nights" (extended version 8:10)/"Silly Love Songs" (Version II)-"No More Lonely Nights" (ballad 4:38) (Paul) (Columbia 44-05077; and on picture disc, 39927). A revised edition of this 12-inch was released in Jan 1985.

Oct 5: Single "No More Lonely Nights" (ballad 4:38)/"No More Lonely Nights" (playout version 3:56) (Paul) (Columbia 38-04581). First U.S. release of shorter playout version. Revised in Jan 1985 with new B side.

- Single "Every Man Has a Woman Who Loves Him" (John)/"It's Alright" (Sean Ono Lennon) (Polydor 881-378-7). Both previously released.

Oct 22: LP *Give My Regards to Broad Street* (Paul) (Columbia SC 39613). Contains the previously released "No More Lonely Nights" (ballad and playout version extended to 4:17) and "Silly Love Songs" (Version II). First U.S. and U.K. release of "Good Day Sunshine" (Version II), "Yesterday" (Version II), "Here, There and Everywhere (Version II), "Wanderlust" (Version II), "Ballroom Dancing" (Version II), "Not Such a Bad Boy," "No Values," "For No One" (Version II), "Eleanor Rigby" (Version II), "The Long and Winding Road" (Version II), and instrumentals from the film score: "Corridor Music" and "Eleanor's Dream." Also issued on CD (CK 39613) and cassette (SCT 39613); CD and cassette add "So Bad" (Version II) and a longer version of "Eleanor's Dream" (4:59 compared to 1:01 on LP). The CD also adds the instrumental, "Goodnight Princess" with a spoken introduction by Paul.

Nov: LP *The British Are Coming* (Silhouette SM-10013). Includes 1966 Ken Douglas interviews released on Oct 14, 1966 on LP *Beatle Views* and material repeated from Silhouette's *Timeless II 1/2*, released in Mar 1983.

Dec 7: Single "Do They Know It's Christmas?"/"Feed the World" (Columbia 38-04749). Includes Christmas messages from Paul and other British rock stars. Proceeds from the sale of the record went to aid starving people in Africa. First U.S. and U.K. release.

Dec 14: 12-inch single "Do They Know It's Christmas?"-"Feed the World"/"Do They Know It's Christmas?" (remix) (Columbia 44-05157). First U.S. and U.K. release of B side; other tracks previously released.

Late that year: LP *The Beatles Talk Downunder (and All Over) Volume 2* (Australia; Raven RVLP 1013). Ed Rudy's Feb 1964 Miami telephone interview with George (with Charlie Murdock dubbing in the questions); WQAM Radio's "Farewell to Miami" (Feb 1964); interview with Bernice Lumb (Mar 1964); Jun 1964 Australia press conference clips; Jun 27, 1965 Rome press conference; Jul 2, 1965 Graham Webb "MBE Chat" in Madrid; Aug 21, 1965 Minneapolis press conference; Jun 1966 Tokyo interview; edited version of Aug 25, 1966 Seattle interviews by Dusty Adams. First U.S. import release of Australian album.

1985

Jan: A very limited (and rare) 12-inch reissue edition (Columbia 44-05077) included "No More Lonely Nights" (special dance mix by Arthur Baker, 6:53 edit)/"No More Lonely Nights" (ballad 4:38)-"Silly Love Songs" (Version II). Revised 7-inch single also released: "No More Lonely Nights" (ballad)/"No More Lonely Nights" (Arthur Baker "Special Dance Mix" 4:20 edit, listed as 4:14) (Paul) (Columbia 38-04581). The U.S. picture sleeve was not changed, and it still listed the original "Playout Version" as the B side. When the Arthur Baker remix had been released earlier in the U.K., the new B side was noted on the record sleeve and label.

Mar 14: Soundtrack LP *Porky's Revenge* (Columbia JS 39983). Contains "I Don't Want to Do It" (George). First release. Also issued on CD (CK 39983).

May: Single "I Don't Want to Do It" (George) (Columbia 38-04887) backed with "Queen of the Hop" by Dave Edmunds. Slightly different mix from previously released LP version.

Jul: LP *The Golden Beatles* (Silhouette S.M. 10015). Contains the Kenny Everett interview of Jun 5–6, 1968, and 1965 open-end promo interview for film *Help!* with questions dubbed in by Wink Martindale. This is not the KFWB promo interview of Jun 5, 1964, also with Martindale, although a tiny clip of it is heard here. Previously released tracks.

Aug 19: LP *Greenpeace* (A&M SP 5091). Includes alternate version of "Save the World" (George) with new vocal track and a remix of the original backing track. First U.S. release.

Nov 18: Single "Spies Like Us" (4:42)/"My Carnival" (3:56) (Paul) (Capitol B-5537). 12-inch single features "Spies Like Us" (party mix, 7:10; alternate mix, 3:56; D.J. version, 3:46)/"My Carnival" (party mix, 6:00) (Capitol V- 15212). First U.S. and U.K. release.

Nov: LP *East Coast Invasion* (Cicadelic CIC LP 1964). First release of 1964 tour interviews by Larry Kane. LP *West Coast Invasion* (Cicadelic CIC LP 1966). First release of Aug 1964 interviews and San Francisco and Los Angeles press conferences.

Dec: LP *The Beatles 'Round the World* (Cicadelic CIC LP 1965). First release of 1963–65 interviews.

■ One-sided 7-inch 33½ RPM paper picture disc single with "Roll Over Beethoven" (from Dec 31, 1962 Star-Club tapes) (Silhouette #1); released as part of package that also included reissues of LPs *The British Are Coming* (SM 10013 on red vinyl) and *The Golden Beatles* (SM 10015 on gold vinyl).

■ LP *Alice in Wonderland* (Ringo) (Kid Stuff DAR-3902 and cassette, DAT-4902). Includes some of Ringo's dialogue from the TV film *Alice in Wonderland* but none of the songs from the film. The LP was issued with a book that featured color stills from the movie, including one of Ringo as the Mock Turtle. First release.

1986

Jan: LP *Unfinished Music #1: Two Virgins* (John) (Apple/Tetragrammaton). Virtually indistinguishable reissue from Out of the Past Records, which had purchased the Tetragrammaton catalog.

Jan 24: LP *John Lennon: Live in New York City* (John) (Capitol SV-12451). First release of recordings from Lennon's Aug 30, 1972 One to One Concerts, with most tracks taken from the afternoon show: "New York City," "It's So Hard," "Woman Is the Nigger of the World," "Well, Well, Well," "Instant Karma (We All Shine On)," "Mother," "Come Together," "Imagine," "Cold Turkey," "Hound Dog," "Give Peace a Chance."

Feb 1: CD *John Lennon: Live in New York City* (John) (Capitol CDP 7 46196 2). See LP release Jan 24.

Feb 8: LP *All Our Loving* (Cicadelic LP-1963). Contains first release of 1964–65 interviews.

May: LP *Imagine* (John) (Capitol SW 3379). Digitally remastered reissue.

Jul 14: Single "Press" (3:35)/"It's Not True" (4:27) (Paul) (Capitol B-5597). First release of 3:35 "video edit" of Bevans/Forward remix of "Press"; first U.S. and U.K. release of "It's Not True" (U.K. running time listed as 4:31). Bevans and Forward are not listed on the label, which states "Produced by Paul McCartney and Hugh Padgham." A 12-inch edition featured "Press" (4:41)/"It's Not True" (5:51)/"Hanglide" (5:18)/"Press" (dub mix 6:28) (Capitol V-15235). First U.S. and U.K. release of this edit of Bevans/Forward "Press" remix (listed as 4:43 in U.K.), "Hanglide," "Press" dub mix, and the Julian

Mendelsohn remix of "It's Not True," featured at 5:51, compared to 5:50 listed on the U.K. 10-inch single release and 5:52 listed on *Press to Play* CD. "Hanglide" was mixed by McCartney and Matt Butler, billed as "Mac 'n' Matt." The dub mix, another variation of the 3Bevans/Forward mix, is listed as 6:30 on the U.K. release.

Jul 23: Single "Twist and Shout"/"There's a Place" (Capitol B-5624). Reissue.

Aug 13: Single "Seaside Woman"/"B Side To Seaside" (Paul/Linda McCartney & Wings billed as Suzy and the Red Stripes) (Capitol B-5608). New, remixed versions of both sides of single first released in 1977; new mixes by Alvin Clark. A 12-inch edition featured extended mixes of both sings (Capitol V 15244).

Aug 22: LP *Press to Play* (Paul) (Capitol PJAS-12475). Contains previously released "Press" (Bevans/Forward) mix 4:41), and first release of "Stranglehold," "Good Times Coming"/"Feel the Sun," "Talk More Talk," "Footprints," "Only Love Remains," "Pretty Little Head," "Move Over Busker," "Angry," "However Absurd." CD release (CDP 7 46269 2) adds three tracks not included on the vinyl LP: first release of "Write Away" (later released as the B side of "Pretty Little Head" in the U.K.), and "Tough on a Tightrope" (later released as the B side of "Only Love Remains"); and previously released "It's Not True" (Julian Mendelsohn remix; 5:52).

Aug: LPs *Things We Said Today* (Cicadelic 1962) and *Not a Second Time* (CICLP-1961), containing 1964–65 interviews and press conferences in Toronto and Los Angeles. First release.

Oct 10: CD *Double Fantasy* (John) (Geffen 2001-2). Contents unchanged.

Oct 27: CD *Menlove Ave.* (John) (Capitol CDP 7 46576 2) and LP (SJ-12533). Posthumous album featuring first release of "Here We Go Again," "Angel Baby" (artificially extended and thus runs longer than on 1975 unauthorized *Roots* album), "My Baby Left Me," and "To Know Her Is to Love Her" from 1973 *Rock 'N' Roll* LP sessions; "Rock and Roll People" from the 1973 *Mind Games* sessions; alternate versions of "Steel and Glass," "Scared," "Old Dirt Road," "Nobody Loves You (When You're Down and Out)," and "Bless You" from the 1974 *Walls and Bridges* sessions. Only "Angel Baby" was previously released, and then only on the unauthorized (and withdrawn) *Roots* album. This extended version is its first authorized release.

Oct 29: Single "Stranglehold" (3:36)/"Angry" (3:36) (Paul) (Capitol B-5636). First U.S. release of "Angry" remix (by Larry Alexander with orchestration by Dave Matthews).

Nov 14: LP *Conspiracy of Hope* (Mercury 830-588-1). Contains Paul's "Pipes of Peace."

Nov: LP *Here There and Everywhere* (Cicadelic 1968). First release of Feb–Mar 1965 interviews taped by Derek Taylor during filming of *Help!* in the Bahamas.

Dec 1: CD *Wings Greatest* (Paul) (Capitol CDP 7 46056 2). Contents unchanged.

1987

Jan 17: Single "Only Love Remains" (4:11)/"Tough on a Tightrope" (4:44) (Paul) (Capitol B-5672). First U.S. release of Jim Boyer remix of A side.

Feb 26: CD release of *Please Please Me* (Capitol/EMI CDP 7 46435 2), *With The Beatles* (CDP 7 46436 2), *A Hard Day's Night* (CDP 7 46437 2), and *Beatles for Sale* (CDP 7 46438 2). Worldwide release of the first four U.K. Beatles albums on compact disc, all four in mono.

Feb: CD *The Beatles Live in Hamburg '62* (KTEL CD 1473). 20 tracks from Dec 31, 1962 Star-Club tapes.

Apr 21: CD *13 Original James Bond Themes* (EMI America 7 46079 2). Contains Wings' "Live and Let Die."

Apr 30: CD release of *Help!* (Capitol/EMI CDP 7 46439 2), *Revolver* (CDP 7 46441 2), *Rubber Soul* (CDP 7 46440 2), all in stereo. *Help!* and *Rubber Soul* remixed by George Martin.

Apr: LP *Moviemania!* (Cicadelic LP-1960). First release of more Feb–Mar 1965 Bahamas interviews.

May 11: LP *Prince's Trust Tenth Anniversary Birthday Party* (Paul) (A&M AMA 3906) and CD (CDA 3906). LP contains Paul's performance of "Get Back" from the Jun 20, 1986 Prince's Trust concert. The U.K. LP included a free bonus single with Paul's other two songs, "Long Tall Sally" and "I Saw Her Standing There"; the single was not issued in the U.S. The CD and cassette releases of the album included "Get Back" and "Long Tall Sally."

May 26: CD *Shaved Fish* (John) (Capitol CDP 7 46642 2). This first release of the CD was withdrawn; the CD was finally released worldwide on May 17, 1988.

Jun 1: CD *Sgt. Pepper's Lonely Hearts Club Band* (Capitol/EMI CDP 7 46442 2). The CD contained the "Inner Groove" and 15 kc tone heard only by dogs; both were present on the original U.K. LP but omitted at that time on the U.S. release. Stereo.

Jul 1: LP *Withnail and I* (George) (DRB-SBL 12590/SBLC 12590; LP/cassette release). Soundtrack LP includes the Beatles' "While My Guitar Gently Weeps."

Jul 21: Capitol Records released its own pressings of the first seven original British Beatles albums, while continuing to offer its own Beatles albums. The imminent end of virtually all vinyl record releases in the U.S. would make the original Capitol albums rarities, since they would not appear on CD. The Capitol issues of the British albums were all taken from the CD digital masters, thus the first four were mono: *Please Please Me* (Capitol CLJ 46435), *With The Beatles* (CLJ 46436), *A Hard Day's Night* (CLJ 46437), *Beatles for Sale* (CLJ 46438), *Help!* (CLJ 46439), *Rubber Soul* (CLJ 46440), *Revolver* (CLJ 46441).

Jul: LP *From Britain with Beat* (Cicadelic LP-1967). First release of 1964–65 interviews.

■ CD *The Beatles: The Early Tapes* (Polydor 823-701-2). Contains 14 Tony Sheridan cuts.

Aug 1: LP *Hear The Beatles Tell All* (Vee Jay PRO-202). Cut-to-shape picture disc reissue of 1964 Beatles interview album. The contents of the original LP have been edited here. Side 1: interview with Lennon is 8:15 (originally 13:00); Side 2: interviews are 7:45 (originally 13:06).

Aug 24: CD releases of *The Beatles* (the "*White Album*") (Capitol/EMI CDS 7 46443 8), double CD, and *Yellow Submarine* (CDP 7 46445 2).

Sep 21: CD *Magical Mystery Tour* (Capitol/EMI CDP 7 48062 2). The entire CD is in stereo. The original 1967 U.S. LP included some songs in mono, and the LP was not released in the U.K. until 1976, when the original U.S. version was issued.

Oct 16: Single "Got My Mind Set on You"/"Lay His Head" (George) (Dark Horse 7-28178) and cassette single (4-28178). First U.S. release of both songs. B side is remixed version also released on special CD and EP issued with George's book *Songs by George Harrison*. Original mix was included on first, unreleased version of George's *Somewhere in England* album.

Oct 19: CD releases *Abbey Road* (Capitol/EMI CDP 7 46446 2) and *Let It Be* (CDP 7 46447 2).

Nov 2: CD *Cloud Nine* (George) (Dark Horse 2-25643) and LP (1-25643). Contains previously released "Got My Mind Set on You." First U.S. and U.K. release of "Cloud 9," "That's What It Takes," "Fish on the Sand," "Just for Today," "This Is Love," "When We Was Fab," "Devil's Radio," "Someplace Else," "Wreck of the Hesperus," "Breath Away From Heaven." "Someplace Else" and "Breath Away From Heaven" first appeared in the film *Shanghai Surprise*; both were rerecorded for the album. Also released on cassette (4-25643).

Dec 1: CD *Band on the Run* (Paul) (Capitol CDP 7 46055 2). Initial releases of the CD omitted "Helen Wheels," which was added to later issues. The first batch had been imported from England, where the CD followed the original U.K. album song line up, thus omitting "Helen Wheels." The original U.S. CD released by Columbia in 1984 did include "Helen Wheels."

Dec 5: CD *All the Best* (Paul) (Capitol/Parlophone CCT 7 48287 2) and double LP (CLW 48287). The configurations of this "greatest hits" album were different in the U.S. and the U.K. The U.K. release includes a new song, "Once Upon a Long Ago," also released in England as a single, but never issued in the U.S., and several other songs omitted from the U.S. release, which includes "Junior's Farm," "Uncle Albert"/"Admiral Halsey," "Coming Up" (live version) (all missing from the U.K. edition), "Jet," "Band on the Run," "Ebony and Ivory," "Listen to What the Man Said," "No More Lonely Nights," "Silly Love Songs," "Let 'Em In," "C Moon," "Live and Let Die," "Another Day," "Goodnight Tonight," "Say Say Say," "With a Little Luck," "My Love." U.S. CD and LP releases are identical.

1988

That year: Capitol changed the label numbers of many of its original-format Beatles albums, the change coinciding with a switch of all records to the purple Capitol dome label. All seven of Capitol's U.S. releases of the

British-format albums switched to the purple label as well. *A Hard Day's Night* (SW-11921), *Let It Be* (SW-11922), and *20 Greatest Hits* (SV-12245) retained their old catalog numbers while appearing on the new label. The following new numbers, all with C1 prefixes for records and C4 for cassettes, appeared: *Sgt. Pepper* (46442), *The Beatles* ("White Album") (46443), *Yellow Submarine* (46445), *Abbey Road* (46446), *Magical Mystery Tour* (48062), *1962–1966* (90435), *1967–1970* (90438), *Meet The Beatles* (90441), *Hey Jude* (90442), *Something New* (90443), *Second Album* (90444), *Beatles VI* (90445), *Beatles '65* (90446), *Yesterday and Today* (90447), *Revolver* (90452), *Rubber Soul* (90453), and *Help!* (90454).

Jan 17: CD releases of *Blast from Your Past* (Ringo) (Capitol CDP 7 46663 2). *McCartney* (CDP 7 46611 2), *Tug of War* (CDP 7 46057 2), *Wings Over America* (CDP 7 46715 2) (double CD), *Ram* (CCT 7 46612 2) (all Paul).

Jan 25: Single "When We Was Fab"/"Zig Zag" (George) (Dark Horse 7-28131). First U.S. and U.K. release of both songs. B side is an instrumental from the 1986 film *Shanghai Surprise.* Also released on cassette single (Dark Horse 9 28131-4).

Feb 21: Double CD *All Things Must Pass* (George) (Capitol CDP 7 46688/9 2). Capitol used Sonic Solutions No Noise System, which was not used on the U.K. release of the CD issued in May 1987. EMI announced it would use the U.S. digital master for future CD pressings in the U.K. Later, Abbey Road engineer Mike Jarratt said that only some songs had undergone the Sonic treatment.

Mar 8: CDs *Past Masters Vol. 1* (Capitol CDP 7 90043-2), *Past Masters Vol. 2* (CDP 7-90044-2). These two CDs contain the remaining Beatles songs not included on the original U.K. Beatles albums and thus not found on the Beatles CDs. Vol. 1: "Love Me Do" (Version I), "From Me to You," "Thank You Girl," "She Loves You," "I'll Get You," "I Want to Hold Your Hand," "This Boy," "Komm, Gib Mir Deine Hand," "Sie Liebt Dich," "Long Tall Sally," "I Call Your Name," "Slow Down," "Matchbox," "I Feel Fine," "She's a Woman," "Bad Boy," "Yes It Is," "I'm Down." Vol. 2: "Day Tripper," "We Can Work It Out," "Paperback Writer," "Rain," "Lady Madonna," "The Inner Light," "Hey Jude," "Revolution" (Version I), "Get Back" (Version I), "Don't Let Me Down," "The Ballad of John and Yoko," "Old Brown Shoe," "Across the Universe" (Version I), "Let It Be" (Version I), "You Know My Name (Look Up the Number)."

Mar 17: CD *Imagine* (John) (Capitol C2 7 46641 2).

That spring: CD *The Silver Beatles* (Teichiku Records) and CD *Raw Energy* (Romance Records SB 18); each contains the usual 12 Decca audition cuts. *Raw Energy* appeared with two label variations, each with different song lineups listed, and was apparently a legal release, although The Beatles sued to stop its sale. Missing, as usual, are the three Lennon/McCartney compositions, "Love of the Loved," "Like Dreamers Do" and "Hello Little Girl."

Mar 22: CD release of *The Best of George Harrison* (George) (Capitol CCT 7 46682 2) and *Mind Games* (John) (CDP 746769-2).

Apr 5: CD *John Lennon: Plastic Ono Band* (John) (Capitol CDP 7 46770-2).

Apr 19: CD release of *Rock 'N' Roll* (Capitol/EMI CDP 7-46707-2) and *Walls and Bridges* (CDP 7 46768-2) (both John).

May 2: Single "This Is Love"/"Breath Away from Heaven" (George) (Dark Horse 7-27913). Also on cassette single (9 27913-4). Both songs previously released.

May 17: CD *Shaved Fish* (John) (Capitol C2 7 46642-2). Second release, the original May 26, 1987 issue having been withdrawn due to poor sound quality. This release was allegedly improved through the use of Sonic Solutions No Noise Processing.

Sep 19: Single "Jealous Guy"/"Give Peace a Chance" (John) (Capitol B 44230). Tie-in to film/LP *Imagine: John Lennon.*

Oct 4: CD *Imagine: John Lennon* (John) (Capitol CDP 7 90803) and double LP (C1-90803). All songs previously released except for first release of "Real Love," a 1980 demo, and "Imagine," a 1971 demo. Other songs include The Beatles' "Twist and Shout" (mono), "Help!" "In My Life," "Strawberry Fields Forever," "A Day in the Life," "Revolution" (Version I), "The Ballad of John and Yoko," "Julia," "Don't Let Me Down," and Lennon's solo titles "Give Peace a Chance" (full single version), "How?" "Imagine" (released version), "God," "Mother" (live; One to One Concert), "Stand by Me," "Jealous Guy," "Woman," "Beautiful Boy (Darling Boy)," "(Just Like) Staring Over." "A Day in the Life" contains a clean intro, rather than the crossfade heard on the *Sgt. Pepper* album.

Oct 10: CD *Water From the Wells of Home* (Johnny Cash; Paul) (Mercury 834778-2) and LP (834778-1). Paul's duet with Johnny Cash on "New Moon over Jamaica" appears on this album, with Paul taking lead vocal during one verse.

Oct 17: Single "Handle with Care"/"Margarita" (George/Traveling Wilburys) (Wilbury 7-27732), CD single (2-27732) and cassette single (1-27732). First U.S. and U.K. release of both songs. All three formats contained the same two songs in the U.S.; the U.K. 3-inch CD single, however, added an extended version of "Handle with Care" not released in the U.S.

Oct 18: CD *Stay Awake* (Ringo) (A&M CD 3918) and LP (SP 3918). Contains first release of Ringo's recording of "When You Wish Upon a Star," with Herb Alpert, part of a medley that closes the album.

■ CD *The Traveling Wilburys Volume One* (George/Traveling Wilburys) (Wilbury/Warner Bros. 2-25796), LP (1-25796) and cassette (4-25796). This mythical group included the following, each of whom appears only under the noted pseudonym: George Harrison (Nelson Wilbury), Roy Orbison (Lefty Wilbury), Bob Dylan (Lucky Wilbury), Tom Petty (Charlie T. Jnr. Wilbury), and Jeff Lynne (Otis Wilbury). No real name appears anywhere on the album. The album was produced by George and Jeff Lynne (billed as Nelson and Otis, of course). Harrison shares lead vocal with Orbison on "Handle with Care," previously released as a single, and he is heard on several other tracks including "End of the Line," on which each of the Wilburys takes a turn at lead vocal. The other titles include "Margarita," "Dirty Word," "Rattled," "Last Night," "Not Alone Any More," "Congratulations," "Heading for the Light," and "Tweeter and the Monkey Man." First release except for previously released "Handle with Care" and "Margarita."

Oct 24: LP *Past Masters* (Capitol/Parlophone C1-91135). Double album previously available only as two separately issued CDs.

Oct 31: *The Beatles* (LP/CD/Cassette boxed sets) (EMI LP: BBX 1; Cassette: TC BBX 1; CD: CD BBX 1). Worldwide EMI release of Beatles boxed sets of albums, CDs, and cassettes. Each set issued in a wooden box with a paperback book and included the *Past Masters* albums. All of these releases included the new digitally remastered versions used on the CD releases, including the first four albums in mono, and the new George Martin remixed *Help!* and *Rubber Soul* albums. All orders to EMI after Oct 10 would be filled with the new versions; the old versions were phased out.

Nov 2: CD *Porky's Revenge* (George) (Mobile Fidelity MFCD 797). Soundtrack album includes Harrison's "I Don't Want to Do It." An earlier CD, released in 1985 by Columbia (CK-39983), was withdrawn in the U.S., although it remained available in Canada and the U.K.

Nov: CD releases of three McCartney albums: *Red Rose Speedway* (Capitol Starline CDM 7 52026 2). Adds the following bonus tracks: "The Mess," "I Lie Around," and "Country Dreamer." *Venus and Mars* (CDM 7 46984 2), with the added bonus tracks "Zoo Gang," "Lunch Box-Odd Sox," and "My Carnival." A 1984 release of the CD in the U.S. on the Columbia label (CK 36801) was only available for a short time and did not contain the extra tracks. *McCartney II* (CDM 7 52024 2), with the bonus tracks "Check My Machine" and "Secret Friend."

Dec 2: CD singles: "From Me to You"/"Thank You Girl" (Capitol/Parlophone C3-44280-2); "Love Me Do" (Version II)/"P.S. I Love You" (C3-44278-2); "She Loves You"/"I'll Get You" (C3-44281-2); "Please Please Me"/"Ask Me Why" (C3-44279-2). Start of 3-inch CD single reissue series including all original Beatles U.K. singles. Once again, EMI mistakenly used the album version of "Love Me Do" (Version II), with Andy White on drums.

1989

Jan 23: Single "End of the Line"/"Congratulations" (George/Wilburys) (Wilbury 7-27637), CD single (2-27637) and cassette single (4-27637). Both songs previously released. U.K. CD and 12-inch singles have extended version of A side; U.S. release contains the shorter LP version on all singles releases.

Jan 30: CD *Double Fantasy* (John) (Capitol CDP 7 91425 2) and LP (EST 2083). Capitol reissue; album originally released on the Geffen label.

Feb 24: CD *Starr Struck: Best of Ringo Starr Vol. 2* (Ringo) (Rhino CD: R2 70135) and LP (R1 70135). CD release adds four songs not included on LP: "Attention," "Who Needs a Heart," *"Hopeless," and "You Belong to Me." Both releases include: "Wrack My Brain," *"In My Car," "Cookin' (in the Kitchen of Love)," *"I Keep Forgettin'," "Hard Times," "Hey! Baby," "A Dose of Rock & Roll," "Private Property," "Can She Do It Like She Dances," "Heart on My Sleeve," "Sure to Fall (in Love With You)," *"She's About a Mover." CD features first U.S. release of four songs (*) from Ringo's *Old Wave* album (LP contained only three, omitting "Hopeless").

Feb: CD single "I Want to Hold Your Hand"/"This Boy" (Capitol C3-44304-2). 3-inch CD single reissue of original U.K. single worldwide.

Mar 21: CD *Paul McCartney CD Gift Set* (Paul) (Capitol; no number). Special gift box edition with four McCartney CDs: *McCartney*, *Red Rose Speedway*, *Ram*, and *McCartney II*.

May 10: Single "My Brave Face"/"Flying to My Home" (Paul) (Capitol B-44367) and cassette single (4JM-44367). First U.S. release of both songs. The single was issued with three label variations in the U.S.: (1) running time on A side listed as 3:17; (2) time listed as 3:16 (both of these have Paul McCartney's name in custom typesetting, different from that used elsewhere on the label); (3) time listed as 3:17 with Paul's name in standard block typeset, the same as other lettering on the label. The Capitol purple dome label came in various shades from light to very dark. Cassette single contains only these two songs; the U.K. cassette single, however, adds "I'm Gonna Be a Wheel Someday" and "Ain't That a Shame," the same two numbers added to the U.K. 12-inch and CD singles.

Jun 5: 12-inch single "Spirit of the Forest" (Ringo) (Virgin 0-96551). Features Ringo doing a few lines of lead vocal, which rotates among a number of different artists during the 5:18 all-star recording released to benefit the Earth Love Fund—Rainforest Appeal in England. Only the 12-inch single was issued in the U.S.; in the U.K. only a 7-inch single was released. First release in U.S. and U.K. on same date.

Jun 6: CD *Flowers in the Dirt* (Paul) (Capitol CDP 7 91653 2), LP (C1-91653) and cassette (C4-91653). CD and cassette add bonus track "Ou Est le Soleil?" omitted from LP. All formats contain previously released "My Brave Face" and first U.S. release of "Rough Ride" (Version I), "You Want Her Too," "Distractions," "We Got Married," "Put It There," "Figure of Eight" (Version I), "This One," "Don't Be Careless Love," "That Day Is Done," "How Many People," and "Motor of Love."

Jun 20: CD releases of Paul's *Wild Life* (Capitol CDM 7 52017 2), with added bonus tracks "Oh Woman, Oh Why," "Mary Had a Little Lamb," and "Little Woman Love"; *Pipes of Peace* (CDP 7 46018 2); *London Town* (CDP 7 48198 2), with added bonus track "Girl's School";

Back to the Egg (CDP 7 48200 2), with added bonus tracks "Daytime Nightime Suffering," "Wonderful Christmastime," and "Rudolph the Red-Nosed Reggae"; *Wings at the Speed of Sound* (CDP 7 48199 2), with bonus tracks "Walking in the Park with Eloise," "Bridge Over the River Suite," and "Sally G."

Jun: CD *Tommy* (Rhino R2 CD-71113); London Symphony Orchestra and Chambre Choir, with Ringo's "Fiddle About" and "Tommy's Holiday Camp."

Jul 1: Single "Got My Mind Set on You"/"When We Was Fab" (George) (Dark Horse 7-21891). "Back to Back Hits" series.

Jul 5: Single "Act Naturally"/"The Key's in the Mailbox" (Ringo/Buck Owens) (Capitol B-44409), cassette single (4JM-44409). First release of A side, a duet by Ringo and Buck Owens; B side is by Owens only.

Jul 26: 12-inch single "Ou Est le Soleil?" (7:02 Shep Pettibone Remix)/"Tub Dub Mix" (4:27)/"Instrumental Mix" (4:25) (Paul) (Capitol: V-15499), also issued on cassette maxi single (Capitol 4V-15499). First release of these remixes of "Ou Est le Soleil?" See "Alternate Versions and Bonus Tracks" section for full details on the various releases of "Ou Est le Soleil?"

Aug 2: Cassette single "This One"/"The First Stone" (Paul) (Capitol 4JM 44438). First U.S. release of B side. This was the only official release of the single in the U.S.

Aug 7: CD singles: "Hello Goodbye"/"I Am the Walrus" (Capitol/Parlophone C3-44317-2); "The Ballad of John and Yoko"/"Old Brown Shoe" (C3-44313-2); "Get Back"/"Don't Let Me Down" (C3-44320-2); "All You Need Is Love"/"Baby You're a Rich Man" (C3-44316-2); "Something"/"Come Together" (C3-44314-2). Three-inch CD reissues of original U.K. singles. This was the first U.S. release of the original mono U.K. single version of "Get Back."

Aug 10: CD *Lethal Weapon 2* (George) (Warner Bros. 2 25985), LP (1 25985), and cassette (4 25985). Soundtrack album contains first release of "Cheer Down," performed by George Harrison.

Aug 24: Single "Cheer Down"/"That's What It Takes" (George) (Warner Bros. 7-22807) and cassette single (Warner Bros. 4-22807). A side from *Lethal Weapon 2* film soundtrack; B side from Harrison's LP *Cloud Nine*.

Aug: CD singles "I Feel Fine"/"She's a Woman" (Capitol/Parlophone C3-44321-2); "Help!"/"I'm Down" (C3-44308-2); "Ticket to Ride"/"Yes It Is" (C3-44307-2); "Can't Buy Me Love"/"You Can't Do That" (C3-44305-2); "A Hard Day's Night"/"Things We Said Today" (C3-44306-2); "Hey Jude"/"Revolution" (C3-44319-2); "Paperback Writer"/"Rain" (C3-44310-2); "Let It Be"/"You Know My Name (Look Up the Number)" (3-44315-2); "Strawberry Fields Forever"/"Penny Lane" (C3-44312-2); "Yellow Submarine"/"Eleanor Rigby" (C3-44311-2); "We Can Work It Out"/"Day Tripper" (C3-44309-2), "Lady Madonna"/"The Inner Light" (C3-44318-2). Three-inch CD reissues of original U.K. singles.

Sep 1: Cassette single "Got My Mind Set on You"/"When We Was Fab" (George) (Dark Horse 9 21891-4; Warner Bros. Back Trax). The first Beatles-related oldies cassette single, part of Warner Brothers' Back Trax cassette series.

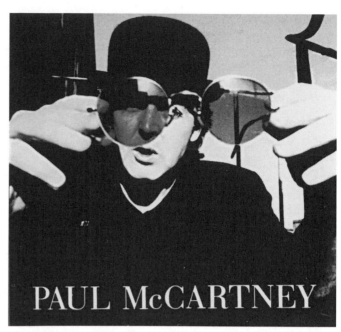

"My Brave Face" (© MPL Communications Ltd.). U.K. 12-inch version. Paul's U.S. 7-inch single appeared with at least three different label variations.

Sep 11: CD single "My Brave Face"/"Flying to My Home"/"I'm Gonna Be a Wheel Someday"/"Ain't That a Shame" (Paul) (Capitol CDP 7 15468 2). First U.S. release of latter two titles, taken from Paul's Soviet album, *CHOBA B CCCP*. It is also the first U.S. Beatles-related 5-inch CD single release. Early CD singles by The Beatles, Harrison, and Wilburys were all 3-inch discs. This 5-inch CD single was released in the U.K. May 8.

Oct 1: CD *Savage Young Beatles* (Romance Records SB-19). Contains eight of the previously released Jun 1961 Hamburg recordings, including The Beatles' "Cry for a Shadow" and Tony Sheridan's "Why," "If You Love Me, Baby," "Sweet Georgia Brown," "Ya Ya," "Ruby Baby," "Let's Dance," "What'd I Say."

■ CD *Act Naturally* (Buck Owens/Ringo) (Capitol CDP 7 92893), LP (C1 92893), and cassette (C4 92893). Includes previously released Ringo/Owens "Act Naturally" duet and other Owens tracks.

Oct 15: Single "Nobody Told Me"/"I'm Stepping Out" (John) (Polydor 883 927-7). Timepieces series.

Oct 17: CD *Best of Dark Horse: 1976–1989* (George) (Dark Horse 25726-2), LP (25726-1) and cassette (25726-4). Compilation album adds first release of two new songs, "Cockamamie Business" and "Poor Little Girl," and features the previously released "Cheer Down," "Blow Away," "That's the Way It Goes," "Wake Up My Love," "Life Itself," "Got My Mind Set on You," "Crackerbox Palace," "Cloud 9," "Here Comes the Moon," "When We Was Fab," "Love Comes to Everyone" and "All Those Years Ago." The CD and cassette editions add "Gone Troppo."

Nov 15: Cassette single "Figure of Eight" (Version II)/"Ou Est le Soleil?" (Pettibone remix 4:06) (Paul)

(Capitol 4JM-44489). First release of "Figure of Eight" (Version II) and of these edits of the two songs. The 4:06 "Ou Est le Soleil?" was not issued in the U.K., and the 3:57 edit of "Figure of Eight" appeared there only on a promo. The U.K. 7-inch vinyl single, not issued in the U.S., featured running times of 5:11 (listed as 5:16) and 4:50 respectively for the A and B sides.

1990

Jan 15: CD *Flowers in the Dirt* (World Tour Pack) (Paul) (EMI CD-PCSDX-106; CD only). This special edition of Paul's album was originally released in the U.K. on Nov 23, 1989 in both CD and LP editions; only the CD edition was imported into the U.S. The pack included a bonus one-track 3-inch CD single with the previously unreleased "Party Party." A one-sided, etched/engraved 7-inch vinyl edition of the same single was issued in the U.K. with the vinyl World Tour Pack. The pack also included a bumper sticker, color poster of the band, tour itinerary, "family tree" of band members, and a set of postcards; CD box also had a 12 × 12 copy of LP cover. The catalog number listed is for the outer box containing the CD and the special bonus single; the CD itself is the same as the original release and retained its original U.K. catalog numbers (7 91653 2 or CD PCSD 106). The 3-inch CD single "Party Party" number is Parlophone CD3R 6238.

Feb 19: CD *The John Lennon Collection* (John) (Capitol CDP 7 91516 2). In addition to the 17 tracks contained on the original U.K. album (15 in U.S.), the CD adds "Move Over Ms. L" and "Cold Turkey," marking the first LP or CD release for "Ms. L." The U.S. release was originally scheduled for Nov 14, 1989 but was postponed when it was learned that the U.K. release had a shortened version of "No. 9 Dream" (reduced by 2 minutes). Capitol claimed it wanted to restore the full version. The CD also contains the complete versions of "Give Peace a Chance" and "Happy Xmas (War Is Over)." The November 1982 U.S. LP release of this collection omitted "Happy Xmas (War Is Over)" and "Stand by Me," but both are included on the CD.

Apr 1: Double CD *Some Time in New York City* (John) (Capitol CDP 7 46782/3 2; outer box lists C2 93850). Contents unchanged. Individual discs numbered 46782 and 46783 respectively, identical to U.K. issue; different number appears on outer cardboard box issued in the U.S. as noted.

■ CD *After the Hurricane: Songs for Montserrat* (Paul) (Ulatradisc UDCD-529). Contains Paul's previously released duet with Stevie Wonder, "Ebony and Ivory." The album was designed to raise relief funds for victims of hurricane Hugo, which struck Montserrat and the southern United States. Other artists on the LP include The Rolling Stones, Elton John, Dire Straits, The Police and Midge Ure.

Apr 15: CD *China Beach: Music & Memories* (John) (SBK K2 93744). Contains John's previously released recording of "Stand by Me" and songs by other artists.

Also issued on LP (SBK K1 93744) and cassette (K4 93744).

Apr: CD *The Last Temptation of Elvis* (Paul) (NME CD 038/039) and double LP (NME 038/039). Includes first U.S. release of McCartney's "It's Now or Never" from the Jul 1987 sessions for his Soviet LP, but omitted from that album. The album also contains 25 additional cover versions of Elvis Presley numbers by a variety of stars. Initial release was made in the U.K. through mail order by *New Musical Express*, with general release following, and was sold in the U.S. as an import.

May 1: Cassette single "Put It There"/"Mama's Little Girl" (Paul) (Capitol 4JM-44570). First U.S. release of B side, recorded during Paul's 1978 *Back to the Egg* sessions; A side previously released.

Jul 1: Single "Handle with Care"/"End of the Line" (George) (Wilbury Records, Warner Bros. 7-21867) and cassette single (9 21867-4). Part of Warner Brothers' "Back-to-Back Hits" vinyl and "Back Trax" cassette singles reissue series.

Jul 24: CD *Nobody's Child: Romanian Angel Appeal* (Traveling Wilburys; George) (Warner Bros. 9 26280-2) and casette (9-26280-4). First U.S. release of George and Paul Simon's "Homeward Bound" duet recorded for NBC-TV's "Saturday Night Live" taped Nov 19, 1976 and aired Nov 20, 1976; and first U.S. release of "With a Little Help from My Friends" from Ringo's Sep 4, 1989 Los Angeles show (omitted on the cassette release). The CD also contains the first U.S. release of "Nobody's Child" by The Traveling Wilburys. Other album tracks include Eric Clapton's recording of George's composition "That Kind of Woman," which he recorded earlier but decided to omit from his *Journeyman* album, and Duane Eddy's "The Trembler," originally released in Oct 1987 on Eddy's album, *Duane Eddy*, and featuring George on slide guitar.

Aug 6: Double CD *Knebworth: The Album* (Paul) (Polydor 847 042-2), double LP (847 042-1) and double cassette (847 042-4). Includes Paul's live versions of "Coming Up" and "Hey Jude" from the Jun 30 Knebworth concert. First release worldwide.

Sep: LP *Press Conferences Madrid/L.A.* (Paul) (Discussion Records). Picture disc LP with Paul's Nov 27, 1989 Los Angeles and Nov 2, 1989 Madrid press conferences. First U.S. release.

Oct 12: CD *Ringo Starr and His All-Starr Band* (Ringo) (Rykodisc RCD 10190), LP (RALP 0190) and cassette (RACS 0190). First U.S. release of the following tracks from Ringo's Sep 3 and 4, 1989 Los Angeles concerts at the Greek Theater: *"It Don't Come Easy," "No No Song," "Honey Don't," "You're Sixteen" and "Photograph." A bonus CD single included only with a U.S. limited deluxe edition of the CD added the first release of *"Act Naturally" and repeated "It Don't Come Easy" from the album. All of the songs are from the Sep 3, 1989 show except (*) from the Sep 4, 1989 performance. The following concert numbers by other members of the band, with Ringo on drums, appear on the album: "Iko

Iko" (Dr. John), "The Weight" (Levon Helm), "Shine Silently" (Nils Lofgren), "Quarter to Three" (Clarence Clemmons), "Raining in My Heart" (Rick Danko), "Will It Go Round in Circles" (Billy Preston) and "Life in the Fast Lane" (Joe Walsh). The bonus CD single also added Walsh's "Rocky Mountain Way." [Note: Both outer and inner cardboard boxes for the deluxe CD edition have the number 90190. The boxes for the standard edition (without the bonus CD single), the CD itself, and the jewel box paper insert listed it as *10190*.] The bonus CD single number is Rykodisc RCD5-1019.

Oct 16: Cassette single "Birthday"/"Good Day Sunshine" (Paul) (Capitol 4JM-44645). First U.S. release of both songs; live versions from Paul's tour. "Good Day Sunshine" is not on *Tripping the Live Fantastic* tour album. "Sunshine" was misspelled "Shunshine" on the cardboard sleeve.

Oct 30: CD *Lennon* (John) (Capitol/EMI CDS 7 95220 2) 4 CDs individually numbered: (95221/2/3/4-2). Four-CD boxed set, issued to commemorate Lennon's 50th birthday and containing 73 songs, all previously released. The set, not issued in vinyl or cassette formats, contains "Give Peace a Chance," "Blue Suede Shoes," "Money," "Dizzy Miss Lizzie" and "Yer Blues" (first CD release of these tracks from the 1969 *Live Peace in Toronto* LP); "Cold Turkey," "Instant Karma!," "Mother," "Hold On," "I Found Out," "Working Class Hero," "Isolation," "Remember," "Love," "Well Well Well," "Look at Me," "God," "My Mummy's Dead," "Power to the People," "Well (Baby Please Don't Go)" (live Jun 6, 1971), "Imagine," "Crippled Inside," " Jealous Guy," "It's So Hard," "Gimme Some Truth," "Oh My Love," "How Do You Sleep?" "How?" "Oh Yoko!" "Happy Xmas (War Is Over)," "Woman Is the Nigger of the World," "New York City," "John Sinclair"; "Come Together" and "Hound Dog" (both live from Aug 30, 1972 One to One Concerts); "Mind Games," "Aisumasen (I'm Sorry)," "One Day (at a Time)," "Intuition," "Out the Blue," "Whatever Gets You Through the Night," "Going Down on Love," "Old Dirt Road," "Bless You," "Scared," "No. 9 Dream," "Surprise Surprise (Sweet Bird of Paradox)," "Steel and Glass," "Nobody Loves You (When You're Down and Out)," "Stand by Me," "Ain't That a Shame," "Do You Want to Dance," "Sweet Little Sixteen," "Slippin' and Slidin'," "Angel Baby" (same artificially extended 3:38 remix released earlier on *Menlove Ave.*), "Just Because," "Whatever Gets You Through the Night," "Lucy in the Sky with Diamonds" and "I Saw Her Standing There" (last three cuts from Nov 28, 1974 Elton John concert; first CD and Capitol Records release of these tracks, and the first U.S. release of the first two titles); "(Just Like) Starting Over," "Cleanup Time," "I'm Losing You," "Beautiful Boy (Darling Boy)," "Watching the Wheels," "Woman," "Dear Yoko," "I'm Stepping Out," "I Don't Wanna Face It," "Nobody Told Me," "Borrowed Time," "(Forgive Me) My Little Flower Princess," "Every Man Has a Woman Who Loves Him" and "Grow Old With Me." According to Capitol Records, the U.S. release was

technically considered an import of the U.K. release since Capitol pressed no copies of its own and imported the set from Europe. Initial copies omitted "Imagine" from the track listing on the box, but these were replaced with corrected ones.

- CD *The Traveling Wilburys Volume 3* (George/Traveling Wilburys) (Wilbury Warner Bros. 9 26324-2), LP (9 26324-1) and cassette (9 26324-4). The Traveling Wilburys' second album, with the tongue-in-cheek "Volume 3" title (there was no Volume 2). The fictitious names of the four surviving Wilburys were changed to Spike (George), Muddy (Tom Petty), Clayton (Jeff Lynne) and Boo (Bob Dylan). There was no replacement for the late Roy Orbison, but the album was dedicated to his Wilbury alter ego, Lefty. George has no solo number on the album, but he does a few lines of lead vocal on "She's My Baby," "The Devil's Been Busy," "Where Were You Last Night?" and "Wilbury Twist." The album also includes "If You Belonged to Me," "Inside Out," "7 Deadly Sins," "Poor House," "Cool Dry Place," "New Blue Moon" and "You Took My Breath Away." First U.S. release of all songs.

Nov 5: Double CD *Tripping the Live Fantastic* (Paul) (Capitol CDP 7 94778 2), triple LP (C1 94778) and double cassette (C4 94778). Songs from Paul's 1989–90 world tour, including several tracks taped during soundchecks. The album begins with "Showtime," a recording of the band being called to the stage. Soundcheck recordings include: "Inner City Madness," "Together," "Crackin' Up," "Matchbox," "Sally," and "Don't Let the Sun Catch You Crying" (the Ray Charles number, not the more familiar Gerry and the Pacemakers hit). The album includes the following songs from different shows: "Figure of Eight," "Jet," "Rough Ride," "Got to Get You into My Life," "Band on the Run," "Birthday" (previously released as a single), "Ebony and Ivory," "We Got Married," "Maybe I'm Amazed," "The Long and Winding Road," "The Fool on the Hill," "Sgt. Pepper's Lonely Hearts Club Band," "Can't Buy Me Love," "Put It There," "Things We Said Today," "Eleanor Rigby," "This One," "My Brave Face," "Back in the USSR," "I Saw Her Standing There," "Twenty Flight Rock," "Coming Up," "Let It Be," "Ain't That a Shame," "Live and Let Die," "If I Were Not upon a Stage" (a comical busk used as a lead-in to "Hey Jude" at many shows), "Hey Jude," "Yesterday," "Get Back," medley "Golden Slumbers"/"Carry That Weight"/"The End." First U.S. and U.K. release, except "Birthday."

Nov 19: CD *Tripping the Live Fantastic: Highlights!* (Paul) (Capitol CDP 7 95379 2) and cassette (C4 95379). Condensed version of Paul's live concert album. The U.K. edition of *Highlights!* included "All My Trials" from Paul's Oct 27, 1989 Milan concert, omitted from the U.S. edition, which featured the previously released "Put It There" instead. The remaining tracks on the U.S. album were *"Got to Get You Into My Life," "Birthday," *"We Got Married," "The Long and Winding Road," "Sgt. Pepper's Lonely Hearts Club Band," "Can't Buy Me

Love," *"Things We Said Today," "Eleanor Rigby," "My Brave Face," *"Back in the USSR," "I Saw Her Standing There," "Coming Up," "Let It Be," "Hey Jude," "Get Back" and medley *"Golden Slumbers"/"Carry That Weight"/"The End." The Columbia House Record Club released an abbreviated 12-track vinyl edition of *Highlights!* in the U.S. that did contain "All My Trials," the only release of the song in the U.S. The vinyl edition omitted five (*) tracks.

1991

Mar 25: Cassette single "Wilbury Twist"/"New Blue Moon" (instrumental) (George/Traveling Wilburys) (Wilbury/Warner Bros. 9 19443-4).

Mar 26: CD *Bad Boy* (Ringo) (Epic EK 35378).

May 6: CD *Ringo* (Ringo) (Capitol CDP 7 95884 2) and cassette (TC-EMS 1386). CD adds bonus tracks "Down and Out," "It Don't Come Easy" and "Early 1970."

May 28: CD *For Our Children* (Walt Disney Records 60616-2). Charity album includes Paul's previously released "Mary Had a Little Lamb."

Jun 4: CD *Unplugged (The Official Bootleg)* (Paul) (Capitol CDP 7 96413 2), cassette (C4-96413). Album taken from Paul's appearance on MTV's "Unplugged" series, videotaped Jan 25 and aired Apr 3 in the U.S. First U.S. release of all tracks: "Be-Bop-a-Lula," "I Lost My Little Girl," "Here, There and Everywhere," "Blue Moon of Kentucky," "We Can Work It Out," "San Francisco Bay Blues," "I've Just Seen a Face," "Every Night," "She's a Woman," "Hi-Heel Sneakers," "And I Love Her," "That Would Be Something," "Blackbird," "Ain't No Sunshine" (vocal: Hamish Stuart), "Good Rockin' Tonight," "Singing the Blues," "Junk" (instrumental). A limited number of vinyl albums were imported from Europe, but the CD was a domestic Capitol pressing.

Jun 11: CD release of George's albums *Somewhere in England* (Dark Horse/Warner Bros. 9 26614-2) and *Gone Troppo* (9 26615-2).

Jun 25: CD releases of George's albums *Thirty Three & 1/3* (Dark Horse/Warner Bros. 9 26612-2) and *George Harrison* (9 26613-2; cassette Apple/Columbia C2T-48216).

Jul 1: Cassette singles set: All 22 original U.K. Beatles singles were issued in cassette format, the first five on

Jul 1, five more each on Aug 5, Sep 3, and Oct 7, and the final two on Nov 4.

Jul 30: CD *The Concert for Bangla Desh* (George/Ringo) (Capitol CDP 7 93265 2; cassette Apple/Columbia C2T-48216).

Late Jul: CD set *Lennon* (John) (Capitol 95220). First official Capitol/U.S. release of this set, originally issued as an import Oct 30, 1990.

Aug: CD *Unfinished Music #1: Two Virgins* (John/Yoko) (Creative Sounds SS1 9999). Possibly unauthorized release; copied from a vinyl copy of the album and of marginal sound quality.

Oct 29: CD CHOBA B CCCP (The Russian Album (Paul) (Capitol CDP 7 97615 2). Worldwide release of album originally issued only on vinyl in the Soviet Union Oct 31, 1988. The CD adds "I'm in Love Again," previously issued only on singles, and includes "Kansas City," "Twenty Flight Rock," "Lawdy Miss Clawdy," "Bring It on Home to Me," "Lucille," "Don't Get Around Much Anymore," "I'm Gonna Be a Wheel Someday," "That's All Right (Mama)," "Summertime," "Ain't That a Shame," "Crackin' Up," "Just Because" and "Midnight Special."

Nov 26: CD *Music from the Motion Picture Curly Sue* (Ringo) (Giant/Warner Bros. 9 24439-2), cassette (9 24439-4). Soundtrack album contains first release of Ringo's "You Never Know."

Dec: CD *Give My Regards to Broad Street* (Paul) (Capitol CDP 7 46043 2). Contents unchanged.

1992

Feb 3: CDs *Living in the Material World* (EMI CDP 7 94110 2), *Dark Horse* (CDP 7 98079 2) and *Extra Texture (Read All About It)* (CDP 7 98080 2) (all George). Contents unchanged.

Apr 28: CD single "Weight of the World,"/"After All These Years,"/"Don't Be Cruel," (Ringo) (Private Music 01005-81003-2). Cassette single contains first two songs only (81003-4).

May 22: CD/cassette *Time Takes Time* (Ringo) (Private Music 01005-82097). First release of "The Weight of the World," "Don't Know a Thing About Love," "Don't Go Where the Road Don't Go," "Golden Blunders," "All in the Name of Love," "I Don't Believe You," "Runaways," "After All These Years," "In a Heartbeat," and "What Goes Around."

U.K. Discography

1962

Jan 5: Single "My Bonnie"/"The Saints" (Polydor NH-66833). First U.K. release of both songs.

Oct 5: Single "Love Me Do" (Version I)/"P.S. I Love You" (Parlophone 45-1 4949). First release of both songs.

1963

Jan 11: Single "Please Please Me"/"Ask Me Why" (Parlophone 45-R 4983). First release of both songs.

Mar 22: LP *Please Please Me* (Parlophone stereo: PCS 3042; mono: PMC 1202). Contains previously released

"Ask Me Why," "Please Please Me" and "P.S. I Love You." First release of "I Saw Her Standing There," "Misery," "Anna," "Chains," "Boys," "Love Me Do" (Version II), "Baby It's You," "Do You Want to Know a Secret," "A Taste of Honey," "There's a Place," "Twist and Shout."

Apr 12: Single "From Me to You"/"Thank You Girl" (Parlophone R 5015). First release of both songs.

Jul 12: EP *My Bonnie* (Polydor EPH-21610). Contains previously released "My Bonnie" and "The Saints," and first U.K. release of "Why" and "Cry for a Shadow."

■ EP *Twist and Shout* (Parlophone GEP 8882). "Twist and Shout," "A Taste of Honey," "Do You Want to

Know a Secret," "There's a Place." All previously released.

Aug 23: Single "She Loves You"/"I'll Get You" (Parlophone R 5055). First release of both songs.

Sep 6: EP *The Beatles Hits* (Parlophone GEP 8880). "From Me to You," "Thank You Girl," "Please Please Me," "Love Me Do" (Version II). All previously released.

Nov 1: EP *The Beatles (No. 1)* (Parlophone GEP 8883). "I Saw Her Standing There," "Misery," "Anna," "Chains." All previously released.

Nov 22: LP *With The Beatles* (Parlophone stereo: PCS 3045; mono: PMC 1206). "All My Loving," "Don't Bother Me," "Little Child," "It Won't Be Long," "All I've Got to Do," "Till There Was You," "Please Mr. Postman," "Roll Over Beethoven," "Hold Me Tight," "You Really Got a Hold on Me," "I Wanna Be Your Man," "Devil in Her Heart," "Not a Second Time," "Money (That's What I Want)." First release of all songs.

Nov 29: Single "I Want to Hold Your Hand"/"This Boy" (Parlophone R 5084). First release of both songs.

Dec 6: *The Beatles Christmas Record* released to fan club.

1964

Jan 31: Single "Sweet Georgia Brown"/"Nobody's Child" (Polydor NH-52906). First release of B side; first U.K. release of A side.

Feb 7: EP *All My Loving* (Parlophone GEP 8891). "All My Loving," "Ask Me Why," "Money," "P.S. I Love You." All previously released.

Feb 28: Single "Why"/"Cry for a Shadow" (Polydor NH-52275). Both previously released.

Mar 20: Single "Can't Buy Me Love"/"You Can't Do That" (Parlophone R 5114). First U.K. release of both songs.

May 29: Single "Ain't She Sweet"/"Take Out Some Insurance on Me Baby" (Polydor NH-52317). First release of both songs.

Jun 19: EP *Long Tall Sally* (Parlophone GEP 8913). First release of "Slow Down" and "Matchbox." First U.K. release of "Long Tall Sally" and "I Call Your Name."

- LP *The Beatles First* (Polydor 236-201). "Ain't She Sweet," "Cry for a Shadow," "My Bonnie," "Take Out Some Insurance on Me Baby," "Sweet Georgia Brown," "The Saints," "Why," "Nobody's Child" and non-Beatles material. All previously released.

Jul 10: LP *A Hard Day's Night* (Parlophone stereo: PCS 3058; mono: PMC 1230). First release of "Anytime at All," "Things We Said Today," "When I Get Home," "I'll Be Back." First U.K. release of "A Hard Day's Night," "I Should Have Known Better," "If I Fell," "I'm Happy Just to Dance with You," "And I Love Her," "Tell Me Why," "I'll Cry Instead" (1:44). Also contains previously released "Can't Buy Me Love."

- Single "A Hard Day's Night"/"Things We Said Today" (Parlophone R 5160). Released same day on LP *A Hard Day's Night*.

Nov 4: EP *Extracts from the Film A Hard Day's Night* (Parlophone GEP 8920). "I Should Have Known Better," "If I Fell," "Tell Me Why," "And I Love Her." All previously released.

Nov 6: EP *Extracts from the Album A Hard Day's Night* (Parlophone GEP 8924). "Anytime at All," "I'll Cry Instead" (1:44), "Things We Said Today," "When I Get Home." All previously released.

Nov 27: Single "I Feel Fine"/"She's a Woman" (Parlophone R 5200). First U.K. release of both songs.

Dec 4: LP *Beatles for Sale* (Parlophone stereo: PCS 3062; mono PMC 1240). "I'm a Loser," "Baby's in Black," "Rock and Roll Music," "I'll Follow the Sun," "Mr. Moonlight," "Kansas City"/"Hey Hey Hey Hey," "Eight Days a Week," "Words of Love," "Honey Don't," "Every Little Thing," "I Don't Want to Spoil the Party," "What You're Doing," "Everybody's Trying to Be My Baby," "No Reply." First release of all songs.

Dec 18: *Another Beatles Christmas Record*. Released to fan club.

1965

Apr 6: EP *Beatles for Sale* (Parlophone GEP 8931). "I'm a Loser," "Rock and Roll Music," "Eight Days a Week," "No Reply." All previously released.

Apr 9: Single "Ticket to Ride"/"Yes It Is" (Parlophone R 5265). First release of both songs.

Jun 4: EP *Beatles for Sale (No. 2)* (Parlophone GEP 8938). "I'll Follow the Sun," "Baby's in Black," "Words of Love," "I Don't Want to Spoil the Party." All previously released.

Jul 23: Single "Help!" (Version I)/"I'm Down" (Parlophone R 5305). First U.K. release of both songs.

Aug 6: LP *Help!* (Parlophone stereo: PCS 3071; mono: PMC 1255). First release of "Help!" (Version II), "The Night Before," "You've Got to Hide Your Love Away," "I Need You," "Another Girl," "You're Going to Lose That Girl," "Act Naturally," "It's Only Love," "I've Just Seen a Face," "Yesterday." First U.K. release of "You Like Me Too Much," "Tell Me What You See," "Dizzy Miss Lizzie." Also contains previously released "Ticket to Ride."

Dec 3: Single "Day Tripper"/"We Can Work It Out" (Parlophone R 5389). First release of both songs.

- LP *Rubber Soul* (Parlophone stereo: PCS 3075; mono: PMC 1267). "Drive My Car," "Norwegian Wood (This Bird Has Flown)," "You Won't See Me," "Nowhere Man," "Think for Yourself," "The Word," "Michelle," "What Goes On?" "Girl," "I'm Looking Through You," "In My Life," "Wait," "If I Needed Someone," "Run for Your Life." First release of all songs.

Dec 6: EP *The Beatles Million Sellers* (aka *Beatles' Golden Discs*) (Parlophone GEP 8946). "She Loves You," "I Want to Hold Your Hand," "Can't Buy Me Love," "I Feel Fine." All previously released.

Dec 17: *The Beatles Third Christmas Record*. Released to fan club.

1966

Mar 4: EP *Yesterday* (Parlophone GEP 8948). "Yesterday," "Act Naturally," "You Like Me Too Much," "It's Only Love." All previously released.

Jun 10: Single "Paperback Writer"/"Rain" (Parlophone R 5452). First U.K. release of both songs.

Jul 8: EP *Nowhere Man* (Parlophone GEP 8952). "Nowhere Man," "Drive My Car," "Michelle," "You Won't See Me." All previously released.

Aug 5: LP *Revolver* (Parlophone stereo: PCS 7009; mono: PMC 7009). First release of "Yellow Submarine" and "Eleanor Rigby" (also released same day in U.S. and U.K. as a single), "Taxman," "Love You To," "Here, There and Everywhere," "She Said She Said," "Good Day Sunshine," "For No One," "I Want to Tell You," "Got to Get You Into My Life," "Tomorrow Never Knows." First U.K. release of "I'm Only Sleeping," "And Your Bird Can Sing," "Dr. Robert."

■ Single "Yellow Submarine"/"Eleanor Rigby" (Parlophone R 5493). Released same day on LP *Revolver*.

Dec 10: LP *A Collection of Beatles Oldies* (Parlophone stereo: PCS 7016; mono: PMC 7016). First U.K. release of "Bad Boy." Remaining contents previously released: "She Loves You," "From Me to You," "We Can Work It Out," "Help!" "Michelle," "Yesterday," "I Feel Fine," "Yellow Submarine," "Can't Buy Me Love," "Day Tripper," "A Hard Day's Night," "Ticket to Ride," "Paperback Writer," "Eleanor Rigby," "I Want to Hold Your Hand."

Dec 16: *The Beatles Fourth Christmas Record*. Released to fan club.

1967

Feb 17: Single "Strawberry Fields Forever"/"Penny Lane" (Parlophone R 5570). First U.K. release of both songs.

May 26: LP *Sgt. Pepper's Lonely Hearts Club Band* (Parlophone stereo: PCS 7027; mono: PMC 7027). "Sgt. Pepper's Lonely Hearts Club Band" (1:59), "With a Little Help from My Friends," "Lucy in the Sky with Diamonds," "Getting Better," "Fixing a Hole," "She's Leaving Home," "Being for the Benefit of Mr. Kite!" "Within You Without You," "When I'm Sixty-Four," "Lovely Rita," "Good Morning Good Morning," "Sgt. Pepper's Lonely Hearts Club Band" (Reprise, 1:20), "A Day in the Life" (also 15 KC tone, and "Inner Groove," not released on U.S. LP, consisting of untitled gibberish heard in the runout groove). First release of all songs. The album was rush-released on May 26, but Jun 1 was the officially announced release date, which has been traditionally observed ever since.

Jul 7: Single "All You Need Is Love"/"Baby, You're a Rich Man" (Parlophone R 5620). First release of both songs.

Aug 4: LP *The Beatles First* (Polydor 236-201). Reissue of LP released Jun 19, 1964; contents unchanged.

Oct 13: Single "How I Won the War" (voice: John Lennon speaking a line of dialogue from the film *How I Won the War*)/non-Beatles B side ("Aftermath") (United Artists UP 1196). First release.

Nov 24: Single "Hello Goodbye"/"I Am the Walrus" (Parlophone R 5655). First release of both songs.

Dec 8: Double EP *Magical Mystery Tour* (Parlophone stereo: SMMT 1; mono: MMT 1). First U.K. release of "Magical Mystery Tour," "Your Mother Should Know," "Fool on the Hill," "Flying," "Blue Jay Way." Also contains previously released "I Am the Walrus" and "Hello Goodbye."

Dec 15: *Christmas Time Is Here Again*. Released to fan club.

1968

Mar 15: Single "Lady Madonna"/"The Inner Light" (Parlophone R 5675). First release of both songs.

Aug 30: Single "Hey Jude"/"Revolution" (Version I) (Apple R 5722). First U.K. release of both songs.

Nov 1: LP *Wonderwall Music* (Apple stereo: SAPCOR 1; mono: APCOR 1). First release of original soundtrack album of film score composed by George.

Nov 22: Double LP *The Beatles* (aka the "*White Album*") (Apple stereo: PCS 7067/8; mono: PMC 7067/8). "Back in the USSR," "Dear Prudence," "Glass Onion," "Ob-La-Di, Ob-La-Da," "Wild Honey Pie," "The Continuing Story of Bungalow Bill," "While My Guitar Gently Weeps," "Happiness Is a Warm Gun," "Martha My Dear," "I'm So Tired," "Blackbird," "Piggies," "Rocky Raccoon," "Don't Pass Me By," "Why Don't We Do It in the Road?" "I Will," "Julia," "Birthday," "Yer Blues," "Mother Nature's Son," "Everybody's Got Something to Hide Except Me and My Monkey," "Sexy Sadie," "Helter Skelter," "Long Long Long," "Revolution 1" (Version II), "Honey Pie," "Savoy Truffle," "Cry Baby Cry," "Revolution 9," "Good Night." First release of all songs.

Nov 29: LP *Unfinished Music No. 1—Two Virgins* (John and Yoko) (Apple SAPCOR 2). Side one: "Two Virgins" (14:02); side two: "Two Virgins" (15:00). First U.K. release.

Dec 20: *The Beatles 1968 Christmas Record*. Includes "Nowhere Man" sung by Tiny Tim. Released to fan club.

1969

Jan 17: LP *Yellow Submarine* (Apple stereo: PCS 7070; mono: PMC 7070). First U.K. release of "Only a Northern Song," "All Together Now," "Hey Bulldog," and "It's All Too Much." Also contains previously released "Yellow Submarine" and "All You Need Is Love."

Apr 11: Single "Get Back" (Version I)/"Don't Let Me Down" (Apple R 5777). First release of both songs.

May 9: LP *Unfinished Music No. 2—Life with The Lions* (John and Yoko) (Zapple 01). "Cambridge 1969," "No Bed for Beatle John," "Baby's Heartbeat," "Two Minutes Silence," "Radio Play." First release.

■ LP *Electronic Sound* (George) (Zapple 02). Side one: "Under the Mersey Wall"; side two: "No Time or Space." First release.

May 30: Single "The Ballad of John and Yoko"/"Old Brown Shoe" (Apple R 5786). First release of both songs.

Jul 4: Single "Give Peace a Chance" (Version I) (John)/"Remember Love" (Yoko) (Apple 13). First release of both songs.

Sep 26: LP *Abbey Road* (Apple PCS 7088). "Come Together," "Something," "Maxwell's Silver Hammer," "Oh! Darling," "Octopus's Garden," "I Want You (She's So Heavy)," "Here Comes the Sun," "Because," "You Never Give Me Your Money," "Sun King," "Mean Mr. Mustard," "Polythene Pam," "She Came in Through the Bathroom Window," "Golden Slumbers/Carry That Weight," "The End," "Her Majesty." First release of all songs.

Oct 24: Single "Cold Turkey" (John)/"Don't Worry Kyoko" (Yoko) (Apple 1001). First U.K. release of both songs.

Oct 31: Single "Something"/"Come Together" (Apple R 5814). Both previously released.

Nov 7: LP *Wedding Album* (John and Yoko) (Apple SAPCOR 11). Side one: "John and Yoko"; side two: "Amsterdam," which includes "John, John (Let's Hope for Peace)," "Bed Peace," "Good Night," "Goodbye Amsterdam Goodbye." First U.K. release.

Dec 12: LP *The Plastic Ono Band Live Peace in Toronto—1969* (John and Plastic Ono Band) (Apple Core 2001). Recorded live Sep 13 in Toronto at the Rock and Roll Revival. "Introduction of the Band," "Blue Suede Shoes," "Money," "Dizzy Miss Lizzie," "Yer Blues," "Cold Turkey," "Give Peace a Chance" (John), and Yoko's "Don't Worry Kyoko" and "John, John (Let's Hope for Peace)." First U.K. and U.S. release.

■ LP *No One's Gonna Change Our World* (EMI Starline SRS 5013). First release of "Across the Universe" (Version I); also contains non-Beatles material. LP released in U.K. only.

Dec 19: *The Beatles Seventh Christmas Record.* Released to fan club.

1970

Feb 6: Single "Instant Karma (We All Shine On)" (John)/"Who Has Seen the Wind?" (Yoko) (Apple 1003). First release of both songs.

Mar 6: Single "Let It Be" (Version I)/"You Know My Name (Look Up the Number)" (Apple R 5833). First release of both songs.

Mar 27: LP *Sentimental Journey* (Ringo) (Apple PCS 7101). "Sentimental Journey," "Night and Day," "Whispering Grass (Don't Tell the Trees)," "Bye Bye Blackbird," "I'm a Fool to Care," "Star Dust," "Blue Turning Grey Over You," "Love Is a Many Splendored Thing," "Dream," "You Always Hurt the One You Love," "Have I Told You Lately That I Love You," "Let the Rest of the World Go By." First release of all songs.

Apr 10: LP *The Magic Christian* (PYE NSPL 28133). Original soundtrack album. "Hunting Scene" (Ringo and Peter Sellers' dialogue from film soundtrack). First U.K. release.

Apr 17: LP *McCartney* (Paul) (Apple PCS 7102). "The Lovely Linda," "That Would Be Something," "Valentine Day," "Every Night," medley: "Hot As Sun"/"Glasses"; "Junk," "Man We Was Lonely," "Oo You," "Momma Miss America," "Teddy Boy," "Singalong Junk," "Maybe I'm Amazed," "Kreen-Akrore," unlisted bit of "Suicide." First release of all songs.

May 8: LP *Let It Be* (Original Soundtrack Album). Deluxe boxed edition with book *Get Back* (Apple PXS1); reissued Nov 6 in standard album sleeve. "Two of Us," "Dig a Pony," "Across the Universe" (Version II), "I Me Mine," "Dig It," "Let It Be" (Version II), "Maggie Mae," "I've Got a Feeling," "The One After 909," "The Long and Winding Road," "For You Blue," "Get Back" (Version II). First release of all songs.

Sep 25: LP *Beaucoups of Blues* (Ringo) (Apple PAS 10002). "Beaucoups of Blues," "Love Don't Last Long," "Fastest Growing Heartache in the West," "Without Her," "Woman of the Night," "I'd Be Talking All the Time," "$15 Draw," "Wine, Women and Loud Happy Songs," "I Wouldn't Have You Any Other Way," "Loser's Lounge," "Waiting," "Silent Homecoming." First release of all songs.

Nov 6: LP *Let It Be* reissued in standard album sleeve (Apple PCS 7096).

Nov 30: Triple LP *All Things Must Pass* (George) (Apple STCH 639). "My Sweet Lord," "Isn't It a Pity" (Version I), "I'd Have You Any Time," "Wah-Wah," "What Is Life," "If Not for You," "Behind That Locked Door," "Let It Down," "Run of the Mill," "Beware of Darkness," "Apple Scruffs," "Ballad of Sir Frankie Crisp (Let It Roll)," "Awaiting on You All," "All Things Must Pass," "I Dig Love," "Art of Dying," "Isn't It a Pity" (Version II), "Hear Me Lord," Apple Jam: "Out of the Blue," "It's Johnny's Birthday," "Plug Me In," "I Remember Jeep," "Thanks for the Pepperoni." First U.K. release of all songs.

Dec 11: LP *John Lennon/Plastic Ono Band* (John) (Apple PCS 7124). "Mother" (5:29 edit), "Hold On (John)," "I Found Out," "Working Class Hero," "Isolation," "Remember," "Love," "Well Well Well," "Look at Me," "God," "My Mummy's Dead." First release of all songs in U.K. and U.S. on same day.

Dec 18: LP *From Then to You* (Apple LYN 2154). Collection of all seven Beatles Christmas records, 1963–69. U.S. title: *Beatles Christmas Album*, released to fan club.

1971

Jan 15: Single "My Sweet Lord"/"What Is Life" (George) (Apple R 5884). Both previously released.

Feb 19: Single "Another Day"/"Oh Woman, Oh Why" (Paul) (Apple R 5889). First release of both songs.

Mar 12: Single "Power to the People" (John)/"Open Your Box" (Yoko) (later retitled "Hirake") (Apple R 5892). First release of both songs.

Apr 9: Single "It Don't Come Easy"/"Early 1970" (Ringo) (Apple R 5898). First release of both songs.

May 28: LP *Ram* (Paul and Linda McCartney) (Apple PAS 10003). "Too Many People," "3 Legs," "Ram On" (Version I), "Dear Boy," "Uncle Albert/Admiral Halsey," "Smile Away," "Heart of the Country," "Monkberry Moon Delight," "Eat at Home," "Long Haired Lady," "Ram On" (Version II; reprise 0:55), "Back Seat of My Car." First U.K. release of all songs.

Jun 8: LP *The Early Years* (Contour 287011). "Ain't She Sweet," "Cry for a Shadow," "My Bonnie," "Take Out Some Insurance on Me, Baby," "Sweet Georgia Brown," "The Saints," "Why," "Nobody's Child." Reissue of LP *The Beatles First* originally released Jun 19, 1964.

Jul 16: Single "God Save Us" (Bill Elliot)/"Do the Oz" (John) (Apple 36). Record credited to The Elastic Oz Band. First U.K. release of both songs.

Jul 30: Single "Bangla Desh"/"Deep Blue" (George) (Apple R 5912). First U.K. release of both songs.

Aug 13: Single "Back Seat of My Car"/"Heart of the Country" (Paul and Linda) (Apple R 5914). Both previously released.

Oct 8: LP *Imagine* (John) (Apple PAS 10004). "Imagine," "Crippled Inside," "Jealous Guy," "It's So Hard," "I Don't Want to Be a Soldier Mama, I Don't Want to Die," "Gimme Some Truth," "Oh My Love," "How Do You Sleep?" "How?" "Oh Yoko." First U.K. release of all songs.

Dec 7: LP *Wild Life* (Wings) (Apple PCS 7142). "Mumbo," "Bip Bop," "Love Is Strange," "Wild Life," "Some People Never Know," "I Am Your Singer," "Bip Bop" (reprise), "Tomorrow," "Dear Friend." First release of all songs in U.K. and U.S. on same day.

1972

Jan 10: Triple LP *The Concert for Bangla Desh* (George, Ringo and others) (Apple STCX 3385). Recorded live Aug 1, 1971: "Wah-Wah," "My Sweet Lord," "Awaiting on You All," "Beware of Darkness" (with Leon Russell), "While My Guitar Gently Weeps," "Here Comes the Sun," "Something," "Bangla Desh" (all by George); "It Don't Come Easy" (by Ringo); also contains additional non-Beatles performances. First U.K. release of these recordings.

Feb 25: Wings' single "Give Ireland Back to the Irish" (vocal and instrumental versions) (Apple R 5936). First release.

Mar 17: Single "Back Off Boogaloo" (Version I)/"Blindman" (Ringo) (Apple R 5944). First release of both songs.

May 12: Wings' single "Mary Had a Little Lamb"/"Little Woman Love" (Apple R 5949). First release of both songs.

Sep 15: Double LP *Some Time in New York City* (John and Yoko, Elephant's Memory and others as noted) (Apple PCSP 716). "Woman Is the Nigger of the World," "Attica State," "New York City," "Sunday Bloody Sunday," "The Luck of the Irish," "John Sinclair," "Angela" (John) and "We're All Water," "Sisters O Sisters," "Born in a Prison" (Ono). Recorded live Dec 15, 1969 at London's Lyceum Ballroom: "Cold Turkey" (John) and "Don't Worry Kyoko" (Ono). Recorded live Jun 6, 1971 at New York's Fillmore East with Frank Zappa and The Mothers of Invention: "Well (Baby Please Don't Go)," "Jamrag," "Scumbag," "Au." First U.K. release of all songs.

Nov 24: Single "Happy Xmas (War Is Over)" (John and Yoko)/"Listen, The Snow Is Falling" (Yoko) (Apple R 5970). First U.K. release A side; B side previously released. Issued on green vinyl.

- Double LP *Tommy* (ODE 99001) by London Symphony Orchestra and Chambre Choir. Contains "Fiddle About" and "Tommy's Holiday Camp" (Ringo). First release of both songs.

Dec 1: Single "Hi Hi Hi"/"C Moon" (Wings) (Apple R 5973). First release of both songs.

1973

Mar 23: Single "My Love"/"The Mess" (Paul and Wings) (Apple R5985). First release of both songs.

Apr 19: Double LP *The Beatles 1962–1966* (Apple PCSP 717). "Love Me Do" (Version II), "Please Please Me," "From Me to You," "She Loves You," "I Want to Hold Your Hand," "All My Loving," "Can't Buy Me Love," "A Hard Day's Night," "And I Love Her," "Eight Days a Week," "I Feel Fine," "Ticket to Ride," "Yesterday", "Help!" (Version II), "You've Got to Hide Your Love Away," "We Can Work It Out," "Day Tripper," "Drive My Car," "Norwegian Wood (This Bird Has Flown)," "Nowhere Man," "Michelle," "In My Life," "Girl," "Paperback Writer," "Eleanor Rigby," "Yellow Submarine." All songs previously released; does not contain James Bond theme that precedes "Help!" on the U.S. release of this LP.

- Double LP *The Beatles 1967–1970* (Apple PCSP 718). "Strawberry Fields Forever," "Penny Lane," "Sgt. Pepper's Lonely Hearts Club Band" (1:59), "With a Little Help from My Friends," "Lucy in the Sky with Diamonds," "A Day in the Life," "All You Need Is Love," "I Am the Walrus," "Hello Goodbye," "The Fool on the Hill," "Magical Mystery Tour," "Lady Madonna," "Hey Jude," "Revolution" (Version I), "Back in the USSR," "While My Guitar Gently Weeps," "Ob-La-Di, Ob-La-Da," "Get Back" (Version I), "Don't Let Me Down," "The Ballad of John and Yoko," "Old Brown Shoe," "Here Comes the Sun," "Come Together," "Something," "Octopus's Garden," "Let It Be" (Version I), "Across the Universe" (Version II), "The Long and Winding Road." All songs previously released.

May 4: LP *Red Rose Speedway* (Paul and Wings) (Apple PCTC 251). Contains previously released "My Love." First U.K. release of "Big Barn Bed," "Get on the Right Thing," "One More Kiss," "Little Lamb Dragonfly," "Single Pigeon," "When the Night," "Loup (1st Indian on the Moon)," medley "Hold Me Tight"/"Lazy Dynamite"/"Hands of Love"/"Power Cut."

May 25: Single "Give Me Love (Give Me Peace on Earth)"/"Miss O'Dell" (George) (Apple R 5988). First U.K. release of both songs. "Miss O'Dell" is unique in that George's fits of giddy laughter are clearly heard during the song, which he did not bother to rerecord.

Jun 1: Single "Live and Let Die"/"I Lie Around" (Wings) (Apple R5987). First release of both songs.

Jun 22: LP *Living in the Material World* (George) (Apple PAS 10006). Contains previously released "Give Me Love (Give Me Peace on Earth)." First U.K. release of "Sue Me, Sue You Blues," "The Light That Has Lighted the World," "Don't Let Me Wait Too Long," "Who Can See It," "Living in the Material World," "The Lord Loves the One (That Loves the Lord)," "Be Here Now," "Try Some, Buy Some," "The Day the World Gets Round," "That Is All."

Jul 6: LP *Live and Let Die* (soundtrack; United Artists UAS 29475). Contains Wings' recording of the title track, previously released.

Oct 19: Single "Photograph"/"Down and Out" (Ringo) (Apple R5992). First U.K. release of both songs.

Oct 26: Single "Helen Wheels"/"Country Dreamer" (Paul and Wings) (Apple R 5993). First release of both songs.

Nov 16: LP *Mind Games* (John) (Apple PCS 7165). "Mind Games," "Meat City," "Tight A$," "Aisumasen (I'm Sorry)," "One Day (at a Time)," "Bring on the Lucie (Freeda Peeple)," "Nutopian International Anthem," "Intuition," "Out the Blue," "Only People," "I Know (I Know)," "You Are Here." First U.K. release of all songs.

■ Single "Mind Games"/"Meat City" (John) (Apple R 5994). Songs released same day on LP *Mind Games*.

Nov 23: LP *Ringo* (Ringo) (Apple PCTC 252). Contains previously released "Photograph." First U.K. release of "I'm the Greatest," "Have You Seen My Baby," "Sunshine Life for Me (Sail Away Raymond)," "You're Sixteen," "Oh My My," "Step Lightly," "Six O'Clock," "Devil Woman," "You and Me (Babe)."

Dec 7: LP *Band on the Run* (Paul and Wings) (Apple PAS 10007). "Band on the Run," "Jet," "Bluebird," "Mrs. Vanderbilt," "Let Me Roll It," "Mamunia," "No Words," "Picasso's Last Words (Drink to Me)," "Nineteen Hundred and Eighty Five." Does not contain "Helen Wheels," previously released, which is on the U.S. release of this album. First U.K. release of all songs.

1974

Feb 8: Single "You're Sixteen"/"Devil Woman" (Ringo) (Apple R 5995). Both previously released.

Feb 15: Single "Jet"/"Let Me Roll It" (Paul and Wings) (Apple R 5996). Both previously released.

May 24: LP *Son of Dracula* (Ringo/Harry Nilsson) (RCA APL 1-0220). Film soundtrack album includes dialogue by Ringo and "Daybreak" (George: cowbell; Ringo: drums) and "At My Front Door" (Ringo: drums). First U.K. release.

Jun 28: Single "Band on the Run"/"Zoo Gang" (Paul and Wings) (Apple R 5997). First release of B side, released only in U.K.; A side previously released.

Oct 4: LP *Walls and Bridges* (John) (Apple PCTC 253). "Whatever Gets You Through the Night," "Beef Jerky," "Going Down on Love," "Old Dirt Road," "What You Got," "Bless You," "Scared," "No. 9 Dream," "Surprise, Surprise (Sweet Bird of Paradox)," "Steel and Glass," "Nobody Loves You (When You're Down and Out)," "Ya Ya" (Version I). First U.K. release of all songs.

■ Single "Whatever Gets You Through the Night"/"Beef Jerky" (John) (Apple R 5998). Both songs released same day on LP *Walls and Bridges*.

Oct 18: Single "Walking in the Park with Eloise"/"Bridge over the River Suite" (Paul, Wings, Floyd Cramer, and Chet Atkins billed as The Country Hams; instrumentals) (EMI 2220). Also released as a 7-inch picture disc. First release of both songs.

Oct 25: Single "Junior's Farm"/"Sally G." (Paul and Wings) (Apple R 5999). Rereleased Feb 7, 1975 with A and B sides reversed. First release of both songs.

Nov 15: LP *Goodnight Vienna* (Ringo) (Apple PCS 7168). First U.K. release of "Only You (and You Alone)" and "Call Me"; first release of "It's All Down to Goodnight Vienna," "Occapella," "Oo Wee," "Husbands and Wives," "Snookeroo," "All by Myself," "No No Song"/"Skokiaan," "Easy for Me," "Goodnight Vienna" (reprise).

■ Single "Only You (and You Alone)"/"Call Me" (Ringo) (Apple R 6000). Both songs released same day on LP *Goodnight Vienna*.

Dec 6: Single "Ding Dong; Ding Dong"/"I Don't Care Anymore" (George) (Apple R 6002). First release A side; first U.K. release B side.

Dec 20: LP *Dark Horse* (George) (Apple PAS 10008). Contains previously released "Ding Dong; Ding Dong." First U.K. release of "Dark Horse," "Hari's on Tour (Express)," "Simply Shady," "So Sad," "Bye Bye, Love," "Maya Love," "Far East Man," "It Is He (Jai Sri Krishna)."

1975

Jan 31: Single "No. 9 Dream"/"What You Got" (John) (Apple R6003). Both previously released.

Feb 21: LP *Rock 'N' Roll* (John) (Apple PCS 7169). "Be-Bop-a-Lula," "Stand by Me," medley "Rip It Up"/"Ready Teddy," "You Can't Catch Me," "Ain't That a Shame," "Do You Want to Dance," "Sweet Little Sixteen," "Slippin' and Slidin'," "Peggy Sue," medley "Bring It On Home to Me"/"Send Me Some Lovin'," "Bony Moronie," "Ya Ya" (Version II), "Just Because." First U.K. release of all songs.

■ Single "Snookeroo"/"Oo Wee" (Ringo) (Apple R 6004). Both previously released.

Feb 24: Single "Philadelphia Freedom" (Elton John)/"I Saw Her Standing There" (John and Elton John, live at Madison Square Garden Nov 28, 1974)

(DJM DJS 354). First release in U.S. and U.K. on same day.

Feb 28: Single "Dark Horse"/"Hari's on Tour (Express)" (George) (Apple R 6001). Both previously released.

Apr 18: Single "Stand By Me"/"Move Over Ms. L" (John) (Apple R 6005). First U.K. release of B side; A side previously released.

May 16: Single "Listen to What the Man Said"/"Love in Song" (Wings) (Capitol R 6006). First release of both songs.

May 30: LP *Venus and Mars* (Wings) (Capitol PCTC 254). Contains previously released "Listen to What the Man Said" and "Love in Song." First U.K. release of "Venus and Mars", "Rock Show," "You Gave Me the Answer," "Magneto and Titanium Man," "Letting Go," "Venus and Mars" (reprise), "Spirits of Ancient Egypt," "Medicine Jar," "Call Me Back Again," medley "Treat Her Gently"/"Lonely Old People," "Crossroads Theme."

Sep 5: Single "Letting Go"/"You Gave Me the Answer" (Wings) (Capitol R 6008). Both previously released.

Sep 12: Single "You"/"World of Stone" (George) (Apple R 6007). First release of both songs.

Oct 3: LP *Extra Texture—Read All About It* (George) (Apple PAS 10009). Contains previously released "You" and "World of Stone." First U.K. release of "The Answer's at the End," "This Guitar (Can't Keep from Crying)," "Ooh Baby (You Know That I Love You)," "A Bit More of You," "Can't Stop Thinking About You," "Tired of Midnight Blue," "Grey Cloudy Lies," "His Name Is Legs (Ladies and Gentlemen)."

Oct 24: LP *Shaved Fish* (John) (Apple PCS 7173). Contains first U.K. and U.S. release of "Give Peace a Chance" (Version II 0.50) recorded live at Madison Square Garden Aug 30, 1972 and previously released "Give Peace a Chance" (Version I shortened from original 4:50 to 0:59), "Cold Turkey," "Instant Karma (We All Shine On)," "Power to the People," "Mother," "Woman Is the Nigger of the World" (shortened from original 5:15 to 4:37), "Imagine," "Whatever Gets You Through the Night," "Mind Games," "No. 9 Dream," "Happy Xmas (War Is Over)."

■ Single "Imagine"/"Working Class Hero" (John) (Apple R 6009). Both previously released.

Nov 28: Single "Venus and Mars"-"Rock Show" (medley)/"Magneto and Titanium Man" (Wings) (Capitol R 6010). All previously released.

Dec 12: LP *Blast from Your Past* (Ringo) (Apple PCS 7170). "You're Sixteen," "No No Song," "It Don't Come Easy," "Photograph," "Back Off Boogaloo" (Version I), "Only You (and You Alone)," "Beaucoups of Blues," "Oh My My," "Early 1970," "I'm the Greatest." All previously released.

1976

Jan 9: Single "Oh My My"/"No No Song" (Ringo) (Apple R 6011). Both previously released.

Feb 6: Single "This Guitar (Can't Keep from Crying)"/"Maya Love" (George) (Apple R 6012). Both previously released.

Mar 6: *The Singles Collection 1962–1970* (EMI; no number). Included 23 U.K. singles: "Love Me Do"/"P.S. I Love You," "Please Please Me"/"Ask Me Why," "From Me to You"/"Thank You Girl," "She Loves You"/"I'll Get You," "Can't Buy Me Love"/"You Can't Do That," "A Hard Day's Night"/"Things We Said Today," "I Feel Fine"/"She's a Woman," "Ticket to Ride"/"Yes It Is," "Hey Jude"/"Revolution," "Paperback Writer"/"Rain," "Penny Lane"/"Strawberry Fields Forever," "Get Back"/"Don't Let Me Down," "Help!"/"I'm Down," "Eleanor Rigby"/"Yellow Submarine," "Let It Be"/"You Know My Name (Look Up the Number)," "I Want to Hold Your Hand"/"This Boy," "All You Need Is Love"/"Baby You're a Rich Man," "Hello Goodbye"/"I Am the Walrus," "Lady Madonna"/"The Inner Light," "Day Tripper"/"We Can Work It Out," "Something"/"Come Together," "The Ballad of John and Yoko"/"Old Brown Shoe" and "Yesterday"/"I Should Have Known Better," the latter not previously released as a single in the U.K. All songs previously released.

Mar 8: Single "Yesterday"/"I Should Have Known Better" (Parlophone R 6013). Both previously released.

Apr 9: LP *Wings at the Speed of Sound* (Wings) (Capitol PAS 10010). "Let 'Em In," "The Note You Never Wrote," "She's My Baby," "Beware My Love," "Wino Junko," "Silly Love Songs" (Version I), "Cook of the House," "Time to Hide," "Must Do Something About It," "San Ferry Anne," "Warm and Beautiful." First U.K. release of all songs.

Apr 30: Single "Silly Love Songs" (Version I)/"Cook of the House" (Wings) (Capitol R 6014). Both previously released.

Jun 4: LP *The Beatles Featuring Tony Sheridan* (Contour CN 2007). Reissue of LP *The Beatles First* released Jun 19, 1964.

Jun 10: Double LP *Rock and Roll Music* (Parlophone PCSP 719). "Twist and Shout," "I Saw Her Standing There," "You Can't Do That," "I Wanna Be Your Man," "I Call Your Name," "Boys," "Long Tall Sally," "Rock and Roll Music," "Slow Down," "Kansas City"/"Hey Hey Hey Hey," "Money," "Bad Boy," "Matchbox," "Roll Over Beethoven," "Dizzy Miss Lizzie," "Anytime at All," "Drive My Car," "Everybody's Trying to Be My Baby," "The Night Before," "I'm Down," "Revolution" (Version I), "Back in the USSR," "Helter Skelter," "Taxman," "Got to Get You Into My Life," "Hey Bulldog," "Birthday," "Get Back" (Version II, listed as Version I). All previously released.

Jun 25: Single "Back in the USSR"/"Twist and Shout" (Parlophone R 6016). Both previously released.

Jul 23: Single "Let 'Em In"/"Beware My Love" (Wings) (Capitol R 6015). Both previously released.

Jul 30: Double LP *The Beatles Tapes* (Polydor 2683-0068). First release of interviews recorded by David Wigg for BBC Radio's "Scene and Heard": Ringo (Jan 21, 1969, Mar 20, 1970 and Jan 3, 1973); George (Mar 4, 1969 and Oct 8, 1969); John (May 8, 1969, Feb 18,

1970 and Oct 25, 1971); Paul (Sep 19, 1969). The recording dates for several of these interviews are listed incorrectly on the record and jacket.

Sep 17: LP *Ringo's Rotogravure* (Ringo) (Polydor 2302-040). "A Dose of Rock and Roll," "Hey Baby," "Pure Gold," "Cryin'," "You Don't Know Me at All," "Cookin' (in the Kitchen of Love)," "I'll Still Love You," "This Be Called a Song," "Las Brisas," "Lady Gaye," "Spooky Weirdness." First release of all songs.

Oct 15: Single "A Dose of Rock and Roll"/"Cryin'" (Ringo) (Polydor 2001 694). Both previously released.

Nov 19: LP *Thirty-Three & 1/3* (George) (Dark Horse K 56319). First U.K. release of "This Song" and "Learning How to Love You." First release of "Woman Don't You Cry for Me," "Dear One," "Beautiful Girl," "See Yourself," "It's What You Value," "True Love," "Pure Smokey," "Crackerbox Palace."

■ Single "This Song"/"Learning How to Love You" (George) (Dark Horse K 16856). Both released same day on *Thirty-Three & 1/3*.

■ LP *Magical Mystery Tour* (Parlophone PCTC 255). "Magical Mystery Tour," "The Fool on the Hill," "Flying," "Blue Jay Way," "Your Mother Should Know," "Hello Goodbye," "I Am the Walrus," "Strawberry Fields Forever," "Penny Lane," "Baby You're a Rich Man," "All You Need Is Love." First U.K. release of album originally issued in the U.S. on Nov 27, 1967; all songs previously released.

Nov 20: LP *The Best of George Harrison* (George) (Parlophone PAS 10011). "Something," "If I Needed Someone," "Here Comes the Sun," "Taxman," "Think for Yourself," "For You Blue," "While My Guitar Gently Weeps," "My Sweet Lord," "Give Me Love (Give Me Peace on Earth)," "You," "Bangla Desh," "Dark Horse," "What Is Life." All previously released.

Nov 29: Single "Hey Baby"/"Lady Gaye" (Ringo) (Polydor 2001699). Both previously released.

Dec 10: Triple LP *Wings Over America* (Wings) (Capitol PCSP 720). "Venus and Mars," "Rock Show," "Jet," "Let Me Roll It," "Spirits of Ancient Egypt," "Medicine Jar," "Maybe I'm Amazed," "Call Me Back Again," "Lady Madonna," "The Long and Winding Road," "Live and Let Die," "Picasso's Last Words," "Richard Cory," "Bluebird," "I've Just Seen a Face," "Blackbird," "Yesterday," "You Gave Me the Answer," "Magneto and Titanium Man," "Go Now," "My Love," "Listen to What the Man Said," "Let 'Em In," "Time to Hide," "Silly Love Songs," "Beware My Love," "Letting Go," "Band on the Run," "Hi Hi Hi," "Soily." First U.K. and U.S. release. Although recorded live during Wings' 1976 North American tour, many tracks were reportedly rerecorded in the studio.

Dec 25: Single "My Sweet Lord"/"What Is Life" (George) (Apple R 5884). Both previously released.

1977

Feb 4: Paul's single "Maybe I'm Amazed"/"Soily" (live versions) (Wings) (Capitol R 6017). Previously released on *Wings Over America*.

Feb 11: Single "True Love"/"Pure Smokey" (George) (Dark Horse K 16896). Both previously released.

Apr 29: LP *Thrillington* (Paul under pseudonym "Percy 'Thrills' Thrillington") (EMI EMC 3175). Instrumental versions of the following songs from Paul's *Ram* album: "Too Many People," "3 Legs," "Ram On," "Dear Boy," "Uncle Albert/Admiral Halsey," "Smile Away," "Heart of the Country," "Monkberry Moon Delight," "Eat at Home," "Long Haired Lady," "Back Seat of My Car." First release.

Apr: Single "Uncle Albert/Admiral Halsey"/"Eat at Home" (Paul under pseudonym "Percy 'Thrills' Thrillington") (EMI 2594). Instrumental versions taken from the *Thrillington* LP.

May 1: Double LP *The Beatles Live! At the Star Club in Hamburg, Germany: 1962* (Lingasong LNL1). "I Saw Her Standing There," "Roll Over Beethoven," "Hippy Hippy Shake," "Sweet Little Sixteen," "Lend Me Your Comb," "Your Feets Too Big," "Twist and Shout," "Mr. Moonlight," "A Taste of Honey," "Besame Mucho," "Reminiscing," "Kansas City"/"Hey Hey Hey Hey," "Nothin' Shakin' (But the Leaves on the Trees)," "To Know Her Is to Love Her," "Little Queenie," "Falling in Love Again," "Ask Me Why," "Be-Bop-a-Lula," "Hallelujah I Love Her So," "Red Sails in the Sunset," "Everybody's Trying to Be My Baby," "Matchbox," "I'm Talking About You," "Shimmy Shake," "Long Tall Sally," "I Remember You." The LP omits "I'm Gonna Sit Right Down and Cry Over You," "Where Have You Been All My Life," "Till There Was You" and "Sheila" from the Star-Club tape. First release of these recordings made Dec 31, 1962.

May 6: LP *The Beatles at the Hollywood Bowl* (Parlophone EMTV 4). "Twist and Shout," "She's a Woman," "Dizzy Miss Lizzie," "Ticket to Ride," "Can't Buy Me Love," *"Things We Said Today," *"Roll Over Beethoven," *"Boys," "A Hard Day's Night," "Help!" *"All My Loving," *"She Loves You," *"Long Tall Sally." First U.K. and U.S. release; recorded live *Aug 23, 1964 and Aug 30, 1965 at the Hollywood Bowl

May 31: Single "It's What You Value"/"Woman Don't You Cry for Me" (George) (Dark Horse K 16967). Both previously released.

Jun 24: Single "Twist and Shout"/"Falling in Love Again" (Lingasong NB.1). From the *Star-Club* LP; both previously released.

Sep 16: Single "Drowning in a Sea of Love"/"Just a Dream" (Ringo) (Polydor 2001 734). A side: first release; B side: first U.K. release.

Sep 20: LP *Ringo the 4th* (Ringo) (Polydor 2310 556). Contains previously released "Drowning in a Sea of Love." First U.K. release of "Wings." First release of "Tango All Night," "Gave It All Up," "Out on the Streets," "Can She Do It Like She Dances," "Sneaking Sally Through the Alley," "It's No Secret," "Gypsies in Flight," "Simple Love Song."

That fall: *The Beatles Collection* (EMI boxed set of 24 Beatles singles; no number). Same as Mar 6, 1976 U.K.

singles set with "Back in the USSR"/"Twist and Shout" added. A 25th single, "Sgt. Pepper's Lonely Hearts Club Band"-"With a Little Help from My Friends"/"A Day in the Life," was added to the set in Jun 1978. The set was deleted in Apr 1981. All songs previously released; set sold via mail order.

Nov 11: Single "Mull of Kintyre"/"Girl's School" (Wings) (Capitol R 6018). First release of both songs.

Nov 19: Double LP *Love Songs* (Parlophone PCSP 721). "Yesterday," "I'll Follow the Sun," "I Need You," "Girl," "In My Life," "Words of Love," "Here, There and Everywhere," "Something," "And I Love Her," "If I Fell," "I'll Be Back," "Tell Me What You See," "Yes It Is," "Michelle," "It's Only Love," "You're Gonna Lose That Girl," "Every Little Thing," "For No One," "She's Leaving Home," "The Long and Winding Road," "This Boy," "Norwegian Wood," "You've Got to Hide Your Love Away," "I Will," "P.S. I Love You." All previously released.

Dec 9: LP *Scouse the Mouse* (Ringo) (Polydor Super 2480 429). "Scouse's Dream," "Running Free," "Living in Pet Shop," "Boat Ride," "Scouse the Mouse," "I Know a Place," "S.O.S.," "A Mouse Like Me." First release of all songs; other songs on the album are by other artists. Released with book.

1978

Jan: LP *Sgt. Pepper's Lonely Hearts Club Band* (Picture Disc) (Parlophone PHO 7027).

Feb 10: LP *All You Need Is Love* (Theatre Projects 9199-995). Contains previously released "All You Need Is Love."

Mar 23: Single "With a Little Luck"/"Backwards Traveller"-"Cuff Link" (Wings) (Parlophone R 6019). First U.K. release.

Mar 31: LP *London Town* (Wings) (Parlophone PAS 10012). Contains previously released "With a Little Luck," "Backwards Traveller" and "Cuff Link." First release of "London Town," "Cafe on the Left Bank," "I'm Carrying," "Children Children," "Girlfriend," "I've Had Enough," "Famous Groupies," "Deliver Your Children," "Name and Address," "Don't Let It Bring You Down," "Morse Moose and the Grey Goose."

Apr 21: LP *Bad Boy* (Ringo) (Polydor Deluxe 2310.599). "Who Needs a Heart," "Bad Boy," "Lipstick Traces," "Heart on My Sleeve," "Where Did Our Love Go," "Hard Times," "Tonight," "Monkey See, Monkey Do," "Old Time Relovin'," "A Man Like Me." First release in U.K.

Jun 16: Single "I've Had Enough"/"Deliver Your Children" (Wings) (Parlophone R 6020). Both previously released.

Jul 21: Single "Tonight"/"Old Time Relovin'" (Ringo) (Polydor 2001 795). Both previously released.

Aug 26: Single "London Town"/"I'm Carrying" (Wings) (Parlophone R 6021). Both previously released.

"I've Had Enough" (© MPL Communications Ltd.). One of Paul's more bizarre picture sleeves.

Sep 30: Single "Sgt. Pepper's Lonely Hearts Club Band"-"With a Little Help from My Friends"/"A Day in the Life" (Parlophone R 6022). All previously released.

■ The following two double LPs were reissued: *The Beatles 1962–1966* (Parlophone PCSPR 717—on red vinyl), *The Beatles 1967–1970* (PCSPB 718—on blue vinyl). Both originally released Apr 19, 1973.

Dec 1: LP *Wings Greatest* (Wings) (Parlophone PCTC 256). "Another Day," "Silly Love Songs" (Version I), "Live and Let Die," "Junior's Farm," "With a Little Luck," "Band on the Run," "Uncle Albert/Admiral Halsey," "Hi Hi Hi," "Let 'Em In," "My Love," "Jet," "Mull of Kintyre." All previously released.

Dec 2: *The Beatles Collection* (EMI BC-13) Set of all 12 original U.K. Beatles LPs plus a *Rarities* LP (different versions of which were included with the U.S. and U.K. sets). Set contains the following Parlophone LPs: *Please Please Me* (PCS 3042), *With The Beatles* (PCS 3045), *A Hard Day's Night* (PCS 3058), *Beatles for Sale* (PCS 3062), *Help!* (PCS 3071), *Rubber Soul* (PCS 3075), *Revolver* (PCS 7009), *Sgt. Pepper's Lonely Hearts Club Band* (PCS 7027), *The Beatles* (aka the "*White Album*") (PCS 7067/8), *Yellow Submarine* (PCS 7070), *Abbey Road* (PCS 7088), *Let It Be* (PCS 7096), *Rarities* (PSL 261). Contents of U.K. *Rarities* LP: "Across the Universe" (Version I), "Yes It Is," "This Boy," "The Inner Light," "I'll Get You," "Thank You Girl," "Komm, Gib Mir Deine Hand," "You Know My Name (Look Up the Number)," "Sie Liebt Dich," "Rain," "She's a Woman," "Matchbox," "I Call Your Name," "Bad Boy," "Slow Down," "I'm Down," "Long Tall Sally." *Rarities* was issued separately Oct 12, 1979. First U.K. release of "Sie Liebt Dich" and "Komm, Gib Mir Deine Hand"; other material previously released.

1979

Early that year: The following LPs were reissued by Parlophone: *The Beatles* (aka the *"White Album"*) (PCS 7067/8—on white vinyl), *Abbey Road* (PCS 7088—on green vinyl), *Let It Be* (PCS 7096—on white vinyl).

Feb 16: LP *George Harrison* (George) (Dark Horse K 56562). "Love Comes to Everyone," "Not Guilty," "Here Comes the Moon," "Soft Hearted Hana," "Blow Away," "Faster," "Dark Sweet Lady," "Your Love Is Forever," "Soft Touch," "If You Believe." First U.K. release of all songs.

■ Single "Blow Away"/"Soft Touch" (George) (Dark Horse K 17327). Released same day on LP *George Harrison*.

Mar 23: Single "Goodnight Tonight"/"Daytime Nighttime Suffering" (Wings) (Parlophone R 6023). First release of both songs.

Apr 3: 12-inch single of Wings' "Goodnight Tonight" (extended version)/"Daytime Nightime Suffering" (Parlophone 12 R 6023). Extended mix of prior release.

Apr 20: Single "Love Comes to Everyone"/"Soft Hearted Hana" (George) (Dark Horse K 17284). Both previously released.

May 4: LP *A Monument to British Rock* (Harvest EMTV 17). Includes previously released "Get Back," "My Sweet Lord" (George) and "Imagine" (John).

May 11: LP *Hey Jude* (aka *The Beatles Again*) (Parlophone PCS 7184). "Can't Buy Me Love," "I Should Have Known Better," "Paperback Writer," "Rain," "Lady Madonna," "Revolution" (Version I), "Hey Jude," "Old Brown Shoe," "Don't Let Me Down," "The Ballad of John and Yoko." All previously released; LP first released in U.S. Feb 26, 1970.

May: LP *Magical Mystery Tour* (PCTC 255—on yellow vinyl).

Jun 1: Single "Old Siam, Sir"/"Spin It On" (Wings) (Parlophone R 6026). First U.K. release of both songs.

Jun 8: LP *Back to the Egg* (Wings) (Parlophone PCTC 257). Contains previously released "Spin It On" and "Old Siam, Sir." First U.K. release of "Reception," "Getting Closer," "We're Open Tonight," "Again and Again and Again," "Arrow Through Me," "Rockestra Theme," "To You," "After the Ball-Million Miles," "Winter Rose"-"Love Awake," "The Broadcast" (which includes the poems "The Sport of Kings" and "The Little Man," both read by Harold Margery, who is not mentioned on the album), "So Glad to See You Here," "Baby's Request."

Jul 30: Single "Faster"/"Your Love Is Forever" (George) (Dark Horse K 17423; and picture disc 17423P). Both previously released.

Aug 10: Single "Seaside Woman"/"B Side to Seaside" (Wings billed as Suzy and the Red Stripes) (A&M AMS 7461).

Aug 16: Single "Getting Closer"/"Baby's Request" (Wings) (Parlophone R 6027). Both previously released.

Aug 17: LP *Instrumental Gems 1959–70* (EMI NUT M22). Includes previously released "Flying."

Oct 12: LP *The Beatles Rarities* (Parlophone PCM 1001). Originally included with the boxed set of LPs released Dec 2, 1978; for contents see that date above. All previously released.

Nov 16: Single "Wonderful Christmastime"/"Rudolph the Red Nosed Reggae" (Paul) (Parlophone R 6029). First release of both songs.

1980

Jan 11: LP *The Summit* (K-TEL NE 1067). Includes Paul's previously released "Jet."

Apr 11: Single "Coming Up" (studio version; Paul)/"Coming Up" (live version; Paul and Wings) and "Lunch Box-Odd Sox" (Paul and Wings) (Parlophone R 6035). First release of all songs.

May 16: LP *McCartney II* (Paul) (Parlophone PCTC 258). Contains previously released "Coming Up" (studio version). First release of "Temporary Secretary," "On the Way," "Waterfalls," "Nobody Knows," "Front Parlour" (instrumental), "Summer's Day Song," "Frozen Jap" (instrumental), "Bogey Music," "Darkroom," "One of These Days."

Jun 13: Single "Waterfalls"/"Check My Machine" (Paul) (Parlophone R 6037). A side previously released; first release of B side.

Jul 18: Single "Seaside Woman"/"B Side to Seaside" (Linda McCartney) (A&M AMS 7548). Reissued in a new picture sleeve and credited to Linda McCartney. Also issued as a 12-inch single (A&M AMSP 7548).

Sep 19: 12-inch single "Temporary Secretary"/"Secret Friend" (Paul) (Parlophone 12 R 6039). A side previously released; first release of B side.

Oct 13: LP *The Beatles Ballads—20 Original Tracks* (Parlophone PCS 7214). "Yesterday," "Norwegian Wood," "Do You Want to Know a Secret," "For No One," "Michelle," "Nowhere Man," "You've Got to Hide Your Love Away," "Across the Universe" (Version I), "All My Loving," "Hey Jude," "Something," "The Fool on the Hill," "Till There Was You," "The Long and Winding Road," "Here Comes the Sun," "Blackbird," "And I Love Her," "She's Leaving Home," "Here, There and Everywhere," "Let It Be" (Version I). All previously released.

Oct 24: Single "(Just Like) Starting Over" (John)/"Kiss Kiss Kiss" (Ono) (Geffen K 79186). First release of both songs.

■ LPs *Rock and Roll Music Vol. I* and *Vol. II* (MFP 50506 and 50507). Reissues of double LP released Jun 10, 1976.

Nov 3: Boxed set *The Beatles Box* (SM 701/8). Set of eight LPs containing 126 previously released Beatles songs; available only from EMI's World Records subsidiary. "Across the Universe" (Version II), "Act Naturally," "All My Loving" (with "hi hat" intro), "All Together Now," "All You Need Is Love," "And I Love Her" (with the extra guitar riffs), "And Your Bird Can Sing," "Another Girl," "Baby You're a Rich Man," "Back in the USSR," "Ballad of John and Yoko," "Because," "Being for the Benefit of Mr. Kite!" "Can't Buy Me Love," "Carry

That Weight," "Come Together," "The Continuing Story of Bungalow Bill," "A Day in the Life," "Day Tripper," "Do You Want to Know a Secret," "Dr. Robert," "Don't Let Me Down," "Don't Pass Me By" (mono), "Drive My Car," "Eight Days a Week," "Eleanor Rigby," "The End," "Every Little Thing," "Fixing a Hole," "The Fool on the Hill," "For No One," "For You Blue," "From Me to You," "Get Back" (Version II), "Girl," "Golden Slumbers," "Good Day Sunshine," "Got to Get You Into My Life," "Happiness Is a Warm Gun," "A Hard Day's Night," "Hello Goodbye," "Her Majesty," "Help!" (Version I), "Here Comes the Sun," "Here, There and Everywhere," "Hey Jude," "I Am the Walrus" (Full, original, unedited version), "I Call Your Name," "I Don't Want to Spoil the Party," "I Feel Fine," "I Need You," "I Saw Her Standing There," "I Should Have Known Better," "I Want to Hold Your Hand," "If I Fell," "I'll Be Back," "I'll Follow the Sun," "I'm a Loser," "I'm Down," "I'm Looking Through You," "I'm Only Sleeping," "I'm So Tired," "In My Life," "It Won't Be Long," "It's Only Love," "I've Just Seen a Face," "Julia," "Kansas City"/"Hey Hey Hey Hey," "Lady Madonna," "Let It Be" (Version II), "The Long and Winding Road," "Long Tall Sally," "Love Me Do" (Version I), "Lovely Rita," "Lucy in the Sky with Diamonds," "Magical Mystery Tour," "Martha My Dear," "Matchbox," "Maxwell's Silver Hammer," "Michelle," "Misery," "Mr. Moonlight," "Money," "The Night Before," "No Reply," "Norwegian Wood," "Nowhere Man," "Ob-La-Di, Ob-La-Da," "Octopus's Garden," "P.S. I Love You," "Paperback Writer," "Penny Lane" (U.S. promo release with extra piccolo trumpet riff), "Piggies," "Please Mr. Postman," "Please Please Me" (stereo version with lyric error), "Rain," "Revolution" (Version I), "Roll Over Beethoven," "Sgt. Pepper's Lonely Hearts Club Band," "She Loves You," "She's a Woman," "She's Leaving Home," "Slow Down," "Something," "Strawberry Fields Forever," "A Taste of Honey," "Taxman," "Tell Me What You See," "Thank You Girl," "Things We Said Today," "This Boy," "Ticket to Ride," "Twist and Shout," "Two of Us," "We Can Work It Out," "When I'm Sixty-Four," "While My Guitar Gently Weeps," "With a Little Help from My Friends," "Yellow Submarine," "Yesterday," "You Can't Do That," "You Like Me Too Much," "You Won't See Me," "Your Mother Should Know," "You're Gonna Lose That Girl," "You've Got to Hide Your Love Away." All songs previously released although some variations are noted in parentheses; See "Alternate Versions and Bonus Tracks" section for details on these and other variations in Beatles releases.

Nov 17: LP *Double Fantasy* (John and Yoko) (Geffen K 99131). Contains previously released "(Just Like) Starting Over" (John) and "Kiss Kiss Kiss" (Yoko). First U.K. and U.S. release of "Cleanup Time," "I'm Losing You," "Beautiful Boy (Darling Boy)," "Watching the Wheels," "Woman," "Dear Yoko" (all by John); and "Every Man Has a Woman Who Loves Him," "Hard Times Are Over," "Give Me Something," "I'm Moving

On," "(Yes) I'm Your Angel," "Beautiful Boys" (all by Yoko).

Nov 27: The following LPs were reissued on the Music For Pleasure label: *Dark Horse* (George) (MFP 50510), *Mind Games* (John) (MFP 50509), *Ringo* (Ringo) (MFP 50508).

Dec 5: Double LP *The Guinness Album: Hits of the 70's* (CBS 10020). Contains " "My Sweet Lord" (George).

1981

Jan 16: Single "Woman" (John)/"Beautiful Boys" (Yoko) (Geffen K 79195). Both previously released.

Feb 20: LP *Hear The Beatles Tell All* (Charly CRU 202). 1964 interviews recorded with The Beatles; album originally released in the U.S. Sep 14, 1964.

Feb 23: LP *The McCartney Interview* (Paul) (Parlophone CHAT 1). Interview with Paul taped by Vic Garbarini of *Musician* magazine recorded in May 1980. First U.K. release.

Mar 13: 7-inch EP *Elton John Band Featuring John Lennon and The Muscle Shoals Horns* (DJM DJS 10965). Live performance by John Lennon and Elton John at New York's Madison Square Garden Nov 28, 1974: "I Saw Her Standing There," "Whatever Gets You Through the Night" and "Lucy in the Sky with Diamonds." First release except "I Saw Her Standing There," previously released on an Elton John single.

Mar 27: Single "Watching the Wheels" (John)/"(Yes) I'm Your Angel" (Ono) (Geffen K 79207). Both previously released.

Apr 3: Double LP *Concerts for the People of Kampuchea* (Atlantic K 60153). Includes live performance by Wings and Rockestra supergroup, recorded Dec 29, 1979: "Got to Get You Into My Life," "Every Night," "Coming Up," "Lucille," "Let It Be," "Rockestra Theme." First U.K. release of these recordings.

May 15: Single "All Those Years Ago"/"Writing's on the Wall" (George) (Dark Horse K 17807). First U.K. release of both songs.

Jun 5: LP *Somewhere in England* (George) (Dark Horse K56870). Contains previously released "All Those Years Ago" and "Writing's on the Wall." First U.K. release of "Blood from a Clone," "Unconsciousness Rules," "Life Itself," "Baltimore Oriole," "Teardrops," "That Which I Have Lost," "Hong Kong Blues," "Save the World."

Jun 15: *John Lennon Boxed Set* (John) (Parlophone JLB8). All albums previously released: *Plastic Ono Band Live Peace in Toronto—1969, John Lennon/Plastic Ono Band, Imagine, Some Time in New York City, Mind Games, Walls and Bridges, Rock 'N' Roll, Shaved Fish.*

Jul 17: LPs *The Beatles—The Early Years (Volumes 1 & 2)* (Phoenix PHX 1004 and 1005). Selections from the Star-Club tape of Dec 31, 1962: Volume 1: "I Saw Her Standing There," "Roll Over Beethoven," "Hippy Hippy Shake," "Sweet Little Sixteen," "Lend Me Your Comb," "Twist and Shout," "Mr. Moonlight," "A Taste of Honey," "Besame Mucho," "Reminiscing." Volume 2: "Nothin'

Shakin' (But the Leaves on the Trees)," "To Know Her Is to Love Her," "Little Queenie," "Falling in Love Again," "Ask Me Why," "Red Sails in the Sunset," "Everybody's Trying to Be My Baby," "Matchbox," "I'm Talking About You," "Shimmy Shake." All previously released.

Jul 31: Single "Teardrops"/"Save the World" (George) (Dark Horse K 17837). Both previously released.

Sep 25: Double LP *The Beatles: Historic Sessions* (Audiofidelity: AFELD 1018). "I'm Gonna Sit Right Down and Cry Over You," "I Saw Her Standing There," "Roll Over Beethoven," "Hippy Hippy Shake," "Sweet Little Sixteen," "Lend Me Your Comb," "Your Feets Too Big," "Twist and Shout," "Mr. Moonlight," "A Taste of Honey," "Besame Mucho," "Reminiscing," "Kansas City"/"Hey Hey Hey Hey," "Where Have You Been All My Life?" "Till There Was You," "Nothin' Shakin' (But the Leaves on the Trees)," "To Know Her Is to Love Her," "Little Queenie," "Falling in Love Again," "Ask Me Why," "Be-Bop-a-Lula," "Hallelujah, I Love Her So," "Sheila," "Red Sails in the Sunset," "Everybody's Trying to Be My Baby," "Matchbox," "I'm Talking About You," "Shimmy Shake," "Long Tall Sally," "I Remember You." Previously released Star-Club recordings of Dec 31, 1962; all 30 tracks were included in a single package for the first time.

Nov 2: LP *Savile's Time Travels (20 Golden Hits of 1963)* (MFP 50541). Includes previously released "Do You Want to Know a Secret."

Nov 13: Single "Wrack My Brain"/"Drumming Is My Madness" (Ringo) (RCA 166). First U.K. release of both songs.

Nov 20: LP *Stop and Smell the Roses* (Ringo) (RCA RCALP 6022). Contains previously released "Wrack My Brain" and "Drumming Is My Madness." First U.K. release of "Attention," "Private Property," "Stop and Take the Time to Smell the Roses," "Dead Giveaway," "You Belong to Me," "Sure to Fall," "Nice Way," "Back Off Boogaloo" (Version II).

Nov 25: The following LPs were reissued on the Music For Pleasure label: *The Best of George Harrison* (George) (MFP 50523), *Rock 'N' Roll* (John) (MFP 50522), *Blast from Your Past* (Ringo) (MFP 50524).

Dec 7: *The Beatles E.P. Collection* (BEP-14) containing all 13 original U.K. EPs and a new EP, *The Beatles* (SGE 1), featuring stereo versions of "She's a Woman" (with an intro countdown), "The Inner Light," and "Baby You're a Rich Man," and a fake stereo version of "This Boy." The other Parlophone EPs are: *Twist and Shout* (8882), *The Beatles Hits* (8880), *The Beatles (No. 1)* (8883), *All My Loving* (8891), *Long Tall Sally* (8913), *Extracts from the Film A Hard Day's Night* (8920), *Extracts from the Album A Hard Day's Night* (8924), *Beatles for Sale* (8931), *Beatles for Sale (No. 2)* (8938), *The Beatles' Million Sellers* (8946), *Yesterday* (8948), *Nowhere Man* (8952), double EP set *Magical Mystery Tour* (SMMT 1). All previously released.

1982

Jan 22: LP *Rare Beatles* (Phoenix PHX 1011). From the Star-Club tapes of Dec 31, 1962: "Be-Bop-a-Lula," "Long Tall Sally," "Your Feet's Too Big," "I'm Gonna Sit Right Down and Cry Over You," "Where Have You Been All My Life," "Sheila," "Hallelujah I Love Her So," "Till There Was You," "Kansas City"/"Hey Hey Hey Hey," "I Remember You." All previously released.

Mar 3: Single "Walking in the Park with Eloise"/"Bridge Over the River Suite" (Wings/Floyd Cramer/Chet Atkins billed as The Country Hams) (EMI 2220). Reissue of Oct 18, 1974 single.

Mar 8: LP *James Bond's Greatest Hits* (Liberty EMTV 007). Includes previously released "Live and Let Die" (Wings).

Mar 29: LP *Reel Music* (Parlophone PCS 7218). "A Hard Day's Night," "I Should Have Known Better," "Can't Buy Me Love," "And I Love Her," "Help!" "You've Got to Hide Your Love Away," "Ticket to Ride," "Magical Mystery Tour," "I Am the Walrus," "Yellow Submarine," "All You Need Is Love," "Let It Be" (Version II), "Get Back" (Version II), "The Long and Winding Road." All previously released.

■ Single "Ebony and Ivory" (Paul and Stevie Wonder)/"Rainclouds" (Paul) (Parlophone R 6054). First release of both songs.

■ 12-inch single "Ebony and Ivory" (Paul solo)/"Rainclouds" (Paul)–"Ebony and Ivory" (Paul and Stevie Wonder) (Parlophone 12 R 6054). First release of "Ebony and Ivory" (solo); others released same day on 7-inch single.

Apr 26: LP *Tug of War* (Paul) (Parlophone PCTC 259). Contains previously released "Ebony and Ivory" (Paul and Stevie Wonder). First U.K. and U.S. release of "Take It Away," "Dress Me Up As a Robber," "Tug of War," "Somebody Who Cares," "What's That You're Doing?" "Here Today," "Ballroom Dancing" (Version I), "The Pound Is Shrinking," "Wanderlust" (Version I), "Get It," "Be What You See."

Apr: LP *First Movement* (Phoenix PHX 339). Contains "Cry for a Shadow," "Take Out Some Insurance on Me, Baby," "Sweet Georgia Brown" and "Why," previously released.

May 1: LP *The Beatles Talk Downunder* (Goughsound Ltd. GP 5001). Interviews and press conferences taped during The Beatles' Jun–Jul 1964 tour of Australia and New Zealand. LP originally released in Australia by Raven Records in 1981 and sold in the U.K. and the U.S. at that time as an import. First official U.K. release.

May 24: Single "The Beatles' Movie Medley"/"I'm Happy Just to Dance with You" (Parlophone R 6055). All previously released.

Jun 21: Single "Take It Away"/"I'll Give You a Ring" (Paul) (Parlophone R 6056). First release of B side; A side previously released.

Jun 25: LP *The Beatle Interviews* (Everest Records CBR 1008). Contains Aug 22, 1964 Vancouver press conference, Aug 11, 1966 Chicago press conference, Aug 25, 1966 Seattle press conference, and Dusty Adams' interview with John. First U.K. release.

Jul 5: 12-inch single "Take It Away" (3:59 edit)/"I'll Give You a Ring"-"Dress Me Up As a Robber" (Paul) (Parlophone 12R 6056). All songs previously released.

Jul 31: 10-inch LP *The Savage Young Beatles* (Charly Records CFM 701). "Why," "Cry for a Shadow," "Take Out Some Insurance on Me, Baby," "Sweet Georgia Brown." Originally released in 1964 in the U.S. as *This Is The Savage Young Beatles*.

Sep 10: LP *The Complete Silver Beatles* (Audiofidelity AFELP 1047). 12 cuts from the Decca audition of Jan 1, 1962: "Three Cool Cats," "Crying, Waiting, Hoping," "Searchin'," "Sheik of Araby," "Money," "To Know Her Is to Love Her," "Take Good Care of My Baby," "Memphis," "Sure to Fall," "Till There Was You," "September in the Rain," "Besame Mucho." First U.K. release of these recordings. None of the tracks was artificially lengthened on this album as some had been on *The Silver Beatles Volume 1* and *Volume 2*, released in the U.S. Sep 27.

Sep 20: Single "Tug of War"/"Get It" (Paul) (Parlophone R6057). Both previously released.

Oct 4: Single "Love Me Do" (Version II)/"P.S. I Love You" (Parlophone 45-R 4949 and picture disc RP 4949). The first in a series of 20th-anniversary commemorative reissues of The Beatles' original U.K. singles. However, this release actually contains the album version of "Love Me Do" rather than Version I, which appeared on the original single and which featured Ringo on drums. A 12-inch single was later released with both versions of the song plus the B side.

Oct 18: LP *The Beatles: 20 Greatest Hits* (Parlophone PCTC 260). "Love Me Do" (Version II), "From Me to You," "She Loves You," "I Want to Hold Your Hand," "Can't Buy Me Love," "A Hard Day's Night," "I Feel Fine," "Ticket to Ride," "Help!" "Day Tripper," "We Can Work It Out," "Paperback Writer," "Yellow Submarine," "Eleanor Rigby," "All You Need Is Love," "Hello Goodbye," "Lady Madonna," "Hey Jude," "Get Back" (Version I), "The Ballad of John and Yoko." All previously released.

Oct 29: Single "Searchin'"-"Money"/"Till There Was You" (Audiofidelity AFS 1). Previously released tracks from the Jan 1, 1962 Decca audition.

■ Single "The Girl Is Mine" (Paul and Michael Jackson)/"Can't Get Outta the Rain" (Michael Jackson) (Epic EPC A2729; and picture disc, Epic EPC A 11-2729). First U.K. release.

Nov 1: 12-inch single "Love Me Do" (Version I)-"P.S. I Love You"/"Love Me Do" (Version II) (Parlophone 12R 4949). Special EMI commemorative issued to remedy error on Oct 4 7-inch reissue that omitted the original single version of "Love Me Do."

■ LP *The John Lennon Collection* (John) (Parlophone EMTV 37). Contains "Happy Xmas (War Is Over)" and "Stand By Me," both omitted from the U.S. version of this LP, and "Give Peace a Chance," "Instant Karma,"

"Power to the People," "Whatever Gets You Through the Night," "No. 9 Dream," "Mind Games," "Love," "Imagine," "Jealous Guy," "(Just Like) Starting Over," "Woman," "I'm Losing You," "Beautiful Boy (Darling Boy)," "Watching the Wheels," "Dear Yoko." All previously released.

Nov 5: Double LP *The Pop Explosion* (Cambra CR 028). Includes "Long Tall Sally," "Till There Was You" and "Mr. Moonlight," from Star-Club tapes.

Nov 8: LP *Gone Troppo* (George) (Dark Horse 923734-1). "Wake Up My Love," "That's the Way It Goes," "I Really Love You," "Greece," "Gone Troppo," "Mystical One," "Unknown Delight," "Baby Don't Run Away," "Dream Away," "Circles." First U.K. release of all songs.

■ Single "Wake Up My Love"/"Greece" (George) (Dark Horse 929864-7). Both released on same day on LP *Gone Troppo*.

Nov 15: Single "Love"/"Gimme Some Truth" (John) (Parlophone R 6059). This is a new remix of "Love"; both songs were previously released.

Dec 3: LP *Thriller* (Michael Jackson) (Epic EPC 85930). Includes previously released duet with Paul, "The Girl Is Mine,"

Dec 6: *The Beatles Singles Collection* (BSC-1); sold through EMI's World Records, this set included 26 U.K. Beatles singles: "Love Me Do" (Version II)/"P.S. I Love You," "Please Please Me"/"Ask Me Why," "From Me to You"/"Thank You Girl," "She Loves You"/"I'll Get You," "I Want to Hold Your Hand"/"This Boy," "Can't Buy Me Love"/"You Can't Do That," "A Hard Day's Night"/"Things We Said Today," "I Feel Fine"/"She's a Woman," "Ticket to Ride"/"Yes It Is," "Help!"/"I'm Down," "Day Tripper"/"We Can Work It Out," "Paperback Writer"/"Rain," "Eleanor Rigby"/"Yellow Submarine," "Penny Lane"/"Strawberry Fields Forever," "All You Need Is Love"/"Baby, You're a Rich Man," "Hello Goodbye"/"I Am the Walrus," "Lady Madonna"/"The Inner Light," "Hey Jude"/"Revolution," "Get Back"/"Don't Let Me Down," "The Ballad of John and Yoko"/"Old Brown Shoe," "Something"/"Come Together," "Let It Be"/"You Know My Name (Look Up the Number)." Also included were the following singles that had been released after 1976: "Yesterday"/"I Should Have Known Better," "Back in the USSR"/"Twist and Shout," "Sgt. Pepper's Lonely Hearts Club Band"— "With a Little Help from My Friends"/"A Day in the Life," "Beatles Movie Medley"/"I'm Happy Just to Dance with You." All previously released.

1983

Jan 10: Single "Please Please Mc"/"Ask Me Why" (Parlophone 45-R 4983 and picture disc RP 4983). 20th-anniversary reissue.

Apr 11: Single "From Me to You"/"Thank You Girl" (Parlophone R 5015 and picture disc RP 5015). 20th-anniversary reissue.

Apr 15: LP *Liverpool 1963–1968* (Charly Records CM 118). Includes "How I Won the War" with a line or two of dialogue by John Lennon, and "America" by Rory Storm and The Hurricanes with Ringo's backing vocals. Previously released tracks.

Jun 6: LP *Savile's Time Travels (20 Golden Hits of 1964)* (MFP 5620). Includes previously released "I Want to Hold Your Hand."

Aug 22: Single "She Loves You"/"I'll Get You" (Parlophone R 5055 and picture disc RP 5055). 20th-anniversary reissue.

Sep 10: LP *20 Greatest Hits* (Phoenix 20 P20 623). Contains "Take Out Some Insurance on Me Baby," "Sweet Georgia Brown," "Why," all from the Jun 1961 Tony Sheridan session plus four of Sheridan's cuts done without The Beatles; and the following 12 cuts from the Decca audition of Jan 1, 1962: "To Know Her Is to Love Her," "Three Cool Cats," "Crying, Waiting, Hoping," "Besame Mucho," "Searchin'," "The Sheik of Araby," "Money," "Take Good Care of My Baby," "Memphis," "Sure to Fall," "Till There Was You" and "September in the Rain." All previously released.

■ LP *20 Great Hits* (Phoenix 20 P20 629). Contains the following tracks from the Star-Club tapes of Dec 31, 1962: "Twist and Shout," "Mr. Moonlight," "A Taste of Honey," "Kansas City"/"Hey Hey Hey Hey," "I Saw Her Standing There," "Roll Over Beethoven," "Hippy Hippy Shake," "Sweet Little Sixteen," "Your Feets Too Big," "Nothin' Shakin' (But the Leaves on the Trees)," "Little Queenie," "Ask Me Why," "Be-Bop-a-Lula," "Hallelujah I Love Her So," "Red Sails in the Sunset," "Everybody's Trying to Be My Baby," "Matchbox," "I'm Talking About You," "Shimmy Shake," "Long Tall Sally." All previously released.

Oct 3: Single "Say Say Say" (Paul and Michael Jackson)/"Ode to a Koala Bear" (Paul) (Parlophone R 6062).

■ 12-inch single (12R 6062) "Say Say Say" (extended dance mix)/"Say Say Say" (instrumental) (both mixed by John "Jellybean" Benitez)—"Ode to a Koala Bear." First U.S. and U.K. release of all titles.

Oct 17: LP *Pipes of Peace* (Paul) (Parlophone PCTC 1652301). Contains previously released "Say Say Say" (with Michael Jackson). First release of "The Man" (also with Michael Jackson), "Pipes of Peace," "The Other Me," "Keep Under Cover," "So Bad" (Version I), "Sweetest Little Show," "Average Person," "Hey Hey," "Tug of Peace," "Through Our Love."

Oct 31: Double LP *Mersey Beat* (Parlophone PCSP 1783293). Includes previously released "She Loves You" and "I Want to Hold Your Hand."

Oct: Reissue of LP *A Collection of Beatles Oldies* (Fame FA 4130811).

Nov 4: Double LP *The Pop Explosion Volume 2* (Cambra CR 103). Includes previously released "Cry for a Shadow" and "Why."

Nov 28: LP *James Bond—13 Original Themes* (Liberty LO 51138). Includes Paul's previously released "Live and Let Die" (Wings).

■ Single "I Want to Hold Your Hand"/"This Boy" (Parlophone R 5084 and picture disc RP 5084). 20th-anniversary reissue.

Dec 5: Single "Pipes of Peace"/"So Bad" (Version I) (Paul) (Parlophone R 6064). Both previously released.

Dec 16: LP *Heart Play—Unfinished Dialogue* (John) (Polydor/PolyGram 817238-1). Contains portions of interviews with Lennon recorded by David Sheff for *Playboy* magazine in Sep 1980. First U.K. release.

Dec 19: LP *The Audition Tapes* (Breakaway BWY 72). From the Jan 1, 1962 Decca audition: "Three Cool Cats," "Crying, Waiting, Hoping," "Besame Mucho," "Searchin'," "Sheik of Araby," "Money," "To Know Her Is to Love Her," "Take Good Care of My Baby," "Memphis," "Sure to Fall," "Till There Was You," "September in the Rain." All previously released.

Dec 30: Three separate LPs, *The Hamburg Tapes Vol. 1, Vol. 2, Vol. 3* (Breakaway Records/Stage 1 Records BWY 85, BWY 86, BWY 87). Each contains 10 cuts from the Star-Club tapes of Dec 31, 1962.

Dec: LP *Beatles* (Audiofidelity PD 339 picture disc). Picture disc reissue of LP *First Movement* (Phoenix PHX 339). "Cry for a Shadow," "Take Out Some Insurance on Me Baby," "Why," "Sweet Georgia Brown."

■ LP *Now That's What I Call Music II* (EMI/Virgin). Contains Paul's previously released "Pipes of Peace."

1984

Jan 6: Three-LP set *The Beatles Historic Sessions* (Audiofidelity PHX 31). Contains the 12 non–Lennon/McCartney songs form the Jan 1, 1962 Decca audition and all 30 tracks from the Star-Club tape of Dec 31, 1962.

Jan 9: Single "Nobody Told Me" (John)/"O'Sanity" (Yoko) (Polydor POSP 700). First U.K. release.

Jan 23: LP *Milk and Honey* (John and Yoko) (Polydor POLH-5). Contains previously released "Nobody Told Me." First U.K. release of "Grow Old with Me," "I Don't Wanna Face It," "Borrowed Time," "I'm Stepping Out," "(Forgive Me) My Little Flower Princess" (John); following six cuts by Yoko: "Sleepless Night," "Don't Be Scared," "O'Sanity" (previously released), "Your Hands," "Let Me Count the Ways," "You're the One." Songs were all recorded Aug/Sep 1980 during the *Double Fantasy* sessions.

Jan 27: CD *Milk and Honey* (John) (Polydor CD 817 160-2). First Beatles-related CD released in the U.K.

Jan: LP set *Original Oldies* (Audiofidelity). Set of 18 LPs that included the following Beatles Star-Club tracks: "I Saw Her Standing There" (Vol. 10: SOS-6010), "Matchbox" (Vol. 14: SOS-6014), "Till There Was You" (Vol. 17: SOS- 6017), "Twist and Shout" (Vol. 18: SOS-6018). All previously released.

Feb 1: LP *The Beatles Talk Downunder* (Goughsound PGP 5001). Picture disc issue of previously released interview album.

Feb 29: CD *Pipes of Peace* (Paul) (EMI CDP 7 46018 2). First U.K. Beatles-related CD release by EMI.

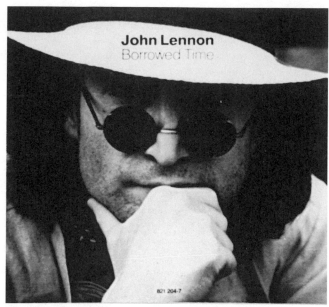

"Borrowed Time" (© PolyGram). The photo from this U.S. single was also used for the U.K. "I'm Stepping Out" single.

Mar 9: Single "Borrowed Time" (John)/"Your Hands" (Yoko) (Polydor POSP 701).

■ 12-inch single "Borrowed Time" (John)/"Your Hands"-"Never Say Goodbye" (Yoko) (Polydor POSPX-701). John's cut previously released.

Mar 12: Singles "Give Peace a Chance"/"Cold Turkey" (John) (EMI Golden 45's G452); "It Don't Come Easy"/"Back Off Boogaloo" (Version I) (Ringo) (G45 13). Previously released tracks.

Mar 16: Limited edition single "Borrowed Time" (John)/"Your Hands" (Yoko) (Polydor POSPG-701—with color foldout poster sleeve; 10,000 copies issued). Previously released.

Mar 19: Single "Can't Buy Me Love"/"You Can't Do That" (Parlophone R5114 and picture disc, RP 5114). 20th-anniversary reissue.

Mar 23: LP *Milk and Honey* (John and Yoko) (Picture Disc-Polydor POLH P5). Previously released.

Apr 2: LPs *McCartney* (Paul) (Fame FA 413100-1); *Wild Life* (Wings) (FA 413101-1).

Jul 2: LP *John Lennon/Plastic Ono Band* (John) (Fame FA 41 3102-1). Reissue.

Jul 9: Single "A Hard Day's Night"/"Things We Said Today" (Parlophone R 5160 and picture disc RP 5160). 20th-anniversary reissue of single.

Jul 15: Single "I'm Stepping Out" (John)/"Sleepless Night" (Ono) (Polydor POSP 702). Also issued as a 12-inch single (Polydor POSPX 702), "I'm Stepping Out" (John)/"Sleepless Night"-"Loneliness" (Yoko). All previously released.

Sep 3: LP *The Beatles at the Hollywood Bowl* (Music For Pleasure; MFP 4156761). Reissue.

Sep 21: LP *Every Man Has a Woman* (Polydor POLH 13). Contains John's harmony vocal from Yoko's previously released recording of "Every Man Has a Woman

Who Loves Him," billed as a Lennon solo version of the song; first U.K. release.

Sep 24: Single "No More Lonely Nights" (ballad 4:38)/"No More Lonely Nights" (playout version 3:56) (Paul) (Parlophone R 6080).

■ 12-inch single (12 R 6080) "No More Lonely Nights" (extended version 8:10)/"Silly Love Songs" (Version II)-"No More Lonely Nights" (ballad 4:38). First release of all songs.

That fall: LP *Tribute to the Cavern Club* (Parlophone CAV 1). Special LP sold at Beatles City exhibit in Liverpool; contains the previously released "Love Me Do," "I Saw Her Standing There," "Twist and Shout," "She Loves You," "Money," "I Want to Hold Your Hand," "Can't Buy Me Love," "A Hard Day's Night" and non-Beatles cuts from the Mersey Beat era.

Oct 8: 12-inch picture disc single (Parlophone 12RP 6080) "No More Lonely Nights" (Paul); contents identical to (12R 6080) issued on Sep 24.

Oct 22: CD *Give My Regards to Broad Street* (Paul) (EMI CDP 7 46043 2), LP (EL 260 278 1), cassette (EL 260 278 0). First McCartney album issued simultaneously on CD, LP and cassette; contains previously released "No More Lonely Nights" (ballad, 4:50 edit; 5:00 on cassette; and playout version extended here to 4:17) and "Silly Love Songs" (Version II). First release of "Good Day Sunshine" (Version II), "Yesterday" (Version II), "Here, There and Everywhere" (Version II), "Wanderlust" (Version II), "Ballroom Dancing" (Version II), "Not Such a Bad Boy," "No Values," "For No One" (Version II), "Eleanor Rigby" (Version II), "The Long and Winding Road" (Version II); also includes "Corridor Music" and "Eleanor's Dream," instrumentals from the film score. CD and cassette add "So Bad" (Version II) and longer version of "Eleanor's Dream" (4:59 compared to 1:01); CD also adds additional instrumental track, "Goodnight Princess," with a spoken intro by Paul.

Oct 29: Single "No More Lonely Nights" (ballad 4:38)/(Arthur Baker Special Dance Mix 4:20 edit) (Paul) (Parlophone R 6080).

■ 12-inch single (12 RA 6080) "No More Lonely Nights" ("extended playout version"—actually the extended version of the Baker Special Dance Mix 6:53 edit)/"No More Lonely Nights" (ballad 4:38)—"Silly Love Songs."

Nov 12: Single "We All Stand Together"/"We All Stand Together" (humming version) (Paul) (Parlophone R 6086). Record is credited to Paul and The Frog Chorus (A side), and The Finchely Frogettes (B side). First release.

Nov 16: Single "Every Man Has a Woman Who Loves Him" (John)/"It's Alright" (Sean Ono Lennon) (Polydor POSP 712). Previously released Lennon track on A side.

■ CD *Every Man Has a Woman* (John) (Polydor 823 490-2). Same as Sep 21 LP release.

■ LP *The Beatles Featuring Tony Sheridan. Hamburg 1961* (Topline TOP 108). Rerelease of *The Savage Young Beatles*; see Jul 31, 1982.

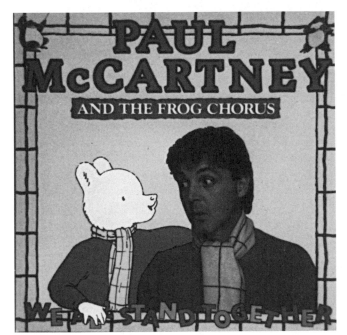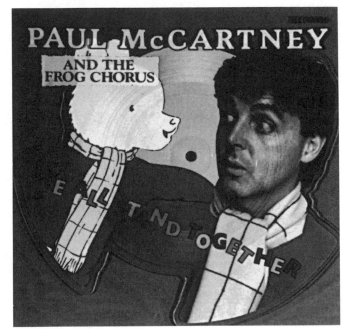

"We All Stand Together" (© MPL Communications Ltd.). Released only in the U.K. in standard 7-inch and cut-to-shape picture disc, "We All Stand Together" is taken from the animated film *Rupert and the Frog Song*.

Nov 26: Single "I Feel Fine"/"She's a Woman" (Parlophone R5200 and picture disc RP 5200). 20th-anniversary reissue of single.

Dec 3: Cut-to-shape picture disc "We All Stand Together"/"We All Stand Together" (humming version) (Paul) (Parlophone RP 6086). Previously released.

Dec 7: Single "Do They Know It's Christmas?"/"Feed the World" (Mercury FEED 1). B side has two brief messages by Paul. First U.K. and U.S. release; record by Band Aid.

Dec 14: 12-inch single "Do They Know It's Christmas?"-"Feed the World"/"Do They Know It's Christmas?" (remix) (Mercury FEED 112); includes Paul's spoken messages. First U.K. and U.S. release of remix.

Dec 18: Volume 26 of Orbis Publishing's 30-LP collection *The History of Rock* consisted of the LPs *A Collection of Beatles Oldies* and *The Beatles at the Hollywood Bowl*.

Dec: CD *The Beatles First* (Polydor 823 701-2). Tony Sheridan tracks on a CD. See *Savage Young Beatles*, Jul 31, 1982.

Late that year: LP *The Beatles Talk Downunder (and all Over) Volume 2* (Australia; Raven RVLP 1013). Ed Rudy's Feb 1964 telephone interview with George, with Charlie Murdock dubbing in the questions; WQAM Radio's "Farewell to Miami" (Feb 1964); interview with Bernice Lumb (Mar 1964); Jun 1964 Australia press conference clips; Jun 1965 Rome press conference excerpt; Jul 2, 1965 Graham Webb Madrid "MBE Chat"; Aug 21, 1965 Minneapolis press conference; Jun 1966 Tokyo interview; edited version of Aug 25, 1966 Seattle interviews by Dusty Adams. First U.K. release; Australian LP sold as an import in U.K. and U.S.

1985

Feb 4: CD release of *Tug of War* (EMI CDP 7 46057 2), *Band on the Run* (CDP 7 46055 2) (without "Helen Wheels"), *Wings Greatest* (CDP 7 46056 2) (all Paul).

Mar 4: Double LP *Words and Music* (Cambra CR 5149). Previously released interview clips and tracks from Decca audition and Star-Club tapes.

Apr 9: Single "Ticket to Ride"/"Yes It Is" (Parlophone R 5265 and picture disc RP 5265). 20th-anniversary reissue.

May 24: Single "You'll Never Walk Alone"/"Messages" by The Crowd (lead vocal: Gerry Marsden) (BRAD 1). B side includes a 17-second spoken message by Paul. First release.

Jun 4: LP *Greenpeace* (FUND 1). Containing first release of an alternate version of George's "Save the World" with a new vocal track and a remix of the original backing track.

Jun 7: 12-inch single "You'll Never Walk Alone" (BRAD 1/12). Extended mix; Paul's spoken message moved to start of A side. Remix of prior release.

Jun 24: Double LP *Rock 'N' Roll Gold* (Cambra CR 5155). Contains "Memphis" and "Money" from Jan 1, 1962 Decca audition and "Matchbox," "Roll Over Beethoven," "Kansas City"/"Hey Hey Hey Hey," "Sweet Little Sixteen" from the Dec 31, 1962 Star-Club tapes. All previously released.

■ Double LP *Saturday Night's Alright* (Cambra CD 5159). Contains the previously released "Money" from the Jan 1, 1962 Decca audition.

Jun: LPs *The Beatles Live! At the Star Club, Hamburg, Germany, 1962 Volume I* (Castle SHLP 130) and *Volume*

II (SHLP 131). Previously released tracks from the Dec 31, 1962 Star-Club tapes.

Jul 1: Soundtrack CD *Porky's Revenge* (Columbia CK 39983) and LP (CBS 70265). Contains "I Don't Want to Do It" (George). First U.K release.

■ LP *Let's Beat It* (Epic EPC 26345). Contains the previously released "Say Say Say" (Paul and Michael Jackson).

Jul 23: Single "Help"/"I'm Down" (Parlophone R 5305 and picture disc RP 5305). 20th-anniversary reissue.

Aug 21: CD *Greenpeace* (George) (Towerbell EMI CD FUND1). CD edition of LP released Jun 4 with George's new version of "Save the World."

Nov 18: Single "Spies Like Us" (4:42)/"My Carnival" (3:56) (Paul) (Parlophone R 6118).

■ 12-inch single "Spies Like Us" (party mix, 7:10; alternate mix, 3:56; D.J. version, 3:46)/"My Carnival" (party mix, 6:00) (Paul) (Parlophone 12R 6118). First U.K. and U.S. release of all recordings.

■ Single "Jealous Guy"/"Going Down on Love" (John) (Parlophone R 6117). Previously released tracks.

■ 12-inch single "Jealous Guy"/"Going Down on Love"-"Oh Yoko!" (John) (Parlophone 12R 6117). Previously released tracks.

■ LP *Now That's What I Call Music: The Christmas Album* (EMI NOX 1). Contains the previously released "Happy Xmas (War Is Over)" (John/Yoko) and "Wonderful Christmastime" (Paul).

Dec 2: Single "We Can Work It Out"/"Day Tripper" (Parlophone R 5389 and picture disc RP 5389). 20th-anniversary reissue.

■ 12-inch picture disc single "Spies Like Us" (Paul) (Parlophone 12 RP 6118). Contents identical to Nov 18 12-inch release (12R 6118).

Dec 9: Seven-inch cut-to-shape picture disc of "Spies Like Us"/"My Carnival" (Paul) (Parlophone RP 6118A). Previously released tracks.

Dec: Single "We All Stand Together"/"We All Stand Together" (humming version) (Paul) (Parlophone R 6086 and picture disc, RP 6086). Reissue.

■ CD *The Beatles Live! At the Star Club in Hamburg, German, 1962* (Teichiku/Overseas Records CD 38CP-44). CD release of all 30 tracks recorded Dec 31, 1962 at the Star-Club.

■ CD *The Beatles First* (Polydor CD 823 701-2). CD release of Tony Sheridan tracks; see Jul 31, 1982.

1986

Feb 24: CD *John Lennon: Live in New York City* (John) (EMI CDP 746196 2) and LP (Parlophone PCS 7301). First U.K. release of live recordings from the Aug 30, 1972 One to One Concerts: "New York City," "It's So Hard," "Woman Is the Nigger of the World," "Well, Well, Well," "Instant Karma (We All Shine On)," "Mother," "Come Together," "Imagine," "Cold Turkey," "Hound Dog," "Give Peace a Chance."

Jun 9: Single "Paperback Writer"/"Rain" (Parlophone R 5452 and picture disc RP 5452). 20th-anniversary reissue.

Jul 7: Single "Seaside Woman"/"B Side to Seaside" (Wings/Linda McCartney billed as Suzy and The Red Stripes) (EMI 5572). Remixed versions, by Alvin Clark, of both sides of single first released in 1977.

■ 12-inch single "Seaside Woman"/"B Side to Seaside" (12 EMI 5572). Extended versions of Alvin Clark remixes of both songs.

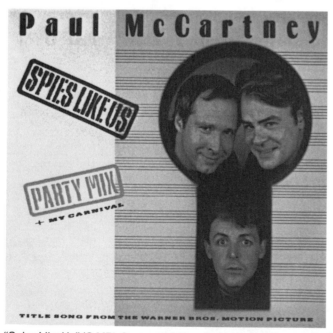

"Spies Like Us" (© MPL Communications Ltd.). Paul's title song for the Warner Bros. film was issued as a standard 7-inch and cut-to-shape picture disc; 12-inch discs were also issued.

■ LP *Now That's What I Call Music: The Summer Album* (EMI/Virgin SUMMER 1). Includes The Beatles' "All You Need Is Love" and "Here Comes the Sun."

Jul 14: Single "Press" (4:20)/"It's Not True" (4:31) (Paul) (Parlophone R 6133). This initial release of the single was available only in England, and only for a few days, before being replaced by a new version. It contains the first release of the original Hugh Padgham mix of "Press," never issued in the U.S.; first U.S. and U.K. release of "It's Not True" (the number stamped in the runout groove is R 6133 A-1). The single was replaced on Jul 20 with one containing the Bevans/Forward mix of "Press," called the "video edit."

■ 12-inch single "Press" (4:43)/"It's Not True" (5:51)/"Hanglide" (5:18)/"Press" (6:30 dub mix) (Paul) (Parlophone 12R 6133). First U.S. and U.K. release of 4:43 edit of Bevans/Forward mix of "Press" (listed as 4:41 in U.S.), "Hanglide," "Press" dub mix, and the Julian Mendelsohn remix of "It's Not True." A few days after the initial release of this 12-inch single, a second edition was released only in the U.K., with the words "Video Soundtrack" added to the picture sleeve. The original edition had 12 R 6133 A-1 stamped into the runout groove, while the second version had 12R 6133 A-3. Otherwise the two editions are identical, and the music was not changed on the discs themselves. The Video Soundtrack version of "Press" is a longer edit of the Bevans/Forward mix. "Hanglide" was mixed by McCartney and Matt Butler, billed as "Mac 'n' Matt." The dub mix of "Press" is another variation of the Bevans/Forward mix.

Jul 20: Single "Press" (3:35)/"It's Not True" (4:31) (Paul) (Parlophone R 6133). This second edition replaced the Hugh Padgham mix of "Press" with the first

"Press" (© MPL Communications Ltd.). The second U.K. edition of this single added the notation "Video Edit."

U.K. release of 3:35 edit of Bevans/Forward mix. The record added the words "Video Edit" to the label and picture sleeve (runout groove on this release stamped R 6133 A-3).

Jul: CD releases *The Golden Beatles* (Overseas Records 32-35), first released on LP in U.S. Jul 1985, and *The Silver Beatles* (30CT-55), with Jan 1, 1962 Decca audition tracks.

Aug 1: LP *Beatles Talk Downunder* (Shanghai Records GP 5001; picture disc). Interview LP originally issued in Australia.

Aug 18: 10-inch single "Press" (4:20)/"It's Not True" (5:50)/"Press" (3:35) (Paul) (Parlophone 10R 6133). Limited edition (6,000 copies) featuring Hugh Padgham and Bevans/Forward mixes of "Press" and extended mix of "It's Not True" by Julian Mendelsohn.

Sep 1: CD *Press to Play* (Paul) (Parlophone CDP 7 46269 2) and LP PCSD 103). Contains the previously released "Press" and first U.K. release of "Stranglehold," "Good Times Coming"/"Feel the Sun," "Talk More Talk," "Footprints," "Only Love Remains," "Pretty Little Head," "Move Over Busker," "Angry" and "However Absurd." The CD adds three bonus tracks not found on LP: First U.K. release of "Write Away" (also released later as the U.K. B side of "Pretty Little Head"), and "Tough on a Tightrope" (later released as the B side of "Only Love Remains"); and previously released "It's Not True" (Julian Mendelsohn remix; 5:52). In the U.K. only, two different versions of the LP were released. The first, of which only about 45,000 copies were pressed, contained the Bevans/Forward mix of "Press," while the second version contained the original Hugh Padgham mix, mistakenly listed as Bevans/Forward. The first release had PCSD 103 B-7-1-1 stamped in the runout groove on side 2; the second release had PCSD 103 B-3U-1-2-1. Thus most U.K. buyers received an LP different from buyers elsewhere in the world, where only copies with the Bevans/Forward mix were issued. The only other releases of the Padgham mix were on the original U.K. 7-inch single, which was quickly replaced with one featuring the Bevans/Forward mix, and on a U.K. limited edition 10-inch single that included both mixes. When the album was reissued in the U.K. on Aug 30, 1988 on the Fame label, the two variations again appeared.

Oct 10: CD *Double Fantasy* (John) (Geffen/WEA 299-131). Contents unchanged.

Oct 27: Single "Pretty Little Head" (3:50)/"Write Away" (3:00) (Paul) (Parlophone R 6145). A side is first release of Larry Alexander remix; B side originally released on *Press to Play* CD.

■ 12-inch single "Pretty Little Head" (6:56)/"Angry"/"Write Away" (Paul) (Parlophone 12R 6145). First release of "Pretty Little Head" 6:56 remix by John "Tokes" Potoker, and 3:36 remix of "Angry" by Larry Alexander with orchestration by Dave Matthews.

■ 12-inch single "Live-in World"-"On the Street"/"Something Better"-"You Know It Makes Sense" (Ringo) (EMI 12AHP 1). Includes first release of Ringo's "You

■ Know It Makes Sense," also released later on LP *The Anti-Heroin Project: It's a Live-in World*. A 7-inch single was also released, without Ringo's song.

Nov 3: LP *Menlove Ave.* (John) (Parlophone PCS 7308). Posthumous album featuring first U.K. release of several Lennon alternate takes and unreleased titles: from the Oct–Dec 1973 *Rock 'N' Roll* LP sessions, "Here We Go Again," "Angel Baby" (artificially extended and thus runs longer than on 1975 unauthorized U.S. *Roots* album), "My Baby Left Me," and "To Know Her Is to Love Her"; from the 1973 *Mind Games* sessions, "Rock and Roll People"; from the 1974 *Walls and Bridges* sessions, alternate versions of "Steel and Glass," "Scared," "Old Dirt Road," "Nobody Loves You (When You're Down and Out)," and "Bless You." "Angel Baby" was previously released on unauthorized (and withdrawn) U.S. *Roots* album. This extended version is its first authorized release and its first U.K. release in any form.

Nov 14: CD *Conspiracy of Hope* (Mercury 839 588-2) and LP (MERH 99), contains Paul's "Pipes of Peace."

Nov 17: Cassette single "Pretty Little Head"/"Angry"/"Write Away" (Paul) (Parlophone TCR 6145). McCartney's first cassette single; contents are the same as U.K. 12-inch single issued Oct 27.

Nov 24: LP *The Anti-Heroin Project: It's a Live-in World* (Paul/Ringo) (EMI AHP-LP 1 and cassette, TC AHP LP 1). Charity double album, originally announced for Nov 1 release, includes first release of Paul's "Simple as That" and Ringo's previously released "You Know It Makes Sense"; Ringo is also present on "Naughty Atom Bomb" (first release) with John Cleese and Bill Oddie, although his presence is difficult to detect and Cleese has no recollection of Ringo's involvement.

Menlove Ave. (© Capitol Records, Inc.). Another posthumous Lennon release, this one featuring alternate *Walls and Bridges* takes and previously unreleased tracks from *Rock 'N' Roll.*

Dec 1: CD *The Christmas Compact Disc* (EMI CDNOX 1). CD edition of *Now: The Christmas Album*, which was also reissued (EMI NOX 1).

■ Single "Only Love Remains" (4:11)/"Tough on a Tightrope" (4:44) (Paul) (Parlophone R 6148). First release of Jim Boyer remix of A side; B side is the original Hugh Padgham mix released on the *Press to Play* CD.

■ 12-inch single "Only Love Remains" (4:11)/"Tough on a Tightrope" (7:03)/"Talk More Talk" (5:56) (Paul) (Parlophone 12R 6148). First release of 7:03 remix of "Tough on a Tightrope" by Julian Mendelsohn, different from the mix found on the *Press to Play* CD and on the B side of the 7-inch single; and of 5:56 remix of "Talk More Talk" by Paul and Jon Jacobs.

1987

Early that year: Double CD *Some Time in New York City* (John) (Parlophone CDP 7 46782/3 2; double box spine number CDS 7 46782 8). This U.K. release was quickly withdrawn due to poor sound quality, and the CD was reissued on Aug 10, 1987.

Jan 30: LP *The Beatles: Interviews II* (Premier Records CBR 1047). Contents same as *The Golden Beatles*, released in U.S. Jul 1985.

Jan: LP *Paul McCartney Interview* (Paul) (Baktabak BAK 2003; picture disc). Picture disc album contains a recording of Chris Salewicz's 1986 *Q* magazine interview with Paul (also published in *Musician*). Later reissued as *Chat with the Stars: Paul McCartney* (ZUFG 003). First release.

Feb 16: Single "Strawberry Fields Forever"/"Penny Lane" (Parlophone R 5570 and picture disc, RP 5570). 20th-anniversary reissue.

Feb 26: Release of CD *Please Please Me* (EMI CDP 7 46435 2), *With The Beatles* (CDP 7 46436 2), *A Hard Day's Night* (CDP 7 46437 2) and *Beatles for Sale* (CDP 46438 2). The first four Beatles albums were released on compact disc worldwide. All were mono, which caused a considerable furor among Beatles fans and audiophiles. See this date in U.S. Discography for details.

Apr 3: CD *Milk and Honey* (John) (Polydor 817-160-2). Contents unchanged.

Apr 13: CD *Menlove Ave.* (John) (EMI CDP 7 46576-2). Contents unchanged.

■ Ladybird Books issued *Rupert the Bear* book/audio cassette pack with Paul's recording of "We All Stand Together" (Pickwick Tell-a-Tale PLBR 212).

Apr 21: CD *13 Original James Bond Hits* (EMI CDP 7 46079 2). Contains Wings' "Live and Let Die."

Apr 24: CD *Prince's Trust Tenth Anniversary Birthday Party* (Paul) (A&M CDA 3906) and LP (AMA 3906). Live recordings from Jun 20, 1986 Prince's Trust Concert. The LP contains "Get Back"; CD adds "Long Tall Sally." The U.K. LP included free bonus single "Long Tall Sally"/"I Saw Her Standing There" (FREE 21) in a separate picture sleeve, thus accounting for all three of Paul's songs; the single was not issued with the U.S. LP.

Apr 27: CDs *Ram* (EMI CDP 7 46612 2) and *McCartney* (7 46611 2) (Paul).

Apr 30: CD release of *Help!* (EMI CDP 7 46439 2), *Revolver* (CDP 7 46441 2) and *Rubber Soul* (CDP 7 46440 2), all in stereo.

May 18: CD *The Best of George Harrison* (George) (EMI CDAS-10011).

■ Double CD *All Things Must Pass* (George) (EMI CDS 7 46688/9 2). Capitol used Sonic Solutions No Noise System on U.S. release, which was not used on the U.K. CD. EMI announced it would use the U.S. digital master for future releases of the CD in the U.K. Later Abbey Road engineer Mike Jarratt said that only some songs had undergone the Sonic treatment.

May 26: CD releases *Rock 'N' Roll* (EMI CDP 7 46707 2), *Imagine* (CDP 7 46641 2), *Shaved Fish* (CDP 7 46642 2) (withdrawn due to poor sound quality and reissued on May 17, 1988) (all John), and CD *Wings over America* (Paul) (Parlophone CDS 7 46715/6 8).

Jun 1: CD *Sgt. Pepper's Lonely Hearts Club Band* (EMI CDP 7 46442 2). Stereo. At last it could almost truly be said that "It was 20 years ago today," as the *Sgt. Pepper's Lonely Hearts Club Band* appeared worldwide on the 20th anniversary of that landmark album's release. The CDs were actually shipped on May 26 (the actual anniversary of *Sgt. Pepper's* original rush-release); the entire Beatles CD release program that began with the four hastily released mono CDs on Feb 26 was built around reaching the *Pepper* 20th anniversary date. The CD contained the "Inner Groove," and the 15 kc tone, heard only by dogs, that were present on the original U.K. LP release, but omitted at that time on the U.S. release.

Jun: CD *Hamburg 1961* (Topline TOP CD 510). Same as LP *Savage Young Beatles*.

Jul 6: Single "All You Need Is Love"/"Baby You're a Rich Man" (Parlophone R 5620 and picture disc RP 5620) and cassette single (Parlophone TCR 5620). This 20th-anniversary reissue did not contain the original mono mix released on the original single but had the separate tracks from the stereo mix combined into one, or a "fake mono" version. First release of a Beatles single in the cassette format.

■ 12-inch single "All You Need Is Love"/"Baby You're a Rich Man" (Parlophone 12R 5620).

Jul 20: CD *Walls and Bridges* (John) (EMI CDP 7 46768 2).

Jul: Cassette set *The Beatles Box* (EMI). A set of eight cassettes in individually numbered boxes, each containing a four-page booklet. Released by EMI's World Records via mail order, the set had originally appeared in 1980 as a boxed edition of eight custom LPs with 126 Beatles songs. The LP set was deleted in 1982.

Aug 3: CD *Mind Games* (John) (EMI CDP 7 46769 2).

■ *The Beatles: The Early Tapes* (Polydor 823 701-2). Tony Sheridan tracks yet again.

Aug 10: Double CD *Some Time in New York City* (John) (EMI CDP 7 46782/3 2; CD box spine number: CDS 7 46782 8).

Prince's Trust Concert—1987 (© The Prince's Trust and A&M Records). U.K.–only album with live numbers by George and Ringo.

Aug 14: Double CD *The Prince's Trust Concert 1987* (George/Ringo) (A&M CDA 1987), double LP (PTA 1987), double cassette (1987). First release of live recordings from the Jun 5 and Jun 6 Prince's Trust Concerts. George: "While My Guitar Gently Weeps," "Here Comes the Sun"; Ringo: "With a Little Help from My Friends." There was no U.S. release.

Aug 24: CD release of *Yellow Submarine* (EMI CDP 7 46445 2) and *The Beatles* (aka the "*White Album*") (CDS 7 46443 8, double CD).

Sep 4: LP *McCartney II* (Paul) (Fame FA-3191). Reissue.

Sep 21: CD *Magical Mystery Tour* (EMI CDP 7 48062 2). Stereo. The original 1967 U.S. LP included some songs in mono, since no stereo mixes for them yet existed. When the album was released in the U.K. in 1976, the same U.S. master was used. A later German release of the album and a U.K. cassette release were all-stereo.

Oct 5: CD releases *Red Rose Speedway* (Paul and Wings) (Fame CD-FA 3193), with bonus tracks "The Mess," "I Lie Around" and "Country Dreamer"; *McCartney II* (Paul) (CD-FA 3191), adds bonus tracks "Check My Machine" and "Secret Friend"; and *Wild Life* (Wings) (CD-FA 3101), adds bonus tracks "Oh Woman, Oh Why," "Mary Had a Little Lamb" and "Little Woman Love."

■ LP *Red Rose Speedway* (Paul) (Fame FA-3193). Reissue.

Oct 12: Single "Got My Mind Set on You"/"Lay His Head" (George) (Dark Horse W 8178). B side is remixed version also released on special CD and EP issued with George's book *Songs by George Harrison*. Original mix was included on first, unreleased version of George's *Somewhere in England* album. First release of both songs.

■ 12-inch single "Got My Mind Set on You" (extended version)/"Got My Mind Set on You" (single version)-"Lay His Head" (Dark Horse W 8178 T and picture disc W 8178 TP). First release of the extended version of "Got My Mind Set on You."

Oct 19: CD releases *Abbey Road* (EMI CDP 7 46446 2) and *Let It Be* (CDP 7 46447 2). Jan 1988 issue of *Beatletter* reported that CDs appeared with original LP numbers, not the CD numbers as listed here (CD-PCS 7088 for *Abbey Road* and CD- PCS-7096 for *Let It Be*).

■ CD *Decca Sessions (1/1/62)* (Topline Records TOP CD 523), LP (TOP 181), and cassette (KTOP 181). Contains the same 12 audition cuts issued many times before, excluding the three Lennon/McCartney compositions; see Sep 10, 1982.

Nov 2: CD *Cloud Nine* (George) (Dark Horse 9 25643-2), LP (WX 123) and cassette (123C). Contains previously released "Got My Mind Set on You." First U.K. and U.S. release of "Cloud 9," "That's What It Takes," "Fish on the Sand," "Just for Today," "This Is Love," "When We Was Fab," "Devil's Radio," "Someplace Else," "Wreck of the Hesperus" and "Breath Away from Heaven." Ringo appears on "When We Was Fab." "Someplace Else" and "Breath Away from Heaven" first appeared in the film *Shanghai Surprise*; both were rerecorded for the album.

■ Double CD *All the Best* (Paul) (Parlophone CD-PMTV 1), double LP (Parlophone PMTV-1) and double cassette (TC-PMTV 1). The configurations of this "greatest hits" album were different in the U.S. and the U.K. The U.K. edition includes the first release of "Once upon a Long Ago" (4:06), also released as a single in the U.K. but unavailable in the U.S. The U.K. album also includes "Mull of Kintyre," "We All Stand Together," "Coming Up" (studio version), "Pipes of Peace" and "Maybe I'm Amazed," all missing from the U.S. release. The U.S. release includes "Junior's Farm," "Uncle Albert/Admiral Halsey" and the live version of "Coming Up," all missing on the U.K. edition. Both editions include "Jet," "Band on the Run," "Ebony and Ivory," "Listen to What the Man Said," "No More Lonely Nights," "Silly Love Songs," "Let 'Em In," "C Moon," "Live and Let Die," "Another Day," "Goodnight Tonight," "Say Say Say," "With a Little Luck" and "My Love." The U.K. CD omits "Maybe I'm Amazed," "Goodnight Tonight" and "With a Little Luck," all of which are on the U.K. LP.

Nov 16: Single "Once upon a Long Ago" (4:12)/"Back on My Feet" (Paul) (Parlophone R 6170). A side previously released on U.K. edition of *All the Best*. First release of B side, co-written by McCartney and Elvis Costello (under his real name, Declan MacManus). Neither song has been released in the U.S.

■ CD single "Once upon a Long Ago" (4:12)/"Back on My Feet"/"Don't Get Around Much Anymore"/"Kansas City" (Paul) (Parlophone CDR 6170). First release of "Don't Get Around Much Anymore" and "Kansas City," both of which would also appear on

"Once upon a Long Ago" (© MPL Communications Ltd.). Another U.K.–only release, issued in several formats.

McCartney's Oct 31, 1988 Soviet LP, *CHOBA B CCCP* (*Back in the USSR*).

■ 12-inch single "Once upon a Long Ago" (long version 4:34)/"Back on My Feet"/"Midnight Special (Prisoner's Song)"/"Don't Get Around Much Anymore" (Paul) (Parlophone 12R 6170). First release of "long version" of "Once upon a Long Ago" and "Midnight Special," another track destined for the *CHOBA* album.

■ Cassettes *Thomas and the Missing Christmas Tree* (Ringo) (Pickwick Tell-A-Tale PLBE 199). Book/cassette pack; narration by Ringo. First release. *Thomas Gift Box* (Ringo) (Pickwick Tell-A-Tale TATGP 13). Contains three *Thomas the Tank Engine & Friends* cassettes and books (PLBE 158, 159 and 160); narration by Ringo. First release.

Nov 19: Cassette album set *The Beatles*. All 13 U.K. Beatles albums were reissued on completely new cassettes, using the same digital masters used for the CD releases. All were manufactured on high-quality XDR tape, replacing earlier U.K. cassette releases, which were notoriously shoddy, and that often had songs in the wrong order compared to the original LPs. The new cassettes were as follows: *Please Please Me* (TC-PMC 1202; mono); *With The Beatles* (TC-PMC 1206; mono); *A Hard Day's Night* (TC-1230; mono); *Beatles for Sale* (TC-PMC 1240; mono); remainder all in stereo: *Help!* (TC-PCS 3071); *Rubber Soul* (TC-PCS 3075); *Revolver* (TC-PCS 7009); *Sgt. Pepper's Lonely Hearts Club Band* (TC-PCS 7027); *Magical Mystery Tour* (TC-PCS 3077); *The Beatles* (TC-2 PCS 4501); *Yellow Submarine* (TC-PCS 7070); *Abbey Road* (TC-PCS 7088); *Let It Be* (TC-PCS 7096). *Pepper* had been available since Jun 1 on the XDR tape.

Nov 20: CD *Conspiracy of Hope* (Stylus Records SMD 743), LP (SMR 743) and cassette (SMC 743). Reissue of Nov 14, 1986 release containing Paul's "Pipes of Peace."

Nov 23: 12-inch single "Once upon a Long Ago" (extended version 6:06)/"Back on My Feet"/"Lawdy Miss Clawdy"/"Kansas City" (Paul) (Parlophone 12 RX 6170). First release of extended version of "Once upon a Long Ago" and "Lawdy Miss Clawdy"; other tracks previously released. LP "Lawdy Miss Clawdy" would later appear on the Soviet LP *CHOBA*.

■ Single "Hello Goodbye"/"I Am the Walrus" (Parlophone R 5655 and picture disc RP 5655) 20th-anniversary reissue.

Dec: Cassette *Thomas the Tank Engine and Friends* (Ringo) (Pickwick PLBE 189–230). Six more book/cassette packages were released with the following *Thomas the Tank Engine* stories narrated by Ringo: "Thomas, Percy and the Coal"/"Saved from Scrap" (PLBE 189); "Thomas and Trevor"/"Duck Takes Charge" (190); "Percy and Harold"/"Percy Takes the Plunge" (223); "Pop Goes the Diesel"/"Dirty Work"/"A Close Shave" (228); "Thomas Comes to Breakfast"/"Boco the Diesel" (229); "Daisy"/"Percy's Predicament"/"Wooly Bear" (230). First release.

Dec 4: Reissue single "Do They Know It's Christmas"/"FEED the World" (Paul) (Feed 1); also issued as a 12-inch single (FEED 112), and 12-inch picture disc (FEED P1).

1988

Jan 4: CD *Press to Play* (Paul) (EMI CDP 7 46269 2). Reissue.

Jan 25: Single "When We Was Fab"/"Zig Zag" (George) (Dark Horse W8131) and cassette single (9 28131-4). First release of both songs in U.K. and U.S. on same date. B side is an instrumental from the 1986 film *Shanghai Surprise*, produced by Harrison's HandMade Films.

■ 12-inch single: "When We Was Fab" (unextended version)-"Zig Zag"/"That's the Way It Goes" (remix)-"When We Was Fab" (reverse ending) (George) (Dark Horse) (W8131T). First release of the "reverse ending" mix of "When We Was Fab," not issued in the U.S. "That's the Way It Goes" is a remix of the track that originally appeared on George's LP *Gone Troppo*.

Jan 29: LP *Withnail and I* (Filmtrax MOMENT 110). Includes The Beatles' "While My Guitar Gently Weeps." Soundtrack LP from film produced by Harrison's HandMade Films.

■ Singles set *A Rare Interview with The Beatles* (Baktabak BAKPAK 1004). A set of four 7-inch picture discs, in a display pack. The records contained clips from the Murray "The K" interviews and the 1966 Seattle press conference. The same recordings were released on the Baktabak CD, *The Beatles Conquer America*, Feb 5. The recordings were previously released in the U.S. in 1982 on the *Timeless II* picture disc.

Feb 1: Single "When We Was Fab"/"Zig Zag" (George) (Dark Horse W 8131 B). Special boxed edition of the single with a cutout of Harrison posed in his 1967 *Sgt. Pepper* uniform and a poster.

Feb 5: CD *The Beatles Conquer America* (Baktabak CBAK 4001; picture disc CD). See Jan 29; this CD should not be confused with the bootleg album of the same title that contains Beatles' performances on "The Ed Sullivan Show" and other selections.

Feb 8: Three-inch CD single (George) (Dark Horse W 8131 CD) and 12-inch picture disc single (W 8131 TP) with same contents as Jan 25 "When We Was Fab" 12-inch release.

Mar 8: CD *Past Masters Vol. 1* (Parlophone CDP 7 90043-2/CD-BPM1) and *Past Masters Vol. 2* (CDP 7-90044-2/CD-BPM2). CDs contain the remaining Beatles songs not included on the original U.K. Beatles albums and thus not found on the Beatles CDs. Volume 1: "Love Me Do" (Version I), "From Me to You," "Thank You Girl," "She Loves You," "I'll Get You," "I Want to Hold Your Hand," "This Boy," "Komm, Gib Mir Deine Hand," "Sie Liebt Dich," "Long Tall Sally," "I Call Your Name," "Slow Down," "Matchbox," "I Feel Fine," "She's a Woman," "Bad Boy," "Yes It Is," "I'm Down." Volume 2: "Day Tripper," "We Can Work It Out," "Paperback Writer," "Rain," "Lady Madonna," "The Inner Light," "Hey Jude," "Revolution" (Version I), "Get Back" (Version I), "Don't Let Me Down," "The Ballad of John and Yoko," "Old Brown Shoe," "Across the Universe" (Version I), "Let It Be" (Version I), "You Know My Name (Look Up the Number)."

Mar 14: Single "Lady Madonna"/"The Inner Light" (Parlophone R 5675 and picture disc RP 5675). 20th-anniversary reissue.

That spring: CD *The Beatles: The Decca Sessions 1.1.62* (Charly/Topline TOP CD 523). Contains songs from The Beatles' Jan 1, 1962 Decca audition; CD was withdrawn following a suit filed by Apple. All CD releases of the Decca audition to date eliminate the three Lennon-McCartney compositions ("Like Dreamers Do," "Love of the Loved" and "Hello Little Girl").

Apr 5: CD *John Lennon/Plastic Ono Band* (John) (EMI CDP 7 46770 2). Worldwide CD release.

May 17: CD *Shaved Fish* (John) (EMI CDP 7 46642 2). Second release; original CD issue was withdrawn due to poor sound quality. This release was reportedly improved through the use of Sonic Solutions No Noise Processing.

Jun 13: Single "This Is Love"/"Breath Away from Heaven" (George) (Dark Horse W 7913).

■ Three-inch CD single "This Is Love"/"Breath Away from Heaven"/"All Those Years Ago"/"Hong Kong Blues" (George) (W 7913 CD).

■ 12-inch single "This Is Love"/"Breath Away from Heaven"/"All Those Years Ago" (George) (W 7913 T).

Jul 11: CD *The Last Word* (John) (Baktabak CBAK 4014; picture disc CD) and LP (Baktabak BAK 2096). Contains 55 minutes of the 150-minute John Lennon interview with RKO Radio taped on Dec 8, 1980, only hours before John's death. A shorter edit was previously released in the U.S. on LP *Reflections and Poetry*.

Aug 4: CD *Beatles Volume II* (Baktabak CBAK 4009; picture disc CD). Interview CD.

Aug 30: Single "Hey Jude"/"Revolution" (Apple R 5722 and picture disc RP 5722). 20th-anniversary reissue.

- 12-inch single "Hey Jude"/"Revolution" (Parlophone 12R 5722) and 12-inch picture disc (Parlophone 12RP 5722), the first official EMI Beatles 12-inch picture disc single release.

- CD *Press to Play* (Paul) (Fame CDFA 3209) and LP (Fame FA 3209). Reissues; the same two versions of the LP that appeared in England when originally released Sep 1, 1986 were pressed for this reissue. See Sep 1, 1986 for details.

Sep: LP *Beatles Volume II* (Baktabak BAK 2108; picture disc). Same contents as Aug 4 CD release.

Oct 10: CD *Imagine: John Lennon* (John) (Parlophone CD-PCSP 722; CDP 7 90808 2) and double LP (PCSP 722). All songs previously released except first U.K. release of "Real Love," a 1980 demo, and a 1971 demo of "Imagine." Other songs include The Beatles' "Twist and Shout" (mono), "Help!" "In My Life," "Strawberry Fields Forever," "A Day in the Life" (clean intro; no *Sgt. Pepper* cross-fade), "Revolution" (Version I), "The Ballad of John and Yoko," "Julia," "Don't Let Me Down" and Lennon's solo titles "Give Peace a Chance" (full single version with count in), "How?" "Imagine" (released version), "God," "Mother" (live; One to One Concert), "Stand by Me," "Jealous Guy," "Woman," "Beautiful Boy (Darling Boy)," "(Just Like) Starting Over."

Oct 17: Single "Handle with Care"/"Margarita" (George/Wilburys) (Wilbury W 7732). Also issued separately in a picture sleeve with a peel-off sticker (W 7732 W). First U.S. and U.K. release.

- Three-inch CD single (W 7332 CD), 10-inch single (W 7732 TE) and 12-inch single (W 7732 T) "Handle with Care" (extended version)/"Margarita" (George/Wilburys). 12-inch was issued in a facsimile of a 78 rpm brown-card stitched sleeve; first release of extended A side mix.

- CD *Venus and Mars* (Paul) (Fame CDFA 3213) and LP (FA 3213). CD includes bonus tracks "Zoo Gang," "Lunch Box-Odd Sox" and "My Carnival."

- CD *Tug of War* (Paul) (Fame CDFA 3210) and LP (FA 3210).

Oct 24: CD *The Traveling Wilburys Volume One* (George/Wilburys) (Wilbury/Warner Bros. K 925796-2) and LP (WX 224). This group included the following personnel, each billed only under the noted pseudonym: George Harrison (Nelson Wilbury), Roy Orbison (Lefty Wilbury), Bob Dylan (Lucky Wilbury), Tom Petty (Charlie T. Jnr. Wilbury) and Jeff Lynne (Otis Wilbury). The album was produced by George and Jeff Lynne (billed as Nelson and Otis Wilbury, of course). Harrison shares lead vocal on "Handle with Care" with Orbison and is heard on several other tracks including "End of the Line." The other titles are "Dirty World," "Rattled," "Last

Night," "Not Alone Any More," "Congratulations," "Heading for the Light," "Margarita," "Tweeter and the Monkey Man." First U.K. release except for previously released "Handle with Care" and "Margarita."

- Double LP *Past Masters* (Parlophone BPM 1). Double album, also released as a double cassette worldwide; previously available only as two separately issued CDs. The double album, CDs and cassette were also included with *The Beatles* boxed sets released worldwide on Oct 31.

- CD *Stay Awake* (Ringo) (A&M CDA 3918) and LP (AMA 3918). Contains first U.K. release of Ringo's "When You Wish upon a Star," recorded with Herb Alpert, part of a medley that closes the album.

Oct 31: LP *The Beatles* (LP/Cassette/CD boxed sets) (EMI LP BBX 1/TC BBX 1/CD BBX 1). Worldwide release of Beatles boxed sets of albums, CDs and cassettes. Each set, issued in a wooden box with a paperback book, included the *Past Masters* albums. All included the new, digitally remastered CD versions of the albums, including the first four albums in mono.

Oct: LP *The Gospel According to: The Beatles* (Baktabak BAK 2108). Contains the 1964 "Beatles Open-End Interview," with Bob Miles dubbing in the questions; 1966 Ken Douglas interview clips, first released in the U.S. on *Beatle-Views*; 1965 *Teen Set* interview clip with John and Paul. Essentially the same material was previously released in the U.S. on *Timeless II 1/2* and *The British Are Coming*.

Nov 2: Star-Club singles set (Baktabak TABOKS 1001). The 30 tracks recorded at the Star-Club on Dec 31, 1962 were reissued yet again, this time on a set of 15 singles, also issued as a boxed set (TABOKS 1001). The singles were numbered STAB 2001 through 2015.

Nov 14: CD *Water from the Wells of Home* (Johnny Cash/Paul) (Mercury 834 778-2), LP (834 778-1) and cassette (834 778-4). First U.K. release of Paul's duet with Johnny Cash, "New Moon over Jamaica," composed by Paul, Cash and Tom T. Hall.

Nov 21: CD *Beatles at the Star Club* (Baktabak CTAB 5001) and double LP (LTAB 5001). All 30 Star-Club tracks recorded Dec 31, 1962.

Nov 28: CD single "Love Me Do"/"P.S. I Love You" (EMI CD3R 4949); "Please Please Me"/"Ask Me Why" (CD3R 4983); "From Me to You"/"Thank You Girl" (CD3R 5015); "She Loves You"/"I'll Get You" (CD3R 5055). First in series of 3-inch CD releases of all 22 original U.K. Beatles singles. Unfortunately, it was not a very good start since, once again, EMI used the album version of "Love Me Do," which features Andy White, not Ringo, on drums. The Ringo version appeared on the original U.K. single; the White version on the *Please Please Me* album.

- Single "Imagine"/"Jealous Guy" (John) (Parlophone R 6199).

- CD single "Imagine"/"Jealous Guy"/"Happy Xmas (War Is Over)" (John) (CDR 6199). *Shaved Fish* version of "Happy Xmas" with a brief bit of "Give Peace a Chance" from the One to One Concert tacked on to the end.

"Imagine"/"Jealous Guy" (© EMI Records Ltd.). U.K. 12-inch single featured the same cover photo as the *Imagine: John Lennon* compilation soundtrack album.

- 12-inch single "Imagine"/"Jealous Guy"/"Happy Xmas (War Is Over)" (John) (12R 6199). Contains full, original single version of "Happy Xmas."
- CD *Now—The Christmas Album* (John/Paul) (EMI CD-NOX-1), LP (NOX 1) and cassette (TC-NOX 1). LP and cassette include Paul's "Wonderful Christmastime" and John's "Happy Xmas (War Is Over)"; CD omits "Happy Xmas"; first CD release of "Wonderful Christmastime."

Dec 5: Single "Imagine"/"Jealous Guy" (John) (Parlophone RP 6199; picture disc). Picture disc edition of 7-inch single; a planned 12-inch picture disc (12RP 6199) was never released.

Dec: CD *The Beatles: The Conversation Disc Series* (ABCD 005; picture disc CD). Contains interview clips first released in the U.S. on *The Beatles 'Round the World* and the *Help!* open-end interview promo.

1989

Jan 23: Three-inch CD singles: "I Want to Hold Your Hand"/"This Boy" (Parlophone CD3R 5084); "Can't Buy Me Love"/"You Can't Do That" (CD3R 5114).

Jan 30: CD *Double Fantasy* (John) (EMI/Capitol CDP 7 91425 2) and LP (EMI/Capitol EST 2083). Originally on the Geffen label, this is a Capitol/EMI reissue.

Feb 20: Single "End of the Line"/"Congratulations" (George/Wilburys) (Wilbury/Warner Bros. W 7367).

- Three-inch CD (W 7637 CD) and 12-inch (W 7637 T) singles "End of the Line" (extended version)/"Congratulations" (George/Wilburys). A second 12-inch (W 7637T W) included Wilburys stickers. First release of extended A side.

Mar 28: LP *The Beatles Conquer America* (Baktabak BAK 2114; picture disc). First released as a picture disc CD Feb 5. Interviews.

Apr 3: Three-inch CD singles: "I Feel Fine"/"She's a Woman" (EMI CD3R 5200); "Help!"/"I'm Down" (CD3R 5305); "Ticket to Ride"/"Yes It Is" (CD3R 5265); "A Hard Day's Night"/"Things We Said Today" (CD3R 5160).

Apr 10: Single "Get Back"/"Don't Let Me Down" (Parlophone R5777 and picture disc, RP 5777). 20th-anniversary reissue.

May 8: Three-inch CD singles: "Paperback Writer"/"Rain" (EMI CD3R 5452); "Yellow Submarine"/"Eleanor Rigby" (CD3R 5493); "Strawberry Fields Forever"/"Penny Lane" (CD3R 5570); "We Can Work It Out"/"Day Tripper" (CD3R 5389).

- Single "My Brave Face"/"Flying to My Home" (Paul) (Parlophone R 6213). First release of both songs.
- CD single (CDR 6213), 12-inch single (12R 6213) and cassette single (TCR 6213) "My Brave Face"/"Flying to My Home"/"I'm Gonna Be A Wheel Someday"/"Ain't That a Shame." First U.K. release of "I'm Gonna Be a Wheel Someday" and "Ain't That a Shame" from Paul's *CHOBA B CCCP* sessions.
- Single "Ferry 'Cross the Mersey" (Paul) (PWL PW 41) and CD single (PWL PWCD 41). Charity single on which Paul alternates lead vocal with Gerry Marsden, Holly Johnson, The Christians and Stock Aitken Waterman.

May 30: Single "Ballad of John and Yoko"/"Old Brown Shoe" (Parlophone R 5786 and picture RP, 5786). 20th-anniversary reissue.

Jun 5: CD *Flowers in the Dirt* (Paul) (Parlophone CDP 7 91653 2), LP (PCSD 106) and cassette (TC-PCSD 106). LP includes previously released "My Brave Face." First release of "Rough Ride" (Version I), "You Want Her Too," "Distractions," "We Got Married," "Put It There," "Figure of Eight" (Version I), "This One," "Don't Be Careless Love," "That Day Is Done," "How Many People," "Motor of Love"; CD and cassette add "Ou Est le Soleil?"

- Three-inch CD singles: "Hello Goodbye"/"I Am the Walrus" (EMI CD3R 5655); "All You Need Is Love"/"Baby You're a Rich Man" (CD3R 5620).
- Single "Spirit of the Forest" (Ringo) (Virgin VS 1191). Issued as a 7-inch single (12-inch in U.S.). First U.K. and U.S. release of charity single released for the benefit of rain forest preservation; Ringo does one line of lead vocal.

Jul 10: Three-inch CD singles: "Lady Madonna"/"The Inner Light" (Parlophone CD3R 5675), "Hey Jude"/"Revolution" (CD3R 5722).

- CD *Wings at the Speed of Sound* (Paul) (EMI CDP 7 48199 2). CD adds bonus tracks "Walking in the Park with Eloise," "Bridge over the River Suite" and "Sally G."

Jul 17: Single "This One"/"The First Stone" (Paul) (Parlophone R 6223). First release of B side.

- Paul's CD single (CDR 6223) and 12-inch (12R 6223) "This One"/"The First Stone"/"I Wanna Cry"/"I'm in

Love Again." First release of latter two titles; "I'm in Love Again" is from *CHOBA* sessions but was originally omitted from that album.

Jul 24: Single "This One"/"The Long and Winding Road" (Version III) (Paul) (Parlophone RX 6223). Special limited boxed edition. First release of a new B side, a new version of "The Long and Winding Road." The box also contained six color postcards of McCartney and his new band members. The record itself was contained in a picture sleeve identical to the one used for the regular U.K. 7-inch release, but with the new B side listed on the back. "The Long and Winding Road" was taken from the soundtrack of the "Put It There" TV special.

- CD *Back to the Egg* (Paul) (EMI CDP 7 48200 2 or CZ 218). The CD adds the following bonus tracks: "Daytime Nightime Suffering," "Wonderful Christmastime" and "Rudolph the Red Nosed Reggae."

Jul 31: 12-inch single "This One"/"The First Stone"/"Good Sign" (6:52) (Paul) (Parlophone 12RX 6223). Second of two U.K. 12-inch "This One" releases. First release of "Good Sign."

Aug 7: Three-inch CD singles "Get Back"/"Don't Let Me Down" (Parlophone CD3R 5777). Contains the original mono U.K. single version of "Get Back," previously available only on the original U.K. single and the 20th-anniversary reissue. "The Ballad of John and Yoko"/"Old Brown Shoe" (CD3R 5786). First of the 3-inch CD Beatles singles to be released in stereo.

Aug 14: LP *Now That's What I Call Music 15* (Paul) (EMI/Virgin/PolyGram NOW/TC-NOW). Double LP, double cassette, double CD. Each includes Paul's "My Brave Face" and the Hillsborough charity recording of "Ferry 'Cross the Mersey," which includes vocals by Paul.

"This One" (© MPL Communications Ltd.). One of the U.K. releases of "This One," featuring the rare B side "Good Sign."

Aug 29: CD *London Town* (Paul) (Fame CD-FA 3223), LP (FA 3223), cassette (TC-FA 3223). CD adds bonus track "Girl's School."

Sep 4: LP/cassette/CD *Lethal Weapon 2* (George) (Warner Bros. 925 985-1/4/2). This soundtrack album contains the first release of "Cheer Down," performed by George Harrison.

- Three-inch CD singles: "Let It Be"/"You Know My Name (Look Up the Number)" (EMI CD3R 5833); "Something"/"Come Together" (CD3R 5814).

Oct 3: CD *Wings at the Speed of Sound* (Paul) (Fame CD-FA 3229), LP (FA 3229) and cassette (TC-FA 3229). Only three months after releasing the full-price CD, EMI deleted it and reissued the CD on the midprice Fame label.

Oct 7: LP *The Beatles Talk Downunder—Volume One* (Baktabak VBAK 3004; picture disc). U.K. release of first half of Australian interview album, previously released in the U.K. in Jun 1982.

Oct 23: CD *The Best of Dark Horse: 1976–1989* (George) (Dark Horse/Warner Bros WX 925), LP (WX 312) and cassette (312 C). Greatest hits compilation adds the first U.K. release of "Cockamamie Business" and "Poor Little Girl." Also contains the previously released "Cheer Down," "Blow Away," "That's the Way It Goes," "Wake Up My Love," "Life Itself," "Got My Mind Set on You," "Crackerbox Palace," "Cloud 9," "Here Comes the Moon," "When We Was Fab," "Love Comes to Everyone" and "All Those Years Ago." The CD and cassette editions added "Gone Troppo."

- CD *The John Lennon Collection* (John) (EMI EMTV 37). In addition to the 17 tracks contained on the original U.K. album release (15 in U.S.), the CD adds "Move Over Ms. L" and "Cold Turkey," the first LP or CD release for "Ms. L." U.K. release had a shortened version of "No. 9 Dream" (reduced by 2 minutes). The CD also contains the complete versions of "Give Peace a Chance" and "Happy Xmas (War Is Over)."

Oct 30: Single "Something"/"Come Together" (Parlophone R 5814 and picture disc RP 5814). 20th-anniversary reissue.

Nov 6: CD single *Beatles CD Singles Set* (EMI CDBSC 1). Complete boxed set of 22 original U.K. Beatles singles in 3-inch CD format, all of which had been released individually during the preceding year. While the CD singles were released individually in the U.S., no boxed set was issued there.

- CD *The '80s—The Album of the Decade* (Paul) (EMI CD-EMTVD 48), LP (EMTVD 48) and cassette (TC-EMTVD 48). Contains Paul's duet with Stevie Wonder, "Ebony and Ivory."

Nov 13: Single "Figure of Eight" (Version II 5:11, listed as 5:16)/"Ou Est le Soleil?" (Pettibone remix, 4:50) (Paul) (Parlophone R 6235) and cassette single (TCR 6235). A new version of "Figure of Eight," with eight different formats of the single eventually released in the U.K. Initial 7-inch release listed only McCartney as the producer; replaced with one listing McCartney, Chris

Hughes and Ross Cullum. First release of "Figure of Eight" (Version II) and of the 5:11 edit, issued in the U.S. only on a promo, and of the Pettibone remix of "Ou Est le Soleil?" and of the 4:50 edit, which was not issued in the U.S.

■ CD single "Figure of Eight" (Version II, 4:01 edit)/"Loveliest Thing"/"The Long and Winding Road" (Version III) (Paul) (Parlophone CDRS 6235; Gatefold). First release of 4:01 D.J. edit of "Figure of Eight" and of "Loveliest Thing"; previously released "The Long and Winding Road." This gatefold edition had an empty space to hold the 3-inch CD single released Nov 20. When this gatefold edition was sold out, a second edition (CDR 6235) was released in a standard jewel box and with identical contents. The 4:01 D.J. edit was only released on these two 5-inch CD singles and on U.K. and U.S. promos.

■ 12-inch single "Figure of Eight" (Version II 5:11, listed as 5:16)/"This One" (Club Lovejoys Mix 6:10) (Paul) (Parlophone 12R 6235). Club Lovejoys Mix was previously available only on a limited edition U.K. 12-inch promo release (12R LOVE 6223A). The same mix was also released on 12-inch in France and Germany.

■ LP/cassette/CD *After the Hurricane: Songs for Montserrat* (Paul) (Chrysalis CHR/ZCHR/CCD 1750). Contains Paul's duet with Stevie Wonder, "Ebony and Ivory."

Nov 17: LP *The Beatles Talk Downunder—Volume Two* (Baktabak VBAK 3006; picture disc). Picture disc LP with second half of LP originally released in Australia and first released in the U.K. in Jun 1982.

Nov 20: 12-inch single "Figure of Eight" (Version II 5:11, listed as 5:16)/"Ou Est le Soleil?" (Pettibone remix 4:50) (Paul) (Parlophone 12RS 6235; etched edition). Limited edition etched/engraved 12-inch disc. Contents same as the original 7-inch single release. The etching is of a flower drawn by Paul.

Nov 23: LP and CD *Flowers in the Dirt* (World Tour Pack) (Paul) (EMI PCSDX and CD-PCSDX 106). A limited edition repackaging included a bonus one-track single with the previously unreleased song, "Party Party"; a 3-inch CD single was issued with the CD box, and a 7-inch etched/engraved single with the vinyl LP edition, each in its own custom picture sleeve (Parlophone R 6238 and CD 3R 6238). The boxes also contained a bumper sticker, color poster of the band, tour itinerary, "family tree" of the band members designed by Pete Frame and a set of postcards; the CD box also included a 12×2 copy of the album cover. Note: The catalog numbers listed here are for the *outer box* containing the LP or CD and the special bonus singles; the CD and LP contained in the boxes are the same as the original releases and retained their original U.K. catalog numbers (LP: PCSD 106; CD: 7916532; short number CD PCSD 106).

Nov 27: Three-inch CD single "Figure of Eight" (Version II)/"Rough Ride" (Version II)/"Ou Est le Soleil?" (Pettibone 4:50 edit) (Parlophone CD3R 6235) (Paul). First release of "Rough Ride" (Version II). Second edi-

"Figure of Eight" (© MPL Communications Ltd.). All sense of reason vanished when *eight* different formats of this McCartney single were issued in the U.K. (three on CD, three on 12-inch, one each on 7-inch and cassette). As usual, a lone cassette single appeared in the U.S.

tion of 5-inch "Figure of Eight" CD single (first issued on Nov 13) also released (CDR 6235) with gatefold cover replaced by standard jewel box.

■ 12-inch single "Figure of Eight" (Version II 5:11, listed as 5:16)/"Ou Est le Soleil?" (7:10 Pettibone remix/"Ou Est le Soleil?" (Tub Dub Mix; 4:27, listed as 4:30) (Paul) (12RX 6235). First release of the full 7:10 Pettibone remix; first U.K. release of "Tub Dub Mix," previously released on U.S. and non-U.K. European 12-inch singles. The 7:10 edit was not released in the U.S.

■ CD *It's Christmas* (John/Paul) (EMI CD-EMTV 49), LP (EMTV 49), cassette (TC-EMTV 49). Contains Paul's "Wonderful Christmastime" and John's "Happy Xmas (War Is Over)."

■ Single "Cheer Down"/"Poor Little Girl" (George) (Dark Horse W 2696), cassette (W 2696C), 12-inch (W 2696T), and CD singles (W 2696CD): "Cheer Down"/"Poor Little Girl"/"Crackerbox Palace."

Dec: *The Royal Concert* CD (Paul/George) (Telstar Records 2TCD 2401) and double LP (STAR 2401). Includes Paul's 1986 "Get Back" and "Long Tall Sally," and George's 1987 performance of "While My Guitar Gently Weeps" and "Here Comes the Sun" from Prince's Trust Concerts.

1990

Jan 12: CD *The Beatles Talk Downunder—Volume One* (Baktabak CBAK 4024). Picture disc CD release. Contents same as picture disc vinyl LP released Oct 7, 1989.
Jan 22: *London and Rome Press Conferences* (Paul) (Wax Records BAND ON THE 1/PM7). Paul's Jun 15,

1989 and Jul 27, 1989 press conferences in Rome and London were released on a variety of limited edition discs. The complete recordings appeared on CD *Press Conferences Rome & London 1989* (BAND ON THE 1CD; limited edition box issued with color sticker and 2 5" × 7" color photos; 500 copies), and on a color vinyl LP *Press Conferences Rome & London 1989* (BAND ON THE 1; 500 copies), which included a 7-inch black vinyl single (PM 7) containing the conclusion of each press conference. Both discs are needed to hear the full recordings. The 7-inch disc was also released separately in at least three different colors of vinyl—red, blue and orange (also as PM 7; 250 copies). A picture disc LP (BAND ON THE 1P; unlimited number) did not contain the complete recordings.

Feb 5: Single "Put It There"/"Mama's Little Girl" (Paul) (Parlophone R 6246), cassette single (TCR 6246). First release of "Mama's Little Girl," which dates from 1978 *Back to the Egg* sessions. CD single (CDR 6246), 12-inch single (12R 6246), 12-inch single (12RS 6246) also included first release of "Same Time Next Year" originally for the film of that title, but omitted from the movie. The two 12-inch singles are identical, but the second one included a free copy of the print drawn by Paul that was used for the cover and added wording on the cover advertising the bonus print.

Feb 19: CD *Act Naturally* (Buck Owens/Ringo) (Capitol CD-EST 2119), LP (Capitol EST 2119) and cassette (TC-EST 2119). Buck Owens album containing first U.K. release of his duet with Ringo on "Act Naturally."

Mar 1: *The Beatles: Adelaide Press Conference 64* (Was Records FAB 7-1 and picture disc FAB 7-1P). Color vinyl and black-and-white picture discs containing identical material from The Beatles' Jun 1964 Adelaide press conference.

Mar 5: Single "Let It Be"/"You Know My Name (Look Up the Number)" (Parlophone R 5833 and picture disc RP 5833). 20th-anniversary reissue, concluding 20th-anniversary U.K. singles reissues. Each reissue was to include both a black vinyl single in a picture sleeve and an accompanying picture disc, but in some cases only the picture discs appear to have been released, although catalog numbers for all the discs were issued. Some picture sleeves in this series were different from those used for the 1982 U.K. singles boxed set, with several of them adding photographs to the backs, different coloring or simply the addition of a UPC bar code. A second run of the picture discs contained some altered pictures on the discs.

Mar 24: CD *The Last Temptation of Elvis* (Paul) (NME CD 038/039), LP (038/039). Includes the first releases of McCartney's "It's Now or Never" from the *CHOBA* sessions, but omitted from that album. The album also contains 25 additional cover versions of Elvis Presley numbers by a variety of stars. Initial release was made through mail order in England's *New Musical Express*.

Apr 17: LP *McCartney* (Paul) (EMI PCS 7102). Special 20th-anniversary reissue; not part of a series but designed to insure that the album remained available, as the Fame budget-line reissue LP was deleted.

May 29: LP *The Northern Beat* (London Records 840 968-1/4/2: LP/cassette/CD). Compilation album sold via TV mail order, contains Beatles' 1961 Hamburg recording of "Ain't She Sweet."

Jun 18: Single "Nobody's Child"/"Lumiere" (George/Wilburys) (Wilbury/Warner Bros. W 9773), cassette single (W 9773C). Charity single featuring first release of The Traveling Wilburys' "Nobody's Child" (George, Bob Dylan, Tom Petty and Jeff Lynne); B side is a Dave Stewart instrumental. "Nobody's Child" was one of the songs recorded in Jun 1961 in Hamburg by Tony Sheridan with The Beatles backing him. The Wilbury version is more faithful to the original country and western flavor of the song. 12-inch single (Wilbury/Warner Bros. W 9773T) and CD single (W 9773CD) also included first release of Ringo's Sep 4, 1989 live concert version of "With a Little Help from My Friends."

Jun: CD *Denny Laine Featuring Paul McCartney* (Denny Laine/Paul) (The Collection OR0069). Budget-line release of Denny Laine's *Japanese Tears* album, with new title designed to capitalize on the inclusion of several McCartney/Wings recordings.

■ EP *Vancouver Press Conference/Interviews 64* (FAB 7-2 and 7-2P; color vinyl and picture disc). Seven-inch black-and-white picture disc and color vinyl EP with excerpts from Aug 11, 1966 Beatles Chicago press conference and one of Murray "The K's" 1964 interviews. Record is mistakenly identified as a 1964 Vancouver press conference.

Jul 2: CD *Nuns on the Run* (George) (LP/cassette/CD: 846 043-1/4/2). Soundtrack album included George's recording of "Blow Away."

Jul 23: CD *Nobody's Child: Romanian Angel Appeal* (George/Wilburys; Ringo) (Warner/WEA 9 26280-2), LP (WEA WX 353), cassette (WX 353C). First release of George and Paul Simon's "Homeward Bound" duet, recorded for U.S. TV's "Saturday Night Live" show Nov 19, 1976, aired Nov 20, 1976 on NBC Television. The CD also contains the previously released "Nobody's Child" by The Traveling Wilburys and Ringo's live version of "With a Little Help from My Friends." Other album tracks include Eric Clapton's recording of George's composition "That Kind of Woman," which he recorded earlier but decided to omit from his *Journeyman* album, and Duane Eddy's "The Trembler," featuring George on slide guitar, originally released on Eddy's album *Duane Eddy*. The LP and cassette omitted Ringo's song.

Jul: Single *Detroit Press Conference* (Paul) (Wax Records PM1P/PM1; picture disc and color vinyl). Paul's Feb 1990 Detroit press conference. First release.

■ LP *Los Angeles, Madrid and Detroit Press Conferences* (Paul) (Wax Records TUGA4), picture disc (TUGA4P), CD (TUGA4CD). Paul's press conferences in Los Angeles (Nov 27, 1989) and Madrid (Nov 2, 1989) on a color vinyl LP with a bonus 7-inch single and picture disc LP. CD only adds Feb 1990 Detroit press conference; first release.

Aug 6: Double CD *Knebworth: The Album* (Paul) (Polydor 843 921-2), double LP (843 921-1), double cassette (843 921-4). First U.K. and U.S. release of Paul's live versions of "Coming Up" and "Hey Jude" from the Jun 30 Knebworth concert.

Aug: Single *Los Angeles, Madrid, Detroit, Rotterdam Press Conferences* (Paul) (Wax Records PM PACK 1). Paul's Nov 1989 Madrid, Rotterdam and Los Angeles press conferences, and his Feb Detroit press conference on a set of four vinyl singles. First release of Rotterdam press conference. Rotterdam also issued separately on 10-inch color vinyl LP *Rotterdam Press Conference* (Wax Records PM10).

■ Single *Seattle Press Conference* (Wax Records FAB7-3 and FAB7-3P). Seven-inch picture disc and color vinyl disc with excerpts from The Beatles' Aug 11, 1966 Chicago and Aug 25, 1966 Seattle press conferences, both previously released.

Sep 7: CD *The Beatles Talk Downunder—Volume Two* (Baktabak CBAK 4034). Contents same as picture disc LP released Nov 17, 1989.

Sep: EP *Tokyo Interviews* (Wax Records FAB7-4 and FAB7-4P). Color vinyl and picture disc editions containing clips from Jun–Jul 1966 Beatles interviews taped in Japan. First release.

Oct 8: CD *Ringo Starr and His All-Starr Band* (Ringo) (EMI CZ 353/CDP 7 95372 2), LP (EMS 1375), cassette (TC-EMS 1375). First release of the following tracks from Ringo's Sep 3–4*, 1989 concerts at the Greek Theater in Los Angeles:* "It Don't Come Easy," "No-No Song," "Honey Don't," "You're Sixteen" and "Photograph." The following concert numbers by other members of the band, with Ringo on drums, were also included: "Iko Iko" (Dr. John), "The Weight" (Levon Helm), "Shine Silently" (Nils Lofgren), "Quarter to Three" (Clarence Clemmons), "Raining in My Heart" (Rick Danko), "Will It Go Round in Circles" (Billy Preston) and "Life in the Fast Lane" (Joe Walsh).

■ Single "Birthday"/"Good Day Sunshine" (Paul) (Parlophone R 6271), cassette single (TCR 6271). First release of both songs; A side later released on *Tripping the Live Fantastic* album. CD single (CDR 6271) and 12-inch single (12R 6271) also included "P.S. Love Me Do"/"Let 'Em In." First release of the latter two tracks, neither of which was included on the *Tripping the Live Fantastic* album, and not issued in the U.S.

Oct 29: CD *The Traveling Wilburys Volume 3* (George/Wilburys) (Wilbury/Warner 7599 26324-2), LP (WX 384), cassette (WX 384C). The Traveling Wilburys' second album, with the tongue-in-cheek "Volume 3" title (there was no Volume 2). The fictitious names of the four surviving Wilburys were changed to Spike (George), Muddy (Tom Petty), Clayton (Jeff Lynne) and Boo (Bob Dylan); there was no replacement for the late Roy Orbison but the album was dedicated to his Wilbury alter ego, Lefty. George has no solo number on this album,

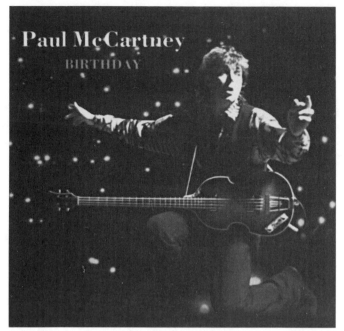

"Birthday" (© MPL Communications Ltd.). This single from Paul was issued in a variety of formats in the U.K. but, as was becoming customary, only on cassette in the U.S.

but he does a few lines of lead vocal on "She's My Baby," "The Devil's Been Busy," "Where Were You Last Night?" and "Wilbury Twist." The album also includes "If You Belonged to Me," "Inside Out," "7 Deadly Sins," "Poor House," "Cool Dry Place," "New Blue Moon" and "You Took My Breath Away." First release of all songs.

Oct 30: CD Boxed Set *Lennon* (John) (EMI CDS 7 95220 2; 4 CDs: 95221/2/3/4-2). Four-CD boxed set, issued to commemorate Lennon's 50th birthday, and containing 73 songs, all previously released; the set was not issued in vinyl or cassette formats, and contains "Give Peace a Chance," "Blue Suede Shoes," "Money," "Dizzy Miss Lizzie," "and "Yer Blues" (first CD release of these tracks from the 1969 LP *Live Peace in Toronto*); "Cold Turkey," "Instant Karma!" "Mother," "Hold On," "I Found Out," "Working Class Hero," "Isolation," "Remember," "Love," "Well Well Well," "Look at Me," "God," "My Mummy's Dead," "Power to the People," "Well (Baby Please Don't Go)" (live Jun 6, 1971), "Imagine," "Crippled Inside," "Jealous Guy," "It's So Hard," "Gimme Some Truth," "Oh My Love," "How Do You Sleep?" "How?" "Oh Yoko!" "Happy Xmas (War Is Over)," "Woman Is the Nigger of the World," "New York City," "John Sinclair," "Come Together," "Hound Dog" (both live from Aug 30, 1972 One to One Concert), "Mind Games," "Aisumasen (I'm Sorry)," "One Day (at a Time)," "Intuition," "Out the Blue," "Whatever Gets You Through the Night," "Going Down on Love," "Old Dirt Road," "Bless You," "Scared," "No. 9 Dream," "Surprise Surprise (Sweet Bird of Paradox)," "Steel and Glass," "Nobody Loves You (When You're Down and Out)," "Stand by Me," "Ain't That a Shame," "Do You Want to

Lennon CD Box (© EMI Records Ltd.). Two of the four CDs in this boxed compilation of 73 Lennon songs.

Dance," "Sweet Little Sixteen," "Slippin' and Slidin'," "Angel Baby" (same artificially extended 3:38 mix released on *Menlove Ave.*), "Just Because," "Whatever Gets You Through the Night," "Lucy in the Sky with Diamonds" and "I Saw Her Standing There" (last three cuts from Nov 28, 1974 Elton John concert at Madison Square Garden, New York; first CD and Capitol Records release of these tracks, and the first U.S. release of the first two numbers in any form), "(Just Like) Starting Over," "Cleanup Time," "I'm Losing You," "Beautiful Boy (Darling Boy)," "Watching the Wheels," "Woman," "Dear Yoko," "I'm Stepping Out," "I Don't Wanna Face It," "Nobody Told Me," "Borrowed Time," "(Forgive Me) My Little Flower Princess," "Every Man Has a Woman Who Loves Him" and "Grow Old with Me." According to Capitol Records, the U.S. release was technically considered an import of the U.K. release. Initial copies omitted "Imagine" from the track listing on the box, but these were replaced with corrected ones.

■ EP *Dallas Press Conference 66* (Wax Gang of 4). Seven-inch color vinyl disc featuring The Beatles' previously released Sep 18, 1964 Dallas press conference, mistakenly dated 1966.

Nov 5: Single "She's My Baby"/"New Blue Moon" (instrumental version) (George/Wilburys) (Wilbury/Warner W 9523) and cassette single (W 9523 C). First release of the instrumental version of "New Blue Moon," not available on *The Traveling Wilburys Volume 3* and not released in the U.S.

■ 12-inch single (W 9523 T) and CD single (W 9523 CD) added first release of "Runaway," not available on *The Traveling Wilburys Volume 3* album, and not released in the U.S.

■ Double CD *Tripping the Live Fantastic* (Paul) (Parlophone CD PCST 73461-2), triple LP (PCST 73461-3), double cassette (TC-PCST 73461-2). Worldwide release of Paul's live 1989–90 concert tour album. Contains several tracks that were not actually performed during the concerts, including "Showtime," the band being called to the stage, recorded especially to start off the album, and the following titles from various soundchecks during the tour: "Inner City Madness" (instrumental), "Together," "Crackin' Up," "Matchbox," "Sally" (an old Gracie Fields number dating from World War II), "If I Were Not Upon a Stage" (a comical busk used as a lead-in to "Hey Jude" at many shows) and "Don't Let the Sun Catch You Crying" (the old Ray Charles number, not the more familiar Gerry and The Pacemakers hit). The album also includes live versions of "Figure of Eight," "Jet," "Rough Ride," "Got to Get You Into My Life," "Band on the Run," "Birthday" (previously released as a single), "Ebony and Ivory," "We Got Married," "Maybe I'm Amazed," "The Long and Winding Road," "The Fool on the Hill," "Sgt. Pepper's Lonely Hearts Club Band," "Can't Buy Me Love," "Put It There," "Things We Said Today," "Eleanor Rigby," "This One," "My Brave Face," "Back in the USSR," "I Saw Her Standing There," "Twenty Flight Rock," "Coming Up," "Let It Be," "Ain't That a Shame," "Live and Let Die," "Hey Jude," "Yesterday," "Get Back," medley "Golden Slumbers"/"Carry That Weight"/"The End."

Nov 12: Double CD *John and Yoko—The Interview* (John) (BBC Radio Collection BBCCD 6002), double cassette (ZBBC 1195). Double CD and double cassette containing Andy Peebles' Dec 6, 1980 interview with John. This is the first official release of the interview, although portions of it had been played on the air many times. The release also adds a small amount of material not heard during the original broadcast and omits the commercially available musical tracks that were aired at that time.

Nov 19: CD *Tripping the Live Fantastic: Highlights!* (Paul) (Parlophone CDP 7 95379 2) and cassette (TC-PCSD 114). A one-CD, condensed version of Paul's live concert tour album. Different versions of *Highlights!* were released in the U.S. and U.K. The British version added the first release of "All My Trials" from Paul's Oct 27, 1989 Milan concert, a song omitted on the U.S. edition of *Highlights!* which featured "Put It There" from the full *Tripping* album instead. A planned abbreviated 12-track vinyl release (PCSD 114) was canceled, making this the first McCartney album not released on vinyl in the U.K. The vinyl edition was issued in the U.S. by Columbia House Record Club; it included "All My Trials," the only U.S. release of the song and the only U.S. or U.K. vinyl edition of *Highlights!* The remaining tracks on the *Highlights!* CD are "Got to Get You Into My Life," "We Got Married," "Things We Said Today," "Back in the USSR," "Birthday," "The Long and Winding Road," "Sgt. Pepper's Lonely Hearts Club Band," "Can't Buy Me Love," "Eleanor Rigby," "My Brave Face," "I Saw Her Standing There," "Coming Up," "Let It Be," "Hey Jude," "Get Back" and the *Abbey Road* medley. The U.K. version of the *Highlights!* CD was also released in Canada, and the vinyl LP was issued in Australia.

Nov 26: Single "All My Trials"/"C Moon" (Paul) (Parlophone R 6278). A side previously released; first release of B side from Oct 26, 1989 Milan soundcheck.

■ 12-inch single (12 R 6278) and CD single (CDR 6278) added "Mull of Kintyre"/"Put It There"; first release of "Mull of Kintyre" from Paul's Jun 23 Glasgow show, not released in the U.S.; "Put It There" is taken from *Tripping the Live Fantastic*.

Dec 3: CD single "All My Trials"/"C Moon"/"Lennon Medley" (Paul) (Parlophone CDRX 6278). First release

"All My Trials" (© MPL Communications Ltd.). The second edition of this U.K. CD single replaced bonus tracks with Paul's live medley of three Lennon compositions (all of them Lennon/McCartney copyrights), "Help!" "Strawberry Fields Forever" and "Give Peace a Chance."

of Lennon medley from Paul's Jun 28 Liverpool concert, comprising "Strawberry Fields Forever"/"Help!"/"Give Peace a Chance." The medley was not released in the U.S.

Dec 14: CD *Testimony* (John) (Magnum Music Group; Thunderbolt CDTB 095). Interview recorded by RKO Radio Dec 8, 1980, just hours before Lennon's death. The interview is often mistakenly listed as having been recorded by Bob Miles, who merely acts as narrator. A shorter edit of the interview was released in Apr 1984 in the U.S. on *Reflections and Poetry*, and in the U.K. on the Baktabak LP and picture disc CD *The Last Word*. *Testimony*, however, runs longer than any of the others at 73:54; the Baktabak CD runs 55:13.

Dec: CD/LP *Liverpool Press Conference June 1990* (Paul) (Wax FORNO1/P1/CD1; color vinyl and picture discs). Paul's Jun 28 Liverpool press conference on picture disc, color vinyl and picture CD boxed edition with three color postcards. First release.

1991

Mar 4: CD *Ringo* (Ringo) (EMI CD-EMS 1386; full CD number: CDP 7 95884 2), cassette (TC EMS 1386). Adds bonus tracks "Down and Out," "It Don't Come Easy" and "Early 1970."

Mar 11: CD *Give My Regards to Broad Street* (Paul) (CDP 7 46043 2), LP (EL 2602781/0) and cassette (EL 2602780). Reissue.

■ CD *Pipes of Peace* (Paul) (EMI CDP 7 46018 2), LP (PCTC 1652301) and cassette (TC PCTC 1652301). Reissue.

■ LP and CD *George Harrison, Ringo Starr—1980's Press Conferences* (George/Ringo) (Wax Records). 1985 interview with George taped in New Zealand, and a Nov 28, 1984 Atlanta press conference with Ringo. The material was released on a color vinyl LP, a picture disc LP and a CD boxed set with two color postcards. First release.

Mar 25: Single "Wilbury Twist"/"New Blue Moon" (instrumental) (George/Traveling Wilburys) (Wilbury/Warner Bros. W0018), cassette single (W0018C); also issued as a 7-inch with several postcards (W0018W). 12-inch single (W0018T) and CD single (W0018CD) added "Cool Dry Place." All previously released.

May 20: CD *Unplugged (The Official Bootleg)* (Paul) (Parlophone CDPCSD 116 and CDP 7964132), LP (EMI/Hispa VOX PCSP 116/796 4131), cassette (PC-PCSP 116). First release; contains part of Paul's Jan 25 performance at Limehouse Studios for MTV's "Unplugged" television series, aired Apr 3 in the U.S. The CD contains "Be-Bop-a-Lula," "I Lost My Little Girl," "Here, There and Everywhere," "Blue Moon of Kentucky," "We Can Work It Out," "San Francisco Bay Blues," "I've Just Seen a Face," "Every Night," "She's a Woman," "Hi-Heel Sneakers," "And I Love Her," "That Would Be Something," "Blackbird," "Ain't No Sunshine" (vocal: Hamish Stuart), "Good Rockin' Tonight," "Singing the Blues," "Junk" (instrumental). LP features Spanish-language liner notes on jacket and label.

Aug 12: Cassette singles set: EMI reissued all 22 original U.K. Beatles singles on cassettes (TCR 4949–TCR 5833).

Aug 19: Double CD *The Concert for Bangla Desh* (Epic 468835-2) and double cassette (468835-4).

Aug: LP *Introspective* (Baktabak LINT 5004) and cassette (MINT 5004). Interview album.

Sep 30: CD *CHOBA B CCCP (The Russian Album)* (Paul) (Parlophone CD-PCSD 117/CDP 7 97615 2). CD release of album originally issued only in the Soviet Union Oct 31, 1988, with "I'm in Love Again" added to the original 13 songs: "Kansas City," "Twenty Flight Rock," "Lawdy Miss Clawdy," "Bring It on Home to Me," "Lucille," "Don't Get Around Much Anymore," "That's All Right (Mama)," "Ain't That a Shame," "Crackin' Up," "Just Because," "Midnight Special," "Summertime" and "I'm Gonna Be a Wheel Someday."

Nov: CD and LP *Press Conferences/1964–1966* (both discs: Discussion REVOL 4). Various press conference clips.

Dec: CD and LP *Paul McCartney: Press Conferences Tokyo/Chicago 1990* (Paul) (both discs: Discussion LMW 281F). Press conferences of Mar 1 and Jul 29, 1990.

1992

Jan 6: CD *Music from the Motion Picture Curly Sue* (Ringo) (Giant/Warner Bros. 7599 24439 2) (cassette: 7599 2 4439 4). Soundtrack album contains the first U.K. release of Ringo's recording of "You Never Know."

Jan 27: CDs *Living in the Material World* (EMI CDP 7 94110 2), *Dark Horse* (CDP 7 98079 2) and *Extra Texture (Read All About It)* (CDP 7 98080 2) (all George); U.K. additional catalog numbers: CD-PAS 10006, CD-PAS 10008 and CD-PAS 10009. Contents unchanged.

May 4: Single "Weight of the World"/"After All These Years" (Private Music 115 392); CD single "Don't Be Cruel" (665 392) added.

May 22: CD *Time Takes Time* (Ringo) (Private Music 262 902; cassette: 412 902). First U.K. and U.S. release of "Weight of the World," "Don't Know a Thing About Love," "Don't Go Where the Road Don't Go," "Golden Blunders," "All in the Name of Love," "I Don't Believe You," "Runaways," "After All These Years," "In a Heartbeat," and "What Goes Around."

Special Release Discography

The records listed in this section contain unique Beatles recordings, not widely available elsewhere, that were sold or issued on a limited basis or only in narrow geographic regions, usually in limited numbers. A few of them are promos given to radio stations at the time the record in question was released to the public. Virtually every Beatles group and solo release was accompanied by one or more such promos, often with stereo and mono versions of the song, sometimes in edited form, in a different mix or with a different running time. Only promos for records that were never actually issued or that feature a unique, otherwise unavailable recording, mix or edit are included in this list, thus eliminating the bulk of promos. Listing and describing all the promos in detail would require a separate book (see Cox and Lindsay).

1964

Early Feb: "The Beatles Open-End Interview" (Capitol Compact 33 PRO 2548/2549). Seven-inch promo issued to disc jockeys to simulate an interview with The Beatles. It appears on U.S. *Timeless II 1/2*, *The British Are Coming*, and U.K. *The Gospel According to: The Beatles*, with the questions dubbed in by Bob Miles. The first two records falsely ascribe it to a Feb 9 interview with Miles.

Feb 16: The Beatles were interviewed at the Deauville Hotel in Miami by Detroit disc jockey Lee Alan; released on a 45 RPM single "A Trip to Miami"/"A Trip to Miami Part 2" (Lee Alan Presents).

Feb: LP *Beatlemania Tour Coverage* (INS Radio News Doc 1). An open-end interview LP produced by Ed Rudy for disc jockeys.

Apr 24: *The Beatles Second Open-End Interview* was recorded and issued as a 7-inch U.S. promo (Capitol Compact 33 PRO-2598/2599); similar to Feb issue.

Jun 5: "You Can't Do That"/"Music City KFWBeatles" (Capitol Custom RB-2637/2638). Includes a Beatles interview by Wink Martindale. Sold in Los Angeles by Wallich's Music City Record Stores and radio station KFWB. A tiny clip from this disc was included on the U.S. LP *The Golden Beatles*.

Jun 26: "A Hard Day's Night" (United Artists SP-2357). A U.S. 7-inch promo with spots and film dialogue.

Sep 14: "The Beatles Introduce New Songs" (Capitol PRO 2720). John introduces Cilla Black's "It's for You"; Paul introduces Peter and Gordon's "I Don't Want to See You Again"; they each sign off as well.

That fall: Seven-inch 45 RPM, "Remember, We Don't Like Them We Love Them" (ZTSC 97436/7). Official IBBB interview by Tom Clay. Disc is labeled "Not for Sale" and was probably distributed to radio stations. The record contains an interview with The Beatles conducted during their 1964 U.S. tour. Clay wonders aloud if Ringo can actually sing and play drums at the same time.

1965

Mar: *Capitol: Silver Platter Service* (Capitol). Promo sampler LP from Capitol containing a four-minute interview with John and Paul.

Aug: "Help! [United Artists Presents . . .]" (United Artists). Promo containing radio spots. An open-end interview with The Beatles promoting the film *Help!* was also released. A copy with Wink Martindale dubbing in the questions was released in the U.S. on LP *The Golden Beatles*. The open-end interview was released in full on a special 7-inch picture disc issued in 1990 with the third edition of *The Beatles Price Guide for American Records*. It also appeared on the Dec 1988 U.K. CD *Beatles: Conversation Series*.

1966

Mar 25: An interview with The Beatles was recorded by Tom Lodge of Radio Caroline and released on the flexi disc "Sound of the Stars" (Lyn 996). The record was offered free to readers of *Disc and Music Echo* magazine and contained interview clips with several stars.

That fall: One-sided LP *I Apologize* (Sterling Products 8893-6481; sold by Chicago newspaper). Contains Beatles' Aug 11 Chicago press conference, including John "apologizing" for his remarks about Christianity.

Oct 14: LP *Beatle Views* (BV-1966). Sold by Ring Around the Pops, an organization for the blind, with proceeds going to the blind. Includes first release of interviews by Ken Douglas from the Aug U.S. tour and portion of previously released Aug 11 press conference.

That year: LP *Beatles Blast at Stadium Described by Erupting Fans* (Audio Journal). Documentary LP of interviews and events surrounding the second Shea Stadium concert Aug 23.

1968

That year: Kenny Everett recorded an interview with The Beatles at Abbey Road during Jun 5–6 recording sessions for "Don't Pass Me By." The interview was heard in edited form on "The Kenny Everett Show" on Jun 9 in the U.K. The interview was commercially released by Apple only in Italy on EP *Una Sensazionale Intervista Con I Beatles (A Sensational Interview with The Beatles)* (Apple DPR-108), one of four 45 RPM EPs contained in a set, each with a different picture sleeve. Although it was subsequently released on other discs (see Jun 5–6, 1968 in "Recording Chronology"), this was the only official Apple release of the interview.

1969

May 29: John was interviewed by telephone by Tom Campbell and Bill Holley of San Francisco radio station KYA during the Montreal bed-in. The interview was issued by the station on a blue vinyl 7-inch 45 RPM disc, "The KYA 1969 Peace Talk" (KYA 1969).

That summer: John and Yoko's Nov 1968 recordings of "No Bed for Beatle John," "Radio Play" and Ono's "Song for John" were issued in the U.S. on a special flexi disc that was Issue 7, Selection 7 of *Aspen* magazine. Slightly different mixes appeared on *Unfinished Music No. 2: Life with the Lions*, released in May.

Dec: (aired early 1970): "John Lennon on Ronnie Hawkins" (Cotillion PR 104/105). Seven-inch 45 RPM vinyl promo contains two Lennon messages for Ronnie Hawkins' "Down in the Alley" "Short Rap" (0:06)/"Long Rap" (1:24).

That year: "Hey Jude" (3:25 edit)/"Revolution" (*Pocket Disc* Apple/Americom 2276/M-221). Unique 3:25 edit of "Hey Jude" issued on 4-inch flexi disc sold in vending machines in the U.S.

1970

May: One-sided promo *Dialogue from The Beatles' Motion Picture "Let It Be"* (Apple Beatles Promo-1970). Disc sent to members of the fan club includes dialogue from the *Let It Be* film soundtrack. "Let It Be" (United Artists ULP 42370) promo containing radio spots for the film also issued.

1971

Feb: "Another Day"/"Oh Woman, Oh Why" (Paul) (Apple PRO 6193/4). This Apple promo has a unique mix of "Oh Woman, Oh Why," including different gunshot effects, not released on any other record.

May: LP *Brung to Ewe By* (Apple SPRO-6210) (Paul). Promo for Paul's *Ram* album includes 15 radio spots and "Now Hear This Song of Mine," sung by Paul.

That year: The *Liverpool Echo* newspaper released the album *Echoes of the Merseyside* (LPDE 101), which featured interview clips taped with many sports and entertainment figures, including a five-second clip of John Lennon. The album's title was later mistaken for an unreleased Beatles song title.

1972

Early that year: A U.K. promo of a Wings' single, "Love Is Strange"/"I Am Your Singer" (Apple R 5932) was distributed, but the single was never released.

Apr 24: John's "Woman Is the Nigger of the World" single was scheduled for U.K. release as Parlophone R 5953, and promos were issued, but the single was never issued there.

1973

Apr: While recording his LP *Ringo*, Ringo recorded a 30-second antidrug radio public service announcement, issued on a special LP *Get Off* (National Association of Progressive Radio Announcers, Inc.; pressed by MCA Records; no number), released to radio stations and containing several messages from various artists.

Nov: LP *Ringo* (Ringo) (Apple SWAL 3413). Promotional copy of LP on which "Six O'Clock" runs 5:26; it is

4:05 on the commercially released LP. The longer version was also released on cassette and 8-track tape releases of the album.

Dec: Promo LP *Radio Interview Special with Paul and Linda McCartney (for Promotional Use with "Band on the Run" Album)* (Capitol/National Features Corp. PRO-2955/6). An open-end interview LP to promote Paul's LP *Band on the Run*.

1974

Jan: "Jet" (Paul) (Promo; Apple P-1871). Contains the full (4:08) version in stereo and a 2:49 edit in mono.

Feb: "Ding Dong, Ding Dong" (George) (Promo; Apple P-1879) contains a 3:12 edit in mono and stereo; that mono mix is different from the official release. There are two different promos with this number. One features the full version (5:09) in stereo and a 3:50 edit in mono; the other contains the 3:50 edit in both stereo and mono.

Apr: "Band on the Run" (Promo: Apple P-1873) (Paul).

Oct 16: A six-second message by John is included on "Happy First Birthday from Cuddley Capital Starring K. Everett Esq. and Everybody Who Is Anybody" (Warner Brothers SAM 20), released in U.K. on the first anniversary of London's Capital Radio.

Nov: "Dark Horse" (George) (Promo; Apple P-1877). Two promos were issued with this number. One has the standard 3:50 edit in mono and stereo; the other has a 2:48 edit in mono and stereo.

- LP *Dark Horse Radio Special* (George) (Dark Horse—No number). Promo LP with George discussing his new Dark Horse record company. Includes songs by other artists.

Dec: "No. 9 Dream" (John) (Promo; Capitol P-1878). Contains a unique 2:58 edit in both stereo and mono; official release runs 4:46.

1975

Mar: "Ain't That a Shame" (stereo/mono versions); "Slippin; and Slidin'" (stereo/mono versions) (John) (Apple P-1883). Two different U.S. promos with this number were issued, each featuring one of the songs in stereo and mono. No official single was ever issued.

Sep: "Letting Go" (Paul) (Promo; Capitol PRO-4145). U.S. promo featured mono and stereo mixes of the song; the mono mix on the promo is a unique one not available on any other disc. The standard single release features a clean introduction rather than the crossfade found on the album release.

1976

Feb: LP *An Introduction to Roy Harper* (Paul) (Chrysalis PRO 620). Promo LP for Harper's LP *When an Old Cricketer Leaves the Crease*. This promo LP includes two tracks with comments by Paul.

Apr: "Silly Love Songs" (5:54)/"Silly Love Songs" (3:28 edit) (Promo; Capitol P-4256) (Paul).

Jun: U.S. promo "Let 'Em In" (3:43)/"Let 'Em In" (5:08) (Paul) (Capitol P-4293). Two promos were released, both with the same number; one contains these two edits in mono, the other in stereo; they are the only releases of the 3:43 edit. Labeling on a French 12-inch edition of the "Let 'Em In"/"Beware My Love" single, with custom leopard-skin labels and sleeve (EMI 2C052-98.062 Y), falsely lists the A and B sides as "Special Disco Mixes," but the French 12-inch contains the standard A and B sides released worldwide.

Sep: "A Dose of Rock & Roll" (Ringo) (Promo; Atlantic 45-3361). Contains edits with and without the introduction.

Nov: Promo LP *Dark Horse Records Presents a Personal Music Dialogue with George Harrison at 33 1/3* (George) (Dark Horse; PRO-649). Promo interview/music LP with George discussing his new LP, *Thirty-Three & 1/3*.

That year: LP *The History of Syracuse Music Vol. VIII/IX* (ECEIP 1015/16/17/18). Includes first release of excerpts from John and Yoko's Syracuse press conference of Oct 8, 1971. Additional excerpts were released in 1980 on *Vol. X/XI*.

1977

Feb: "Maybe I'm Amazed" (Paul) (Promo; Capitol PRO-8570/1). Contains mono and stereo mixes of a 3:43 edit. 12-inch promo (PRO-8574) contains stereo and mono mixes of both the full (5:11) version and the 3:43 edit.

Oct: "Drowning in a Sea of Love" (Ringo) (Promo; Atlantic 3412). Contains full (5:08) version and a 3:39 edit.

Nov: U.S. promo "Mull of Kintyre" (3:31 edit)/"Girl's School" (3:19 edit) (Paul) (Capitol SPRO 8746/7).

That year: "Original Beatles Medley" (Disconet Vol. 9 Program 9 MWDN402A; reissued in 1979 as Volume 4, program 2). Issued to subscribers of Disconet D.J. service. The medley, produced by Ray Lenahan, includes "Day Tripper," "Taxman," "Birthday," "Dizzy Miss Lizzie," "A Hard Day's Night," "I Should Have Known Better," "Got to Get You Into My Life," "All My Loving," "I Saw Her Standing There," "Magical Mystery Tour," "Rock & Roll Music" and "Slow Down."

1978

Mar: "With a Little Luck" (Paul) (Promo; Capitol PRO-8812). Contains a 3:13 edit in both mono and stereo; full version runs 5:45.

Apr: "Lipstick Traces" (Ringo) (Promo; Portrait 6-70015). Contains mono and stereo mixes of the song; the mono side is a unique mix.

Aug: "London Town" (Paul) (Promo; Capitol P-4625). Contains full (4:10) version in mono and a 3:48 edit in stereo.

1979

That year: LP *The Warner Brothers Music Show: Monty Python Examines "The Life of Brian"* (Warner Bros. WBMS 110). Includes comments by George.

■ Double LP *The Ultimate Radio Bootleg Vol. III* (Mercury MK 2-121). Contains an Apr 18, 1964 telephone interview with The Beatles by Art Roberts and Ron Riley of Chicago radio station WLS.

1980

May: Double LP set *The McCartney Interview* (Paul) (Columbia A25-821). Released to radio stations to promote *McCartney II*. One disc is identical to the commercially released interview LP; the other disc contains only McCartney's answers, making it an open-end interview LP.
Jul: "Waterfalls" (Paul) (Promo; Columbia 1-11335). Contains the full (4:41) version and a 3:22 edit.
Oct: U.S. 12-inch promo "(Just Like) Starting Over" (John)/"Kiss Kiss Kiss" (Yoko) (Geffen PRO-A-919), features an otherwise unreleased longer version of A side (4:17), the result of a longer fadeout.
That year: "The David Peel Interview" (Orange OR-70078 PD; 7-inch picture disc), a mid-1972 interview with John by an unknown person concerning David Peel; also features non-Beatles track by Peel and the Apple Band. At least part of the interview also appears on *John Lennon: A Day on the Radio* (NBC 83-49), *John Lennon for President* (Orange 005) and *The John Lennon Interview* (Orange 70079 PD).
■ LP *The History of Syracuse Music Vol. X/XI* (ECEIP 1019/20/21/22). Contains first release of additional excerpts from John and Yoko's Oct 8, 1971 Syracuse press conference. Other excerpts had been released on *Vol. VIII/IX* in 1976.

1981

Apr: "Rockshow" (Paul); 7-inch promo for film *Rockshow*; one-sided disc with two 60-second radio spots and one 30-second spot (Miramax Films).

1982

Middle of Mar: Capitol pressed following single for release with LP *Reel Music*: "The Beatles Movie Medley"/"Fab 4 on Film (Beatles Talk About *Hard Day's Night*)" (Capitol B 5100). Due to legal problems, the single was withdrawn, but it had already been released on 12-inch (Capitol SPRO-9758) and 7-inch (PB-5100) promos. This was the only release of the B side, recorded May 24, 1964.
Oct: "The Girl Is Mine" (Paul and M. Jackson) (Promo; Epic 34-03288). Two promos released with same number; one contains full (3:41) version on both sides; the other features a 3:32 edit that eliminates Paul's dialogue with Jackson; label lists this as "New Edited Version."
■ "OUI Presents The Silver Beatles: 'Like Dreamers Do'/'Love of the Loved'" (Backstage Records). Each side of the flexi disc contains both songs from the Decca audition of Jan 1, 1962. Offered free by mail from *Oui* magazine in its Oct 1982 issue. These are two of the three Lennon/McCartney compositions omitted from most releases of the Decca material.

1983

Apr 15: LP *Liverpool 1963–1968* (U.K.) Contains "How I Won the War," with some of John's lines from the film, "America" by Rory Storm and The Hurricanes (with Ringo's backing vocal).
Jun 16: During the summer of 1982 Ringo recorded *"In My Car," "As Far as We Can Go," *"Hopeless," "Alibi," "Be My Baby," *"She's About a Mover," *"I Keep Forgettin'," "Picture Show Life," "Everybody's in a Hurry But Me" (instrumental), "I'm Going Down," all released on the album *Old Wave* on Jun 16 in Germany (Bellaphon/Boardwalk 260.16.029) and Jun 24 in Canada (RCA/Canada DXL 1-3233). There has been no U.S. or U.K. release of these songs to date except (*), released in the U.S. Feb 24, 1989 on the CD *Starr Struck: Best of Ringo Starr Vol. 2* (LP contained only three of these songs, omitting "Hopeless"). *Old Wave* was also released in Brazil, Mexico, Japan, South Africa, Australia and New Zealand. A single, "In My Car"/"As Far as We Can Go," was also released in Germany (Bellaphon/Boardwalk 100.16.012). All releases, except Germany, were on the RCA label.
Late that year: A poor audio quality CD release of *Abbey Road* was issued in Japan by EMI-Toshiba several years before official EMI Beatles CDs were released and was, technically, the first Beatles CD (Odeon CP 35-3016). It was deleted in 1985.

1984

Jan: A U.S. promo for the rerelease of "I Want to Hold Your Hand" (Capitol 7-PRO-9076) was issued containing both mono and stereo versions of the song.
Feb: EP *The Carroll James Interview with The Beatles* (Carroll James CJEP 3301). Washington, D.C. interview of Feb 11, 1964; released in the U.S. via mail order.
■ Cassette *Historic Interviews: The Beatles' First Day in America* (Robbins' Nest Inc. and Beatlefest Inc.). Contains interviews taped by Fred Robbins on Feb 7, 1964.
Mar: "I'm Stepping Out" (Promo; Polydor 821-107-7 DJ). Contains standard (4:06) version and a 3:33 edit.
May 11: "Borrowed Time" (John) (Promo; Polydor 821-204-7 DJ). Contains full (4:30) version and a 3:45 edit.
Jun 9: LP *De Bietels Tussen de Bollen* (*The Beatles Among the Bulbs*) (Beatles Unlimited BU-1-1984), issued via mail order by "Beatles Unlimited," the Dutch Beatles Fan Club. The album included a Jun 5, 1964 Beatles press conference and an interview on Dutch TV, where they also mimed to released recordings of "She Loves You," "All My Loving," "Twist and Shout," "Roll Over Beethoven," "Long Tall Sally" and "Can't Buy Me Love." The album also contains instrumentals and audience singalong from The Beatles' Jun 6, 1964 evening concert at Blokker Exhibition Hall. The Beatles' vocals are not actually heard on these recordings, which are taken from the Dutch AVRO-KRO-VARA Radio/TV broadcast tapes and Polygon Movie archives: "I Saw Her Standing There," "I Want to Hold Your Hand," "All My Loving,"

"She Loves You," "Twist and Shout" and a very short excerpt of "Long Tall Sally."

Oct 29: A special version of Paul's "No More Lonely Nights" (Arthur Baker's Mole Mix) was released in the U.K. to D.J.s only on a one-sided 12-inch promo with a white label (Parlophone 12 R DJ 6080).

1986

Early that year: "Imagine"/"Come Together" (John) (Capitol SPRO 9585/6). A U.S. 12-inch promo with John's live versions of these songs taken from the LP *John Lennon: Live in New York City*; no single was actually released. The promo came in a plain cover with a special sticker.

Feb 3: *The Mixes* LP (DMC 37/2) for Feb 1986 in the U.K. included a special disco mix Beatles medley called "From Us to You," running 5:24, that included parts of "From Me to You," "Day Tripper," "I Want to Hold Your Hand," "Please Please Me," "She Loves You," "A Hard Day's Night," "Back in the USSR," "Eight Days a Week" and "Help!" These LPs were released monthly, only to disco clubs, by Disco Mix Club; only 3,000 copies of this disc were pressed.

May: Yet another remix of Paul's "No More Lonely Nights" (7:17) appeared in the U.S. on a disco D.J.-only 12-inch released by "Hot Trax" (Columbia). This special dance edit was mixed by San Francisco disc jockey Warren Sanford.

Middle of that year: *The Beatles Live! The Beatles' First Radio Interview 27 October 1962* (LYN 17148). Flexi disc issued free with Mark Lewisohn's book *The Beatles Live!* contains the first known recorded interview with The Beatles, taped Oct 27, 1962 and aired the following day on a hospital radio station.

Jul 1: Heineken beer marketed a Beatles cassette, *Only The Beatles*, available in the U.K. by mail order. "Love Me Do," "Twist and Shout," "She Loves You," "This Boy" (fake stereo, despite claim that it is real stereo), "Eight Days a Week," "All My Loving"; (side two): "Ticket to Ride," "Yes It Is," "Ob-La-Di, Ob-La-Da," "Lucy in the Sky with Diamonds," "And I Love Her," "Strawberry Fields Forever." Includes the first stereo release of "Yes It Is," which later appeared on *Past Masters*. The Beatles, through Apple, sued on Jul 18 to halt sale of this cassette.

Jul: "Press" (Paul) (Capitol 7-PRO-9765/6). Second U.S. 7-inch promo includes unique 4:07 edit, and released 3:35 edit.

That fall: "Rock & Roll People" (John) (Capitol SPRO 9917). U.S. 12-inch promo issued as a tie-in to the *Menlove Ave.* LP; no single was ever actually issued.

■ *A Tribute to John Lennon* (John) (1986 The Quaker Oats Company). One of five paper picture discs in a series called "Great Moments in Rock 'N Roll" given away with Quaker Granola Dipps; 5¼-inch 33 1/3 RPM disc with excerpts of "Nobody Told Me," "I'm Stepping Out," "Woman," "I Don't Wanna Face It" and "Beautiful Boy (Darling Boy)," and a narration about

John. Picture is of the Imagine mosaic in New York's "Strawberry Fields" section of Central Park.

That year: LP *The History of Syracuse Music Vol. XII/XIII* (Blue Wave Records 105). Complete recording of John and Yoko's Oct 8, 1971 Syracuse press conference, different parts of which had been previously released on *Vol. VIII/IX* (1976) and *Vol. X/XI* (1980).

1987

Mar 23 (U.K.), Mar 24 (U.S.): "Let It Be" (Ferry Aid) U.K. and U.S. 7-inch and U.S. 12-inch (U.S. Profile PRO-5147/7147; U.K. Sun AID 1). A new version of "Let It Be" was recorded in London by a group of rock stars to raise funds for the victims of the Mar 6 Zeebrugge ferry disaster. Paul gave the group permission to use The Beatles' original, released version for the opening of the charity record. It was released as a 7-inch single in the U.S. and U.K., and as a 12-inch single only in the U.S. with two longer remixed versions of the recording. The U.S. releases had a slightly different picture sleeve with a replacement photo of McCartney found to be more flattering than the one used on the U.K. sleeve.

Apr 24: Single "Long Tall Sally"/"I Saw Her Standing There" (Paul) (A&M FREE 21). This 7-inch vinyl single was released only in the U.K. as a free bonus, in a separate picture sleeve, with the vinyl LP *Prince's Trust Tenth Anniversary Birthday Party*. Both songs were recorded live by Paul Jun 20, 1986, but neither was included on the LP, although "Long Tall Sally" was added to the CD release. All releases of the album included Paul's "Get Back."

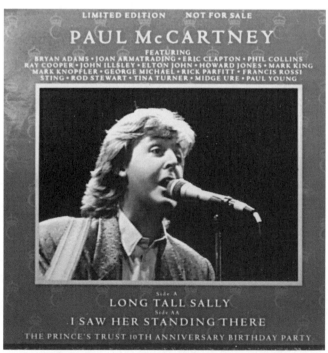

"Long Tall Sally"/"I Saw Her Standing There" (© Prince's Trust and A&M Records). The U.K. edition of the 1986 *Prince's Trust* album included this free bonus single with two additional live McCartney numbers; it was not issued in the U.S.

Dec: *Yulesville* (George) (Warner Brothers PRO-A-2896; red vinyl). U.S. promo LP issued by Warner Brothers contains a 7-second holiday greeting from George, one of several holiday messages from many of Warner's recording artists.

Late that year: "Devil's Radio (Gossip)" (George) (Dark Horse PRO-A 2889). U.S. 12-inch promo with a special picture cover; no single was ever officially released.

1988

Feb 15: *Songs by George Harrison* (George) (SGHCD 777). Special four-song vinyl EP and CD included with George's limited edition book, *Songs by George Harrison*. The special 5-inch CD and 7-inch vinyl EP (purchasers chose one) contained three previously unreleased Harrison songs: "Sat Singing" and "Flying Hour," both recorded for the *Somewhere in England* album but omitted from the release, plus "For You Blue" from George's Dec 13, 1974 concert at the Capitol Center in Largo, Maryland. The fourth song, "Lay His Head," was also left over from the original *Somewhere in England* album and had been released as the B side of "Got My Mind Set on You." The three *Somewhere in England* tracks were remixed for this release and differ from the original mixes done for that LP.

- "Cloud 9" (George) (Dark Horse PRO-CD-2924). A promo CD of George's "Cloud 9" was issued in the U.S. but no official single was ever released. The promo came with a booklet.

That spring: *The Best of Dick James* (Polygram SACD-072). Promo-only CD with three Beatles songs never before released on CD in stereo: "Please Please Me," "Ask Me Why"

and "Don't Bother Me." These are the only three Beatles titles to which James had retained publishing rights.

Sep: "Twist and Shout" (Ultimix #20; side F). U.S. D.J. 12-inch single featured an otherwise unavailable remix of The Beatles' recording of "Twist and Shout" (5:20). The record was issued to D.J.s and clubs only as part of a three-record set sold by Ultimix.

Oct 31: LP *CHOBA B CCCP* (*Back in the USSR* or *Again in the USSR*) (Paul) (Soviet Union) (Melodiya A60 00415 006). This album was originally released only in the Soviet Union and only in vinyl LP form. Several variations were released with a variety of labels and cover art. The first version contained 11 songs: "Kansas City," "Twenty Flight Rock," "Lawdy Miss Clawdy," "Bring It on Home to Me," "Lucille," "Don't Get Around Much Anymore," "That's All Right (Mama)," "Ain't That a Shame," "Crackin' Up," "Just Because" and "Midnight Special." The second version, released on Dec 24, had 13 songs, adding "I'm Gonna Be a Wheel Someday" and "Summertime." McCartney's fan club gave free copies of that version to selected club members. A rare pressing of the album contained 12 songs, adding "Summertime" to the original 11. This was not an intentional pressing, however, and was the result of a production error at one Soviet plant when converting from the original 11-song version to the 13-song second edition. A few thousand 12-track copies were accidentally pressed when one side of the 11-song version was coupled with the other side of the 13-song version. The 12-song variation, however, is considered highly collectible and valuable. The entire album was ultimately issued on CD Sep 30, 1991 in the U.K. and Oct 29, 1981 in the U.S., with a 14th track, "I'm in Love Again," added.

Nov 14: *HandMade Films Music: The 10th Anniversary* (George) (AVM 1126859). A U.K. promo-only CD release with 21 cuts running a total of 79 minutes; includes George's recordings of "Dream Away" and "Someplace Else," and a medley from the film *Water*, including "Freedom" (with George on guitar). A limited run of 1,000 copies of this CD was reportedly made. It is different from the scheduled commercial release of a 10th anniversary HandMade LP, which remains unreleased.

Nov 28: CD single "Imagine"/"Jealous Guy"/"Happy Xmas"/"Give Peace a Chance" (John) (Parlophone CDR 6199). The U.K. release of this CD single did not contain the full version of "Give Peace a Chance," but rather the same short clip from the One to One Concert that appears on the LP *Shaved Fish*, added at the end of "Happy Xmas." EMI again released the CD single in Europe, but not in the U.K., on Nov 19, 1990 with the full version of "Give Peace a Chance" (EMI 2041542).

Dec 1: *Winter Warnerland* (George) (Warner Bros. PRO-A-3328; and CD PRO-CD-3328). Warner Brothers released double LP and CD promo sampler, which included a 28-second holiday greeting from George, as Nelson Wilbury, called "Holiday I.D."

Late that year: "Stand by Me" (John) (Capitol SPRO-79453). A U.S. 12-inch promo of John's "Stand by Me" was issued by Capitol in a white jacket featuring a sticker

"Devil's Radio" (© Dark Horse Records). Although issued as a U.S. 12-inch promo with this unique cover photo, no "Devil's Radio" single was ever released.

that announced this as the second single from *Imagine: John Lennon*, but no single was actually released.

1989

Early that year: "Last Night" (George/Wilburys) (Wilbury/Warner Bros. PRO-CD-3337). A 5-inch promo CD of The Traveling Wilburys' "Last Night" was released in the U.S., but no single was ever officially released.

Mar 1: LP *HandMade Films' 10th Anniversary Album* (George) (AVM/AVMC/AVMCD 2002: double LP/cassette/CD). Unreleased to date, originally scheduled for U.K. release on this date. The album was to have included Harrison's "Dream Away" (LP version), "The Hottest Gong in Town," from the film *Shanghai Surprise*, the title song from *Shanghai Surprise*, "Freedom" from the film *Water*, which features Harrison, Eric Clapton and Ringo, and a previously unreleased song. It was subsequently announced that the album was indefinitely postponed, and it has not appeared to date. The album should not be confused with the promo CD *HandMade Films Music: The 10th Anniversary* (AVM 1126859), issued Nov 14, 1988.

Jul: "Good Sign" (6:52)/(7:22 Groove Mix) (Paul) (Parlophone GOOD 1). U.K. promo-only 12-inch single featuring Paul's "Good Sign," also released on U.K. 12-inch "This One" single (12RX 6223), and the otherwise unreleased "Groove Mix." Only 500 copies of this limited edition promo were reportedly issued to British club/disco DJs. McCartney's name and MPL insignia were not on the labels or sleeves, and a limited number of pressings with plain white labels were also issued.

Aug 2: "This One" (Paul) (Capitol 7PRO-79700). Seven-inch 45 RPM vinyl promo of Paul's "This One" was issued in the U.S., very likely the last Paul McCartney vinyl single that will ever be released in that country; the single was officially issued there on only cassette. The release coincided with Capitol's announcement that it was discontinuing most 7-inch vinyl singles; a vinyl single was released in Canada (Capitol B-44438). To date, no subsequent U.S. McCartney 7-inch vinyl release of any kind has appeared. Seven-inch vinyl test pressings of "Figure of Eight" (featuring the long 12-inch U.K. version) were circulated in Nov 1989 with blank white labels (7PRO-79889), but no corresponding promo or vinyl single was released.

Aug: "Ou Est Le Soleil?" (Paul) (Disconet Vol 11 Program 9 MWDN 1109 B; Side B). Includes a 6:57 disco version of the song called "Dennis Muyet Edit." It also notes "special thanks: Frank Murray." Disconet provided the discs to D.J. subscribers of its service. The mix appeared again in Mar 1991 on a Disconet CD sampler.

That fall: Several promos of Paul's "Figure of Eight" (Version II) were issued: (1) U.K. 7-inch vinyl promo with labels indicating two different edits (3:59 and 3:57 edits listed) (Parlophone RDJ 6235A); (2) U.K. 7-inch promo (4:01, listed as 4:03)/"Ou Est Le Soleil?" (3:57) (Parlophone RDJ 6235). This edit of "Figure of Eight" was also released officially in England on both editions of the "Figure of Eight" 5-inch CD single. The promo B side is a rare 3:57 edit. (3) U.S. promo 5-inch CD single with two edits (4:01 and 5:11 edits) (Capitol DPRO-79871).

- "Ou Est le Soleil?" (Paul) (Capitol DPRO-79836). U.S. promo 5-inch CD with a unique 4:15 edit of the Shep Pettibone remix.

- Seven-inch vinyl test pressings of "Figure of Eight" were circulated in the U.S. with blank white labels (7PRO-79889), but no promo or vinyl single was released in the U.S.

Oct 9: *Seattle Press Conference (8/21/64)* (Topaz T-1353). Special limited edition 7-inch single with Beatles Seattle press conference of Aug 21, 1964.

Oct 10: "Poor Little Girl" (George) (Dark Horse PRO-CD-3775). U.S. promo CD with George's "Poor Little Girl" contains a 3:25 edit and the 4:32 *The Best of Dark Horse: 1976–1989* edit. No official single was released in the U.S.

Nov 10: *Hitmakers Top 40 CD Sampler* (Paul) (Capitol Vol. 29, Nov 10, 1989). The time listed for "Figure of Eight" (Version II) on this promo CD sampler is 3:59, but the actual time is 4:01, the same edit released on both issues of the U.K. 5-inch CD single.

Nov 23: Single "Party Party" (Paul) (Parlophone R 6238) and 3-inch CD single (CD3R 6238). One-track single issued as an etched 7-inch and 3-inch picture disc CD single included with vinyl LP and CD editions of the *Flowers in the Dirt* World Tour Pack. The 7-inch single was etched on its blank side. Both singles issued in custom picture sleeves.

Nov 27: "Party Party" (6:21 Forest mix)/(5:36 Tour Pack Version) (Paul) (Parlophone 12RDJ 6238). Limited Edition U.K. 12-inch promo released only to club D.J.s. This was the only release of the 6:21 remix.

"This One" (© MPL Communications Ltd.). Paul's 7-inch vinyl promo issued in the U.S.

"Party Party" (© MPL Communications Ltd.). This single was issued only as a one-sided etched 7-inch vinyl and 3-inch picture disc CD bonus included with World Tour pack editions of *Flowers in the Dirt*.

That year: *Gold Disc 3* (Century 21). Promo-only CD with true stereo version of "And I Love Her" as well as an excerpt of the mono version.

1990

Feb 13: A 5-inch promo CD (Capitol DPRO-79979) was released in the U.S. with a unique edit of Paul's "We Got Married" (4:00, listed as 3:42) and the *Flowers in the Dirt* version; no U.S. single was released.

Feb 20: *Paul McCartney Rocks* (Paul) (Capitol DPRO-79987). Five-inch promo-only CD picture disc issued in the U.S. with 10 McCartney and Wings songs: "Figure of Eight" (Version II; 4:01 edit, listed as 3:59), "We Got Married" (4:55), "Rough Ride" (Version I 4:43), "Band on the Run" (5:15), "Uncle

Paul McCartney Rocks (© MPL Communications Ltd.). A unique U.S. promo-only CD album with several rare tracks and unique mixes.

Albert/Admiral Halsey" (4:50), "Live and Let Die" (3:15), "Party Party" (3:40 edit), "I Wanna Cry" (4:40), "Junior's Farm" (4:20) and "Don't Get Around Much Anymore" (2:51). This was the only release of the 3:40 edit of "Party Party."

Mar 24: "It's Now or Never" (Paul) (10-inch vinyl promo: NME PRO 10-1990; 5-inch CD promo: NME CD PRO 1990). Ten-inch vinyl and 5-inch CD U.K. promos of Paul's "It's Now or Never," also released on the U.K. album *The Last Temptation of Elvis*.

Mar: *The Beatles Open-End Interview: A Hard Day's Night* (Cicadelic-BIOdisc 001). Special picture disc issued with book *Picture Discs of the World Price Guide*.

Late Mar: *Flowers in the Dirt* (Paul) (Japan Double CD Pack) (Japan: EMI/Odeon TOCP 6118-9). Special Japan-only release containing both the standard *Flowers in the Dirt* CD plus a bonus CD with the only official release of "P.S. Love Me Do" (3:40); (a live concert version was released only in the U.K. as a bonus track on 12-inch and CD "Birthday" singles). The rest of the bonus CD contains a 28-second spoken message from Paul, "The Long and Winding Road" (Version III 3:51), "Loveliest Thing" (3:59), "Rough Ride" (Version II 4:53), "Ou Est le Soleil?" (4:50 U.K. 7-inch Pettibone remix), "Mama's Little Girl" (3:41), "Same Time Next Year" (3:06) and "Party Party" (5:35).

Jun: *Help! Open-End Interview '65: The Beatles and Radio WFUN* (Cicadelic Records/Beatles Price Guide). Special edition of open-end interview promo originally released in connection with The Beatles' film *Help!* in 1965. This reissue was included with the third edition of *The Beatles Price Guide For American Records*. The disc adds material omitted from the original release.

Oct 8: "She's My Baby" (George/Wilburys) (album version 3:12) (Wilbury/Warner Bros. PRO-CD-4518). U.S. 5-inch promo CD; no single was actually released in the U.S.

Oct 12: CD single "Act Naturally"/"It Don't Come Easy"/ "Rocky Mountain Way"/"The Weight" (Ringo/Joe Walsh)

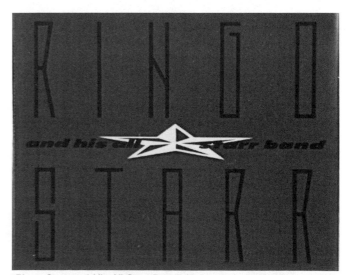

"Ringo Starr and His All-Starr Band" (© Monteco B.V.). For once U.S. buyers got something not issued in the U.K.; this four-track bonus CD single was included with Rykodisc's deluxe edition of the CD and included two tracks omitted from the album, one of them Ringo's "Act Naturally."

(Rykodisc RCD5-1019). Bonus 5-inch CD single included only with the U.S. deluxe limited edition CD *Ringo Starr and His All-Starr Band*. "Act Naturally" (Ringo) and "Rocky Mountain Way" (Joe Walsh) were omitted from the album and were not released in the U.K.

Dec: EMI released the special 16-track promotional CD sampler *Christmas Fun and Great New Hits for '91* (CD XMAS 1), which included a 10-second Christmas greeting from Paul, not available elsewhere, as an introduction to his live version of "The Long and Winding Road" from *Tripping the Live Fantastic*.

1991

Early that year: U.S. 5-inch promo CD "Good Golly Miss Molly" (by Little Richard)/"Good Golly Miss Molly" (by John Goodman) (Polydor CDP 399) from *King Ralph* film soundtrack. Ringo joined Little Richard, Tom Petty and Jeff Lynne (who produced the Little Richard version) on this otherwise unreleased recording, a remake of Little Richard's classic. There is no Beatles involvement in the Goodman version.

Mar: "Ou Est le Soleil?" (Paul) (Disconet Dennis Muyet Edit, 6:57) released on CD sampler *Dance Classics Volume*

#3 (Disconet DN-03). This mix was previously released by Disconet.

■ Promo CD single "Inside Out" (George/Traveling Wilburys) (Wilbury/Warner Bros. PRO-CD-4652) issued in the U.S.; no single was actually released.

That spring: LP *Tripping the Live Fantastic Highlights!* (Paul) Columbia House Record Club edition (Capitol C1-595379). Offered to U.S. club members under license from Capitol Records, this abbreviated 12-track vinyl edition of *Highlights!* contained the only U.S. release of Paul's live version of "All My Trials." The 17-track Capitol CD *Highlights!* did not contain that song, but the U.K. edition did, as did several U.K. singles. This LP is the only U.S. or U.K. vinyl release of *Highlights!* and the only U.S. release of "All My Trials."

Nov 12: Promo CD single "You Never Know" (Ringo) (Giant/Warner Bros. PRO-CD-5153). Issued in U.S.; contains Ringo's recording, otherwise available only on the soundtrack album *Music from the Motion Picture Curly Sue*; no single was actually released.

Nov 20: Special Japan issue of CD *Paul McCartney's Liverpool Oratorio* included a six-minute spoken message by Paul (Toshiba-EMI) on a 3-inch CD.

Alternate Versions and Bonus Tracks

Over the years many Beatles songs have been released in more than one version. The differences range from slight variations in the stereo and mono mixes to completely different recordings of the same song. Seven Beatles tracks have never been released in stereo: both versions of "Love Me Do," "I'll Get You," "Only a Northern Song," "P.S. I Love You," "She Loves You" and "You Know My Name (Look Up the Number)." Still, other songs originally appeared only on singles or as bonus tracks on multisong 12-inch and CD singles, which are the modern equivalent of the old 7-inch 45 RPM EP.

This section alphabetically lists all of The Beatles' songs released in more than one version and songs that were not included on albums. Most solo ex-Beatles nonalbum titles that later appeared on various "greatest hits" compilations have been omitted, although some are included where there is something of additional interest about them. The solo compilation albums include John's *Shaved Fish*, *The John Lennon Collection*, *Imagine: John Lennon* and the CD boxed *Lennon* set; George's *The Best of George Harrison* and *The Best of Dark Horse 1976–1989*; Paul's *Wings Greatest* and *All the Best*; and Ringo's *Blast From Your Past* and *Starr-Struck*.

Many live concert recordings by The Beatles, both group and solo, have been released, most of them in album form. Only those live recordings that did not originally appear on such albums have been included in the following list. A few live tracks that were released only in one country, only on singles or in limited editions are included. The Beatles live concert albums are (by The Beatles): *The Beatles at the Hollywood Bowl*; (by John Lennon): *The Plastic Ono Band—Live Peace in Toronto 1969*, *John Lennon: Live in New York City*; (by Paul McCartney): *Wings over America*, *Tripping the Live Fantastic*, *Tripping the Live Fantastic Highlights!*, *Unplugged (the Official Bootleg)*, *Concerts for the People of Kampuchea* (one side of LP); (by George Harrison and Ringo Starr): *The Concert for Bangla Desh*; (by Ringo Starr): *Ringo Starr and His All-Starr Band*.

"Across the Universe" (Version I 3:41; Version II 3:51). Prior to Version II's released on *Let It Be*, an alternate

mix of this recording, Version I, was included on the U.K. charity LP *No One's Gonna Change Our World* with bird sound effects included. Version I is also included on both *Rarities* albums and on *Past Masters*. Both versions are taken from the same recording. There is no mono release of either version.

"Act Naturally" (Ringo and Buck Owens). Ringo's duet with Owens appeared on a single, released only in the U.S., and on Owens' *Act Naturally* album in the U.S. and U.K.

"Act Naturally" (Ringo, live). Live concert version released only in the U.S. on bonus CD single issued with deluxe CD edition of *Ringo Starr and His All-Starr Band*.

"Ain't She Sweet." Recorded during the Hamburg sessions, when The Beatles also backed Tony Sheridan. The mono mix contains additional drum overdubs not included on the stereo mix.

"All My Loving." The opening high-hat cymbal countdown was cut from almost all releases but does appear on *The Beatles Box* and the German LPs *Beatles Greatest* and *With The Beatles* and on a German single.

"All My Trials" (Paul, live). A live concert version of this song was released on the U.K. edition of the CD *Tripping the Live Fantastic Highlights!*, and on U.K. 7-inch, cassette, 12-inch, and two different 5-inch CD singles. In the U.S., the song appeared only on the Columbia House Record Club vinyl LP edition of *Highlights!*

"All You Need Is Love" (Version I [mono] 3:57; Version II [stereo] 3:48). The mono version is longer than the stereo version due to a longer fadeout. The mono version has two repeats of "Greensleeves" during the fade, while the stereo version has only one. The U.K. 20th anniversary reissue single actually has the stereo version with the separate tracks mixed together to simulate mono. The original singles and the U.S. LP *Magical Mystery Tour* (also released in the U.K.) contain the mono mix. The *Yellow Submarine* album and CD *Magical Mystery Tour* feature the stereo version. (Note: an alternate mono mix [3:44] was used in the *Yellow Submarine* film.)

"And I Love Her." All British releases of this song, mono and stereo, have Paul's vocal double-tracked except on the two lines starting with "Bright are the stars that shine . . ." A vocal noise (perhaps a cough) is heard just before the instrumental break, and Paul ends the song on a lingering crooning note. The U.S. *A Hard Day's Night* album (released only in mono) and the U.S. mono release of LP *Something New* have the song almost totally single-tracked, and the cough and crooning ending are missing. The U.S. stereo *Something New* album has the double-track mix heard on the British albums. Another variation of "And I Love Her," also the double-tracked version, appeared on the German *Something New* album and on the U.S. LP *Rarities*, both in stereo. That version is a bit longer as it includes six (rather than four) repeats of the closing guitar riff.

"Angel Baby" (John) (Version I 3:03; Version II [artificially extended] 3:41). The song first appeared on the unauthorized *Roots* album (Version I). It was artificially extended to 3:41 when it was released on *Menlove Ave.*, where a repeat of the chorus was edited in before the final verse (Version II). The *Menlove Ave.* version also appeared on the boxed CD set *Lennon*.

"Angry" (Paul). Two different mixes were released: 3:35 Hugh Padgham mix: on LP *Press to Play*; 3:36 Larry Alexander remix on U.K. 12-inch "Pretty Little Head" single and the U.S. 7-inch "Stranglehold" single.

"Anytime at All" (Version I [U.S. mono]; Version II [all others]). The U.S. mono release is missing the piano, most noticeably during the instrumental break, that is present on all other releases of this song.

"Baby You're a Rich Man" (Version I [stereo] 2:58; Version II [mono] 3:04). The mono version has a slightly longer fadeout. The stereo mix was somewhat rare prior to release of the CD *Magical Mystery Tour*. It had appeared earlier on the German release of the album, the U.K. cassette edition and *The Beatles* bonus EP issued with the U.K. boxed EP set. The original single, U.S. and U.K. *Magical Mystery Tour* albums and the U.K. *The Beatles Box* all contained the mono mix.

"Back in the USSR" (Version I [mono]; Version II [stereo]). The airplane sounds used throughout the recording occur in different places on the stereo and mono releases of *The Beatles*.

"Back Off Boogaloo" (Ringo) (Version I 3:21; Version II 3:16). Version I appeared on a single with "Blindman"; Version II was released on *Stop and Smell the Roses*.

"Back on My Feet" (Paul). B side of U.K.-only single "Once upon a Long Ago," released on 7-inch, 5-inch CD and two separate 12-inch singles.

"Bad Boy." Originally released in the U.S. on the *Beatles VI* album, the song was released in the U.K. much later on *A Collection of Beatles Oldies*. It appears on *Past Masters* in stereo. Ringo recorded a completely different song, also titled "Bad Boy," for his *Bad Boy* album.

"Ballroom Dancing" (Paul) (Version I 4:06; Version II 4:36). Version I appeared on *Tug of War*; Version II was released on *Give My Regards to Broad Street*.

"Band on the Run" (Paul) (Version I 5:09; Version II 3:50). Version I is the official release; Version II appears on two different U.S. promos, one of which features mono and stereo mixes.

"Beware My Love" (Paul) (Version I 6:25; Version II 6:05). This song runs 6:25 on the *Wings at the Speed of Sound* album and 6:05 on the single release, where the song begins later with the acoustic guitar notes. The German single, however, included the 6:25 album version. A French 12-inch release of the "Let 'Em In"/"Beware My Love" single, with custom leopard-skin labels and sleeve, mistakenly lists the two songs as "Special Disco Mixes" (EMI 2C052-98.062 Y).

"Bip Bop" (Paul) (Version I, vocal; Version II, instrumental reprise). The song appears twice on Paul's LP *Wild Life*, once as an instrumental reprise. The reprise was not listed on the album until the CD edition appeared.

"Birthday" (Version I [mono]); Version II [stereo]). The stereo version has additional vocals at the end of the second chorus.

"Blackbird" (Version I [mono]; Version II [stereo]). The bird effects are quite different on mono and stereo releases.

"Bless You" (John). Two different versions were released, the original on *Walls and Bridges*, an outtake on *Menlove Ave.*

"Blindman" (Ringo). Released only as a single with "Back Off Boogaloo."

"Blue Jay Way" (Version I [mono]; Version II [stereo]). The mono release omits the reversed backing vocals that appear on the stereo version.

"Borrowed Time" (John) (Version I 4:30; Version II 3:45). Version I is the official release; Version II was issued on a U.S. promo.

"Bridge over the River Suite" (Paul). Originally released only as a single with "Walking in the Park with Eloise," the song added to the CD *Wings at the Speed of Sound* as a bonus track.

"C Moon" (Paul). A preconcert soundcheck of this song was released only in the U.K. with "All My Trials" on 7-inch, cassette, 12-inch and two different CD singles; it was not released in the U.S. This should not be confused with Paul's original studio recording of the song, which originally appeared only on a single with "Hi Hi Hi" but was later issued on the U.S. and U.K. *All the Best* albums.

"Check My Machine" (Paul). Originally released only as a single with "Waterfalls," it was added to the CD *McCartney II* as a bonus track.

CHOBA B CCCP (English translation: *Back in the USSR* or *Again in the USSR*) (Paul). This album was originally released only in the Soviet Union, although several songs appeared as bonus tracks on U.S. or U.K. singles. The Soviet album appeared in 11- and 13-track editions. A 14-track CD version was issued in 1991 in the U.K. and U.S.

"Coming Up" (Paul) (Studio Version 3:49; Live Version I 3:51; Live Version II 4:55). The studio version was included on the *McCartney II* album, and it was issued with Live Version I on a single with "Lunch Box-Odd Sox." In the U.S., a special one-sided single with Live Version I was included with the album. Live Version I also appeared on the U.S. edition of the *All the Best* album. Live Version II is from Paul's 1990 Knebworth concert appearance and was released only on *Knebworth: The Album*.

"Coochy-Coochy" (Ringo). Released in the U.S. only as a single with "Beaucoups of Blues."

"Country Dreamer" (Paul). Originally released only as a single with "Helen Wheels," it was included as a bonus track on the CD *Red Rose Speedway*.

"Dark Horse" (George) (Version I 3:50; Version II 2:48). Version I is the official release; Version II appeared on a U.S. promo in mono and stereo.

"A Day in the Life." All releases feature the crossfade from "Sgt. Pepper's Lonely Hearts Club Band (reprise)" into this song except the *Imagine: John Lennon* compilation soundtrack album, which features a clean introduction. Singles released in 1978 featured a fake "clean intro" manufactured by simply lopping off the crossfade and beginning the song several beats later.

"Daytime Nightime Suffering" (Paul). Originally released only as a single with "Goodnight Tonight," the song was added to the CD *Back to the Egg* as a bonus track.

"Day Tripper" (Stereo Version I; Stereo Version II). Two different stereo mixes were released; Version I, appears on *Past Masters* and the U.K. LP *A Collection of Beatles Oldies* and has the guitar opening in both channels. Version II, is found on *The Beatles 1962–1966*, the U.S. *Yesterday and Today* and U.K. *The Beatles Box* and *20 Greatest Hits*; it begins with the guitar only in one channel before switching to two-channel.

"Deep Blue" (George). Released only as a single with "Bangla Desh."

"Ding Dong, Ding Dong" (George) (Version I 3:39; Version II 3:12). Version I is the official release; Version II appeared on a U.S. promo in both mono and stereo; the mono mix was different from the official release.

"Don't Pass Me By" (Version I [stereo] 3:52; Version II [mono] 3:45). The stereo version is slower and thus runs longer. The fiddle ending is different on the mono and stereo releases.

"Do the Oz" (John). Released only as a single with Bill Elliot's "God Save Us" (record credited to The Elastic Oz Band).

"Down and Out" (Ringo). Originally released only as a single with "Photograph," the song was added to the CD *Ringo* as a bonus track.

"Dream Away" (George) (Version I, film mix; Version II, LP mix). Version I is shorter and appeared in the film *Time Bandits* where it was played over the film's closing titles. Version II, a noticeably different mix, was released on *Gone Troppo*.

"Drowning in a Sea of Love" (Ringo) (Version I 5:08; Version II 3:39). Version I is the official release; Version II appeared on a U.S. promo.

"Dr. Robert" (Version I [U.S. mono]; Version II [all others]). Some talking is heard at the very end on the U.S. mono *Yesterday and Today* album; it is missing on all other releases of the song.

"Ebony and Ivory" (Paul) (Version I, duet 3:41; Version II, solo 3:41). Paul's duet with Stevie Wonder appears on *Tug of War*. His solo version was only released on a 12-inch single that also included the duet version and "Rainclouds."

"Eleanor Rigby" (Version I by The Beatles, 2:11; Version II by Paul, 2:07). The Beatles' original appeared on *Revolver*; Paul's remake is on *Give My Regards to Broad Street*.

"Eleanor's Dream" (Paul). This instrumental music from *Give My Regards to Broad Street* runs only 1:01 on the LP release but 4:59 on the CD and cassette editions.

"End of the Line" (George/Wilburys) (Version I 3:30; Version II [extended version] 5:31). Version I was released on *The Traveling Wilburys Volume One* and on 7-inch and cassette singles. Version II is a special extended mix released only in the U.K. on 12-inch and 3-inch CD singles.

"Ferry 'Cross the Mersey" (Paul). Originally released only in the U.K. as a charity 7-inch vinyl and 5-inch CD single; includes vocal solo by Paul. It is also on the U.K. LP *Now That's What I Call Music 15* and U.K. CD compilation *Hit Factory #3: The Best of Stock-Aitken-Waterman*.

"Figure of Eight" (Paul) (Version I, LP 3:23; Version II, several edits). Two completely different recordings of this song were released. The first appeared on the *Flowers in the Dirt* album. The second was released in a variety of edits on several singles: 3:57 edit: U.S. cassette single, U.S. CD promo (DPRO 79836) and U.K. 7-inch promo (RDJ 6235A); 4:01 edit: U.K. 5-inch CD single (both editions), U.S. 5-inch CD promo *Paul McCartney Rocks* (listed as 3:59), U.S. 5-inch promo CD (DPRO 79871, listed as 4:03) and U.K. 7-inch promo (RDJ 6235, listed as 4:03); 3:59 edit: U.K. 7-inch promo (RDJ 6235A); 5:11 edit (almost always listed as 5:16): U.K. 7-inch single, U.K. cassette single, U.K. 3-inch CD single, U.K. 12-inch singles (all 3 releases) and U.S. 5-inch promo CD (DPRO 79871).

"The First Stone" (Paul). Released only on U.K. 7-inch, two 12-inch (12R and 12RX 6223) and CD "This One" singles, and U.S. cassette single.

"Flying Hour" (George). Omitted from the original, unreleased version of the *Somewhere in England* album, a remix of this track was officially released on bonus 7-inch vinyl and 5-inch CD EP *Songs by George Harrison*, issued with George's book.

"Flying to My Home" (Paul). Released with "My Brave Face" on U.S. and U.K. 7-inch, cassette and CD singles, and on U.K. 12-inch single.

"For No One" (Version I by The Beatles, 2:03; Version II by Paul, 1:56). The Beatles' version appeared on *Revolver*; Paul's version is on *Give My Regards to Broad Street*.

"For You Blue" (George, live version). Recorded at George's 1974 Largo, Maryland concert, released only on the free bonus 7-inch vinyl and 5-inch CD EP *Songs by George Harrison*, issued with George's book.

"From Me to You" (Version I [mono]; Version II [stereo]). The mono version includes harmonica in the intro that was mixed out on the stereo release. The mono version appears on *Past Masters, A Collection of Beatles Oldies* (mono edition), *Jolly What! The Beatles and Frank Ifield on Stage*, original single with "Thank You Girl" and reissues, U.S. Vee Jay and Capitol Starline singles backed with "Please Please Me" and the U.K. EP *Beatles Hits*; the stereo version is found on *The Beatles 1962–1966*, *The Beatles Box* and U.K. *20 Greatest Hits*, and stereo edition of *A Collection of Beatles Oldies*.

"Get Back" (Version I [single] 3:11; Version II [LP *Let It Be*] 3:09). Both versions are noticeably different mixes of the same recording. Version II includes John's "Sweet Loretta Fart . . ." spoken lines, spliced on just before the song begins, and his "I'd Like to thank you . . ." speech from the Jan 30, 1969 rooftop concert, spliced onto the end. The opening and closing were not present on the single release. At least one Capitol single release, a reissue on the black rainbow label, contains the *album* version (matrix number: S-45-X-1-2490-46843 G-13). Other black rainbow label editions include the original single version, released with two different matrix numbers stamped into the runout groove (S45 X46843 2490 W11 #1) and (S45-X46843 2490 W12 #2). Version I was released in mono only on the original U.K. single, the 20th-anniversary single and the 3-inch CD single. The original U.S. single and all reissues are stereo, as are the versions on *The Beatles 1967–1970* and U.S. *20 Greatest Hits*.

"Get Back" (Paul, live version). Live performance at 1986 Prince's Trust show, released only on *The Prince's Trust 10th Anniversary Birthday Party* and *The Royal Concert*.

"The Girl Is Mine" (Paul and M. Jackson) (Version I 3:41; Version II 3:32). Version I is the official release; Version II appeared on a U.S. promo with the McCartney/Jackson dialogue edited out.

"Girl's School" (Paul) (Version I 4:31; Version II 3:19). Originally released only as a single with "Mull of Kintyre," the song was added to the CD *London Town* as a bonus track. Version I is the official release; Version II was issued on a U.S. promo and also appeared on European releases of the CD.

"Give Ireland Back to the Irish" (Paul). Vocal and instrumental versions of this song appeared only on a single.

"Give Peace a Chance" (John) (Version I 4:49; Version II 0:50; Version III 1:00): Version I was released as a single. Versions II and III are different excerpts from the Aug 30, 1972 One to One Concert performance of the song that were released on the *Shaved Fish* and *John Lennon: Live in New York City* albums respectively. The original single included John's count-in, which was omitted on the U.S. release but restored on the *Imagine: John Lennon* film soundtrack compilation album and on *The John Lennon Collection*.

"Good Day Sunshine" (Version I by The Beatles, 2:08; Version II by Paul, 1:43). The Beatles recorded the song for *Revolver*; Paul's version appeared on *Give My Regards to Broad Street*.

"Good Day Sunshine" (Paul, live version). A live concert version of the song was released only on "Birthday" (live) singles, which appeared in 7-inch, cassette, 12-inch and CD formats in the U.K. but only as a cassette single in the U.S.

"Goodnight Princess" (Paul). An instrumental track with a spoken introduction by Paul, released only on the CD edition of *Give My Regards to Broad Street*.

"Goodnight Tonight" (Paul) (Version I 4:15; Version II 7:25). Version I was originally released only as a single with "Daytime Nightime Suffering." It later appeared on the U.S. and U.K. *All the Best* LPs and on the U.S. CD (it was omitted from the U.K. CD). Version II, an extended mix, was released only on a 12-inch single.

"Good Sign" (Paul) (Version I, U.K. 12-inch; Version II, U.K. promo). Version I was released only in the U.K. on a "This One" 12-inch single (12RX 6223). Version II is a unique 7:22 "Groove Mix," released only on a U.K. 12- inch promo (GOOD 1).

"Got My Mind Set on You" (George) (Version I, 3:50; Version II [extended version] 5:17). Version I was released on *Cloud Nine* and 7-inch and cassette singles. Version II is a special extended mix with a unique Harrison guitar solo that was released only in the U.K. on a 12-inch single.

"Got to Get You into My Life" (Version I [mono]; Version II [stereo]). Paul's lines during the fadeout appear to be from different takes on the mono and stereo releases and are noticeably different.

"Handle with Care" (George/Wilburys) (Version I 3:20; Version II [extended version] 5:16). Version I is the original mix that appeared on *The Traveling Wilburys Volume One* and on 7-inch, cassette and U.S. 3-inch CD singles. Version II is an extended mix that was released only in the U.K. on 12-inch, 10-inch and 3-inch CD singles.

"Hanglide" (instrumental) (Paul). Released only on U.S. and U.K. "Press" 12-inch singles.

"A Hard Day's Night" (Version I [mono]; Version II [stereo]). The stereo mix is a few seconds longer than the mono mix. The stereo and mono U.S. *A Hard Day's Night* albums both contained mono versions of The Beatles' songs, including the title track. The album was released in both stereo and mono in the U.K. and the song was subsequently released in stereo on several other albums, none of which has appeared on CD to date. The song also appears in stereo on non-U.S. editions of *The Beatles 1962–1966* and on *Reel Music*, *20 Greatest Hits*, *A Collection of Beatles Oldies* and *The Beatles Box*.

"Helen Wheels" (Paul). Included on the original U.S. *Band on the Run* album but omitted on the U.K. version; also released as a single. Initial U.K. CD releases of *Band on the Run* also omitted the song, but it was restored on subsequent issues of the CD and included on all U.S. CDs.

"Help!" (Version I [mono] 2:16; Version II [stereo] 2:16). The mono and stereo versions contain the same instrumental track but different vocals. The different versions were issued in the U.K. on the mono and stereo releases of the *Help!* album. In the U.S., however, the stereo mix was used for both the mono and stereo releases of the *Help!* album. The mono mix was released in the U.S. only on a single; it also appeared on the U.S. *Rarities* and U.K. *The Beatles Box*. The U.S. *Help!* and *The Beatles 1962–1966* add "The James Bond Theme" before the start of the song.

"Helter Skelter" (Version I [stereo] 4:33; Version II [mono] 3:38). The stereo version includes a fadeout/fade-in ending and Ringo's "I've got blisters on my fingers" line, which is omitted on the mono version. As with much of the "*White Album*," this track sounds faster in mono than in stereo.

"Here Comes the Sun" (George, live version). Live version from Jun 1987 Prince's Trust shows, released only in the U.K. on *The Prince's Trust Concert 1987* and *The Royal Concert* albums.

"Here, There and Everywhere" (Version I by Beatles, 2:29; Version II by Paul, 1:44). The Beatles' version is on *Revolver*; Paul's is on *Give My Regards to Broad Street*.

"Hey Jude." Originally released as a mono single, the song subsequently appeared in stereo on several compilation albums and on Capitol reissues of the single in the U.S. U.K. reissues, including the 20th-anniversary vinyl and 3-inch CD singles, are mono; it is available in CD format in stereo on *Past Masters*. The song was drastically shortened to 5:05 on the U.S. LP *20 Greatest Hits*, and it appeared in a unique 3:25 edit on a 4-inch flexi disc sold by Pocket Disc in vending machines in the U.S. The full stereo version appears on *The Beatles 1967–1970*, *Beatles Ballads*, *Hey Jude* and U.K. *20 Greatest Hits*. A live version of Paul's performance of the song at the Knebworth Concert was released only on *Knebworth: The Album*.

"Homeward Bound" (George). George's duet with Paul Simon recorded for "Saturday Night Live" was released only on the album *Nobody's Child: Romanian Angel Appeal*.

"Honey Pie" (Version I [mono]; Version II [stereo]). The stereo mix has a shorter guitar solo than the mono release.

"I Am the Walrus" (Several variations). All releases include four repeats of the organ introduction, except the stereo edition of the U.K. EP *Magical Mystery Tour*, which has six repeats. That version also appeared on the LPs *The Beatles 1967–1970* and *Reel Music*. The

U.S. mono single adds four extra beats before the "yellow matter custard" line that are missing from all other releases. All releases of the song switch to mono toward the end when the radio broadcast begins. A full version including the six organ repeats and the four extra beats is on *The Beatles Box* and the U.S. *Rarities* album.

"I Call Your Name" (Version I [mono]; Version II [stereo]; Version III [Ringo solo/video]). The guitar intro is different on the stereo and mono versions. The bell sound heard in the intro begins sooner on the mono release than it does on stereo release; it begins sooner on the U.S. stereo release than on the U.K. stereo version. The U.S. stereo mix is found on *The Beatles Second Album*; the U.K. stereo mix is on *Past Masters*, *Rock and Roll Music* and *The Beatles Box*. The mono mix is on the U.K. *Rarities* and the original U.K. EP *Long Tall Sally*. Version III was recorded and filmed by Ringo for the May 1990 Liverpool Lennon tribute concert, where it was originally screened, and has thus far been released only on the concert videocassette.

"I Don't Care Anymore" (George). Released only as a single with "Dark Horse."

"I Don't Want to Do It" (George) (Version I, on *Porky's Revenge* soundtrack album; Version II, released on U.S. single). The two versions represent noticeably different mixes of the same recording.

"I Feel Fine" (Version I [Stereo I]; Version II [stereo II]; Version III [mono]). Some (not all) stereo releases include a very brief bit of whispering just before the song begins and the sound of a hi hat cymbal closing just after the song begins. Both sounds are heard on the non-U.S. editions of *The Beatles 1962–1966* and on the U.K. *The Beatles Box*. The stereo version without the whispering is found on *Past Masters*, *A Collection of Beatles Oldies* and *20 Greatest Hits*. The mono version is on the original single and reissues, including the 3-inch CD single, and the U.S. edition of *The Beatles 1962–1966*, U.S. *Beatles '65* and original U.K. EP *Beatles Million Sellers* (aka *Golden Discs*).

"If I Fell" (Version I [mono]; Version II [stereo]). John's opening vocal solo is single-tracked in mono; double-tracked in stereo.

"I Lie Around" (Paul). Originally released only as a single with "Live and Let Die," it was added as a bonus track to the CD *Red Rose Speedway*.

"I'll Cry Instead" (Version I 1:44; Version II 2:04). Version I appears on all U.K. releases and on the U.S. stereo *Something New* album. Version II was released on the U.S. *A Hard Day's Night* album and the mono edition of *Something New*. Version II appears to be an early mix of the song intended for the film *A Hard Day's Night*. Although omitted from the film, Version II was used for the prologue of the videocassette edition, where it was played over a series of still photographs. The song was recorded in two separate parts that were later edited together, with two differ-

ent edits finding their way into release, and thus onto this page.

"I'll Give You a Ring" (Paul). Released only on 7-inch and 12-inch "Take It Away" singles.

"Imagine" (John) (Version I [studio recording]; Version II [demo]). Version I was released as a single and on the *Imagine* album. Version II, a demo, was released as a bonus track on the *Imagine: John Lennon* soundtrack compilation album.

"I'm in Love Again" (Paul). Originally released only in the U.K. on 12-inch and CD "This One" singles. Recorded during sessions for the Soviet release *CHOBA B CCCP* but omitted from that album, it was added to the CD, released in the U.K. on Sep 30, 1991 and the U.S. on Oct 29, 1991.

"I'm Looking Through You." The U.S. stereo release of *Rubber Soul* includes two false starts omitted on all other releases of this song.

"I'm Only Sleeping" (Version I [stereo I]; Version II [Stereo II]; Version III [mono I]; Version IV [mono II]). Four different mixes of this recording have been released, all of which include the same Lennon vocal. The differences are almost entirely in the location of the backward guitar effects. These effects appear in different places on the U.S. *Yesterday and Today* and U.K. *Revolver* stereo releases. On the U.S. mono releases, the effects appear in different places than on either stereo release. They are missing in some places, added in others and begin either earlier or later in still other places. The U.S. LP *Rarities* has the U.K. stereo *Revolver* version. The fourth (and rarest) mix, was released on U.K. mono *Revolver* LP and French EP *Strawberry Fields Forever* (Odeon MEO-134) with the backward guitar effects in different places than on the other releases.

"I'm Stepping Out" (John). (Version I 4:06); Version II 3:33). Version I is the official release; Version II appeared on a U.S. promo.

"I Saw Her Standing There" (John, Version I; Paul, Version II). In addition to The Beatles' original version, John performed this song with Elton John at Elton's Nov 1974 Madison Square Garden concert. That version appeared as the B side of Elton's "Philadelphia Freedom" single, on a U.K. EP, a European Elton John album and various foreign singles. It also appeared on the CD boxed set *Lennon*. Paul also performed the song live, also with Elton John on stage, at the 1986 Prince's Trust show. Paul's version was issued on a bonus single included only with U.K. release of LP *The Prince's Trust 10th Anniversary Birthday Party*.

"I Should Have Known Better" (Version I [stereo]; Version II [mono]). The stereo release has a brief interruption of the harmonica intro; the mono version has a complete harmonica introduction. The stereo version also contains four repeats of the closing "You love me too" line, compared to three on the mono release.

It appears in stereo on *Reel Music*, *Hey Jude*, U.K. *A Hard Day's Night* and a 1976 U.K. stereo single; the mono version is on U.S. *A Hard Day's Night*, U.K. mono *A Hard Day's Night*, CD *A Hard Day's Night* and on a single backed with "A Hard Day's Night."

"Isn't It a Pity" (George) (Version I 7:10; Version II 4:46). Both versions are on the *All Things Must Pass* album.

"It's All Down to Goodnight Vienna" (Ringo) (Version I 2:32; Version II [reprise] 1:15). Both versions are on Ringo's LP *Goodnight Vienna*. The two versions were combined in a special edit released only on the U.S. edition of the "Goodnight Vienna" single; other editions throughout the world did not add the reprise. The original titles on initial album pressings were "Goodnight Vienna" and "Goodnight Vienna" (reprise). Reissue pressings changed the title of Version I to "It's All Down to Goodnight Vienna."

"It's Not True" (Paul) (Version I [single]; Version II [remix]). Version I originally appeared as the B side of "Press." Version II, a remix by Julian Mendelsohn, was released as a bonus track on the CD *Press to Play* and on U.K. 12-inch and 10-inch singles. Version I: U.S. 7-inch single (4:27) and U.K. 7-inch single (4:31); Version II, Julian Mendelsohn remix: U.S. and U.K. 12-inch single (5:51), U.K. 10-inch single (5:50) and CD *Press to Play* (5:52).

"It's Now Or Never" (Paul). Recorded during sessions for the Soviet *CHOBA B CCCP* album but omitted from that LP and the later CD release, the song was released only on the U.K. charity album *The Last Temptation of Elvis* and on U.K. promos. The LP was sold in the U.S. as an import.

"I Wanna Cry" (Paul). Released only on U.K. 12-inch and CD "This One" singles, and on U.S. promo-only CD *Paul McCartney Rocks*.

"I Want to Hold Your Hand" (Version I [Stereo I]; Version II [Stereo II]; Version III [mono]). The Australian reissue single features a more primitive stereo mix (Stereo I) with vocals on the right and instruments on the left. The same mix appears on the Australian *The 23 Number Ones* album. Other stereo releases have the Stereo II version, with the vocals in the middle, including the 1984 U.S. Capitol promo, *Past Masters*, *A Collection of Beatles Oldies*, *The Beatles Box*, *20 Greatest Hits* and non-U.S. editions of *The Beatles 1962–1966*. The original mono single mix (Version III) is on the 3-inch CD single, *Meet The Beatles*, U.K. EP *Beatles Million Sellers*, Capitol 1984 reissue promo (mono and stereo sides) and the U.S. edition of *The Beatles 1962–1966*. Some sources claim that there is a slightly different third stereo mix, also with centered vocals.

"Jet" (Paul) (Version I 4:08; Version II 2:49). Version I is the official release; Version II appeared on a U.S. promo in mono.

"Just a Dream" (Ringo). Released only on two different singles, one with "Wings," and the other with "Drowning in a Sea of Love."

"(Just Like) Starting Over" (John) (Version I 3:55; Version II 4:17). Version I is on all commercial releases; Version II, with a longer fadeout, is on a U.S. 12-inch promo.

"Komm, Gib Mir Deine Hand." German-language version of "I Want to Hold Your Hand," originally released in Germany on mono single backed with "Sie Liebt Dich" (Odeon 22671). It also appears in mono on reissue German single (Odeon 1 C006-04204 M), *Past Masters* and U.S. mono *Something New* and German *Something New*. The stereo mix on U.S. *Something New* includes a word spoken by someone just before the song begins and a shout by one of The Beatles before they begin singing; both of these are missing from the stereo mix that appears on the U.K. *Rarities* album.

"Lay His Head" (George). Dropped from the original version of the *Somewhere in England* album, a remix of this song was released on 7-inch, cassette and 12-inch "Got my Mind Set on You" singles and on the bonus 7-inch vinyl and 5-inch CD EP *Songs by George Harrison*, released with George's book. It also appeared on a Japanese 3-inch CD single.

"Lennon Medley" (Paul, live). A live concert medley comprising "Strawberry Fields Forever"/"Help!"/ "Give Peace a Chance" was released only in the U.K. on the second edition of the "All My Trials" CD single.

"Let 'Em In" (Paul) (Version I, studio recording in 3:43 and 5:08 edits; Version II, live). Version I appeared on Paul's *Wings at the Speed of Sound* and on a single. U.S. stereo and mono promos featured a unique 3:43 edit, unavailable elsewhere, and the standard edit released on the album and single (5:08). Labeling on a French 12-inch edition of the "Let 'Em In"/"Beware My Love" single, with custom leopard-skin labels and sleeve (EMI 2C052-98.062 Y), mistakenly lists the A and B sides as "Special Disco Mixes," but they are the standard A and B sides. Version II is a live concert recording released only in the U.K. as a bonus track on 12-inch and CD "Birthday" singles.

"Let It Be" (Version I, single 3:50; Version II, *Let It Be* album 4:01). The two versions are different mixes of the same recording. The album version includes three repeats of the "Let It Be" chorus at the end, two of them ending with "There will be an answer . . ." while the single contains only two repeats. A mono mix of "Let It Be" was released only on a Japanese single.

"Letting Go" (Paul) (Version I [LP]; Version II [promo single mix]). Released on *Venus and Mars*, a unique mono mix of the song with a clean introduction appeared only on a U.S. 7-inch promo single. That promo also featured the standard version in stereo.

"Lipstick Traces" (Ringo) (Version I [official release]; Version II [alternate mono mix]). In addition to Version I, the official release, a unique mono mix, Version II, was issued on a U.S. promo.

"Little Woman Love" (Paul). Originally released only as a single with "Mary Had a Little Lamb," the song was added to the CD *Wild Life* as a bonus track.

"London Town" (Paul) (Version I 4:10; Version II 3:48). Version I is the official release; Version II appeared in stereo on a U.S. promo, which also featured a mono mix of Version I.

"The Long and Winding Road" (Version I by Beatles 3:40; Version II by Paul 3:47; Version III by Paul 3:50). The Beatles' original version appeared on *Let It Be*. Version II was released on Paul's *Give My Regards to Broad Street* album. Version III, from the *Put It There* documentary film, appeared in the U.K. as the B side of a limited boxed edition reissue of Paul's "This One" single. Version III was also released on the U.K. "Figure of Eight" 5-inch CD single and on the Japanese double CD pack *Flowers in the Dirt*.

"Long, Long, Long." George's double-tracked vocal is noticeably out of synch on the mono release of *The Beatles*.

"Long Tall Sally" (Paul, live). Live 1986 performance at the Prince's Trust show, issued on a bonus single included only with U.K. release of LP *The Prince's Trust 10th Anniversary Birthday Party*, on the CD release of that album and on U.K. album *The Royal Concert*.

"Love" (John) (LP Version 3:17; U.K. Single Version 3:12). This song was included on *John Lennon/Plastic Ono Band* but was remixed and edited for release on the U.K. single. John's vocal is faded in on the LP but begins at full volume on the single.

"Loveliest Thing" (Paul). Released only on U.K. "Figure of Eight" 5-inch CD single and Japanese double CD pack *Flowers in the Dirt*.

"Love Me Do" (Version I 2:22; Version II 2:19). The original U.K. single (Version I, with Ringo on drums) is a completely different recording than the one released on the U.K. LP (Version II) *Please Please Me*. Version II, which features session man Andy White on drums, also appeared on almost all subsequent releases, singles and albums. A special 20th-anniversary U.K. 12-inch single release included both versions and "P.S. I Love You." The original 7-inch single was also reissued at that time, but that disc contained the album version, as did the single included in the U.K. *Singles Collection* and the 3-inch CD single. Version I appeared again on *Past Masters*. It is also on the U.S. *Rarities* album and the U.K. *Beatles Box*. There is no stereo release of either recording.

"Lucy in the Sky with Diamonds" (Version I, Beatles; Version II, live Lennon performance). On The Beatles; original recording of this song, John's vocal has a noticeable echo on the mono release (absent in stereo), which gives the song a dreamier quality. John also performed the song live with Elton John in Nov 1974, and that version was released on a U.K. EP, on several European singles and on a European Elton John album. The song also appeared on the 1990 CD set *Lennon*.

"Lunch Box-Odd Sox" (Paul). An instrumental originally released only as a single with "Coming Up," it was added to the CD *Venus and Mars* as a bonus track.

"Mama's Little Girl" (Paul). B side of Paul's U.K. 7-inch and U.S./U.K. cassette "Put It There" singles; also on U.K. 12-inch and CD singles and Japanese double CD pack *Flowers in the Dirt*.

"Mary Had a Little Lamb" (Paul). Originally released only as a single with "Little Woman Love," it was added to the CD *Wild Life* as a bonus track. It also appeared on the U.S. charity CD *For Our Children*.

"Matchbox" (Version I [mono]; Version II [stereo]). Ringo's double-tracked vocal is slightly out of synch on the stereo release, and there are different guitar solos on the mono and stereo versions. The stereo version is found on *Past Masters*, *Rock and Roll Music*, *The Beatles Box* and U.S. *Something New*; it is in mono on U.K. EP *Long Tall Sally*, U.K. *Rarities*, mono edition of *Something New* and U.S. single backed with "Slow Down."

"Maybe I'm Amazed" (Paul) (Version I 5:11; Version II 3:43). Version I is the official release; Version II appeared on 7-inch and 12-inch U.S. promos in mono and stereo. The 12-inch also featured mono and stereo mixes of Version I.

"The Mess" (Paul, live). This live concert track originally appeared as a single with "My Love" and was later added to the CD *Red Rose Speedway* as a bonus track.

"Miss O'Dell" (George). Released only as a single with "Give Me Love," complete with George's outbursts of laughter.

"Money" (Version I [stereo]; Version II [mono]). The guitar heard prominently in the opening on the stereo release is missing on the mono version. The mono and stereo piano intros are different, and instrumentation is somewhat different throughout on the two mixes. Despite its more sophisticated sound, the stereo version of this song was not created from four-track masters. It was recorded on the same two-track equipment used for all of the songs on The Beatles' first two albums. Two separate two-track masters were used to create the stereo mix of "Money," making it sound more balanced in stereo than any of the other stereo mixes from those first two albums. It appears in mono on the CD *With The Beatles*. The original album was issued in both stereo and mono editions, and the stereo mix appeared on the Mobile Fidelity half-speed master edition. The stereo and mono releases appeared on the respective U.S. *The Beatles Second Album* releases.

"Mother" (John) (Version I 5:29; Version II 3:55). Version I was released on *John Lennon/Plastic Ono Band*; Version II, a shortened edit, was released as a single.

"Move Over Ms. L" (John). Originally released only as a single with "Stand by Me," the song was later added to the CD edition of *The John Lennon Collection*; it was not included on the LP edition.

"Mull of Kintyre" (Paul) (Version I 4:41; Version II 3:31; Version III live). Versions I and II are different edits of the original studio recording. Version I is the official release; Version II appeared on a U.S. promo. Version III is a live concert performance released only in the U.K. on 12-inch and first edition CD "All My Trials" singles. It was replaced on the second edition of the CD by the "Lennon Medley."

"Mumbo" (Paul) (Version I [vocal]; Version II [reprise jam]). Version I appears as the first track on Paul's *Wild Life* album; Version II, a brief reprise instrumental jam of the song, appeared at the end of the album following "Dear Friend." The reprise was omitted from Columbia reissues of *Wild Life* that appeared in the 1980s. It was never formally credited on the album until the CD edition was issued.

"My Bonnie" (by Tony Sheridan with The Beatles as a backing group). Recorded in Hamburg in Jun 1961, the song was originally released in two different editions, one featuring a German-language introduction (0:35), the other an English introduction (0:32). Subsequent releases eliminated the introductions. Both introductions appeared on a 1985 Dutch Fan Club single.

"My Carnival" (Paul) (Version I 3:56; Version II [Party Mix] 6:00). Version I was released on the "Spies Like Us" 7-inch single, Version II was issued on the 12-inch single. Version I was also added to the CD *Venus and Mars* as a bonus track.

"Naughty Atom Bomb" (Ringo). Recorded with John Cleese and Bill Oddie, released only on U.K. charity LP *The Anti-Heroin Project: It's a Live-in World*.

"New Blue Moon" (George/Wilburys) (Version I [vocal]; Version II [instrumental]). Version I appeared on *The Traveling Wilburys Volume 3*. Version II, the instrumental track from that recording, was released only in the U.K. on 7- inch, cassette, 12-inch and CD "She's My Baby" and "Wilbury Twist" singles.

"New Moon over Jamaica" (Paul). This duet by Paul and Johnny Cash appeared only on Cash's album, *Water from the Wells of Home*. Paul does not have merely a supporting role on the song; at one point he takes lead vocal. He also produced the record and co-wrote the song with Cash and Tom T. Hall.

"Nobody Loves You (When You're Down and Out)" (John). Two different versions were released, the original on *Walls and Bridges* and an outtake on *Menlove Ave.*

"Nobody's Child" (George/Wilburys). Released in the U.K. on 7-inch, 12-inch and CD singles; released in U.S. and U.K. on *Nobody's Child: The Romanian Angel Appeal* album. Tony Sheridan also recorded this song, in 1961, with The Beatles backing him.

"No More Lonely Nights" (Paul) (Ballad Version, 4:38 edit on single, 4:50 edit on LP; Playout/Extended Version, 3:56 edit on 7-inch single, 4:17 edit on LP, 8:10 edit on first edition 12-inch single; Arthur Baker remix [4:20 and 6:53 edits]). Rather than the usual remix, the playout or extended version is a completely different recording from the ballad version. The different versions were released on the following records: *Ballad* 4:38 edit: U.S. and U.K. 7-inch and 12-inch singles; 4:50 edit: *Give My Regards to Broad Street* album; 5:00 edit: *Broad Street* cassette.

Playout, 3:56 edit: U.S. and U.K. 7-inch single; 4:17 edit: *Give My Regards to Broad Street* album; 8:10 extended mix: U.S. and U.K. first edition 12-inch singles; 5:11 edit: *Broad Street* cassette; 7:17 mix: 12-inch "Hot Trax" D.J.-only issue mixed by San Francisco D.J. Warren Sanford;

Special Dance Mix (Arthur Baker remix), 4:20 edit: U.S. and U.K. second edition 7-inch single (listed as 4:14 on U.S. single), and U.K. LP *Now That's What I Call Music 4*; 6:53 edit: U.S. and U.K. second edition 12-inch singles (listed as "Extended Playout Version" on U.K. 12-inch). Both edits were issued on a U.S. 12-inch promo.

"Mole Mix" (Arthur Baker remix), 8:54: only on U.K. one-sided 12-inch promo.

"No. 9 Dream" (John) (Version I 4:46; Version II 2:58). Version I is the official release; Version II was issued on a U.S. promo in stereo and mono and on European editions of the CD *Walls and Bridges*.

"Norwegian Wood (This Bird Has Flown)" (Version I [stereo I]; Version II [stereo II]; Version III [mono]). Stereo I is on the *Rubber Soul* album; an alternate stereo mix (Stereo II) with centered vocals is on U.K. *The Beatles Ballads*. A cough is heard shortly after the line "She told me to sit anywhere" on the mono release, but it was mixed out on the stereo version.

"Ob-La-Di, Ob-La-Da" (Version I [stereo]; Version II [mono]). The hand clapping heard in the stereo intro is missing on the mono release. The mono mix was also released on a 1976 U.S. promo with the stereo version on the flip side.

"Ode to a Koala Bear" (Paul). Released only on 7-inch and 12-inch "Say Say Say" singles.

"Oh Woman, Oh Why" (Paul) (Version I, official release; Version II, U.S. promo). Version I was originally released only as a single as the B side of "Another Day"; it was added to the CD *Wild Life* as a bonus track. The U.S. promo release (Version II), also the B side of "Another Day," is a completely different mix and includes gunshot effects in different places.

"Old Dirt Road" (John). Two different versions were released, the original on *Walls and Bridges* and an outtake on *Menlove Ave.*

"Old Time Relovin'" (Ringo) (Version I 4:16; Version II 3:29). Version I appeared on Ringo's *Bad Boy* album; Version II was issued on a single.

"Once Upon a Long Ago" (Paul). Released only in the U.K. on several singles and as a bonus track on the U.K. edition of the *All the Best* album. The song appeared in the following different mixes: U.K. 7-inch and CD single (4:12); U.K. *All the Best* album (4:06); first U.K. 12-inch single (12R 6170) (4:34 long version); second U.K. 12-inch (12RX 6170) (6:06 extended version).

"Only Love Remains" (Paul). The following different edits of this song were released: 4:13 Hugh Padgham mix: LP *Press to Play*; 4:11 Jim Boyer remix: U.S. and U.K. 7-inch single and U.K. 12-inch single.

"Ou Est le Soleil?" (Paul) (Version I [album mix]; Version II [Pettibone remix]). Originally a bonus track issued on the *Flowers in the Dirt* CD and cassette releases (Version I), the song was remixed by Shep Pettibone (Version II) and issued in several different edits, as listed below: Shep Pettibone remix (Version II): 7:02 edit: U.S. and non-U.K. Europe 12-inch and cassette maxi single. *Instrumental mix*: U.S./Europe 12-inch and cassette maxi single (listed as 4:25); U.K. 12-inch promo (listed as 4:30; 12 SOL1). *Tub Dub Mix*: U.S./Europe 12-inch and cassette maxi single (listed as 4:27); U.K. 12-inch "Figure of Eight" single (12RX 6235) (listed as 4:30); U.K. 12-inch promo (12 SOL 1) (listed as 4:30). *7:10 edit*: U.K. 12-inch "Figure of Eight" single (12RX 6235). *4:50 edit*: On following "Figure of Eight" singles: U.K. 7-inch and 12-inch (12RS 6235) singles, U.K. cassette single, U.K. 3-inch CD single (CD3R 6235). Also on Japan double CD pack *Flowers in the Dirt*. *4:06 edit*: U.S. cassette single. *4:15 edit*: U.S. promo 5-inch CD (79836). *3:57 edit*: U.K. 7-inch promo. *6:57 edit*: U.K. Disconet Dennis Muyet edit; D.J. remix.

"Party Party" (Paul) (Version I 5:36; Version II 3:40; Version III 6:21 Bruce Forest mix). All versions are different edits of the same recording. Version I was released on bonus 7-inch vinyl and 3-inch CD singles included with *Flowers in the Dirt* World Tour Packs; it is also found on the Japanese double CD pack *Flowers in the Dirt*. Version II was released only on the U.S. promo CD *Paul McCartney Rocks*. Version III was released only in the U.K. on a 12-inch promo issued to club D.J.s; that promo also included Version I.

"Penny Lane" (Version I [released mono mix]; Version II [U.S. promo mono mix]; Version III [original stereo mix]; Version IV [alternate stereo mix]). The original single was issued only in mono (Version I). A different mono mix, done at EMI in England expressly for the U.S. (Version II), was issued only on a U.S. promo and includes a piccolo trumpet riff at the end, which was eliminated from all other releases. The song was also issued in a separate stereo mix (Version III). The U.S. *Rarities* album and U.K. *The Beatles Box* feature Ver-

sion IV—the stereo mix with the mono trumpet ending edited on (copied from the U.S. promo). Version I (original mono without the trumpet ending) is found on singles, U.S. and U.K. LPs *Magical Mystery Tour* and the U.S. *The Beatles 1967–1970* album. The original stereo release (Version III, without the spliced-on trumpet ending) appears on U.S. *20 Greatest Hits*, non-U.S. releases of *The Beatles 1967–1970*, the German *Magical Mystery Tour* cassette and the CD *Magical Mystery Tour*. The stereo mix also features a few extra beats after the fire engine bell.

"Piggies" (Version I [stereo]; Version II [mono]). The pig noises are noticeably different on the mono and stereo releases of *The Beatles*.

"Please Please Me" (Version I [stereo] 2:00; Version II [mono] 2:00). On the stereo release, John makes a mistake in the lyric in the final verse and chuckles briefly over this in the chorus that follows. Neither the mistake nor the chuckle are heard on the mono release, which is a different mix containing at least parts of a different recording of the song. The stereo version was released on the original stereo edition of *Please Please Me* in the U.K. and on the U.S. Vee Jay albums and Capitol's *The Early Beatles* and *The Beatles 1962–1966*. Only the mono edition of "Please Please Me" has been issued on CD. The stereo version is also found on the Japanese Beatles EP set, but there the tracks have been mixed together to simulate mono, as was done in the U.S. with *The Early Beatles* mono album.

"Poor Little Girl" (George). Released as a bonus track on *The Best of Dark Horse 1976–1989* and on U.K. 7-inch, cassette, 12-inch and 3-inch CD singles with "Cheer Down." The song appeared in the following edits: 3:25: U.S. promo CD (no official U.S. single was issued). 4:30: *Best of Dark Horse* (vinyl LP, listed as 4:31), and U.K. 7-inch and cassette singles. 4:32: CD *Best of Dark Horse*, and U.S. promo CD. 4:34: U.K. 3-inch CD and 12-inch singles.

"Press" (Paul) (Version I, Hugh Padgham mix; Version II, Bevans/Forward mix; Version III, Dub Mix). Although they were not identified anywhere on the sleeves or labels, two different editions of the *Press to Play* album were released in the U.K. The first featured Version II of "Press," while the second contained Version I; both editions listed it as Version II. The only way to distinguish the two editions was by the matrix numbers stamped in the runout groove on side 2 (Version I: PCSD 103 B-3U-1-2-1; Version II: PCSD 103 B-7-1-1). The U.S. album and all CD releases of *Press to Play* contain Version II. The different versions were released on the following discs in the edited lengths noted:

Version I (Padgham mix): first edition U.K. 7-inch single (3:57; listed as 4:20); second U.K. pressing of LP *Press to Play* (4:17); U.K. 10-inch single (4:22, listed as 4:20).

Version II (Bevans/Forward mix): CD *Press to Play*

(4:45); U.S. *Press to Play* (4:41); first U.K. pressing of *Press to Play* (4:37, listed as 4:41); U.K. 12-inch single (4:45, listed as 4:43; a second edition of the U.K. 12-inch added the words "video soundtrack" to the cover). U.S. 12-inch single (4:41); U.S. 7-inch single (3:35); second edition of U.K. 7-inch single (3:39, listed as 3:35; U.K. picture sleeve added words "video edit"); U.K. 10-inch single (3:36 "video edit"); second U.S. 7-inch promo (3:35 and unique 4:07 edit).

Dub Mix (6:28): U.S. and U.K. 12-inch single.

"Pretty Little Head" (Paul). Three noticeably different mixes of the song were released: LP *Press to Play*: 5:14 Hugh Padgham mix; 7-inch U.K. single: 3:50 Larry Alexander mix; 12-inch U.K. single: 6:56 John "Tokes" Potoker remix.

"P.S. Love Me Do" (Paul, Version I, studio version; Version II, live). Version I of this new arrangement of The Beatles' "Love Me Do" and "P.S. I Love You" was released only in Japan on the double CD pack *Flowers in the Dirt*. Version II, a live concert version, was released only in the U.K. as a bonus track on 12-inch and CD "Birthday" (live) singles.

"Rainclouds" (Paul). Released only on 7-inch and 12-inch "Ebony and Ivory" singles.

"Ram On" (Paul) (Version I 2:30; Version II [reprise] 0:55). Both versions are on Paul's *Ram* album.

"Real Love" (John). Home-recorded demo released as a bonus track on the *Imagine: John Lennon* compilation soundtrack album. The same recording was released under its original copyrighted title, "Girls and Boys," on the CD boxed set *Lennon*.

"Revolution" (Version I 3:22, released on single; Version II, titled "Revolution 1," released on LP *The Beatles*). The single and album versions are completely different recordings. Version I, the single version, originally appeared only in mono. It is available on CD in stereo on *Past Masters* and in mono on 3-inch CD single. The album version (Version II) was released in mono on the U.K. mono edition of *The Beatles* (no mono version of *The Beatles* was issued in the U.S.). Thus there are two completely different versions of this song, and each exists in different stereo and mono mixes. Version I also appears in stereo on *Hey Jude*, *The Beatles 1967–1970*, *Rock and Roll Music* and *The Beatles Box*.

"Rough Ride" (Paul) (Version I 4:43; Version II 4:53). There are two completely different recordings of this song. Version I is on *Flowers in the Dirt*; Version II is on the U.K. 3-inch CD single "Figure of Eight" and the Japanese double CD pack *Flowers in the Dirt*.

"Rudolph the Red-Nosed Reggae" (Paul). Originally released as a single with "Wonderful Christmastime," the song was added to the CD *Back to the Egg* as a bonus track. On the original single the song appeared in mono (the A side was stereo), but subsequent pressings and all album releases are stereo.

"Runaway" (George/Wilburys). Released only in the U.K. as a bonus track on Traveling Wilburys 12-inch and CD "She's My Baby" singles. Vocal is by Jeff Lynne.

"Sally G." (Paul). Originally released only as a single with "Junior's Farm," the song was added to the CD *Wings at the Speed of Sound* as a bonus track.

"Same Time Next Year" (Paul). Bonus track included with U.K. 12-inch and CD "Put It There" singles and on Japanese double CD pack *Flowers in the Dirt*.

"Sat Singing" (George). Omitted from the *Somewhere in England* album, a remix was released on bonus 7-inch vinyl and 5-inch CD EP *Songs by George Harrison* issued with George's book.

"Save the World" (George) (Version I, on *Somewhere in England*; Version II on *Greenpeace*). George completely rerecorded his vocal and remixed this track for the 1985 *Greenpeace* charity album (Version II).

"Say Say Say" (Paul/Michael Jackson) (Version I 3:55; Version II [remix] 5:40; Version III [instrumental] 7:00). Version I originally appeared on *Pipes of Peace* and on a 7-inch single. Versions II and III, both mixed by John "Jellybean" Benitez, were issued on a 12-inch single.

"Scared" (John). Two different versions were released, the original on *Walls and Bridges* and an outtake on *Menlove Ave.*

"Secret Friend" (Paul). Originally released only in the U.K. as a single with "Temporary Secretary," the song was added to the CD *McCartney II* as a bonus track.

"Sexy Sadie" (Version I [mono]; Version II [stereo]). Ringo taps his tambourine twice during the intro on the stereo release but only once on the mono version.

"Sgt. Pepper Inner Groove." Actually an untitled bit of audio gibberish, combined with the sound of a whistle audible only to dogs, that was placed in the runout groove on the original U.K. *Sgt. Pepper* album but omitted on the U.S. release. These two gems were restored on the CD release of the album. The gibberish also appeared on the U.S. *Rarities* album, where it was titled "Sgt. Pepper Inner Groove."

"Sgt. Pepper's Lonely Hearts Club Band" (Version I [mono]; Version II [stereo]). Heard at the start of the *Sgt. Pepper* album, the mono version features more prominent lead guitar work toward the end, which is barely audible on the stereo release.

"Sgt. Pepper's Lonely Hearts Club Band" (reprise) (Version I [mono]; Version II [stereo]). The audience sounds begin more abruptly on the mono release, there is a longer drum introduction with four extra drum beats before the count-in, some words spoken by John and some audience laughter, all missing from the stereo release. Paul's ad lib at the end, almost inaudible in stereo, is quite clear on the mono release. The transition from "Good Morning Good Morning" is sloppier than on the stereo release and lacks the smooth transition from the chicken sound to that of a guitar.

"She's a Woman." Originally released in mono as the B side of "I Feel Fine," the song appears in true stereo on *Beatles '65*, *The Beatles Box* and *Past Masters*. The mono version appears on a 3-inch CD single and on the U.K. *Rarities* album. The stereo version released on the special EP *The Beatles*, issued with the U.K. *The Beatles EP Collection*, adds a count-in that is missing on all other releases. It was originally thought that the count-in was added on for this release and that it was not part of the original recording. However, EMI officials have claimed that it was on the original tape of this recording.

"She's Leaving Home" (Version I [mono]; Version II [stereo]). The song is noticeably slowed down on the stereo release of *Sgt. Pepper* and sounds much faster in mono.

"Sie Liebt Dich." German-language version of "She Loves You," originally released in mono on a German single backed with "Komm, Gib Mir Deine Hand" (Odeon 22671), and on a U.S. single backed with "I'll Get You." The original German single was still available as a reissue as late as 1976 (Odeon 1-C006-04204-M). It also appears in mono on *Past Masters* and in stereo on both the U.S. and U.K. *Rarities* albums.

"Silly Love Songs" (Paul) (Version I 5:54; Version II 3:28; Version III [remake] 4:29). Paul's original version was officially released at 5:54 on *Wings at the Speed of Sound*. Version II, a shorter edit of that recording, was issued on a U.S. promo. Version III was a completely new recording for *Give My Regards to Broad Street*.

"Simple As That" (Paul). Released only on U.K. charity LP *The Anti-Heroin Project: It's a Live-in World*.

"Six O'Clock" (Ringo). (Version I 4:05; Version II 5:26). Version I released on *Ringo* LP; Version II on cassette, 8-track, and some promo copies of LP.

"Slow Down" (Version I [mono]; Version II [stereo]). There is an extra shout by John at the end on the stereo release that is missing on the mono version. Originally in mono on the EP *Long Tall Sally*, it is available on CD in stereo on *Past Masters*. It also appears in stereo on *Rock and Roll Music*, *The Beatles Box* and *Something New*. It appears in mono on U.K. EP *Long Tall Sally*, U.K. *Rarities*, U.S. mono *Something New* and on a U.S. single backed with "Matchbox."

"So Bad" (Paul) (Version I 3:18; Version II 3:10). Version I is on LP *Pipes of Peace*; Version II was released only on the CD and cassette editions of *Give My Regards to Broad Street*.

"Spies Like Us" (Paul) (Version I [7-inch] 4:42; Version II [Party Mix] 7:10; Version III [Alternate Mix] 3:56; Version IV [D.J. Version] 3:46). Released only as a single in the U.S. and U.K., Version I appeared on a 7-inch edition; the other versions were issued on the 12-inch edition.

"Spirit of the Forest" (Ringo). Ringo is one of several artists taking a line or two of lead vocal on this charity record, released as a 7-inch single in the U.K. and a 12-inch single in the U.S.

"Stand by Me" (George and Ringo, live). George and Ringo joined in on Ben E. King's performance of this song at the Jun 5, 1987 Prince's Trust show but did not participate in the number at the Jun 6 show. The Jun 6 version (*without* George and Ringo) is on the LP *Prince's Trust: 1987 All-Star Concert*, released only in the U.K.

"Steel and Glass" (John). Two different versions were released, the original on *Walls and Bridges* and an outtake on *Menlove Ave.*

"Strawberry Fields Forever" (several variations). The song fades down and back up twice toward the end. On the mono and U.S. stereo mixes, the song does not completely fade out the first time, although it fades slightly more on the U.S. stereo mix. On the German stereo (released elsewhere as well), the first fadeout is a complete one. Also, John's "cranberry sauce" line is heard twice at the very end only on the German stereo mix; it is heard once on other releases. On the German release, John's voice is not as slowed down and many of the backward effects and instrumental riffs are in different places. The German stereo mix was also released on the CD *Magical Mystery Tour* and on U.K. and Japanese *The Beatles 1967–1970*.

"Sweet George Brown" (Version I: original Jun 1961 Sheridan recording with The Beatles; Version II: Sheridan Dec 1961 remake [no Beatles involvement]; Version III: Sheridan rerecorded vocal using original Beatles backing track). One of the Jun 1961 Tony Sheridan Hamburg recordings on which The Beatles served as backing group. At least two different versions of the song have been released (Versions II and III), and there is serious speculation that the original Beatles-related recording is actually an extremely rare third version (Version I). According to the theory, Version I is the untouched original recorded by Sheridan with The Beatles in Jun 1961 and released in Oct 1961 on the German EP *Ya Ya* (Polydor EPH 21485); it was reportedly reissued on a Swedish fan club disc in 1982. Version II is a completely different straight rendition of the song recorded by Sheridan, without The Beatles, in Dec 1961. That version is also quite rare, but it is found on several early German discs and on a Bulgarian album (Polydor BTA-1789). Version III is yet another Sheridan remake, this one recorded in 1963, in which the original Beatles backing track was again used but over which Sheridan recorded a new vocal with revised lyrics in which he makes reference to The Beatles' haircuts and makes a comical remark to the piano player. Version III is the most commonly available version and has appeared on all reissues of the Sheridan material. The three-version theory was put forth by an article by Peter Ingham and Toru Mitsui. Also see liner notes and recording session information included with CD *The Beatles—First* (Polydor 823 701-2 YH).

"Take It Away" (Paul) (Version I 4:13; Version II 3:59). Version I appears on *Tug of War*; Version II, a shorter edit, was released on 7-inch and 12-inch singles. The single features a clean opening; the opening is sequed from the previous track on the *Tug of War* album.

"Talk More Talk" (Paul). Two different mixes were issued: 5:18 Padgham mix on *Press to Play*; 5:56 McCartney/John Jacobs remix on U.K. 12-inch "Only Love Remains" single.

"Taxman" (Version I [mono]; Version II [stereo]). On the mono release of the *Revolver* album, the cowbell starts during the second verse; on the stereo release it does not begin until the middle of the second "I'm the taxman" chorus.

"Teardrops" (George) (Version I 4:04; Version II 3:20). Version I is found on *Somewhere in England*; Version II is a shorter edit issued as a single.

"Tell Me Why" (Version I [mono]; Version II [stereo]). John's brief solo vocals are single-tracked on the mono release of the U.K. *A Hard Day's Night* album, but double-tracked on the stereo release; only the mono version has been issued on CD. The stereo version also appeared on the U.S. *Something New* album.

"Thank You Girl" (Version I [mono]; Version II [stereo]). The stereo version, available only on the U.S. *The Beatles Second Album* and the German *Beatles Beat*, has added harmonica riffs toward the middle and at the end that are missing on the mono release, which is found on *Past Masters*, 3-inch CD single, Vee Jay and Parlophone singles backed with "From Me to You," Vee Jay single backed with "Do You Want To Know a Secret?" U.K. *Rarities, Jolly What! The Beatles and Frank Ifield on Stage*, U.K. EP *The Beatles' Hits* and *The Beatles Box*.

"That's The Way It Goes" (George) (Version I [original mix]); Version II [remix]). Version I appeared on the LP *Gone Troppo*. Version II, a remix, was released on U.K. CD and 12-inch "When We Was Fab" singles.

"This Guitar (Can't Keep from Crying)" (George) (Version I 4:11; Version II 3:49). Version I was issued on *Extra Texture—Read All About It*; Version II is a shorter edit issued as a single.

"This One" (Paul) (Version I 4:10; Version II [Club Lovejoys Mix] 6:10). These variations were released as follows: Version I: *Flowers in the Dirt*, U.K. 7-inch and cassette singles, U.S. cassette single, U.S. 7-inch promo, U.K. 5-inch CD single, U.K. 12-inch single (12RX 6223); Version II: U.K. D.J. 12-inch promo (12 R LOVE 6223A), U.K. 12-inch "Figure of Eight" single (12R 6235).

"Tomorrow Never Knows" (Version I [mono]; Version II [stereo]). The mono and stereo releases have different backward tape effects.

"Tough on a Tightrope" (Paul). The following different mixes of this recording were released: 4:44 High Padgham mix: U.S. and U.K. 7-inch "Only Love Remains" singles, CD *Press to Play*. 7:03 Julian Mendelsohn remix: U.K. 12-inch "Only Love Remains" single.

"Twist and Shout." A unique 5:20 mix of this Beatles recording was released in the U.S. by Ultimix on a Club D.J. 12-inch single, issued as part of a three-record set.

"Venus and Mars" (Paul) (Version I 1:16; Version II 2:03). Both versions are on LP *Venus and Mars*.

"Venus and Mars"/"Rock Show" (Paul). Special reedited coupling of these two songs released only as a single. "Rock Show" appears in a shortened edit on the single. Mono and stereo mixes of the single were issued on a U.S. promo.

"Walking in the Park with Eloise" (Paul). Instrumental originally released only as a single; it was added to the CD *Wings at the Speed of Sound* as a bonus track.

"Wanderlust" (Paul) (Version I 3:50; Version II 2:48). Version I appears on *Tug of War*; Version II is on *Give My Regards to Broad Street*.

"Waterfalls" (Paul) (Version I 4:41; Version II 3:22). Version I is the official release; Version II was issued on a U.S. promo.

"We All Stand Together" (Paul) (Vocal Version 4:13; Humming Version 2:23). This song is heard in the animated film *Rupert and the Frog Song* and was released only in the U.K. as a single. The A side features Paul's vocal (by Paul and the Frog Chorus); the B side is a humming rendition (by Paul and the Finchley Frogettes). The A side was also released on the U.K. edition of Paul's *All the Best* album.

"We Got Married" (Paul) (Version I [LP] 4:55; Version II [U.S. promo] edit 4:00, listed as 3:42). U.S. promo CD single has a unique 4:00 edit (listed as 3:42) as well as the 4:55 LP *Flowers in the Dirt* version.

"What Goes On" (Version I [mono]; Version II [stereo]). The mono mix on the U.S. *Yesterday and Today* and the U.K. *Rubber Soul* albums is missing some of the lead guitar at the end, just before the final guitar chord. The full lead guitar part is heard on the stereo releases of those two albums.

"When I Get Home" (Version I [U.S. mono]; Version II [all others]). John's line "Till I walk out that door" comes in sooner on the U.S. mono *Something New* album than on any other U.S. or U.K. stereo or mono release of the song.

"When We Was Fab" (George) (Version I 3:55; Version II [reverse ending] 5:17). Version I is the original mix that appeared on the LP *Cloud Nine* and on 7-inch and cassette singles. Version II is a special "reverse ending" remix that was released only in the U.K. on 3-inch CD and 12-inch singles. Version I also appears on the 12-inch and CD singles, where it is labeled "unextended mix."

"When You Wish Upon a Star" (Ringo). Released only on the *Stay Awake* album of Disney songs by various artists.

"While My Guitar Gently Weeps" (Version I [mono]; Version II [stereo]; Version III [George, live]). Most of George's vocal sounds heard at the end of the song on the stereo release of *The Beatles* (aka the "*White Album*") are missing on the mono edition. Version III is George's live performance at the Jun 1987 Prince's Trust shows, released only in U.K. on *The Prince's Trust Concert 1987* and *The Royal Concert* albums.

"Why Don't We Do It in the Road (Version I [mono]; Version II [stereo]). The hand clapping heard during the intro on the stereo version is missing on the mono release of *The Beatles*.

"With a Little Help from My Friends" (Ringo, live Version I and live Version II). Version I is from Jun 1987 Prince's Trust shows, released only in U.K. on concert album *The Prince's Trust Concert 1987*. Version II was recorded at Ringo's Sep 4, 1989 Los Angeles concert; released on U.K. 12-inch and CD "Nobody's Child" singles and in the U.S. and U.K. on the CD *Nobody's Child: Romanian Angel Appeal* but omitted from the LP and cassette editions of the album.

"With a Little Luck" (Paul) (Version I 5:45; Version II 3:13). Version I is the official release; Version II was issued in mono and stereo on a U.S. promo.

"Woman Is the Nigger of the World" (John) (Version I [original 5:15 edit]; Version II [4:37 edit]). Version I is on *Some Time in New York City*; it was edited down to 4:37 for the LP *Shaved Fish* (Version II).

"Wonderful Christmastime" (Paul). Originally released only as a single with "Rudolph the Red Nosed Reggae," the song was added to the CD *Back to the Egg* as a bonus track. It also appears on the U.K. *Now—The Christmas Album*.

"The Word" (Stereo I and Stereo II). The U.S. stereo edition of *Rubber Soul* has most of the vocal only in the right channel (Stereo I); the U.K. stereo album has the vocal in both channels (Stereo II).

"Words of Love" (Version I [mono] 2:11; Version II [stereo] 2:02). As indicated, the mono version is noticeably longer than the stereo.

"Wrack My Brain" (Ringo) (Version I [standard mix]; Version II [Canadian single mix]). An alternate mix

was issued on the Canadian single. The original mix was released on U.S. and U.K. singles and on *Stop and Smell the Roses*.

"Write Away" (Paul). Released only as a bonus track on the CD *Press to Play* and on U.K. 7-inch, 12-inch and cassette "Pretty Little Head" singles.

"Ya Ya" (John) (Version I 1:06; Version II 2:17). Version I was released on *Walls and Bridges*; Version II on *Rock 'N' Roll*.

"Yellow Submarine" (Version I [mono]; Version II [stereo]). The opening on the mono release includes a guitar chord missing from the stereo release. On the mono version, John's shouted repeats of Ringo's lines begin one line sooner and are louder than on the stereo version. The respective versions were released on the mono and stereo editions of *Revolver*; the mono mix was also released on a single. The stereo version also appears on the *Yellow Submarine* album; that stereo mix was also used for the U.K. mono release of *Yellow Submarine* (the album was not released in mono in the U.S.).

"Yesterday" (Version I by The Beatles, 2:04; Version II by Paul, 1:43). The Beatles' version appeared in the U.K. on the *Help!* album and in the U.S. as a single and on *Yesterday and Today*. Paul's version was released on *Give My Regards to Broad Street*.

"You Know It Makes Sense" (Ringo). Released only in the U.K. on the album *Anti-Heroin Project: It's a Live-in World* and on a 12-inch single.

"You Never Know" (Ringo). Recorded for the 1991 film *Curly Sue* and played over the film's closing credits. Released only on the soundtrack album *Music from the Motion Picture Curly Sue* and on a U.S. promo CD.

"Zig Zag" (George). Instrumental released on U.S. and U.K. 7-inch and cassette "When We Was Fab" singles, and featured on U.K. 3-inch CD and 12-inch singles.

"Zoo Gang" (Paul). An instrumental originally released only in the U.K. as a single with "Band on the Run," it was added to the CD *Venus and Mars* as a bonus track.

Notable Album Variations

The U.K. *Please Please Me*, *With The Beatles*, *A Hard Day's Night* and *Beatles for Sale* albums were issued on CD in mono only. Thus stereo versions of most of the songs on those albums are not yet available on CD. Similarly, the mono versions of the other albums have not been issued on CD, and it is highly unlikely that they ever will be.

The Beatles (aka the "*White Album*"). The mono version of this album, released only in England, is markedly different from its stereo counterpart released throughout the world. Most notably, the mono release runs faster since many of the tracks were slowed down on the stereo release. Two noticeably different tracks, "Helter Skelter" and "Don't Pass Me By," were lifted from

the mono release for the U.S. LP *Rarities*, but there are equally obvious differences on other tracks as well, including "Long, Long, Long," "Piggies" and others.

A Hard Day's Night. The much-maligned U.S. release of this album appears to contain the actual soundtrack recordings used in the film *A Hard Day's Night*. All U.S. releases of the album contain mono versions of The

Beatles' songs, although the stereo edition does feature stereo versions of George Martin's instrumental titles. Of particular note are "And I Love Her" and "I'll Cry Instead," both described in detail in the "Alternate Versions and Bonus Tracks" section. Unlike the U.S. album, the U.K. LP includes none of the film's incidental background music. See Lewisohn (1988) for specific information on mono mixes prepared specifically for the film soundtrack between Mar 3 and Jun 22, 1964.

Magical Mystery Tour. Originally released only in the U.S. as a 12-inch LP (a double EP with fewer songs was issued in the U.K.). Three songs appeared in mono on both the mono and stereo releases of the album: "All You Need Is Love," "Penny Lane" and "Baby You're a Rich Man." The reason for this was quite simple: No stereo mixes had been prepared at the time Capitol compiled the album. The German *Magical Mystery Tour*, a U.K. cassette edition and the CD, all released later, feature stereo versions of all the songs. When the album was first issued in the U.K. in 1976, the original Capitol master was used, thus the same three songs appeared in mono. The same master was again used for the Mobile Fidelity half-speed master edition. The final U.S. Capitol pressing was all stereo (serial number changed to C1-48062).

Help! and *The Early Beatles.* The mono releases of both of these U.S. albums actually contained the stereo mixes with the separate tracks mixed together to simulate mono.

Yesterday and Today. Original stereo pressings contained mono mixes of several songs; later pressings were all stereo.

Abbey Road, Let It Be and *Yellow Submarine.* No real mono mixes of these albums exist. A mono version of *Yellow Submarine* was released in the U.K., but it was simply the stereo mix with the tracks combined to simulate mono, rather than a unique, separate mono mix.

Bootlegs and Unreleased Recordings

This section lists all known unreleased Beatles recordings, most of which are available on bootleg records. Each entry lists the date of the event, describes the recorded material and lists bootleg records, where available, on which it can be found. Bootlegged material is typically recycled many times on different records, not always in equal sound quality. Many duplicative bootleg records are omitted where more complete bootlegs of improved sound quality have appeared. For more information on unreleased Beatles recordings, see King (1988, 1989) and Walker in the references, and *Belmo's Beatleg News* and *The 910*. Among the more recent, better sounding bootlegs are the 13-album *Beatles at the Beeb*, *Ultra Rare Trax*, *Unsurpassed Masters* and *Lost Lennon Tapes* series. Several bootlegs of complete albums that were scheduled for release but were ultimately canceled have appeared, including *Sessions*, *Get Back*, *Cold Cuts* and original versions of *Somewhere in England* and *McCartney II*.

A few different bootlegs in this listing have the same title and are thus followed by a number to identify them: CD: *Sessions* (CD-1: Disques du Monde, CD-2: Toasted/Condor; CD-3: bogus "EMI" label); CD: *Yer Blues* (CD-1: Vigotone; CD-2: Library Products); *Beatles at the Beeb (3 LP)* refers to copies of the 1982 radio special "The Beatles at the Becb"; *Sgt. Pepper (9 LP)* refers to copies of the 1984 syndicated radio special "Sgt. Pepper's Lonely Hearts Club Band: A History of the Beatle Years 1962–1970."

The chronology is followed by a list of unreleased song titles and composers.

Chronology

1958

That year: The Quarrymen made a recording of "That'll Be the Day," backed with "In Spite of All the Danger." The only known original copy is owned by Paul McCartney, and he played part of the former during "The Real Buddy Holly Story" TV special. All bootlegs are taken from the film, and no complete version has yet appeared. *Lost Lennon Tapes Volume Eight* has the longest version; it also appears on *Lost Lennon Tapes 1* (CD) and the latter adds Paul's acoustic takes of "Love Me Do" and "Words of Love" from the same TV special. Paul eventually had "That'll Be the Day" and "In Spite of All the Danger" digitally remastered and had 50 copies of the single pressed as Christmas gifts for friends.

1960

Aug 17–Nov 20: The Beatles taped themselves during a rehearsal session in Germany (often listed as a spring 1960 Liverpool recording). The tape includes the following song titles: "I'll Follow the Sun," "Hallelujah I Love Her So," "The One After 909" (two versions), "Movin' and Groovin'," "I Will Always Be in Love with You," "Matchbox," "Wildcat" (often mistitled "You Just Don't Understand"), "That's When Your Heartaches Begin," "Rebel Rouser," "Hello Little Girl." Other, speculative titles that have been suggested for several unidentified songs on the tape are "I Don't Know," "Come on People," "You'll Be Mine," "Some Days," "Well Darling" and "You Must Write Every Day." All but "Rebel Rouser," "I Don't Know" and "Come on People" are on *The Quarrymen Rehearse with Stu Sutcliff* [sic] *Spring 1960*, also released as *The Quarrymen at Home* (LP and CD). *Liverpool May 1960* contains the three missing songs, but mainly comprises a large number of unidentified instrumentals; it also includes "I'll Follow the Sun," "Hallelujah I Love Her So," one version of "The One After 909" and a longer edit of "Movin' and Groovin'." An additional title, "The World Is Waiting for the Sunrise," appeared only on the *1989 Beatleg News Christmas Record*.

Oct 15: As a backing group for Walter Eymond (stage name "Lu Walters") of Rory Storm and The Hurricanes, The Beatles recorded "Summertime" in Hamburg. Ringo substituted for Pete Best on drums on this occasion. Two additional numbers were recorded by Eymond, "Fever" and "September Song," also with Ringo on drums but without the other Beatles.

1960–61: Early Lennon/McCartney compositions include the following: "I Fancy Me Chances," "Tip of My Tongue," "I Lost My Little Girl" (the first song ever written by Paul), "Just Fun," "Keep Looking That Way," "Long Black Train" (Lennon), "Looking Glass" (instrumental), "That's My Woman," "Thinking of Linking," "Too Bad About Sorrows," "Winston's Walk" (instrumental), "Years Roll Along," "Pinwheel Twist," "I'm in Love" and "Nobody I Know." No early Beatles recordings of these songs have surfaced, but some of the songs were revived by the group during the *Let It Be* filming sessions of Jan 1969, and some of those recordings have appeared on bootlegs.

1961

Jun 22–24: Tony Sheridan claims that he and Paul co-authored the unreleased song "Tell Me If You Can" during this period.

That year: Several titles of unreleased Beatles numbers were noted during the Aug 28, 1968 auction at Sotheby's including several written by Stu Sutcliffe; these include "Ooh, Ooh, Ooh," "Yea Cos Your a Sure Fire Bet to Win My Lips [sic]" and "Everybody's Ever Got Somebody Caring." The same auction offered a 1961 Beatles playlist written by Harrison that included "Reelin' and Rockin'," "Long Tall Sally," "Sticks and Stones," "More Than I Can Say," "Jambalaya," "I Know," "Hi Heel Sneakers," "Summertime" and "Let's Stomp."

1962

Jan 1: The 15 songs recorded by The Beatles at their audition for Decca Records have been legitimately released (see Recording Chronology), but are sometimes artificially extended on those records. All 15, in their original form, are on *The Silver Beatles/Original Decca Tapes* (CD) and *The Decca Tapes*.

Mar 7: The Beatles recorded "Dream Baby," "Memphis" and "Please Mr. Postman," all aired the following day on BBC Radio's "Teenager's Turn (Here We Go)." All three are on *The Lost Beebs*, *The Beatles at the Beeb W/Pete Best* and *Meet the Beeb*.

Mar: The Beatles recorded themselves rehearsing a few songs, reportedly at the Cavern Club. The date of the session is not certain, but the quality of their playing as well as the choice of material would seem to place this as earlier rather than later that year, although the recordings are also thought to have originated in Oct. The songs include "I Saw Her Standing There," "The One After 909" (two versions) and "Catswalk" (later retitled "Cat Call") (two versions). The unedited tape is on *The Cavern Tapes Circa 1962* (CD), *The Silver Beatles/Original Decca Tapes* (CD) and *Cavern Club Rehearsals* (CD). John sings "I begged her not to *leave*" instead of "I begged her not to *go*" on one version of "The One After 909."

Jun 6: The Beatles' first recording session at EMI is of special interest since it was the only one at EMI in which drummer Pete Best took part. The Beatles recorded "Love Me Do," "P.S. I Love You," "Ask Me Why" and "Besame Mucho." Apparently only "Besame Mucho" has survived; the other tapes were erased or destroyed. That recording was scheduled for official release by EMI in 1985 on the ultimately scrapped *Sessions* album, and it appears on *Ultra Rare Trax Volume 1*, *Back Track* (CD), *Sessions* (LP, CD-1, CD-2) and *Unsurpassed Masters Volume 1*.

Jun 11: The Beatles recorded an appearance on BBC Radio's "Here We Go," aired Jun 15, and sang "Ask Me Why," "Besame Mucho" and "A Picture of You"; they also reportedly recorded "Sheila" but, if they did, it was cut from the broadcast. The first three songs are on *The Lost Beebs*, *Meet the Beeb* and *The Beatles at the Beeb W/Pete Best*.

Jul 1: A Gene Vincent Cavern Club performance of "What'd I Say" is said to feature The Beatles as his backing group. The track appears on the Gene Vincent bootleg, *Rarities*. Vincent had his own backing group and at least one member—a saxophonist—can be heard on this cut, but the relatively unknown Beatles may have joined in (they had worked with Vincent in Hamburg).

Jul: A crude 1¾ IPS tape of a Beatles Cavern Club performance was recorded by a fan and includes "Hey! Baby," "If You Gotta Made a Fool of Somebody," "Hippy Hippy Shake," "Please Mr. Postman," "Roll Over Beethoven," "Ask Me Why," "Sharing You," "Your Feets Too Big," "Words of Love," "Till There Was You," "Dizzy Miss Lizzie," "I Forgot to Remember to Forget," "Matchbox" (vocal by Pete Best), "Shimmy Shake," "Memphis," "Young Blood" and "Dream Baby." Paul purchased the tape at Sotheby's auction for £2,100 on Aug 29, 1985.

Aug 22: The Beatles were filmed at the Cavern Club by Granada TV for a show called "Know the North," scheduled to be aired on Nov 7. The segment was reportedly not aired due to the film's poor sound quality. The group sang "Some Other Guy" and "Kansas City"/"Hey Hey Hey Hey." According to different reports, film of the second song was destroyed, or its soundtrack was. "Some Other Guy" appears on *The Beatles Live in United Kingdom* (CD), *The Real Early Beatles* and several other bootlegs, all taken from the film soundtrack. Both bootlegs also include the same recording from an acetate made from the soundtrack.

Sep 4: The Beatles recorded "How Do You Do It." The song was scheduled to appear on EMI's 1985 *Sessions* album, where the ending was edited so that the first of three repeats of "Wish I knew how you do it to me, I'd do it to you" was replaced with "Wish I knew how you do it to me, but I haven't a clue," taken from the second verse. It appears in that form on bootlegs of *Sessions* (LP, CD-1, CD-2). The original, pre-edit recording appears on *Ultra Rare Trax 1* (CD), *Back Track* (CD), *Not for Sale* (LP and CD), *Unsurpassed Masters 1* (CD) and *Sessions* (CD-3).

Sep 11: The Beatles recorded a slow version of "Please Please Me" at EMI's Abbey Road studio, but the tape was destroyed and no copies are known to exist.

Nov 26: The Beatles recorded "Tip of My Tongue," but the tape was destroyed and no copies are known to exist.

Dec 17: The Beatles appeared live on Granada Television's "People and Places" show. "A Taste of Honey," reportedly from this show, is on the *1989 Beatleg News Christmas Record*.

Dec 31: In addition to the number and variety of commercially released recordings of The Beatles' Star-Club performance on this date, some additional recordings from the show have surfaced only on bootlegs. Whether these are actually different recordings from the released ones or simply the original, untouched versions is unknown. The commercial versions underwent a variety

Not for Sale (bootleg). Many unreleased Beatles tracks were first heard on this album.

of editing and mixing and appear in different form on various legitimate releases. Original, unedited tapes of several songs are on *The Beatles Vs. the Third Reich* and *Mach Shau*, including "I'm Talking About You," "Till There Was You," "Where Have You Been All My Life?" "A Taste of Honey," "Lend Me Your Comb," "Your Feet's Too Big," "To Know Her Is to Love Her," "Everybody's Trying to Be My Baby," "Matchbox," "Little Queenie," "Nothin' Shakin' (But the Leaves on the Trees)" and "Roll Over Beethoven" (which includes a false start). A short bit of "Red Hot," another track reportedly from the Star-Club performance, is found on *The Beatles Vs. Don Ho* and *When It Says Beatles*. Finally, a different Star-Club version of "I Saw Her Standing There" appeared on the *1989 Beatleg News Christmas Record*.

1963

Jan 22: The Beatles recorded songs for BBC Radio's "Saturday Club" show, aired Jan 26, and sang "Some Other Guy," "Keep Your Hands Off My Baby," "Beautiful Dreamer," "Love Me Do" and "Please Please Me." The first three songs are found on *Meet the Beeb* and *Beatles at the Beeb W/Pete Best*.

Feb 11: "I Saw Her Standing There" was recorded under the working title "Seventeen"; takes 1–12 were cut on this date. *Unsurpassed Masters 1* (CD) has takes 6–9 and takes 11 and 12. Take 2 is on *Ultra Rare Trax 1* (CD), *Unsurpassed Masters 6 (CD), Back Track* (CD) and *Sessions* (CD-2); take 3 is on *Unsurpassed 6*; take 10 is on *Hold Me Tight* (CD), *Ultra Rare Trax 3 & 4, Back Track Part Three* (CD) and *Ultra Rare Trax 3* (CD).

- The Beatles recorded "A Taste of Honey" in six takes, the released version being take 7, an overdub onto take

5. The basic take is on *Ultra Rare Trax 3 & 4*, *Ultra Rare Trax 4* (CD), *Hold Me Tight* (CD) and *Back Track Part Three* (CD); the take on *Unsurpassed Masters 1* (CD) is listed as take 6.

- The Beatles recorded "There's a Place" with take 13 used for release. An unknown take and take 11 are on *Hold Me Tight* (CD), *Ultra Rare Trax 3 & 4*; *Ultra Rare Trax 2* (CD) and *Back Track* (CDs; *Parts One, Two*, and *Three*) have a false start (take 3) immediately followed by take 4, which includes a fadeout. *Unsurpassed Masters 1* (CD) has take 5 (false start), take 6, take 12 (harmonica overdub; false start); and take 13 (harmonica overdub; the released take).

- The Beatles recorded 13 unreleased takes of "Hold Me Tight," but the tapes were destroyed and no copies are known to exist.

- The Beatles recorded "Do You Want to Know a Secret." *Back Track* (CD) has an alternate take. Take 8 (the released take) is on *Unsurpassed Masters 1* (CD), *Ultra Rare Trax 3 & 4, Back Track Part Three* (CD), *Hold Me Tight* (CD) and *Ultra Rare Trax 4* (CD). Take 7, without echo, is on *Sessions* (CD-3) *Unsurpassed 7* (CD) and *Not for Sale* (fades out on LP but not on CD).

- The Beatles recorded 11 takes of "Misery," completed at a Feb 20 overdub session. Take 1 is on *Ultra Rare Trax 2* (CD), *Back Track* (CD) and *Sessions* (CD-2). *Ultra Rare Trax 3 & 4, Hold Me Tight* (CD), *Unsurpassed Masters 1* (CD) and *Back Track Part Two* (CD) all have takes 2–5 (all false starts) and take 6.

Mar 5: Four takes and one edit piece of "The One After 909" were recorded on this date. Take 2 is in stereo on *Ultra Rare Trax 1* (CD) and *Back Track* (CD); *Unsurpassed Masters 1* (CD) has a false start, take 1 (a breakdown) and take 2 (with left and right channels reversed). A different take appears in mono on *Unsurpassed 7* and *File Under*; it is also on all copies of *Sessions* with a different guitar solo.

- The Beatles recorded "From Me to You." *Ultra Rare Trax 1* (CD), *Back Track* (CD) and *Sessions* (CD-2) contain an alternate take with Paul's countdown. *Unsurpassed Masters 1* has takes 1, 2 and 8–13. *Unsurpassed 6* has takes 6 and 7.

- The Beatles recorded "Thank You Girl." *Unsurpassed Masters 1* (CD) has takes 2–4 and 7–13; *Unsurpassed 6* has take 1. All are edit pieces, except 2 and 3 (false starts), and 4 (ending fades). The released version is an edit of several takes.

Mar 16: The Beatles appeared live on BBC Radio's "Saturday Club" and sang "I Saw Her Standing There," "Misery," "Too Much Monkey Business," "I'm Talking About You," "Please Please Me" and "The Hippy Hippy Shake." All are on *Meet the Beeb* and *Beatles at the Beeb W/Pete Best*.

Apr 1: The Beatles recorded an appearance on BBC Radio's "Side by Side" show, aired May 13. They did the show's theme with The Karl Denver Trio, and "Long Tall Sally," "A Taste of Honey," "Chains," "Thank You Girl," "Boys" and "From Me to You." The last track is not bootlegged; all of the other songs, including the theme, are on *Beatles at the Beeb 2* and *Radio Active 2* (CD).

Apr 3: The Beatles recorded an appearance on BBC Radio's "Easy Beat," aired Apr 7, and sang "Please Please Me," "Misery" and "From Me to You." The latter song, introduced by Gerry Marsden of The Pacemakers, is on *Meet the Beeb* and *Beatles at the Beeb W/Pete Best*.

Apr 4: The Beatles recorded an appearance on BBC Radio's "Side by Side" show, aired Jun 24. They did the show's theme song with The Karl Denver Trio, and sang "Too Much Monkey Business," "I'll Be on My Way," "Boys," "From Me to You" and "Love Me Do," with the last title still not bootlegged. The other songs and the theme are all on *Beatles at the Beeb 1*, *Radio Active 1* (CD) and *Beatles at the Beeb* (CD).

Apr 18: During the live broadcast "Swinging Sound '63," transmitted from Royal Albert Hall, The Beatles sang "Twist and Shout" and "From Me to You." Both songs are on *Beatles at the Beeb 1* and *Radio Active 1* (CD).

Middle of May: John recorded a demo of "Bad to Me," to be recorded the following month by Billy J. Kramer. John's demo appears on *Acetates* (CD), *File Under* and *Not for Sale* (LP and CD).

May 21: The Beatles recorded songs for BBC Radio's "Saturday Club," aired May 25, including "I Saw Her Standing There," "Do You Want to Know a Secret," "Boys," "Long Tall Sally," "From Me to You" and "Money." All of the songs are on *Beatles at the Beeb 1*, *Radio Active 1* (CD) and *Beatles at the Beeb* (CD).

■ The Beatles recorded songs for BBC Radio's "Steppin' Out," aired Jun 3, including "Please Please Me," "I Saw Her Standing There," "Roll Over Beethoven," "Thank You Girl," "From Me to You" and "Twist and Shout"; the last title was cut from the broadcast; the first two songs are found on *Radio Active Volume 1* (CD) and *Beatles at the Beeb 1*.

May 24: The theme for The Beatles' "Pop Go The Beatles" BBC Radio series was recorded by The Lorne Gibson Trio backed by The Beatles, who never actually sang the song; Gibson himself was reportedly absent from the session. The theme appears on many bootlegs, which are listed under the many entries for this series.

■ The Beatles recorded an appearance on "Pop Go The Beatles," aired Jun 4. They sang "From Me to You," "Everybody's Trying to Be My Baby," "Do You Want to Know a Secret," "You Really Got a Hold on Me," "Misery" and "The Hippy Hippy Shake." The first title has not been bootlegged; numbers 2, 3 and 4 are on *Beatles at the Beeb 2* and *Radio Active 2* (CD); numbers 3, 4, 5 and 6 are on *Studio Sessions Volume One* and *The Last Beetle Record*.

Jun 1: The Beatles recorded the Jun 11 edition of "Pop Go The Beatles" and sang "Too Much Monkey Business," "I Got to Find My Baby," "Young Blood," "Baby It's You," "Till There Was You" and "Love Me Do." All of the songs, including the theme, are on *Beatles at the Beeb 2* and *Radio Active 2* (CD).

■ The Beatles recorded the Jun 18 edition of "Pop Go The Beatles" and sang "A Shot of Rhythm and Blues," "Memphis," "A Taste of Honey," "Sure to Fall," "Money," "Happy Birthday to You" and "From Me to You"; the final song is not bootlegged. All of the others, and the theme, are on *Beatles at the Beeb 3* and *Radio Active 3* (CD).

Jun 17: The Beatles recorded an appearance on "Pop Go The Beatles," aired Jun 25, and sang "Anna," "I Saw Her Standing There," "Boys," "Chains," "P.S. I Love You" and "Twist and Shout." They also recorded "A Taste of Honey," but it was cut from the broadcast. All of the other songs are on *Beatles at the Beeb 3* and *Radio Active 3* (CD) including the theme.

Jun 19: The Beatles recorded an appearance on BBC Radio's "Easy Beat," aired Jun 23, and sang "Some Other Guy," "A Taste of Honey," "Thank You Girl" and "From Me to You." All of the songs are on *Beatles at the Beeb 1*, *Radio Active 1* (CD) and *Beatles at the Beeb* (CD).

Jun 24: The Beatles recorded songs for the Jun 29 edition of "Saturday Club" for BBC Radio, including (1) "I Got to Find My Baby," (2) "Memphis," (3) "From Me to You," (4) "Roll Over Beethoven," (5) "Money" and (6) "Till There Was You." The first four are on *Beatles at the Beeb 2* and *Radio Active 2* (CD); numbers 3, 4, 5 and 6 are on *Studio Sessions 1*.

Middle of that year: A reel-to-reel tape of George composing "Don't Bother Me" was auctioned at Sotheby's in 1989 but did not sell. The tape also reportedly contains some guitar exercises recorded at a Bournemouth hotel in Aug 1963.

Jul 2: The Beatles recorded an appearance on "Pop Go The Beatles," aired Jul 16, and sang "That's All Right (Mama)," "Carol," "Soldier of Love," "Lend Me Your Comb," "Clarabella" and "There's a Place." They also recorded "Three Cool Cats," "Sweet Little Sixteen" and "Ask Me Why," all cut from the broadcast. All of the other songs, including the theme, are on *Beatles at the Beeb 3*, *Radio Active 3* (CD) and *Beatles at the Beeb* (CD).

Jul 10: The Beatles recorded the Jul 23 edition of "Pop Go The Beatles," and sang (1) "Sweet Little Sixteen," (2) "Nothin' Shakin' (But the Leaves on the Trees)," (3) "Lonesome Tears in My Eyes," (4) "So How Come No One Loves Me," (5) "Love Me Do" and (6) "A Taste of Honey." All but the final song have been bootlegged, and all but number 5 are on *Beatles at the Beeb 4* and *Radio Active 4* (CD); 5 is on *The Lost Beebs*.

■ The Beatles recorded the Jul 30 edition of "Pop Go The Beatles," and sang "Memphis," "Do You Want to Know a Secret," "Till There Was You," "Matchbox," "Please Mr. Postman" and "The Hippy Hippy Shake." All of the songs are on *Beatles at the Beeb 4* and *Radio Active 4* (CD).

Jul 16: The Beatles recorded "Pop Go The Beatles," aired Aug 6, and sang "I'm Gonna Sit Right Down and Cry Over You," "Crying, Waiting, Hoping," "Kansas City"/"Hey Hey Hey Hey," "To Know Her Is to Love Her," "The Honeymoon Song" and "Twist and Shout." All six are on *Beatles at the Beeb 4* and *Radio Active 4* (CD).

- The Beatles recorded "Pop Go The Beatles," aired Aug 13, and sang "Long Tall Sally," "Please Please Me," "I Got a Woman," "She Loves You," "You Really Got a Hold on Me" and "I'll Get You." All six songs are on *Beatles at the Beeb 5* and *Radio Active 5* (CD). Only one version of "She Loves You" was recorded on Jul 16, and the same recording was used for both the Aug 13 and Aug 20 editions of "Pop Go The Beatles."

- The Beatles recorded "Pop Go The Beatles," aired Aug 20, the third edition of that show to be recorded on this date. For the Aug 20 program, they recorded "She Loves You," "Words of Love," "Glad All Over," "I Just Don't Understand," "(There's a) Devil in Her Heart" and "Slow Down." The same recording of "She Loves You" was used for both the Aug 13 and Aug 20 editions of the series. All of the songs are on *Beatles at the Beeb 5* and *Radio Active 5* (CD).

Jul 17: The Beatles recorded an appearance on BBC Radio's "Easy Beat," aired Jul 21. They sang "I Saw Her Standing There," "A Shot of Rhythm and Blues," "There's a Place" and "Twist and Shout." All four are on *Beatles at the Beeb W/Pete Best*.

Jul 18: The Beatles recorded some unreleased takes of "Till There Was You."

Jul 22–27: The Beatles made several recordings on a reel-to-reel machine with Gerry Marsden, of The Pacemakers, during their six-day stint at the Odeon Cinema in Weston-super-Mare. The tapes feature readings from the Bible and "There Is a Green Hill," sung by the entire group. Gerry, George and John are also heard asking directions from inside a car.

Jul 24: A reel-to-reel tape made at Abbey Road during The Fourmost's recording of "Hello Little Girl," with The Beatles present, was auctioned at Sotheby's in 1989 for £5,720.

Jul 30: The Beatles recorded an interview with Phil Tate, aired Aug 30 on BBC Radio's "Non Stop Pop" show. It appears in part on *Meet the Beeb*.

- Two unreleased takes of "It Won't Be Long" are on the same reel-to-reel tape containing the Jul 24 Fourmost's recording of "Hello Little Girl."

Aug 1: The Beatles recorded the Aug 27 edition of "Pop Go The Beatles" and sang (1) "Ooh! My Soul," (2) "Don't Ever Change," (3) "Anna," (4) "A Shot of Rhythm and Blues," (5) "Twist and Shout" and (6) "She Loves You." The final song is not bootlegged; numbers 1, 2 and 5 are on *Beatles at the Beeb 5* and *Radio Active 5* (CD); numbers 2 and 4 are on *BBC, Beatles at the Beeb* (3 LP) and *From Us to You* (CD).

- The Beatles recorded the Sep 3 edition of "Pop Go The Beatles" and sang (1) "I'll Get You," (2) "Money," (3) "There's a Place," (4) "Honey Don't" (with lead vocal by John rather than Ringo), (5) "Roll Over Beethoven" and (6) "From Me to You." They also recorded "Lucille," "Baby It's You" and "She Loves You," all cut from the broadcast. Numbers 1 and 6 have not been bootlegged; numbers 3, 4 and 5 are on *Beatles at the Beeb 5* and *Radio Active 5* (CD); number 2 is on *The Lost Beebs*.

Aug 27–28: The Beatles recorded an appearance on the BBC TV documentary *The Mersey Sound*, aired Oct 9 in London and the North and on Nov 13 nationwide. The concert portion was filmed at a private concert before an invited audience at Southport's Little Theatre on Aug 27. "She Loves You" from that performance appears on *Live in the United Kingdom 1962–65* (CD) and the *1989 Beatleg News Christmas Record*; film of the number was aired in the U.S. on "The Jack Paar Show" on Jan 3, 1964. The Beatles also mimed to "Twist and Shout" and "Love Me Do."

Sep 3: The Beatles recorded three different editions of "Pop Go The Beatles," aired Sep 10, 17 and 24 respectively. For the Sep 10 show they sang (1) "Too Much Monkey Business," (2) "Till There Was You," (3) "Love Me Do," (4) "She Loves You," (5) "I'll Get You," (6) "A Taste of Honey" and (7) "The Hippy Hippy Shake." All of the songs except number 2, which is not bootlegged, are on *Beatles at the Beeb 6* and *Radio Active 6* (CD). For the Sep 17 show, they sang "Chains," "You Really Got a Hold on Me," "Misery," "Lucille," "From Me to You" and "Boys." They also recorded "A Taste of Honey," which was cut from the broadcast. All of the other songs are on *Beatles at the Beeb 6* and *Radio Active 6* (CD). For the Sep 24 show, they sang "I Saw Her Standing There," "Sure to Fall," "She Loves You," "Ask Me Why," "(There's a) 2Devil in Her Heart" (actually an excerpt from the released recording) and "Twist and Shout." All of the songs are on *Beatles at the Beeb 6* and *Radio Active 6* (CD). The same Sep 3 recording of "She Loves You" was used for both the Sep 10 and Sep 24 editions of "Pop Go The Beatles."

Sep 7: The Beatles recorded an appearance for BBC's "Saturday Club," aired Oct 5, and sang (1) "I Saw Her Standing There," (2) "Memphis," (3) "Happy Birthday," (4) "Lucille," (5) "I'll Get You," all of which have been bootlegged, and (6) "She Loves You," which has not. The first four appear on *Beatles at the Beeb 7* and *Radio Active 7* (CD); 2, 4, 5 and 6 are on *From Us to You* (CD). "She Loves You" appears to be the same recording aired on the Dec 21 "Saturday Club." (See *Belmo's Beatleg News* vol. 3, no. 6.)

Sep 12: The Beatles recorded "Hold Me Tight." Take 26 is on *Ultra Rare Trax 3 & 4, Hold Me Tight* (CD), and *Unsurpassed 7* (CD) (with a false start). *Unsurpassed Masters 1* (CD) has takes 22 and 23 (both false starts) and take 24. The released version is an edit of takes 26 and 29.

- The Beatles recorded "Don't Bother Me" (the song had been started the previous day). Takes 11 and 12 (both false starts) and take 13, before the final overdubs, are on *Unsurpassed Masters 1* (CD); take 10 is on *Unsurpassed 6* (CD).

Oct 4: The Beatles were seen doing "Twist and Shout," "She Loves You" and "I'll Get You" on the UK TV show "Ready, Steady, Go!" The group merely mimed to their released recordings of these songs. The first two numbers were released on the videocassette *Ready, Steady, Go! Volume 2*; "She Loves You" appears on the bootleg album *Ready Steady Go!*

Oct 13: The Beatles appeared live on ATV's "Sunday Night at the London Palladium" singing "From Me to You," "I'll Get You," "She Loves You" and "Twist and

Beatles at the Beeb Volume 7 (bootleg). Another in the 13-volume bootleg series that made most earlier "Beeb" bootlegs obsolete.

Shout." Although a tape of the performance exists, it has not appeared on bootleg to date. For many years it was thought that the group did "I Want to Hold Your Hand," "This Boy," "All My Loving" and "Money" during this performance, but they did not. Live versions of those songs from an unknown source are on *ABC Manchester*, *Sunday Night at the London Palladium* and *London*; "This Boy" and "All My Loving" are on *The Beatles*.

Oct 16: The Beatles recorded an appearance on BBC Radio's "Easy Beat," aired Oct 20, and sang "I Saw Her Standing There," "Love Me Do," "Please Please Me," "From Me to You" and "She Loves You." All five songs are on *Beatles at the Beeb 7* and *Radio Active 7* (CD). John also recorded a demo of "I'm in Love" for *The Fourmost*.

Oct 24: The Beatles' show at Stockholm's Karlaplan Studio was recorded and aired later on Swedish radio's "Pop '63" show. It is an excellent performance, and some very good bootlegs of it are available, including *Stars of '63* (CD) and *Johnny and The Moondogs*. The Beatles sang "From Me to You," "I Saw Her Standing There," "Roll Over Beethoven," "Money," "She Loves You," "Twist and Shout" and "You Really Got a Hold on Me." An interview from the session is on *Both Sides*. The concert has often been mistakenly identified as the Nov 3 Swedish TV show "Drop In," recorded Oct 30.

Oct 30: The Beatles recorded an appearance on the Swedish television show "Drop In," aired Nov 3. They sang "She Loves You," "Twist and Shout," "Long Tall Sally" and "I Saw Her Standing There"; these numbers have been identified as those found, in poor sound quality, on the bootleg LP *Stockholm*.

Nov 4: The Beatles appeared live at the Royal Variety Show, filmed at the Prince of Wales Theatre, London, televised

on Nov 10. They sang "From Me to You," "She Loves You," "Till There Was You" and "Twist and Shout." All of the songs are on *Live in the United Kingdom 1962–65* (CD), *Radio Active 7* (CD), and *Beatles at the Beeb 7*.

Nov 20: The Beatles performed live at the ABC Cinema, Ardwick, Manchester, singing "She Loves You" and "Twist and Shout." The performance was filmed in color by Pathe and released to British movie houses beginning Dec 22 as an 8½-minute clip titled *The Beatles Come to Town*. The film, from which bootlegs are taken, also included a clip of the released version of "From Me to You." The performance is found on *ABC Manchester* and *Recovered Tracks*, but the bootlegs, like the film, contain the released version of "From Me to You." The first two songs, along with 13 seconds of an instrumental version of "From Me to You," are on *Live in the United Kingdom 1962–65* (CD).

Dec 2: The Beatles recorded an appearance on the "Morecambe and Wise Show" at ATV studios, aired Apr 18, 1964, and sang "On Moonlight Bay," "I Want to Hold Your Hand," "All My Loving" and "This Boy." "On Moonlight Bay" appears on the *1989 Beatleg News Christmas Record*.

Dec 7: The Beatles' afternoon concert at the Empire Theatre in Liverpool was filmed by BBC and a 30-minute special was aired that evening titled "It's the Beatles!" The film included "From Me to You," "I Saw Her Standing There," "All My Loving," "Roll Over Beethoven," "Boys," "Till There Was You," "She Loves You," "This Boy," "I Want to Hold Your Hand," "Money" and "Twist and Shout"; a 19-second instrumental version of "From Me to You" was also played. The performance appears on *Live in the United Kingdom 1962–65* (CD), *Youngblood* and other bootlegs.

Dec 10: During an interview in Doncaster, John recited his poem "The Neville Club," which appears on *Lost Lennon Tapes 6*.

The Lost Lennon Tapes Vol. 6 (bootleg). Although listeners were able to tape this unprecedented radio series, bootleggers still did a brisk business selling the rare Lennon recordings.

Dec 15: The Beatles taped an appearance on a special Christmas version of "Thank Your Lucky Stars," aired Dec 21 on U.K. television. They delivered a brief, informal Christmas message, which is found on *The Beatles Vs. Don Ho*, and mimed to "All My Loving," "Twist and Shout," "She Loves You" and "I Want to Hold Your Hand."

Dec 17: The Beatles recorded an appearance on "Saturday Club," aired Dec 21, and sang (1) "All My Loving," (2) "This Boy," (3) "I Want to Hold Your Hand," (4) "Till There Was You," (5) "Roll Over Beethoven" and (6) "She Loves You." They also read some Christmas messages to their fans, did a 7-second parody of "All I Want for Christmas Is a Beatle" (sung as "All I Want for Christmas Is a Bottle") and did a medley of one line each from "Love Me Do," "Please Please Me," "From Me to You," "She Loves You," "I Want to Hold Your Hand" and "Rudolph the Red-Nosed Reindeer" played over a repeated riff from "Shazam!" The medley, termed "Crimble" medley, and numbers 2–6 are on *Beatles at the Beeb 8* and *Radio Active 8* (CD); number 1 has not been bootlegged. This recording of "She Loves You" appears to be the same one used on the Oct 5 "Saturday Club." The recording of "I Want to Hold Your Hand" was used again on the Feb 15, 1964 edition of "Saturday Club."

Dec 18: The Beatles recorded the first of five "From Us to You" holiday BBC Radio specials. This one aired Dec 26 and featured "From Us to You" (a version of "From Me to You" used as the theme for each of these shows), "Tie Me Kangaroo Down, Sport" (parody version with host Rolf Harris), "She Loves You," "All My Loving," "Roll Over Beethoven," "Till There Was You," "Boys," "Money," "I Saw Her Standing There" and "I Want to Hold Your Hand." All of the songs are on *Beatles at the Beeb 8* and *Radio Active 8* (CD).

That year: A reel-to-reel tape made by The Beatles sometime during 1963 was put up for auction, but did not sell, at Sotheby's in 1989. The tape reportedly features John and Paul singing "Tell Me True," "Over the Rainbow," instrumentals including "Michelle" (calling the dating of the tape into question), "Three Coins in the Fountain," "Rockin' and Rollin'" ("Reelin' and Rockin'"?) and the recitation of nursery rhymes.

1964

Early that year: A reel-to-reel tape dated as early 1964 was auctioned at Sotheby's in 1989 but did not sell. The tape features John doing several demo takes of "If I Fell" outside of the studio. Paul also cut at least one demo of "A World Without Love," not on the Sotheby's tape, for Peter and Gordon, which is now owned by Peter Asher.

Jan 7: The Beatles recorded an appearance for BBC Radio's "Saturday Club," aired Feb 15, and sang "All My Loving," "Money," "The Hippy Hippy Shake," "I Want to Hold Your Hand" (from Dec 21 "Saturday Club"), "Roll Over Beethoven," "Johnny B. Goode" and "I Wanna Be Your Man." All of the songs in excellent sound

quality are on *Beatles at the Beeb 9* and *Radio Active 9* (CD).

Jan 12: The Beatles appeared live on the U.K. TV show "Sunday Night at the London Palladium" for the second time. Five songs from the performance are on *Live in the United Kingdom 1962–65* (CD): "I Want to Hold Your Hand," "This Boy," "All My Loving," "Money" and "Twist and Shout."

Jan 16–Feb 4: In Paris, John and Paul completed writing "One and One Is Two," later recorded by The Strangers with Mike Shannon and released in the U.K. only on May 8. They reportedly taped at least four demos in Paris, one of which has some spoken messages from John and Paul. One of the demos, taped by Paul, appears on *Acetates* (CD) and *Ultra Rare Trax 3 & 4*.

■ The Beatles performed in the Olympia Theatre, Paris for 20 consecutive days doing two and sometimes three shows per day. A Jan 19 performance was taped for ORTF-Radio, and ORTF-TV filmed one of the Jan 22 shows; likely the bootlegs come from one of these sources. Five songs are on *The Beatles a Paris* and *Live in Paris 1964 and in San Francisco 1966* (CD): "From Me to You," "This Boy," "I Want to Hold Your Hand," "She Loves You" and "Twist and Shout."

Jan 24: The Beatles recorded an interview for the British Forces Network, broadcast later to troops stationed in West Germany. Excerpts are found on *Re-Introducing The Beatles*.

Jan 29: Recording of "Can't Buy Me Love" was completed in four takes while The Beatles were in Paris and was done at the same session at which they recorded their two German-language releases. Take 1 includes backing vocals by George and John that were discarded by take 4, the released version. An alternate take is on *Ultra Rare Trax 2* (CD), *Back Track* (CD), *Sessions* (CD-2), and (with a false start) on *Unsurpassed Masters 7*.

Feb 7–8: Interviews with Murray "The K" and one of his Beatles spots from New York's WINS radio were broadcast in the U.K. on BBC's Feb 8 edition of "Saturday Club." A phone call from Brian Matthew to The Beatles was also heard and is found on *Withered Beatles* and on *Beatles at the Beeb 8* and *Radio Active 8* (CD), and slowed down on *The Lost Beebs*.

Feb 9: In New York, The Beatles appeared live on "The Ed Sullivan Show." They performed "All My Loving," "Till There Was You," "She Loves You," "I Saw Her Standing There" and "I Want to Hold Your Hand." *The Beatles Conquer America* has all of the songs; most of that bootleg was copied onto *Live in the USA 1964–65* (CD), which is missing some tracks available on the vinyl LP.

■ The Beatles taped performances of "Twist and Shout," "Please Please Me" and "I Want to Hold Your Hand," seen on "The Ed Sullivan Show" on Feb 23; on *The Beatles Conquer America*; the first two songs only are on *Live in USA 1964–65* (CD).

Feb 11: The Beatles' first U.S. concert took place at the Coliseum in Washington, D.C. They sang "Roll Over Beethoven," "From Me to You," "I Saw Her Standing

There," "This Boy," "All My Loving," "I Wanna Be Your Man," "Please Please Me," "Till There Was You," "She Loves You," "I Want to Hold Your Hand," "Twist and Shout" and "Long Tall Sally." The show was filmed by CBS and seen at closed-circuit theater locations on Mar 14 and 15. The first 10 songs are on *Beatles: Vancouver '64/Washington '64* (CD), *First U.S. Concert* and *First U.S. Performance.*

Feb 12: While there is no record at EMI of The Beatles' Carnegie Hall concert being recorded on this date, an EMI official has stated that a recording of the show was made. He may have been referring to a tape made by a member of The Beatles' entourage from the audience, similar to the one made by Tony Barrow at The Beatles' last concert on Aug 29, 1966 in Candlestick Park, San Francisco.

Feb 16: The Beatles held a dress rehearsal before a live audience, videotaped during the afternoon, and in the evening made their second live appearance on "The Ed Sullivan Show." At both appearances they performed "She Loves You," "This Boy," "All My Loving," "I Saw Her Standing There," "From Me to You" and "I Want to Hold Your Hand." By far the best bootleg of the Sullivan shows is *The Beatles Conquer America*, on which the Feb 16 afternoon performance is featured (Paul can be heard bidding the audience "Good afternoon" after "This Boy"; during the evening performance he said "Good evening" at the same point). The evening performance is on *The Ed Sullivan Show CBS TV Studio-Demo Copy* and *Ed's Really Big Beatles Blast*. The Beatles also rehearsed for this show on the previous day, Feb 15.

Feb 21: The Beatles were filmed while improvising a tune called "Guitar Blues," which is seen in the documentary film *What's Happening: The Beatles in the U.S.A.* and appears on *The Beatles Vs. Don Ho.*

The Beatles Conquer America (bootleg). This album contains all of the initial Ed Sullivan appearances, except for the Feb 16 evening telecast, in correct order and in good sound quality.

Feb 22: The Beatles were interviewed by telephone by Brian Matthew from London's Heathrow Airport upon their return to England, aired on this date on "Saturday Club"; on *Beatles at the Beeb 9*, and *Radio Active 9* (CD).

Feb 23: At Teddington Studios, London, The Beatles filmed an appearance for ABC television's "Big Night Out," aired in the U.K. on Feb 29. The group mimed to their recordings of "Please Mr. Postman," "All My Loving," "I Wanna Be Your Man," "Till There Was You" and "I Want to Hold Your Hand." They also appeared in some comic skits. The entire appearance is on *London* (listed as Aug 1, 1965) and *Sunday Night at the London Palladium.*

Feb 28: The Beatles recorded the second of five holiday specials titled "From Us to You," aired Mar 30, and sang "All My Loving," "Roll Over Beethoven," "This Boy," "Till There Was You," "I Wanna Be Your Man," "Please Mr. Postman," "Can't Buy Me Love" and "You Can't Do That." All of the songs and the theme are on *Beatles at the Beeb 9* and *Radio Active 9* (CD).

Mar 2–Apr 24: The Beatles filmed their first feature-length movie, *A Hard Day's Night*. The entire film soundtrack, including dialogue, appears on *Cinelogue 3—A Hard Day's Night*, *A Hard Day's Night* and *Bactrax*. A film clip of The Beatles singing "You Can't Do That," done for the film but cut from the released print, was seen in the U.S. on "The Ed Sullivan Show" on May 24 following a film clip of Sullivan interviewing The Beatles on the film set. This film clip has frequently been mistakenly identified as being from The Beatles' Apr 26 *New Musical Express* Poll-Winners' show.

Mar 20: The Beatles mimed to their recordings of "Can't Buy Me Love" and "You Can't Do That" during a live appearance on the Associated-Rediffusion TV show, "Ready, Steady, Go!" Both songs are on the bootleg album *Ready Steady Go!* and the appearance was released on the video *Ready, Steady, Go Volume 1.*

Mar 31: The Beatles recorded an appearance on BBC Radio's "Saturday Club," aired Apr 4, and sang "Everybody's Trying to Be My Baby," "I Call Your Name," "I Got a Woman," "You Can't Do That," "Can't Buy Me Love," "Sure to Fall" and "Long Tall Sally." All of the songs are on *Beatles at the Beeb 10* (CD and LP).

Apr 16: The Beatles recorded "A Hard Day's Night" in nine takes, five of them complete runthroughs, with take 9 the keeper. *Ultra Rare Trax 2* (CD), *Back Track* (CD) and *Sessions* (CD-2) have an alternate complete take. *Unsurpassed Masters 2* (CD) has takes 6 (a breakdown) and 7. Takes 2 and 3, both false starts, are on *Abbey Road Show 1983* (CD), which also has the released take 9 with a count-in.

Apr 19: The Beatles recorded songs for a soundtrack for the Associated-Rediffusion television special, "Around the Beatles," which was aired on May 6. They sang "Can't Buy Me Love," "I Wanna Be Your Man," "Long Tall Sally," medley "Love Me Do"/"Please Please Me"/"From Me to You"/"She Loves You"/"I Want to Hold Your Hand," "Roll Over Beethoven," "Shout" and "Twist and Shout." Rehearsals for the special were held on Apr 27 with the actual filming done before a live audience on the following day. During filming of the musical concert sequence on Apr 28, The Beatles mimed to the recordings made on Apr 19. The musical portion of the show was released on the home video *The Beatles Live! Ready, Steady, Go Special Edition*, while a comic Shakespearean sketch from the show was released in the U.S. on the videocassette *Fun with The Fab Four*. While The Beatles' songs were prerecorded in the studio, audience screaming sound effects were added to the soundtrack for the actual broadcast. Most bootlegs are taken from that soundtrack, thus they include the audience effects. *Not Guilty* contains the entire mono prerecorded performance, without the audience effects; *Ready Steady Go! Cinelogue 6* and *Around The Beatles* feature the entire performance as it was aired, with the audience effects.

Apr 26: The Beatles performed at the *New Musical Express* 1963–1964 Annual Poll-Winners' All-Star Concert at Empire Pool, Wembley, England. They sang "She Loves You," "You Can't Do That," "Twist and Shout," "Long Tall Sally" and "Can't Buy Me Love." All but the last song are on *Beatles at the Beeb 13* and *Live in the United Kingdom 1962–65* (CD). The performance was filmed and aired in England by ABC-TV on May 10 on one of two "Big Beat '64" specials and was repeated Nov 8.

May 1: The Beatles recorded the third of their five "From Us to You" holiday specials for BBC Radio, which aired on May 18. They sang the theme, "I Saw Her Standing There," "Kansas City"/"Hey Hey Hey Hey," "Whit Monday to You" (a variation of "Happy Birthday"), "I Forgot to Remember to Forget," "You Can't Do That," "Sure to Fall," "Can't Buy Me Love," "Matchbox" and "Honey Don't" (with lead vocal by John Lennon). All of the songs are on *Beatles at the Beeb 10* (LP and CD).

May 24: An interview with George, Paul and Ringo concerning the filming of *A Hard Day's Night* was released in Mar 1982 in the U.S. only on promo copies of "The Beatles Movie Medley," where it was listed as "Fab Four on Film" (Capitol PB-5100 and SPRO-9758). Commercial copies intended for release were also pressed (Capitol B-5100), but these were never officially issued. "The Beatles Movie Medley" was finally released, but with the B side changed to "I'm Happy Just to Dance with You" (original version). "Fab Four on Film" also appears on *The Beatles Conquer America*.

Jun 4: The Beatles began a world tour with two concerts at K.B. Hallen, in Denmark. Ringo, who was ill, was replaced temporarily by drummer Jimmy Nicol for the first five dates of this tour. They sang "I Saw Her Standing There," "I Want to Hold Your Hand," "You Can't Do That," "All My Loving," "She Loves You," "Till There Was You," "Roll Over Beethoven," "Can't Buy Me Love," "This Boy" and "Twist and Shout." During the first Copenhagen show, the first two songs were reversed. Eight songs from the evening show are on *John, Paul, George & Jimmy*. They are copied onto *Danmark and Nederland June 1964*, which adds "I Saw Her Standing There" in very poor sound quality, taken from some other source.

Jun 5: The Beatles taped an appearance for VARA-TV at its Treslong Studio in Hellegom, the Netherlands. The show aired on Jun 8 on network Nederland-1 as the TV special "The Beatles" and was repeated Jul 18. The Beatles mimed to released recordings, but their microphones were also on, so a double-track effect was created. They did "She Love You," "All My Loving," "Twist and Shout," "Roll Over Beethoven," "Long Tall Sally" and "Can't Buy Me Love." Apparently, The Beatles left the stage before the final number was completed, and the recording played on while only dancing teenagers could be seen on television. All of the songs are on *John, Paul, George & Jimmy* and *Danmark & Nederland June 1964*. An interview clip from this show is on *Beatles Vs. Don Ho*. The interview, an airport press conference, the taping of the TV show as aired on VARA-Radio, including a clip of "Twist and Shout," and the TV broadcast were released on the Dutch fan club album, *De Bietels Tussen De Bollen* on Jun 9, 1984.

Jun 10: George composed the unreleased song "You'll Know What to Do." No recordings have surfaced.

Jun 12: The Beatles' concert at Adelaide's Centennial Hall, probably taken from a Jun 13 TV broadcast, is on *A Doll's House, 300,000 Beatles Fans Can't Be Wrong* (LP and CD) and *Australia 1964* (CD). Songs were the same as the Jun 15 Melbourne show except that "You Can't Do That" was replaced with "Twist and Shout."

Jun 15–17: The Beatles did two shows on each of three dates, six shows in all, at Melbourne's Festival Hall; they sang (1) "I Saw Her Standing There," (2) "I Want to Hold Your Hand," (3) "You Can't Do That," (4) "All My Loving," (5) "She Loves You," (6) "Till There Was You," (7) "Roll Over Beethoven," (8) "Can't Buy Me Love," (9) "This Boy" and (10) "Long Tall Sally." All 10 songs from the Jun 16 show, as aired on the Jul 1 Australian TV special, "The Beatles Sing for Shell," are on *Live in Melbourne 1964 and Paris 1965* (CD). Nine songs are on *Australia 1964* (CD), which adds numbers 1, 4 and 8 from the Jun 17 show and mistakenly lists them as the Jun 18 Sydney show. Songs from Jun 17 are on *Eight Arms to Hold You* (2 cuts) and *Great to Have You with Us* (3 cuts, mistakenly listed as Sydney show).

Jun 16: Melbourne interviews with The Beatles are on *Live in Melbourne Australia 7/16/64*.

Jul 14: The Beatles recorded an appearance for BBC Radio's "Top Gear," aired Jul 16, and sang "Long Tall Sally," "And I Love Her," "A Hard Day's Night," "Things We Said Today," "If I Fell" and "You Can't Do That." The released version of "I Should Have Known Better" also appears on bootlegs and may have been mimed by The Beatles. All of the songs are on *Beatles at the Beeb 11* (LP and CD). Two promos for this program, one recorded by Paul and one by George and Ringo, were aired on episode 9 of "The Beeb's Lost Beatles Tapes."

Jul 17: The Beatles recorded the fourth in their "From Us to You" BBC Radio holiday specials, and the last one to bear that title. The show aired on Aug 3. Several recordings that were cut from the broadcast have been bootlegged. "I Should Have Known Better" (false start) and the aired version without harmonica, and an instrumental take of "I'm Happy Just to Dance with You" are on *From Us to You—A Parlophone Rehearsal Session*. The entire Aug 3 broadcast is also on that bootleg and *Beatles at the Beeb 11* (LP and CD). The song lineup on the broadcast was "Long Tall Sally," "If I Fell," "I'm Happy Just to Dance with You," "Things We Said Today," "I Should Have Known Better," "Boys," "A Hard Day's Night" and "Kansas City"/"Hey Hey Hey Hey." There is some questions as to whether "Kansas City"/"Hey Hey Hey Hey" was actually used on the broadcast. Many references omit mention of it, and one theory has it as another song that was recorded for the show but cut from the broadcast. *Beatles at the Beeb 11* appears to have the entire broadcast intact, and it includes that number, thus indicating that somewhere along the way the title simply got dropped inadvertently from written listings.

Aug 14: The Beatles recorded "Leave My Kitten Alone," an unreleased track that was to have been included on EMI's canceled 1985 *Sessions* album and issued as a single. Five takes were recorded, with take 2 being a breakdown and take 4 a false start. Take 5 is on *Ultra Rare Trax 2* (CD), *Back Track* (CD), *Not for Sale* (LP and CD), *File Under*, *Sessions* (LP, CD-1, CD-2, CD-3) and *Unsurpassed Masters 2* (CD). The false start (take 4) is on *File Under* and *Not for Sale* (LP only). Takes 1 and 2 of "I'm a Loser," are on *Unsurpassed 6*; take 3 on *Unsurpassed 7*.

"Leave My Kitten Alone" (bootleg). Single slated for release in 1985 with the *Sessions* album but, like the album, ultimately scrapped. It is hard to understand why The Beatles never issued this outstanding recording with its magnificent Lennon vocal.

Aug 22: The Beatles performed live at Empire Stadium, Vancouver, and sang "Twist and Shout," "You Can't Do That," "All My Loving," "She Loves You," "Things We Said Today," "Roll Over Beethoven," "Can't Buy Me Love," "If I Fell," "I Want to Hold Your Hand," "Boys," "A Hard Day's Night" and "Long Tall Sally," all of which are found on *Vancouver '64/Washington '64* and *Vancouver 1964*.

Aug 23: The Beatles performed their first Hollywood Bowl concert in Los Angeles. Songs were the same as at the Aug 22 Vancouver show. "Things We Said Today," "Roll Over Beethoven," "Boys," "All My Loving," "She Loves You" and "Long Tall Sally" were officially released on *The Beatles at the Hollywood Bowl*; a short excerpt of "Twist and Shout" appeared on Capitol Records' 1964 documentary LP *The Beatles Story*. All 12 songs are on *Get Yer Yeah Yeahs Out, Back in 1964 at the Hollywood Bowl* and many other bootlegs.

Sep 2: The Beatles performed a concert in Philadelphia's Convention Hall, singing the same songs done on Aug 22. Bootlegs often list recordings apparently made at this show as an Atlanta, Georgia concert but the consensus now is that the bootlegs are from the Philadelphia show (often referred to as the "Whiskey Flats" tapes); it appears on *Look What We Found* (CD) and *Perfect Beat* (CD).

Oct 3: The Beatles recorded three songs at the Granville Theatre, Fulham, which were aired on the U.S. TV show "Shindig" on Jan 20, 1965: "Boys," "I'm a Loser" and "Kansas City." All three are on *The Beatles Conquer America, Live in USA 1964–1965* (CD) and *Live in the United Kingdom 1962–65* (CD). Apparently they did not record a version of "House of the Rising Sun," despite reports that they had done so, but John seems to have ad-libbed a brief acoustic version during The Beatles' warmup prior to the performance.

Oct 8: The Beatles recorded "She's a Woman" in seven takes, with take 6 the keeper. Take 2 with a false start is on *Ultra Rare Trax 1* (CD) and *Back Track* (CD); take 7 and a false start are on *Unsurpassed Masters 2* (CD), *Hold Me Tight* (CD), *Back Track Part Two* (CD), *Ultra Rare 3 & 4, Strawberry Fields Forever* (CD) and *Sessions* (CD-2).

Oct 18: The Beatles recorded "I Feel Fine" in nine takes. Take 9, a vocal overdub onto take 7, was used for release. Takes 6 (rhythm track) and 9 are on *Ultra Rare Trax 3 & 4, Hold Me Tight* (CD), *Back Track Part Two* (CD) and *Unsurpassed Masters 2* (CD); take 5 is on *Unsurpassed 7*.

Oct 26: A 29-second outtake of Paul recording his speech for The Beatles' second annual Christmas record is on *Sgt. Pepper* (9 LP).

Nov 17: The Beatles recorded an appearance on BBC Radio's "Top Gear" show, aired Nov 26, and sang (1) "I'm a Loser," (2) "Honey Don't" (with Ringo taking over lead vocal from John by this time), (3) "She's a Woman," (4) "Everybody's Trying to Be My Baby," (5) "I'll Follow the Sun" and (6) "I Feel Fine." All of the songs are on *Beatles at the Beeb 12*. The recordings of numbers 1, 3, 4 and 6 were used again on the Dec 26 "Saturday Club" broadcast and again for the BBC's overseas show, "Top of the Pops." A false start of "I Feel Fine" and an excerpt of the raw final take, before Lennon's vocal was double-tracked, were aired on episode 1 of "The Beeb's Lost Beatles Tapes." The false start was also aired on episode 9, but with feedback added. The same episode featured the overdubbing of Lennon's vocal on the final version.

Nov 23: The Beatles recorded an appearance on "Ready, Steady, Go!" aired Nov 27, miming to released recordings of "Baby's in Black," "She's a Woman" and "Kansas City"/"Hey Hey Hey Hey." This was reportedly the first time that any group appeared on this program in a prerecorded segment; the show normally aired live. All three songs are on *Ready Steady Go!*

Nov 25: The Beatles recorded two songs for BBC Radio's "Saturday Club," aired Dec 26: "Rock and Roll Music" and "Kansas City"/"Hey Hey Hey Hey." The Dec 26 broadcast also used the following numbers, recorded on Nov 17 and first aired on the Nov 26 "Top Gear" show: "I'm a Loser," "Everybody's Trying to Be My Baby," "I Feel Fine" and "She's a Woman." The two shows, as originally aired, are on *Beatles at the Beeb 12*.

1965

Feb 15: The Beatles recorded "Ticket to Ride," with Lennon adding his vocal and other overdubs onto take 2, which appears on *Ultra Rare Trax 3 & 4*, *Hold Me Tight* (CD), *Ultra Rare Trax 3* (CD), *Back Track Part Two* (CD) and *Sgt. Pepper* (9 LP).

Feb 16: The Beatles recorded "Yes It Is" in 14 takes, all of them rhythm tracks. Take 14 was chosen for release and the vocals were overdubbed onto it. Takes 1, 2 and 14, all with vocal overdubs heard, are on *Ultra Rare Trax 3 & 4*. Takes 1 and 2 are on *Unsurpassed Masters 2* (CD) and *Hold Me Tight* (CD).

Feb 18: The Beatles recorded "If You've Got Trouble," unreleased but intended for inclusion on EMI's scrapped 1985 *Sessions* album. The recording appears on several bootlegs and has been edited to varying degrees on almost all of them. The complete recording is in stereo on *Unsurpassed Masters Volume 2* (CD) (2:50), and in mono on *Not for Sale* (LP) (2:41). It is found in a shorter edit (1:45) on *File Under*. It runs 2:24 on *Sessions* (LP, CD-1, CD-2, CD-3) in a different mix where the first verse is omitted, which is how EMI intended to release it on *Sessions*. The same mix appears on *Ultra Rare Trax Volume 1* (CD) (edited to 2:17), *Not Guilty* (CD), *Not for Sale* (CD) and *Back Track* (CD).

Feb 19: An alternate mix of "You're Going to Lose That Girl" is on *Not Guilty*.

Feb 20: The Beatles recorded two takes of the unreleased song "That Means a Lot." They recorded the song again on Mar 30. Take 2 from Feb 20 was planned for official release by EMI on its scrapped 1985 *Sessions* album and is found on *Ultra Rare Trax 2* (CD), *Back Track* (CD), *Unsurpassed Masters 2* (CD), *Sessions* (LP, CD-1, CD-2, CD-3), *File Under* and *It Was 20 Years Ago Today*.

Mar 30: The Beatles recorded five takes of the unreleased song "That Means a Lot." None of these takes has appeared on bootlegs to date; it is a noticeably different arrangement from the recordings cut on Feb 20.

Apr 11: The Beatles sang "She's a Woman," "Ticket to Ride," "Long Tall Sally," "I Feel Fine" and "Baby's in Black" at the *New Musical Express* 1965–65 Annual Poll-Winners' All-Star Concert, aired Apr 18 in the U.K. on ABC-TV's "Big Beat '65" show. The first three songs are on *Dig It*, *Beatles at the Beeb 13* and *Live in the United Kingdom 1962–65* (CD).

Apr 13: Twelve takes of the song "Help!" were cut on this date; takes 1–5 were all rhythm tracks; take 5 is complete; takes 1–5 are on *Ultra Rare Trax 3 & 4*, *Hold Me Tight* (CD) and *Back Track Part Two* (CD). The released stereo version, with Lennon's count-in added, is on *Classified Document Volume 3* and *Sgt. Pepper* (9 LP). Take 8 is on *Unsurpassed 6* (CD).

May 13: The entire *Help!* film soundtrack is on *Cinelogue 4*.

May 20: The Beatles recorded BBC Radio's "The Beatles (Invite You to Take a Ticket to Ride)," aired Jun 7. This was the last BBC Radio show with songs especially recorded by The Beatles, the last in their series of five holiday specials and the only one without the "From Us to You" title. They sang "Ticket to Ride" (short version), "Everybody's Trying to Be My Baby," "I'm a Loser," "The Night Before," "Honey Don't," "Dizzy Miss Lizzie," "She's a Woman" and "Ticket to Ride" (long version). All of the songs are on *Beatles at the Beeb 13*.

May: John's very brief bit in D.A. Pennebacker's Bob Dylan documentary film *Eat the Document* appears on *Teddy Boy*, *Come Back Johnny* and *Lifting Material from the World*. The full sequence shot for the film, but almost entirely cut from the final print, is on *Lost Lennon Tapes 8* (LP) and *2* (CD). Some bootlegs title the track "A Comment to a Bleary-Eyed Bob Dylan." The film should not be confused with a similar Dylan documentary, *Don't Look Back*, also filmed by Pennebacker.

Jun 14: An acetate with an alternate, unreleased mix of "Yesterday," once owned by Beatles publisher Dick James, was auctioned for £770 at Sotheby's in 1989. The recording reportedly features different effects on Paul's vocal.

Jun 16: John recorded an interview for BBC Radio's "The World of Books," aired Jul 3. He read his poem "The Fat Budgie," which is found on *It's All Too Much* and *Four Sides of the Circle*.

Jun 18: John appeared live on BBC 1's "Tonight" show to promote his book, *A Spaniard in the Works*. He read "We Must Not Forget the General Erection" and "The Wumberlog (Or, The Magic Dog)," both of which appear on *Lost Lennon Tapes 3* (LP) and *2* (CD). A recording of John reading "The National Health Cow," also taped around this time, is on *It's All Too Much*, *Four Sides Of The Circle*, *Not For Sale* (LP) and *Sgt. Pepper* (9 LP).

Jun 20: The Beatles did two shows at the Palais des Sports, Paris. The second show was filmed by French TV and transmitted live by radio station Europe 1. Each

Les Beatles à Paris (bootleg). One of many live Beatles group and solo concert recordings, a staple for many bootleggers.

show featured the same 12 songs: "Twist and Shout," "She's a Woman," *"I'm a Loser," *"Can't Buy Me Love," "Baby's in Black," *"I Wanna Be Your Man," *"A Hard Day's Night," "Everybody's Trying to Be My Baby," *"Rock & Roll Music," *"I Feel Fine," *"Ticket to Ride" and *"Long Tall Sally." Except for the evening performance of "I Feel Fine," of which only a fragment has been bootlegged, both complete shows are on *Live in Paris 1965* (CD); *The Original Beatles Live* (CD) replaces the fragment with a repeat of the afternoon performance, but is otherwise complete. Eight songs from the afternoon show (*) and all but the partial recording of "I Feel Fine" from the evening show are on *Les Beatles a Paris* and *Palais des Sports Paris* (CD). The entire evening show is on *Live in Melbourne 1964 and Paris 1965* (CD) and *Live at the Paris Olympia*, both of which include the fragment of "I Feel Fine."

Jun 24: "Twist and Shout," "She's a Woman" and "I'm a Loser" from one of The Beatles' shows in Italy are on *Live in Italy* (EP), *Live Tracks—Previously Italian E.P.* (EP) and *Beatles 4 Ever*.

Jun 27–28: The Beatles played two shows per day on each of these dates at the Teatro Adriano in Rome; songs were the same as at the Jun 20 Paris show. A poor-quality audience recording of one show is on *Rome Italy 1965*; all but "Rock & Roll Music" are on *Roma*.

Aug 1: The Beatles appeared live on the U.K. TV show "Blackpool Night Out" broadcast from the ABC Theatre in Blackpool and did six numbers: "I Feel Fine," "I'm Down," "Act Naturally," "Ticket to Ride," "Yesterday" and "Help!" All six are on *Live in the United Kingdom 1962–65* (CD), *Stockholm 1964* and *Stockholm and Blackpool*. The Beatles also did "I Do Like to Be Beside the Seaside," but it has not appeared on any bootlegs to date.

Aug 14: The Beatles recorded six songs exclusively for the Sep 12 Ed Sullivan show: "I Feel Fine," "I'm Down," "Act Naturally," "Ticket to Ride," "Yesterday" and "Help!" All six are on *The Beatles Conquer America* and *Live in USA 1964–1965* (CD).

Aug 15: The Beatles performed their landmark Shea Stadium concert in Flushing Meadow, New York. Most bootlegs are taken from the concert film *The Beatles at Shea Stadium*. The released recording of "Act Naturally" was substituted for the live version on the film soundtrack. The Beatles sang "She's a Woman," "Everybody's Trying to Be My Baby," "Twist and Shout," "Act Naturally," "I Feel Fine," "Dizzy Miss Lizzie," "Ticket to Ride," "Can't Buy Me Love," "Baby's in Black," "A Hard Day's Night," "Help!" and "I'm Down." The last song is repeated twice during the telecast of the film, which omits the first two songs. All 10 of the film's songs are found on *Cavern Club, Battle, Shea . . . At Last* and other boots.

Aug 19: The Beatles performed two concerts at Sam Houston Coliseum, Houston, Texas. The songs were the same as those done at their Aug 15 Shea Stadium concert except that "Act Naturally" was replaced with "I Wanna Be Your Man." Full day and evening concerts are both on *Sam Houston Coliseum* (CD), *Live from the Sam Houston Coliseum* and *Texan Troubadours*.

Aug 21: Part of The Beatles' concert at Metropolitan Stadium in Minneapolis, Minnesota is on *Visit to Minneapolis* (EP). Audio from local TV news footage is also included. Part of the video portion is on the videocassette *Fun With the Fab Four*.

Aug 23: Part of an interview with John and Paul recorded by Capitol's *Teen Set* magazine is heard on *The Beatles Vs. Don Ho*.

Aug 29: Capitol recorded The Beatles' concert at the Hollywood Bowl on this date, but technical failures, including a problem with Paul's microphone, rendered the tapes useless. None of the numbers from this show has appeared to date on any official or bootleg records.

Aug 30: While some of The Beatles' songs from their Hollywood Bowl concert on this date were officially released on *The Beatles at the Hollywood Bowl*, the following numbers remain unreleased: "I Feel Fine," "Everybody's Trying to Be My Baby," "Baby's in Black," "I Wanna Be Your Man" and "I'm Down."

Oct 12: The Beatles cut take 1 of "Norwegian Wood (This Bird Has Flown)," which was discarded, the final version being recorded on Oct 21. Take 1 is on *Ultra Rare Trax 5 & 6*, *Not Guilty* (CD), *Sessions* (CD-2), *Unsurpassed Masters 2* (CD) and *Back Track Part Two* (CD).

Oct 16: The Beatles cut "Day Tripper." Takes 1 and 2 were breakdowns of the rhythm track with take 3 the keeper, and the vocal was overdubbed onto that take. *Ultra Rare Trax 3 & 4*, *Hold Me Tight* (CD), *Back Track Part Two* (CD) and *Unsurpassed Masters 2* (CD) have all three takes. An alternate mix of the released version, without the echo, is on *Sgt. Pepper* (9 LP).

Oct 20: The Beatles recorded "We Can Work It Out." *Ultra Rare Trax 3 & 4*, *Hold Me Tight* (CD), *Unsurpassed Masters 2* (CD) and *Back Track Part Two* (CD) have takes 1 (a rhythm track breakdown) and take 2 (heard here with Paul's count-in and a fadeout). Take 2 is on *Ultra Rare Trax 2* (CD) and *Back Track* (CD). A McCartney demo, cut short where Lennon taped over it, is on *Nothing But Aging*; the demo and a rough mix were heard on episode 45 of "The Lost Lennon Tapes".

Oct 21: The Beatles recorded "Norwegian Wood (This Bird Has Flown)," with take 4 the keeper. Take 4, with two false starts, is on *Ultra Rare Trax 2* (CD), *Not Guilty* (CD), *Ultra Rare Trax 3* (CD) and *Back Track* (CD). In addition to the false starts, these bootlegs include John's closing, "I showed ya." An unreleased instrumental take of "Nowhere Man" was also recorded.

Oct 24: The Beatles recorded unreleased take 1 of "I'm Looking Through You," with the middle section missing. It appears on *Ultra Rare Trax 1* (CD), *Back Track* (CD), *Unsurpassed Masters 2* (CD), *Not Guilty* (CD) and *Sessions* (LP, CD-1, CD-2, CD-3); it sounds slowed down on *Sessions*, which also adds a fadeout.

Oct 28: A rough mix of "We Can Work It Out" was made for The Beatles to mime to during the taping of an appearance on Granada TV's special *The Music of Lennon and McCartney*, videotaped Nov 1 and 2.

Oct 29: The Beatles recorded vocal overdubs for "We Can Work It Out"; one for release and one for the Granada TV special. Two separate mixes of "Day Tripper" were made on this date for the same purposes.

Nov 4: The Beatles recorded two takes of "12-Bar Original," an unreleased instrumental. A mono mix of take 2 (6:36) was made on Nov 30. Bootlegs include *Acetates* (CD), *Ultra Rare Trax 3 & 4*, *Hold Me Tight* (CD), *Back Track Part Three* (CD), *Lost Lennon Tapes 20* and *Unsurpassed Masters 2* (CD). In a late 1990 interview, Ringo recalled that all four Beatles had composed the number, that at least two different mixes existed and that he had an acetate of one of them.

Nov 8: A brief a cappella rehearsal of the harmony vocals for "Think for Yourself," taped on this date, was used in the film *Yellow Submarine*. It appears on *By George, The Beatles Vs. Don Ho*. *Cinelogue 2* contains the entire film soundtrack. About 15 minutes of additional dialogue called "Beatles Speech" is on *Unsurpassed Masters 7* (CD).

Dec 2: Promotional films of "We Can Work It Out" and "Day Tripper," in which The Beatles mimed to the released recordings, were aired on BBC's "Top of the Pops." Apparently, several different film clips of each song were done. Both songs are on *Forest Hills Tennis Stadium* and *On Stage*; the clips were also aired on Jan 3, 1966 in the U.S. on the "Hullabaloo" TV show.

Dec 10: "I'll Follow the Sun" from The Beatles' show at the Hammersmith Odeon is on *Rarer Than Rare*.

Dec: Paul recorded and cut only four copies (one for each of The Beatles) of a special disc, *Paul's Christmas Album*.

1966

Mar: Lennon cut several demos of "She Said She Said," most of them under the working title "He Said He Said"; two appear on *Lost Lennon Tapes 2*.

Apr 6–7: An unreleased alternate mix of "Tomorrow Never Knows" is on *Lost Lennon Tapes 9*, *Not for Sale* (CD) and *Unsurpassed Masters 3* (CD).

Apr 13–14: The Beatles recorded "Paperback Writer" in two takes, the first being a breakdown. Numerous overdubs were added over the two-day period. The released basic take 2, with Paul's count-in, without the echo effects on the vocal, and no fadeout is on *Ultra Rare Trax 5 & 6*, *Not Guilty* (CD), *Unsurpassed Masters 3* (CD) and *Back Track Part Two* (CD), which include a breakdown, and *Ultra Rare Trax 1* (CD) and *Back Track* (CD). The same take is heard with the count-in and fadeout and without echo on *Not for Sale* (LP and CD) and *Sessions* (CD-3).

Apr 14–16: The Beatles recorded "Rain" in five takes, with only the fifth including Lennon's vocal. Take 7, a reduction mix that was used for release, is heard on *Ultra Rare Trax 5 & 6*, *Not Guilty* (CD) and *Unsurpassed Masters 3* (CD).

Apr 20: The Beatles recorded unreleased versions of "Taxman" and "And Your Bird Can Sing."

May 19–20: The Beatles filmed promotional clips for "Paperback Writer" and "Rain," in which they mimed to the released recordings. The films were aired in the U.K. on "Top of the Pops" on Jun 2 and in the U.S. on "The

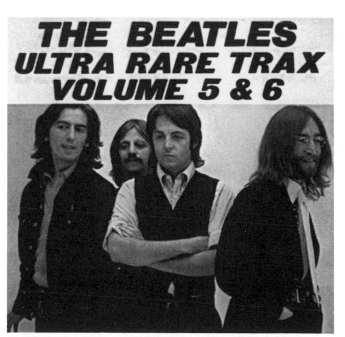

Ultra Rare Trax Volume 5&6 (bootleg). The "Ultra Rare Trax" series marked a revolution in Beatles bootlegs, offering superb sound quality and many previously unheard studio outtakes.

Ed Sullivan Show" on Jun 5. The "Ed Sullivan" telecast is on *ABC Manchester*, *Backtrax*, and *Supertracks 2*.

Jun 23: George's acceptance speech, in German, for the 1966 Bravo award is on *Beatles 4 Ever*, *Live at the Circus Crone* and *The Live Beatles . . . June 24th, 1966*.

Jun 24: The Beatles performed two shows at the Circus-Krone-Bau in Munich, Germany, the second one being filmed by the German national TV station, ZDF. The film includes "Rock and Roll Music," "She's a Woman" (only a few seconds' worth), "Baby's in Black," "I Feel Fine," "Yesterday," "Nowhere Man" and "I'm Down." The Beatles also did "Day Tripper," "If I Needed Someone," "I Wanna Be Your Man" and "Paperback Writer." All of the filmed songs are on *Look What We Found* (CD) and *London Melbourne Munchen* (CD).

Jun 30–Jul 2: The Beatles did five concerts at Nippon Budokan Hall, Tokyo; one on Jun 30 and two each on Jul 1 and 2. The Jun 30 show was filmed in color by Japanese TV (NTV) and aired the following day. One of the Jul 2 shows was also filmed but not aired. The songs done at both of these shows were the same as those done on Jun 24. Both shows are on *Live in Japan 1964* (CD) and *The Original Beatles Live* (CD). *Five Nights in a Judo Arena* has all 11 songs in good sound quality. The Jun 30 show is on *The Live Beatles: Tokio* [sic] *July 2, 1966* (a quasi-legal Italian CD with the wrong date listed). Interviews taped with The Beatles during their visit to Tokyo are on *Welcome The Beatles* and *Beatles '66* (EP).

Aug 29: The last scheduled Beatles concert took place at Candlestick Park, San Francisco, California. They sang "Rock & Roll Music," "She's a Woman," "If I Needed Someone," "Day Tripper," "Baby's in Black," "I Feel Fine," "Yesterday," "I Wanna Be Your Man," "Nowhere Man," "Paperback Writer" and "Long Tall Sally." An audiocassette recording of the show was made by Beatles' press officer Tony Barrow, but the 30-minute tape ran out before The Beatles completed their final number. The recording is on *Live in Paris 1964 and In San Francisco 1966* (CD) and *Candlestick Park*. Before leaving the stage, The Beatles began playing "In My Life," but then, for no apparent reason, stopped abruptly and left the stage.

Early Nov: Four Lennon demos of "Strawberry Fields Forever" are on *Back Track Part Three* (CD); one is found on *Lost Lennon Tapes 3* and *Lost Lennon 2* (CD); the other three are on *Lost Lennon Tapes Volume One*; another demo is on *Nothing But Aging*.

Nov 24–Dec 29: The Beatles recorded John Lennon's "Strawberry Fields Forever." The full history of the recording is traced in detail by Lewisohn (1988); also see Nov 28, 1966 in Recording Chronology. The released version was an edit containing parts of two different takes (7 and 26). The recording history is largely contained on *Unsurpassed Masters 3* (CD), *Ultra Rare 5 & 6* (takes 1, 2, 3, 4, 5, 6, 7, 25 [rhythm track] and 26).

Nov 25: An unedited clip of the song "Everywhere It's Christmas," recorded for *The Beatles Fourth Christmas Record* (aka "Pantomime: Everywhere It's Christmas") is on *Sgt. Pepper* (9 LP).

Dec 6: The Beatles recorded several Christmas messages at Abbey Road for the British pirate stations Radio London and Radio Caroline.

Dec 29–Jan 17, 1967: The Beatles recorded Paul's "Penny Lane" during Dec and resumed overdub sessions between Jan 4 and 17, 1967. Take 9 was used for the commercially released version, but a piccolo trumpet solo included on the original mono mix sent to the U.S., and used there only on a promo release, was cut from all commercially released versions. Mono remix 9 of this take is on *Ultra Rare Trax 1* (CD), *Back Track* (CD) and *Not Guilty* (CD); mono remix 11, the one used for the U.S. promo, is on *1967*. A Jan 9, 1967 overdub session was heard on "The Lost Lennon Tapes" radio series, episode 111, along with an unreleased trumpet-ending mix.

1967

Early that year: John cut a demo of "You Know My Name (Look Up the Number)," which is found on *Lost Lennon Tapes 3* and *Lost Lennon Tapes 2* (CD).

Jan 5: The Beatles recorded a 14-minute experimental sound effects track for the "Carnival of Light."

Jan 19–Feb 22: The Beatles recorded "A Day in the Life." The bootlegs *Acetates* (CD), *1967*, *It Was 20 Years Ago Today* and *Classified Document* have an unreleased mono version (4:20) from Jan 20 when Paul recorded his first vocal solo, redone on Feb 3. On this first, discarded try, Paul begins laughing during his vocal and then says, "Oh, shit." The orchestral overdubs, recorded Feb 10, are missing, as is the final piano chord, recorded Feb 22. The track ends abruptly following some wild piano chords. *Ultra Rare Trax 5 & 6*, *Not Guilty* (CD) and *Unsurpassed Masters 3* (CD) contain alternate stereo mixes of the released version. Both have a 19-second false start (RS 5) and a stereo version (RS 6) that cuts off just as Paul's vocal begins. *Unsurpassed 3* also adds a third version listed as edits of takes 6 and 7.

Early Feb: A Lennon demo of "Good Morning, Good Morning" is on *Lost Lennon Tapes 4* and *Lost Lennon Tapes 2* (CD).

Feb 22: The Beatles recorded the unreleased "Anything" (aka "Drum Track"), a 22:10 track of Ringo drumming and playing tambourine and congas.

Mar 20: A spoken-word tape titled "Beatle Talk," recorded at Abbey Road, was removed from the studio by George Martin; contents unknown.

Apr 21: Mono mixes were done for "Only a Northern Song." On Oct 29, 1968, fake stereo remixes from mono mix 6 were made, one of them being released on the *Yellow Submarine* album. No true stereo mix of the song has ever been released. A clean mono mix of the song appears on *Casualties* and *1967*.

May: The Beatles were interviewed by Kenny Everett at a dinner party at Brian Epstein's home in Belgravia. Some of the taped interview may have been used on Everett's May 20 "Where It's At" radio broadcast showcasing *Sgt. Pepper*.

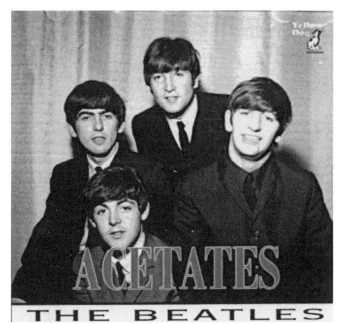

Acetates (bootleg). Bootleg CD with 13 Beatles demos and alternate takes.

May 4: Mono remix 7 of "Magical Mystery Tour," the version used in the film but not released on any official records, is on *Acetates* (CD), *Dig It* and *1967*. Both the released version and the soundtrack mix were taken from take 9.

May 9: The Beatles recorded an untitled 16-minute rambling instrumental jam.

May 25–Jun 2: The Beatles recorded "It's All Too Much," with most of the vocals and rhythm tracks done on May 25 and 26. A mono mix for the *Yellow Submarine* film soundtrack was done on Oct 12 (mono remix 1) and contains an extra verse missing from the released version. The final mono and stereo mixes were done on Oct 16 and 17, 1968. The film version is on *1967* and *Strawberry Fields Forever* (LP and CD). A shortened edit of this version, without the extra verse, is on *Off White* (CD). A rough, prefinal mix running 8:54 has surfaced on an underground tape. Near the end of a May 26 recording of the song, George went into "Sorrow," once a hit for The Merseys.

Jun 1–2: The Beatles recorded lengthy, rambling instrumental jams on both of these days.

Jun 14–25: The Beatles recorded "All You Need Is Love." One of two remixes made on Jun 21 was given to the BBC to be used on the Jun 25 "Our World" TV special. For the live satellite "Our World" broadcast, take 58 was recorded on the air with The Beatles playing to the previously recorded rhythm track, take 10. The "live" part of the broadcast consisted of the vocals, bass guitar, lead guitar solo in the middle eight, drums and the orchestra. The Beatles ran through the song once on the air before the final take with the orchestra was done. After the broadcast, some additional overdubbing was done, including some of Lennon's final, released vocal

and Ringo's opening snare drumroll. *Ultra Rare Trax 5 & 6*, *Not Guilty* (CD) and *Strawberry Fields Forever* (LP and CD) feature the TV broadcast exactly as it was heard at the time, with part of the first runthrough. *Unsurpassed Masters 3* (CD) has the complete TV broadcast with narration. The broadcast version is also found on *1967*, *Ultra Rare Trax 4* (CD) and *Beatles Vs. Don Ho*. A different mono mix (also from take 58) was used for the *Yellow Submarine* film soundtrack and is shorter than the single by 13 seconds (at 3:44).

Aug 22: An alternate mono mix of "Your Mother Should Know," with no bass or organ and with different backing vocals, is on *Acetates* (CD) and *Not for Sale* (LP and CD) and, with the commercially released ending tacked on, *1967*.

Sep 5–6: The Beatles recorded "I Am the Walrus." Although many overdubs were later added, most of the recording took place on these two days. Acetates were made from a mono mix done on Sep 6 (mono remix 4); that unreleased mix is found on *Acetates* (CD), *Ultra Rare Trax 2* (CD), *Not Guilty* (CD), *Back Track* (CD), *Sessions* (CD-3), *1967* and *Casualties*. Alternate rhythm takes are on *Unsurpassed Masters 3* and *6* (CDs).

Sep 6: Actual recording of "Fool on the Hill" did not begin until Sep 25, but on this date Paul recorded a mono two-track demo of the song at the piano. It is found on *Acetates* (CD), *1967*, *Not Guilty* (CD), *Ultra Rare Trax 1* (CD), *Back Track* (CD), *Sessions* (CD-3) and *Strawberry Fields Forever* (LP and CD). An alternate mono mix of "Blue Jay Way" is on *Acetates*.

Sep 8: The Beatles recorded the instrumental "Flying," at this point titled "Aerial Tour Instrumental," with overdubs completed on Sep 28. Six takes were done on Sep 8, with take 6 adding bizarre backward organ tracks. Overdubs were added and a mono mix made and pressed onto acetates; it includes the backward organs and the jazz band ending, reportedly taken from an unidentified record and cut from the released version. That mix is found on *Lost Lennon Tapes 9*, *Lost Lennon Tapes 3* (CD), *Back Track* (CD) and *Unsurpassed Masters 3* (CD).

Sep 16: The Beatles recorded an unreleased remake of "Your Mother Should Know" (11 takes).

Oct 2: Take 1, the first of 14 instrumental/rhythm takes done on this date for "Hello Goodbye," is on *Ultra Rare Trax 5 & 6*, *Not Guilty* (CD), *Unsurpassed Masters 3* (CD) and *Back Track Part Two* (CD). The song's working title at this stage was "Hello Hello," and it was completed at subsequent sessions.

Oct 12: The instrumental "Shirley's Wild Accordion," composed by John and Paul, was recorded under the working title "Accordion (Wild)." Beatle participation on this recording was minimal, although John served as producer for the first time in the group's recording history, and Paul and Ringo did add some overdubs. The recording, featuring accordion players Shirley Evans and Reg Wale, was never released. It was to have been used as incidental music in the *Magical Mystery Tour* film, but it was never used.

Oct: The Beatles composed and recorded, outside of EMI's studios, their instrumental composition "Jessie's Dream," which was used as background music in the *Magical Mystery Tour* film. It is on *Cinelogue 5*.

Nov 24: A prerecorded interview with John, taped by Kenny Everett and Chris Denning, was aired on BBC Radio One's "Where It's At." Excerpts are on *Tragical History Tour/Dr. Pepper*; part of the interview was heard during episode 14 of "The Beeb's Lost Beatles Tapes."

Nov 28: A full version of "Christmas Time (Is Here Again)" (6:37), recorded on this date for the 1967 Christmas fan club record, is on *Acetates* (CD), *File Under, Nothing Is Real* and *1967*. An abbreviated edit (0:52), originally intended for release on the canceled 1985 "Ob-La-Di, Ob-La-Da" single, is also on *Sessions* (LP, CD-1, CD-2), *Dig It* and *Ob-La-Di, Ob-La-Da* (LP and EP).

Dec 12: Paul and Kenny Everett recorded the song "All Together on the Wireless Machine" for one of Everett's radio shows, with Paul on piano and doing some minimal vocals behind Everett. It is on *Cavern Days*, *A Doll's House*, *Their Greatest Unreleased* and several other bootlegs. "Bye Bye Bye," often mentioned in connection with "All Together on the Wireless Machine," may not involve The Beatles at all, although some authorities think Paul and Linda may have performed on it. It is found on *Cavern Days* and *Their Greatest Unreleased*.

Dec 26: The entire film soundtrack from *Magical Mystery Tour* is on *Cinelogue 5—Magical Mystery Tour*, which is made obsolete by the vastly superior sound quality found on legitimate laser disc and videocassette releases of the film.

Late that year: John's demos of "Cry Baby Cry" are on *Nothing But Aging*. "Daddy's Little Sunshine Boy," a Ringo studio ad lib, is on *Lost Lennon Tapes 2* and *Lost Lennon Tapes 3* (CD). Another recording involving John and Ringo, perhaps from around this time, is "Chi Chi's Cafe," a comical improvisation. That track is found on *Lost Lennon 11*. Ringo's "Sailor Come Back to Me" and John's "El Tango Terrible."

1968

That year: An interview with The Beatles recorded by two fans was auctioned many years later and purchased by the Hard Rock Cafe chain.

Feb: A Lennon demo of "Hey Bulldog" is on *Nothing But Aging*. Paul's demo of "Step Inside Love," written for and recorded by Cilla Black, is on *Cavern Days*, *A Doll's House*, *Their Greatest Unreleased* and other boots.

Feb 3 & 6: The Beatles recorded "Lady Madonna." John and George originally did scat backing vocals while chewing Marmite-flavored potato chips, but that overdub was eventually discarded. Several bootlegs feature playbacks of the overdub sessions. A commonly heard cut reveals someone (probably Paul himself) beginning what sounds like an attempt to record a second vocal

over the first, but this quickly breaks down with a burst of laughter. That laughing opening is included on *Off White* and *Dig It*, where the song is found in an early mono mix missing most of the later overdubs. A stereo mix of the song, essentially at the same stage of development, is found on *Ultra Rare Trax 5 & 6*, *Not Guilty* (CD) and *Back Track Part Three* (CD), and includes alternate handclap overdubs. The track includes John's comical "Lady Madonna" uttered at the end. It is missing the opening count-in, however, which is included on the otherwise inferior mono mix. *Unsurpassed Masters 4* (CD) includes two playbacks of this same take, with the laughter opening, but they are both cut short after a few seconds and the tape is heard being rewound. The complete stereo mix of the released version of the song is also heard.

Feb 4 & 8: The Beatles recorded "Across the Universe." Two unreleased mono mixes were done on Feb 8. A mono mix found on *Lost Lennon Tapes 3*, *Lost Lennon Tapes 2* (CD), *Unsurpassed Masters 4* (CD), *Ultra Rare Trax 3* (CD) and *Back Track Part Three* (CD) is referred to as the "Hums Wild" version due to The Beatles adding a 15-second take of humming as an overdub at the conclusion of the Feb 4 sessions. The mix also features backward electric guitar, which was later erased along with the humming. A different mono mix is on *Some Other Guy*. Final instrumental overdubs were done on Feb 8. The Beatles never recorded the song again. The versions officially released on *No One's Gonna Change Our World* in Dec 1969 and on the *Let It Be* album in 1970 were both taken from this same original recording, although they are two very different stereo mixes. An alternate stereo mix is found on *Dig It* and *Not for Sale* (CD). That mix, like the "Hums Wild" mono mix, retains

Dig It! (bootleg). Another early breakthrough bootleg, predating *Ultra Rare Trax*, with several previously unheard nuggets.

the backward guitar effects and John's remark, "You're right Richie," that precedes the start of the song.

Feb 6: Ringo appeared live on Cilla Black's BBC-TV show "Cilla." The two did a duet of "Act Naturally" and also did "Do You Like Me (Just a Little Bit)?" The first number is on *Rizz Off!*; the second on the *1989 Beatleg News Christmas Record*.

Late Feb: A jam session that included The Beatles, The Beach Boys, Donovan and others was filmed and aired at a later date on Italian television. The broadcast, which lasted about 10 minutes, is on *Nothing But Aging* and includes "When the Saints Go Marching In," "You Are My Sunshine," "Jingle Bells," "She'll Be Coming Around the Mountain," "Blowing in the Wind," "Hare Krishna Mantra" and "Catch the Wind" (sung by Donovan).

Mar 15: In Rishikesh, India, The Beatles sang "Happy Birthday" to Mike Love of The Beach Boys and "Thank You Guru Dev" (aka "Spiritual Regeneration" and "Indian Rope Trick"). The songs were done as a medley and appear on *Indian Rope Trick* and *Strawberry Fields Forever* (LP and CD).

May 15: John and Paul wre interviewed by Joe Garagiola on the "Tonight" show in the U.S. (Garagiola was substituting for regular host Johnny Carson). Part of the interview can be found on *The Little Red Album* and *Sgt. Pepper* (9 LP).

■ John and Paul were interviewed on "Newsfront" on PBS in the U.S. Nearly 20 minutes of their appearance is on *The Little Red Album*.

May 20: The Beatles began rehearsal sessions at George's home in Esher during which they recorded demos of virtually all of the songs that they would record for *The Beatles* (aka the "*White Album*"). The session included (1) "Mother Nature's Son," (2) "Not Guilty," (3) "Back in the USSR," (4) "Julia," (vocal), (5) "Piggies," (6) "Dear Prudence," (7) "Child of Nature" (which became "Jealous Guy"), (8) "Julia" (instrumental), (9) "The Continuing Story of Bungalow Bill," (10) "Sexy Sadie," (11) "Revolution," (12) "I'm So Tired," (13) "Cry Baby Cry," (14) "What's the New Mary Jane," (15) "Yer Blues," (16) "Everybody's Got Something to Hide Except Me and My Monkey," (17) "Ob-La-Di, Ob-La-Da," (18) "While My Guitar Gently Weeps," (19) "Blackbird," (20) "Rocky Raccoon," (21) "Junk" (then titled "Jubilee"), (22) "Sour Milk Sea," (23) "Honey Pie" and (24) "Circles." All but number 4 arc on *Unsurpassed Demos* (CD) (which substitutes a different vocal demo of "Julia"). Numbers 1–7 and 9–16 are in better sound quality, but with "Not Guilty" cut from 3:10 to 0:50, on *The 1968 Demos* (CD). Numbers 6–16 are on *Lost Lennon Tapes 9*; numbers 1–5 appear on *The Beatles* (EP-1). Three different Lennon vocal demos of "Julia" from this period have surfaced. All three are on *The 1968 Demos* (CD). One appears on *Look at Me* (CD) and *The Beatles* (EP-1); another is found on *Lost Lennon 3* and *9*; a third is on *Serve Yourself* (CD), *Unsurpassed Demos* (CD) and *Lost Lennon 11*. The instrumental take is only on *Unsurpassed Demos* (CD). John's demo of "The Happy Rishikesh Song," from

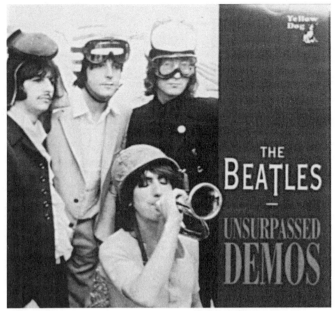

Unsurpassed Demos (bootleg). The full May 1968 Beatle rehearsal for the "*White Album*" at George's Esher home, including some unreleased titles.

around this time but apparently not from the Esher sessions, is on *Lost Lennon 1* and *Watching the Wheels* (CD). Paul would later record "Junk" for his *McCartney* album, and John would record "Jealous Guy" for *Imagine*. George would later record "Not Guilty" and "Circles" in Apr 1978, the former released on his 1979 LP *George Harrison* and the latter held over for release on his 1982 album *Gone Troppo*. The May 1968 "Circles" demo is very likely the source of erroneous reports of the existence of an unreleased Beatles recording called "Colliding Circles." "Sour Milk Sea" and "What's the New Mary Jane" were never released by The Beatles, although they did record the latter, and George gave the former to Jackie Lomax.

Jun 11: An alternate mono mix of the released version of "Blackbird," without the bird sound effects, is on *Unsurpassed Masters 4* (CD).

Jul 3–5: Alternate take 5 version of "Ob-La-Di, Ob-La-Da" was slated for official release by EMI in 1985 as the B side of the canceled "Leave My Kitten Alone" single. That take is on *Sessions* (CD-1, CD-2), in mono *Ultra Rare Trax 3* (CD), *Off White* (CD) and *Dig It*, and on *Unsurpassed 6* (CD); a different mix is on *Unsurpassed 7* (CD).

Jul 10: The basic mono mix of "Revolution" (single version) with most overdubs missing, is on *Lost Lennon Tapes 4*, with the opening and last beat (in stereo) edited on to (understandably) cover "Lost Lennon Tapes" radio show voiceover. Another edit is on *Unsurpassed Masters 7* (CD).

Jul 15: An unreleased mono mix of "Ob-La-Di, Ob-La-Da" is on *Unsurpassed Masters 4* (CD). The track includes Paul's final lead vocal, recorded on this date, and the final backing vocals recorded on Jul 9. The unreleased mix includes a false start. It also features John adding "I'm sure" after he says "Thank you" at the end. Although this is a mono mix, it includes the handclaps from the intro released only on the stereo version.

Jul 18: The Beatles recorded three lengthy alternate unreleased takes of "Helter Skelter": take 1 (10:40), take 2 (12:35) and take 3 (27:11). The released version was not recorded until Sep 9.

Jul 19: Lennon is heard doing an impromptu ballad about The Beatles' late manager, dubbed "Brian Epstein Blues" by the bootleggers who released the recording on *Unsurpassed Masters 4* (CD). The group also recorded an unreleased 6-minute instrumental version of "Summertime" and a take of "Sexy Sadie" with off-color lyrics.

Jul 22: An alternate mono mix of "Don't Pass Me By" is on *Unsurpassed Masters 4* (CD). The mix runs 4:08, compared to the 3:40 released mono mix. The tinkling-piano introduction on the released version is also on this bootlegged mix. That edit piece was not recorded until Jul 22, so the alternate mix must date from no earlier, thus it cannot be one of four mono mixes done on Jul 12. However, only one mono mix of the song is noted following Jul 22, and that is the released mix completed on Oct 11. This is one of the songs reportedly included on a tape of mono "*White Album*" tracks given to actor Peter Sellers by Ringo. The mix was manufactured using an earlier, longer take of the song, but adding the piano introduction from the released version. It is made longer primarily by a repeat of the "I listen for your footsteps" verse, cut from the released version.

- A mono mix of "Good Night," virtually identical to the released one but with a minor edit after the second verse, is on *Unsurpassed Masters 4* (CD), taken from a tape of mono mixes given to Peter Sellers by Ringo. The very end is a bit different as Ringo's final "Good night" is clearer and some voices are just barely heard in the background.

Jul 23: A slightly different mono mix of "Everybody's Got Something to Hide Except Me and My Monkey" is on *Unsurpassed Masters 4* (CD). The mix includes the Lennon released vocal recorded on this date and the backing vocal overdubs; it was another mix used by Ringo for his Peter Sellers tape.

Jul 25: George recorded an unreleased acoustic version of "While My Guitar Gently Weeps." This take was edited for the 1985 EMI-planned *Sessions* album, where an artificial ending was created by repeating the same two guitar licks and cutting George's actual final note. The track appears that way on bootleg copies of *Sessions* (LP, CD-1, CD-2, CD-3) and on *Ultra Rare Trax 3*. The unedited, original version is on *Unsurpassed Masters 7* (CD) *Nothing Is Real*, *Off White*, *Abbey Road Show 1983* (CD).

Jul 29: The Beatles recorded unreleased rehearsals of "Hey Jude" including complete takes running 6:21, 4:30 and 5:25.

Jul 30: The Beatles were filmed at EMI rehearsing "Hey Jude" by the National Music Council of Great Britain for a film titled *Music!* which was reportedly aired in Aug 1968 on the U.K. TV show "Experiment in Television." The finished film contained about 2:30 of the footage shot at this session, including one of at least two unreleased versions of "Hey Jude," and Paul busking a line from "St. Louis Blues" ("I hate to see the evening sun go down"); both titles appear on *Not Guilty* (CD), *Sessions* (CD-2), *Back Track Part Two* (CD) and *Ultra Rare Trax 5 & 6*. A second unreleased take of "Hey Jude" (5:01), omitted from the released film, is heard on *Unsurpassed Masters 4* (CD), where John can be heard raucously joining in in the background. The take is followed by an impromptu busk called "Las Vegas Jude," comprising a few improvised lines, which is followed by the same "St. Louis Blues" excerpt described above.

Jul: An alternate acoustic version of "Helter Skelter" was recorded and aired on Dutch television's "Vara Puntje" on Sep 27. It is found on the *1989 Beatleg News Christmas Record*.

Jul–Aug: During recording sessions for *The Beatles* album, The Beatles compiled three tapes containing studio outtakes and conversation. The Beatles kept the tapes for their personal collections and titled them "Beatles Chat." During those sessions The Beatles also worked on songs that would not be recorded for release until later, including "Something," "Let It Be" and "The Long and Winding Road." Paul recorded a demo of the latter, which he kept.

Aug 7–12: George recorded the unreleased song "Not Guilty," cutting 102 takes (with only 21 complete), nearly all of them rhythm tracks during Aug 7 and 8. A reduction mix was made and overdubs added on Aug 9. Harrison's lead vocal was finally added on Aug 12. The song was never released, but George recorded it again for his 1979 LP *George Harrison*. Several mixes of the unreleased version have been bootlegged. A mono mix done on Aug 12 has appeared on several boots, but in the best sound quality on *Unsurpassed Masters 4* (CD). Virtually an identical mono mix, apparently taken from an acetate with a resultant drop in sound quality, is on *Not Guilty* and *Nothing Is Real*. A stereo mix was prepared for EMI's scrapped 1985 *Sessions* album, and it is on all *Sessions* bootlegs, *Unsurpassed 6* (CD) and *Ultra Rare Trax 3* (CD). In that remix, the song has been slowed down and edited to eliminate the verse beginning with the lines "Not guilty, of being in your street . . ." that follow the first guitar break. Another stereo mix, also slowed down, but without the *Sessions* edit, is found on *Unsurpassed 7* (CD), *Ultra Rare Trax 5 & 6*, *Not Guilty* (CD), *Ultra Rare Trax 4* (CD) and *Back Track Part Three* (CD).

Aug 13: The Beatles recorded a spontaneous instrumental jam between takes 8 and 9 of "Yer Blues." It was added to one of the tapes of collected "*White Album*" outtakes, this one titled "Various Adlibs."

Aug 14: John, George and Yoko recorded "What's the New Mary Jane?" which remains unreleased. Four takes were cut on this date, one of them a breakdown, the other three running 2:35, 3:45 and 6:35. At the end of takes 2 and 4 a handbell and a xylophone are heard; take 4 has someone rustling paper into the microphone; John's "Let's hear it, before we get taken away!" is at the end of take 4, which is widely bootlegged. A mono remix of take 4, made on this date, was faded at 3:15. Two more mono mixes from take 4 were done on Sep 26; two stereo remixes were done on Oct 14; three new stereo mixes were done on Sep 11, 1969. On Nov 26, 1969 additional remixes were done and more overdubs added simultaneously, and considerable editing and remixing was done on the same day as preparation for the song's release on a single (APPLES 1002) with "You Know My Name (Look Up the Number)," a release that never took place although a Dec 5, 1969 release date was announced. Lennon's own mono acetate, without complete overdubs, was aired on episode 140 of "The Lost Lennon Tapes" radio series. The basic take 4 from Aug 14 is on *Not Guilty* (CD), *Ultra Rare Trax 5 & 6*, *Back Track Part Three* (CD) and, with the vocal mixed forward more, on *Unsurpassed Masters 4* (CD); stereo remix 4 is on *Mary Jane* and *Strawberry Fields Forever*. Stereo remix 5 is on *Four Sides of the Circle*, *The Toy Boy* and *The Little Red Album*. Both stereo mixes 4 and 5 are on a 12-inch bootleg single, "What a Shame Mary Jane Had a Pain at the Party." A completely new stereo mix was done for the scrapped 1985 *Sessions* album, and it appears on all bootlegs of that album and on *Unsurpassed 6* (CD).

Aug 15: *Unsurpassed Masters 4* (CD) includes a murkier copy of the mono mix of "Rocky Raccoon," which was officially released on the U.K.-only mono edition of *The Beatles* (aka the "*White Album*").

Aug 20: Additional mono mixes of *The Beatles* tracks later included on the tape compiled by Ringo for actor Peter Sellers are found on *Unsurpassed Masters 4* (CD) and include "Mother Nature's Son," "Wild Honey Pie" and "Yer Blues." All three are essentially the same as those released on the U.K.-only mono release of *The Beatles*.

- Paul recorded the unreleased "Etcetera" at Abbey Road and kept the tape. There are no known copies of the recording other than Paul's.

Aug 21: An alternate mono mix of "Sexy Sadie," one of five done on this date, appears on *Unsurpassed Masters 4* (CD).

Aug 23: Only one mono mix of "Back in the USSR" was made at EMI studios, completed on this date, and released on the U.K.-only mono version of *The Beatles*. Essentially the same mix appears on *Unsurpassed Masters 4* (CD), but without the noticeable handclaps, also largely missing from the more common stereo release, and with different airplane effects at the end. Since no official alternate mono mix exists, this appears to have been the mix used by Ringo for the tape he gave to Peter Sellers. Ringo did not do the mix himself on this date, since he had announced that he was quitting The Beatles a day earlier and was not even in the studio. The tape compiled for Sellers must have been assembled at a later date.

Aug 28–30: An alternate take of "Dear Prudence," recorded at Trident Studios, is on *Lost Lennon Tapes 6* and *Strawberry Fields Forever* (CD).

That summer: John recorded the unreleased, rambling, narrative-style "The Maharishi Song," a critical summation of his experience with the title character while in India, and "I Want You" with Yoko (not The Beatles' song of that title), also largely improvised. Both recordings are on *The 1968 Demos* (CD).

Sep 4: The Beatles shot promotional films for "Hey Jude" and "Revolution." They also did a short ad lib of "It's Now or Never" during the filming. These filmed performances contain new vocals recorded specifically for the films over previously recorded studio backing tracks. About 300 people from the David Frost audience joined The Beatles on stage for the chorus of "Hey Jude," which is on *Strawberry Fields Forever*. "Revolution" is on *Nothing Is Real* and *It's All Too Much*. Both tracks are on *The Last Album*, *Top of the Pops*, *Live in Europe* and *U.S. TV Casts* and *Nassau Coliseum*. "It's Now or Never" is also on *Strawberry Fields Forever* (LP and CD). Several takes were filmed and various edits were done, some of which have appeared on underground videocassettes.

Sep 5: The Beatles recorded unreleased alternate takes of "While My Guitar Gently Weeps." The released version was a complete remake. Take 40 cut on this date evolved into a jam that included "Lady Madonna," with Paul doing lead vocal on both songs. Part of this was added to one of the "Beatle Chat" compilation tapes assembled during the "*White Album*" sessions.

Sep 16: During recording of "I Will," Paul, John and Ringo (George was absent) lapsed into an untitled im-

Strawberry Fields Forever (bootleg). An early bootleg compilation of several interesting alternate takes and mixes.

provisation that lasted 2:21, listed as take 19 of "I Will." A small bit of it, the "Can you take me back" ditty, was used on *The Beatles* (aka the *"White Album"*) between "Cry Baby Cry" and "Revolution 9." Additional outtakes from this date included a stab at "Step Inside Love," written by Paul for Cilla Black, a 3:48 improvisation called "Los Paranoius," long erroneously thought to be a working title for "Sun King," and "The Way You Look Tonight," an improvised tune derived from "I Will," not the more famous song of the same title released by The Lettermen in 1961.

Oct–Nov: John cut an acoustic demo of "Everybody Had a Hard Year," a song he never actually finished but which was later incorporated into "I've Got a Feeling." John's demo (1:33), on which he uses the word "Everyone" rather than "Everybody," is on *The 1968 Demos* (CD), *Lost Lennon Tapes 4* and *Lost Lennon Tapes 2* (CD). Another take, in which John switches to the lyric "Everybody," is on *Johnny Moondog* (0:54).

Nov: The full, unedited recordings of John's poems "Yuck and Yono" and "Once Upon a Pool Table," from *The Beatles 1968 Christmas Record*, were aired on episode 101 of "The Lost Lennon Tapes" radio series.

Nov–Jan 1969: During sessions for Mary Hopkin's *Post Card* album, produced by Paul and for which Donovan Leitch wrote several songs, Paul and Donovan were recorded running through several songs including "Heather," "Blackbird" (both written by McCartney), "How Do You Do," "The Unicorn," "Lalena," "Mr. Wind," "The Walrus and the Carpenter" and "Land of Gisch" (all Donovan songs). All of the songs appear on *Sunshine Supermen* and *No. 3 Abbey Road*.

Dec 10–11: The Rolling Stones' unreleased film, *Rock and Roll Circus*, was filmed on Dec 11, with rehearsals held the previous day. A rehearsal of "Yer Blues," as well as an ad-lib improvisation of the song by John and Mick Jagger, both taped either at the rehearsal or during the next day's filming, are on *Lost Lennon Tapes 13* and *18*, *Lost Lennon Tapes 1* (CD) and *Yer Blues* (CD-1 and CD-2). The vocal on the rehearsal take is barely audible, and only the instrumental track is clearly heard. The track runs 1:29 on *Lost Lennon 13* and a full 4:00 on *Lost Lennon 18*. The Lennon/Jagger ad lib is also found on *Strawberry Fields Forever* (LP and CD) and *Ultra Rare Trax 4* (CD). The final version included in the film was done by John, Eric Clapton (lead guitar), Keith Richards (bass), Mitch Mitchell (drums) and Rick Gretch (violin) and is found in varying lengths on several bootlegs, a number of them exceeding 8 minutes: *Snaps 'n' Trax, Yin Yang, Working Class Hero, Ultra Rare Trax 4* (CD), *Johnny Moondog* and *Once Upon a Time*. The full original running time is reportedly 8:47. Not all bootlegs feature the stereo mix. In addition to an edited mix of the song, a jam session recorded during the filming, nominally titled "Dirty Mac Jam," is also on *Yer Blues* (CD-1 and CD-2); the jam only is on *Lost Lennon Tapes 8*.

Dec: Lennon recorded a demo of "A Case of the Blues," a song he is also heard rehearsing during the following month's *Let It Be* film sessions. While he never released the song, the demo can be found on *The 1968 Demos* (CD), *Lost Lennon Tapes 10, Lost Lennon Tapes 1* (CD), *Not for Sale* (CD) and *Back Track Part Three* (CD). John also cut some demos of "Don't Let Me Down" at this time, two of which are on *The 1968 Demos* (CD); one is on *Lost Lennon Tapes 17* and *The Beatles* (EP-1); the other is found on *Lost Lennon Tapes 18*. Two demos of "Oh My Love" are on *The 1968 Demos* (CD); one is on *My Love Will Turn You On* (CD).

Late that year–early 1969: Paul cut a demo of "Goodbye" for Mary Hopkin. The demo is on *Acetates* (CD) and *Not for Sale* (LP and CD).

1969

Let It Be Song Titles

Date and Song Title	Get Back I	Get Back II	Let It Be
Jan 30: "The One After 909"	X	X	X
Jan 22: "Rocker"	X	X	
Jan 22: "Save the Last Dance for Me"	X	X	
Jan 22: "Don't Let Me Down"	X	X	
Jan 24: "Dig a Pony"	X	X	
Jan 30: "Dig a Pony"			X
Jan 24: "I've Got a Feeling"	X	X	
Jan 30: "I've Got a Feeling"			X
Jan 27–28: "Get Back"	X	X	X
Jan 25: "For You Blue"	X	X	X
Jan 24: "Teddy Boy"	X		
Jan 24: "Two of Us"	X	X	
Jan 31: "Two of Us"			X
Jan 24: "Maggie Mae"	X	X	X
Jan 26: "Dig It"	X	X	X
Jan 31, Apr 30: "Let It Be"	X	X	
Jan 31, Jan 4, 1970: "Let It Be"			X
Jan 31: "Long and Winding Road"	X	X	X
Jan 28: "Get Back" (reprise)	X	X	
Jan 3, 1970: "I Me Mine"		X	X
Feb 4–8, 1968: "Across the Universe"		X	X

Jan 2–31: The Beatles spent virtually the entire month filming and recording what would become the *Let It Be* movie and album. A considerable amount of material from both the Twickenham (Jan 26) and Apple (Jan 20–31) sessions has appeared on bootlegs.

At the conclusion of the *Get Back* sessions, Glyn Johns, an independent engineer hired by EMI for this project, mixed two different versions of the *Get Back* album (on May 28 and on Jan 5, 1970), neither of which was ever officially released, although the first (*Get Back I*) was widely bootlegged under a variety of titles. Two examples are *Get Back with Don't Let Me Down and 9 Other Songs* (LP: bogus "Apple" PCS 7080/Black Bird Records; CD: bogus "EMI/Parlophone" CDP 7 48003 2), and *Get Back with Let It Be and 11 Other Songs* (LP: bogus "Apple"/no number; black label; also released on Tonto TO 643, and on CD: Disques Du Monde GB 87 1969). Reports that these bootlegs were copies of promotional *Get Back* albums sent to radio stations are false. The project was later turned over to Phil Spector, who conducted radical remixing sessions in producing the final album, released as *Let It Be* in conjunction with the film that bore the same title. Although many of the same original recordings were used by both Johns and Spector, the *Get Back* mixes are far different from those found on *Let It Be*.

Recordings found only on bootlegs constitute a large body of material. To detail each song title and each bootleg on which they appear would require a book in itself, so large is the number of unauthorized releases. (See Schweighard and Sulpy.) To give the reader a general idea of what exists and where it can be found, the following breakdown identifies the material recorded and lists the smallest number of bootlegs necessary in order to obtain virtually all of it. Many if not most of the more obscure song titles that appear here represent little more than a line or two busked by The Beatles. In some cases, one member of the group merely recites or shouts the title.

Lewisohn (1988) provides information that enables us to piece together the three albums and to identify which recordings appear on each of them. The song titles and recording dates in the table on page 224 are followed by an "X" under the title of each album on which they appear. Unless otherwise noted, recording dates took place in 1969. The recordings are listed again later in this section under their respective recording dates, where details about the different edits and mixes used on the different releases are also noted.

Jan 2–16: The following titles from the Twickenham sessions can be found on *The Get Back Journals*, an 11-album set that incorporates the unreleased *Get Back* album (Glyn Johns' first mix), *The Black Album* (3 LP) and most of the following: all three *Sweet Apple Trax* double albums, *Almost Grown*, *Singing the Blues* and *I Had a Dream*. The *Get Back Journals* material, except for the unreleased *Get Back* album, is duplicated on the following double albums, where the tracks have been reordered: *Commonwealth*, *Kool Wax*, *Magtrax*, *Goldmine* and *Y'Orite Wack*; a considerable amount of it appears on the bootleg CDs *Songs From the Past Volumes 3, 4 & 5*. Additional material is on *'69 Rehearsals* (3 CDs) and *Get Back and 22 Other Songs* (CD). With the

exception of the *Get Back* album, the titles included on these bootlegs are as follows (many titles, especially those actually being rehearsed for the *Get Back* album, are repeated a number of times and exist in several different versions, including those mentioned earlier): "Across the Universe," "All Along the Watchtower," "All Shook Up," "All Things Must Pass," "Almost Grown," "Around and Around," "Baa Baa Black Sheep," "Back Seat of My Car," "Bad Boy," "The Ball of Inverary," "Be-Bop-a-Lula," "Blowin' in the Wind," "Blue Suede Shoes," "Bring It on Home to Me," "Bring It to Jerome," "Cathy's Clown," "Child of Nature" (working title and version of "Jealous Guy"), "Chopsticks," "Crackin' Up," "(There's a) Devil in Her Heart," "Domino," "Don't Let Me Down," "Every Night," "Fools Like Me," "For You Blue," "Get Back," "Gimme Some Truth," "Good Rockin' Tonight," "Hare Krishna Mantra," "Harry Lime" (aka "Third Man Theme"), "Help!" "Hi Heel Sneakers," "Hippy Hippy Shake," "Hitch Hike," "Honey Hush," "House of the Rising Sun," "I Me Mine," "I Shall Be Released," "I Threw It All Away," "I'm Ready," "I'm So Tired" (with Paul doing lead vocal), "I've Got a Feeling," "Jambalaya," "Jazz Piano Song," "Johnny B. Goode," "Just Fun," "Lady Jane," "Let It Be," "Little Eddie," "Little Queenie," "The Long and Winding Road," "Long Tall Sally," "Love Is a Swingin' Thing," "Lucille," "Mama You Been on My Mind," "Maxwell's Silver Hammer," "Mean Mr. Mustard," "Midnight Special," "Milkcow Blues," "Money," "Move It," "New Orleans," "Norwegian Wood," "Ob-La-Di, Ob-La-Da," "Octopus's Garden," "The One After 909," "Papa's Got a Brand New Bag," "Penina," "Please Please Me", "Polythene Pam," "A Pretty Girl Is Like a Melody," "Queen of the Hop," "Reach Out, I'll Be There," "Rock and Roll Music," "Roll Over Beethoven," "(I Can't Get No) Satisfaction," "Save the Last Dance for Me," "School Day," "She Came in Through the Bathroom Window," "She Said She Said," "Short Fat Fanny," "Shout!" "Soldier of Love," "Stand By Me," "Sun King," "Suzy Parker," "Sweet Little Sixteen," "Take This Hammer," "Tea for Two," "Teddy Boy," "Tennessee," "Thirty Days," "Three Cool Cats," "Time Is Tight," "Too Bad About Sorrows," "Tutti Frutti," "Two of Us," "Watch Your Step," "What Do You Wanna Make Those Eyes at Me For?" "When I'm Sixty-Four," "When Irish Eyes Are Smiling," "Where Have You Been All My Life?" "Whole Lotta Shakin' Goin' On," "Why Don't We Do It in the Road," "Woman" (McCartney), "Won't You Please Say Goodbye," "You Can't Do That," "You Win Again," "Your True Love," "You're Going to Lose That Girl" and "You've Got Me Thinking."

A compilation tape (most of it on *Get Back and 220 Other Songs*) (CD) containing selected songs from the Twickenham sessions was auctioned at Sotheby's in 1990 and included the following titles, some of them speculative: 3"Tomorrow Never Comes," "Won't You Please Say Goodbye," "Bring It on Home to Me," "Hitch Hike," "You Can't Do That," "Short Fat Fanny," "Midnight Special," "What Do You Want to Make Those Eyes at Me For," "Low Down Blues Machine," "What'd I Say," "Thirty Days," "Hi-Heel Sneakers," medley "Don't Be Cruel"/"In the Middle of an Island," an instrumental jam, medley "Brazil"/"The Animal & Famous Persons Jam"/"Groovin'," "It's Only Make Believe," "My Baby Left Me," "That's All Right (Mama)," "Hallelujah, I Love Her So," "Little Queenie," "When Irish Eyes Are Smiling," "Queen of the Hop," "Gilly Gilly Ossenfeffer Katzeneleen Bogen by the Sea," "Blue Suede Shoes," "Good Rockin' Tonight," "Forty Days," "Too Bad About Sorrows," "Maggie Mae" (an unreleased, long version), "I Fancy Me Chances," "Digging My Potatoes," "Rock Island Line," "Michael Row Your Boat Ashore," "Rock-a-Bye Baby" (instrumental), "Singing the Blues," medley "Maybelline"/"You Can't Catch Me," "Brown Eyed Handsome Man," "Short Fat Fanny," "Sweet Little Sixteen," "Around and Around," "Almost Grown," "School Day," "Stand by Me," "I Lost My Little Girl" (McCartney's first composition, sung here by John), "There Once Was a Beautiful Girl," "I'm Talking About You," "High School Confidential," "Great Balls of Fire," medley "Don't Let the Sun Catch You Crying"/"Sexy Sadie," "Blue Suede Shoes," "Hava Nagila," medley "Moving Along the River Rhine"/"The Long and Winding Road," "I Got to Find My Baby," "Vacation Time," "Maybe Baby," "Peggy Sue Got Married," "Thinking of Linking," "Crying, Waiting, Hoping" and "Mailman, Bring Me No More Blues." Some of these titles have been bootlegged and are mentioned elsewhere in this section, but many of them are unavailable.

Speculative titles for other unidentified songs heard during these sessions include: "All I Want Is You," "Go Johnny Go," "Commonwealth"/"Get Off"/"White Power"/"Enoch Powell"/"No Pakistanis" (all speculative working titles of various experiments that eventually became "Get Back"), "Early in the Morning" (different from the Darin/Harris composition, which is found on *Bye Bye Love*), "If Tomorrow Ever Comes," "It's for You," "I've Got My Blue Fingers," "Look Out," "Madman a Comin'," "Negro in Reserve"/"Hole in My Heart," "Ramblin' Woman Blues," "Shakin' in the Sixties," "Thinking That You Love Me," "This Song of Love," "Wake Up in the Morning," "Watching Rainbows," "When You're Drunk You Think of Me," "The William Smith Boogie," "You Got Me Going" and "You Got the Message."

The following bootlegs feature additional titles: *The Real Case Has Just Begun* and *Soundcheck* (most of this also appears on CD *Songs from the Past Volume 1*): "Act Naturally," "Crying, Waiting, Hoping," "Don't Let the Sun Catch You Crying," "Get Back" (in German), "Great Balls of Fire," "Hava Nagila," "I Want You (She's So Heavy)," "I'm Talking About You," "I've Got a Feeling," "The Inner Light" (with Lennon doing lead vocal), "Jo Jo Gun," "Let It Down," "Little Yellow Pills," "The Long and Winding Road," "Maybe Baby," "The One After 909," "Piece of My Heart," "Rainy Day Women #12 & 35," "Sexy Sadie," "Strawberry Fields Forever" (instrumental), "Suicide," "Two of Us" and "Vacation Time" (listed as "The Real Case Has Just Begun"). Speculative titles for unidentified songs are "There Once Was a Beautiful Girl," "Moving Along the River Rhine" (an improvised blues number by Paul that

goes into "The Long and Winding Road") and "Once Upon a Time."

Code Name Russia (largely duplicated on CD *Songs from the Past Volume 2*): "Another Day," "I've Got a Feeling" (a cappella), "Hello Dolly," "Please Mrs. Henry," "I Bought a Picasso," "Brown Eyed Handsome Man," "Well . . . All Right," "Every Little Thing," "Piece of My Heart," "Sabre Dance," "Frere Jacques," "It Ain't Me Babe," "Two of Us," "Hear Me Lord," "Lady Madonna," "What'd I Say," "Till There Was You," "Shout," "A Shot of Rhythm and Blues," "(You're So Square) Baby I Don't Care," "Across the Universe," "Hello Muddah, Hello Fadduh," "Jenny Jenny," "Slippin' and Slidin'," "That'll Be the Day," "Don't Be Cruel" and "In the Middle of an Island" (sometimes listed as "Tiny Bossanova"). Speculative titles for unidentified songs include "Taking a Trip to Carolina" and "Low-down Blues."

File Under: "Bo Diddley," "Dig a Pony," "Hey Little Girl (in the High School Sweater)," "Not Fade Away," "Kansas City."

Singing the Blues: "Digging My Potatoes," "Hello Goodbye," "Rock Island Line," "Singing the Blues," "Kansas City."

Bye Bye Love: "Early in the Morning," "Gimme Some Lovin'," "London Bridge Is Falling Down." There are also some tracks with experimental guitar feedback.

In a Play Anyway and *Cinelogue 1* contain the entire *Let It Be* film soundtrack, which includes: "Paul's Piano Theme" (actually the untitled opening of the film), "Don't Let Me Down," "Maxwell's Silver Hammer," "Two of Us," "I've Got a Feeling," "Oh! Darling" (only two

Get Back (bootleg). An unreleased album of the Jan 1969 recordings, mixed by Glyn Johns. The tracks were later remixed by Phil Spector and issued as *Let It Be*. The *Get Back* cover was later used on the "Red" and "Blue" collections.

lines), Paul recites lines from "Just Fun" and mentions "Too Bad About Sorrows" as an early Lennon/McCartney song, "The One After 909," "Jazz Piano Song," "Get Back" (just a false start), "Across the Universe," "Dig a Pony," "Suzy Parker," "I Me Mine," "For You Blue," "Besame Mucho," "Octopus's Garden," "You Really Got a Hold on Me," "The Long and Winding Road," medley/jam "Rip It Up"/"Shake, Rattle and Roll"/"Kansas City"/"Miss Ann"/"Lawdy Miss Clawdy," "Dig It," "Two of Us," "Let It Be," "The Long and Winding Road" (second time); from rooftop concert: "Get Back," "Don't Let Me Down," "I've Got a Feeling," "The One After 909," "Dig a Pony" and "Get Back" (reprise). Filmed material comes from both the Twickenham sessions and the later Apple Studio sessions.

Other song titles and some of the bootlegs on which they can be found are "A Case of the Blues," "Gone Gone Gone" (both on *Almost Grown*), "Hot as Sun" (*Revolting*), "Her Majesty" (*Dig It*, CD), "A Quick One While He's Away" (*Beatles Vs. Don Ho*), different takes of "Don't Let Me Down" and "Two of Us" (*Songs from the Past*, CD).

Dozens of albums, far too numerous to list here, contain recordings from the *Let It Be* sessions.

Jan 22: Joined for the first time by Billy Preston, who remained with them for the remainder of the *Get Back* sessions, The Beatles recorded a song called "Rocker," which includes a bit from "I'm Ready"; it is also known as "Instrumental 42" and "Link Track." They also recorded "Save the Last Dance for Me" and a version of "Don't Let Me Down." All three songs are on Glyn John's first *Get Back* album mix and on the bootlegged versions of it noted above, and on *Get Back Journals*. Paul also did a very brief runthrough of Canned Heat's "Going Up the Country" and was heard doing "She Came in Through the Bathroom Window," then known as "Bathroom Window," which would be recorded later for the *Abbey Road* album.

Jan 23: An untitled one-minute blues instrumental improvisation was recorded in which Billy Preston's electric piano predominates.

Jan 24: The Beatles recorded two takes of "Dig It" (Version I), which is sometimes called "Can You Dig It." One take appears on *Classified Document Volume 3* and *Songs from the Past Volume 2* (CD). Less than one minute of it is on *The Real Case Has Just Begun* and *Soundcheck*. That take can be identified by John's "Hot Rod Cow" line. The second take was heard on episode 74 of "The Lost Lennon Tapes" radio series. Lewisohn (1988) lists these recordings as one take, but it appears to break down almost completely after 3:59, stops, and then begins again and continues for another 4:45.

- The Beatles cut versions of "Maggie Mae," "Two of Us," "Dig a Pony," "Teddy Boy" and "I've Got a Feeling." This is the same version of "Maggie Mae" released on the *Let It Be* album. All of the songs are on the unreleased *Get Back* album (first mix) and bootlegged copies of it. Most of them, and an alternate take

of "I've Got a Feeling" are on *Celluloid Rock* (CD) and *Singing the Blues*.

Jan 25: A brief bit of The Beatles doing "Bye Bye Love" is on *Bye Bye Love*. The Beatles also recorded an untitled jam. The versions of George's "For You Blue," also recorded, that appear on the *Let It Be* and *Get Back* albums represent noticeably different mixes—so different that they appear to be completely different recordings. The most obvious difference is the absence of George's spoken lines during the instrumental break on *Get Back* that are heard on *Let It Be*. Lewisohn (1988), however, clearly indicates that the same take was used for both albums. The track underwent heavy editing and remixing by Phil Spector for the *Let It Be* release.

Jan 26: The Beatles recorded Version II of "Dig It," the more common version. While the full track runs 12:25, it only begins to fade in after 8:27 on the unreleased *Get Back* album; the tiny bit released on *Let It Be* runs from 8:52 to 9:41. Although the full 12:25 recording is not available thus far, several bootlegs contain long versions in excess of 8 minutes, while others contain various edits; the records include *Celluloid Rock* (CD) (8:25) and *Dig It* (LP and CD; 8:22). The song runs 3:26 in the *Let It Be* film.

- The Beatles did an extended jam/medley that included "Rip It Up," "Shake, Rattle, and Roll," "Kansas City," "Miss Ann," "Lawdy Miss Clawdy," "Blue Suede Shoes" and "You Really Got a Hold on Me." The medley was included in the *Let It Be* film and is heard on *Celluloid Rock* (CD), *Singing the Blues* and *Circuit Songs*; all but "Blue Suede Shoes" are on *In a Play Anyway* and *Cinelogue 1*. The Beatles also did a largely instrumental version of "Tracks of My Tears," and George did a then-untitled 3:03 demo of "Isn't It a Pity," which he would later record for his *All Things Must Pass* album.

- Ringo worked on "Octopus's Garden," as seen in the *Let It Be* film. However, no studio recording of the song was made until the *Abbey Road* album. It has survived only on the film and bootlegs taken directly from the soundtrack, including *In a Play Anyway*, *Cinelogue 1* and *Get Back Journals*.

Jan 27: The Beatles were heard doing Jimmy McCracklin's "The Walk" and an alternate version of "Oh! Darling." The first number is on *Celluloid Rock* (CD), *Singing the Blues*, *Get Back to Toronto* and other bootlegs. The second title appears on *The Real Case Has Just Begun* and *Soundcheck*. "Oh! Darling" was later recorded for the *Abbey Road* album. This runthrough breaks down about halfway through. Several unreleased takes of "Get Back" were also recorded; one is on *Celluloid Rock* (CD). The Beatles also engaged in an untitled 10:54 jam.

Jan 27–28: The Beatles recorded several takes of "Get Back" on both of these dates, and it is not clear which date produced the released version. The different single and album mixes both fade out early before Paul's mock laughter is heard, but that unreleased ending was used during the closing credits in the *Let It Be* film and also appeared at the end of the *Get Back* album.

Jan 28: The Beatles recorded a 2:20 unreleased bluesy take of "Love Me Do" and unreleased takes of "Dig a Pony" and "The One After 909" and a rehearsal of "Teddy Boy."

Jan 29: The Beatles did a short version of "Besame Mucho," which appeared in the *Let It Be* film. The group also did Buddy Holly's "Mailman, Bring Me No More Blues," which appears on *Unsurpassed Masters 6* (CD), *Ultra Rare Trax 4* (CD), *Strawberry Fields Forever* (CD), *Songs from the Past* (CD), *The Real Case Has Just Begun* and *It Was 20 Years Ago Today*. A special remix and edit (1:52) of the song was created for the scraped *Sessions* album, and it appears in that form on *Sessions* (LP, CD-1, CD-2) and, shortened to 1:22, on *Mailman Blues*. The original track runs 1:44; it was extended for *Sessions* by creating an instrumental opening, beginning the song with the middle verse ("She wrote me only one sad line"), and going to the first verse after the instrumental break. The closing lines are the same, but the song fades out before they are completely heard on *Sessions*. Other unreleased tracks from this date include "Not Fade Away," "The One After 909," "Teddy Boy" and "I Want You," later recorded for *Abbey Road* as "I Want You (She's So Heavy)."

Jan 30: The Beatles' final public appearance as a group took place on the roof of the Apple building. Approximately half of this 42-minute set was seen as the conclusion of the *Let It Be* film. The following songs, taken directly from the film soundtrack, have been bootlegged: "Get Back" (2 versions), "Don't Let Me Down," "Dig a Pony," "The One After 909" and "I've Got a Feeling," all of which appear on *In a Play Anyway* and *Cinelogue 1*. The two versions of "Get Back" actually represent three different takes done on the roof that day. In the *Let It Be* film, the first two takes were edited together to create a single take for the movie; what appears to be the second version in the film is actually the third rooftop take. That final take is complete in the movie but was not used on the *Let It Be* or *Get Back* albums. "I've Got a Feeling," "The One After 909" and "Dig a Pony" are the same versions that were released on the *Let It Be* album, although the last title was edited by Phil Spector; "The One After 909" was also used on *Get Back*, and thus appears on bootlegs of that album as well. The rooftop version of "Don't Let Me Down" seen in the film is at least the third identifiable take available to collectors; the Jan 22 recording appears on bootlegs of the *Get Back* album, and the Jan 28 take was officially released as a single. Yet another rooftop take of that song remains completely unreleased along with a number of other tracks from the 42-minute set, including a short bit of "God Save the Queen," and another take of "I've Got a Feeling."

Jan 31: The released versions of "Two of Us" (take 12), "The Long and Winding Road" (take 19) and "Let It Be" (take 27) were cut; all but "Two of Us" were also used on the unreleased *Get Back* album (which used the Jan 24 take of "Two of Us"). "Let It Be," in fact, exists in three

different mixes, all taken from the same Jan 31 recording. The first appears on the *Get Back* album, the second as a single with overdubs added on Apr 30 and the third on the *Let It Be* album, with overdubs added on Jan 4, 1970. Both overdub sessions added lead guitar solos by Harrison; the single and *Get Back* mixes feature the Apr 30 solo, while the *Let It Be* album includes that of Jan 4, 1970. The brass and cello overdubs (from Jan 4, 1970) are more noticeable on *Let It Be* than on the single, and they are missing entirely on *Get Back*. An alternate take of "Let It Be" is on *Get Back to Toronto* and *Celluloid Rock* (CD). The Beatles also recorded a version of "Lady Madonna," still unavailable, that evolved into an extended jam. Unreleased takes of "Let It Be," "The Long and Winding Road," and "Two of Us" are on *'69 Rehearsals Vol. 2* (CD); other takes are found in *In a Play Anyway* and *Cinelogue 1*. The *Get Back* mixes of "Let It Be" (take 27) and "The Long and Winding Road" (take 19) appear on bootlegs of that album and *Get Back Journals*.

Feb 22: The Beatles recorded 35 rhythm track takes for "I Want You (She's So Heavy)," then known only as "I Want You." John recorded a guide vocal on this date, but one unreleased take with Paul on lead vocal is found on *Rough Notes*, *I Had A Dream* and *Both Sides*.

Feb 25: George recorded unreleased versions of "Old Brown Shoe," "All Things Must Pass" and "Something" without the other Beatles at Abbey Road. Later versions of these songs were officially released. Demo take 1 of "Something" is on *Acetates* (CD).

Mar 10: Glyn Johns mixed eleven songs from the *Get Back* sessions and prepared an acetate for The Beatles. The acetate appears to have found its way to America where it was aired by several radio stations as early as Sep 1969. Parts of it also appeared on early stereo bootlegs, including *Kum Back* and *Get Back to Toronto*. The acetate contains an alternate version of "Let It Be" and the same versions of several songs later used on the unreleased *Get Back* albums prepared by Johns, including "Get Back," "Teddy Boy," "Two of Us," "Dig a Pony," "I've Got a Feeling," "Don't Let Me Down," and "For You Blue." It also features "The Walk," which was omitted from *Get Back*. All but "Get Back" and "I've Got a Feeling" appear in excellent mono on *Celluloid Rock* (CD). The original acetate also contained "The Long and Winding Road" and "Get Back" (reprise). "Rocker" and "Save the Last Dance For Me," also mixed on this date, were omitted from the acetate.

Mar 25–31: During an interview with Akiva Noff of Israeli radio, John did an impromptu version of "I Want You (She's So Heavy)," ending it with "Hello Israel." The interview reportedly took place at the Amsterdam bed-in, but may have been done slightly before it or during a May 26 Toronto interview held just prior to the Montreal bed-in. The excerpt appears on *Dig It* and *Goodnight Vienna*. The Noff radio interview also included Lennon singing "Jerusalaim," [sic] written by Noff himself, and the traditional "Hava Nagila," both found on *Johnny Moondog* and *Goodnight Vienna*. An original ditty called "Radio Peace" is found on *Yin Yang*, and an impromptu version of the *"White Album"* track "Good Night" is on *The Toy Boy* and *The Little Red Album*. Runthroughs of The Beatles' "Don't Let Me Down" and "Those Were the Days," also apparently from the Amsterdam bed-in, but also reported as originating during a fall 1968 Lennon press conference, are on *Cavern Days*, *Recovered Tracks* and several other boots.

Apr 16: George recorded 13 unreleased takes of the rhythm track for "Something."

Apr 20–26: A studio version of "Oh! Darling" with an alternate McCartney lead vocal is on *Unsurpassed Masters 5* (CD), *No. 3 Abbey Road* and other bootlegs. During Apr 20 recording of "Oh! Darling" The Beatles lapsed into a jam that included some of Joe South's "Games People Play."

May 6: An unreleased studio take of "You Never Give Me Your Money" features guitar, piano, drums and Paul's guide vocal. Other overdubs, added later, are missing, including backing vocals, bass and chimes. The recording eventually drifts into a jam and runs 5:48. This is a mono mix, like many bootlegged Abbey Road alternate takes and mixes, which is interesting since no mono mixes of any *Abbey Road* songs were officially released. The recording is found on *Unsurpassed Masters 5* (CD), *No. 3 Abbey Road* and other bootlegs.

May 25: A pre–bed-in recording of "Give Peace a Chance" was taped at the King Edward Hotel in Toronto during an interview with John. It was aired on Episode 96 of "The Lost Lennon Tapes" radio series.

May 26: John recorded an improvised song called "Get It Together" during the Montreal bed-in. It was aired on episode 164 of "The Lost Lennon Tapes" radio series. An acoustic demo of "Because" is heard in the film *Bed-In*, released on home video.

Jun 1: John and his entourage recorded rehearsals of "Give Peace a Chance" in the Montreal bed-in hotel room prior to cutting the released version. One rehearsal is on *Beatles Vs. Don Ho* and *Twice in a Lifetime*. It appeared in vastly improved sound quality on episode 93 of "The Lost Lennon Tapes" radio series. A second rehearsal take was aired on episode 94 and another very brief take is on *Dreaming of the Past* (CD); episode 96 aired the complete released version with before and after talking added from the film *Bed-In*. Another acoustic version, found on *Classified Document Volume Two*, is preceded by spoken messages read by John and Yoko in Japanese.

Jul 2: An early take of "Golden Slumbers"/"Carry That Weight" runs over three minutes, includes only piano, drums, bass and McCartney's guide vocal, and is clearly different from the released one. This appears to be an edit of takes 13 and 15, still called take 13. The recording is mono and is found on *Unsurpassed Masters 5* (CD), *No. 3 Abbey Road* and other boots.

■ The released version of "Her Majesty" is missing the final guitar chord on the *Abbey Road* album due to an editing mistake on that album. The song is heard with the final chord intact on *Unsurpassed Masters 5* (CD), *No. 3 Abbey Road*, *Casualties* and other bootlegs.

Jul 9–11: A prefinal mix of "Maxwell's Silver Hammer" has a distinctive drum opening but is missing some overdubs, including synthesizer. The mix is found on *Unsurpassed Masters 5* (CD), *No. 3 Abbey Road* and other boots.

Jul 11: A reduction take (37) of George's recording of "Something," with an alternate vocal, is heard in various lengths on several different bootlegs, including *Unsurpassed Masters 5* (CD) and *No. 3 Abbey Road*.

Jul 17: A prefinal mix of "Octopus's Garden" appears to be from this date since the piano overdub has been added, but not the other overdubs done on this date. It is on *Unsurpassed Masters 5* (CD), in lesser sound quality on *No. 3 Abbey Road* and other boots.

Jul 17–22: One of Paul's unreleased lead vocals for "Oh! Darling," is on *Dig It* and other boots. This is Paul's vocal overdub track only, and no instrumentation is heard, so the song sounds a cappella. He recorded discarded lead vocals for the song on Apr 26, 1969 and Jul 17, 18 and 22, 1969. The final, released lead vocal was taped on Jul 23, 1969.

Jul 24: Paul's demo of "Come and Get It" was scheduled for released on EMI's scrapped 1985 *Sessions* album. The demo was recorded for Badfinger, who would record the song the following week with Paul serving as producer. Paul's demo can be heard on *Unsurpassed Masters 7* (CD), *Sessions* (LP, CD-1, CD-2), *File Under* and *Both Sides*. During recording of "Sun King"/"Mean Mr. Mustard" The Beatles lapsed into a jam that included "Ain't She Sweet," "Who Slapped John?" and "Be-Bop-a-Lula."

Jul 30: A mono copy of the initial mix of the *Abbey Road* medley, prepared on this date, appears on *Unsurpassed Masters 5* (CD), listed as "A Huge Melody" (Parts 1 and 2), with "Her Majesty" omitted and including some alternate vocals, and "The End" without vocals (which were added later).

Aug 1–4: The Beatles' harmony vocal only, without the instrumental track, for "Because" is found on *Unsurpassed Masters 6* (CD), *Ultra Rare Trax 5 & 6*, *Not Guilty* (CD), *Lost Lennon Tapes 14* and *Back Track Part Three* (CD). Take 16, harpsichord, vocals and synthesizer, is found on *Both Sides* and *Abbey Road Show 1983* (CD).

Aug 14: During *Abbey Road* sessions, a short, bouncy version of "Mean Mr. Mustard" was recorded, possibly during an interview with John recorded by Kenny Everett. It is found on *Cavern Days*, *Those Were the Days* and *Abbey Road Revisited*.

Aug: John recorded an instrumental called "Rock Peace." No recording of the song has surfaced to date.

Early Sep: John cut several demos of "Cold Turkey." The first demo take is on *Lost Lennon Tapes 17* and *Gone from This Place* (CD); the third, and final, demo is on *Lost Lennon 20*.

Sep 25: An alternate studio take of John's "Cold Turkey" is found on *Lost Lennon Tapes 7*.

Oct 2: John was interviewed on BBC Radio and discussed the *Abbey Road* album. Segments from the interview are sandwiched between tracks from the album, including several alternate versions listed above, on *Abbey Road Talks*.

Oct 27: Ringo recorded the unreleased "Bei Mir Bist Du Schon," once a hit for The Andrews Sisters. The outtake has been erroneously listed as "Buy Me a Beer, Mr. Shane," "My Mere Bits of Shame" and "Barney McShane."

Oct 31: George, Eric Clapton, Ric Grech and Denny Laine recorded unreleased tracks at Olympic Sound Studios in London.

Late Oct: A Lennon-Ono recording called "John & Yoko's Happy Xmas Ditty" may date from around this time when the two recorded material for *The Beatles 1969 Christmas Record*. It is found on *Lost Lennon Tapes 12*.

Dec 8: Ringo recorded new vocals for "Octopus's Garden" for the Dec 24 George Martin television special, "With a Little Help from My Friends" aired on the IBA network.

Dec 10: The Delaney and Bonnie and Friends concert at the Falkoner Theater, Copenhagen, Denmark, featuring George on second rhythm guitar, is on the bootleg album *Falconer*. George had played several shows with the group beginning on Dec 2. Songs included "Poor Elijah"/"Tribute to Johnson," "Don't Know Why," "Where There's a Will There's a Way," "You're My Girl," "That's What My Man Is For," "Comin' Home," medley "Tutti Frutti"/"The Girl Can't Help It"/"Long Tall Sally"/"Jenny Jenny."

Dec 17: During a Toronto press conference John and Yoko delivered a "Christmas/Peace Message," which is found on *Get Back to Toronto*.

Dec 29: In Denmark, the Lennons were taped at a press conference where they joined in on "O Kristelighed" ("O Christianity"), written nearly 100 years earlier by a Danish priest named Grundtvig. Two impromptu performances of the song were done; a short excerpt from one appears on *Both Sides*, where it is listed as "Christmas Song."

Dec 30: ITV aired a one-hour special called *Man of the Decade*, featuring segments on John Lennon, Mao Tse-Tung and John F. Kennedy. The 20-minute segment on Lennon featured a new interview with him; excerpts are on *Twice in a Lifetime*.

1970

Jan 3: Alternate stereo mixes of "I Me Mine," recorded on this date, appear on *Acetates* (CD), *Not for Sale* (LP and CD), *Sessions* (CD-3) and *File Under*. These mixes run 1:34 and were prepared before Phil Spector began his remixing, during which the song was extended to 2:25.

■ During recording of "I Me Mine," George, Paul and Ringo broke into an unreleased version of "Peggy Sue Got Married" with George doing the vocal. They led into the song with an instrumental jam.

Feb 3–Mar 13: During sessions for *Sentimental Journey* Ringo recorded the unreleased numbers "Autumn Leaves" and "I'll Be Seeing You."

Feb 11: John, Yoko, Klaus Voorman, Alan White and Mal Evans performed "Instant Karma!" for BBC-TV's "Top of the Pops," aired the following day. The track appears on *Christmas Message*, *Some Other Guy* and in edited form on *A Doll's House*.

Mar 15: Ringo filmed a promotional clip for the title track from his *Sentimental Journey* album. The clip was seen on "The David Frost Show" on Mar 29 and on "The Ed Sullivan Show" on May 17. The soundtrack, a different mix with some alternate vocals, is found on *Richie and His Pals/Scouse the Mouse*.

May 1: George and Bob Dylan recorded together during sessions held in Nashville for Dylan's *Self Portrait* album. The bootlegs *Harrison and Dylan Meet J. Cash* and *Bob Dylan Meets George Harrison and Johnny Cash* include the following titles from this session: "Song to Woody," "Mama, You Been on My Mind," a loose jam listed as "Justo" including bits of "Don't Think Twice, It's All Right" and "Corinna Corinna" (one line by George), which goes into "Yesterday," "Just Like Tom Thumb's Blues," "Da Do Ron Ron" and "One Too Many Mornings." The "Justo" jam and "Yesterday" are on *Classified Document Volume Three*. Recordings of Dylan and Harrison doing "I'd Have You Anytime" and "Every Time Somebody Comes to Town," quite probably from this date too, are also found on *Harrison and Dylan Meet J. Cash*. An alternate Dylan take of "If Not for You" with George on slide guitar was recorded on this date and officially released in Mar 1991 on Dylan's *Bootleg Series* boxed set; it also appears on *Traveling Wilburys Vol. 4 1/2* (CD).

May 26–Aug: George began work on "I Don't Want to Do It" during the *All Things Must Pass* sessions, recording demos of the song at this time. He would record it for official release in late 1984 with Dave Edmunds producing.

That summer: Lennon recorded several demos prior to studio sessions for his *John Lennon/Plastic Ono Band* album. "Well Well Well" is on *Look at Me* (CD) and *Lost Lennon Tapes 20*; "Love" is on *Yer Blues* (CD-1) and *Lost Lennon 18*; "Look at Me" is on *Look at Me* (CD) and *Lost Lennon Tapes 20*; "Mother" is on *Lost Lennon Tapes 16* and *Yer Blues* (CD-1). One demo of "My Mummy's Dead" is on *Look at Me* (CD) and *Lost Lennon Tapes 20*; a different demo was aired on episode 92 of "The Lost Lennon Tapes" radio series. Episode 85 included a demo of "How." One demo of "I Found Out" is on *Lost Lennon Tapes 12* while another is on *Vol. 13, News of the Day* (CD) and *Gone from This Place* (CD).

Jul 26: John cut several demos of "God"; demo take 2 is complete on *My Love Will Turn You On* (CD) and edited on *Lost Lennon Tapes 1*. Another demo appears on *Lost Lennon Tapes 12*, *Lost Lennon Tapes 2* (CD) and *Gone from This Place* (CD). Still another demo is on *Lost Lennon Tapes 21*.

Lost Lennon Tapes Vol. 13 (bootleg). As long as the radio series continued, bootleggers continued to package the rare Lennon recordings.

Sep 26–Oct 27: A rare, longer mix of John's "I Found Out," released only on the Australian edition of *Plastic Ono Band* is on *Lost Lennon Tapes 11* and *Look at Me* (CD). A different alternate mix is found on *Serve Yourself* (CD). An early take of "Mother" is found on *Yer Blues* (CD-2), *News of the Day* (CD) and *Lost Lennon Tapes 11*. John also cut two acoustic demos of the unreleased "When a Boy Meets a Girl," one of which is on *Lost Sleepy Blind Lemon Lennon Album* (CD) and *Look at Me* (CD). An acetate of alternate take 4 of "Well Well Well" and a rough mix of "Look at Me" are also found on *Look at Me* (CD); the latter is on *Dreaming of the Past* (CD); "Well Well Well" is also on *Lost Lennon Tapes 20*. Session outtakes, with Ringo also performing, include "Matchbox," "Hound Dog," "Don't Be Cruel" and "Honey Don't," all of which appear on *Watching the Wheels* (CD) and *Lost Lennon Tapes 6*. A studio jam of "That's All Right (Mama)" was heard on episode 116 of the radio series.

That fall: Ringo recorded a special song for John's 30th birthday; it is heard on *Lost Lennon Tapes 11*.

Late that year: John recorded a number of home demos during this period, including an early stab at "I'm the Greatest." Lennon would ultimately give the song to Ringo in 1973 for his LP *Ringo*. Other home demos from the period include "I Promise" and "Make Love Not War" (an early version of "Mind Games"), both of which appear on *Mind Games (Alternates & Demos)* (CD) and with the "I'm the Greatest" demo on *Lost Lennon Tapes 2*. Another demo was aired on episode 200 of "The Lost Lennon Tapes" radio series. "Make Love Not War" also appears on *News of the Day* (CD). An excerpt of a demo of "Sally and Billy" and a final demo of the song, recorded in the late 1970s, are on *Lost Lennon Tapes 10*.

A piano demo of "Oh Yoko!" is on *Lost Lennon Tapes 13*; an acoustic demo is on *My Love Will Turn You On* (CD). An ad lib of "Help!" is on *Lost Lennon Tapes 3* and *Lost Lennon Tapes 2* (CD). An early piano/vocal demo of "Rock & Roll People" is on *My Love Will Turn You On* (CD). A piano demo medley of "How?"/"Child of Nature"/"Oh! Yoko" was aired on episode 206 of the radio series. A composing demo of "How?" is on *Lost Lennon Tapes 13*, and *My Love Will Turn You On* (CD), opening with a line from The Impressions' "People Get Ready"; another demo is on *Lost Lennon Tapes 21*. The earliest known demo of "Aisemussen," under the working title "Call My Name," also from this period, is on *Mind Games (Alternates & Demos)* (CD) and *Lost Lennon Tapes 19*. A demo of the unreleased "I'll Make You Happy" was heard on episode 182.

■ An interview was taped with Paul including discussion of Jimi Hendrix's death; it is heard on *Can You Please Crawl Out Your Window*.

1971

Jan 22: An alternate take of "Power to the People" is on *Lost Lennon Tapes 18*. A second alternate take, with a count-in and false start, is on *Watching the Wheels* (CD) and *Lost Lennon Tapes 19*. A third alternate take is on *Lost Lennon Tapes 1*. A fourth alternate take is found on *Look at Me* (CD) and *Lost Lennon Tapes 4*.

Jun 1: John recorded a studio demo vocal of "God Save Us." The released version has Bill Elliot's vocal dubbed over Lennon's with the same instrumental backing track. John's demo is on *Gone from This Place* (CD) and *Lost Lennon Tapes 1* and *8*. John's original home acoustic demo of this song is on *Dreaming of the Past* (CD), *Lost Lennon Tapes 5* and *Johnny "L"* (CD).

Jun 6: A full version of John's live recording of "Well (Baby Please Don't Go)" is on *Randomonium*, an album included in *Mystery Box*, a 10-LP bootleg boxed set of Frank Zappa material. This is the same recording commercially released on *Some Time in New York City*, but this is the full, unedited version, which runs 7:14, compared to the released version, which is 3:44 (listed as 5:00 on the album).

Jun–Jul: John recorded most of his *Imagine* album. Saxophone overdubs recorded on Jul 4 by King Curtis for "It's So Hard" and "I Don't Want to Be a Soldier . . ." were heard on episode 107 of "The Lost Lennon Tapes." The following alternate takes have surfaced: "Oh Yoko!" "Gimme Some Truth," "How?" "Oh My Love," "How Do You Sleep?" "Imagine," "San Francisco Bay Blues." All are on *Lost Lennon Tapes 14* and *Imagine: The Alternate Album* (LP and CD); the latter adds alternate takes of "Jealous Guy" and "It's So Hard." Some of the songs are on CDs *Imagine—The Sessions*, *News of the Day*, *Serve Yourself*, *Look at Me* and *Watching the Wheels*. The following additional alternate takes are also on CD *Imagine—The Sessions*: "Imagine," "Crippled Inside," "It's So Hard," "Jealous Guy," "How?" "I Don't Want to Be a Soldier," "How Do You Sleep?" (different take),

"Well (Baby Please Don't Go)" (a studio outtake) and "Oh My Love." Some of these songs are on *Lost Lennon Tapes 2, 5, 10, 11, 12, 15* and *17,* and CDs *Johnny "L," Serve Yourself, Watching the Wheels, News of the Day, Lost Sleepy Blind Lemon Lennon* and *Gone from This Place.* The "Imagine" demo, edited to 1:24 on *Imagine: John Lennon,* runs a full 2:55 on *Imagine: The Sessions* (CD) and *Lost Lennon Tapes 21.* A different rehearsal take of "How Do You Sleep?" is on *Lost Lennon Tapes 15* and *Watching the Wheels* (CD); an alternate take is on *Serve Yourself* (CD) and *Lost Lennon Tapes 18;* a different alternate take of "Jealous Guy" is on *Lost Lennon Tapes 17;* another alternate take of "Oh Yoko!" is on *My Love Will Turn You On* (CD) and *Lost Lennon Tapes 19.* Another take of "Imagine" is on *Dreaming of the Past* (CD). The following alternate takes were aired on "The Lost Lennon Tapes" radio series on the episodes noted in parentheses: "Imagine" (rough mix; 84), "Oh My Love" (87), "It's So Hard" (91); an untitled jam was aired on episode 87.

Jul: John cut a studio demo of "I'm the Greatest," which is on *Lost Lennon Tapes 1* (CD), *Gone from This Place* (CD), *Imagine—The Sessions* (CD) and *Lost Lennon Tapes 2.* A second, more complete Lennon demo is on *Lost Lennon Tapes 15.*

Jul 16: John made a statement in support of *Oz* magazine and sang "The End of the Road" during a press conference dealing with the *Oz* magazine obscenity case in England, timed to coincide with the release of the "God Save Us." John signed off as "Radio Free Widnes." The recording was released as a flexi disc included with *Oz* magazine at the time and is reproduced in its entirety on *Lost Lennon Tapes 16;* the song only is found on *Lost Lennon Tapes 1.*

Aug 1: George, Ringo and several other performers appeared at two Concerts for Bangla Desh at New York's Madison Square Garden, New York. The evening concert was officially released on *The Concert for Bangla Desh.* Unreleased Dylan numbers "Love Minus Zero" and "A Hard Rain's Gonna Fall" are on *Traveling Wilburys Vol. 4 1/2* (CD). Unreleased portions from the afternoon and evening shows are on *Concert for Bangla Desh, The Greatest Show on Earth, George Harrison—Bob Dylan—Leon Russell—Eric Clapton* and *Madison Square Garden—August 1st 1971.*

Late summer: Extremely short clips of Paul doing "Bip Bop," "Hey Diddle" and "Lucille," filmed around this time, were seen in the 90-minute *Wings over the World* television special, first broadcast on Mar 16, 1979 by CBS-TV in the U.S. "Lucille" is from Wings' first rehearsal session. The recordings, largely obscured by a McCartney voiceover, are on *In the 1970s. . . .* A different Wings version of "Lucille," also possibly from this period, is on *Great to Have You with Us* and *Sunshine Supermen.*

Sep: Paul's unreleased recording of "Tragedy" may date from *Wild Life* sessions held during this period. Two different mixes with different vocals have appeared; one

is on *Cold Cuts* and *Hot Hits and Cold Cuts (Second Mix)* (CD); the other is on *Cold Cuts (Another Early Version)* and *Hot Hits and Cold Cuts* (CD).

- John and Yoko recorded the soundtrack for their film *Clock* in a room at the St. Regis Hotel in New York. John's versions of "Rave On," "Not Fade Away," "Maybe Baby," "Heartbeat," "Peggy Sue Got Married" and "Peggy Sue" are all on *Lost Lennon Tapes 8* (LP) and *1* (CD). "New York City" (1:17) is on *Lost Lennon Tapes 10.* "Mailman, Bring Me No More Blues" is on *Lost Lennon Tapes 17.* "Honey Don't," "Glad All Over" and "Lend Me Your Comb" are on *Look at Me* (CD) and *Lost Lennon Tapes 20* with a Duane Eddy jam that includes "Shazam!," "Raunchy" and other numbers. "J.J.," later rewritten to become "Angela," is on *Serve Yourself* (CD).

That fall: Lennon made a home recording of "Send Me Some Lovin'," which is found on *Dreaming of the Past* (CD) and *The Lost Lennon Tapes 10.* An acoustic demo of "Woman Is the Nigger of the World" is also on *Lost Lennon Tapes 10,* and on *News of the Day* (CD); the earliest known demo of that song is on *Lost Lennon Tapes 20.* Episode 84 of "The Lost Lennon Tapes" included the first demo takes of "Attica State." A demo of "New York City" is on *Lost Lennon Tapes 12* and *News of the Day* (CD); *Lost Lennon Tapes 15* includes demos of "Bring on the Lucie (Freeda Peeple)" and "People" (another early incarnation of "Angela" with different lyrics); the latter song is also on *Lost Sleepy Blind Lemon Lennon* (CD) and the former is on *Mind Games (Alternates & Demos)* (CD). John's only known recording of the unreleased "Pill" is on *Gone from This Place* (CD) and *Lost Lennon Tapes 13.* Five demo takes of the unreleased "Call My Name" (only one complete) are on *Lost Lennon Tapes 19* and *Mind Games (Alternates & Demos)* (CD).

Oct 9: John's 31st birthday was celebrated in a Syracuse hotel room with a jam session that included Ringo, Yoko, Phil Spector, Klaus Voorman, Allan Ginsberg, Jim Keltner and possibly Eric Clapton, Mal Evans and Neil Aspinall. Songs included: "What'd I Say," "Yellow Submarine," "On Top of Old Smokey," "Goodnight Irene," "He's Got the Whole World in His Hands," "Like a Rolling Stone," "Twist and Shout," "Louie Louie," "La Bamba," "Bring It on Home to Me," "Yesterday," "Tandoori Chicken," "Power to the People," "Maybe Baby," "Peggy Sue," "My Baby Left Me," "Blue Suede Shoes," "Crippled Inside" (twice), "Give Peace a Chance," "Uncle Albert/Admiral Halsey" (twice), "Happy Birthday to You," "My Sweet Lord" (Harrison). *John Lennon's 31st Birthday Party* (CD) adds "Imagine" (Spector vocal) and "Oh Yoko!," both missing from *Let's Have a Party* (LP and CD), which contains all of the other titles. Lennon and Ono were also interviewed by a Japanese journalist, part of which was aired on episode 88 of "The Lost Lennon Tapes" where it was dubbed "the argument interview," owing to an unusual degree of acrimony between the two.

Middle of Oct: Lennon cut a demo of "Happy Xmas (War Is Over)" sometime prior to the recording of the released version on Oct 28 and 29. The demo is on *Serve Yourself* (CD) and *Lost Lennon Tapes 12*.

Oct 28–29: A prefinal mix of "Happy Xmas (War Is Over)" without the choir and other overdubs is on *Dreaming of the Past* (CD).

Nov 12: John recorded home demo takes of "Luck of the Irish." Two takes are on *Lost Lennon Tapes 4* (CD) and *Lost Lennon Tapes 2* (LP). Two different demos are on *Lost Lennon Tapes 15*, one of which also appears on *Yer Blues* (CD-1). A different demo was aired on episode 169 of "The Lost Lennon Tapes" radio series.

Dec 3: George appeared on "The David Frost Show" in the U.S. Some clips are on *Beatles Vs. Don Ho* and *Classified Document Volume Three*.

Dec 10: John and Yoko appeared at a benefit concert for John Sinclair in Ann Arbor, Michigan. John sang "John Sinclair," "Attica State" and "Luck of the Irish," and Yoko did "Sisters O Sisters." Lennon's three songs are on *The Live Lennon Tapes* (CD), *Lost Lennon Tapes 4* (LP) and *5* (CD). A film of the event, titled *Ten for Two*, was also shot. During an informal jam at his hotel room, John played slide guitar on "Chords of Fame," sung by Phil Ochs, and aired on episode 148 of "The Lost Lennon Tapes."

Dec 17: John appeared at a benefit concert for the families of those killed during the Attica Prison uprising. He sang "Imagine" and "Attica State"; Yoko did "Sisters O Sisters." "Imagine" is found on *Yin Yang*, *Johnny Moondog* and *The Live Lennon Tapes* (CD).

1972

Early that year: John Lennon reportedly gave approximately 25 hours of unreleased Lennon tapes to Bruce Bierman during the recording of David Peel's *The Pope Smokes Dope* album, produced by Lennon. Bierman claimed that the tapes contained Beatles rehearsals, outtakes and unreleased Lennon compositions.

Jan 13: John and Yoko were guests on "The David Frost Show" in the U.S. and sang "John Sinclair," "Attica State," "The Luck of the Irish" and "Sisters O Sisters." The Lennons were backed by David Peel and the Lower East Side Band. The first two songs are on *Telecasts* and *The Live Lennon Tapes* (CD).

Feb 1: An unreleased filmed Wings rehearsal of "Give Ireland Back to the Irish" is on *In the 1970s*. The recording reportedly comes from a screening on "The David Frost Show" of May 21, 1975, which was itself borrowed from an earlier telecast on an ABC-TV news report.

Feb 9: An audience tape of Wings' Nottingham University concert has circulated. The tape contains "Blue Moon of Kentucky," "Give Ireland Back to the Irish," "Help Me," "Say Darling," "Wild Life," "Bip Bop," "Henry's Blues," "The Mess" (which Paul notes had already been played earlier), "My Love," "Lucille" and "Long Tall Sally."

Feb 11: Wings performed live at Hull University. The entire show is on *First Live Show Spring 72* and *Live at Hull University*, including "Lucille," "Give Ireland Back to the Irish," a bit of "Turkey in the Straw," "Blue Moon of Kentucky," "Seaside Woman," "Help Me," "Some People Never Know," "The Mess," "Bip Bop," "Say Darling," "Smile Away," "My Love," a bit of "The Grand Old Duke of York," "Henry's Blues," "Wild Life," "Give Ireland Back to the Irish" (reprise), "The Mess" (reprise), "Lucille" (reprise). Part of the show is on *Belgium 1972* and *Naturescapes*.

Feb 14–18: John and Yoko were guest hosts for a week on "The Mike Douglas Show." Over the five-day period they sang "It's So Hard" (Feb 14), "Imagine" (Feb 17) and "Luck of the Irish" (Feb 18); Ono did "Midsummer New York" (Feb 15), "Sisters O Sisters" (Feb 16), "Sakura" (Feb 18). On Feb 16 John greeted special guest Chuck Berry, calling him "my hero," and the two dueted on the Berry classics "Johnny B. Goode" and "Memphis." All of the songs are on *Telecasts* and *The Live Lennon Tapes* (CD).

Mar 1–20: During the *Some Time in New York City* sessions, Lennon and Elephant's Memory ran through a number of unreleased rock standards, including "Don't Be Cruel," "Hound Dog" and "Send Me Some Lovin'," all of which are found on *Lost Lennon Tapes 12* and *Yer Blues* (CD-2); "Roll Over Beethoven," "Whole Lotta Shakin' Going On," and "It'll Be Me" are on *Lost Lennon Tapes 8* (LP) and *1* (CD); a short jam of "Not Fade Away" is on *Lost Lennon Tapes 6*. "Ain't That a Shame" and "Caribbean" are on *Lost Sleepy Blind Lemon Lennon Album* (CD). An unreleased take of "Woman Is the Nigger of the World" was aired on episode 83 of "The Lost Lennon Tapes"; episode 168 included a rehearsal of "Attica State."

Telecasts (bootleg). An interesting collection of early 1972 Lennon TV appearances.

Middle of Mar: During sessions for *Red Rose Speedway*, Wings recorded Denny Laine's "I Would Only Smile," which was cut from the album but was later remixed and released on Laine's album, *Japanese Tears*. It appears in its original form on *Cold Cuts: Another Early Version* and *Hot Hits & Cold Cuts* (CD), and in its released mix on *Suitable for Framing*. "Mama's Little Girl" was also reportedly recorded. A version officially released in 1990 may be from this period, or from the 1978 *Back to the Egg* sessions. The 1972 track may simply have been remixed in 1978, or a completely new recording made at that time.

May 11: Lennon and Ono appeared on "The Dick Cavett Show," singing "Woman Is the Nigger of the World"; Ono did "We're All Water." Both songs are on *Telecasts* and *The Live Lennon Tapes* (CD).

That summer: Lennon ran through acoustic versions of "Rock Island Line," "Well (Baby Please Don't Go)," "Peggy Sue" and "Maybe Baby" reportedly during a television news segment. The medley is on *Come Back Johnny* and *Teddy Boy*.

Jul 9: Wings began a European tour with a show at the Centre Culturelle in Chateau Valonne, France. An unidentified "1882" from the tour is on *A Doll's House*; an unidentified performance of "Best Friend" appears on *Cold Cuts* and *Hot Hits and Cold Cuts (Second Mix)* (CD).

Jul 19: Wings did a concert at the Offenbach Halle in Frankfurt, Germany. "1882," "I Would Only Smile," "Blue Moon of Kentucky," "Best Friend," "I Am Your Singer," "Say You Don't Mind," "Henry's Blues" and "Seaside Woman" are on *Live in Hanover Germany 1972*; "Bip Bop," "Smile Away," "Give Ireland Back to the Irish," "The Mess" and "Mary Had a Little Lamb" are on *Oriental Nightfish*.

Jul 22: Wings performed a concert at the Pavilion in Montreaux, Switzerland. Songs included "Bip Bop," "Smile Away," "Mumbo," "Give Ireland Back to the Irish," "1882," "I Would Only Smile," "Blue Moon of Kentucky," "The Mess," "Best Friend," "Soily," "I Am Your Singer," "Say You Don't Mind," "Henry's Blues," "Seaside Woman," "Wild Life," "My Love," "Mary Had a Little Lamb," "Maybe I'm Amazed," "Hi Hi Hi" and "Long Tall Sally." The concert is on *Wings over Switzerland* (CD) and *Wings Over Switzerland—Live in Montreux 1973* [sic].

Aug 7: "Eat at Home," "Mumbo," "Best Friend," "1882" and "I Would Only Smile" from Wings' Stockholm show appear on *Oriental Nightfish*, taken from a poor-quality audience recording.

Aug 11: "My Love" from Wings' concert in Lund, Sweden, is on *God Jul 1972* (translation: *Happy Xmas 1972*).

Aug 14: Wings' concert at the Vejlby Risskov Hallen in Arhus, Denmark is on *Wings Over Denmark 1972*.

Aug 17: The following songs, taken from a radio broadcast of Wings' Rotterdam show, are on *Complaint to the Queen*: "Eat at Home," "Smile Away," "1882," "I Would Only Smile," "Blue Moon of Kentucky," "Best Friend" and "Seaside Woman."

Aug 18: The first of at least three rehearsals for Lennon's Aug 20 One to One Concerts was recorded and included the following titles, in various stages of completeness: "Cold Turkey," "Born in a Prison," "Give Peace a Chance," "Come Together" (vocal and instrumental versions), "Well Well Well," "Mother," "New York City," "Instant Karma," "It's So Hard," "Sisters O Sisters," "Woman Is the Nigger of the World," "Don't Worry Kyoko," "It's Only Make Believe," "Open Your Box," "Tequila," "We're All Water," "Move on Fast," "Roll Over Beethoven," "Unchained Melody" and an ad lib of Ringo's "Back Off Boogaloo," all of which appear on *One and One and One Is Three*, released as three separate albums rather than as a single set; part of the recording is on *Willowbrook Rehearsals*. Another version of "Tequila" and "Bunny Hop" (a loose jam) are on *Classified Document Volume Three* and *Goodnight Vienna*. A brief breakdown of "New York City," cut off by Lennon himself, is on *Lost Lennon Tapes 8*. A much longer alternate version was heard on episode 19 of "The Lost Lennon Tapes." Some radio spots recorded for the concert are on *Lost Lennon Tapes 3* (LP) and *1* (CD).

Aug 19: "Hi Hi Hi" from the soundcheck preceding Wings' Netherlands show is on *Complaint to the Queen*.

Aug 20: During an Amsterdam radio interview, Paul sang an impromptu ditty christened "Complain to the Queen," which is found on *Complaint to the Queen* and *Suitable for Framing*.

Aug 20–21: Wings performed concerts on each of these dates at the Concertgebouw, Amsterdam, the Netherlands. "I Am Your Singer" from the first show and "The Mess" (later commercially released as the B side of "My Love") from the second are on *Complaint to the Queen*.

Aug 21–22: John conducted additional rehearsals for his One to One Concerts with Elephant's Memory. A 7:37 rehearsal of "Give Peace a Chance" is on *Yer Blues* (CD-2). "The Lost Lennon Tapes" radio series aired "Hound Dog" and "Long Tall Sally" from Aug 21 and "Well Well Well" from Aug 22. "Honky Tonk" and Ono's "Mind Train" were also aired.

Aug 22: A portion of Wings' Antwerp concert is on *Cottonfields* (CD), which includes "Best Friend," "Soily," "I Am Your Singer," "Seaside Woman," "Say You Don't Mind," "Henry's Blues," "Give Ireland Back to the Irish," "Cottonfields" and "My Love." A tape of the entire show has circulated, but the CD offers much improved sound.

Aug 30: John and Yoko did two shows at Madison Square Garden, New York, the One to One Benefit Concerts. Lennon sang "New York City," "Cold Turkey," "Come Together," "Hound Dog," "Imagine," "Instant Karma," "Mother," "It's So Hard," "Well Well Well" and "Woman Is the Nigger of the World." "Give Peace a Chance" closed the evening show and included all of the concert's performers, Stevie Wonder, Roberta Flack and Sha Na Na among them. It is not known if the number was done at the afternoon show, however, and no afternoon recording of the song has ever surfaced. Some bootlegged tracks are taken from a Dec 14 ABC-TV special that included several numbers, and from a broadcast on the U.S. syndicated radio series "The King Biscuit Flower Hour." Most of Lennon's evening show is on *Come Back Johnny*, which is missing only "Imagine" and "Give Peace a Chance," both of which are found on *A Hard Road* and *Plop Plop . . . Fizz Fizz*. No complete version of "Give Peace a Chance" has appeared, although different parts of it are found on the officially released *Live in New York City* album and video, on the bootlegs noted and also on the LP *Shaved Fish*, where a short bit is tacked onto the end of "Happy Xmas (War Is Over)." Most of the afternoon show was officially released with many songs in edited form on *Live in New York City*.

Sep 6: John and Yoko appeared live on the U.S. "Jerry Lewis Muscular Dystrophy Telethon" and sang "Imagine" and a reggae version of "Give Peace a Chance." The appearance is found on *Angel Baby/John Winston Lennon* and *Classified Document Volume Two*.

Nov 2: A copyright was registered for "You've Gotta Stay with Me," written by Paul L. Woodall (words, music, arrangement) and George Harrison (music and arrangement). No publishing company is listed on the copyright and it is not certain that this is The Beatles' George Harrison. George reportedly worked with Cilla Black on unreleased recordings of this song and "I'll Still Love You" during Aug 1972 with Ringo and Eric Clapton. "I'll Still Love You," written by Harrison and originally copyrighted under the title "When Every Song Is Sung," was later recorded by Ringo for his *Ringo's Rotogravure* album.

Dec: George cut a demo of "Sue Me, Sue You Blues," later recorded during Jan–Apr 1973 sessions for *Living in the Material World*. The demo is on *Onothimagen*.

Onothimagen (bootleg). A double-LP collection of Harrison rarities.

1973

Mar 10: Ringo recorded a radio antidrug spot called "Get Off," found on *Richie and His Pals/Scouse the Mouse*.

Middle of Mar: During taping for his TV special "James Paul McCartney," Paul did an unreleased acoustic medley of "Bluebird"/"Mama's Little Girl"/"Michelle"/"Heart of the Country," which was not included in the special but is found on *Lifting Material From the World* and *20X4*. A similar medley, without "Mama's Little Girl," was used in the TV special and comprised "Blackbird"/"Bluebird"/"Michelle"/"Heart of the Country."

Mar 18: Paul and Wings performed a live set before an invited audience at ATV's Boreham Wood Studios for the "James Paul McCartney" TV special, aired Apr 16. The set included "Big Barn Bed," "The Mess," "Maybe I'm Amazed" and "Long Tall Sally." All four are on *James Paul McCartney*. "Big Barn Bed" may actually have been recorded and filmed in the studio with the film edited to make it seem part of the live performance.

That spring: John recorded several demos prior to *Mind Games* sessions. These included one of "I Know (I Know)" on *Dreaming of the Past* (CD) and *Mind Games (Alternate & Demos)* (CD); two other demos were aired on episodes 75 and 104 of "The Lost Lennon Tapes" radio series; a demo of "Mind Games" was aired on episode 24. One demo of "Meat City," under the working title "Shoe Shine," is on *Dreaming of the Past* (CD) and *Mind Games (Alternates & Demos)* (CD); another was heard on episode 125; another take, part of the medley "Just Gotta Give Me Some Rock & Roll"/"Shoe Shine" is found on *Serve Yourself* (CD) and *Mind Games (Alternates & Demos)* (CD), and *Lost Lennon Tapes 18*. An acoustic demo of "Tight A$" is also on *Mind Games (Alternates & Demos)* (CD), *Serve Yourself* and *Lost Lennon Tapes 7*. One acoustic demo of "Rock and Roll People" is on *Lost Lennon Tapes 5*. A piano demo of "Intuition" is on *Lost Lennon Tapes 19* and *Mind Games (Alternates & Demos)* (CD); another was heard on episode 209.

Apr 1–15: During sessions for the *Ringo* album in Los Angeles, John, George and Ringo cut several studio demo takes of "I'm the Greatest" with John doing lead vocal on his own composition. Although Lennon had been working on this song for more than two years, initially planning to record it himself, he now gave the song to the former Beatles drummer. Bootlegs of various portions of these studio sessions have appeared. The complete session tape includes at least nine takes, several of which are breakdowns. The full session, running nearly 18 minutes, is on *Serve Yourself*, *Snap Shots*, *Soundcheck* and *Something Precious and Rare* (CD). Parts of the session are on the 12-inch single "Je Suis Le Plus Mieux," *Look at Me* (CD), and *The Toy Boy*.

Apr 16: Paul's "James Paul McCartney" TV special was aired on ABC-TV in the U.S. and included four songs recorded live on Mar 18 (see that date above). The show also included an acoustic medley of "Blackbird"/"Bluebird"/"Michelle"/"Heart of the Country." The following

James Paul McCartney (bootleg). One of several bootlegs of Paul's 1973 special.

numbers were also performed: "Mary Had a Little Lamb," "Little Woman Love"/"C Moon," "My Love," "Uncle Albert" (the "Admiral Halsey" part was cut), "Gotta Sing, Gotta Dance," "Live and Let Die" and "Yesterday." The U.K. broadcast also included "Hi Hi Hi." The entire program as aired in the U.S. is on *James Paul McCartney* (LP and CD).

Apr 16–30: Several prefinal mixes, alternate takes and edits from sessions for Ringo's album, *Ringo* are found on *With a Little Help from My Friends*, which includes "I'm the Greatest," "Have You Seen My Baby," "Photograph," "Sunshine Life for Me (Sail Away Raymond)," "You're Sixteen," "Oh My My" and "Six O'Clock."

May 1: A copyright was registered for the unreleased song "Only One More Kiss," written by Paul McCartney.

May 12: Paul was interviewed by Dave Simons following Wings' concert at the New Theatre in Oxford. The interview appears on *Give Ireland Back to the Irish?* (CD).

May 19: Wings performed a concert at Leeds University. "Soily," "Big Barn Bed," "When the Night," "Wild Life," "Seaside Woman," "Little Woman Love"/"C Moon," "Live and Let Die," "Maybe I'm Amazed," "My Love," "Go Now" and "The Mess" are on *Leeds, England*; "Long Tall Sally" and "Say You Don't Mind" were also performed.

May 23: Wings performed at the Odeon Cinema in Edinburgh, Scotland. Songs were the same as May 19; most of the show is on *Paul McCartney in Scotland* and *Scotland—73*.

Jul 10: The final show of Wings' 1973 tour took place at the City Hall in Newcastle-upon-Tyne. Songs were similar to May 19; most of the show is on *Live in Newcastle, 1973*.

Jul–Aug: An alternate mix of John's "Bring on the Lucie (Freeda Peeple)" is on *Lost Lennon Tapes 15*, *Mind Games (Alternates & Demos)* (CD) and *Yer Blues* (CD-1). A rough mix of "Only People" with kazoo overdub is also on *Lost Lennon Tapes 15*; a slightly different mix is on *Yer Blues* (CD-1) and *Mind Games (Alternates & Demos)* (CD); a different mix, without kazoo, is on *Dreaming of the Past* (CD). An alternate take of "Out the Blue" with organ overdub appears on *News of the Day* (CD) and *Lost Lennon Tapes 13*; a different mix is on *Yer Blues* (CD-1), *Mind Games (Alternate & Demos)* (CD), and *Lost Lennon Tapes 18*. An alternate take of "Aisemussen" is on *Watching the Wheels* (CD), *Mind Games (Alternates & Demos)* (CD) and *Lost Lennon Tapes 19*. An alternate take of "Mind Games" is on *Lost Lennon Tapes 7* and *Watching the Wheels* (CD); the basic track with Lennon's guide vocal is on *Mind Games (Alternates & Demos)* (CD). An alternate take of "I Know (I Know)" is on *Lost Lennon Tapes 18*; an alternate take of "Intuition" is on *Lost Lennon Tapes 19*; both are also on *Mind Games (Alternates & Demos)* (CD). An alternate take of "Tight A$" (take 4) is on *Dreaming of the Past* (CD) and *Mind Games (Alternates & Demos)* (CD). A pre-final mix of "Meat City" is on *My Love Will Turn You On* (CD) and *Mind Games (Alternates & Demos)* (CD). An alternate take of "One Day (At a Time)" is on *My Love Will Turn You On* (CD) and *Mind Games (Alternates & Demos)* (CD).

Aug 4: Lennon recorded "Rock and Roll People." Unreleased take 5, from the same tape containing the version released on *Menlove Ave.*, is on *Watching the Wheels* (CD) and *Lost Lennon Tapes 6*. Another unreleased take is found on *Lost Lennon Tapes 15* and *Yer Blues* (CD-1). Unreleased take 7 is on *My Love Will Turn You On* (CD).

Aug 10–Sep 22: During *Band on the Run* sessions Wings recorded "Oriental Nightfish," with Linda McCartney doing lead vocal. The song was used as the soundtrack for the animated short *Oriental Nightfish*, released in May 1978, and later released on the *Rupert and the Frog Song* home video. "Oriental Nightfish" appears on *Cold Cuts: Another Early Version* and *Hot Hits & Cold Cuts* (CD).

Oct–Dec: During *Rock 'N' Roll* sessions, John recorded "Here We Go Again," co-written with Phil Spector. A demo appears in shortened form on *Lost Lennon Tapes 1*. In this form, the middle is cut out and the ending lopped off. The full demo, in better sound quality, is on *Dreaming of the Past* (CD) and *Lost Lennon Tapes 6*. The song was officially released on *Menlove Ave.* Lennon also cut an embarrassingly drunken version of "Just Because," which appears on *You Should'a Been There* and *Winston O'Boogie*. Outtakes of "You Can't Catch Me" and "Sweet Little Sixteen" are on *Lost Lennon Tapes 6*. An alternate take of the first title was aired on episode 128 of "The Lost Lennon Tapes" and an alternate take of the second is on *Lost Lennon Tapes 22*. An unreleased vocal for "Ain't That a Shame" appears on *You Should'a Been There* and *The May Pang Tapes*. An alternate take of "Bony Maronie" is found on *Yer Blues* (CD-1) and *Lost Lennon Tapes 18*. John also recorded "Angel Baby," which was omitted from *Rock 'N' Roll* but included on the unauthorized Feb 1975 mail-order release, *John Lennon Sings the Great Rock & Roll Hits [Roots]*. It appears on bootlegs of that album and on *The Toy Boy* and *You Should'a Been There*. The song was officially released on *Menlove Ave.* and again in 1990 on the CD boxed set *Lennon*, where it was artificially extended by adding a repeat of the chorus before the final verse. The *Roots* version runs 3:03 while the *Menlove Ave.* version is 3:41 (listed as 3:39). John also recorded "Be My Baby," which was released only on the *Roots* album. The version on that album was actually manufactured from two different takes, one of which appears in full on *Lost Lennon Tapes 18*, *Watching the Wheels* (CD) and in poorer sound quality on *You Should'a Been There*. Only *You Should'a Been There* retains the full ending, and that bootleg also contains the *Roots* version. The alternate version is much longer and has a greatly extended fadeout. The entire instrumental track from that take appears to have been used for the final version, but the vocal during the first half was not released; the vocal during the second part was retained on the *Roots* version.

Dec: During a studio jam session, Lennon produced a Mick Jagger recording of "Too Many Cooks," which remains unreleased but appears on *Both Sides*, *Great to Have You with Us* and *Snaps 'n' Trax*.

1974

Early that year: A Lennon acoustic demo of "What You Got" is on *Yer Blues* (CD-1) and *Lost Lennon Tapes 19*.

Mar–Apr: John cut three demo takes of "Mucho Mungo" for Harry Nilsson while producing the latter's *Pussy Cats* album. All three takes are on *Yin Yang* and *Johnny Moondog*. Take 2 is on *Lost Sleepy Blind Lemon Lennon* (CD) and *Look at Me* (CD). A different demo is found on *Lost Lennon Tapes 12*.

■ John and Paul both participated in a lengthy jam, including "Midnight Special" in Los Angeles. Other participants included Harry Nilsson, Stevie Wonder, Jesse Ed Davis, Danny Kortchmar, Linda McCartney and May Pang, on *A Toot and a Snore 74* (CD).

Jun 19: A copyright was registered for the unreleased "Where Are You Going?" written by Ringo and Billy Lawrie.

Middle of that year: Paul taped demos of several songs that he and Wings would later record for *Venus and Mars*. The demos include "Letting Go," "Call Me Back Again," "Lunch Box-Odd Sox," "Lonely Old People," "Treat Her Gently" and "You Gave Me the Answer"; they are found on *Rock Show* (EP).

Early that summer: John recorded the earliest known demo of "Surprise Surprise (Sweet Bird of Paradox)," found on *Lost Lennon Tapes 17* and *Watching the Wheels* (CD). Another demo is found on *Lost Lennon Tapes One*, while still another is heard on *Lost Lennon Tapes 10*. A demo of "No. 9 Dream" is found on *Yer Blues* (CD-1) and *Lost Lennon Tapes 13*; a different demo, under the working title "So Long," is on *Look at Me* (CD) and *Lost Lennon Tapes 20*. A demo of "Whatever Gets You Through the Night" is on *Lost Lennon Tapes 3* and *Dreaming of the Past* (CD); two additional demos were aired on episodes 12 and 104 of "The Lost Lennon Tapes." One demo of "Move Over Ms. L" is on *Lost Lennon Tapes 15* and *My Love Will Turn You On* (CD), while a second demo is on *Lost Lennon Tapes 16* and *Yer Blues* (CD-1); both of them are on *Yer Blues* (CD-2). An acoustic demo of "Going Down on Love" was aired on episode 138 of "The Lost Lennon Tapes."

Jun–Jul: Unreleased songs from Wings' Nashville sessions include "Hey Diddle," which is found on *Cold Cuts* and on *Hot Hits and Cold Cuts (Second Mix)* (CD) and, in a different mix, on *Cold Cuts: Another Early Version* and *Hot Hits & Cold Cuts* (CD). "Wide Prairie," "Send Me the Heart" and two takes of the instrumental "Proud Mum" are also heard on the latter two bootlegs. Denny Laine later recorded a new vocal for "Send Me the Heart" and released the song on his *Japanese Tears* album. That version is also found on *Suitable for Framing*.

Jul 14–15: Several rehearsals, outtakes, and prefinal mixes of songs John recorded during *Walls and Bridges* sessions have surfaced, most of them reportedly recorded during this two-day period. *Something Precious and Rare* (LP and CD) features alternate versions of 10 songs, including "Steel and Glass," "Going Down on Love," "Move Over Ms. L," "Surprise Surprise (Sweet Bird of Paradox)," "Beef Jerky," "Scared," "Old Dirt Road," "Bless You," "Whatever Gets You Through the Night" and "Nobody Loves You (When You're Down and Out)." Five of these tracks were officially released in edited form on the posthumous Lennon album, *Menlove Ave.* (see table below). On *Menlove Ave.* some vocalization during the instrumental break on "Steel and Glass" was eliminated. "Move Over Ms. L" features clearly understood lyrics, unlike the released version that appears on the B side of John's "Stand by Me" single. A rehearsal of "Move Over Ms. L" is on *Yer Blues* (CD-2), while unreleased take 3 is on *Lost Lennon Tapes 17* and *Dreaming of the Past* (CD) (recorded Jul 15). A rehearsal of "Going Down on Love" (Jul 14) is on *Gone from This Place* (CD). The first studio rehearsal of "Whatever Gets You Through the Night" was aired on episode 104 of "The Lost Lennon Tapes" radio series; a different rehearsal is on *Lost Lennon Tapes 10* and *Yer Blues* (CD-2). An alternate take of "Steel and Glass" is on *Serve Yourself* (CD), while a rehearsal of "Bless You" (Jul 14) is on *Lost Lennon Tapes 17* and *Yer Blues* (CD-2). An unreleased mix of "No. 9 Dream" was aired on episode 128 of the radio series; another mix was heard on episode 81. During this period John also wrote "Incantation" with Roy Cicala, but no recording of the song has surfaced; a copyright for the title was registered on Nov 15.

Song Title	Something Precious & Rare	Menlove Ave.
"Steel and Glass"	5:18	4:09
"Scared"	4:55	4:15
"Old Dirt Road"	4:45	3:51
"Bless You"	5:30	4:01
"Nobody Loves You (When You're Down & Out)"	5:13	4:27

That summer: John cut a demo of "It's All Down to Goodnight Vienna" for Ringo, who then recorded the song for his *Goodnight Vienna* LP. John's demo is on *Lost Lennon Tapes 1*, *Goodnight Vienna* and *Johnny Moondog*. John later flew to Los Angeles to assist in Ringo's recording, and brought his demo. While there, John cut a demo of "Only You," after which Ringo recorded his vocal over John's for release on *Goodnight Vienna*. John's demo is heard on *Yer Blues* (CD-2) and *Lost Lennon Tapes 10*. The same demo appears on *Classified Document Volume Three*, where an additional spoken verse by Ringo is added.

Jul 21: The bootleg album *Off the Walls* contains a recording of John and others listening to studio playbacks of *Walls and Bridges* tracks before final overdubbing and mixing. The recording includes versions of "Bless You," "Move Over Ms. L," "Scared," "Surprise Surprise (Sweet Bird of Paradox)," "Whatever Gets You Through the Night," "Going Down on Love," "Nobody Loves You (When You're Down and Out)," "What You Got," "Old Dirt Road" and "Steel and Glass."

Sep 27: Some of John's commercials for "Tobias Casuals," done during his stint as a guest D.J. on KHJ-AM in Los Angeles, are on *Lost Lennon Tapes 10, 12, 13, 14* and *16*; *Volume 15* features one of his Tower Records spots. Excerpts of the KHJ stint were heard on "The Lost Lennon Tapes" radio series and are on *Snap Shots*, *Stereo Walk* and *Broadcasts*.

Sep 28: Part of John's appearance as a guest D.J. on WNEW-FM, New York, with D.J. Dennis Elsas, is on *Listen to This Picture Record*; more segments were aired on "The Lost Lennon Tapes" radio series.

That summer–fall: Paul and Wings filmed recording sessions in Nashville and London intended for release under the title, *One Hand Clapping*, but the film was never released. According to bootleg videos of the film, it was directed by David Litchfield and videotaped at EMI in the fall of 1974. Song titles include "One Hand Clapping" (instrumental theme), "Jet" (same version heard twice on some bootlegs), "Soily" (two versions), "Little Woman Love"/"C Moon," "Let Me Roll It," "Wild Life," "Band on the Run," "My Love," "Nineteen Hundred and Eighty Five," "Live and Let Die," "Hi Hi Hi," "Go Now," "Maybe I'm Amazed," "Bluebird," "Blackbird" and the promo film soundtrack from "Junior's Farm." The film also features a section with Paul at the piano doing "Suicide," "Let's Love," "Sitting at the Piano" (probably an improvisation), "All of You" and "I'll Give You a Ring." Paul's Feb 1975 live New Orleans performance of "Baby Face" with the Tuxedo Jazz Band is also seen in the film. The piano set and "Baby Face" are on *All the Rest* (CD) and *And All the Rest* (LP). All of the other songs, except "Blackbird," are on *One Hand Clapping* (LP and CD). Paul also shot the unreleased film *The Backyard*, originally part of *One Hand Clapping*, including "Blackpool," "Blackbird," "Country Dreamer," "Twenty Flight Rock," "Peggy Sue," "I'm Gonna Love You Too," "Sweet Little Sixteen," "Loving You," "We're Gonna Move" and "Blue Moon of Kentucky." An audio tape with all of the songs has circulated, and the "Peggy Sue" footage was seen in *The Paul McCartney Special*, which was released on home video. *The Backyard* film has also circulated on underground video. A few of the songs are on *Classified Document*.

Sep–Oct: Several unreleased takes of George's song "Dark Horse" have been bootlegged. An early acoustic demo that finds George in fine voice is heard on *Onothimagen*. A later electric guitar alternate take with drum appears to be a rehearsal for Harrison's 1974 tour, his voice already hoarse. That take is found on *By George*. A third take (1:52), reportedly from the unreleased concert film, is on *Somewhere in Utopia*; but no audience sounds are heard. A demo of "Ding Dong, Ding Dong" from this period is found on *Somewhere in Utopia*.

Oct 21–25: John rerecorded vocals for several songs released on his *Rock 'N' Roll* album. Unreleased recordings include "Do You Want to Dance?" "Be-Bop-a-Lula," "Slippin' and Slidin'," "Stand by Me," "Send Me Some Lovin'," "Ya Ya," "Peggy Sue," medley "Rip It Up"/"Ready Teddy" and "Bring It on Home to Me." John also cut outtakes of "That'll Be the Day," "Thirty Days," "C'mon Everybody" and a jam session that included about 44 seconds of Link Wray's "Rumble" and about 9 seconds of Led Zeppelin's "Whole Lotta Love," none of which were released on the album but which are found, along with the other titles, on *You Should'a Been There*. A different take of "Rip It Up"/"Ready Teddy" is on *Lost Lennon Tapes 16*; a rough mix of "Peggy Sue" is on *Dreaming of the Past* (CD) and *Lost Lennon Tapes 17*.

Nov 2: George opened his North American tour with a concert at the Pacific Coliseum in Vancouver, B.C. Song titles included "Dark Horse," "For You Blue," "Give Me Love," "Hari's on Tour," Lennon's "In My Life," "Maya Love," "My Sweet Lord," "Something," "Sound Stage of Mind," "Sue Me Sue You Blues," "What Is Life" and "While My Guitar Gently Weeps." Billy Preston, Tom Scott and Ravi Shankar also performed at this concert. *George Harrison 1974* also includes the Monty Python number, "The Lumberjack Song" (mistitled "All Right as a Lumberjack"), which is not from this concert but is very likely from George's guest appearance with the group at New York's City Center on Apr 20, 1976 during which the song was done (George produced the group's

1975 studio recording of the song). An audience tape of most of the show is on *Live in Vancouver*.

Nov 4: George performed at the Seattle Center Coliseum, Seattle, Washington. The show is on *George Harrison 1974*.

Nov 10: George performed a concert at the Long Beach Arena, Long Beach, California. "While My Guitar Gently Weeps," "Something," "Sue Me Sue You Blues," "For You Blue," "Give Me Love," "In My Life," "Maya Love" and "My Sweet Lord" are on *Let's Hear One for Lord Buddha* and *On Tour 1974*.

Nov 15: A copyright was registered for the unreleased song "Incantation," written by John and Roy Cicala during John's summer 1974 *Walls and Bridges* sessions.

Nov 22: George performed a concert in Fort Worth, Texas. Songs are the same as those listed under Nov 2. All but "What Is Life" are on *Hari's on Tour* (CD), which adds Billy Preston's "Will It Go Round in Circles."

Nov 24: Lennon and Elton John rehearsed songs that they would perform together at Elton's Nov 28 Thanksgiving concert at New York's Madison Square Garden. "I Saw Her Standing There" from the rehearsal is on *The Toy Boy*.

Nov 26: George performed at the Louisiana State University Assembly Center in Baton Rouge, Louisiana. (See Nov 2 song titles.) Most of the show is on *George Harrison: Baton Rouge*.

Nov 27: Paul and Linda sang backing vocals on "Mine for Me" for Rod Stewart during a live performance at the Odeon Cinema, Lewisham, South London. Paul had written the song for Stewart, who had released a studio version of it. The live performance was aired on "Midnight Special" in the U.S. on Apr 25, 1975 and appears on the bootleg *Oriental Nightfish*.

Nov 30: George did two shows in Chicago, Illinois; excerpts from one show are on *Chicago 11 30 74*.

Nov: Paul began recording sessions for his *Venus and Mars* album with basic tracks for "Love in Song," "Letting Go" and "Medicine Jar." Rough mixes of the recordings are found on *Venus*.

Dec 9: John was interviewed by Howard Cossell on "Monday Night Football" in the U.S. The clip appears on *Come Back Johnny*.

Dec 13: George's Largo, Maryland show is on *Live Washington '74* (CD), including all songs listed under Nov 2, 1974 except "Sound Stage of Mind." The CD includes Tom Scott's "Tomcat" and Billy Preston's "Will It Go 'Round in Circles."

Dec 15: George did two shows at the Nassau Coliseum in Uniondale, Long Island, New York. The evening show is on *Last Live Concert*. (See Nov 2 song titles.) A Billy Preston number, "Outa-Space," was added.

Dec 20: George ended his North American tour with a concert at New York's Madison Square Garden, portions of which are on *Excerpts from Three Major Concerts*.

Dec–Feb 1975: John cut several demos of "Tennessee." The song went through a number of later incarnations under different titles, including "Memories" and "Howling at the Moon," with different lyrics. Part of "Memories" later evolved into "Watching the Wheels." Demo takes 1 and 4 of "Tennessee" are on *Lost Lennon Tapes 1*; take 4 only is on *Dreaming of the Past* (CD). Other working titles for the song reportedly include "Emotional Wreck" and "People." Lennon also wrote the unreleased "Popcorn" during this period.

Late that year: George sang "I Don't Care Anymore," "Far East Man" and "Awaiting on You All" during an appearance on "Rock Around the World" on U.K. radio with Alan Freeman. All three songs were prerecorded and are found on *By George*; the second and third are on *Somewhere in Utopia*; the first only is on *Onothimagen*.

1975

Jan 16–Feb 24: Rough, prefinal mixes, some with different vocals, from Paul's New Orleans sessions for *Venus and Mars* appear on *Venus* and include "Venus and Mars" (instrumental version), "Rock Show," "Venus and Mars Reprise," "Listen to What the Man Said," medley "Treat Her Gently"/"Lonely Old People" and "Crossroads Theme." A slightly different mix of "Lunch Box-Odd Sox" appears on *Cold Cuts (Another Early Version)* and *Hot Hits & Cold Cuts* (CD). During sessions for *Venus and Mars*, Paul recorded the unreleased songs "Karate Chaos" and "Sea Dance" (an instrumental). Both songs have copyright dates of Jun 16. "Karate Chaos" may be an instrumental from Paul's score for the 1974 documentary film *Empty Hand*, shot at a karate tournament featuring Wings' drummer Geoff Britton.

Feb 12: Paul and Wings were filmed by a New Orleans television news crew while recording "My Carnival." The TV film version is on *20X4*, *Four Sides of the Circle* and

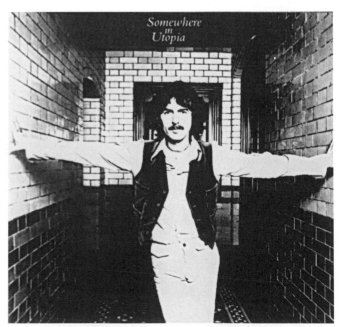

Somewhere in Utopia (bootleg). A follow-up to *Onothimagen*, this bootleg double LP features more Harrison rarities.

Snaps 'n' Trax. An unreleased mix is found on *Cold Cuts* and *Hot Hits and Cold Cuts (Second Mix)* (CD); a second alternate mix is on *Cold Cuts (Another Early Version)* and *Hot Hits & Cold Cuts* (CD). In New Orleans, Paul performed a live version of "Baby Face" with The Tuxedo Jazz Band. The number was filmed and included in the unreleased film, *One Hand Clapping*. It also appears on *All the Rest* (CD) and *And All the Rest* (LP).

Feb: An instrumental version of "Tomorrow," a vocal version of which had originally appear on Paul's *Wild Life* album in Aug 1971, is on *Cold Cuts (Another Early Version)*. A copyright for the instrumental is dated Feb 1975.

Mar: During an interview, John sang one line ("Voulez Vous Coucher Avec Moi Ce Soir") from Labelle's hit "Lady Marmalade." The clip is found on *Working Class Hero* and *Snap Shots*.

■ Paul held final sessions for his *Venus and Mars* album in Los Angeles. A prefinal mix of the album appears on the bootleg *Mars* and includes "Venus and Mars," "Rock Show," "Love in Song," "You Gave Me the Answer," "Magneto and Titanium Man," "Letting Go," "Medicine Jar," "Venus and Mars Reprise," "Spirits of Ancient Egypt" (with a different lead vocal), "Call Me Back Again," "Listen to What the Man Said," medley "Treat Her Gently"/"Lonely Old People," "Crossroads Theme" and "Lunch Box-Odd Sox."

Apr 18: John appeared on BBC-TV's "Old Grey Whistle Test" where he was interviewed and sang "Stand by Me" and "Slippin' and Slidin'." Both songs are on *Working Class Hero* and *Yin Yang*. The appearance was prerecorded in New York.

Apr 28: Ringo appeared on "The Smothers Brothers Comedy Hour" on U.S. TV and sang "No No Song" with Tom and Dick Smothers. It is heard on *Richie and His Pals/Scouse the Mouse*.

■ John and his lawyer, Leon Wildes, were interviewed by Tom Snyder on "The Tomorrow Show" on NBC-TV in the U.S. The interview appears on *Doctor Winston O'Boogie on the Tomorrow Show* and *All We Need is John*. A commercial videotape of the show was also released.

Jun 13: John appeared in a prerecorded segment of the ABC-TV special "A Salute to Sir Lew Grade," in honor of the head of Britain's Associated Communications, in the U.S., marking his last live stage appearance. His performance included "Slippin' and Slidin'," "Imagine" and "Stand by Me," although only the first two numbers were aired. All three songs, taken from an audience recording, are on *Snap Shots* and *Goodnight Vienna*; the first two songs, taken from the broadcast, are on *Plop Plop . . . Fizz Fizz*. John's backing group wore two-faced masks during this performance, an expression of John's opinion of Sir Lew, and he billed himself and the band as "John Lennon and Etcetera."

Sep 9: Wings opened a world tour with a show at the Gaumont Cinema in Southampton. Unidentified performances of "I've Just Seen a Face" and "Blackbird" from the tour are on *Four Sides of the Circle*.

Nov 1: Wings began a tour of Australia with a concert at the Entertainment Centre in Perth. Songs on this portion of the tour included: "Venus and Mars," "Rock Show," "Jet," "Let Me Roll It," medley "Little Woman Love"/"C Moon," "Maybe I'm Amazed," "Lady Madonna," "The Long and Winding Road," "Live and Let Die," "Picasso's Last Words," "Bluebird," "I've Just Seen a Face," "Blackbird," "Yesterday," "You Gave Me the Answer," "Magneto and Titanium Man," "Call Me Back Again," "My Love," "Listen to What the Man Said," "Letting Go," "Junior's Farm," "Band on the Run," "Hi Hi Hi" and "Soily." Portions of the show, taken from a Nov 2 radio broadcast on Australian station 3XY, are on *Paul McCartney and Wings Fly South*.

Nov 4–5: "Junior's Farm" from Paul's Nov 4 show at the Apollo Stadium, Adelaide is on *Classified Document*. "Junior's Farm" and "Little Woman Love"/"C Moon" from Nov 5 are on *A Doll's House*.

Nov 13: Wings played the Myer Music Bowl in Melbourne, Australia. *Paul McCartney and Wings Fly South* and *Fly South* feature part of the show, including "Waltzing Matilda" (a comical busk used as a lead in to the next song). The bootlegs are apparently taken from an Australian telecast of part of the show.

Dec 26: George sang "The Pirate Song" during a prerecorded broadcast of "Rutland Weekend Television." The song appears on *By George* and *Onothimagen*.

Early–middle of that year: Paul recorded the unreleased "Thank You Darling," "Great Cock and Seagull Race," "When I Was in Paris" and "Rode All Night," the latter possibly a working title for "Giddy," later given to Roger Daltrey.

Late 1975–early 1976: John cut an acoustic home recording of "Mucho Mungo," found on *Lost Lennon Tapes Tapes 1*. It is odd that Lennon would cut another demo of the song, originally written in 1974 for Harry Nilsson's *Pussy Cats* album.

Mid-1970s: A number of undated, unreleased Lennon demos and home recordings have been bootlegged, most of which appear to have originated during the middle or late 1970s, sometimes referred to as John's "house husband" period. *Lost Lennon Tapes 4* features two takes of "Brown Eyed Handsome Man," slow and fast versions (Lennon lapses into "Get Back"), "I'm a Man," "Lord Take This Makeup Off of Me" (a parody of Dylan's "Knockin' on Heaven's Door") and a medley of "Beyond the Sea"/"Blue Moon"/"Young Love." The Dylan parody is also on *Dreaming of the Past* (CD). Two takes of "Rock Island Line" were cut; an electric take is on *Lost Lennon Tapes 5*; an acoustic take is heard on *Lost Lennon Tapes 1* and *Gone from This Place* (CD). John's final demo of "Sally and Billy" is on *Lost Lennon Tapes 10* and *News of the Day* (CD). Take 2 was aired on episode 201 of "The Lost Lennon Tapes" radio series. "Howling at the Moon," a later development of "Tennessee," recorded with electric guitar and rhythm box, is on *Lost Lennon*

Tapes 11 and *Lost Sleepy Blind Lemon Lennon* (CD). That song would undergo further development, appearing next as "Memories" in the late 1970s. An untitled blues instrumental from this period was aired on episode 5 of the radio series.

1976

Jan 1: During an interview recorded by Elliot Mintz, John twice ad-libbed a few lines from "As Time Goes By" and discussed "What's the New Mary Jane," doing one line from the chorus. Both excerpts are on *The Toy Boy*. Some bootlegs add the "Mary Jane" comments before the Aug 14, 1968 song itself is played.

Mar 21: Wings performed at the Falkoner Theatre in Copenhagen, Denmark. The songs were the same as those listed under Nov 1, 1975, except that "Little Woman Love"/"C Moon" and "Junior's Farm" were dropped, and "Beware My Love," "Let 'Em In," "Medicine Jar," "Richard Cory," "Silly Love Songs," "Spirits of Ancient Egypt" and "Time to Hide" were added. The show is on *In Concert in Copenhagen*, *Great Dane* and *The Copenhagen Concert*.

Mar 26: Part of Wings' Paris show is on *Wings Live Paris Mar 26/76*.

Apr: John's first demo of "Cookin' (In the Kitchen of Love)," recorded for Ringo's *Rotogravure* sessions, is on *Lost Sleepy Blind Lemon Lennon* (CD) and *Lost Lennon Tapes 19*; another demo on *Lost Lennon Tapes 3*; still another is on *Serve Yourself*.

May 3–Jun 23: Wings toured North America. Tracks from several shows have been bootlegged. Fort Worth (May 3, *Ft. Worth/Seattle* and *First American Concert*), Toronto (May 9, *Maple Leaf Gardens*), Largo, Maryland (May 15, *Light As a Feather* [part 1], *Wings Over America—Landing Gear Down* [part 2], *9 MM. Automatic* [part 3]), Atlanta (May 19, *Wings Over Atlanta*), Boston (May 22, *Wings*), Madison Square Garden, New York (May 25, *Classified Document*), Chicago (Jun 1, *Wings*), Seattle (Jun 10, *Kingdome 6/10/76*), San Francisco (Jun 14, *Zoo Gang*, *Wings over Frisco*), San Diego (Jun 16, *Wings*, *Oriental Nightfish*) and Los Angeles (Jun 21, *Wings at the Forum* and *Wings—L.A. Forum*; Jun 23, *Wings from the Wings*).

Jun 28: Paul and Wings were interviewed by Geraldo Rivera on "Goodnight America." The broadcast also included clips of "Band on the Run" and "Yesterday" shot at Wings' Jun 10 Seattle concert. This TV appearance is found on *Ft. Worth/Seattle*.

That summer: Prefinal mixes of songs released on Denny Laine's *Holly Days* album appear on *2 Buddies on Holly Days* (CD). Paul played virtually all the instruments on this album, provided backing vocals and produced the sessions. Bootlegged songs are: "Heartbeat," "Moondreams," "Rave On," "I'm Gonna Love You Too," "Fool's Paradise," medley "It's So Easy"/"Listen to Me," "Listen to Me" (instrumental track only) and "Look at Me."

Oct 29: Ringo recorded the unreleased "I Can Hear You Calling" at Atlantic's New York studios.

Nov 19: George recorded "Homeward Bound," "Here Comes the Sun," "Bye Bye Love," "Rock Island Line," a few seconds each of "Yesterday" and "Bridge over Troubled Water," and "Don't Let Me Wait Too Long" for "Saturday Night Live," aired Nov 20 on NBC. Only the first two songs were aired on the show. "Homeward Bound" was officially released worldwide on Jul 24, 1990 on the charity album *Nobody's Child: Romanian Angel Appeal*. All but "Don't Let Me Wait Too Long" are on *Somewhere in Utopia*.

1977

Early–middle of that year: Wings cut an unreleased recording of "Boil Crisis." A different fall 1980 recording has been bootlegged.

Early that year: George recorded a message for a Warner Brothers promo film intended for viewing by the company's sales personnel. Harrison added a line from "Go Your Own Way"; the appearance is on *Classified Document Volume Two* and *Great to Have You with Us*.

Feb 5: Ringo recorded the unreleased songs "Lover Please" and "Wild Shining Stars" at Cherokee Studios in Los Angeles.

May: An underground tape containing outtakes and alternate mixes of songs from Paul's *London Town* album has circulated, and includes an unreleased Denny Laine song (speculative title, *"Find a Way"), *"I'm Carrying," *"Deliver Your Children," *"I've Had Enough," *"With a Little Luck," *"Famous Groupies," *"Don't Let It Bring You Down," *"Backwards Traveller," "Cuff Link," "London Town," *"Cafe on the Left Bank," "Children Children," "Girlfriend," "Name and Address" and *"Morse Moose and the Grey Goose." Some songs (*) appear in far better sound quality, and at the correct speed, on the bootleg CD *London Town Roughs and Demos*, which also adds an otherwise unreleased McCartney rendition of the classic "After You've Gone." During *London Town* sessions aboard the yacht *Fair Carol*, Paul recorded the instrumental "El Toro Passing."

Jun 1977: Ringo recorded an alternate take of "Just a Dream" and the unreleased songs "Party" and "Birmingham" at Cherokee Studios in Los Angeles. The released version of "Just a Dream" was recorded in New York at Atlantic Studios in Jun 1977. During those sessions, he also recorded the unreleased songs "By Your Side," "Duet-Nancy & Ringo" and "Nancy, Ringo, Vinnie & Friends."

That fall: Two Lennon demos of "Mirror Mirror (on the Wall)" are on *Lost Lennon Tapes 6*.

Oct: Paul taped an interview with Melvin Bragg, aired on the first broadcast of London Weekend Television's "The South Bank Show," broadcast on Jan 14, 1978. During the interview, an unidentified Wings rehearsal of "Lucille" was heard along with versions of "I Lost My Little Girl," "Michelle," "Yesterday," "Maybe I'm Amazed," "Too Bad About Sorrows," "Mull of Kintyre" and an improvisation called "Melvin Bragg." All of these excerpts are found on *Sunshine Supermen*.

That year: Ringo recorded two versions each of the songs "Simple Life" and "I Love My Suit," which were used in a total of four commercials in Japan for Simple Life leisure suits, in which he also appeared. Both songs are on *Ognir Rrats Greatest Hits*.

Dec–Jan 1978: During *London Town* sessions, Paul recorded the unreleased song "Waterspout," one of his most infectious tunes. He planned to release it on the *Cold Cuts* album early in 1981 but canceled the LP following John's death. The bootleg of *Cold Cuts* contains the best-quality version of this noteworthy McCartney outtake. It also appears on *All the Rest* (CD), *And All the Rest* (LP) and in a different mix on *Hot Hits and Cold Cuts (Second Mix)* (CD). An instrumental version, perhaps just the basic rhythm track, is on *2 Buddies on Holly Days* (CD).

Late that year–early 1978: John's demo take 1 of "One of the Boys" is on *Lost Sleepy Blind Lemon Lennon* (CD) and *Lost Lennon Tapes 19*; take 2 is found on *Lost Lennon Tapes 7*.

1978

Early that year: Paul recorded a number of songs, many of them unreleased, while seated at the piano at home. The date of this tape, often called "The Piano Tapes," is not certain. The tape includes "Million Miles," "Mull of Kintyre," "I'll Give You a Ring," "Getting Closer," "Rockestra Theme," "Letting Go," "Call Me Back Again," "Treat Her Gently," "Lonely Old People," "You Gave Me the Answer," "Girlfriend," "I Lost My Little Girl," "Blackpool" and "Suicide." Titles of the following songs are really speculation and include "You Know It's True," "Woman Kind," "Sea," "In My Dreams," "Waiting for the Sun to Shine," "She's Got It Bad," "Sunshine in Your Hair," "It Can Be Done," "Love Is" and "Partners in Crime." Only "I Lost My Little Girl" has been bootlegged so far, appearing on *Classified Document Volume Three*. A different version of "Sea" is heard on the bootleg CD *Rupert*, from Paul's late 1970s recording sessions for a planned *Rupert the Bear* full-length film.

Apr 17: Ringo appeared on the U.S. TV show "The Mike Douglas Show"; a clip from the interview is on *Beatles Vs. Don Ho*.

Apr 26: Ringo appeared in his own one-hour TV special "Ringo," on NBC-TV in the U.S. The special was a modern comic/musical version of Mark Twain's *The Prince and the Pauper*, with a cameo appearance and narration by George Harrison. Songs included new versions of "I'm the Greatest," "Act Naturally" (with a special intro), "Yellow Submarine," "You're Sixteen" (a duet with Carrie Fisher), "With a Little Help from My Friends" and a concert segment including "Heart on My

Sleeve," "Hard Times" and "A Man Like Me." Ringo ad-libbed a line or two from "Octopus's Garden" as well, and his released recordings of "It Don't Come Easy" and "Oh My My" were also heard during the show. All of the new musical selections, some in edited form, are on *Ognir Rrats Greatest Hits*.

Jun 29–Jul 27: During *Back to the Egg* sessions, Paul and Wings recorded alternate versions of "Arrow Through Me," medley "Winter Rose"/"Love Awake" and "Old Siam Sir," which appear on *Scrambled Egg* (EP) along with Wings' "Maisie," later released on Laurence Juber's solo LP *Standard Time*. A rough mix of most of the *Back to the Egg* album appears on *Eggs Up*. Wings also recorded the unreleased "Cage," omitted from *Back to the Egg* but later included on *Cold Cuts*. It appears on bootlegs of that album and *Hot Hits and Cold Cuts (Second Mix)* (CD), *All the Rest* (CD), *And All the Rest* (LP, where it appears twice) and in a slightly rougher mix on *Eggs Up*. These sessions may also have yielded "Mama's Little Girl" (see Middle of Mar 1972), included on *Cold Cuts* and finally released officially as the B side of Paul's "Put It There" single in Feb 1990. It is found on *Cold Cuts* and *Hot Hits and Cold Cuts (Second Mix)* (CD), and in a different stereo mix on *Cold Cuts (Another Early Version)*, and *Hot Hits & Cold Cuts* (CD). Two film songs were recorded during this period as well. "Did We Meet Somewhere Before" was intended for the film *Heaven Can Wait* but was not used. Instead, a small bit of it was heard in the film *Rock and Roll High School*. "Same Time Next Year" was cut for the film of the same title but was not used in that movie (it was officially

Ognir Rrats Greatest Hits (bootleg). The cover was actually used as a prop on Ringo's 1978 TV special, and it was adopted by bootleggers for a package of musical tracks from that show. Unscrupulous dealers have been known to sell these bootleg covers as "authentic" props from the show itself.

Cold Cuts (bootleg). Paul has fiddled with this album of leftover tracks several times. This version, appropriated by bootleggers, was apparently slated for early 1981 release but was canceled by Paul in the wake of John's death.

released in Feb 1990). Both recordings were originally scheduled for release on *Cold Cuts*, and they appear on the *Cold Cuts* bootlegs listed above. Paul also recorded the unreleased "Crawl of the Wild" with Dave Mason. A Wings studio jam, possibly from around this time, has appeared on *Rock and Roll* (CD). Several titles remain unidentified but the songs include "Young Love," "Whole Lotta Shakin' Goin' On," "I'm Gonna Be a Wheel Someday," "Twenty Flight Rock," "Little Queenie," "The Fool," "Take Your Time" and "I'm Walking." Possible titles of the other songs are "Sail Away on the Sea of Love," "Judy," "No Disgrace," "If I Can't Share It with You" and "You're Doin' Your Daddy Wrong."

Middle of that year: According to Wings' Laurence Juber, Wings recorded an early version of "Ballroom Dancing" during *Back to the Egg* sessions.

Jul 23: An alternate mix of the released version of "Spin It On" appears on *Eggs Up*.

Sep 11–20: Wings recorded alternate versions of "The Broadcast" and "Reception"; these tracks, along with alternate mixes of "We're Open Tonight" and "After the Ball-Million Miles," are on *Eggs Up*. Wings also recorded "Weep for Love," officially released on Denny Laine's solo LP *Japanese Tears*. It also appears on *Suitable for Framing*.

Oct 3: Alternate mixes of "Rockestra Theme" and "So Glad to See You Here" are on *Eggs Up*.

Oct–Nov: During the final recording sessions for *Back to the Egg*, an alternate version of "Getting Closer," found on *Eggs Up*, was recorded. Paul also recorded "Robbers Ball," "Night Out" and "A Love for You," all found on bootleg copies of *Cold Cuts* and on *Hot Hits*

and Cold Cuts (Second Mix) (CD). Another version of "Night Out" is found on *Cold Cuts (Another Early Version)* and *Hot Hits & Cold Cuts* (CD).

Late Nov: Lennon ad-libbed a Dylan parody while watching a TV news broadcast around this time. He simply used the news reports to create spontaneous lyrics. The track is known as "News of the Day (from Reuters)" and appears on *Lost Lennon Tapes 4* (LP), *Lost Lennon Tapes 1* (CD), and *News of the Day* (CD).

Late Dec: An early mix of Paul's "Daytime Nightime Suffering" is on *Classified Document Volume Two*. An alternate take of the song appears on *Hot Hits and Cold Cuts (Second Mix)* (CD).

1979

That summer: Paul recorded his LP *McCartney II*, originally pressed as a double album and containing several unreleased songs. *McCartney II* was finally released as a single LP, but test pressings of the double album version were made and later appeared as the bootleg *The Lost McCartney Album*. It includes the unreleased titles "All You Horseriders" heard in the MPL documentary film *Blankit's First Show*, aired Jul 12, 1986 in the U.K., "Blue Sway," "Mr. H Atom," "You Know I'll Get You Baby" and "Bogey Wobble." The remaining tracks are followed by running times of the unreleased and released versions respectively: "Front Parlor (5:06, 3:31), "Frozen Jap" (5:30, 3:38), "Temporary Secretary" (3:05, 3:13), "On the Way" (3:27, 3:36), "Summer's Day Song" (instrumental, 3:16; with vocal, 3:24; the bootleg features the instrumental track only, which also appeared on *Raving On*, (3:25), "Darkroom"

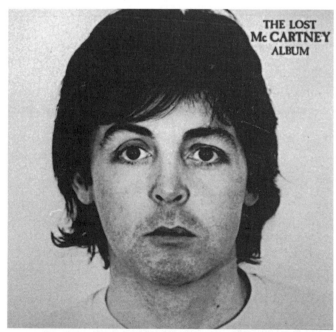

The Lost McCartney Album (bootleg). Bootleggers filched the original double-LP *McCartney II* master as well as the cover from the released version, and topped off their illegal package with liner notes poached from a *Goldmine* article penned by the author.

(3:28, 2:18), "One of These Days" (3:26, 3:34), "Bogey Music" (3:17, 3:25), "I Need Love" (4:29, 4:42; the title was changed to "Waterfalls" on the released album); an edited version of "Waterfalls" (3:25), copied from the promotional video (the only version with an added electric piano part), is on *Suitable for Framing*; "Nobody Knows" (2:44, 2:50), and "Coming Up" (5:26, 3:51; the studio version). The original double LP also includes two songs that McCartney ultimately released only as B sides: "Secret Friend" (10:05, 10:20) and "Check My Machine" (8:39, 5:44).

Sep 5: John began tape-recording his memoirs, delivering a verbal history of his youth and negative opinions on the contemporary recordings of Paul McCartney, Mick Jagger and Bob Dylan, particularly Dylan's "Gotta Serve Somebody"; Lennon referred to the three as "company men."

Sep 14: Wings performed during a Buddy Holly Week concert at the Hammersmith Odeon in London, Paul singing "It's So Easy" and "Bo Diddley"; Denny Laine did "Raining in My Heart" with Don Everly. All three songs are on *2 Buddies on Holly Days* (CD).

Oct 30–Oct 30, 1980: During the initial sessions for his *Somewhere in England* album, George recorded four songs that were included on an early pressing of the album but that were cut from the released version. Three of those songs, "Lay His Head" (recorded Apr 1980), "Flying Hour" (recorded Mar 1978) and "Sat Singing" (recorded Mar 1980), were officially released on Feb 15, 1988 on a special vinyl EP and CD, *Songs by George Harrison*, which was available only with George's limited edition book of the same title; the songs were remixed for that release, and the same mix of "Lay His Head" appeared as the B side of George's 1987 "Got my Mind Set on You" single. The fourth song, "Tears of the World," remains unreleased. The original mixes of all four songs appear on *Onothimagen*, *By George* and bootleg copies of the original, unreleased version of the *Somewhere in England* album. The three 1988 remixes from *Songs by George Harrison* appear on *Somewhere in Utopia*.

Nov 25: The following songs from Wings' Liverpool show are on *Wings over Tokyo*: "Got to Get You into My Life," "Getting Closer," "Every Night," "Again and Again and Again," "I've Had Enough," "No Words," "Old Siam Sir," "Maybe I'm Amazed," "The Fool on the Hill," "Let It Be," "Hot as Sun," "Spin It On," "Twenty Flight Rock," "Go Now," "Arrow Through Me," "Wonderful Christmastime," "Coming Up," "Goodnight Tonight," "Yesterday," "Mull of Kintyre" and "Band on the Run."

Dec 5: Paul appeared on the "Tomorrow" TV show in the U.S. and sang abbreviated versions of "Silly Love Songs," "Spin It On," "Wonderful Christmastime," "With a Little Luck" and "Yesterday." The appearance is found on *Yesterday and Tomorrow*.

Dec 7: Wings performed at the Empire Pool in Wembley, England. The song lineup was the same as that listed under Nov 25 but with "Cook of the House" and "Baby Face" added; the show is found on *Wings over Wembley*.

Dec 29: While only a few Wings and Rockestra numbers were officially released on the *Concerts for the People of Kampuchea*, the entire set has appeared on the bootlegs *Cold Turkey for Kampuchea*, also released as two picture discs called *Kampuchea Volume I* and *Volume II* and on *Concerts for Kampuchea*. The song lineup was the same as that listed under Nov 25 except that the bootlegs add "Cook of the House" and drop "Wonderful Christmastime." "Let It Be" was moved to the Rockestra set, which also added "Rockestra Theme" and "Lucille."

Late 1970s: Paul recorded an entire album for a full-length *Rupert the Bear* animated film to be shot by Oscar Grillo. The film was never made, but test pressings of Paul's album later appeared on the bootleg CD *Rupert*, which included the following songs with Paul's between-songs narration: "Rupert Song" (with vocal), "Tippi Tippi Toes," "Flying Horses," "When the Wind Is Blowing" (some scat vocals can be heard), "The Castle of the King of the Birds," "Sunshine Sometime" (with vocal), medley "Sea"/"Cornish Water" (with vocal), "Storm" (with vocal; essentially a different arrangement of "Sea"), "Nutwood Scene," "Walking in the Meadow" (with some vocal), "Sea Melody" and a reprise of "Rupert Song." "We All Stand Together," used in the 1984 short *Rupert and the Frog Song*, also appears here. It is the same demo version heard on *Tug of War Demos and More*. Paul recorded another new Rupert song with George Martin during Dec 14–19, 1987. One or two songs sound similar to some of those on Paul's early 1978 demo session, sometimes called "The Piano Tapes," and "Sea" is clearly on that tape, with slightly different lyrics; its title was once thought to be either "Lucy" or "Around the World."

■ John recorded several demos of "Real Life"; one is found on *Lost Lennon Tapes 5*; a different demo is on *Look at Me* (CD) and *Lost Lennon Tapes 20*; a third demo was aired on episode 115 of "The Lost Lennon Tapes" radio series. Lennon would incorporate parts of "Real Life" into "Real Love," and the song would influence his later composition "I'm Stepping Out." A piano demo of "Real Love" is on *Lost Lennon Tapes 13* and *Gone from This Place* (CD) and begins with Lennon saying "Real Love, take one." Other demos were aired on episodes 115, 169 and 180 of "The Lost Lennon Tapes," including demos with the working titles "Baby Make Love to You" and "That's the Way the World Is."

■ John recorded several other demos during this period, including several working titles that gradually evolved into "(Just Like) Starting Over," later recorded for the *Double Fantasy* album. "My Life" was the song's earliest known incarnation, and piano demo take 1 and acoustic take 3 are on *Lost Lennon Tapes 5*; demo take 2 is on *Lost Lennon Tapes 22*; other demos were heard on episode 180. One demo of "Don't Be Crazy," the next stage of the song's development, is on *Lost Lennon Tapes 5* and the first piano demo was aired on episode 116. That song gradually became "The Worst Is Over," and demo take 1 of that title is on *Lost Sleepy*

Blind Lemon Lennon Album (CD); another demo is on *Lost Lennon Tapes 15*, and still another was aired on episode 90 of "The Lost Lennon Tapes." "I'm Crazy," a prototype of "I'm Losing You," is on *Lost Lennon Tapes 16*; a piano demo of "I'm Losing You," under the working title "Strangers Room," is on *Lost Lennon Tapes 10*; a different demo is on *Lost Lennon Tapes 3*. A different piano demo of "Strangers Room" is on *Lost Lennon Tapes 16* and *Serve Yourself* (CD); still another one was aired on episode 122. A demo of "Nobody Told Me," under the working title "Everybody's Talking Nobody's Talking" is on *Lost Lennon Tapes 11* and *News of the Day* (CD). An early demo of "I Don't Wanna Face It" is on *Lost Lennon Tapes 23*, and a country and western style take of the song was heard on episode 105. Piano demo take 2 of "Memories," an update of Lennon's earlier unreleased "Tennessee," is on *Lost Lennon Tapes 11*, *Lost Sleepy Blind Lemon Lennon* (CD) and *Gone from This Place* (CD); the first known demo take was aired on episode 108. Another demo, with double-tracked vocal, was aired on episode 201. An amusing clip of Lennon and his son Sean doing "With a Little Help from My Friends" is on *Lost Lennon Tapes 1*. "Down in Cuba" is on *Lost Lennon Tapes 10*; "Corrine, Corrina," largely an improvised Lennon lyric parodying Bob Dylan's composition, itself an adaptation and unique arrangement of "Corrina, Corrina," is on *Lost Lennon Tapes 8*, *Lost Lennon Tapes 2* (CD), *Yer Blues* (CD-2) and *Serve Yourself* (CD). Other recordings from this period include "Cathy's Clown" and "You Send Me" (both on episode 145), "Too Much Monkey Business" (episode 148) and "Many Rivers to Cross," on *Serve Yourself* (CD). An electric take of "John Henry"/"I Ain't Got Time" is on *Lost Sleepy Blind Lemon Lennon* (CD), *Lost Lennon Tapes 13* and partially on *Yer Blues* (CD-1). An acoustic take of "John Henry" is on *Lost Lennon Tapes 1*.

1980

Jun–Jul: John spent several weeks in Bermuda with his son Sean, during which he cut a number of demos of songs that would later be recorded during the *Double Fantasy/Milk and Honey* sessions. "Beautiful Boy (Darling Boy)" (take 1) is on *Yer Blues* (CD-2), *Dreaming of the Past* (CD) and *Lost Lennon Tapes 3* and more complete on *Lost Lennon Tapes 11*. John introduces it as "take 1 of 'Darling Boy,' now known as 'Beautiful Boy.'" A different Bermuda demo (2:36) with Lennon repeating "close your eyes" twice at the start, is on *Lost Lennon Tapes 1*. Still another demo, with double-tracked guitar, is on *Lost Lennon Tapes 16* and *News of the Day* (CD). "Dear Yoko" is on *Lost Lennon Tapes 7*. A different demo is on *Lost Lennon Tapes 17* and *Yer Blues* (CD-2). One demo of "Woman" is on *Lost Lennon Tapes 1*, while another one is on *News of the Day* (CD) and *Lost Lennon Tapes 6*. Another demo of "Woman," with double-tracked vocal, was heard on episode 22 of "The Lost Lennon Tapes." "I'm Losing You" is on *Gone from This*

Place (CD) and *Lost Lennon Tapes 11*. "I Don't Wanna Face It," with double-tracked vocal, is on *Lost Lennon Tapes 7*, while "Watching the Wheels" and "Borrowed Time" are on *Lost Lennon Tapes 10*; "Watching the Wheels" only is on *Yer Blues* (CD-2) and *Watching the Wheels* (CD). "Borrowed Time" is complete on *Lost Lennon Tapes 10* and is distinguished by its opening where Lennon strums a chord and says, "Welcome to Bermuda." It is shortened on *My Love Will Turn You On* (CD). A different demo of "Borrowed Time" is on *Lost Lennon Tapes 17*, *Yer Blues* (CD-2) and *Watching the Wheels*.

Middle of that year: Another group of Lennon demos reportedly originated during this post-Bermuda period, most of them cut in preparation for the *Double Fantasy* sessions. Two piano demos of "Watching the Wheels," one a 15-second breakdown, appear on *Lost Lennon Tapes 7*, while another lasting 38 seconds is on *Lost Lennon Tapes 3*. An acoustic demo (1:44) also appears on *Lost Lennon Tapes 3*. An electric "blues" style demo is on *Lost Lennon Tapes 20* and *22* and *Serve Yourself* (CD). Another ("$50 million take") is on *My Love Will Turn You On* (CD); another was heard on episode 163 of "The Lost Lennon Tapes." Two piano demos of "Cleanup Time" have appeared, one on *Lost Lennon Tapes 7*, the other on *Lost Lennon Tapes 1*. Both takes are characterized by the line "Show those mothers how to do it," which is repeated throughout; another demo is on *Yer Blues* (CD-1) and *Lost Lennon Tapes 16*. One demo of "I'm Losing You" appears on *Lost Lennon Tapes 10*, while another is on *Lost Lennon Tapes 3*. Demo take 3 of "(Just Like) Starting Over" is on *Lost Lennon Tapes 2* and *Gone from This Place* (CD). *Dreaming of the Past* (CD) features the first of three acoustic demos with drum machine and different lyrics. Demo take 1 of "Dear Yoko" is on *Lost Lennon Tapes 13*, and a completed demo of "I'm Stepping Out" is found on *News of the Day* (CD) and *Lost Lennon Tapes 7*. Two demo takes were aired on episode 120. Double-tracked demos of "I'm Stepping Out" and "Woman" are on *Lost Lennon Tapes 16*; another demo of "Woman" is on *Dreaming of the Past* (CD); another is on *My Love Will Turn You On* (CD). Demos of "Beautiful Boy (Darling Boy)" are on *Lost Lennon Tapes 22* and *23*; another, with "She Runs Them Around In Circles," was heard on episode 165; a double-tracked demo of "Nobody Told Me" ("for Ringo") with acoustic guitar overdub is on *My Love Will Turn You On* (CD); demo take 3 of "(Forgive Me) My Little Flower Princess" is on *Lost Lennon Tapes 15* and *Yer Blues* (CD-1). *Look at Me* (CD) features a medley of "Memories"/"Howling at the Moon"/"Across the River"/"Beautiful Boy (Darling Boy)"/"Club Dakota Rap." The unreleased "I Watch Your Face," with Lennon lapsing into "Raining in My Heart," is on *Lost Lennon Tapes 22*. John was heard singing "She'll Be Coming Around the Mountain" on episode 167. Some lines of a poem, tentatively titled "'Twas a Night Like Ethel Merman," are heard on *Lost Lennon Tapes 4*.

- A video shot by John at home has circulated among collectors; John does two versions of "Dear Yoko," which he introduces as "Oh Yoko."

Jul 7–31: Ringo's unreleased album *Can't Fight Lightning*, which was later released in slightly different form as *Stop and Smell the Roses*, has been bootlegged. The original album includes the unreleased songs "Can't Fight Lightning," "Brandy" and "Waking Up," which were replaced on the released album with "Drumming Is My Madness," "Sure to Fall" and "Back Off Boogaloo" (Version 2). The remaining tracks are virtually identical to the released versions with two exceptions. "Dead Giveaway" is considerably longer on the bootleg (5:24) and was edited for release (4:29, listed as 3:24). A guitar overdub was added to the released version. Another version, or mix, of "Dead Giveaway" (5:16), with a count-in by someone other than Ringo, possibly Ron Wood, appears on the bootleg *Rizz Off!* and sounds closer to the released version. Both bootlegs include the "Runny Noses, Baggy Trousers" lines, mixed out of the released version. "Stop and Take the Time to Smell the Roses" fades about 10 seconds earlier on the bootleg but includes a lyric about a Ford Cortina that was cut from the released version.

Aug 4–Sep 8: A number of alternate takes and mixes form John's *Double Fantasy/Milk and Honey* sessions have surfaced. An enormous amount of recorded material from these sessions exists since virtually every moment that Lennon spent in the studio was taped.

The first vocal take of "(Just Like) Starting Over" and a rough mix is on *Lost Lennon Tapes 5*. An alternate take is on *My Love Will Turn You On* (CD); episode 21 of "The Lost Lennon Tapes" featured a studio work session. The recording had a long, extended fadeout on the U.S. promo single (4:17), and that edit appears on *Lost Lennon Tapes 13*.

An early mix of "Beautiful Boy (Darling Boy)" is on *Lost Lennon Tapes 11* and *Serve Yourself* (CD). An alternate take is on *Lost Lennon Tapes 23*, and the first studio runthrough was heard on episode 92. An acoustic take was aired on episode 190.

An alternate version of "Cleanup Time," consisting mostly of in-studio talking, appears on *Lost Lennon Tapes 3* and an alternate mix is on *Lost Lennon Tapes 4* and *Gone from This Place* (CD). Another take with guide vocal is on *Look at Me* (CD); take 7, an unreleased mix of the instrumental track, is on *Dreaming of the Past* (CD); the first two studio rehearsals are on *Lost Lennon Tapes 23*; episode 136 featured Lennon reciting the lyrics during playback.

Lost Lennon Tapes 11 and *News of the Day* (CD) feature a rough mix of "Nobody Told Me"; the basic track with Lennon's vocal was aired on episode 106.

Alternate mixes of "I Don't Wanna Face It" are on *Classified Document* and *Fulfilling the Fantasies*; a demo ("For Ringo") was aired on episode 173.

An unreleased take of "Woman" is on *Lost Lennon Tapes 7* and *Serve Yourself* (CD). It runs longer on *Classified Document* but lacks Lennon's count-in; Lennon gets some lyrics reversed on this take, singing "*Your* life is in *my* hands." *Lost Lennon Tapes 7* also features an isolated vocal overdub.

A rough mix of "I'm Losing You" is on *Lost Lennon Tapes 17* and *Yer Blues* (CD-1). An outtake featuring Rick Neilsen and Bun E. Carlos of Cheap Trick was

Starr-Struck (© Rhino Records) and *Can't Fight Lightning* (bootleg). While the cover of Rhino's greatest hits package was not the most imaginative, it did not stop bootleggers from using it for an unauthorized edition of Ringo's *Can't Fight Lightning*, which was altered considerably before its release as *Stop and Smell the Roses*.

heard on episode 158; another take is on *Fulfilling the Fantasies*.

An alternate take of "Watching the Wheels" with different lyrics is on *Look at Me* (CD) and with a different count-in and opening, on *My Love Will Turn You On* (CD).

An alternate take of "Dear Yoko" is on *Lost Lennon Tapes 13* and *Gone from This Place* (CD); another is on *Serve Yourself* (CD) and *Dreaming of the Past* (CD). Two others were aired on episode 161.

A rough mix of "(Forgive Me) My Little Flower Princess" is on *Lost Lennon Tapes 16* and *Watching the Wheels* (CD).

A duet mix of "Every Man Has a Woman Who Loves Him," featuring Lennon and Ono, is on *Lost Lennon Tapes 2*.

A short studio ad lib of "Maggie Mae" appears on *Lost Lennon 6*. "Only the Lonely" is heard on *Lost Lennon Tapes 16* and *Sleepy Blind Lemon Lennon* (CD).

Aug 6: Take 2 of "I'm Stepping Out" is on *Lost Lennon Tapes 23*; "The Lost Lennon Tapes" episode 120 featured unreleased take 8. A different early take is on *Lost Lennon Tapes 15*, while the first studio take is on *Look at Me* (CD) and *Lost Lennon Tapes 20*. The full, unedited tape of the released version is on *Gone from This Place* (CD).

Aug 7: An alternate mix of "Borrowed Time" is on *Lost Lennon Tapes 12* and *Gone from This Place* (CD). John's final vocal heard from the vocal booth, and a guitar overdub is on *Lost Lennon Tapes 18*. *Fulfilling the Fantasies* and episode 119 of "The Lost Lennon Tapes" feature alternate takes of the song. Episode 74 featured excerpts of John running through the guitar chords from "Gone from This Place" on Aug 7 and Aug 24. He would return to that song later in the year.

Aug 18: Recordings made during a videotaping session by John are on *Before Play* and, with between-takes talking edited out, on *Winston O'Boogie*. John ad-libbed bits of the following songs: "C'mon Everybody," "Rip It Up," "I'm a Man," "Be-Bop-a-Lula," "12-Bar Blues," "Dream Lover," "Stay," "Mystery Train," "Blues in the Night," "She's a Woman," "(Just Like) Starting Over" and "I'm Losing You."

That fall: Paul laid down a set of demos, possibly in preparation for his *Tug of War* and *Pipes of Peace* sessions, although some of the songs did not appear on either album and five of them remain unreleased. The songs include "Take Her Back Jack" (1:33), "The Unbelievable Experience" (1:41), "Boil Crisis" (3:50), also recorded (but unreleased) by Wings in 1977, "Here's the Chord, Roy" (3:48) and "Seems Like Old Times" (4:00); and demos of "Average Person" (3:46), "Dress Me Up as a Robber" (three takes, or "segments," 1:00, 1:52, 0:31), "The Pound Is Sinking" (two takes: 2:23 and 2:08, possibly started as two completely different songs, one of them initially titled "Hear Me Lover"), "Sweetest Little Show" (2:48), "Ebony and Ivory" (1:36), "Wanderlust" (1:37), "We All Stand Together" (3:47), "Ballroom Dancing" (1:51), "Take It Away" (5:11) and "Keep Under

Cover" (3:27), heard twice on the original tape. All are on *Rude Studio Demos* (CD) and *Tug of War Demos and More*.

■ John returned to "Real Love" (aka "Girls and Boys"), which he had begun working on in the late 1970s and recorded at least seven new demo takes. One acoustic demo, during which he lapses into "Isolation," is on *Lost Lennon Tapes 1*. Acoustic demo take 4 is on *Yer Blues* (CD-1) and *Lost Lennon Tapes 19*; take 5 is on *Lost Lennon Tapes 23*. Another demo was aired on episode 134 of "The Lost Lennon Tapes."

■ John recorded several demos at this time, many of them for a planned musical tentatively titled *The Ballad of John and Yoko*. The titles include "Gone from This Place," found on *Lost Lennon Tapes 12* and *Gone from This Place* (CD); another demo is on *Lost Lennon Tapes 17*, *Lost Sleepy Blind Lemon Lennon* (CD) and *Watching the Wheels* (CD). "She Is a Friend of Dororthy's" also reportedly from the mid-1970s, is found on *Lost Lennon Tapes 13*; take 7 is on *Lost Sleepy Blind Lemon Lennon* (CD) and *Look at Me* (CD). "Whatever Happened to . . .?" is on *Lost Lennon Tapes 3* and *News of the Day* (CD). "Life Begins at Forty," a country and western number reportedly written for Ringo, is on *Lost Lennon Tapes One*. Three demo takes of "Free as a Bird" were recorded; one is on *Lost Sleepy Blind Lemon Lennon* (CD), *Watching the Wheels* (CD) and *Lost Lennon Tapes 19*; another demo was aired on episode 128 of "The Lost Lennon Tapes." An ad lib loosely titled "Down in Eastern Australia I Met Her" is on *Lost Lennon Tapes 2*. "Not For Love Nor Money" (listed as "Illusions") is on *Lost Lennon Tapes 23*. A group of songs referred to collectively as "Sea Ditties," also on *Lost Lennon Tapes 2*, includes "My Old Man's a Dustman," "I Do Like to Be Beside the Seaside," "Leaning on a Lamp-Post" and "Mr. Wu's a Window Cleaner Now." Another of Lennon's Dylan parodies, this one tentatively titled "The Best Things in Life Are Free," is on *Lost Lennon Tapes 8*. A demo of "He Got the Blues" is on *Lost Sleepy Blind Lemon Lennon* (CD) and *Lost Lennon Tapes 20*. Demos of "Help Me to Help Myself" were aired on episodes 150 and 180, a demo of "Boat Song" was heard on episode 150 of "The Lost Lennon Tapes," and "Pedro the Fisherman" on episode 185. The following songs from this period have been copyrighted in Lennon's name: "I Don't Want to Lose You," "Hold On, I'm Coming," "Dream Time," "Man Is Half of Woman (Woman Is Half of Man)" and "Don't Be Afraid."

■ John recorded many demo versions of "Serve Yourself," a parody of Bob Dylan's "Gotta Serve Somebody." One version, notable for its obscene lyrics, appears on *Johnny Moondog*, *Yin Yang*, *Serve Yourself* and on a bootleg single. Other, sanitized takes appear as follows: *Lost Lennon Tapes 4*, *Gone from This Place* (CD), *Lost Lennon Tapes 8*, *Lost Lennon Tapes 12* and *Last Sleepy Blind Lemon Lennon* (CD) (first "phallic worshipers" take); *My Love Will Turn You On* (CD);

"Serve Yourself" (bootleg). A bootleg single with the expletive-laced version of this unreleased Lennon song, a response to Bob Dylan's "Gotta Serve Somebody."

episode 99 of "The Lost Lennon Tapes" (second "phallic worshipers" take); episode 128; episode 170; and episode 86 (the final take, recorded Nov 14). Some demos reportedly date from as early as spring 1980.

Early Nov: A Lennon acoustic demo of the unreleased "Dear John" is on *Lost Lennon Tapes 3*. This is one of the last songs Lennon composed, perhaps the very last. He goes into the lyrics of "September Song" on the demo, which are all the more poignant given the events that were soon to follow.

Nov 14: During one of his final home taping sessions, John recorded several demos. An unfinished electric demo of "You Saved My Soul (with Your True Love)" is on *Lost Sleepy Blind Lemon Lennon* (CD); another take is on *Dreaming of the Past* (CD). *Lost Lennon Tapes 23* features "Pop Is the Name of the Game," and the final demo of "You Saved My Soul," including lyrics from "Serve Yourself."

Dec: George recorded "Dream Away" for the *Time Bandits* film soundtrack; the recording was later remixed for Harrison's LP *Gone Troppo*. The original film soundtrack version is on *By George* and *Onothimagen*.

That year: George reportedly wrote the unreleased song "Sooty Goes to Hawaii."

1981

Feb 16–18: An alternate mix of Paul's "Take It Away" with a longer fadeout ending is found on *Suitable for Framing*.

Feb 21–25: While recording in Montserrat, Paul and Carl Perkins co-wrote the unreleased song "My Old Friend," and unreleased takes of "Honey Don't," "Boppin'

the Blues," "Lend Me Your Comb," "Cut Across Shorty," "When the Saints Go Marching In" and "Red Sails in the Sunset." No recordings have surfaced to date.

Dec 12: Ringo appeared on the BBC 1 TV show, "Parkinson"; he was interviewed and joined in on an impromptu version of "Singing the Blues," which is found in *Classified Document Volume Two*.

1982

Jan 30: Paul appeared on BBC Radio Four's "Desert Island Discs" where he sang along with parts of The Coasters' recording of "Searchin'" and John's "Beautiful Boy (Darling Boy)." Both excerpts are on *Great to Have You with Us*.

Mar 7: BBC Radio aired a two-hour special called "The Beatles at the Beeb" including most of the original recordings, or portions of them, that The Beatles had made exclusively for BBC Radio shows. The special was syndicated in the U.S. during the Memorial Day weekend beginning May 31. Bootleg copies of this three-LP set have appeared; the same three discs are included in the five-LP set *So Much Younger Then*.

Jun 23: Paul filmed a promo clip for "Take It Away" before a live audience of his U.K. Fan Club. During the short concert he also sang "Bo Diddley," "Peggy Sue," "Twenty Flight Rock," "Lucille," "Send Me Some Lovin'," "Reelin' and Rockin'," and he played the instrumental "Theme from Hill Street Blues."

Sep 28: Ringo recorded a televised appearance for "Parkinson in Australia," aired Oct 8. He played drums and did some vocals on "Honey Don't" and a medley of "Honey Don't"/"Blue Suede Shoes," sung by Glenn Shorrock. The appearance is on *Classified Document Volume Two*.

Nov 5–May 8, 1983: During filming of *Give My Regards to Broad Street*, a documentary on the making of the film was also shot and aired Oct 14, 1984 in the U.K. on "The South Bank Show" and was also seen on U.S. TV. "For No One" is on *Great to Have You with Us* and *Classified Document*. "No Values" and "Wanderlust," taken directly from the film soundtrack of *Give My Regards to Broad Street*, are on *Great to Have You with Us* and *Twice in a Lifetime* respectively.

Late that year: Paul discussed his partnership with John during an interview that appears on the 45 RPM EP "Paul McCartney Talks About His Dear Friend John Lennon."

■ A poor-quality prefinal mix of the released version of "Pipes of Peace" is on *Classified Document Volume Two*, with a synthesizer ending cut from the released version.

1983

That spring: Paul recorded "Twice in a Lifetime," which appeared under the closing credits in the 1985 film of the same title. Paul's recording is on *All the Rest* (CD), *And All the Rest* (LP) and *Twice in a Lifetime*.

Jun 4–Nov 26: Ringo hosted the U.S. syndicated radio series "Ringo's Yellow Submarine." A segment with Ringo dubbing in the questions to the 1964 "Beatles

Open-End Interview" promo record is found on *Classified Document Volume Three*.

Jun 17: A BBC Radio One interview with Paul and Paul singing the Radio One jingle are on *Both Sides*.

Jul 18: Audience recordings of "The Beatles at Abbey Road" show are on *The Beatles Live at Abbey Road Studios*, *The Beatles in Abbey Road* and in improved sound quality on *Abbey Road Show 1983* (CD).

1984

Feb: A planned single that would have included Paul and Michael Jackson's "The Man" backed with the unreleased "Blackpool" was canceled. The record was to have been issued in both 7-inch and 12-inch formats (Parlophone R and 12R 6066). "Blackpool" may be the same song heard in the unreleased mid-1975 McCartney film *The Backyard*. The 12-inch release would also have contained an unreleased instrumental version of "The Man."

Jun 9: Paul appeared live on London Weekend Television's "Aspel & Company." He joined Tracey Ullman for a duet of "That'll Be the Day," found on *All the Rest* (CD), *And All the Rest* (LP) and *Great to Have You with Us*. The latter adds a 6-second bit of Paul busking "I Lost My Little Girl."

That summer: Paul recorded a demo of "On the Wings of a Nightingale," which he had written for The Everly Brothers, who recorded the song with Paul on guitar; Paul remixed the released version. The demo appears on *All the Rest* (CD) and *And All the Rest* (LP).

Dec 8: Ringo appeared on "Saturday Night Live" in the U.S. on NBC-TV, doing the opening monologue and a few comic sketches. He joined Billy Crystal, who impersonated Sammy Davis, Jr. in a medley of "With a Little Help from My Friends," "What Kind of Fool Am I?" "Act Naturally," "I've Gotta Be Me," "Octopus's Garden," "Photograph," "Yellow Submarine" and a reprise of "With a Little Help from My Friends." Ringo also sang along with the theme from "The Jeffersons" TV show, "Movin' on Up," with Jim Belushi. All of the musical selections are on *Rizz Off!*

Dec 14: George appeared as a surprise guest with Deep Purple on stage in Sydney, Australia, and joined the band on "Lucille," which appears on *A Nightmare Is Also a Dream*.

Late that year: George recorded the unreleased "Abandoned Love," written by Bob Dylan; it is heard on *Onothimagen*.

- Paul recorded the unreleased "Lindiana" during brief sessions co-produced by David Foster.

1985

Mar–May: A tape of Paul doing several songs from *Press to Play* includes the unreleased "Yvonne," and medley "Good Times Coming"/"Feel the Sun," "It's Not True," "Footprints," "Move Over Busker," "Press" (a slower version), "Write Away," "Tough on a Tightrope," "Talk More Talk," "Pretty Little Head," "However Ab-

surd" and Stranglehold." All of the songs are on *Played to Press*.

Early May: Ringo recorded "Nonsense," written by Steve Allen, for the TV film *Alice in Wonderland*; the song is on *Rizz Off!*

Jul 14: The day after he sang "Let It Be" at the Live Aid concert, Paul recorded a studio version of the song for use as an overdub for the live performance if it should ever be released; it never was.

Sep 12: Paul appeared on BBC 2 as host of the MPL/BBC special, "Buddy Holly," later released on home video as *The Real Buddy Holly Story*. He played the 1958 Quarry Men recording of "That'll Be the Day" and did a brief acoustic line or two from "Love Me Do" and "Words of Love," all found on *That'll Be the Day* and *Twice in a Lifetime*.

Oct 21: George and Ringo taped an appearance for the TV special "Blue Suede Shoes: A Rockabilly Session with Carl Perkins and Friends," aired Jan 1, 1986 in the U.K. and Jan 5, 1986 in the U.S. George sang "Everybody's Trying to Be My Baby," "Glad All Over," shared lead vocal on "Your True Love" and contributed backing vocals and guitar on "Blue Suede Shoes" (doing lead vocal on the encore), "Gone, Gone, Gone," "Whole Lotta Shakin' Goin' On" and a medley including "That's All Right (Mama)," "Blue Moon of Kentucky" and "Night Train to Memphis." Ringo sang "Honey Don't," shared lead vocal with Carl and Eric Clapton on "Matchbox" and played drums throughout the show and tambourine during the medley. All of George's songs are found on *Onothimagen* and *Look Back*; Ringo's two are on *Rizz Off!* and *Look Back*. "Right String But the Wrong Yo Yo" and "Sure to Fall" were performed but were cut from the broadcast.

That year: George reportedly wrote the unreleased song "Shelter in Your Love" with Alvin Lee; no recordings of it have appeared.

1986

Mar 15: George made a surprise appearance at the Heartbeat '86 charity concert at the National Exhibition Centre in Birmingham. He joined Robert Plant and Denny Laine on "Money" and a ragged rendition of "Johnny B. Goode"; the latter title is found on *Somewhere in Utopia*.

Jul: Paul recorded an alternate vocal for "Press" while being filmed for a BBC-TV special, released in 1989 on home video as *The Paul McCartney Special*. That recording is on *All the Rest* (CD) and *And All the Rest* (LP).

- George wrote and recorded several songs for the *Shanghai Surprise* film soundtrack. "Shanghai Surprise" (a Harrison duet with Vicki Brown), "Someplace Else" and "Breath Away from Heaven" are on *Onothimagen*. "Someplace Else" and "Breath Away from Heaven" were later re-recorded for George's *Cloud Nine* album. "Hottest Gong in Town," also from the film, was aired Dec 12, 1987 on a BBC Radio One

Cloud Nine special. "Twelve Bar Bali," an instrumental, was also used in the film.

Aug 25–29: Paul recorded some unreleased songs in New York with members of Billy Joel's band; Phil Ramone acted as producer.

Sep: Paul composed a song for his wife's birthday titled simply "Linda" and recorded two versions. Only one copy of a special single was pressed with one version of the song on each side, one a Latin-style arrangement, the other a big-band version.

Nov 24: Paul performed "Only Love Remains" at the Royal Variety Show. The song appears on *Played to Press* (CD).

Dec: Ringo filmed and recorded several television and radio commercials for Sun Country Wine Coolers and appeared in magazine ads for the product. Three different radio commercials appear on *Rizz Off!*

1987

Jan 5: At the start of his *Cloud Nine* album sessions, George recorded the unreleased song "Vatican P2 Blues."

Feb: Ringo recorded songs for a planned album at Chips Moman's 3 Alarm Studio in Memphis, Tennessee, with Moman serving as producer. A second set of sessions were held in late Apr. The album reportedly included the song titles "Shoo-Be-Doo-Be-Doo-Da- Day," "Some Kind of Wonderful," "Beat Patrol," "Ain't That a Shame," "Whiskey and Soda" and "I Can Help"; the sessions were videotaped as well. In mid-1989 Ringo successfully sued Moman to halt a planned rush release of this album.

Feb 19: George, Bob Dylan, John Fogerty and Jesse Ed Davis joined Taj Mahal on stage during his performance at the Palomino Club in North Hollywood. Most of the songs from the session are on *Live! The Silver Wilburys* (CD). The session was also videotaped on the house video system; underground copies of the tape contain the entire performance. Those on the CD include all of George's vocals: "Matchbox" (with Taj Mahal; George goes into "Gone Gone Gone" at one point), "Honey Don't," "Blue Suede Shoes" (with Fogerty), "Watching the River Flow," "Peggy Sue" (with Dylan) and "Dizzy Miss Lizzie." The other tracks on the CD are "Farther on Down the Road," "Lucille," "Johnny B. Goode," "Twist and Shout," "Knock on Wood," "Midnight Hour," "Proud Mary" and "Willie and the Hand Jive."

Late Apr: Ringo held additional recording sessions with Chips Moman at 3 Alarm Studios and Sun Studios in Memphis. Bob Dylan participated in at least one recording on Apr 29. A total of 16 songs were recorded during the Feb and Apr sessions, 12 of them written by others exclusively for Ringo.

Jun 2–30: Paul recorded an entire album, produced by Phil Ramone, that remains unreleased. Three of the unreleased Ramone-produced tracks may be "Love Come Tumbling Down," "Beautiful Night" and "Return to Pepperland," all copyrighted Aug 21. Paul reportedly worked on three Ramone-produced tracks with George Martin on Jul 1; these may be the three.

Jun–Jul: Paul recorded a special version of "Sgt. Pepper's Lonely Hearts Club Band" in honor of U.K. disc jockey Alan Freeman's 60th birthday. The song was aired on Jul 6 by Capitol Radio in London.

Jul 20–21: "I Saw Her Standing There" from Paul's oldies sessions for *CHOBA B CCCP* remains unreleased.

Aug: Paul completed mixing and editing another version of his unreleased *Cold Cuts* album with producer Chris Thomas and engineer Bill Price.

Sep 9: During a London party in honor of Buddy Holly Week, Paul sang loose versions of "What'd I Say," "Mean Woman Blues" and "Twenty Flight Rock."

That summer–fall: Paul and Elvis Costello recorded "Lovers That Never Were," the first song that they had written together but not the first of their collaborations to be recorded. The song remains unreleased. Other unreleased McCartney/MacManus songs from this period include "So Like Candy" and "Playboy to a Man," which Costello later recorded for his *Mighty Like a Rose* album.

Oct 17: George joined Bob Dylan on stage for "Rainy Day Women #12 & 35" during Dylan's Wembley concert.

Nov 17: Paul taped a performance of "Once Upon a Long Ago" before an audience of children, aired Nov 24 in the U.K. During the taping, Paul did ad-lib instrumental versions of "Ob-La-Di, Ob-La-Da," "C-Moon," "What'd I Say" and "Sailor's Hornpipe."

Nov 19: Paul and Linda taped an appearance as the only guests on the "Wogan" U.K. TV show, aired the following day. They performed "Jet" with an unidentified band. They were interviewed, premiered the video of "Once Upon a Long Ago" and closed with a live version of "Listen to What the Man Said." The recording of "Listen to What the Man Said" was used again for a Feb 22, 1988 live telecast, during which Paul mimed to the recording; it can be heard, along with this performance of "Jet," on *All the Rest* (CD) and *And All the Rest* (LP).

Nov 27: Paul appeared live on "The Last Resort with Jonathan Ross" on BBC Channel 4. Paul played lead guitar on a live version of "Don't Get Around Much Anymore" with Steve Nieve and the Playboys, resident band on this show, played "I Saw Her Standing There" and closed with "Lawdy Miss Clawdy." There was also a brief riff from "Spin It On." All three songs are on *It's Now or Never* (CD), *All the Rest* (CD) and *And All the Rest* (LP).

Dec 14–19: Paul recorded a new Rupert the Bear song with George Martin.

1988

Jan 20: George and Ringo joined other stars in an informal jam at the Rock & Roll Hall of Fame induction ceremony that included "I Saw Her Standing There." George did one line on "All Along the Watchtower." An underground tape of the entire ceremony, including the jam, has circulated and includes "Twist and Shout," "Stand by Me," "Stop in the Name of Love, " "Whole

Lotta Shakin' Goin' On," "Hound Dog," "Honey Hush," "Barbara Ann," "Blue Bayou" and "(I Can't Get No) Satisfaction."

Feb 10: George appeared live on "Rockline" on KLOS radio, Los Angeles. Besides being interviewed and taking phone calls from the audience, George, who sounded slightly intoxicated, sang an impromptu acoustic medley of "Here Comes the Sun"/"The Bells of Rhymney"/"Mr. Tambourine Man"/"Here Comes the Sun" (reprise). He also sang various-length versions of "Take Me As I Am (or Let Me Go)," "That's All Right (Mama)," "Let It Be Me," "Something" and "Every Grain of Sand." All of the musical tracks are on *Somewhere in Utopia*.

Late Mar: George wrote a song for one of a series of five-minute U.K. TV animated shorts called "Bunburys." The series was scheduled to air late in 1992, when a video and album were also to be issued.

Middle of May: About 20 minutes of prefinal mixes from sessions for *The Traveling Wilburys Vol. One* appears on *The Traveling Wilburys Vol. 2*. Titles include "End of the Line," "Heading for the Light" (instrumental), "Rattled," "Dirty World," "Congratulations," "Handle with Care" and "Last Night." The recordings represent the basic tracks without final overdubs. "Dirty World" has a different Bob Dylan vocal; "Rattled" appears to be a completely different take; Roy Orbison is missing on "End of the Line" and the vocals appear to be different.

Early summer: Paul recorded the unreleased song "Indigo Moon."

1989

Mar 25–May 13: A series of eight one-hour shows, *McCartney on McCartney*, was aired in the U.K. and began with a long McCartney interview during which Paul sang a short bit of "I Lost My Little Girl"; the ad lib appears on *Wings over Denmark 1972* and *And All the Rest*.

May 18: On the West German TV show "Mensch Meir," McCartney did "Put It There" and "Figure of Eight," both of which are found on *And All the Rest*.

May 19: Paul mimed to unreleased versions of "Figure of Eight" (much longer than the released version) and "My Brave Face" on BBC 1's "Wogan." The recordings were made specifically for this appearance.

May 24: McCartney appeared live on NED 2's "Countdown" show, aired on Dutch television. Paul sang "How Many People" and did an impromptu jam; he also mimed to "My Brave Face." The appearance is on *And All the Rest*; "How Many People" is on *Live Rarities*.

Jun 13: Ringo appeared on stage with Bob Dylan at the latter's concert at Les Arenes in Frejus, France and joined in on two songs.

Jun 15: Paul recorded new versions of "This One" and "My Brave Face" before a live audience at the Teatro Delle Vittorie in Rome. He mimed to the recordings on

the following day's broadcast of the "Saint Vincent Estate '89" show, aired by RAI TV in Italy.

Jul 26–27: Paul performed two surprise concerts at London's Playhouse Theatre before invited audiences. Songs included "Figure of Eight," "Jet," "Rough Ride," "Got to Get You into My Life," "Band on the Run," "We Got Married," "Put It There," "Hello Goodbye" (ending only), "Things We Said Today," "Can't Buy Me Love," "Summertime," "I Saw Her Standing There," "This One," "My Brave Face," introduction of the band, "Twenty Flight Rock," "The Long and Winding Road," "Ain't That a Shame," "Let It Be"; encore: "Coming Up." On Jul 27 Paul held a press conference at London's Playhouse Theatre to formally announce his world tour. He also performed four songs: "Midnight Special," "Coming Up," "Twenty Flight Rock" and "This One."

Aug 5: "Back Off Boogaloo" from Ringo's Holmdel, New Jersey show is on *A Little Live* (EP).

Aug 13: "It Don't Come Easy" and "No No Song" from Ringo's Wantaugh, New York show are on *A Little Live* (EP).

Aug 24: Westwood One Radio in the U.S. carried McCartney's press conference from the Lyceum Theater, New York, preceded by a brief performance by Paul and his band that included "Figure of Eight," "This One" and "Coming Up." At the start of the broadcast, the band could be heard rehearsing "Blue Suede Shoes" and "Matchbox." All five songs are on *And All the Rest*. Later that evening, Paul performed a live show at the Lyceum for an invited audience, including "Figure of Eight," "This One," "Jet," "Rough Ride," "Got to Get You into My Life," "Band on the Run," "We Got Married," "Put It There," "Things We Said Today," "Summertime," "Can't Buy Me Love," "I Saw Her Standing There," "My Brave Face," "Twenty Flight Rock," "The Long and Winding Road," "Ain't That a Shame," "Let It Be" and an encore of "Coming Up."

Sep 2: *Live from the Pacific Amphitheater* includes several songs from Ringo's Costa Mesa show: "It Don't Come Easy," "No No Song," "Yellow Submarine," "Act Naturally," "Honey Don't," "I Wanna Be Your Man," "Boys," "Happy Birthday," "Photograph," "You're Sixteen" and "With a Little Help from My Friends."

Sep 3: Ringo was seen live on the Jerry Lewis Muscular Dystrophy Telethon in the U.S. singing "Boys" during his show at the Greek Theater in Los Angeles. The song appeared on the *1989 Beatleg News Christmas Record*.

Sep 28: Paul's unreleased "Church Mice" was one of several prerecorded instrumentals played at each of his concerts prior to the start of the show.

Sep 30: Paul's show at Stockholm's Johanneshovs Isstadion is on *The Paul McCartney World Tour*, issued on colored vinyl and packaged with a cover slick, badge, poster and other inserts. It contains the entire concert: "Figure of Eight," "Jet," "Rough Ride," "Got to Get You into My Life," "Band on the Run," "Ebony and Ivory," "We Got Married," "Maybe I'm Amazed," "The Long and Winding Road," "The Fool on the Hill," "Sgt. Pepper's

Lonely Hearts Club Band" and reprise, "Good Day Sunshine," "Can't Buy Me Love," "Put It There," "Things We Said Today," "Eleanor Rigby," "This One," "My Brave Face," "Back in the USSR," "I Saw Her Standing There," "Twenty Flight Rock," "Coming Up," "Let It Be," "Ain't That a Shame," "Live and Let Die," "Hey Jude," "Yesterday," "Get Back," medley "Golden Slumbers"/"Carry That Weight"/"The End."

Oct 3–Apr 4, 1990: Songs from several of Paul's concerts have been bootlegged: Hamburg (Oct 3, CD *Friends of the Earth World Tour 1989/90*), Paris (Oct 9, CD *Live in Paris 1989*; Oct 10 or 11, *Live in Paris, 1989, Vols. 1 & 2*), Rome (Oct 4, *Dirty Italian Flowers*, one song), Milan (Oct 26, *Dirty Italian Flowers*, entire show; Oct 27, *Dirty Italian Flowers*, partial; unedited "All My Trials" on *Live Rarities*), Rotterdam (Nov 8, *Tiptoe Through the Tulips* entire show), Los Angeles (Nov 23, *Back in the U.S.A, Nov 23, 1989*, entire show; Nov 27, *Yesterday, Today and McCartney*, entire show including "Ebony and Ivory—encore with Stevie Wonder; Nov 28, *Once in a Lifetime*, a few songs), New York (Dec 12, *Madison Square Garden December 1989*, most of the show; Dec 15, *Paul 12/15/89*, entire show including "Jingle Bells"), Tokyo (Mar 7, 1990, *Little Live Rarities* EP, "P.S. Love Me Do" only), Berkeley (Mar 31, 1990, *Live Rarities*, "P.S. Love Me Do"; "Let 'Em In"), and Tempe, Arizona (Apr 4, 1990, *Live Rarities*, same 2 songs as Berkeley).

Nov 23: Paul's Los Angeles Forum soundcheck included "C Moon," "Party Party," "Can't Take My Eyes Off You," "Crackin' Up," "Matchbox" and "Don't Let the Sun Catch You Crying." Band members reported that the Rolling Stones' "Honky Tonk Woman" had also been done with Paul on drums.

1990

Mar 31: Paul's Berkeley soundcheck included "Blue Suede Shoes," "Matchbox," "Just Because," "Don't Let the Sun Catch You Crying," "C Moon" and "Satin Doll."

Late Mar: Ringo joined Joe Walsh, Tom Petty, Jeff Lynne and Jim Keltner to record and film a new version of "I Call Your Name," screened during the May 5 John Lennon Scholarship Concert in Liverpool. The concert was aired in syndication on U.S. and U.K. television on Dec 8, the tenth anniversary of John's death. Ringo's song appears on *A Little Live* (EP). The video was officially released in the U.K. Apr 15, 1991 on the videocassette *Lennon: A Tribute*, issued later in the U.S.

Late Apr–middle of May: Several outtakes and alternate mixes from recording sessions for *The Traveling Wilburys Volume 3* appear on *Traveling Wilburys: Volume 4 1/2* (CD). Most notable is an unreleased George Harrison song, "Maxine," apparently the only all-Harrison song from these sessions, and Bob Dylan's unreleased "Like a Ship." There are also alternate takes and prefinal mixes of "Inside Out," "Where Were You Last Night," "You Took My Breath Away" (with a completely unreleased verse and with Jeff Lynne doing some of Tom Petty's lines), "If You Belonged to Me," "Poor House," "She's My Baby" (with

different lyrics and vocals), "The Devil's Been Busy" (including some different vocals), "Wilbury Twist" (a different take), "7 Deadly Sins," "New Blue Moon," "Cool Dry Place" and "Runaway" (released only on U.K. 12-inch and CD singles), with no fadeout. Most of the songs are missing some overdubs and range from alternate takes to prefinal mixes. CD adds outtakes "I'm Gone," "Borderline," "Sirens" (all by Jeff Lynne), and "Born in Time" (Dylan).

Jun 28: BBC Radio's 75-minute broadcast of Paul's Liverpool concert appears on *Liverpool—June 1990* (CD).

Jun 30: The syndicated radio broadcast of Paul's set at the Knebworth Concert appears on *Knebworth 1990, The Mac Attack* and *The Knebworth Album* (CD).

Nov: Paul recorded several unknown demos in preparation for a new album.

Dec 14: The U.K. newspaper *The Independent* reported that Paul had resumed writing with Elvis Costello and that three new McCartney/MacManus compositions were penned during this month.

1991

Jan 25: "Mean Woman Blues," "Matchbox," "Midnight Special," "The Fool" and "Things We Said Today" from Paul's TV performance for MTV's "Unplugged" show (aired Apr 3) were not released on *Unplugged: The Official Bootleg*, nor were they aired on the television broadcast.

Mar 3: George took the stage at a convention of George Formby fans held at the Winter Gardens in Blackpool. Armed with a ukulele, he sang Formby's "In My Little Snapshot Album." No known recordings of the performance have surfaced, although amateur home videos were taken. George also participated in a closing group play-and-singalong on this date and on the previous night.

May 8–Jul 24: Paul and his band appeared at the following venues: Zeleste Club, Barcelona, Spain (May 8); the Mean Fiddler Club, London (May 10); Teatro Tendo, Naples, Italy (Jun 5); Cornwall Coliseum, St. Austell, U.K. (Jun 7); Cliffs Pavilion, Westcliff, U.K. (Jul 19); and the Falkoner Theatre, Copenhagen, Denmark (Jul 24). Two 45-minute sets were performed at each show, one acoustic and one electric. On May 8 and 10 the first set included "Mean Woman Blues," "Be-Bop-a-Lula," "We Can Work It Out," "San Francisco Bay Blues," "Every Night," "Here, There and Everywhere," "That Would Be Something," "And I Love Her," "She's a Woman," "I Lost My Little Girl," "Ain't No Sunshine," "I've Just Seen a Face" and "Good Rockin' Tonight." Second set: "My Brave Face," "Band on the Run," "Ebony and Ivory," "I Saw Her Standing There," "Coming Up," "Get Back," "The Long and Winding Road," "Ain't That a Shame," "Let It Be" and encores of "Can't Buy Me Love" and the world tour medley/jam version of "Sgt. Pepper's Lonely Hearts Club Band." Paul added three songs to his Jun 5 and 7 acoustic sets: "Hi-Heel Sneakers," a 30-second instrumental version of "The World Is Waiting for the Sunrise" and a completely new McCartney song, "Down to the River." The song lineup on Jul 19 and 24 was the same as May 8 except that "Down to the River," "Hi-Heel Sneakers," and "Twenty Flight Rock" were added while "And I Love Her" and "My Brave Face" were dropped. The Jul 19 show, including poetry reading segment by Adrian Mitchell (not done at the other shows) is on *Southend Surprise*.

Unreleased Song Titles

Many titles recorded by The Beatles were never commercially released. The titles and composers appear below.

"Abandoned Love" (Dylan)
"Across the River" (Lennon)
"After You've Gone" (Creamer/Layton)
"All Along the Watchtower" (Dylan)
"All I Want Is You" (Lennon/McCartney) (different from "Dig a Pony")
"All of You" (McCartney?)
"All Right" (Starkey)
"All Shook Up" (Blackwell/Presley)
"All Things Must Pass" (Harrison) (Beatles version)
"All Together on the Wireless Machine" (Everett)
"All You Horseriders" (McCartney)
"Almost Grown" (Berry)
"Anything" (aka "Drum Track") (Starkey?)
"Around and Around" (Berry)
"As Time Goes By" (Hupfeld) (one or two lines ad-libbed during interview)
"Autumn Leaves" (Kosma/Mercer)
"Baa Baa Blacksheep" (traditional)
"Baby Face" (Davis/Akst)
"Back Seat of My Car" (McCartney) (Beatles version)
"Bad to Me" (Lennon/McCartney)
"The Ball of Inverary" (traditional)
"Barbara Ann" (Fassert)
"Beat Patrol"
    (? unreleased Ringo title from Moman sessions)
"Beautiful Dreamer" (Foster)
"Beautiful Night" (McCartney)
"Because I Love You" (Lennon/McCartney) (aka "Wake Up in the Morning"; *Let It Be* outtake)
"Bei Mir Bist Du Schon" (Secunda/Shalom)
"The Bells of Rhymney" (Davies/Seeger; traditional?)
"Best Friend" (McCartney)
"Beyond the Sea" (Trenet/Lawrence)
"Birmingham" (Starkey? unreleased 1977 recording)
"Blackpool" (McCartney)
"Blowing in the Wind" (Dylan)
"Blue Bayou" (Orbison/Melson)
"Blue Moon" (Rodgers/Hart)
"Blue Sway" (McCartney)
"Blues in the Night" (Arlen)
"Blue Suede Shoes" (Perkins)
"Boat Song" (Lennon)
"Bo Diddley" (McDaniel)
"Bogey Wobble" (McCartney)
"Boil Crisis" (McCartney)

"Boppin' the Blues" (Perkins)
"Borderline" (Lynne)
"Born In Time" (Dylan)
"Brandy" (Nilsson? unregistered, unreleased Ringo title)
"Brazil" (Soares/Allen)
"Brian Epstein Blues"
    (actually an untitled Lennon studio improvisation)
"Bridge over Troubled Waters" (Simon)
"Bring It on Home to Me" (Cooke)
"Bring It to Jerome" (McDaniel)
"Brown Eyed Handsome Man" (Berry)
"Bunny Hop" (Twomey/Wise/Weisman)
"Bye Bye Bye" (Lennon/McCartney?)
"Bye Bye Love" (Bryant/Bryant)
"By Your Side" (Starkey? 1977 unreleased recording)
"Cage" (McCartney)
"Call My Name" (Lennon)
"Can't Fight Lightning" (Starkey?/Bach?)
"Can't Take My Eyes Off You" (Crewe/Gaudio)
"Caribbean" (Torok)
"Carol" (Berry)
"A Case of the Blues" (Lennon)
"Castle of the King" (McCartney)
"Catch the Wind" (Leitch)
"Cathy's Clown" (Everly/Everly)
"Catswalk" (McCartney) (later retitled "Cat Call")
"Chicago" (Fisher)
"Chi Chi's Cafe" (Lennon)
"Chopsticks" (public domain)
"Chords of Fame" (Ochs)
"Church Mice" (McCartney)
"Clarabella" (Pingatore)
"Club Dakota Rap" (Lennon)
"C'mon Everybody" (Cochran/Capehart)
"Come and Get It" (McCartney)
"Corrina, Corrina" (Dylan adaptation/arrangement of "Corrine, Corrina" [Williams/Chatman/Parrish] done by Lennon, largely with improvised lyrics)
"Cottonfields" (Ledbetter)
"Crawl of the Wild" (McCartney/Mason?)
"Cut Across Shorty" (Wilkin/Walker)
"Daddy's Little Sunshine Boy" (Starkey improvisation?)
"Da Do Ron Ron" (Spector/Greenwich/Berry)
"Dear John" (Lennon)
"Did We Meet Somewhere Before?" (McCartney)

"Digging My Potatoes" (traditional)

"Domino" (Ferrari) (mistitled "Da De Da" on bootlegs)

"Don't Be Afraid" (Lennon) (possibly mistaken copyright intended for "Don't Be Crazy" [below] filed erroneously)

"Don't Be Crazy" (Lennon)

"Don't Be Cruel" (Blackwell/Presley)

"Don't Ever Change" (Goffin/King)

"Don't Think Twice, It's All Right" (Dylan)

"Down in Cuba" (Lennon)

"Down in Eastern Australia I Met Her" (aka "Nonsense Song") (Lennon?)

"Do You Like Me (Just a Little Bit)?" (Ayer)

"Down to the River" (McCartney)

"Dream Baby" (Walker)

"Dream Lover" (Darin)

"Dream Time" (Lennon)

"Duet—Nancy & Ringo" (generic title; unreleased 1977 recording)

"Early in the Morning" (Darin/Harris)

"1882" (McCartney)

"El Tango Terrible" (Lennon)

"El Toro Passing" (McCartney)

"The End of the Road" (Lauder)

"Every Grain of Sand" (Dylan)

"Every Night" (Beatles version)

"Every Time Somebody Comes to Town" (Harrison/Dylan?)

"Fever" (Davenport/Cooley)

"Flying Horse" (McCartney)

"The Fool" (Ford)

"Fools Like Me" (Clement/Maddux)

"Forty Days" (Berry)

"Free as a Bird" (Lennon)

"Frère Jacques" (French traditional)

"Get Back" (Lennon/McCartney) (under working titles "Commonwealth Song," "Get Off/White Power," "White Power Promenade," "Enoch Powell," "No Pakistanis")

"Get It Together" (Lennon)

"Gilly Gilly Ossenfeffer Katzenellen Bogen by the Sea" (Hoffman/Wayne)

"Gimme Some Lovin'" (Carter)

"Gimme Some Truth" (Lennon) (Beatles version)

"Girls and Boys" (Lennon) (also copyrighted as "Real Love")

"Glad All Over" (Shroeder/Tepper/Bennett)

"God Save Us" (Lennon/Ono)

"Going Up the Country" (Wilson)

"Gone from This Place" (Lennon)

"Gone Gone Gone" (Perkins)

"Goodbye" (Lennon/McCartney)

"Good Golly, Miss Molly" (Blackwell/Marascalco)

"Goodnight Irene" (Ledbetter/Lomax)

"Good Rockin' Tonight" (Brown)

"Gotta Sing, Gotta Dance" (McCartney)

"Go Your Own Way" (Alexander)

"Great Balls of Fire" (Hammer/Blackwell)

"Groovin'" (King, Bethea)

"Guitar Blues" (Harrison)

"Happy Birthday to You" (Hill/Hill)

"The Happy Rishikesh Song" (Lennon)

"Hare Krishna Mantra" (Mukunda Das Adhikary)

"Hava Nagila" (traditional)

"Hear Me Lord" (Harrison) (Beatles version)

"Heartbeat" (Montgomery/Petty)

"Heather" (McCartney)

"He Got the Blues" (Lennon)

"Hello Dolly" (Herman)

"Hello Muddah, Hello Fadduh" (Sherman/Busch)

"Help Me" (Williamson/Bass) (Paul; early 1972 U.K. university tour)

"Help Me to Help Myself" (Lennon)

"Henry's Blues" (Bellinger) or "Henry's Blue" (McCulloch)

"Here's the Chord, Roy" (McCartney)

"He's Got the Whole World in His Hands" (London/Henry)

"Hey! Baby" (Channel/Cobb)

"Hey Diddle" (McCartney)

"Hey Little Girl (in the High School Sweater)" (Blackwell/B. Stevenson)

"High School Confidential" (Lewis/Hargrave)

"The Hippy Hippy Shake" (Romero)

"Hitch Hike" (Gaye/W. Stevenson/Paul)

"Hold On, I'm Coming" (Lennon)

"Honey Hush" (Turner)

"The Honeymoon Song" (Theodorakis/Sansom)

"Honky Tonk Woman" (Jagger/Richards)

"Hot as Sun" (McCartney) (Beatles version)

"Hottest Gong in Town" (Harrison)

"Hound Dog" (Leiber/Stoller)

"The House of the Rising Sun" (Ray/White/Holmes)

"How Do You Do" (Leitch)

"How Do You Do It?" (Murray)

"Howling at the Moon" (Lennon) (variation of Lennon's "Memories" and "Tennessee")

"Hully Gully" (Smith/Goldsmith)

"I Ain't Got Time" (Eddins)

"I Bought a Picasso" (McCartney?)

"I Can Hear You Calling" (Oct 29, 1976 unreleased) (Starkey?)

"I Can Help" (Starkey?)

"(I Can't Get No) Satisfaction" (Richards/Jagger)

"I Do Like to Be Beside the Seaside" (Glover/Kind)

"I Don't Want to Lose You" (Lennon)

"I Fancy Me Chances" (Lennon/McCartney)

"I Forgot to Remember to Forget" (Kesler/Feathers)

"If You Gotta Make a Fool of Somebody" (Clark)

"If You've Got Trouble" (McCartney; vocal by Ringo)

"I Got a Woman" (Charles/Richards)

"I Got to Find My Baby" (Berry)

"I Just Don't Understand" (Wilkin/Westberry)

"I Know" (Wright)

"I'll Be on My Way" (Lennon/McCartney)

"I'll Be Seeing You" (Brown/Egan/Whiting)

"I'll Make You Happy" (Lennon)
"I'm a Man" (McDaniel)
"I'm Crazy" (Lennon)
"I'm Gone" (Lynne)
"I'm Gonna Love You Too" (Mauldin/Petty/Sullivan)
"I'm Gonna Sit Right Down and Cry Over You"
   (Thomas/Biggs)
"I'm Ready" (King/Durand/Robichaux)
"I'm Talking About You" (Berry)
"I'm Walking'" (Domino/Bartholomew)
"Incantation" (Lennon/Cicala)
"Indigo Moon" (McCartney)
"In My Little Snapshot Album" (Formby)
"The Inner Light" (Harrison)
   (Beatles version with Lennon vocal)
"In Spite of All the Danger" (McCartney/Harrison)
"In the Middle of an Island" (Acquaviva/Varnick)
"I Shall Be Released" (Dylan)
"Isn't It a Pity" (Harrison) (Beatles version)
"It Ain't Me Babe" (Dylan)
"It'll Be Me" (Clement)
"I Threw It All Away" (Dylan)
"I Want You" (Lennon/Ono)
   (not The Beatles song; improvised lyric)
"I Want You, I Need You, I Love You" (Mysels/Kosloff)
"I Watch Your Face" (Lennon)
"I Will Always Be in Love with You" (QMEN at home)
"I Would Only Smile" (Laine)
"It's for You" (Lennon/McCartney)
"It's Hard to Be Lovers" (Starkey/Allison)
"It's Only Make Believe" (Twitty/Nance)
"It's So Easy" (Holly/Petty)
"It's So Long" (Sass)
"Jambalaya" (Williams)
"Jazz Piano Song" (McCartney/Starkey)
"Jealous Guy" (Lennon) (Beatles version)
"Jenny Jenny" (Johnson/Penniman)
"Jerusalaim" (Noff?)
"Jessie's Dream"
   (Lennon/McCartney/Harrison/Starkey?)
"Jingle Bells" (traditional)
"J.J." (Lennon)
"John Henry" (traditional)
"Johnny B. Goode" (Berry)
"Jo Jo Gun" (Berry)
"Just Fun" (Lennon/McCartney)
"Karate Chaos" (McCartney)
"Keep Looking That Way" (Lennon/McCartney)
"Keep Your Hands Off My Baby" (Goffin/King)
"La Bamba" (traditional; arr: Valens)
"Lady Jane" (Jagger/Richards)
"Lady Marmalade" (Crewe/Nolan)
"Lalena" (Leitch)
"Land of Gisch" (Leitch)
"Lawdy Miss Clawdy" (Price)
"Leaning on a Lamp Post" (Gay)
"Leave My Kitten Alone" (John/McDougal/Turner)
"Lend Me Your Comb" (Twomey/Wise/Weissman)

"Let It Be Me" (Trent/Minnier)
"Let It Down" (Harrison) (Beatles *Let It Be* version)
"Let's Love" (McCartney)
"Let's Stomp" (Feldman/Goldstein/Gottehrer)
"Life Begins at Forty" (Lennon)
"Like a Rolling Stone" (Dylan)
"Like a Ship" (Dylan; *Wilburys 3* outtake)
"Linda" (McCartney)
"Lindiana" (McCartney)
"Listen to Me" (Hardin/Petty)
"Little Eddie" (Lennon/McCartney)
"Little Yellow Pills" (Lomax)
"Lonesome Tears in My Eyes"
   (Burnette/Burnette/Burlison/Mortimer)
"Long Black Train" (Lennon; see Lewisohn [1986], p. 25)
"Look at Me" (Holly/Petty/Allison)
"Looking Glass" (Lennon/McCartney)
"Louie Louie" (Berry)
"Love Come Tumbling Down" (McCartney)
"A Love for You" (McCartney)
"Love Is a Swingin' Thing" (Jordan)
"Lover Please" (1977 unreleased recording) (Starkey?)
"Lovers That Never Were" (McCartney/MacManus)
"Loving You" (Leiber/Stoller)
"Low Down Blues" (Williams)
"Lucille" (Penniman/Collins)
"Mailman, Bring Me No More Blues"
   (Roberts/Katz/Clayton)
"Madman" (or "Madman-a-Coming")
   (Lennon/McCartney)
"The Maharishi Song" (Lennon)
"Maisie" (Jubber)
"Mama You Been on My Mind" (Dylan)
"Man Is Half of Woman (Woman Is Half of Man)"
   (Lennon)
"Many Rivers to Cross" (Cliff)
"Maxine" (Harrison)
"Maybe Baby" (Petty/Holly)
"Maybelline" (Berry)
"Mean Woman Blues" (Demetrius)
"Memories" (Lennon)
"Michael Row Your Boat Ashore" (traditional)
"Midnight Special" (traditional; arr: Ledbetter/Lomax)
"Milkcow Blues" (Arnold)
"Mine for Me" (McCartney)
"Mirror Mirror (on the Wall)" (Lennon)
"Miss Ann" (Johnson/Penniman)
"Mister Tambourine Man" (Dylan)
"Moondreams" (Petty)
"Moovin' 'n' Groovin'" (Eddy/Hazelwood)
"More Than I Can Say" (Allison/Curtis)
"Moving Along the River Rhine" (McCartney *Let It Be*
   sessions improvisation; goes into lyrics from "The
   Long and Winding Road")
"Move It" (Donaldson)
"Mr. H. Atom" (McCartney)
"Mr. Wind" (Leitch)

"Mr. Wu's a Window Cleaner Now" (Formby/Gifford/Cliffe)
"Mucho Mungo" (Lennon)
"My Life" (Lennon)
"My Old Friend" (McCartney/Perkins)
"My Old Man's a Dustman" (traditional; arrangement: Donegan)
"Mystery Train" (Parker/Phillips)
"Nancy, Ringo, Vinnie & Friends" (generic title of unreleased recording)
"Negro in Reserve" (Lennon/McCartney) (aka "Hole in My Heart")
"New Orleans" (Guida/Royster)
"News of the Day (from Reuters)" (Lennon; improvisation)
"Night Out" (McCartney)
"Night Train to Memphis" (Smith/Hughes/Bradley)
"Nonsense" (Allen)
"Not Fade Away" (Petty/Hardin)
"Not for Love Nor Money" (Lennon)
"Nutwood Scene" (McCartney)
"O Kristelighed" ("O Christianity") (Grundtvig)
"One and One Is Two" (Lennon/McCartney)
"One Hand Clapping" (McCartney)
"One of the Boys" (Lennon)
"One Too Many Mornings" (Dylan)
"Only One More Kiss" (McCartney)
"Only the Lonely" (Orbison/Melson)
"On Moonlight Bay" (Kennon/Tobin)
"On the Wings of a Nightingale" (McCartney)
"On Top of Old Smokey" (traditional)
"Ooh! My Soul" (Penniman)
"Oriental Nightfish" (L. McCartney)
"Over the Rainbow" (Arlen/Harburg)
"Papa's Got a Brand New Bag" (Brown)
"Party" (Starkey/Nilsson)
"Peggy Sue Got Married" (Holly)
"Penina" (McCartney)
"People" (Lennon)
"Piano Theme" (played by Paul at the start of the film *Let It Be*)
"A Picture of You" (Beveridge/Oakman)
"Piece of My Heart" (Ragavoy/Berns)
"Pill" (Lennon)
"Pinwheel Twist" (Lennon/McCartney)
"The Pirate Song" (Harrison/Idle)
"Please Mrs. Henry" (Dylan)
"Pop Is the Name of the Game" (Lennon) (aka "Popcorn"?)
"A Pretty Girl Is Like a Melody" (Berlin)
"Proud Mum" (McCartney)
"Queen of the Hop" (Harris/Darin)
"A Quick One While He's Away" (Townshend)
"Radio Peace" (Lennon/Ono)
"Raining in My Heart" (Bryant/Bryant)
"Rainy Day Women #12 & 35" (Dylan)
"Ramrod" (Casey)
"Raunchy" (Justis/Manker)

"Rave On" (West/Tilghman/Petty)
"Reach Out (I'll Be There)" (Holland/Dozier/Holland)
"Real Life" (Lennon)
"Real Love" (Lennon) (also copyrighted as "Girls and Boys")
"Rebel Rouser" (Eddy/Hazelwood)
"Red Hot" (Emerson)
"Reelin' and Rockin'" (Berry)
"Return to Pepperland" (McCartney)
"Rip It Up" (Blackwell/Marascalco)
"Road Runner" (McDaniel)
"Robber's Ball" (McCartney)
"Rock Island Line" (Ledbetter)
"Rock Peace" (Lennon)
"Rocker" (aka "Instrumental No. 42" or "Link Track"; includes a bit of "I'm Ready") (Lennon/McCartney/Harrison/Starkey)
"Rudolph the Red-Nosed Reindeer" (Marks)
"Rumble" (Wray/Cooper)
"Rupert Song" (McCartney)
"Sailor Come Back to Me" (Ringo improvisation?)
"Sally and Billy" (Lennon)
"Satin Doll" (Mercer/Ellington/Strayhorn)
"Save the Last Dance for Me" (Pomus/Shuman)
"Say Darling" (McCartney) (early 1972 U.K. university tour only)
"Say You Don't Mind" (Laine)
"School Day" (Berry)
"Sea Dance" (McCartney) (instrumental; may be same song listed as "Sea Melody" or "Sea"/"Cornish Water" on *Rupert* bootleg CD. "Sea Dance" copyrighted Jun 16, 1975 [Paul and Linda McCartney])
"Seems Like Old Times" (McCartney)
"Send Me the Heart" (McCartney/Laine)
"September Song" (Anderson/Weill)
"Serve Yourself" (Lennon)
"Shake, Rattle, and Roll" (Calhoun)
"Shakin' in the Sixties" (Lennon improvisation during *Let It Be*)
"Shanghai Surprise" (Harrison)
"Sharing You" (Goffin/King)
"Shazam" (Eddy/Hazelwood)
"Sheila" (Roe)
"She Is a Friend of Dorothy's" (Lennon)
"She'll Be Coming Around the Mountain" (traditional)
"Shelter in Your Love" (Harrison/Lee; no copyright registered)
"She Runs Them Around in Circles" (Lennon)
"Shimmy Shimmy" (Massey/Schubert)
"Shirley's Wild Accordion" (aka "Accordion [Wild]") (Evans/Wall?)
"Shoo-Be-Doo-Be-Doo-Da-Day" (?) (speculative title of unreleased Ringo song)
"Short Fat Fanny" (Williams)
"A Shot of Rhythm and Blues" (Thompson)
"Shout!" (Isley/Isley/Isley)
"Side by Side" (Wood)

"Singing the Blues" (Endsley)
"Sirens" (Lynne)
"Sitting at the Piano" (McCartney?)
"So How Come No One Loves Me" (Bryant/Bryant)
"Soldier of Love" (Cason/Moon)
"Some Kind of Wonderful" (unreleased Ringo title?)
"Some Other Guy" (Leiber/Stoller/Barrett)
"Someone Nice Like You" (Lennon/McCartney)
   (*Let It Be* outtake)
"Song to Woody" (Dylan)
"Sooty Goes to Hawaii" (Harrison)
"Sound Stage of Mind" (Harrison)
"Sour Milk Sea" (Harrison)
"St. Louis Blues" (Handy)
"Stand by Me" (King/Leiber/Stoller)
"Stay" (Williams)
"Step Inside Love" (Lennon/McCartney)
"Stop in the Name of Love" (Holland/Dozier/Holland)
"Storm" (McCartney)
"Sunshine Sometime" (McCartney)
"Suzy Parker" (Lennon/McCartney/Harrison/Starkey)
"Sweet Little Sixteen" (Berry)
"Take Her Back Jack" (McCartney)
"Take Me as I Am (Or Let Me Go)" (Bryant)
"Take Your Time" (Petty/Holly)
"Tandoori Chicken" (Harrison/Spector)
"Tea for Two" (Youmans/Caesar) (instrumental
   during "Let It Be")
"Tears of the World" (Harrison)
"Teddy Boy" (McCartney)
   (Beatles version; *Let It Be* outtake)
"Tell Me True" (Howard)
"Tennessee" (Perkins)
"Tennessee" (Lennon) (completely different from the
   Perkins song)
"Tequila" (Rio)
"Thank You Guru Dev" (aka "Indian Rope Trick" or
   "Spiritual Regeneration" (Lennon/McCartney?)
"That'll Be the Day" (Allison/Holly/Petty)
"That Means a Lot" (Lennon/McCartney)
"That's All Right (Mama)" (Crudup)
"That's When Your Heartaches Begin"
   (Raskin/Brown/Fisher)
"Theme from 'Hill Street Blues'" (Post)
"There Is a Green Hill" (traditional?)
"There Once Was a Beautiful Girl" (?) (*Let It Be* outtake)
"Thinking of Linking" (Lennon/McCartney)
"Think It Over" (Holly/Allison/Petty)
"The Third Man Theme" (Karas)
"Thirty Days" (Berry)
"This Old Hammer" (or "Take This Hammer")
   (traditional)
"Those Were the Days" (Raskin)
"Three Coins in the Fountain" (Styne/Cahn)
"Tie Me Kangaroo Down, Sport" (Harris)
"Time Is Right" (Jones)
"Tip of My Tongue" (Lennon/McCartney)
"Tippi Tippi Toes" (McCartney)

"Tomorrow" (McCartney) (instrumental version)
"Tomorrow Never Comes" (?) (very brief bit during
   Let It Be)
"Too Bad About Sorrows" (Lennon/McCartney)
"Too Much Monkey Business" (Berry)
"Tracks of My Tears" (Robinson/Moore/Tarplin)
"Tragedy" (Burch/Nelson)
"Turkey in the Straw" (traditional)
"Tutti Frutti" (Penniman/LaBostrie/Lubin)
"Twas a Night Like Ethel Merman" (Lennon; poem)
"Twelve-Bar Bali" (Harrison)
"12-Bar Original"
   ((Lennon/McCartney/Harrison/Starkey)
"Twice in a Lifetime" (McCartney)
"The Unbelievable Experience" (McCartney)
"Unchained Melody" (North/Zaret)
"The Unicorn" (Leitch)
"Vacation Time" (Berry) (listed as "Real Case Has Just
   Begun")
"Vatican P2 Blues" (Harrison)
"Wake Up in the Morning" (Lennon/McCartney? *Let It
   Be* outtake; also listed as "Because I Love You")
"Waking Up" (Nilsson/Starkey?)
"The Walk" (McCracklin/Garlic)
"Walking in the Meadow" (McCartney)
"The Walrus and the Carpenter" (poem by Lewis Carroll,
   ne Charles Lutwidge Dodgson; music by Leitch)
"Waltzing Matilda" (traditional)
"Watching Rainbows" (Lennon)
"Watching the River Flow" (Dylan)
"Watch Your Step" (Nadel)
"Waterspout" (McCartney)
"Weep for Love" (Laine)
"Well . . . All Right" (Holly/Allison/Petty/Mauldin)
"We're Gonna Move" (Presley/Matson)
"What'd I Say" (Charles)
"What Do You Want to Make Those Eyes at Me For?"
   (McCarthy/Johnson/Monaco; new piano part by
   John Lane, a pseudonym for Joe Levin)
"What Kind of Fool Am I?" (Bricusse/Newley)
"Whatever Happened to . . ." (Lennon)
"What's the New Mary Jane" (Lennon/McCartney)
"When a Boy Meets a Girl" (Lennon)
"When Irish Eyes Are Smiling" (traditional)
"When the Wind Is Blowing" (McCartney)
"Where Are You Going?" (Starkey/Lawrie)
"Where Have You Been All My Life?" (Mann/Weil)
"Whiskey and Soda" (Ringo outtake from Moman
   sessions?)
"Whole Lotta Love" (Page/Plant/Jones/Bonham)
"Whole Lotta Shakin' Goin' On" (Williams/David)
"Wide Prairie" (McCartney)
"Wildcat" (Venuti/Lang)
"Wild Shining Stars" (unreleased 1977 Ringo recording)
"Winston's Walk" (Lennon/McCartney)
"Woman" (McCartney under pseudonym "Bernard Webb")
"Won't You Please Say Goodbye" (?) (*Let It Be* outtake)
"Words of Love" (Holly)

"The World Is Waiting for the Sunrise"
   (Lockhart/Seitz)
"The Worst Is Over" (Lennon)
"Yakety Yak" (Leiber/Stoller)
"Years Roll Along" (Lennon/McCartney)
"You Are My Sunshine" (Davis/Mitchell)
"You'll Know What to Do" (Harrison)
"You Know I'll Get You Baby" (McCartney)
"Young Blood" (Leiber/Stoller/Pomus)
"Young Love" (Joyner/Cartey)

"(You're So Square) Baby I Don't Care"
   (Leiber/Stoller)
"Your True Love" (Perkins)
"You Saved My Soul (with Your True Love)" (Lennon)
"You Send Me" (Cooke)
"You've Got Me Thinking" (Lomax) (*Let It Be* outtake)
"You've Gotta Stay" (Harrison/Woodall)
"You Win Again" (Williams) ("Let It Be" outtake)
"Yvonne" (McCartney)

Appendix A:
The Beatles as Supporting Players

The Beatles wrote a number of songs that they never recorded commercially themselves but that were recorded by other artists. Twenty of these given-away songs (preceded by an * below) were included on an album titled *The Songs Lennon and McCartney Gave Away* (U.K. Apr 18, 1979 EMI NUT 18). The Beatles also produced and/or performed on many recordings by other artists.

The songs listed below are in chronological order by release date, like the "Discography" sections, and include the name of the Beatle composer in parentheses (where appropriate), followed by the name of the artist who recorded the song, Beatles musical or production credit and the dates of the record's release in the U.S. and U.K. For Lennon/McCartney compositions, the initial of the one who actually wrote the song is listed in parentheses after the composer's name (J for John, P for Paul). The Beatles often performed their guest roles under pseudonyms (John billing himself as "Dr. Winston O'Boogie," for example), and these names are also noted. Some of the entries show ex-Beatles supporting other ex- Beatles. While these releases also appear in the main sections of this book, they are included here to acknowledge these supporting roles and credits.

*"I'll Be on My Way" (Lennon/McCartney) (P); Billy J. Kramer with The Dakotas; released U.K. Apr 26, 1963; U.S. Jun 10, 1963.

*"Bad to Me" (Lennon/McCartney) (J); Billy J. Kramer with The Dakotas; released U.K. Jul 27, 1963; U.S. Sep 23, 1963.

*"Tip of My Tongue" (Lennon/McCartney) (P); Tommy Quickly; released U.K. only Jul 30, 1963.

*"Hello Little Girl" (Lennon/McCartney) (J); The Fourmost; released U.K. Aug 30, 1963; U.S. Nov 15, 1963.

*"Love of the Loved" (Lennon/McCartney) (P); Cilla Black; released U.K. only Sep 27, 1963.

*"I'll Keep You Satisfied" (Lennon/McCartney) (P); Billy J. Kramer with The Dakotas; released U.K. Nov 1, 1963; U.S. Nov 11, 1963.

*"I'm in Love" (Lennon/McCartney) (J); The Fourmost; released U.K. Nov 15, 1963; U.S. Feb 10, 1964.

*"A World Without Love" (Lennon/McCartney) (P); Peter & Gordon; released U.K. Feb 28, 1964; U.S. Apr 27, 1964 (also see live version, Jul 24, 1964).

*"One and One Is Two" (Lennon/McCartney) (P); The Strangers with Mike Shannon; released U.K. only May 8, 1964.

*"Nobody I Know" (Lennon/McCartney) (P); Peter & Gordon; released U.K. May 29, 1964; U.S. Jun 15, 1964.

*"Like Dreamers Do" (Lennon/McCartney) (P); The Applejacks; released U.K. Jun 5, 1964; U.S. Jul 6, 1964.

*"From a Window" (Lennon/McCartney) (P); Billy J. Kramer with The Dakotas; released U.K. Jul 17, 1964; U.S. Aug 12, 1964.

"A World Without Love" (Lennon/McCartney) (P); Peter & Gordon (live version on LP *Tribute to Michael Holiday*); U.K. only Jul 24, 1964.

*"It's for You" (Lennon/McCartney) (J/P; Paul: piano); Cilla Black; released U.K. Jul 31, 1964; U.S. Aug 17, 1964.

*"I Don't Want to See You Again" (Lennon/McCartney) (P); Peter & Gordon; released U.K. Sep 11, 1964; U.S. Sep 21, 1964.

"It's You"; Alma Cogan (Paul: tambourine); released U.K. only Sep 30, 1964.

"America"; Rory Storm & The Hurricanes (Ringo: backing vocals); released U.K. only Nov 13, 1964.

*"That Means a Lot" (Lennon/McCartney) (P); P.J. Proby; released U.S. Jul 5, 1965; U.K. Sep 17, 1965.

"You've Got to Hide Your Love Away" (Lennon/McCartney) (J); The Silkie; (John/Paul: producers); (Paul: guitar; George: tambourine); released U.K. Sep 10, 1965; U.S. Sep 20, 1965.

*"Woman" (McCartney [billed as "Bernard Webb"]); Peter & Gordon; released U.S. Jan 10, 1966; U.K. Feb 11, 1966.

"Got to Get You into My Life" (Lennon/McCartney) (P); Cliff Bennett & The Rebel Rousers (Paul: co-producer); released U.K. Aug 5, 1966; U.S. Aug 29, 1966.

"Mellow Yellow"; Donovan (Paul: vocal); released U.S. Oct 24, 1966; U.K. Feb 1967.

"From Head to Toe"; The Escorts (Paul: tambourine); released U.K. only Nov 18, 1966.

"Love in the Open Air"/"Theme From *The Family Way*" (McCartney); The George Martin Orchestra; released U.K. Dec 23, 1966; A side only, U.S. Apr 24, 1967.

Soundtrack LP *The Family Way* (McCartney); The George Martin Orchestra; released U.K. Jan 6, 1967; U.S. Jun 12, 1967.

*"Step Inside Love" (Lennon/McCartney) (P); Cilla Black; released U.S. May 6, 1967; U.K. May 8, 1968.

"We Love You"; The Rolling Stones (John/Paul: vocals); released U.K. Aug 18, 1967; U.S. Aug 28, 1967.

"Vegetables"; The Beach Boys (Paul: munching sounds; released U.S. Sep 18, 1967; U.K. Nov 20, 1967.

*"Cat Call" (aka "Catswalk") (McCartney); The Chris Barber Band; released U.K. only Oct 20, 1967.

"Dear Delilah"; Grapefruit (Paul and John: producers); U.K. Jan 19, 1968.

"And the Sun Will Shine"; Paul Jones (Paul: drums); released U.K. only Mar 8, 1968.

LP McGough and McGear; Roger McGough and Mike McGear (Paul: producer); released U.K. only May 17, 1968.

"Sour Milk Sea" (Harrison)/"The Eagle Laughs at You" (George: producer); Jackie Lomax; released U.S. Aug 26, 1968; U.K. Sep 6, 1968.

"Thingumybob" (Lennon/McCartney) (P);/"Yellow Submarine" (Lennon/McCartney) (P) (Paul: producer); John Foster & Songs Ltd. Black Dyke Mills Band; released U.S. Aug 26, 1968; U.K. Sep 6, 1968.

"Those Were the Days"/"Turn Turn Turn"; Mary Hopkin (Paul: producer); released U.S. Aug 26, 1968; U.K. Aug 30, 1968.

"I'm the Urban Spaceman"; Bonzo Dog Band (Paul [as "Apollo C. Vermouth"]: producer); released U.K. Oct 11, 1968; U.S. Dec 18, 1968.

LP Wonderwall Music (Harrison); George Harrison (Ringo: drums); released U.K. Nov 1, 1968; U.S. Dec 2, 1968 (film score).

"Atlantis"; Donovan (Paul: tambourine, vocals); released U.K. only Nov 22, 1968.

"Carolina in My Mind"; James Taylor (Paul: bass; George: harmony vocals); on LP James Taylor; released U.K. Dec 6, 1968; U.S. Feb 17, 1969.

"Badge" (Harrison/Clapton); Cream on LP Goodbye (George [as "L'Angelo Misterioso"]: guitar); released U.S. Feb 5, 1969; U.K. Feb 28, 1969.

"Rosetta" The Fourmost (Paul: producer); released U.K. only Feb 21, 1969.

LP Post Card; Mary Hopkin (Paul: producer); released U.K. Feb 21, 1969; U.S. Mar 3, 1969.

LP Is This What You Want? Jackie Lomax (George: producer; guitar: Paul; Ringo: drums); released U.K. Mar 21, 1969; U.S. May 19, 1969.

"Goodbye" (Lennon/McCartney) (P)/"Sparrow"; Mary Hopkin (Paul: producer); released U.K. Mar 28, 1969; U.S. Apr 7, 1969.

"Thumbin' a Ride"; Jackie Lomax (Paul: producer); released U.S. Jun 2, 1969; U.K. Feb 6, 1970.

"My Dark Hour"; The Steve Miller Band (Paul [as "Paul Ramon"]): bass, drums, vocals); U.S. Jun 16, 1969; U.K. Jul 18, 1969.

"Charity Bubbles"/"Goose"; Scaffold (Paul: lead guitar); released U.K. only Jun 27, 1969.

"That's the Way God Planned It"/"What About You?" Billy Preston (George: producer); released U.K. Jun 27, 1969; U.S. Jul 7, 1969.

*"Penina" (McCartney); Carlos Mendes; released Portugal only Jul 18, 1969.

"Hare Krishna Mantra"/"Prayer to the Spiritual Masters"; Radha Krishna Temple of London (George: producer); released U.S. Aug 22, 1969; U.K. Aug 29, 1969.

LP That's the Way God Planned It; Billy Preston (George: producer); released U.K. Aug 22, 1969; U.S. Sep 10, 1969.

"Never Tell Your Mother She's Out of Tune"; Jack Bruce on LP Songs for a Tailor (George [as "L'Angelo Misterioso"]: guitar); released U.K. Aug 29, 1969; U.S. Oct 6, 1969.

"Cold Turkey" (Lennon)/"Don't Worry Kyoko" (studio version); John Lennon/Yoko Ono and Plastic Ono Band (Ringo: drums; George: guitar); U.S. Oct 20, 1969; U.K. Oct 24, 1969.

"Come and Get It" (McCartney); Badfinger (Paul: producer); released U.K. Dec 5, 1969; U.S. Jan 12, 1970.

"All That I've Got"; Billy Preston (George: producer); released U.K. Jan 30, 1970; U.S. Feb 16, 1970.

"How the Web Was Woven"; Jackie Lomax (George: producer); U.K. Feb 6, 1970; U.S. Mar 9, 1970.

"Instant Karma" (Lennon) (George: guitar)/"Who Has Seen the Wind?" John Lennon/Yoko Ono (John: producer B side); released U.K. Feb 6, 1970; U.S. Feb 20, 1970.

"Ain't That Cute" (Harrison/Troy)/"Vaya Con Dios"; Doris Troy; (George: producer; guitar on B side) released U.K. Feb 13, 1970; U.S. Mar 16, 1970.

"Govinda"/"Govinda Jai Jai"; The Radha Krishna Temple of London (George: producer); released U.K. Mar 6, 1970; U.S. Mar 24, 1970.

LP Leon Russell; Leon Russell (George: guitar; Ringo: drums); released U.S. Mar 23, 1970; U.K. Apr 24, 1970.

"Star Dust"; Ringo on LP Sentimental Journey (Paul: arrangement); released U.K. Mar 27, 1970; U.S. Apr 24, 1970.

LP Delaney and Bonnie on Tour; Delaney and Bonnie Bramlett (George: guitar); released U.S. Apr 7, 1970; U.K. Jun 19, 1970.

"Que Sera Sera"/"Fields of St. Etienne"; Mary Hopkin (Paul: producer); harmony vocal on B side; released U.S. Jun 15, 1970; U.K. Nov 24, 1972.

"Jacob's Ladder" (adaptation: Harrison/Troy)/"Get Back" (Lennon/McCartney) (P); Doris Troy (George: arrangement A side; guitar B side); released U.K. Aug 28, 1970; U.S. Sep 21, 1970.

"My Sweet Lord" (Harrison)/"Long as I Got My Baby"; Billy Preston (George/Preston: producers); released U.K. only Sep 4, 1970.

"Gonna Get My Baby Back" (Harrison/Troy/Starkey, "You Give Me Joy Joy" (Harrison/Starkey/Troy/Stills), "Give Me Back My Dynamite" (Harrison/Troy); Doris

Troy on LP *Doris Troy* (George: guitar; Ringo: drums throughout LP); released U.K. Sep 11, 1970; U.S. Nov 9, 1970.

"Sing One for the Lord" (Harrison/Preston); Billy Preston on LP *Encouraging Words* (George/Preston: LP producers); released U.K. Sep 11, 1970; U.S. Nov 9, 1970.

"Tell the Truth"; Derek and The Dominoes (George: guitar); released U.S. Sep 14, 1970. Released Apr 18, 1988 in U.S. and U.K. on Eric Clapton's *Crossroads* boxed set.

"I'm Your Spiritual Breadman"; Ashton, Gardner and Dyke on LP *The Worst of Ashton, Gardner and Dyke* (U.S. title: *Ashton, Gardner and Dyke*) (George [as "George O'Hara Smith"]: guitar); released U.S. Sep 28, 1970; U.K. Feb, 5, 1971.

"To a Flame" and "We Are Not Helpless"; Stephen Stills on LP *Stephen Stills* (Ringo [as "Richie"]: drums); released U.S. Nov 23, 1970; U.K. Nov 27, 1970.

LP *All Things Must Pass*; George Harrison (Ringo: drums); released U.S. Nov 27, 1970; U.K. Nov 30, 1970.

LP *John Lennon/Plastic Ono Band*; John Lennon/Plastic Ono Band (John/Ono/Spector: co-producers; Ringo: drums); released U.S. and U.K. Dec 11, 1970.

LP *Yoko Ono/Plastic Ono Band*; Yoko Ono/Plastic Ono Band (John: guitar; John/Ono: producers); released U.K. and U.S. Dec 11, 1970.

"Open Your Box" (aka "Hirake"); Yoko Ono (John/Ono: producers); released U.K. Mar 12, 1971; U.S. Sep 20, 1971.

"It Don't Come Easy"/"Early 1970"; Ringo Starr (George: producer; A side, guitar); released U.K. Apr 9, 1971; U.S. Apr 16, 1971.

"Try Some Buy Some" (Harrison)/"Tandoori Chicken" (Harrison/Spector); Ronnie Spector (George/Spector: producers); released U.K. Apr 16, 1971; U.S. Apr 19, 1971.

LP *The Radha Krishna Temple*; The Radha Krishna Temple (George: producer); released U.S. May 21, 1971; U.K. May 28, 1971.

"Stand for Our Rights"/"I Can't See the Reason"; Gary Wright (George: guitar); U.K. May 28, 1971; U.S. Nov 1, 1971.

"God Save Us" (Lennon/Ono); Bill Elliot and The Elastic Oz Band (John/Yoko/Evans/Spector: producers); released U.S. Jul 7, 1971; U.K. Jul 16, 1971.

"I Ain't Superstitious"; Howlin' Wolf on LP *The London Howlin' Wolf Sessions* (Ringo [as "Richie"]: drums); released U.S. Jul 26, 1971; U.K. Aug 20, 1971.

"Joi Bangla-Oh Bhaugowan"/"Raga Mishra"; Ravi Shankar (George: producer); released U.S. Aug 9, 1971; U.K. Aug 27, 1971.

LP *Imagine*; John Lennon (George: dobro, guitars); released U.S. Sep 9, 1971; U.K. Oct 8, 1971.

LP *Fly*; Yoko Ono/Plastic Ono Band (John/Yoko: producers; John: guitar, piano, organ; Ringo: drums); U.K. Sep 20, 1971; U.K. Dec 3, 1971.

"Ghetto Woman," "Wet Hayshark," "Part-Time Love"; B.B. King on LP *B.B. King in London* (Ringo: drums); released U.S. Oct 11, 1971; U.K. Nov 19, 1971.

LP *Footprint*; Gary Wright (George [as "George O'Hara"]: guitar); released U.S. Nov 1, 1971; U.K. Jan 21, 1972.

LP *I Wrote a Simple Song*; Billy Preston (George [as "George H."]: lead guitar); released U.S. Nov 8, 1971; U.K. Jan 14, 1972.

"Day After Day"; Badfinger (George: producer); released U.S. Nov 10, 1971; U.K. Jan 14, 1972.

Soundtrack LP *Raga*; Ravi Shankar (George: producer); released U.S. only Dec 7, 1971.

"I'd Die Babe," "Name of the Game," "Suitcase"; Badfinger on LP *Straight Up* (George: producer); released U.S. Dec 13, 1971; U.K. Feb 11, 1972.

"The Holdup" (Version I) (Harrison/Bromberg); David Bromberg on LP *David Bromberg*; released U.S. Feb 16, 1972; U.K. Jun 2, 1972.

"Oo Wee Baby, I Love You"; Bobby Hatfield (Ringo: drums); released U.S. Mar 1, 1972; U.K. Mar 10, 1972.

"Back Off Boogaloo"/"Blindman"; Ringo Starr (George: producer; A side, guitar); released U.K. Mar 17, 1972; U.S. Mar 20, 1972.

"Bored as Butterscotch" (P. McCartney [as "Friend"]/McGear/McGough); Mike McGear on LP *Woman*; released U.K. only Apr 21, 1972.

LP *The Pope Smokes Dope*; David Peel and The Lower East Side Band (John/Yoko: producers); released U.S. only Apr 28, 1972.

"The Lodger," "Alright"; Peter Frampton on LP *Wind of Change* (Ringo: drums); released U.K. May 26, 1972; U.S. Jul 10, 1972.

"Cold Turkey" (Lennon); "Don't Worry Kyoko" (live versions); John/Ono and Plastic Ono Band with Elephant's Memory on LP *Some Time in New York City*; (George [as "George Harrisong"]: guitar); released U.S. Jun 12, 1972; U.K. Sep 15, 1972.

LP *Bobby Keys*; Bobby Keys (George: guitar; Ringo: drums); released U.K. only Jul 7, 1972.

"You're Breaking My Heart" (George [as "George Harrysong"]: guitar), "Take 54," "Spaceman," "At My Front Door," "Ambush," "The Most Beautiful World in the World" (Ringo [as "Richie Snare"]: drums; Harry Nilsson on LP *Son of Schmilsson*; released U.S. Jul 10, 1972; U.K. Jul 28, 1972.

LP *Elephant's Memory*; Elephant's Memory (John/Yoko: producers; John: guitar, keyboards, percussion, vocals); released U.S. Sep 18, 1972; U.K. Nov 10, 1972.

"Sweet Music," "Another Thought"; Lon and Derrek Van Eaton on LP *Brother* (George: producer; Ringo: drums); released U.S. Sep 22, 1972; U.K. Feb 9, 1973.

"Night Owl"; Carly Simon on LP *No Secrets* (Paul: vocals); released U.S. Nov 3, 1972; U.K. Dec 15, 1972.

"Lovely Lady," "Nothin' Gonna Get You Down" and "Doing the Right Thing" (George: guitar); "If I Had Time" (George: vocal); Rudy Romero on LP *To the World*; released U.S. and U.K. Dec 1, 1972.

LP *Approximately Infinite Universe*; Yoko Ono/Plastic Ono Band/Elephant's Memory (John [as "Joel Nohnn"]: guitar; John/Yoko: producers); released U.S. Jan 8, 1973; U.K. Feb 16, 1973.

LP *In Concert 1972*; Ravi Shankar and Ali Akbar Khan (George/Hussein/McDonald: producers); released U.S. Jan 22, 1973; U.K. Apr 13, 1973.

LP *The Tin Man Was a Dreamer*; Nicky Hopkins (George [as "George O'Hara"]: guitar); released U.S. Apr 23, 1973; U.K. Jul 27, 1973.

LP *Living in the Material World"*; George Harrison (Ringo: drums); released U.S. May 30, 1973; U.K. Jun 22, 1973.

"Basketball Jones Featuring Tyrone Shoelaces"; Cheech and Chong (George: guitar); released U.S. Aug 20, 1973; U.K. Sep 28, 1973.

"Badge" (live version) (Harrison/Clapton); Eric Clapton on LP *Eric Clapton's Rainbow Concert*; released U.S. Sep 10, 1973; U.K. Oct 26, 1973.

"Photograph" (Harrison/Starkey)/"Down and Out"; Ringo Starr (George: guitar, vocals A side; Harrison/Perry: producers B side); released U.S. Sep 24, 1973; U.K. Oct 19, 1973.

"If You've Got Love"; Dave Mason on LP *It's Like You Never Left* (George [as "Son of Harry"]: guitar); released U.S. Oct 29, 1973; U.K. Nov 2, 1973.

LP *Ringo*; Ringo Starr: "I'm the Greatest" (Lennon) (John: piano, vocal; George: guitar); "Six O'Clock" (P. and L. McCartney) (Paul: piano, synthesizer, vocals, string and flute arrangement); "Sunshine Life for Me" (Harrison) (George: guitar, vocal); "You and Me (Babe)" (Harrison/Evans) (George: guitars); "You're Sixteen" (Paul: mouth and sax solo); released U.S. Nov 2, 1973; U.K. Nov 23, 1973.

"So Sad" (Harrison); Alvin Lee and Mylon Lefevre on LP *On the Road to Freedom*; released U.K. Nov 2, 1973; U.S. Dec 7, 1973.

LP *Feeling the Space*; Yoko Ono/Plastic Ono Band (John [as "John O'Cean"]: guitar, vocal); released U.S. Nov 2, 1973; U.K. Nov 16, 1973.

"Rock and Roller" (Starkey/Lawrie); Billy Lawrie; released U.K. only Nov 9, 1973.

"The Holdup" (Version II) (Harrison/Bromberg); David Bromberg on LP *Wanted—Dead or Alive*; released U.S. only Jan 7, 1974.

"Daybreak" (George: cow bell; Ringo: drums); "At My Front Door" (Ringo: drums); Harry Nilsson on LP *Son of Dracula* and on a single; released U.S. (on single) Mar 25, 1974; U.K. (on LP) May 24, 1974; album also contains some of Ringo's dialogue.

"Liverpool Lou"/"Ten Years After on Strawberry Jam" (both P. and L. McCartney); Scaffold (Paul: producer); released U.K. May 24, 1974; U.S. Jul 29, 1974.

LP *Land's End*; Jimmy Webb (Ringo: drums); released U.S. Jun 3, 1974; U.K. Jul 5, 1974.

"God Bless California"; Thornton Fradkin and Ungar and The Big Band (Paul: bass, vocals); released U.S. only Jun 17, 1974; also released Jul 1974 on U.S. on LP *Pass on This Side*.

"Rock 'n' Roll Music Now"/"Let It All Fall Down"; James Taylor (Paul: vocals); released U.K. Jun 28, 1974; U.S. Jul 2, 1974.

"Fourth of July" (McCartney); John Christie; released U.K. Jun 28, 1974; U.S. Jul 1, 1974.

"Mucho Mungo" (Lennon); Harry Nilsson on LP *Pussy Cats* (John: LP producer; Ringo: drums throughout LP); released U.S. Aug 19, 1974; U.K. Aug 30, 1974.

"Change"; "Never Say Goodbye" (Paul: synthesizer); "Star Song" (Paul: vocals); Adam Faith; released U.S. Sep 2, 1974; U.K. Sep 20, 1974.

"Leave It" (McCartney)/"Sweet Baby" (McCartney/McGear); Mike McGear (Paul: producer); released U.K. Sep 6, 1974; U.S. Oct 28, 1974.

"I Am Missing You"/"Lust"; Ravi Shankar Family and Friends (George: producer); released U.K. Sep 13, 1974; U.S. Nov 6, 1974.

LP *The Place I Love*; Splinter (George: producer; and [as "Hari Georgeson"]: guitars, bass, dobro, mandolin; [as "P. Roducer"]: harmonium and synthesizer; [as "Jai Raj Harisein"]: percussion); released U.K. Sep 20, 1974; U.S. Sep 25, 1974.

LP *Shankar Family and Friends*; Ravi Shankar Family and Friends (George: producer; auto harp and [as "Hari Georgeson"]: guitars; Ringo: drums); released U.K. Sep 20, 1974; U.S. Oct 7, 1974.

"What Do We Really Know" (McCartney); "The Casket" (McCartney/McGough); the following by McCartney/McGear: "Norton," "Have You Got Problems," "Rainbow Lady," "Simply Love You," "Givin' Grease a Ride," "The Man Who Found God on the Moon"; Mike McGear on LP *McGear* (Paul: producer); released U.K. Sep 27, 1974; U.S. Oct 14, 1974.

"Mine for Me" (McCartney); Rod Stewart on LP *Smiler*; released U.K. Sep 27, 1974; U.S. Oct 7, 1974.

"Let's Love" (McCartney); Peggy Lee (Paul: producer); released U.S. Oct 1, 1974; U.K. Oct 25, 1974.

"It's All Down to Goodnight Vienna" (Lennon) (John: piano); "All by Myself" (John: guitar); "Only You" (John: acoustic guitar); Ringo Starr on LP *Goodnight Vienna*; released U.K. Nov 15, 1974; U.S. Nov 18, 1974.

"Lucy in the Sky with Diamonds" (Lennon/McCartney) (J)/"One Day at a Time"; Elton John (John [as "Dr. Winston O'Boogie"]: guitar both sides; vocals A side); released U.K. Nov 15, 1974; U.S. Nov 18, 1974.

"Rock 'n' Roll People" (Lennon) (also see live version Feb 9, 1976); Johnny Winter on LP *John Dawson Winter III*; released U.S. Nov 25, 1974; U.K. Feb 7, 1975.

"So Sad"; "Ding Dong, Ding Dong"; George Harrison on LP *Dark Horse* (Ringo: drums); released U.S. Dec 9, 1974; U.K. Dec 20, 1974.

LP *In the Presence of the Lord*; All Occasion Brass Band (Ringo: unspecified contribution); released U.S. 1974.

"Sea Breezes"/"Givin' Grease a Ride" Mike McGear (Paul: producer); released U.K. only Feb 7, 1975.

"Step Lightly" (Starkey); David Hentschel on LP *Sta*rtling Music* (Ringo [as "R.S."]: finger clicks); released U.S. Feb 17, 1975; U.K. Apr 18, 1975.

"Fame" (Lennon/Bowie/Alomar; John: guitar, backing vocal) (studio version; also see live version Sep 25, 1978); "Across the Universe" (Lennon/McCartney) (John: guitar); David Bowie on LP *Young Americans*; released U.S. Mar 10, 1975; U.K. Mar 28, 1975. Several remixes of "Fame" were issued in 1990, one on the *Pretty Woman* soundtrack album, and others on the CD single *Fame 90* in the U.S. The single was included as a bonus with Rykodisc's 1991 edition of Bowie's CD *Young Americans*.

"Kojak Columbo"; Harry Nilsson (Ringo: drums); released U.S. Mar 10, 1975; U.K. Mar 28, 1975.

"Solid Gold" (Ringo: announcer); "Together" (Ringo: drums; rap); Keith Moon on LP *Two Sides of the Moon*; released U.S. Mar 17, 1975; U.K. May 23, 1975.

"Good for God"; Harry Nilsson on LP *Duit on Mon Dei* (Ringo: vocals); released U.S. Mar 21, 1975; U.K. Mar 28, 1975.

"More and More"; Carly Simon on LP *Playing Possum* (Ringo: drums); released U.S. Apr 21, 1975; U.K. Jun 6, 1975.

"As I Come of Age"; Stephen Stills on LP *Stills* (Ringo [as "English Ritchie"]: drums); released U.S. Jun 17, 1975; U.K. Jul 4, 1975.

"That's Life"; Billy Preston on LP *It's My Pleasure* (George [as "Hari Georgeson"]: guitar); released U.S. Jun 20, 1975; U.K. Jul 19, 1975.

"Dance the Do" (McCartney/McGear); Mike McGear (Paul: producer); released U.K. only July 4, 1975.

"Make Love Not War"; Peter Skellern on LP *Hard Times* (George: guitar); released U.K. only Sep 26, 1975.

"Lonely Man"; Splinter on LP *Harder to Live* (George/Scott: producers; George [as "Hari Georgeson"]: guitar); released U.S. Oct 6, 1975; U.K. Oct 24, 1975.

"Lumberjack Song"; Monty Python's Flying Circus (George [as "George 'Onothimagen' Harrison"]: producer); released U.K. only Nov 14, 1975.

"Simply Love You" (McCartney/Mike McGear)/"What Do We Really Know" (McCartney); Mike McGear (Paul: producer); released U.K. only Nov 14, 1975.

"Appolonia (Foxtrata)"; Tom Scott on LP *New York Connection* (George: slide guitar); released U.S. Dec 8, 1975; U.K. Apr 2, 1976.

LP *Hollywood Be Thy Name*; Dr. John (Ringo: Master of Ceremonies); released U.S. 1975.

LP *Ravi Shankar's Music Festival from India*; Ravi Shankar (George: producer); released U.S. Feb 6, 1976; U.K. Mar 19, 1976.

"Rock 'n' Roll People" (Lennon) (live version; also see studio version, Nov 25, 1974); Johnny Winter on LP *Johnny Winter Captured Live*; released U.S. Feb 9, 1976; U.K. Mar 12, 1976.

"Don't You Remember When"; Vera Lynn (Ringo: tambourine); released U.K. only Feb 20, 1976.

"Band of Steel" (Starkey) (Ringo: drums, vocals); "Good Days Are Rollin' In"; "Ramblin' Cocaine Blues" (Ringo: drums); Guthrie Thomas on LP *Lies and Alibies*; released U.S. only May 3, 1976.

"Wishing I Could" (George: vocal); "Direct Me" (George: slide guitar); Larry Hosford on LP *Crosswords*; released U.K. Jul 6, 1976; U.S. Aug 2, 1976.

"Zindy Lou"; "S.O.S."; Manhattan Transfer on LP *Coming Out* (Ringo: drums); released U.K. Aug 27, 1976; U.S. Aug 30, 1976.

medley: "It's So Easy"/"Listen to Me"/"I'm Lookin' for Someone to Love"; Denny Laine (Paul: producer, guitar, drums, piano, vocals); released U.K. Sep 3, 1976; U.S. Oct 4, 1976.

"Cookin' (in the Kitchen of Love)" (Lennon) (John: piano); "Pure Gold" (McCartney) (Paul: vocals); "I'll Still Love You" (Harrison); Ringo Starr on LP *Ringo's Rotogravure*; released U.K. Sep 17, 1976; U.S. Sep 27, 1976.

"Men's Room, L.A."; Kinky Friedman on LP *Lasso from El Paso* (Ringo: voice of Jesus); released U.S. Nov 5, 1976; U.K. Feb 25, 1977.

"A Thousand Miles Away"; Harry Nilsson on LP *That's the Way It Is* (Ringo: announcer); released U.S. and U.K. 1976.

"One of Those Days in England" (Part 1); Roy Harper (Paul: vocals); released U.K. Feb 4, 1977; U.S. Mar 21, 1977.

"Moondreams"/"Heartbeat"; Denny Laine (Paul: producer); released U.K. Apr 15, 1977; U.S. May 19, 1977.

"Good News"; Attitudes on LP *Good News* (Ringo: drums); released U.S. May 5, 1977; U.K. Jun 3, 1977.

LP *Holly Days*; Denny Laine (Paul: producer, drums, guitar, piano, vocals); released U.K. May 6, 1977; U.S. May 19, 1977.

"Giddy" (McCartney); Roger Daltrey on LP *One of the Boys* released U.K. May 13, 1977; U.S. Jun 16, 1977.

"Round and Round"/"I'll Bend for You"; Splinter (George: guitar); released U.S. only Sep 6, 1977.

"Born in Captivity"; "You Angel You"; The Alpha Band on LP *Spark in the Dark* (Ringo: drums); released U.S. only Sep 26, 1977.

LP *Two Man Band*; Splinter (George/Morgan: executive producers; George: guitar); released U.S. Oct 3, 1977; U.K. Oct 7, 1977.

"Have a Drink on Me"; "Ham 'n' Eggs"; Lonnie Donegan on LP *Puttin' on the Style* (Ringo: drums); released U.S. Jan 9, 1978; U.K. Jan 27, 1978.

"I Shall Be Released"; "Ending Jam"; The Band and Friends on LP *The Last Waltz* (Ringo: drums); released U.S. Apr 10, 1978; U.K. Apr 14, 1978.

"Tomorrow"; "Crowds of You" Kate Robbins (Paul: producer); released U.K. only Jun 30, 1978.

"The Last Time"; Daryl Hall and John Oates on LP *Along the Red Ledge* (George: guitar); released U.S. Aug 21, 1978; U.K. Sep 29, 1978.

"Fame" (live version) (Lennon/Bowie/Alomar); David Bowie on LP *Stage*; released U.S. and U.K. Sep 25, 1978.

"Always Look at the Bright Side of Life"; Monty Python on soundtrack LP *Monty Python's Life of Brian* (mixed by George and Phil MacDonald); released U.S. Oct 8, 1979; U.K. Nov 9, 1979.

"Get Well Soon"; Kevin Godley and Lol Creme on LP *Freeze Frame* (Paul: vocals); released U.K. Nov 30, 1979; U.S. Jan 21, 1980.

LP *Troublemaker*; Ian McLagan (Ringo: drums); released U.S. Dec 10, 1979; U.K. Feb 15, 1980.

"Old Dirt Road" (Lennon/Nilsson); "How Long Can Disco On" (Starkey/Nilsson); "I've Got It" (Ringo: drums on all three tracks); Harry Nilsson on LP *Flash Harry*; released U.S. and U.K. Sep 5, 1980.

"Send Me the Heart" (McCartney/Laine) (Paul: bass); "Weep for Love" (Paul/Linda McCartney: vocals); "I Would Only Smile" (by Wings); Denny Laine and Friends on LP *Japanese Tears*; released U.K. Dec 5, 1980; U.S. Aug 8, 1983.

"Walking on Thin Ice (for John)"/"It Happened" (John: guitar, keyboards, vocals; co-producer both sides; editing/remixing B side); Yoko Ono; released U.S. Feb 6, 1981; U.K. Feb 20, 1981.

"All Those Years Ago" (Harrison); George Harrison (Ringo: drums; Paul/Linda McCartney: vocals); released U.S. May 11, 1981; U.K. May 15, 1981.

LP *Somewhere in England*; George Harrison (Ringo: drums); released U.S. Jun 1, 1981; U.K. Jun 5, 1981.

"Walk a Thin Line"; Mick Fleetwood on LP *The Visitor* (George: guitars/vocals); released U.S. and U.K. Jun 30, 1981.

"Heart of Mine"; Bob Dylan on LP *Shot of Love* (Ringo: tom tom); released U.S. Aug 10, 1981; U.K. Aug 21, 1981.

LP *Stop and Smell the Roses*; Ringo Starr: "Private Property" (McCartney) (Paul: producer, bass, piano, vocals); "Attention" (McCartney) (Paul: producer, bass, piano, percussion); "Sure to Fall" (Paul: producer, bass, piano, vocals); "Wrack My Brain" (Harrison) (George: producer, vocals, guitar); "You Belong to Me" (George: producer, lead guitar); released U.S. Oct 27, 1981; U.K. Nov 20, 1981.

"Mineral Man"; Gary Brooker on LP *Lead Me to the Water* (George: guitar); released U.K. Mar 1, 1982; U.S. Aug 9, 1982.

"Take It Away" (McCartney); Paul McCartney on LP *Tug of War* (Ringo: drums); released U.S. and U.K. Apr 26, 1982.

"Maisie"; Laurence Juber on LP *Standard Time* (Paul: bass); released U.S. only Jul 9, 1982.

"Never Say Goodbye"; Yoko Ono on LP *It's Alright* (John: shout); released U.S. Nov 2, 1982; U.K. Nov 26, 1982.

LP *Pipes of Peace*; Paul McCartney (Ringo: drums); released U.K. Oct, 17, 1983; U.S. Oct 26, 1983.

"Paul McCartney's Theme from *The Honorary Consul*" (McCartney); John Williams; released U.K. only Dec 19, 1983.

LP *Like No Other*; Guthrie Thomas (Ringo: drums); released U.S. 1983.

"On the Wings of a Nightingale" (McCartney); The Everly Brothers (Paul: guitar; remix); released U.K. Aug 24, 1984; U.K. Oct 5, 1984.

LP *Give My Regards to Broad Street*; Paul McCartney (Ringo: drums); released U.S. and U.K. Oct 22, 1984.

"Celebration" (Harrison/Moran); Jimmy Helms (George: guitar)/"Freedom"; Billy Connolly and Christopher Tumming and The Singing Rebels band (George: guitar; Ringo: drums); released U.K. only May 31, 1985.

"California Calling"; The Beach Boys on LP *The Beach Boys* (Ringo: drums); released U.S. and U.K. Jun 10, 1985.

"Focus of Attention" (Harrison/Clement/Moran); Jimmy Helms on soundtrack LP *Water* (George: guitar); released U.K. only Jun 28, 1985. LP also includes "Freedom" and "Celebration."

"Sun City"; Artists United Against Apartheid (Ringo: drums); released U.S. and U.K. Nov 11, 1985.

"Talk Don't Bother Me"; Alvin Lee on LP *Detroit Diesel* (George: slide guitar); released U.S. only Aug 1986.

"Children of the Sky"; Mike Batt's concept LP *The Hunting of the Snark* (George: lead guitar); released U.K. only Nov 17, 1986 (also released as a single in U.K. Nov 7, 1986; recorded Jan 26, 1985).

"Back in the USSR" (live); The Beach Boys on mail-order album *Fourth of July: A Rockin' Celebration of America* (Ringo: drums); released U.S. only Dec 1986 (recorded live Jul 4, 1984).

CD *Tana Mana*; Ravi Shankar (George: autoharp; synthesizer); released U.S. Jun 1987; U.K. Feb 9, 1990.

LP *Duane Eddy*; Duane Eddy: "Rockestra Theme" (McCartney) (Paul: producer, bass, backing vocals); "Theme for Something Really Important" (George: slide guitar); "The Trembler" (George: slide guitar); released U.S. Jun 19, 1987; U.K. Oct 12, 1987. "Rockestra Theme" also released in U.K. as a single and in a McCartney/Bevans remix on a U.K. 12-inch single.

"When We Was Fab"; George Harrison on *Cloud Nine* (Ringo: drums); released U.S. and U.K. Nov 12, 1987.

LP set *Crossroads*; Eric Clapton: "Roll It Over" (George: guitar and vocals); released U.S. and U.K. Apr 18, 1988; also includes previously released "Tell the Truth" (George: guitar) and "Badge" (Harrison/Clapton) (George: guitar).

"Love's a State of Mind"; Sylvia Griffin (George: slide guitar); released U.K. only May 27, 1988.

"T-Shirt"; The Crickets (Paul: piano, backing vocals, producer); released U.S. Aug 29, 1988; U.K. Sep 5, 1988 (also released on LP Oct 1988).

"(I Don't Wanna) Hold Back"; Gary Wright on album *Who I Am* (George: slide guitar solo); released U.S. Sep 21, 1988; U.K. Dec 2, 1988.

"Children in Need"; Spirit of Play (Paul: bass; co-producer); released U.K. only Nov 1988.

"Oh Lord, Why Lord"; Jim Capaldi on LP *Some Come Running* (George: guitar); released U.S. Nov 1, 1988; U.K. Feb 13, 1989.

"Sweet Music" (George and Ringo: unspecified musical contribution; George: producer); "Get Happy" (Ringo: unspecified contribution); Derek Van Eaton on LP *Give a Little Love*; released U.S. only Dec 1988 by the Boy Scouts of America.

"A Love So Beautiful"; Roy Orbison on LP *Mystery Girl* (George: acoustic guitar); released U.K. Jan 30, 1989; U.S. Feb 1, 1989. Although he is not credited, George apparently contributed backing vocals on "You Got It" on this album, also released as a single.

"Pads, Paws and Claws" (McCartney/MacManus); "Veronica" (McCartney/MacManus; Paul: bass); ". . . This Town . . ." (Paul: bass); Elvis Costello on LP *Spike*; released U.S. and U.K. Feb 6, 1989.

"I Won't Back Down"; Tom Petty on LP *Full Moon Fever* (George: acoustic guitar; backing vocals); released U.S. Apr 24, 1989; U.K. Jun 26, 1989 (also released as a single).

"Leave a Light On" (George: slide guitar, including solo); "Deep Deep Ocean" (George: 6-string bass; 12-string guitar); Belinda Carlisle on LP *Runaway Horses*; released U.S. Oct 9, 1989; U.K. Oct 23, 1989; first title also released as a single Oct 2, 1989 in U.S. and Oct 16, 1989 in U.K.

"Run So Far" (Harrison); Eric Clapton on LP *Journeyman* (George: guitar; vocal harmony); released U.K. Nov 8, 1989; U.S. Nov 9, 1989.

"That Kind of Woman" (Harrison); Gary Moore on LP *Still Got the Blues* (George: slide guitar; rhythm guitar; backing vocals); released U.K. Mar 26, 1990; U.S. Jun 11, 1990.

"Take Away the Sadness"; Jim Horn on LP *Work It Out* (George: guitar); released U.S. only Mar 1990.

"While My Guitar Gently Weeps" (Harrison); Jeff Healey Band on LP *Hell to Pay* (George: backing vocals; acoustic guitar); released U.S. May 25, 1990; U.K. May 29, 1990.

"Every Little Thing" (not The Beatles song); Jeff Lynne (George: acoustic guitar; backing vocals); released U.S. and U.K. Jun 11, 1990 (also released on LP *Armchair Theatre*).

"Lift Me Up," "September Song," "Stormy Weather" (George: slide guitar; acoustic guitar; also harmony and backing vocals on last title); Jeff Lynne on LP *Armchair Theatre*, released U.S. Jun 12, 1990; U.K. Jul 2, 1990 (album also contains previously released "Every Little Thing" with George on acoustic guitar and backing vocals).

"That Kind of Woman" (Harrison); Eric Clapton on LP *Nobody's Child: Romanian Angel Appeal* album; released U.S. and U.K. Jul 24, 1990.

"Under the Red Sky"; Bob Dylan on LP *Under the Red Sky* (George: slide guitar); released U.S. Sep 11, 1990; U.K. Sep 17, 1990.

"Lu Le La"; Vicki Brown on album *About Love and Life* (George: slide guitar); released continental Europe only Dec 1990.

"Hurdy Gurdy Man" (Leitch/Harrison). Donovan live version on CD *The Classics Live*; released U.S. and U.K. 1990. Donovan restored a verse on this live version, written by George but omitted from Donovan's original 1968 studio recording.

Promo 5-inch CD single "Good Golly Miss Molly"; Little Richard (Ringo: drums); issued in U.S. in early 1991; recording is a completely new version of Little Richard's classic from the *King Ralph* film soundtrack and also features John Goodman's performance of the same song. There was no official release of the recording.

"Walkin' Nerve" (Ringo: drums); "Bein' Angry" (Ringo: vocals); Nils Lofgren on album *Silver Lining*; released U.S. Mar 6, 1991; U.K. Apr 22, 1991. Ringo also appears in Lofgren's "Valentine" video but does not play on that track.

"If Not for You"; Bob Dylan on boxed set *The Bootleg Series Volumes 1–3 [Rare and Unreleased] 1961–1991* (George: slide guitar); released U.S. and U.K. Mar 26, 1991 (recorded May 1, 1970).

LP *Mighty Like a Rose*; Elvis Costello: "So Like Candy" (McCartney/MacManus); "Playboy to a Man" (McCartney/MacManus); released U.S. Apr 30, 1991; U.K. May 13, 1991.

Apr 1991: Ringo reportedly performed on one or more tracks for a still-untitled Taj Mahal album produced by Skip Drinkwater for the Private Music label; the sessions were held in Los Angeles.

Paul McCartney's Liverpool Oratorio (McCartney/Davis); performed live by the Royal Liverpool Philharmonic, conducted by Paul's co-composer Carl Davis, on Jun 28, 1991 in Liverpool; released U.K. Oct 7, 1991; U.S. Oct 22, 1991. Single "The World You're Coming Into"/"Tres Conejos," from the Oratorio; released U.K. only Sep 20, 1991; single "Save the Child"/"The Drinking Song" released U.S. Nov 12, 1991; U.K. Nov 18, 1991.

"Tutti Frutti"; "Children of the Revolution" (Ringo: drums); on film soundtrack album *Born to Boogie—The Motion Picture*; released U.K. Nov 4, 1991.

"Hello Little Girl" (Lennon/McCartney); Gerry and The Pacemakers (previously unreleased original 1963 recording), on CD *The Best of Gerry and The Pacemakers—The Definitive Collection*; released in U.S. Nov 1991.

"I'm in Love" (Lennon/McCartney); Billy J. Kramer (previously unreleased original 1963 recording); on CD *The Best of Billy J. Kramer—The Definitive Collection*; released in U.S. Nov 1991.

"Don't Break the Promises" (McCartney/Stewart); 10cc; on album *Meanwhile*; released in U.S. and U.K. Apr 1992.

Appendix B: Videocassettes and Laser Discs

Many Beatles performances have been released on home videocassettes and an increasing number are appearing on laser video discs. The following alphabetical list summarizes those films, television appearances, concerts and other events that have appeared on commercial videos. Those issued on laser disc are noted (*). Some releases are no longer available.

Alice in Wonderland (Ringo): 1985 U.S. made-for-TV movie, featuring Ringo as the Mock Turtle.

The Beatles: Alone and Together: 1990 documentary comprising newsreel footage. (Also released as *The Legend Continues*).

*The Beatles: The First U.S. Visit: An 83-minute documentary, officially released by Apple in 1991, containing footage from The Beatles' Feb 1964 visit to America shot by Albert Maysles. Video features excerpts from the Washington, D.C. concert and the Ed Sullivan shows.

The Beatles Live in Japan: Released in Japan in 1984 by The Beatles Collector's Shop, contains The Beatles' first 1966 Tokyo concert.

*The Beatles Live!—Ready, Steady, Go! Special Edition: 1989 release of the musical portion of the *Around The Beatles* special.

*Blue Suede Shoes: A Rockabilly Session (George/Ringo): 1986 TV special hosted by Carl Perkins with several numbers by George and Ringo.

Born to Boogie—The Movie (Ringo): 1972 documentary film about Marc Bolan, directed by Ringo, and in which Ringo appears, performing on "Tutti Frutti" and "Children of the Revolution." Most of the film was shot at a T. Rex concert.

British Rock: The First Wave: TV documentary including the following footage of The Beatles: clips from the color Pathé film shot live in Manchester in Nov 1963; The Beatles' Swedish TV appearance of Oct 1963; two songs from *New Musical Express* Poll Winner's Concerts ("Can't Buy Me Love" from 1964 and "She's a Woman" from 1965); one song from the Feb 1964 Washington, D.C. concert; part of John's Aug 11, 1966 "Apology" press conference; the Apple Boutique opening party; and the premiere of the film *Yellow Submarine*.

A Bunch of Videos and Some Other Stuff (George/Ringo): 1989 collection of Tom Petty videos, including "I Won't Back Down" with George and Ringo.

*Casey Kasem's Rock 'n' Roll Gold Mine: The Sixties: 1989 compilation includes mid-1960s interview clips with The Beatles.

*Caveman (Ringo): 1981 film starring Ringo and his then future wife, Barbara Bach.

*Checking Out (George): George makes a cameo appearance in this 1989 film produced by his HandMade Films company.

*The Compleat Beatles: 1982 documentary of the group's history from its formation to breakup.

*Concert for Bangla Desh (George/Ringo): Film of 1971 concert. Issued on laser disc in Japan.

Cool Cats: 1989 compilation including some footage of The Beatles.

The Family Way (Paul): 1966 film with score composed by Paul.

Fun with The Fab Four: 1987 compilation of black and white newsreel footage; no musical segments. Includes Shakespearean sketch from *Around The Beatles*.

*Get Back (Paul): 1991 film of Paul's 1989–90 world tour, directed by Richard Lester.

*Give My Regards to Broad Street (Paul): Paul's 1984 feature film.

Greatest Rock 'n Roll Legends—Elvis & The Fab Four: 1991 compilation of news footage and an interview with author Howard DeWitt.

*Greenpeace: Non-Toxic Video Hits (George): Includes video for George's "Save the World"; George does not appear in the video.

*A Hard Day's Night: The Beatles' first feature film (1964).

*Help!: The Beatles second feature film (1965).

History of The Beatles: A 60-minute collection of various TV and concert clips and newsreel footage. Contains an excellent-quality copy of one of The Beatles' 1966 Tokyo shows in color.

The Honorary Consul (Paul): 1983 film with musical score composed by Paul (U.S. title: *Beyond the Limit*).

*How I Won the War (John): Lennon's 1967 solo film debut in which he portrayed Musketeer Gripweed.

*Imagine (John): John's 1971 film featuring videos for songs from his *Imagine* album.

Imagine: John Lennon (John): 1988 theatrically released documentary film.

I Wanna Hold Your Hand: 1978 film built around The Beatles' first visit to America and appearance on "The Ed Sullivan Show." The film includes Beatles recordings and scenes of them being viewed on TV during the Sullivan performance.

John and Yoko—The Bed-in: All We Are Saying Is Give Peace a Chance (John): 1990 release of Lennon/Ono self-produced film of the May–Jun 1969 Montreal bed-in. The film includes an unreleased acoustic version of "Because" and the recording of "Give Peace a Chance." Laser disc issued in U.K. and Japan.

John Lennon & the Plastic Ono Band: Live Rock & Roll Revival, Toronto (John): 1989 edited version of D.A. Pennebaker film of Lennon's Sep 13, 1969 Toronto concert. It shortens the performances of the other artists on the bill but includes all of the Plastic Ono Band's appearance. Originally released in 1970 as *Sweet Toronto* during limited preview showings, but on general release in 1972 its title was changed to *Keep on Rockin'* and Lennon's footage was eliminated for legal reasons. The video runs 55 minutes, compared to the film's original 140 minute running time. Other performers seen include Jerry Lee Lewis, Little Richard and Chuck Berry.

The John Lennon Interview (John): Dec 9, 1980 rebroadcast of John's appearance on the Apr 28, 1975 edition of "The Tomorrow Show" with John and his lawyer, Leon Wildes, interviewed by Tom Snyder.

John Lennon Live: A 30-minute documentary of Yoko Ono recording with Elephant's Memory, with John sitting in. The tape was later withdrawn from the market.

John Lennon: Live in New York City (John): Film of Lennon's 1972 New York One to One concert.

John Lennon: The Beatles and Beyond: Contains excerpts from "What's Happening: The Beatles in the U.S.A.," "The Beatles Come to Town," "The Beatles at Shea Stadium" and "Man of the Decade."

The Kids Are Alright (Ringo): 1979 documentary film about The Who, including footage of Ringo.

Knebworth: The Event (Volume One) (Paul): Includes four McCartney numbers ("Coming Up," "Birthday," "Hey Jude" and "Can't Buy Me Love") from the Jun 30, 1990 concert.

The Last Waltz (Ringo): 1978 documentary of The Band's final concert, filmed on Nov 24, 1976 at the Winterland in San Francisco. Ringo is seen joining in during part of the performance.

Lennon: A Tribute: (Paul/Ringo). Filmed at the May 5, 1990 Liverpool memorial concert for John, during which new videos for "I Call Your Name" (Ringo) and "P.S. Love Me Do" (Paul) premiered.

Let It Be: The Beatles' final group feature film, released in 1970 but filmed during recording sessions in Jan 1969.

Lethal Weapon 2" (George): 1989 film includes George's "Cheer Down."

Lisztomania (Ringo): 1975 film in which Ringo portrays the Pope.

Live and Let Die (Paul): 1973 James Bond film includes Wings' recording of the title song.

Live at Shea Stadium and *Live in Tokyo, Japan*: Early, apparently legitimate releases of Beatles concert films by MEDA (forerunner of Media Home Entertainment). MEDA later complied with Apple's request that the videos be withdrawn. These and other Beatles concert films subsequently appeared on illegal, poor-quality videocassettes.

The Long Good Friday (George): 1980 film produced by Harrison's HandMade Films with George as executive producer.

Magical Mystery Tour: The Beatles' 1967 television film with remastered digital hi-fi stereo soundtrack, mixed by George Martin, and scene-by-scene color correction. Prior to the official release, a poor copy of the film had been issued on cassette by MEDA.

The Magic Christian (Ringo): 1969 film features Ringo and the song "Come and Get It," composed by McCartney, sung by Badfinger.

Monty Python's Life of Brian (George): 1979 film includes cameo appearance by George.

Music, Memories & Milestones: 1988 compilation includes clips from The Beatles' MBE press conference, airport scenes, the Aug 11, 1966 Chicago press conference, John and Yoko's Montreal bed-in and other scenes.

My Love Is Bigger Than a Cadillac (Paul): 1990 film about The Crickets includes a brief appearance by Paul talking with members of Buddy Holly's former group.

Once Upon a Video (Paul): (1988) Released on cassette just about everywhere but in North America and on laser disc in Japan, it includes videos for "Once Upon a Long Ago," "Stranglehold," "Pretty Little Head," "We All Stand Together" and U.K. TV spots for Paul's *All the Best* album and the *Rupert and the Frog Song* film.

Parkfield Entertainment Pathé Newsreel Series: 1990 release of a series of 40 videotapes issued in the U.S. by Parkfield Entertainment including a tape of Pathé weekly newsreel footage for each year beginning with 1930 and running through 1969. The tapes for 1963 through 1969 inclusive each have Beatles footage. 1963: Variety Club awards luncheon, Sep 1963; 1964: Kennedy Airport arrival and press conference; return to London Airport and press conference; 1965: airport shots; receiving Radio Caroline award from Simon Dee on *Help!* film set; Sep return to London Airport; Oct 26 at Buckingham Palace; 1966: arrival at London Airport from far east tour; 1967: no Beatles footage, but views of Lennon's car and Weybridge home; 1968: Rishikesh, India and 1964 flashback footage; 1969: Paul and Linda's wedding.

Paul McCartney's Liverpool Oratorio (Paul): (1991) Video shot at the Jun 28, 1991 world premiere of the Oratorio, attended by Paul and conducted by his co-composer, Carl Davis.

The Paul McCartney Special (Paul): 1986 BBC/MPL co-produced TV special. Includes an interview with McCartney taped in Jul 1986 by Richard Skinner at Abbey Road Studio #2 and older footage of Paul.

The Point (Ringo): Harry Nilsson's 1971 animated film, originally aired as a TV special with narration by Dustin Hoffman. Ringo recorded the narration for the video release.

Porky's Revenge! (George): 1985 film includes George's song "I Don't Want to Do It," composed by Bob Dylan.

Princess Daisy (Ringo): 1981 U.S. made-for-TV movie, aired in two parts, featuring Ringo and Barbara Bach.

The Prince's Trust Rock Gala (George/Ringo): Film includes George and Ringo performing live at the 1987 concerts. Laser disc issued in Japan.

Prince's Trust 10th Anniversary Birthday Party (Paul). Includes three numbers done by Paul at the 1986 concert.

A *Private Function* (George): 1985 film produced by George's HandMade Films with George as co-executive producer.

Put It There (Paul): 65-minute version of 50-minute TV special shot mostly during a Feb–Apr 1989 McCartney rehearsal session, also including footage of McCartney working with Elvis Costello during summer and fall of 1987. Includes rough versions and alternate takes of several songs and complete versions of five songs that were edited in the TV broadcast. Original cassette packaging boasted four additional songs not included in the TV broadcast, but in fact only one, "Fool on the Hill," was included; packaging in the U.S. was corrected.

Queen: Magic Years (3-volume videocassette): Footage of Paul appears on Volume 1, "The Foundations," and of Ringo on Volume 2, "Live Killers in the Making."

Ready, Steady, Go!—The Beatles: A Japanese compilation *Ready Steady Go!* video with *all* of The Beatles' appearances plus footage missing from the three videos listed above, including "It Won't Be Long," "I'll Get You" and "I Feel Fine" plus additional interview clips.

Ready, Steady, Go! Volume 1: Includes Beatles' live appearance on the U.K. TV show on Mar 20, 1964, miming to released recordings.

Ready, Steady, Go! Volume 2: Includes Beatles' Oct 4, 1963 live appearance on the U.K. TV show, miming to released recordings.

Ready, Steady, Go! Volume 3: Includes Beatles' Nov 27, 1964 appearance, during which they mimed to released recordings.

The Real Buddy Holly Story (Paul): 1987 90-minute version of 60-minute TV special, *The Real Buddy Holly Story*. Includes acoustic numbers by Paul and playing part of 1958 Quarry Men recording "That'll Be the Day."

Ringo Starr and His All-Starr Band (Ringo): Ringo's Sep 3, 1989 show at the Greek Theater in Los Angeles. U.S. cassette and laser disc run 90 minutes and include all of Ringo's songs except "You're Sixteen." A 60-minute cassette was issued only in U.K.

The Road: 1990 compilation contains Beatles newsreel footage.

Rock and Roll High School (Paul): 1979 film, featuring The Ramones, includes Paul's unreleased recording "Did We Meet Somewhere Before."

Rock 'N' Roll—The Greatest Years: 1971 (George/Ringo): 1989 compilation includes George's "My Sweet Lord" from 1971 concert for Bangla Desh, and Ringo's promo film for "It Don't Come Easy," the first commercial release of a Ringo promo film.

Rockshow (Paul): 1980 documentary mostly filmed during Wings' 1976 Seattle show.

Rupert and the Frog Song (Paul): 1984 animated short produced by Paul's MPL company and including McCartney's "We All Stand Together." Video also includes animated shorts "Seaside Woman" and "Oriental Nightfish."

The Rutles (aka *All You Need Is Cash*): Far and away the most celebrated of all Beatles spoofs, the brain child of Eric Idle and Neil Innes includes a cameo appearance by George Harrison as a television reporter. *All You Need Is Cash* originally aired as a TV special in the U.S. on Mar 22, 1978.

Sextette (Ringo): Ringo is featured in this 1978 film, the last ever done by Mae West.

Shanghai Surprise (George): 1986 film produced by George's HandMade Films, and easily the company's biggest flop, includes a score co-composed by Harrison and his unreleased recordings of the title song (a duet with Vicki Brown) and a bit of "The Hottest Gong in Town," "Twelve Bar Bali," plus alternate versions or mixes of "Breath Away from Heaven" and "Someplace Else," different versions of which appeared on George's *Cloud Nine* album as well and "Zig Zag," an instrumental that was later released as a B side.

Spies Like Us (Paul): 1985 film includes Paul's recording of the title song played over the closing credits.

Terry O'Neill: His England, His Ireland: 1990 video includes an excerpt from the Nov 20, 1963 Pathé News footage of The Beatles' performance in Manchester.

That'll Be the Day (Ringo): 1974 film with Ringo in a featured role.

Thomas the Tank Engine and Friends (Ringo): Several video cassettes have been issued with these 1980s-filmed stories narrated by Ringo. Originally aired in the U.K., they were aired with rerecorded narration in the U.S. on the PBS TV series "Shining Time Station," in which Ringo appeared as the 18-inch-tall Mr. Conductor. Releases include compilation video *Better Late Than Never and Other Stories*.

*Time Bandits (George): 1981 film produced by George's HandMade Films with music by Harrison, including an alternate mix of "Dream Away," later released on his *Gone Troppo* album.

*Tommy (Ringo): 1975 film of The Who's rock opera featuring Ringo.

*25 X 5: The Further Adventures of The Rolling Stones: 1989 documentary of The Rolling Stones' career includes several Beatles film clips.

Twice in a Lifetime (Paul): 1985 film includes Paul's unreleased recording of the title song played over the closing credits.

200 Motels (Ringo): 1971 Frank Zappa movie featuring Ringo.

Water (George/Ringo): 1985 film produced by George's HandMade Films and featuring George and Ringo with Eric Clapton during the "Freedom" musical number by Billy Connolly, Christopher Tumming and The Singing Rebels Band. "Celebration" and "Focus of Attention" were co-written by George and performed in the film by Jimmy Helms with George on guitar.

Willie and The Poor Boys—The Video (Ringo): Ringo appeared in a nonmusical cameo in this 1985 video, released to raise funds for ARMS (Action Research into Multiple Sclerosis) and originated by Bill Wyman of The Rolling Stones.

Wonderwall (George): 1969 film with score composed by Harrison.

*Yellow Submarine: Celebrated 1968 animated film containing Beatles songs and a cameo appearance by the group at the end. The voices of The Beatles during the film were recorded by actors. Video release featured a digitally enhanced stereo hi-fi soundtrack. The U.S. print was used for all video releases, and the "Hey Bulldog" number is thus omitted.

Yesterday—The Beatles: collection of assorted newsreel footage.

*Yoko Ono: Then and Now (John/Yoko): 1990 U.K. release of documentary film including footage of Lennon and The Beatles.

References

Castleman, Harry, and Podrazik, Walter J. *All Together Now* (Ballantine Books, 1975; now published by Popular Culture Ink.)

———. *The Beatles Again?* (Pierian Press, 1977; now published by Popular Culture Ink.)

———. *The End of The Beatles?* (Pierian Press, 1985; now published by Popular Culture Ink.)

Cox, Perry, and Lindsay, Joe. *The Beatles Price Guide for American Records*, 3rd ed. (Perry Cox Ent./BIOdisc, 1990).

Davies, Hunter. *The Beatles*, 2d rev. ed. (McGraw-Hill, 1985).

Guzek, Arno, and Mattoon, C. "Recordings of: John, Paul, George, and Ringo" (manuscript, 1977).

Harry, Bill. *Beatlemania: An Illustrated Filmography* (Virgin, 1984).

Ingham, Peter, and Mitsui, Toru. "The Search for 'Sweet Georgia Brown': A Case of Discographical Detection." *Popular Music*, 6, 3 (1987: 273–290).

King, LRE (pseudonym). *Do You Want to Know a Secret?* (Storyteller Productions, 1988).

———. *Fixing a Hole* (Storyteller Productions, 1989).

———. *Help!—A Companion to The Beatles Recording Sessions* (Storyteller Productiosn, 1989).

Lewisohn, Mark. *The Beatles Live!* (Henry Holt, 1986).

———. *The Beatles Recording Sessions* (Harmony, 1988).

———. *The Beatles Day by Day* (Harmony, 1989).

McCabe, Peter and Schonfeld, Robert D. *John Lennon: For the Record* (Bantam Books, 1984).

Norman, Philip. *Shout! The Beatles in Their Generation* (Warner Books, 1981).

Pang, May and Edwards, Henry. *Loving John* (Warner Books, 1983).

Robertson, John (pseudonym). *The Art & Music of John Lennon* (Birch Lane Press, 1990).

Schaffner, Nicholas. *The Beatles Forever* (McGraw-Hill, 1977).

Schweighardt, Ray, and Sulpy, Doug. *Drugs, Divorce and a Slipping Image: The Beatles Get Back Sessions* (manuscript, 1992; in press).

Stannard, Neville. *The Long and Winding Road* (Avon, 1982).

———. *Working Class Heroes* (Virgin, 1983).

Walker, Bob, ed. *Hot Wacks Book XIV* (Hot Wacks Press, 1990).

Wallgren, Mark. *The Beatles on Record* (Fireside, 1982).

Wiener, Allen J. "John Lennon: The Solo Years." *Goldmine*, June 3, 1988.

———. "The Lennon-Spector *Rock 'N' Roll* Sessions." *Goldmine*, July 1, 1988.

———. "The Lost McCartney Album." *Goldmine*, February 24, 1989.

Wiener, Jon. *Come Together* (Random House, 1984).

Recommended Periodicals

Beatlefan, The Goody Press, P.O. Box 33515, Decatur, GA 30033

Beatles Book Monthly, Beat Publications, 45 St. Mary's Road, Ealing, London W5 5RQ, England

Beatletter, P.O. Box 13, St. Clair Shores, MI 48080

Belmo's Beatleg News, c/o Storyteller Productions, P.O. Box 77513, Tucson, AZ 85703

Club Sandwich (Paul McCartney's fan club newsletter), P.O. Box 4 UP; London W1A 4UP, England

Goldmine, 700 E. State Street, Iola, WI 54990

Good Day Sunshine, c/o Charles F. Rosenay, 397 Edgewood Avenue, New Haven CT 06511

The Harrison Alliance, 67 Cypress Street, Bristol, CT 06010

The 910, P.O. Box 751, New Monmouth, NJ 07748

Record Collector, Beat Publications, 43-45 St. Mary's Road, Ealing, London W5 5RQ, England

Also of interest:

Beatlefest, P.O. Box 436, Westwood, NJ 07675
Holds U.S. National Beatles Conventions several times a year in the New York, Los Angeles and Chicago areas.

Title Index

(Song titles appear in roman; all other titles are in italics. Albums in a numbered series such as *The Lost Lennon Tapes* are listed numerically; all others are listed alphabetically.)